Springer Texts in Business and Economics

More information about this series at http://www.springer.com/series/10099

Tim Mazzarol • Sophie Reboud

Entrepreneurship and Innovation

Theory, Practice and Context

Fourth Edition

Springer

Tim Mazzarol
University of Western Australia
Crawley, WA, Australia

Sophie Reboud
Burgundy School of Business
Dijon, France

ISSN 2192-4333 ISSN 2192-4341 (electronic)
Springer Texts in Business and Economics
ISBN 978-981-13-9411-9 ISBN 978-981-13-9412-6 (eBook)
https://doi.org/10.1007/978-981-13-9412-6

This Springer imprint is published by the registered company Springer Nature Singapore Pte Ltd.
The registered company address is: 152 Beach Road, #21-01/04 Gateway East, Singapore 189721, Singapore

Contents

List of Figures

List of Tables

1 Entrepreneurship as a Social and Economic Process

1.1 Introduction

> Nobody talks about entrepreneurship as survival, but that's exactly what it is and what nurtures creative thinking (Anita Roddick, founder of The Body Shop).

This chapter examines the social and economic process underpinning entrepreneurship activity and the impacts of entrepreneurial activity on global, national and local economies. In particular, it focuses on defining key concepts such as enterprise, entrepreneurship, entrepreneurs and innovation. Entrepreneurship and innovation are now recognised as being among the key elements in the process of economic development and vital to the ability of a nation's economy to maintain competitiveness. According to the Organisation for Economic Co-operation and Development (OECD) entrepreneurship and innovation are the essential tools for dealing with many of the world's social and economic challenges.

> **For example,** … Policies to strengthen entrepreneurship and increase the innovation capabilities of SMEs should be one of the main planks of government innovation strategies. Furthermore, government should target SMEs and entrepreneurship as a major potential source of new jobs in the recovery from recession (OECD 2010a).

Government interest in entrepreneurship and innovation is driven by the desire to maintain economic growth and the creation of jobs. The Global Financial Crisis (GFC) of 2007–2009, like the Great Depression of 1929–1939, impacted most of the world's economies, triggering negative GDP growth, high rates of unemployment, the collapse of companies and the failure of banks (OECD 2016). However, even without these traumatic economic crises, the overall trend in the late twentieth and early twenty-first centuries has been a steady decline in full-time employment

T. Mazzarol, S. Reboud, *Entrepreneurship and Innovation*, Springer Texts in Business and Economics, https://doi.org/10.1007/978-981-13-9412-6_1

within large organisations, and their replacement with new jobs created by self-employment and small, high-growth *gazelle* firms (Brännback et al. 2014).

For example, over the period from 1980 to 1999, the major Fortune 500 companies in the United States (US) lost 5 million jobs due to downsizing. However, this massive loss of jobs was offset by the creation of 34 million new jobs, created by entrepreneurial activity (GEM 1999). From 1980 to 2005 nearly all net job creation within the US was generated by firms aged less than 5 years (OECD 2010a), while in 2007 over two-thirds of all net new jobs created there were within such firms (Haltiwanger et al. 2009).

The future of work is also changing, with a rise in the proportion of self-employed, but non-employing sole traders known as 'nano enterprises' (McKeown and Phillips 2014; ASBFEO 2017). These are the independent contractors, independent professionals (iPros), and freelancers working within the so-called 'gig economy' (McKeown et al. 2018). In the United States, this 'gig economy' was estimated in 2016 to comprise between 600,000 to more than 1.9 million people (Brinkley 2016). Although in some industries it represented around 34% of the workforce (Bracha et al. 2015). This is a pattern found in other nations. For example, freelancer non-employing nano enterprises comprise around 61% of the 2.12 million registered businesses in Australia (ASBFEO 2017). While such entrepreneurial employment remains at around 8.7% of total employment in Australia, it is forecast to grow (Productivity Commission 2017).

Another major factor likely to impact employment and stimulate entrepreneurship and innovation is the rise of what has been described as the 4th Industrial Revolution, or *Industrie 4.0* (Kagermann et al. 2013). This involves the convergence of a range of digital technologies into cyber physical systems, comprising such things as artificial intelligence (AI), machine learning, the Internet-of-Things (IoT), cloud computing, big data, blockchain and cobotics (Xu et al. 2018). This technological revolution will have a major impact on labour markets and poses a risk to a significant number of jobs (Liao et al. 2017). For example, within the mining and metals industry, it has been estimated that this digital disruption will result in the loss of around 5% of the current workforce or more than 330,000 jobs by 2025 (WEF 2017).

It is in response to such potential job loss that entrepreneurship and innovation have an important role to play. Not only is entrepreneurial activity important to job creation, but the long-term economic growth of the world's economies is strongly dependent upon innovation within industry. Economic analysis indicates that a strong and positive relationship exists between: (i) the levels of national investment in R&D and the number of patents generated within an economy, and (ii) the level of economic and employment growth (OECD 2010b). Entrepreneurship is a strategic process that starts at the individual level and moves through the organisational level to the macro environment.

> **It is a process,** … supported by collaborative networks across government, education and institutions. Capturing opportunities and converting them into marketable propositions… (Kuratko and Hodgetts 2004).

Entrepreneurship is found in all sectors and within all organisations. The majority (70%) of new enterprises provide products and services into competitive existing markets with relatively mature technologies, while 7% of new entrepreneurs create a new market niche if successful (Hindle and Rushworth 2004). Entrepreneurs have been identified as playing at least five key roles in an economy (OECD 2010a):

1. *Disruptor.* Entrepreneurs seek opportunities to disrupt market equilibrium through the introduction of new products, processes and marketing techniques. They are a key agent of innovation and a 'creative destroyer' (Schumpeter 1934).
2. *Opportunity identification.* Entrepreneurs possess the alertness, noted by Kirzner (1997), to spot commercial opportunities and then take on the challenge of bringing them to market.
3. *Risk taker.* Entrepreneurs assume a willingness to launch new ventures and engage in the commercialisation of innovations which by their nature are risky. However, their ability to deal with uncertainty and ambiguity allows them to take on risks that might not enable innovations to proceed (Knight 1933).
4. *Resource shifter.* Entrepreneurs enhance the productivity within the economy by finding new ways to configure resources to achieve superior growth and wealth creation (Drucker 1985).
5. *Breakthrough innovator.* Finally, entrepreneurs who engage in market disruptive innovation can lead a process of achieving new breakthrough's in technology, business or marketing approaches (Baumol 1968).

Methods used to measure the impact of entrepreneurial activity on the economy include the number of start-up efforts, the incorporation of firms, changes in net tax returns filed, and the amount of self-employment. Entrepreneurial firms contribute to economies in terms of economic renewal, and enabling individuals to enter the social and economic mainstream.

1.2 The Benefits of Entrepreneurial Activity

The growth of interest in entrepreneurial behaviour can be traced to the 1970s when many of the world's industrialised nations began to experience a major change in their economic fortunes (Gibb 1988). New technologies and the expansion of key competitor countries such as Japan saw the decline of traditional manufacturing industries across the developed world. Accompanying this downsizing in the manufacturing sector was a rise in the services sector, which increasingly employed the majority of workers in these post-industrial economies. Many large firms began to outsource or sub-contract services to smaller companies, a process that accelerated in the 1990s. Management buy-outs became more common within the corporate sector, as did the desire by many employees to have greater independence and job flexibility. The arrival of new information technologies from the 1980s also assisted the growth of entrepreneurship, partly through the creation of entirely new industries that allowed the emergence of new entrepreneurs and partly through the decentralisation that such new information and communications technologies (ICTs) allowed (Drucker 2002). As noted above, the pace of technological change and its ability to both disrupt existing industries, potentially destroying many jobs, and create opportunities for new industries and job generating businesses is significant (Schwab 2016, 2018).

Levels of entrepreneurial activity around the world can be measured by global research that suggests 43% of the adult population surveyed across 54 countries believed they had identified good opportunities for starting up a new business within the next 6 months. Further, around 70% of people surveyed across these countries held entrepreneurs in high regard (GEM 2018). This varies across regions, with North Americans being more likely than Europeans to view self-employment, or new venture creation as an attractive career option (Kuratko and Hodgetts 2004). In general, entrepreneurs are more fulfilled by their work than people who work for others. Self-employed people have also been found to be more satisfied with their jobs (Hindle and Rushworth 2004).

While small business creation is not the only measure of entrepreneurship, it provides a useful indicator of the contribution this type of activity can make to an economy. Across the 33 countries that comprise the OECD small- to medium-sized enterprises (SMEs) represent around 99% of all businesses, approximately two-thirds of all the employment, and over a half of all the value added (OECD 2010a).

The annual Global Entrepreneurship Monitor (GEM) study monitors the level of entrepreneurial activity in 54 countries. It classifies countries into three types:

- *Factor-driven economies.* This group of countries includes developing economies in which much of the productive activity is focused on agriculture within largely rural populations with a high level of subsistence farming.
- *Efficiency-driven economies.* This group of countries have a high level of industrialisation and rely heavily on manufacturing within scale-intensive industries.
- *Innovation-driven economies.* This group of countries have a post-industrial industry base that is more focused on services and knowledge intensive businesses with high levels of R&D investment and innovation (GEM 2018).

Within factor-driven economies, the focus of government policy needs to be placed on creating conditions that can foster the growth of sustainable businesses, with investments in basic education and health (Bosma and Levie 2010). In the factor-driven economies, two thirds of working-age adults believe entrepreneurship is a good career choice, with a similar proportion stating that entrepreneurs capture substantial media attention. Even more have high regard for this activity, with nearly three-fourths stating that entrepreneurs have high status in their societies. These results indicate that entrepreneurs are visible and well-regarded, and are considered to have good careers (Kelley et al. 2016).

In efficiency-driven economies, the focus shifts to encouraging economies of scale and employment productivity. They show a different pattern in terms of perception of entrepreneurship. Like the factor-driven economies, two thirds believe entrepreneurship is a good career choice. The other two indicators, however, are lower than in the factor driven economies. This suggests that, relative to the factor driven economies, people believe it's a good work option, even if entrepreneurs are slightly less visible and somewhat less admired than in the factor-driven world (Kelley et al. 2016).

The innovation-driven economies require support for new product development and market access (Bosma and Levie 2010). A third pattern can be seen in this group as for the perception of entrepreneurship. Here, working age adults are about as likely as those in the efficiency-driven group to think entrepreneurs have high status and are represented positively in the media. However, little more than half consider starting a business a good career choice. Implied here is that other options may be more attractive, even if entrepreneurs receive a reasonable amount of respect and attention (Kelley et al. 2016).

A major focus for the GEM is new venture creation within these economies, and the attitudes, activity and aspirations of the entrepreneurs who are planning to found or have founded such businesses. The level of new venture creation within each of the three types of economy is measured by a Total early-stage Entrepreneurial Activity (TEA) score, which is the proportion of people aged between 18 and 64 years who are engaged in a new business as an owner-manager or in activities to establish such a venture as nascent entrepreneurs. It also measures the proportion ownership of established businesses and the rate of discontinuances of businesses (Kelley et al. 2016).

As illustrated in Table 1.1, the rate of early-stage entrepreneurial activity (TEA rate) was much higher in North America than Europe, with Africa, Asia and Oceania somewhere in the middle. By comparison, the rate at which businesses were discontinued was significantly lower in Europe than the other regions. Also, noticeable about these figures is the much higher rate of business ownership in Africa, which reflects greater reliance on self-employment within those countries.

What we can draw from these figures is that for people in factor-driven developing economies, entrepreneurship is often a necessity due to less stable employment conditions and welfare support systems. The rates of discontinuation within these economies is high and often due to illness, lack of access to funding or even civil unrest (Bosma and Levie 2010). By contrast, the more advanced economies enjoy greater survival rates for new business ventures, even though their total start-up activity levels are lower. A principle reason given for a business to cease trading is 'lack of profitability' (GEM 2018).

1.3 Necessity and Opportunity Entrepreneurs

The GEM classifies entrepreneurs into two types: necessity and opportunity driven. Necessity entrepreneurs are those who enter self-employment out of a lack of choice, usually because they have lost a waged job and have no alternatives. Such people are common in countries that have low levels of social welfare. By contrast, the opportunity entrepreneur is a person who follows a specific idea or opportunity out of choice that they have identified as delivering benefits.

Table 1.1 Ranking of six stages of entrepreneurial activity by region, GEM 2017 (% of population aged 18–64 years)

Region	Nascent entrepreneurship rate	New business ownership rate	Early-stage entrepreneurial activity (TEA)	Entrepreneurial employee activity (EEA)	Established business ownership rate	Discontinuation of businesses (% adult pop.)
Africa	7.3	6.6	13.7	0.9	11.9	6.9
Asia & Oceania	6.2	7.1	13.0	3.1	9.7	5.5
Latin America & Caribbean	11.7	7.3	18.5	1.6	8.3	5.2
Europe	5.1	3.1	8.1	4.4	7.0	2.9
North America	10.3	6.3	16.2	7.9	7.0	5.5

Source: GEM (2018)

According to the GEM, of the majority of early stage entrepreneurial activity is opportunity driven and the rest necessity driven.

For example, … Most entrepreneurs around the world are opportunity-motivated. In the factor and efficiency-driven economies, 69% of entrepreneurs stated they chose to pursue an opportunity as a basis for their entrepreneurial motivations, rather than starting out of necessity. The innovation-driven economies show a higher proportion of opportunity motivated entrepreneurs, at 78% (Kelley et al. 2016, p. 8).

Not surprisingly, the opportunity entrepreneur is more likely to be found in developed economies.

For example, … At a regional level, necessity-driven entrepreneurship is highest in Africa and Latin America and the Caribbean, where 30% of entrepreneurs, on average, cite this motive. Particularly high levels of necessity motives can be seen in economies from these regions: Guatemala, Panama, Brazil and Egypt (more than 40%). The highest level of necessity-based activity, however, is in Macedonia, where over half the entrepreneurs started out of necessity (Kelley et al. 2016, p. 18).

As many of opportunity driven entrepreneurs usually seek an improvement of their situation (increased independence, through increased income (versus maintaining their income), GEM has created an additional category: the improvement-driven opportunity entrepreneurs and created the Motivational Index. This index shows that there are, on average, more than twice as many IDO (Opportunity) entrepreneurs as necessity driven ones. Further, as illustrated in Fig. 1.1, business start-ups in North America were 5.2 times more likely to be driven by opportunity than necessity, and more than 3 times more likely in Europe, Asia and Oceania. However, in Africa necessity was just as likely as opportunity to motivate self-employment and new venture creation, due to the lack of alternative employment and social welfare support.

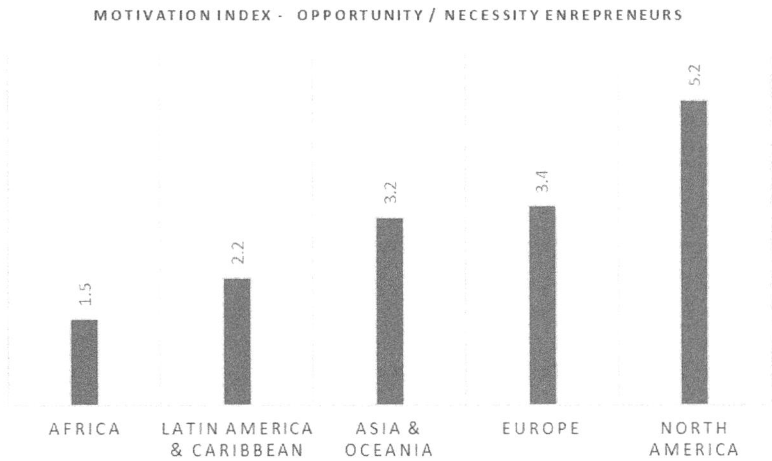

Fig. 1.1 Motivation for Early-Stage Entrepreneurship in 54 GEM countries in 2017 – Relative number of Opportunity to Necessity Entrepreneurs by Region. (Source: GEM 2018)

Table 1.2 Development phase averages for male and female total entrepreneurial activity (TEA) and necessity proportion of TEA in 54 economies, GEM 2017

Phase of economic development	Factor-driven	Efficiency-driven	Innovation-driven
Male TEA (% of adult male population)	16.6%	16.9%	11.3%
Female TEA (% of adult female population)	16.2%	12.8%	7.1%
Ratio of female/male TEA	1.00	0.80	0.60
Male TEA necessity (% of TEA males	23.8%	23.2%	16.1%
Female TEA necessity (% of TEA females)	23.2%	30.9%	19.1%
Ratio of female/male TEA necessity	1.00	1.30	1.20

Source: GEM (2018)

As shown in Table 1.2, male and female necessity entrepreneurial activity is broadly equal across all kinds of economies. However, in the more developed innovation-driven economies, male TEA scores are significantly higher, compared to the almost identical TEA scores for men and women in factor-driven economies. This reflects the need for many women in less-developed economies to engage in self-employment or micro-businesses due to lack of alternative employment. However, it can be more difficult for women to launch and operate business ventures in countries where bank loans and property ownership are often restricted to men. The pattern is often reversed in more developed economies (Pilat and Baygan 2001).

1.4 Attitudes Towards Entrepreneurship as a Career

The GEM study examines the societal values relating to entrepreneurship as held by the adult population aged between 18 and 64 years. As illustrated in Fig. 1.2, this examines three core issues: (i) whether entrepreneurship is considered a good choice as a career; (ii) whether entrepreneurs have high social status; and (iii) whether the media gives high attention to entrepreneurs.

It can be seen from Fig. 1.2 that an average of 63% of people surveyed felt that entrepreneurship was a good career choice, although this was slightly lower (57%) within innovation-driven economies. The view that entrepreneurs have high social status was held by 69% of respondents, with the strongest agreement found in factor-driven (72%) and innovation-driven (70%) economies. An average of 60% of all people surveyed felt that entrepreneurs are given high attention within the media, and this was broadly the same across all types of economy.

In relation to how people view their own capacity for entrepreneurship, the GEM study asks a range of questions about how they feel they can identify a suitable entrepreneurial opportunity, their capability to pursue this, whether they have a fear of failure likely to hold them back, and whether they have an intention to pursue their opportunity in the near future. Figure 1.3 illustrates the results of these questions across the three different types of economy. It can be seen that in terms of identifying potential opportunities there were no significant differences between the

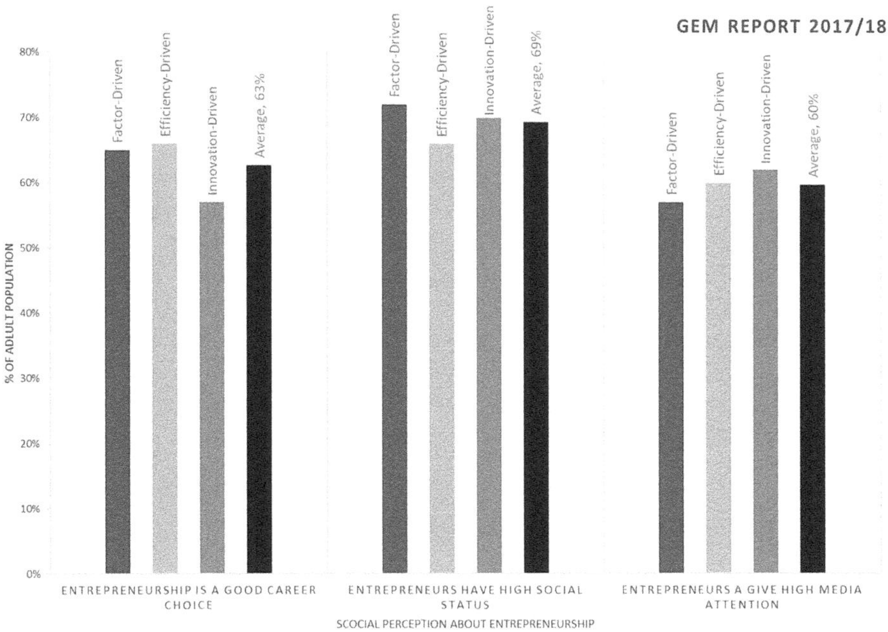

Fig. 1.2 Societal values about entrepreneurship in 52 GEM countries in 2017 – (% of adult population). (Source: GEM 2018)

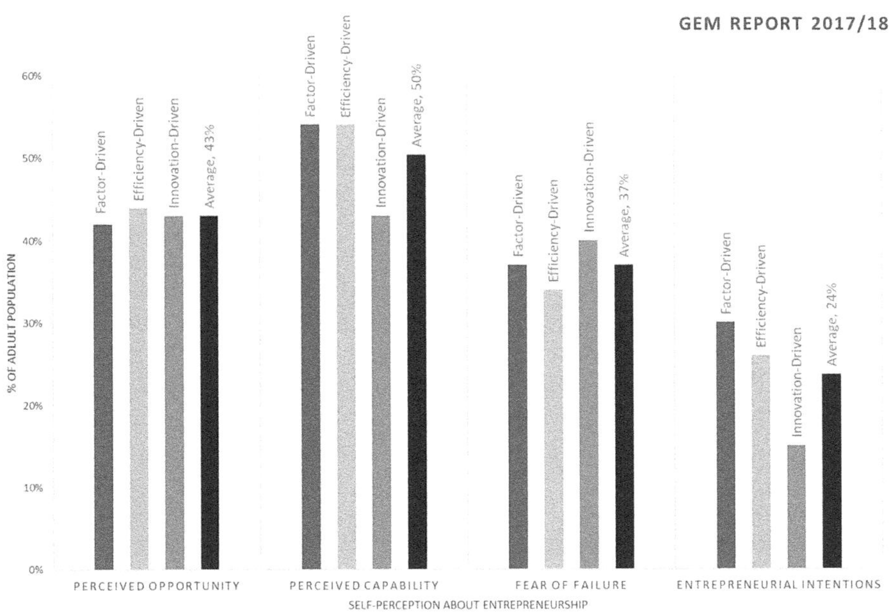

Fig. 1.3 Entrepreneurial attributes and self-perceptions in 54 GEM countries in 2017. (Source: GEM 2018)

groups. The average was also relatively low at 43%. In terms of perceived capability, an average of half all people surveyed felt that they had the capability to pursue an entrepreneurial opportunity if they tried. However, this was lower for people from innovation-driven economies (43%), as opposed to those from factor-driven or efficiency-driven economies where 54% of both groups felt they had such capability. With respect to fear of failure as an impediment to pursuing an entrepreneurial opportunity, an average of 32% of people expressed such fear. This was most prominent within innovation-driven economies, which might be due to this group having more alternatives to self-employment (GEM 2018). Finally, it can be seen that in relation to peoples' intentions to actually pursue their opportunity, an average of only 24% indicated that they would be likely to take action. It can be seen that this was much higher in factor-driven (30%) and efficiency-driven (26%) economies than in innovation-driven (15%) ones. Again, this might be explained in relation to the latter having more alternative options in well-paid employment.

1.5 The Pursuit of High-Growth Firms

Of particular interest to governments is the ability of entrepreneurial firms to achieve high rates of growth. The OECD defines high-growth firms as: *all enterprises with average growth greater than 20 percentage per annum, over a three-year period, and with more employees than at the beginning of the observation period* (OECD 2010c). Growth is thus measured by the number of employees and by turnover (OECD 2010c). Such firms are often referred to as *gazelles* if they not only have high rates of growth but are also less than 5 years old. During the 1990s, around 4% of companies in the US were *gazelles* experiencing sales growth rates of over 20% per annum. Such fast-growing firms are rare within most economies and are riskier that other small firms, as they rely on very innovative and uncertain projects. Their contribution to economic growth is controversial (Coad et al. 2014; Nightingale and Coad 2014).

It is worth noting that these *gazelle* firms were not all high technology, venture capital-supported ventures operating within global markets. Nevertheless, in the United States these small entrepreneurial firms were able to generate twice as many innovations per employee as their larger counterparts (Kuratko and Hodgetts 2004). Innovation-driven economies are more likely to generate *gazelles* than their counterparts in factor or efficiency-driven economies due to the role played by greater R&D investment and technology. Firms in the innovation-driven economies are more likely to develop than adopt new technologies. *Gazelles* in less advanced economies are more likely to be achieving growth from export activity (OECD 2010c).

1.6 Global Trends in Entrepreneurship and Innovation

Research undertaken by the OECD (2010a) identified several key global trends taking place in entrepreneurship and innovation. These can be summarised as follows.

1.6.1 Shift from a 'Managed' to an 'Entrepreneurial Economy'

As defined by Thurik (2009), there have been three major phases in the history of innovation. The first took place in the early decades of the twentieth century with the emergence of entrepreneurs, such as Henry Ford, who changed the nature of industrial organisation in a process of what the economist Schumpeter (1934) described as 'creative destruction'. During the period from the 1940s to the 1970s innovation was dominated by large corporations in what was a 'managed economy'. However, from the late 1970s there was a shift into a post-industrial era and the emergence of an 'entrepreneurial economy' in which small firms have played a much greater role in innovation and economic growth. This has now accelerated with the coming of the 4th Industrial Revolution.

1.6.2 Rise of the 'Knowledge Economy'

Another key trend has been the shift from an economy in which value lies with tangible assets to one in which value is found within intangibles. Knowledge that can be transformed into commercially valuable intellectual property (IP) and licensed or leveraged into global supply chains has become the key for wealth creation in many firms (Sveiby 1997). Small entrepreneurial firms already have greater access to information and communications technologies (ICT) and enhanced digital systems than at any time in history. These technologies are already rapidly transforming industries and must be embraced and adopted by SMEs if they are to successfully compete. However, most small firms, even in developed economies, are lagging in their adoption and use of digital technologies that can allow them to capture value from the knowledge economy (OECD 2005a; Moeuf et al. 2018).

1.6.3 Strategically Networked Innovation

In conjunction with the emergence of the knowledge-based economy has been a trend towards strategic alliances as a framework for innovation. Jarillo (1993) observed that, during the twentieth century, large firms had transformed from vertically integrated structures in which all operations were undertaken in-house to outsourced businesses with large sub-contractor networks. This initially was driven by a desire for cost efficiencies, but in the 1990s it began to take the form of strategic alliances in which collaborative innovation based on knowledge exchange was the primary focus.

1.6.4 Globalisation

With the end of the Cold War in 1989 and the emergence of China and India as major trading economies during the 1990s, the world has become increasingly interconnected. The emergence of the strategic network as a key source of innovation has accelerated the level of international collaboration, and the emergence of new information and communications technologies (ICT) have made it easier for small firms to internationalise.

1.6.5 Low, Mid and High-Technology Innovation

While much attention has been given to what has been described as the *Silicon Valley Business Model*, or high-technology business venture, there is an increasing awareness that the majority of firms are engaged in low to mid-technology sectors. A high-tech business is one that invests greater than 5% of its annual turnover into R&D, compared to a low-tech firm which invests less than 3%, or a mid-tech firm that invests between 3% and 5% (Hirsch-Kreinsen et al. 2008). Many low-tech industries are services that comprise the majority of all businesses in advanced economies. These firms can be in retailing, construction and education, while mid-tech firms can be in automotive, electronics and chemicals manufacturing. Such firms have the ability to be highly innovative, with enhanced use of ICT and new approaches to marketing.

1.6.6 Social Entrepreneurship and Innovation

Another major trend is in the growing recognition of social entrepreneurship and innovation as distinct areas of activity. Social entrepreneurs are found in the not-for-profit sector and seek to alleviate economic and social imbalance within society through innovative and enterprising mechanisms. An example is that of Muhammad Yunus, an economist from Bangladesh who founded the Grameen Bank which provides micro-loans to the poor. Grameen Bank was founded in 1983, and lends primarily to women who use the money to found micro-enterprises. This bank has proven very successful and has helped to alleviate poverty for tens of millions.

> **For example,** … The social entrepreneur neither anticipates nor organises to create substantial financial profit for his or her investors…or for himself or herself. Instead, the social entrepreneur aims for value in the form of large-scale, transformational benefit that accrues either to a significant segment of society or to society at large (Martin and Osberg 2007, p. 34).

1.7 What Is an Entrepreneur?

The word 'entrepreneur' is derived from the French verb *entreprendre* which means 'to undertake', i.e. to undertake organisation or management and to assume business risks. The term 'entrepreneur' was first used by Richard Cantillon, who defined entrepreneurs as those individuals who bear the risk of buying at certain prices and selling at uncertain prices (Messeghem and Torrès 2015). Schumpeter (1934) expanded this definition beyond the concept of a businessman trading goods or services to incorporate innovation. Schumpeter argued that entrepreneurship is a process by which the economy moves forward through the act of creative disruption or innovation. This definition placed innovation at the very centre of entrepreneurial behaviour.

How to Spot an Entrepreneur?

An agent of change. An entrepreneur is a person who historically has brought new ideas or products to market with the ability to create wealth and employment.

Motivation. An entrepreneur has individual motivation and the capacity to identify an opportunity and pursue it to economic success regardless of the resources that are under their control.

Converting opportunity. An entrepreneur converts opportunities into marketable ideas, often assuming risks, implementing the idea and realising any rewards.

Creating new ventures. An entrepreneur is often found starting a company of their own (entrepreneur) or working in an organisation on a new project (intrapreneur).

Economists such as Hirschman (1958) argued that the development of an economy depends upon entrepreneurs marshalling and enlisting hidden, scattered or badly-used resources, further expanding the definition of the entrepreneur as an individual with the ability to identify opportunities and to marshal and organise resources in new and inventive ways. These definitions refer to the *individual* entrepreneur rather than the *process* of entrepreneurship, as it is in essence the individual that undertakes entrepreneurial activities.

The term entrepreneur has more recently been applied to individuals who start new businesses as well as to those who innovate. However, definitions of who is or who isn't an entrepreneur can often limit the scope of the concept. Therefore, definitions that consider the identification and exploitation of opportunities, the marshalling of resources and the satisfying of a felt need within the market provide a more inclusive approach to understanding the entrepreneur.

1.8 The Entrepreneurship Domain

As illustrated in Fig. 1.4, the domain of entrepreneurship comprises at least seven elements. The first three involve the recognition, exploration and exploitation of future opportunities. The next four comprise the creation of new ventures, the creation of new products or components, the creation of new markets or even industries, and the creation of wealth.

This ability to identify opportunities for such activities lies at the heart of the concept of entrepreneurship. Kirzner (1997) suggests that the equilibrium of economic markets is disrupted by the entrepreneur's ability to challenge the *status quo*

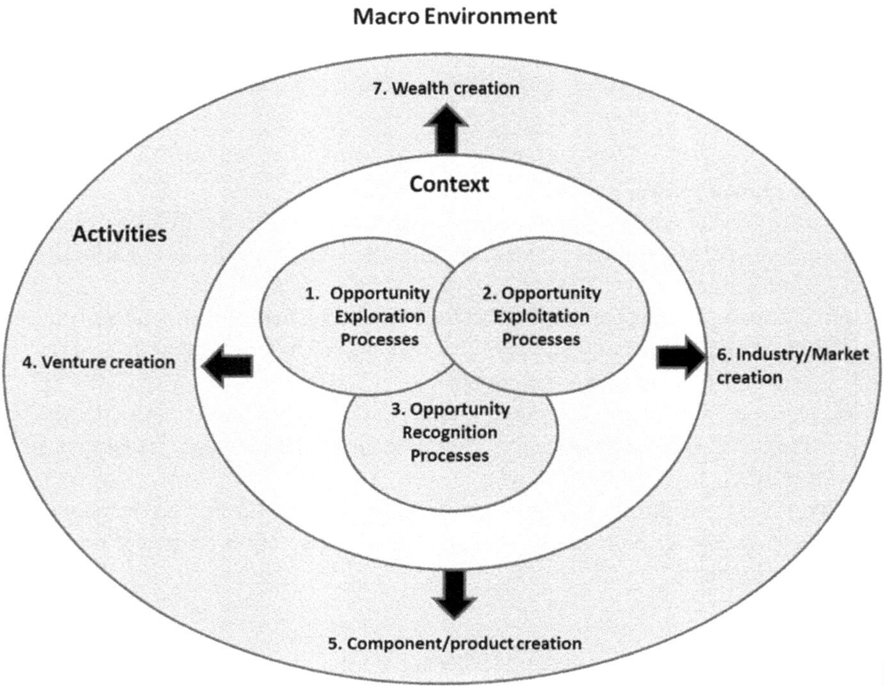

Fig. 1.4 The entrepreneurship domain. (Source: Brush et al. 2003)

by being alert to the discovery of opportunities for innovative new products, processes or markets. This 'entrepreneurial alertness' is not just a result of chance or luck, and is more than just the outcome of routine searching for information.

Entrepreneurs engage in a process of entrepreneurial discovery in which the search process is largely rational and involves specialised knowledge. For many entrepreneurs, the key is not that they have such specialised knowledge, but that they can identify the use of this knowledge to exploit market opportunities. The skills of the entrepreneur are their ability to marshal the specialist skills and knowledge of others and to configure resources for commercial benefit (Alvarez and Busenitz 2001).

According to Timmons (1999), the entrepreneur can be distinguished from inventors, managers and what he refers to as 'promoters' by their ability to combine high levels of creativity and innovation with high levels of general management skill, business know-how and networking.

Figure 1.5 illustrates this typology. It can be seen that inventors, who are often skilled technicians or scientists, possess high levels of creativity and innovative capacity, but they lack the management skills, networks and business acumen to commercialise their ideas. By contrast, the manager administrator is possessed of managerial competencies but often lacks the creativity and innovativeness to pursue entrepreneurial projects. Finally, the 'promoter' is the individual who lacks both the technical or creative skills as well as the managerial competencies. However, they often promote business initiatives without any real capacity to deliver on their promises.

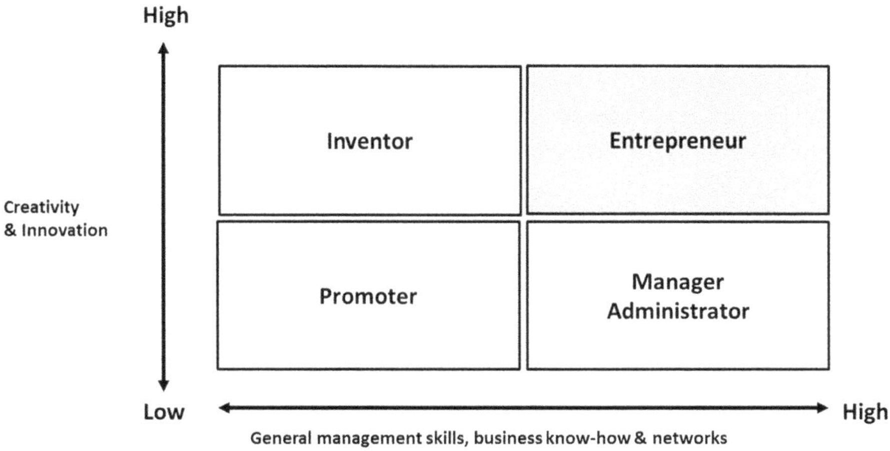

Fig. 1.5 Who is the real entrepreneur? (Source: Timmons 1999)

1.9 Defining Entrepreneurship

The complexity of entrepreneurship has led some to suggest that it is futile to try to find a single definition (Gartner et al. 1988). However, entrepreneurship has been defined in the following terms:

> Entrepreneurship is an activity that involves the discovery, evaluation and exploitation of opportunities to introduce new goods and services, ways of organising, markets, processes and raw materials through organising efforts that previously had not existed (Venkataraman 1997; Shane and Venkataraman 2000).

According to Shane (2003), this definition should be expanded to include the additional concepts of 'self-employment', by which a person undertakes work for personal profit rather than wages paid to them by others, and 'the foundation of a new business'. This latter concept includes the establishment of any for-profit or not-for-profit venture that did not previously exist. Also, linked to entrepreneurship definitions is the concept of performance, which can be in turn measured in terms of the survival, growth and profitability of the venture.

Entrepreneurship is a complex and multifaceted concept that has resulted in numerous definitions. In an attempt to provide a more precise definition, the OECD-Eurostat approach built on a theoretical foundation to define entrepreneurs, entrepreneurship and entrepreneurial activity as follows:

- *Entrepreneurs* – are those persons (business owners) who seek to generate value through the creation or expansion of economic activity by identifying and exploiting new products, processes or markets.
- *Entrepreneurial activity* – is enterprising human action in pursuit of the generation of value through the creation or expansion of economic activity by identifying and exploiting new products, processes or markets.

- *Entrepreneurship* – is the phenomenon associated with entrepreneurial activity (OECD 2009a).

It can be seen from these definitions that entrepreneurship is focused on the creation or expansion of economic activities through the development of new products, process or markets.

Other commonly-used terms are ‘enterprise’, ‘enterprise culture’ and ‘enterprise attributes’ that encompass a concept that is wider than entrepreneurship. These terms can be defined as follows:

- *Enterprise* – is the exercise of enterprise attributes in any task or environment.
- *Enterprise culture* – is a set of values, attitudes and beliefs supporting the exercise in the community of independent entrepreneurial behaviour in a business context.
- *Enterprise attributes* – include initiative, strong persuasive powers, moderate risk taking, flexibility, creativity, autonomy, problem-solving ability, need for achievement, imagination, leadership and hard work (Gibb 1988).

1.10 Managers, Entrepreneurs and Entrepreneurial Managers

Stevenson and Jarillo (1990) have suggested that entrepreneurial management within organisations is likely to be reflected by the following behaviours and outcomes:

1. Entrepreneurial firms pursue opportunity regardless of resources currently controlled.
2. The pursuit of opportunities is dependent upon the attitude of team members.
3. Entrepreneurial behaviour is positively correlated with the efforts of individuals in a position to identify opportunities.
4. Entrepreneurial firms lessen the negative consequences of failure when opportunities are pursued.
5. Entrepreneurial behaviour will be a function of team members’ ability to exploit opportunities.
6. Entrepreneurial firms facilitate internal and external networks, and allow gradual allocation and sharing of resources.

A key point of difference between the conventional corporate manager and the entrepreneurial manager is the ability to seek new opportunities and to use innovation to create dynamic growth within the firm. By contrast, the corporate manager is more about maintaining the *status quo* and ensuring efficiency of existing operations. The flexibility and high levels of innovation found in smaller entrepreneurial *gazelle* companies, however, are also required by larger corporations.

Gibb (1988) compares entrepreneurial and corporate managers in terms of their management styles. Entrepreneurial managers tend to operate well within a flat organisational structure, and tend to challenge owner legitimacy. They need to trust others for rewards, and they develop organic relationships over time. Corporate managers tend to operate well in a hierarchical organisational structure, under clear authority with clearly defined reward systems and rational structures. Entrepreneurs are also viewed as individuals who recognise opportunities, where others see chaos, to create the future (Kuratko and Hodgetts 2004).

Figure 1.6 illustrates some of the differences between the entrepreneurial and corporate style of manager. As can be seen, the corporate manager is focused on formality in planning and measuring success against resource acquisition and control. By contrast, the entrepreneurial manager is more concerned with an informal, market opportunity seeking approach.

Figure 1.7 illustrates the key factors identified by Gibb (1988) as being essential to the success of an independent entrepreneurial venture. These elements are crucial to the success of small firms, and reflect a situation where the ownership of the firm is held by the entrepreneur or entrepreneurial team who owns and manages the venture. For larger firms this issue of ownership is often a major challenge, and this is why many large corporations have provided generous share portfolios to CEOs and share ownership schemes to employees. However, these do not always offer the same level of risk – or the same level of return – to those who are engaged in the process.

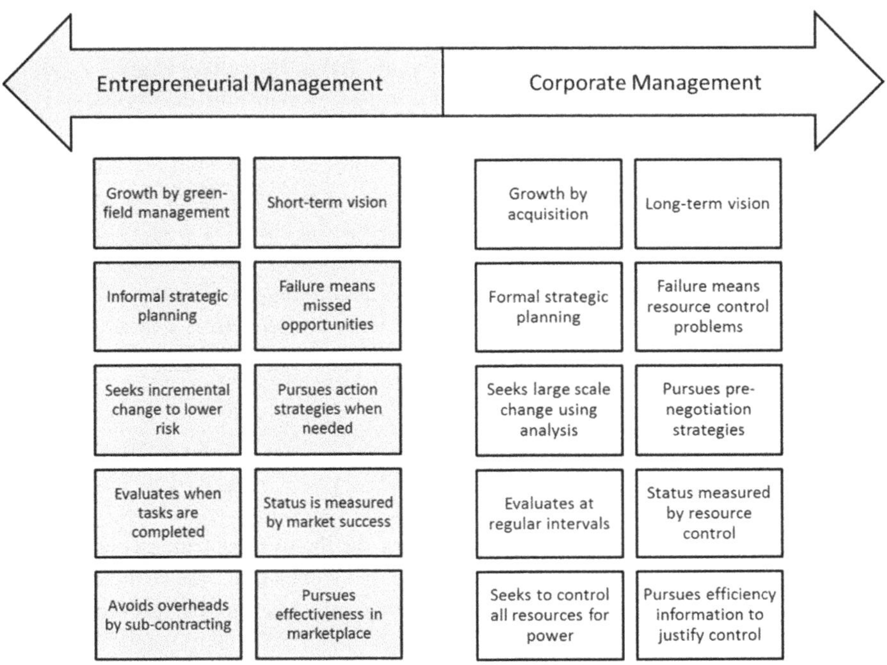

Fig. 1.6 Entrepreneurial vs. corporate management. (Source: Gibb 1988)

Fig. 1.7 Success in new ventures. (Source: Gibb 1988)

1.10.1 Entrepreneurs and Small Business

The process of launching a new business venture is often associated with entrepreneurship. There is little doubt that the launch of a new 'green fields' venture – or even the purchase of an established 'going concern' business – is in many ways an entrepreneurial behaviour. However, the two areas of entrepreneurship and small business management are conceptually different (Carland et al. 1984).

Entrepreneurial vs. Small Business Ventures

Small business venture. Any business that is independently owned and operated, not dominant in its field, and does not engage in any new marketing or innovative practices.

Entrepreneurial venture. A business that engages in at least one of Schumpeter's four categories of behaviour; that is, the principal goals of an entrepreneurial venture are profitability and growth and the business is characterised by innovative strategic practices.

Small business owner. An individual who establishes and manages a business for the principal purpose of furthering personal goals. Their business is their primary source of income and they view the business as an extension of them.

Entrepreneur. An individual who establishes and manages a business for the principal purposes of profit and growth. The entrepreneur is characterised principally by innovative behaviour and uses strategic management practices in their business.

Source: Carland et al. (1984).

On the one hand, entrepreneurship focuses on theoretical frameworks within which to understand entrepreneurs and the various forces that create, motivate and sustain their behaviour, in which ever context they may operate. On the other, small business management is frequently about the technical skills associated with business planning, financial, marketing and human resource management and their specificities in the context of a small structure (Solomon et al. 1999).

While the entrepreneur and the entrepreneurial venture are focused on innovation, profit and growth, the small business owner-manager is often more concerned with lifestyle and security. Small business owners can be entrepreneurial, while many entrepreneurs can own and manage large business enterprises. The distinction between these two areas is important, although it is also not always clearly defined.

By its nature, entrepreneurship involves creating new opportunities and leading change. The behaviours required of entrepreneurs are influenced by environment and by the degree of uncertainty or complexity encountered. Different environments demand different coping behaviours. The basic conditions under which small businesses operate stimulate enterprising behaviour.

However, not all small business owners are entrepreneurs. Michael Gerber (1993) has argued in his *E-Myth: Most Businesses Don't Work and What to Do About It* that most of the people who launch a new business venture are not *entrepreneurs*, rather they are *technicians*. For example, a plumber may start his own business, but may retire many years later having made little more than wages.

1.11 Defining Innovation

Innovation plays an integral role in entrepreneurial activities. Schumpeter (1934) introduced the concept of innovation as 'creative destruction' to the definition of entrepreneurship. He argued that 'new combinations' of behaviour create 'enterprise', and that the individuals who carry out this process are entrepreneurs. These combinations include the introduction of new goods, the quality of those goods, the method of production, the opening a new market, new sources of supply, and the new organisation of an industry.

Definitions of Innovation

Product innovation. Product innovation is the introduction of a good or service that is new or significantly improved with respect to its characteristics or intended uses. This includes significant improvements in technical specifications, components and materials, incorporated software, user friendliness or other functional characteristics.

Process innovation. Process innovation is the implementation of a new or significantly improved product or delivery method. This includes significant changes in techniques, equipment and/or software.

Marketing innovation. Marketing innovation is the implementation of a new marketing method involving significant changes in product design or packaging, product placement, product promotion or pricing.

Organisational innovation. Organisational innovation is the implementation of a new organisational method in a firm's business practices, workplace organisation or external relations.

Source: OECD (2005b).

Drucker (1985) suggests that innovation is a process that involves a set of principles:

1. Managers should be action oriented, and actively searching for new ideas and opportunities.
2. Innovations should be simple and easily understood by those who would be asked to adopt them.
3. Such innovations should also be customer focused, as this would make it more likely that the end-user would accept it.
4. It is better to start small and to build and develop the innovation from a modest base with planned incremental growth.
5. Any new idea should seek to fulfil a niche in the market and aim to dominate this niche.
6. Innovations need to be trialled, tested and reviewed to work out any flaws in the original design.
7. There are lessons to be learnt from failure that may in turn give rise to opportunities.
8. Innovation development, while dynamic, needs to be planned and should follow a milestone schedule.
9. Within firms it is important to reward successful new ideas as a way of encouraging others to do the same.
10. There is no substitute for sheer hard work.

Drucker (1985) supports the notion that innovation is central to identifying entrepreneurs and entrepreneurial behaviour, suggesting that successful entrepreneurs share a commitment to innovation. Innovation as a process of focused change in an enterprise's social or economic potential is the tool by which entrepreneurs create wealth (Drucker 1985).

1.12 Types of Innovation

According to Tushman and Nadler (1986) there are at least two kinds of innovation: product and process. The first deals with the design and development of new products and services or the improvement of existing ones, while the second deals with the way a product is made or a service is provided. Within each of these two categories are three *degrees* of innovation: (i) incremental; (ii) synthetic, and (iii) discontinuous.

Most product innovations are incremental, involving minor changes or enhancements to existing technologies. These are usually made in response to increasing competition, or in response to customer feedback. Once a new product is launched and established, the process of incremental improvement throughout its lifecycle is usually ongoing. In a similar manner, incremental process innovation seeks to continuously improve quality or lower costs via enhanced productivity or reduced cost.

	Product	Process
Incremental	Incremental product change.	Learning by doing.
Synthetic	Dominant designs DC-3, Boeing 707, IBM 360.	Major process improvements. Rotary kiln in cement manufacturing.
Discontinuous	Vacuum tubes to transistors. Piston to jet engines.	Individual wafer to planar process in semiconductor. Float-glass process.

Small

↕

Substantial Learning

Fig. 1.8 Types of innovation. (Source: Tushman and Nadler 1986)

As shown in Fig. 1.8, synthetic innovation involves the ability to combine existing ideas or technologies in creative ways to produce new products or processes. In the 1930s, the Douglas DC-3 incorporated the existing technologies already available within the aircraft industry, but did so in a combination that was superior to all other transport aircraft at the time. Boeing followed a similar approach in the 1960s with its B-707 airliner, and IBM did this during the same period with its 360 family of mainframe computers. Synthetic process innovations usually involve major advances in manufacturing or production e.g. rotary kilns in cement manufacturing.

The discontinuous innovation category of product or process involves radical new ideas that provide breakthrough technologies and advance industries to new levels. Examples include the shift from vacuum tubes to transistors, from pistons to jet engines in product innovation, from individual wafers to planar process in semiconductor manufacture, and from continuous grinding and polishing to float glass manufacturing.

In order to enhance the measurement of innovation, the Oslo Manual published by the OECD (2005b) has defined innovation into product and process categories, but also marketing and organisational categories. This reflects the breadth of areas in which innovation can occur. It can be technological in nature, encompassing new products and processes, or it can be non-technological and focused on new approaches to marketing and the administration and structuring of the organisation. There is a lot of different typologies of innovations, using different names for different categories of innovations and different criteria to define them (Garcia and Calantone 2002).

Innovation must contain a degree of novelty, and the type of innovation can be new to the firm, to the market or to the world. For example, it can be a new technological process adopted by a firm for the first time, but one that is already in use in other businesses. It is therefore new to the firm but not to the market or world. For

Type	Description	Examples
Invention	Totally new product, service or process.	Airplane – Wright bros. Light bulb – Edison. Telephone – A G Bell.
Extension	New use of existing product, service or process.	McDonald's – Kroc. Atari – Bushnell. Holiday Inn – Wilson.
Duplication	Creative replication of existing concept.	Wal-Mart – department store Pizza Hut – pizza parlor.
Synthesis	Combination of existing concepts into new use.	Federal Express – Fred Smith Merrill Lynch – home equity financing.

Fig. 1.9 A typology of innovation. (Source: Kuratko and Hodgetts 2004)

an innovation to be new to the market or the world implies a degree of novelty that is significant (OECD 2009b).

By nature, innovation can be both radical and incremental, with the former often disrupting established industries and requiring old technologies to be replaced by new. Figure 1.9 illustrates a classification of different *types* of innovation. These included four types: invention, extension, duplication and synthesis (Kuratko and Hodgetts 2004). Invention involves a completely new product or process, such as the invention of the electric light or the aeroplane during the nineteenth century. An extension takes an existing concept and develops it further, such as Ray Kroc with McDonald's, while duplication sees the replication of a well-established concept but places it into a market that has previously not had such a product or process. Finally, the concept of synthesis involves combining existing concepts into new arrangements that offer a completely new paradigm.

1.13 Innovation Lifecycles

Tushman and Nadler (1986) mapped the product and process innovations of various industries over time and developed a generalised model for how such innovations work. As shown in Fig. 1.10, during the introductory or 'emergence' stage of the lifecycle there is usually a high level of product innovation, and various competing types of product are frequently found within the market offering different 'standards' (e.g. Microsoft Windows, Apple Mac OS X and Linux in computer operating systems). Learning requirements within the firm are high.

During the growth stage, a dominant design frequently emerges that offers superior price, quality or design features. Once accepted by the market as the 'standard', the emphasis shifts from product to process innovation (Suárez and Utterback 1995). Learning requirements within the firm remain high as the need to mass produce the new products becomes the dominant focus.

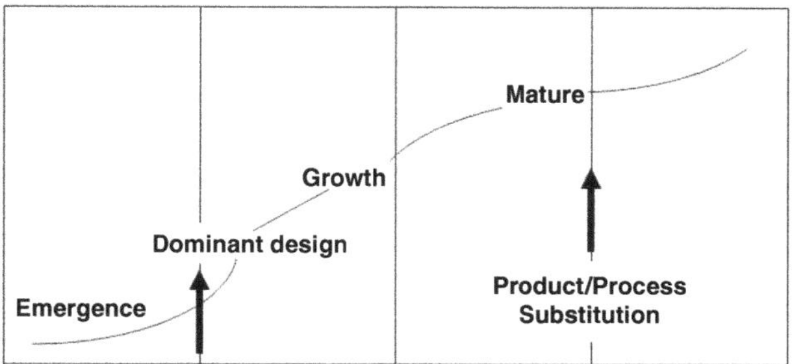

Dominant innovation types	Major Product Minor Process	Major Process Minor Product	Minor Product Minor Process	Major Product Minor Process
Learning requirements	High	High	Low	High

Fig. 1.10 Innovation lifecycles. (Source: Tushman and Nadler 1986)

Throughout the growth phase, the dominant product design replaces alternatives and eventually matures. Product and process innovation during this period are usually minor and incremental with lower learning requirements. The firm is focused on efficiency of production and distribution as it consolidates the market. Profits can be reaped during this period.

The dominant technology is likely to remain in place within the industry until challenged by a new emergent substitution threat, or the impact of external shocks such as government regulation. This triggers a new wave of product innovation and may eventually replace the dominant technology. Learning requirements are high for the firm.

Examples of Innovation Lifecycles

IBM's product innovation problems

During the 1960s IBM was the dominant player in the computing industry. Its experience with the 360 mainframe computers helped the company become the global leader in mainframe computing by the end of that decade. However, during the 1970s and 1980s technological changes in the form of mini-computers (Digital/NEC), super computers (Cray), and personal micro-computers (Apple) seriously challenged its leadership. This led IBM to create the IBM PC, but it lost the leadership of this technology to other companies and was in serious trouble by the 1990s. IBM's primary mistake was not seeing these new emerging technologies as serious threats to its existing business.

(continued)

Nokia's missed opportunities

Nokia Corporation entered the mobile phone industry in the 1990s and by 2006 was the world's market leader. However, despite its success and global reputation, the company found its ability to meet the challenge posed by the smartphone too difficult. The launch of the Apple iPhone in 2007 disrupted the existing mobile telephony market making traditional 2G phones obsolete. Even though Nokia had identified the emergence of the smartphone as a technological trend, it did not move fast enough to configure its product innovation pipeline to match Apple and other competitors such as Samsung. By 2012–2013 Nokia had lost billions and sold its mobile phone business to Microsoft at a bargain price.

Sources: Heller (1994), Mazzarol (2013).

1.14 Sources of Innovation

Successful innovations are simple and focused, requiring work and ingenuity. Drucker (1985) suggests that sources of innovation can come from some or all of the following:

- *Unexpected occurrences*. For example, IBM sold computers designed for banks to libraries – opening up new market opportunities. Also, the unexpected failure of the Ford Edsel car laid the foundations for future company successes, allowing Ford to compete with General Motors and leading to the design of the Mustang. Accessing opportunities in this area requires attention to be paid to failures and problems, and turning failures into opportunities.
- *Incongruities*. It is important to seek ideas within the existing process and economic realities of established industries. For example, steel manufacturing has matured and few dollars can be found for new investment. Shipping is also a mature sector. However, mini-mills for steel production and roll-on-roll-off ships to maximise time spent at sea are two examples of innovations. Both of these required a shift in *viewpoint* rather than technologies. Overnight package delivery by Federal Express is another example.
- *Process needs*. The combination of the invention of the Linotype fast newspaper printing machine and the emergence of the advertising industry allowed news to be distributed cheaply. In a similar manner, sugar-free and caffeine-free products, or the microwave oven adapted existing innovations to new processes to fill new market opportunities.
- *Industry and market changes*. Opportunities rarely fit in with the way an industry has traditionally approached the market. For example, Bio clip (the chemical shearing of sheep) or home health care offer new innovations.

- *Demographic changes*. The rate at which a population ages or changes its ethnic composition often has known lead times, but these are frequently neglected. The building of rest homes for the elderly is a trend in Australia in the face of such change. And, for example, robotics is used in Japan to fill in gaps due to a decline of blue-collar workers.
- *Changes in perception.* The exercise, health and diet industries have all seen innovation opportunities due to a growing concern for fitness among the ageing and frequently overweight population of the developed world.
- *New knowledge.* Basic research and invention – scientific, technical or social – often have the longest lead times of any innovation. For example, because new radical innovation takes a long time to commercialise, and because it involves high risk, it is important that any innovation of this kind possess the potential to be a platform intellectual property (IP). Once a patent is secured, the platform IP can generate a string of inventions and cumulative business opportunities.

The origin of the innovation is also an increasingly discussed point, as more and more firms try to find external inspiration for their innovative process.

> **For example,** ... A new breed of innovation—open innovation—is forcing firms to reassess their leadership positions, which reflect the performance outcomes of their business strategies. It is timely to juxtapose some new phenomena in innovation with the traditional academic view of business strategy (Chesbrough and Appleyard 2007, p. 57).

Firms have thus developed different strategies of securing ideas from external sources, but also of selling their innovation results to external actors, resulting in a greater porosity of the firm's frontiers (West and Bogers 2014).

1.14.1 Encouraging Entrepreneurship and Innovation

The importance of entrepreneurial activity to the economic development of national economies is now widely acknowledged by governments throughout the world. It is now common for governments to have well-defined policies and programs designed to stimulate entrepreneurship and to support the growth of small firms. In Europe, the 2003 *Green Paper – Entrepreneurship in Europe* (European Commission 2003) recommended a three-pronged approach to the enhancement of entrepreneurship. The first requirement was the need to reduce barriers to business development and growth, particularly within the small firms' sector. Such barriers include a lack of access to markets, lack of early stage venture financing, and poor management skills. This fosters the creation of entrepreneurial ecosystems providing, as a system, all the elements fostering the development of small firms (Mazzarol 2014).

Taxation and other compliance burdens were also viewed as a major impediment that required reform. This was the second area of need, with a call for taxation to reflect the risk and rewards of entrepreneurship. Finally, there was a perceived need to foster a more positive attitude toward entrepreneurs within the community.

Innovation is also viewed as a key area of importance for government policy. As noted earlier, innovation enhances the long run growth of the economy and has beneficial effects on labour productivity and job creation. Governments seek to stimulate innovation in order to secure a 'double dividend' in which they achieve short term economic growth and long-term reform of their national economies (OECD 2010a).

1.15 National Innovation Systems

An important focus for many national governments over the past 30 years has been the strengthening of their national innovation systems (NIS) whereby public investment in R&D leads to enhanced innovation and commercialisation in industry (Balzat and Hanusch 2004).

> **For example,** … A national innovation system is a set of distinct institutions which jointly and individually contribute to the development and diffusion of new technologies and which provides the framework within which governments form and implement policies to influence the innovation process. As such it is a system of interconnected institutions to create, store and transfer the knowledge, skills and artefacts which define new technologies (Metcalfe 1995, p. 412).

While the design of specific NIS varies from country to country, most comprise at least two broad elements. The first is a common innovation infrastructure (e.g. the technological sophistication of the country, investment in R&D, government support for innovation). The second is the cluster specific environment for innovation (e.g. competitive rivalry, ease of exit and entry, supplier/buyer power) found within the industries in which the firms are operating (Porter and Stern 2001).

The concept of the NIS was introduced by Lundvall (1985, 1998) and further developed by Freeman (1987) who analysed the success of the Japanese economy in terms of R&D and technology. The structure of NIS varies from country to country although their primary goal is to grow the overall level of R&D investment and commercialisation activity through a combination of direct government funding to basic research plus R&D tax concessions, technology transfer from public to private sectors, provision of common user infrastructure, intellectual property rights protection, and mechanisms to facilitate collaboration and venture capital investment (Johnson 2001; Trott 2007).

According to Johnson and Jacobsson (2000), the NIS has at least five distinct functions:

1. the creation of new knowledge;
2. focusing of research processes within the national scientific community;
3. facilitating access to resources and funding;
4. facilitating the development of positive externalities; and
5. facilitating market creation and development.

Park (2001) illustrates the application of these NIS principles to the South Korean economy within the context of national industry policy. The Korean War (1950–1953) left Korea devastated and the economy of the South was largely dependent on agriculture. In 1962, the first 5-Year Economic Development Plan was launched, targeting the creation of export-driven industrialisation. The focus was on large-scale enterprise and labour-intensive industries such as textiles, clothing and footwear.

In the 1970s, this program was extended to heavy industries e.g. chemicals, shipbuilding, automotive and petrochemicals. This fostered the rise of the *chaebol* system of industrial conglomerates and facilitated a transition, in the 1980s, into semiconductors and high-technology industries. During the 1990s, the Korean economy shifted to a more knowledge intensive model. The *Chaebols* created industrial cities that concentrated skilled labour as well as R&D centres and investment.

National and local governments sought to attract investment and skilled labour through the provision of infrastructure and education facilities. The Korea Institute of Science and Technology (KIST) and the Korea Advanced Institute of Science (KAIS) were established in the 1960s to foster R&D and to develop the basic technological foundations of the Korean state. During the 1970s, government policy focused on expanding the education system in applied technical and engineering disciplines. Government-funded R&D institutes were founded with strong links to local universities.

From the 1980s, the private sector began to replace the government in total R&D investment. Initially this was driven by the *Chaebols,* but in the 1990s it shifted to a series of regional innovation clusters comprising SMEs who forged cooperative networks within the *chaebol* supply chain (Park 2001).

More recently the idea has emerged that regional development could be enhanced by the implementation of "Economic Gardening" (EG). This originated in Littleton, Colorado, USA in 1989 as part of an entrepreneurial stimulation program (Gibbons 2010). This aims to encourage and facilitate the growth of existing SMEs rather than trying to create new ones. It is commonly targeted at regional economies with support to local firms. The concept of "gardening" was chosen to reflect the focus it has on the cultivation of existing businesses in an area, rather than the "hunting and gathering" approach typically associated with regional economic development, which seeks to attract large *'footloose'* companies into the region. It is still focused on encouraging entrepreneurship and innovation (Burgess 1996).

This type of regional economic development relies heavily on the development of networks, support to existing small firms, and the targeting of businesses that have moved beyond start-up and early-stage growth and have the potential and the desire to scale up. Such firms will need to employ innovation and entrepreneurial managerial approaches to achieve this growth. They will also need to grow outside their immediate regions and usually focus on national or international markets. However, the philosophy behind EG is that locally owned, home-grown companies are less likely to leave the area, taking jobs with them, when economic conditions change (Braun et al. 2014).

1.16 Strategies to Encourage Entrepreneurship

Gibb (1988) has suggested that entrepreneurship can be encouraged or facilitated by allowing people more opportunities to work in small- to medium-sized firms, or by taking greater responsibility for the operations of smaller sub-units of larger firms. If people have had parents, relatives or friends who have been self-employed, this can also encourage entrepreneurship. Some cultures also appear to foster more small business ownership, and this too can generate higher levels of entrepreneurial activity. The context also is of great importance and can contribute to stimulate entrepreneurial activity and innovation (Autio et al. 2014).

Figure 1.11 shows the key elements that are likely to contribute to fostering an entrepreneurial culture within the community. As can be seen, these include providing ample examples of successful small firms or entrepreneurs as well as an opportunity for people – and particularly children – to work inside entrepreneurial ventures and even practice enterprise activities. Learning how small firms operate and learning about the challenges that owner-managers from such businesses face is also likely to deliver positive benefits within a child's education. Finally, there is a need to foster active networks of people who can mutually support each other, and upon whom the nascent or novice entrepreneur can call for assistance or advice when required (Gibb 1988).

According to Venkataraman (2004), entrepreneurship, particularly that involving technological innovation, can be fostered in regions through the existence of seven intangibles:

1. *Focal points capable of producing novel ideas.* These can be R&D centres at universities or other public or privately-funded research organisations.
2. *Role models.* Role models can be a pool of local successful entrepreneurs who can serve as role models for nascent and novice entrepreneurs;
3. *Informal entrepreneurship forums.* These can be environments where local entrepreneurs can meet and exchange ideas and information, and where they can network with each other in socially convivial atmosphere;

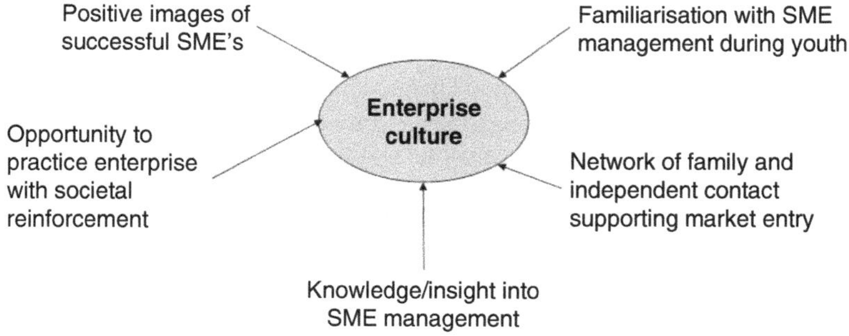

Fig. 1.11 Creating an enterprise culture. (Source: Gibb 1988)

4. *The creation of region-specific ideas.* Rather than seek to emulate what is already being done in other locations, regions need to develop their own original innovations;
5. *Safety nets.* The risks associated with entrepreneurial innovation are high and there needs to be a tolerance of failure and opportunities for entrepreneurs who have failed to restart new ventures building on the lessons they have learnt.
6. *Gateways to larger markets.* There must be access for local entrepreneurs to larger national or international markets as they seek to commercialise their innovations. The removal of trade barriers and the provision of high-quality telecommunications and transportation infrastructure are critical.
7. *Executive leadership.* Entrepreneurial ventures also need high quality management teams with the skills and experience to help the company grow.

The OECD (2010a) recommends the fostering of entrepreneurship through a strategy based on education and training. This is designed to address all levels of the education and training system from school level to university and industry or firm level programs.

OECD Agenda for Entrepreneurship Learning

- Build up entrepreneurship education in universities and higher education institutions.
- Strengthen vocational education and training programs for small business owner-managers and their employees.
- Embed teaching of an entrepreneurship mindset in school curricula and provide teacher training and support materials.
- Reinforce training in SMEs via in-company projects.
- Increase the use of informal learning sources.
- Strengthen local skills ecosystems through the engagement of employers, unions and individuals.

Source: OECD (2010a).

1.17 Strategies to Encourage Innovation

As discussed above, governments around the world are seeking to foster innovation within their economies through their NIS with a combination of direct and in-direct investments. It is now recognised that innovation and entrepreneurship are closely aligned and that programs that foster one are beneficial to the other. There has also been a shift from the previous focus on large scale enterprises towards SMEs.

The OECD (2010d) has outlined a strategy for encouraging innovation that is not only focused on science and technology. A principle of this strategy is that people should be empowered to innovate. This recognises the need to invest in human capital via the education and training system. Teacher education and support within science and technology fields – and the role of universities, technical training colleges and vocational schools – are highlighted. This includes entrepreneurship education and the opening up of the labour market to skilled immigrants. Consumer education should also focus on encouraging the diffusion of new technologies by enabling people to make informed choices.

A second principle of the strategy is that innovation in firms must be unleashed through enhanced support to start-ups and SMEs. There is a need to support innovative SMEs through reductions in business establishment costs, market entry barriers, access to financing, protection of IP rights, and reforms of the taxation and bankruptcy laws. A third principle of the strategy is that the creation, diffusion and application of knowledge are essential to the ability of firms and countries to innovate. There is a need for efficient communications networks with state-of-the-art broadband and ICT services, rail, road, air and sea transport systems. Also, of importance are the protection of IP rights and the effectiveness of the national patent systems. The OECD (2010d) suggests that innovation is a potential key to solving many of the world's problems, including climate change, poverty and economic stagnation. However, government policies must be focused on stimulating innovation.

OECD Recommendations to Encourage Innovation

- There must be a more strategic focus on the role of government innovation policy to deliver stronger, cleaner and fairer growth.
- Policies must be broadened to encourage innovation in areas that are not just focused on science and technology.
- Education and training systems need to be designed to empower people to be creative and engage in innovation.
- Government policy should focus on supporting SMEs and their role in generating breakthrough innovations and new jobs.
- There should be recognition of the fundamental role of scientific research to enable radical innovation and to provide a foundation for future innovation.
- The diffusion and application of knowledge should be improved via well-functioning networks and markets.
- Government should invest in high-speed broadband networks as they are now a key platform for innovation.
- There should be new approaches and governance mechanisms for international co-operation in science and technology to help address global challenges and to share costs and risks.
- Attention should be given to developing frameworks for measuring the broader, more networked concept of innovation and its impacts in order to guide policy-making.

Source: OECD (2010d)

References

Alvarez, S. A., & Busenitz, L. W. (2001). The entrepreneurship of resource-based theory. *Journal of Management, 27*(12), 755–775.

ASBFEO. (2017). *Small business counts: Small business in the Australian economy*. Australian Government, Canberra, Australian Small Business and Family Enterprise Ombudsman (ASBFEO).

Autio, E., Kenney, M., Mustar, P., Siegel, D., & Wright, M. (2014). Entrepreneurial innovation: The importance of context. *Research Policy, 43*(7), 1097–1108.

Balzat, M., & Hanusch, H. (2004). Recent trends in the research on national innovation systems. *Journal of Evolutionary Economics, 14*(2), 197–210.

Baumol, W. J. (1968). Entrepreneurship in economic theory. *American Economic Review, 58*(2), 64–71.

Bosma, N., & Levie, J. (2010). *Global Entrepreneurship Monitor: 2009 executive report*. Babson Park/Santiago: Babson College and Universidad del Desarrollo.

Bracha, A., Burke, M. A., & Khachiyan, A. (2015). *Changing patterns in informal work participation in the United States 2013–2015*. Federal Reserve Bank of Boston: Current Policy Perspectives.

Brännback, M., Carsrud, A. L., & Kiviluoto, N. (2014). *Understanding the myth of high growth firms: The theory of the greater fool* (Springer Briefs in Business). New York/Dordrecht/Heidelberg/London: Springer.

Braun, P., Harman, J., & Paton, F. (2014). Economic gardening: Capacity building for stronger regions. *Journal of Economic and Social Policy, 16*(1), 1–27.

Brinkley, I. (2016). *In search of the gig economy*, August, Lancaster University, The Work Foundation.

Brush, C. G., Duhaime, I. M., Gartner, W. B., Stewart, A., Katz, J., Hitt, M., Alvarez, S. A., Meyer, D., & Venkataraman. (2003). Doctoral education in entrepreneurship. *Journal of Management, 29*(3), 309–311.

Burgess, P. (1996). *The high performance community as an economic development model*. Denver, February, Draft Paper, Center for the New West.

Carland, J. W., Hoy, F., Boulton, W. R., & Carland, J. A. C. (1984). Differentiating entrepreneurs from small business owners: A conceptualization. *Academy of Management Review, 9*(2), 354–359.

Chesbrough, H. W., & Appleyard, M. M. (2007). Open innovation and strategy. *California Management Review, 50*(1), 57–76.

Coad, A., Daunfeldt, S.-O., Hölzl, W., Johansson, D., & Nightingale, P. (2014). High-growth firms: Introduction to the special section. *Industrial and Corporate Change, 23*(1), 91–112.

Drucker, P. (1985). *Innovation and entrepreneurship*. Oxford: Butterworth-Heinemann.

Drucker, P. (2002). The discipline of innovation. *Harvard Business Review, 80*(8), 95–106.

European Commission. (2003). *Green paper – Entrepreneurship in Europe*. Commission of the European Communities: Brussels.

Freeman, C. (1987). *Technology and economic performance: Lessons from Japan*. London: Pinter.

Garcia, R., & Calantone, R. (2002). A critical look at technological innovation typology and innovativeness terminology: A literature review. *Journal of Product Innovation Management, 19*(2), 110–132.

Gartner, W. B., Carland, J. W., Hoy, F., & Carland, J. A. (1988). Who is the entrepreneur? Is the wrong question. *American Journal of Small Business, 12*(4), 11–23.

GEM. (1999). *Global Entrepreneurship Monitor: National entrepreneurship assessment – United States of America* (p. 4). Kansas City: Kauffman Centre for Entrepreneurial Leadership.

GEM. (2018). *Global Entrepreneurship Monitor: Global report 2017/18*. Regents Park, London: Global Entrepreneurship Research Association (GERA), London Business School. www.gem-consortium.org

Gibb, A. (1988). The enterprise culture: Threat or opportunity? *Management Decision, 26*(4), 5–12.
Gibbons, C. (2010). Economic gardening. *Economic Development Journal, 9*(3), 5–11.
Haltiwanger, J., Jarmin, R., & Miranda, J. (2009). *Business dynamics and statistics briefing: Jobs created from business start-ups in the United States*. Ewing Marion Kauffman Foundation: Kansas City.
Heller, R. (1994). *The fate of IBM*. London: Little Brown & Co.
Hindle, K., & Rushworth, S. (2004). *GEM – Global entrepreneurship monitor, a study of Australian entrepreneurship in 2003, Westpac GEM*. Australia: Swinburne University of Technology.
Hirsch-Kreinsen, H., Hahn, K., & Jacobsen, D. (2008). The low-tech issue. In H. Hirsch-Kreinsen & D. Jacobsen (Eds.), *Innovation in low-tech firms and industries* (pp. 3–24). Edward Elgar: Cheltenham.
Hirschman. (1958). *The strategy of economic development*. New Haven: Yale University Press.
Jarillo, J. C. (1993). *Strategic networks: Creating the borderless organization*. Oxford: Butterworth-Heinemann.
Johnson, A., (2001). *Functions in innovation systems approaches*. Communication at DRUID conference “Nelson & Winter”, Aalborg, June.
Johnson, A., & Jacobsson, S. (2000). *The emergence of a growth industry: A comparative analysis of the German, Dutch and Swedish wind turbine industry*. J.A. Schumpeter Society conference, Change, Development and Transformation, University of Manchester, UK.
Kagermann, H., Wahlster, W., & Helbig, J. (2013). *Recommendations for implementing the strategic initiative INDUSTRIE 4.0*. Berlin, Industrie 4.0 Working Group of Acatech.
Kelley, D., Singer, S., & Herrington, M. (2016). GEM 2015/16 global report, GEM Global Entrepreneurship Monitor, Babson College, Universidad del Desarrollo, Universiti Tun Abdul Razak, Tecnológico de Monterrey, International Council for Small Business (ICSB): GEM Consortium.
Kirzner, I. (1997). Entrepreneurial discovery and the competitive market process: An Austrian approach. *Journal of Economic Literature, 35*(1), 60–85.
Knight, F. H. (1933). *Risk, uncertainty and profit*. London: London School of Economics and Political Science.
Kuratko, D., & Hodgetts, R. (2004). *Entrepreneurship: Theory, process, practice* (6th ed.). Thomson South-Western: Mason Ohio.
Liao, Y., Deschamps, F., Loures, E., & Ramos, L. (2017). Past, present and future of industry 4.0 – a systematic literature review and research agenda proposal. *International Journal of Production Research, 55*(12), 3609–3629.
Lundvall, B.-Å. (1985). Product innovation and user-producer interaction, industrial development. In *Research series 31*. Aalborg: Aalborg University Press.
Lundvall, B.-Å. (1998). Why study national systems and national styles of innovations? *Technology Analysis & Strategic Management, 10*(4), 407.
Martin, R. L., & Osberg, S. (2007). *Social entrepreneurship: The case for definition* (Stanford social innovation review). Stanford University.
Mazzarol, T. (2013). *Nokia sells out – Case study*. www.cemi.com.au. Centre for Entrepreneurial Management and Innovation (CEMI).
Mazzarol, T. (2014). *Growing and sustaining entrepreneurial ecosystems: What they are and the role of government policy*. White Paper Small Enterprise Australia and New Zealand, SEAANZ: 18 pages.
McKeown, T., & Phillips, K. (2014). *Growing and sustaining entrepreneurial ecosystems: Recognising the importance of the ‘Nano-Business’*, White Paper WP03-2014. www.seaanz.org, Small Enterprise Association of Australia and New Zealand (SEAANZ).
McKeown, T., Mazzarol, T., Rice, J., Soutar, G., Hanson, B., & Adapa, S. (2018). *Inspiring future workplaces: An Australian and NZ small business perspective*. www.seaanz.org, Small Enterprise Association of Australia and New Zealand (SEAANZ).
Messeghem, K., & Torrès, O. (2015). *Les grands auteurs en entrepreneuriat et PME*. Cormelles le Royal (F), Editions EMS.

Metcalfe, J. S. (1995). Technology systems and technology policy in an evolutionary framework. *Cambridge Journal of Economics, 19*(1), 25–46.

Moeuf, A., Pellerin, R., Lamouri, S., Tamayo-Giraldo, S., & Barbaray, R. (2018). The industrial management of SMEs in the era of industry 4.0. *International Journal of Production Research, 56*(3), 1118–1136.

Nightingale, P., & Coad, A. (2014). Muppets and gazelles: Political and methodological biases in entrepreneurship research. *Industrial and Corporate Change, 23*(1), 113–143.

OECD. (2005a). *SME entrepreneurship outlook 2005*. www.oecd.org/bookshop. Organisation for Economic Co-operation and Development.

OECD. (2005b). *Oslo manual: The measurement of scientific and technological activities: Proposed guidelines for collecting and interpreting technological innovation data*. Oslo: Organisation of Economic Co-operation and Development, European Union, Eurostat.

OECD. (2009a). *Measuring entrepreneurship: A collection of indicators*. Paris: OECD-Eurostat Entrepreneurship Indicators Programme.

OECD. (2009b). *Innovation in firms: A microeconomic perspective*. Paris: Organisation for Economic, Co-operation and Development.

OECD. (2010a). *SMEs, entrepreneurship and innovation*. Paris: Organisation for Economic Co-operation and Development.

OECD. (2010b). *OECD economic outlook*. Paris: Organisation for Economic Co-operation and Development.

OECD. (2010c). *High-growth enterprises: What governments can do to make a difference*. Paris: Organisation for Economic Co-operation and Development.

OECD. (2010d). *The OECD innovation strategy: Getting a head start on tomorrow*. Paris: Organisation for Economic Co-operation and Development.

OECD. (2016). *Financing SMEs and entrepreneurs 2016: An OECD scoreboard*. Paris: Organisation for Economic Co-operation and Development (OECD) Publishing.

Park, S. O. (2001). Regional innovation strategies in the knowledge-based economy. *GeoJournal, 53*(1), 29–38.

Pilat, D., & Baygan, G. (2001). *Statistics on women's entrepreneurship*. Paris: Organisation for Economic Co-Operation and Development.

Porter, M. E., & Stern, S. (2001). Innovation: Location matters. *MIT Sloan Management Review, 42*(4), 28–36.

Productivity Commission. (2017). *Shifting the dial: 5 year productivity review* (Supporting paper no. 8: Upskilling and retraining). Canberra: Australian Government, Productivity Commission.

Schumpeter, J. (1934). *The theory of economic development*. New York: Harvard University Press.

Schwab, K. (2016). *The fourth industrial revolution*. London: Portfolio Penguin.

Schwab, K. (2018). *Shaping the fourth industrial revolution*. Geneva: World Economic Forum. www.weforum.org

Shane, S. (2003). *A general theory of entrepreneurship: The individual-opportunity nexus*. Cheltenham/Northampton: Edward Elgar Publishing.

Shane, S., & Venkataraman, S. (2000). The promise of entrepreneurship as a field of research. *Academy of Management Review, 26*(1), 13–17.

Solomon, G., Tarabishy, A., Winslow, E., & D'Onofrio, S. (1999). *A comparison of the empirical investigation into entrepreneurship education in the United States and internationally*. Innovation and Economic Development: The Role of Entrepreneurship and Small and Medium Enterprises, Naples, Italy., Conference Proceedings, 44th ICSB World Conference, 20–23 June.

Stevenson, H., & Jarillo, J. (1990). A paradigm of entrepreneurship: Entrepreneurial management. *Strategic Management Journal, 11*(Special Issue), 17–27.

Suárez, F. F., & Utterback, J. M. (1995). Dominant designs and the survival of firms. *Strategic Management Journal, 16*(6), 415–430.

Sveiby, K.-E. (1997). *The new organizational wealth*. San Francisco: Berret-Koehler.

Thurik, R. (2009). Chapter 10: Entreprenomics: Entrepreneurship, economic growth and policy. In Z. Acs, D. Audretsch, & R. Strom (Eds.), *Entrepreneurship, growth and public policy* (pp. 219–249). Cambridge: Cambridge University Press.

Timmons, J. (1999). *New venture creation: Entrepreneurship for the 21st century* (5th ed.). McGraw-Hill International Editions.

Trott, P. (2007). "Book review: The management of technology and innovation: A strategic approach", edited by Margaret White and Garry Bruton. *R&D Management, 37*(4), 379–380.

Tushman, M., & Nadler, D. (1986). Organizing for innovation. *California Management Review, 28*(3), 74–92.

Venkataraman, S. (1997). The distinctive domain of entrepreneurship research: An editor's perspective'. In J. Katz & R. Brockhaus (Eds.), *Advances in entrepreneurship, firm emergence, and growth* (Vol. 3, pp. 119–138). Greenwich: JAI Press.

Venkataraman, S. (2004). Regional transformation through technological entrepreneurship. *Journal of Business Venturing, 19*(1), 153–167.

WEF. (2017). *Digital transformative initiative: Mining and metals industry*. www.reports.weforum.org, World Economic Forum.

West, J., & Bogers, M. (2014). Leveraging external sources of innovation: A review of research on open innovation. *Journal of Product Innovation Management, 31*(4), 814–831.

Xu, L. D., Xu, E. L., & Li, L. (2018). Industry 4.0: State of the art and future trends. *International Journal of Production Research, 56*(8), 2941–2962.

2 The Entrepreneur

2.1 Introduction

> I put my balls on the line and I thought – I am just going for it. I have self-belief that no matter what happens there will always be opportunities. You don't always need money to do them, but it helps a lot.
>
> Source: Andrew, entrepreneur and successful property developer.

This chapter examines some of the psychological and social trait theories of entrepreneurship as well as environmental factors likely to trigger enterprising behaviour. Also examined are the roles of creativity and achievement drive, plus concepts for evaluating individual entrepreneurial traits. The chapter also overviews the concept of entrepreneurial orientation.

A particular focus of this chapter is to assess enterprise tendencies by using the *General Enterprise Tendencies* (GET) test developed by Sally Caird at The Open University in the United Kingdom. Interest in identifying entrepreneurs in terms of their traits and behaviour has been generated by the notion of a link between economic growth and business start-ups. Entrepreneurs are often viewed as being radically different from the mainstream, and yet still difficult to characterise. The impetus behind exploring the characteristics of entrepreneurs stems from the vast array of definitions employed in the literature. Despite their shortcomings, psychological tests may be used to identify entrepreneurial types, to compare the enterprising nature of individuals, and to establish differences between entrepreneurs (Caird 1993). However, it should be noted that there is no test that can identify an entrepreneur and the GET test only measures enterprise tendencies, not whether a person is or is not an entrepreneur.

T. Mazzarol, S. Reboud, *Entrepreneurship and Innovation*, Springer Texts in Business and Economics, https://doi.org/10.1007/978-981-13-9412-6_2

2.2 Common Characteristics of Entrepreneurs

An entrepreneur is an enterprising person with enterprising attributes or traits (Gibb 1988). Some individuals appear to be innately more enterprising than others, whilst some develop enterprising attributes through education and experience. Some of the key attributes that define enterprising behaviour are initiative, flexibility, strong powers of persuasion, the ability to take acceptable risks, creativity, autonomy, problem-solving ability, the need for achievement, imagination, leadership, strong belief in making your own destiny, and the capacity for hard work (Gibb 1988).

Research into the factors associated with entrepreneurship and new venture creation has focused on the combination of personality traits and the environment. Early empirical research was very much focused on the psychological characteristics of business founders, although that research was not closely linked to contemporary developments in psychology. During the 1950s and 1960s major studies were undertaken by researchers in psychology and sociology seeking to understand the characteristics and determinants of entrepreneurship (Landström et al. 2012).

A trait approach was often adopted, and almost endless lists of entrepreneurial traits were suggested (Hornaday 1982). For example, factors such as need for achievement (McClelland 1961), risk- taking propensity (Brockhaus 1980), locus of control (Brockhaus 1982), tolerance of ambiguity (Schere 1982), and desire for personal control (Greenberger and Sexton 1988) have all been identified and examined as possible traits associated with entrepreneurial behaviour. This approach eventually reached a dead end, as it could only partially answer the question: 'What makes people found new firms?' (Landström et al. 2012).

It has been convincingly argued that personal background characteristics have a more reliable influence on the decision to found one's own firm than psychological traits (Reynolds 1991; Stanworth et al. 1989). Discussion has also addressed numerous other background factors linked to the personality, e.g. previous employment (Storey 1982; Ronstadt 1988); family background (Scott and Twomey 1988; Matthews and Moser 1995); gender (Buttner and Rosen 1989; Kolvereid et al. 1993); education (Storey 1982); ethnic membership (Aldrich 1980; Aldrich and Waldinger 1990); and religion (Weber 1930).

A response to the limited success of the trait approach has been to view enterprise creation in context. One way of doing this is to apply a more aggregate level of analysis and to look for regional or national level variables that can explain variations in the rate of new enterprise formation (Aldrich 1990). This approach has been relatively successful, and fairly strong relationships have been established. Specht (1993) distinguished five main contextual factors affecting organisation formation, and these include: social, economic, political, infrastructure development, and market emergence factors. This recognises the importance of environmental context on the entrepreneurial process.

In essence, the research that has been undertaken into entrepreneurship and the factors that motivate or trigger it suggests that combinations of internal and external forces are at work (Shane 2003). Although some personality related characteristics or traits appear to be strongly associated with entrepreneurs, they usually need to be placed into an environmental context and linked to a triggering event. From the internal perspective, Kuratko and Hodgetts (1998) identify 17 characteristics likely either to be found among entrepreneurs or at least to be associated with the process of enterprise. These are discussed as follows.

1. *Commitment, determination and perseverance.* New ventures and their sustained growth require commitment and a willingness to persist in the face of obstacles. Entrepreneurs are often willing to take on challenges and find ways to overcome problems – even when others have decided to give up.
2. *Drive to achieve.* A major characteristic of entrepreneurs is their ability to set goals and strive to achieve them. The sense of satisfaction that comes from seeing their goals achieved and dreams fulfilled is often a major motivator for entrepreneurial people.
3. *Opportunity orientation.* Identifying potential opportunities for new ventures, innovations or initiatives is a hallmark of entrepreneurs. The entrepreneur is recognised as being good at environmental scanning and screening potential opportunities (Bhide 1994).
4. *Persistent problem-solving.* Entrepreneurs are typically faced with new problems in which they are learning how to do things for the first time, or actually doing things that have not previously been done. This means that they are continuously faced with problems to solve and must possess or develop skills in this area.
5. *Internal locus of control.* An internal locus of control suggests that the person believes they are responsible for their own destiny and not dependent upon others or in the hands of fate. Most entrepreneurial people have strong self-belief and the sense that they make their own luck.
6. *Calculated risk taking.* The launch of a new business venture or the development of a new innovation is frequently associated with risk. For entrepreneurs, the need to accept and learn to deal with risk is a major attribute. However, entrepreneurs are calculated in their risk taking rather than simply being risk-taking gamblers, and should be viewed as able to successfully manage risk.
7. *Tolerance for failure.* Risk taking implies that there is the chance of failure, and many new ventures and innovations do not succeed. The entrepreneurial person is likely to be ready to accept failure as a process of learning and to accept a trial and error approach to their life. Many of the most successful entrepreneurs in the US have experienced one or more business failures in their past (Sexton and Seale 1997).
8. *Creativity and innovativeness.* The desire to create has been found to be a major motivating factor in the formation of new business ventures (Mazzarol et al. 2001). Creativity is also the key source of innovation, and it is not uncommon to find that many entrepreneurs are also creative individuals.
9. *Self-confidence and optimism.* A strong belief in oneself and a positive or optimistic outlook is an important quality for entrepreneurs to possess. In difficult times when risks are high and there is a high level of uncertainty, such optimism and self-confidence is a valued way of maintaining focus and motivation.

10. *Team building.* A key capability of the entrepreneur is the ability to build and lead teams. Few successful business ventures and new innovations have been developed by single individuals working alone. It is vital for the entrepreneur to know how to seek help and how to attract to their cause people who can assist.
11. *Initiative and responsibility.* Any business venture that is to grow beyond a micro-enterprise will require its leadership to demonstrate a strong sense of initiative and to accept responsibility. Entrepreneurs are able to accept responsibilities and are proactive rather than passive in dealing with issues.
12. *Seeking feedback.* The ability to accept constructive criticism and to look for assistance and advice is a feature of successful entrepreneurs. For example, the willingness to find and use professional business advisors has been demonstrated to be associated with enhanced profitability and success among small business owners (Kent 1994).
13. *Tolerance for ambiguity.* By its nature, entrepreneurship involves trying new ideas and launching new business ventures. Frequently this involves breaking new ground or doing things that have not been tried before. The entrepreneur must therefore have a high tolerance for ambiguity and feel comfortable operating in uncertain environments.
14. *Integrity and reliability.* Some of the issues that have blighted the image of the entrepreneur are that of integrity and honesty. While there have been examples of so-called 'entrepreneurs' who used their business ventures to build their own wealth at the expense of investors, these cases are still a minority. The majority of entrepreneurs have a high level of personal integrity and use their word as their bond. They have learnt that they must win the trust of others to achieve their goals, and that dishonesty will mean a closing off of such support.
15. *High energy level.* The ability to take on new business ventures and to lead change requires a lot of work, and entrepreneurs are typically very busy people with heavy workloads. Stamina and the capacity to work long hours means that entrepreneurs will need high energy levels.
16. *Vision.* A common feature among many entrepreneurs is their strong sense of vision, i.e. having a focus and direction for their venture and for their own personal ambitions. Also important is their ability to share this vision with others to enlist their support to the cause.
17. *Independence.* Finally, most entrepreneurs are characterised by a desire for autonomy and a capacity to undertake complex and difficult tasks independently of others. A key motivator for people wanting to start their own business is a desire to work for themselves (Volery et al. 1997).

These attributes are not isolated only to entrepreneurs, but are found among a wide spread of the population. These enterprising behaviours, skills and attributes can be demonstrated by most people to some degree. Some people will be more enterprising than others. Each will have a different mix of enterprising attributes, and these behaviours and skills can be used in a variety of contexts – not just business or small business.

2.3 Are Entrepreneurs Born or Made?

A strong emphasis within the field of entrepreneurship research has been placed on the causes of entrepreneurial behaviour, conceptualising entrepreneurship as the psychological characteristic of individuals (Stevenson and Jarillo 1990). This research theme can be traced back to Collins and Moore (1964) who identified the need for independence as a core trait of entrepreneurs. The psychological trait theory of entrepreneurship has been expanded by numerous researchers over the last 30 years and now incorporates locus of control and risk-tendency (Brockhaus 1980; Brockhaus and Horwitz 1985).

Entrepreneurial Traits

- Recognising and taking advantage of opportunities
- Resourceful
- Creative
- Visionary
- Independent thinking
- Hard working
- Optimistic
- Innovative
- Willing to take risks
- Able to provide leadership for others

Entrepreneurs have been noted for their need for achievement and their willingness to take calculated risks to achieve their goals, as well as having a tolerance for ambiguity, an internal locus of control (the ability to view the future as being within your own control), an ability to set goals, and self-efficacy (a belief in your ability to take on a task and succeed) (Cunningham and Lischeron 1991; Shane et al. 2003).

A common trait among entrepreneurial people is their desire to achieve, and they display a high need to work hard and achieve something meaningful. Need for achievement (McClelland 1961) may act as a trigger for entrepreneurial behaviour in certain circumstances, but is not always a good predictor. Entrepreneurial activity also involves the measurement and taking of risks regarding financial success, career progressions, family relationships and personal wellbeing (Liles 1974; Saracheck 1978). Entrepreneurs frequently show a preference for moderate risk-taking under conditions of limited control.

Despite the emphasis on trait theories in entrepreneurship research, this approach has been criticised because of the difficulties of making a causal link between psychological traits and entrepreneurial behaviour (Cooper et al. 1988), and its ties to small business management. However, certain psychological trait research can provide important insights into the antecedents to entrepreneurial behaviour. Nevertheless, it is not true that some people are natural born entrepreneurs. In fact, everyone has the capacity for entrepreneurial behaviour, what they need to become entrepreneurial is the right conditions and motivation.

2.4 Entrepreneurial Motivation

Brockhaus (1987) found that around 60% of entrepreneurs decide to start a business before they decide upon what type of business they want to create. Many are motivated by unsatisfactory employment. Motives for starting a new venture include the desire for autonomy, for feedback, greater financial returns, the desire for completion of a task, and the identification of unexplored opportunities. Necessity entrepreneurs may be less likely to create new products, as the basis for their motivation tends to be unemployment or underemployment rather than the pull of an exciting opportunity (Shapero 1985). However, job dissatisfaction, while a potential motivator for venture creation, remains at odds with the concept of the entrepreneur as an innovator..

Morrison (2000) views entrepreneurial motivation as having its foundations in the person and their intuition, as well as in society and in the culture, arguing that culture is much more holistic than a simple economic function. Culture is a critical component of entrepreneurial behaviour because it helps to form an individual's attitude towards entrepreneurship (Vernon-Wortzel and Wortzel 1987).

A favourable environment for entrepreneurial behaviour combines social, political and education attributes with values entrepreneurship (Timmons 1999). The conditioning of children through the education system and the reinforcement of attitudes by family members impacts the development of characteristics associated with entrepreneurial behaviour.

Entrepreneurship tends to pervade family life, placing family background at the centre of the development of entrepreneurial traits. If the entrepreneur has experience of the outcomes of entrepreneurship through family ties, they are likely to be more prepared for their own activities. Family support of entrepreneurial activities can help to sustain a venture (Deakin 1996). Extended family can also play an important role in providing access to funds and markets. Additionally, entrepreneurial activities tend to be fostered in those countries with egalitarian, democratic societies (e.g. US and Australia) (Morrison 2000).

Greenberger and Sexton (1988) also suggest that new business ventures are fostered by several key factors. The first of these is entrepreneurial vision, where the vision or idea of the prospective business becomes a key focus for the nascent entrepreneur. Having a specific goal and agenda for accomplishment, usually an abstract image, such a vision may be formed into intentions and strategic orientation. Essentially, if you can visualise something, you can usually achieve it. Also important is the desire for control by the nascent entrepreneur. An individual's perception of the relationship between their actions and outcomes is important. If a person feels that they cannot control their own destiny, they will not adopt a particularly entrepreneurial orientation.

Other potentially important influences are internal and external factors working within the nascent entrepreneur and their immediate environment. The ability of a person to identify opportunity, believe in their ability to manage a firm effectively, possess expertise that can be developed into a venture, and the capacity to then develop a product or process for a niche market is critical. External influences may involve a precipitating event such as forced redundancy or the freedom that might come from seeing children leave home. Family support and a supportive social and professional environment are also important (Greenberger and Sexton 1988).

2.5 Models of Entrepreneurial Motivation

Academic research has sought to understand the nature of entrepreneurial motivation with the development and testing of conceptual models. The model of entrepreneurial motivation (Naffziger et al. 1994) illustrated in Fig. 2.1 highlights the role that motivation and ego-drive play in the establishment of a new business venture. The model assumes that an entrepreneur's willingness to establish a business will be triggered by the interaction between personal characteristics, environment and goals. These will be mediated by the nature of the business environment and, if all conditions are right, the idea will form. The entrepreneur will make a choice to initiate their venture via an assessment of the levels of risk they face. If the expected rewards (both intrinsic and extrinsic) are suitably encouraging, they will develop their plan and engage in the venture. If they do not continue to see the returns for effort, the venture may be abandoned.

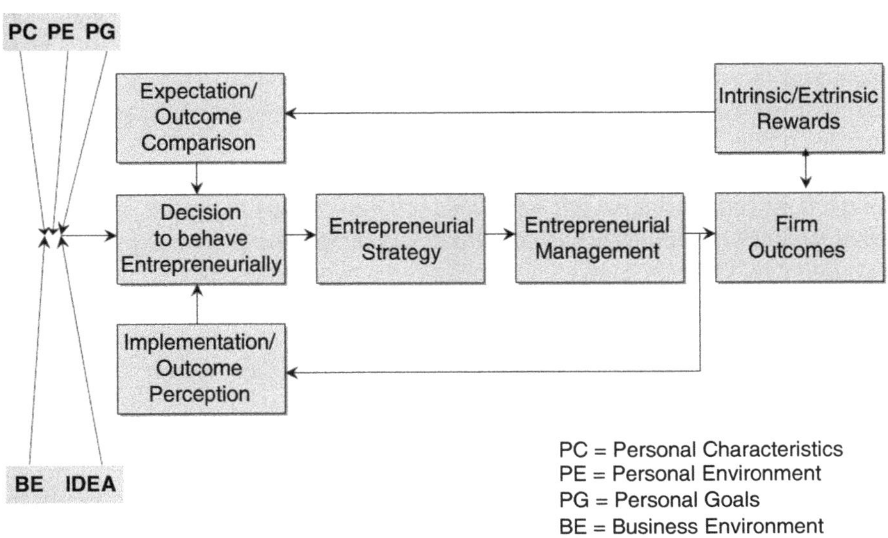

Fig. 2.1 Model of entrepreneurial motivation. (Source: Naffziger et al. 1994)

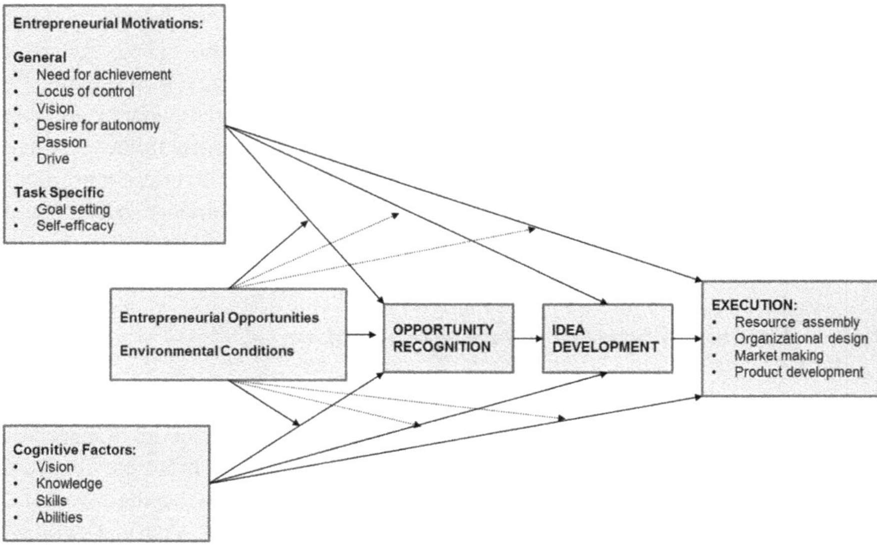

Fig. 2.2 Model of entrepreneurial motivation and the entrepreneurship process. (Source: Shane et al. 2003)

Shane et al. (2003) developed their own model of how entrepreneurial motivation operates within the entrepreneurship process. This is reproduced in Fig. 2.2. It can be seen that the elements that comprise entrepreneurial behaviour are both general and task specific. The general enterprise tendencies encompass the things already discussed such as achievement drive, possession of an internal locus of control, desire for autonomy, and the vision, passion and drive to fulfil ambitions. The task-specific factors are associated with the individual's ability to set goals and to have sufficient self-efficacy to feel that they can achieve them if they try. Other important factors are the cognitive makeup of the individual. This includes their ability to set a vision for their future, as well as the knowledge, skills and abilities to convert their dream into reality.

With these antecedents working on the individual's motivation, there must then be the right entrepreneurial opportunities for the individual to pursue and the right environmental conditions to enable them to take action to explore and exploit these opportunities. Once the individual recognises the opportunity, they need to develop the idea into a product, process or marketing concept that can be commercialised, and they will usually need to create a business venture to bring the idea to market if they don't possess this entity already. In order to execute their venture, the individual will need to assemble resources (e.g. money, people and equipment), establish and organise the business model, and commence development of the product and its eventual marketing.

When examining why individuals start new ventures and how they differ from those who do not, motivation is a critical component to be considered. Any model of new venture creation must therefore consider the characteristics of the individual entrepreneur. The motivation model shows that entrepreneurial behaviour is a result of the interaction of personal characteristics, environment, goals and motivations, and the business environment or existence of a viable business idea. The individual compares perceptions of probable outcomes with personal expectations, then analyses the relationship between the entrepreneurial behaviour they would implement and the expected outcomes. The individual's perceptions are finally compared with actual or perceived firm outcomes, and future behaviour is based on the results of these comparisons. When outcomes meet, or exceed expectations, behaviour is positively reinforced. If outcomes fail to meet expectations, motivation is lowered, impacting the decision to continue to behave entrepreneurially. The perceptions held by the individual affect succeeding strategies, implementation and management.

2.6 Factors Influencing Entrepreneurial Behaviour

Early research into entrepreneurial behaviour highlighted the importance of goal directed behaviour and achievement drive as well as the ability to take calculated risks (Palmer 1971). The behavioural characteristics associated with entrepreneurship were identified by Hornaday and Bunker (1970) to include such things as proactivity, self-confidence, a desire to be your own boss, a need to accomplish things, tenacity, self-motivation, risk-taking, the pursuit of greater financial returns, adaptability, common sense and even luck.

Cunningham and Lischeron (1990) view entrepreneurship as a reiterative process, assuming that some risk is born by the individual entrepreneur, and that rewards can be accrued to them. Figure 2.3 illustrates this perspective. It can be seen that the process associated with entrepreneurial behaviour is an iterative one in which opportunities are recognised and followed in a manner that requires active management of new ventures. As environmental change occurs, the entrepreneur

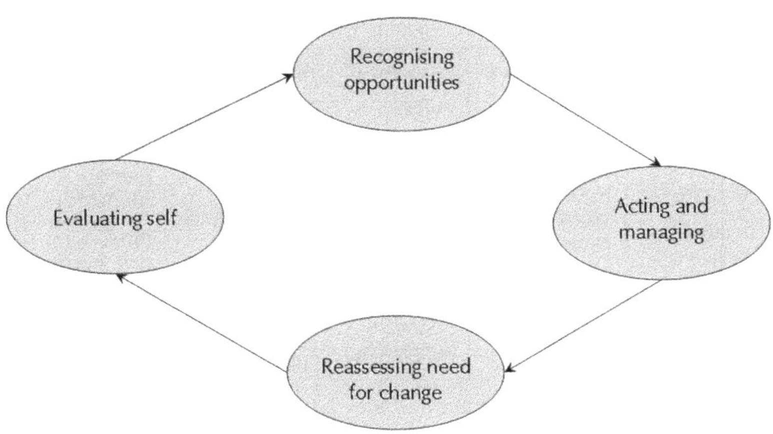

Fig. 2.3 Entrepreneurial behaviour. (Source: Cunningham and Lischeron 1990)

assesses their circumstances and seeks new ways to exploit opportunities – perhaps even evaluating their own personal role and function. Entrepreneurial behaviour is therefore a personal choice to initiate the process of establishing a venture and thereby changing the state of the market in some way. It is also a holistic and dynamic process (Bygrave and Hofer 1991).

The iterative process that defines entrepreneurial behaviour is essentially one of 'learning by doing', in which the entrepreneur tests their ideas against the market and assesses the merits of their idea, innovation or new venture against the feedback they receive from the market and their own self-evaluation (Cope and Watts 2000).

2.7 The Influence of Life Stage on Entrepreneurial Learning and Behaviour

Gibb (1988) has suggested that people experience different influences on them at different stages of life that might serve to shape or trigger entrepreneurial behaviour. Figure 2.4 illustrates this process. It can be seen that in childhood and adolescence, the key influences are parents and family, educational experiences, and the career path chosen. Children and adolescents with parents who are small business owners will be able to gain first-hand experience of how a business operates, and may be encouraged to enter the family business or even start their own. However, many also find the long hours, low social status and stress associated with small business a turn off, and may even be discouraged by parents from following their lead. Adolescents may find that their peer group plays a more prominent role in shaping future career paths. Where the focus among the peer group is on academic success and entry into the established professions via university, there may be less interest in entrepreneurship.

Stage of Life				
Childhood	**Adolescence**	**Early Adult**	**Middle Adult**	**Late Adult**
Family Class. Work. Education. Values & goals.	Family vocational preference. Vocational education choice. Education values & goals. Friends & community.	Further education choice. Class ranking Residual and own family influence. Friends & community.	Work & class mobility. Work. Own family & friends. Job satisfaction. Social interaction.	Class & wealth. Family situation. Work opportun's. Job satisfaction. Retirement facilities.

Fig. 2.4 Influences on entrepreneurial behaviour. (Source: Gibb 1988)

In a study on the entrepreneurial learning experiences of a group of 13 entrepreneurs, Rae (2000) found that their careers developed through a series of five distinct life stages:

1. *Early life* – family background, education and adolescence.
2. *Early career* – first jobs, vocational and professional training.
3. *Engaging and entering a venture* – selecting, starting, acquiring and joining.
4. *Growing a venture* – taking control, driving, leading, and developing people.
5. *Moving out and on from a venture* – selling, leaving, and finding new opportunities.

The experiences these individuals gained from their entrepreneurial activities built on each other to create a personal theory of how they should or could behave in a given situation, and whether or not they were likely to succeed.

Figure 2.5 illustrates the conceptual model developed by Rae (2000) to explain the entrepreneurial learning process taking place within these individuals. As shown, the personal theory developed over time. It was reinforced by the person's knowledge of their capabilities, and was tested via active learning by doing and by the relationships they formed with others. These elements served to strengthen the individual's confidence and self-belief, which in turn was the basis of their values and motivation to strive for ambitious goals. Where they were successful,

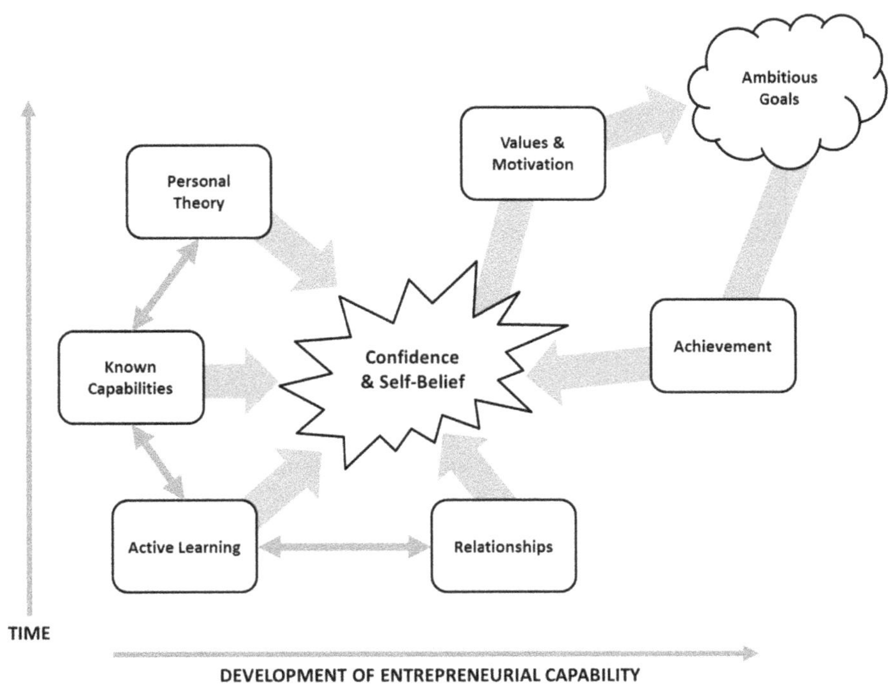

Fig. 2.5 A conceptual model of entrepreneurial learning. (Source: Rae 2000)

their achievements fed back into their confidence and self-belief (Rae and Carswell 2001).

As people enter adult life, they may find their enterprising behaviour shaped by social position, employment experiences, and their social grouping. Many who are able to enter secure, well-paid employment may avoid starting their own business and see little opportunity to do so. Once people have their own children or a lifestyle to support, they may not wish to risk the uncertainty of income associated with self-employment. Women are often less likely to take on a new business venture due to the commitments of pregnancy and child rearing (Mazzarol et al. 1999).

There is no ideal age for an entrepreneur, or for anyone, to start a new business venture. Many people enter self-employment either in their early years out of a desire to follow an opportunity, or because they lacked alternatives later in life. Older people of middle age are increasingly entering self-employment through a desire to do their own thing and achieve a sense of freedom and self-fulfilment. The significant downsizing associated with major corporate restructuring during the 1990s forced many people into early retirement. Being too young to retire and too old to start at the bottom of the heap in a new career, many people started up their own business using their skills and savings.

As discussed in Chap. 1, the Global Financial Crisis of 2007–2009 led to a rise in unemployment in many countries and a significant shedding of jobs in many of the larger firms across the US and Europe (OECD 2010a). Within many countries, the only significant new employment growth was from new business start-ups. Across the OECD group of countries, the SME sector has contributed to approximately 75% of all employment – with a range from 53% in the UK to 89% in Greece (OECD 2010b). As most SME are non-employing micro-enterprises, this suggests that self-employment and entrepreneurship is being experienced by millions of people throughout the world.

2.8 Measuring Entrepreneurial Characteristics

Many tests have been used to measure or assess entrepreneurial behaviour. Caird (1993) describes five main tests that have been used over previous years.

The Thematic Apperception Test (TAT). This test was developed by McClelland (1961) to measure a person's need for achievement, need for power and need for affiliation. McClelland's research found that entrepreneurs tended to have high need for achievement and high need for power, but low need for affiliation.

Edwards Personal Preference Schedule (EPPS). Using Maslow's (1987) needs hierarchy, this test found entrepreneurs exhibited high needs for achievement and abasement. Need for autonomy was found to be the strongest motivation for the establishment of a business.

Honey and Mumford Measure of Learning Styles. Honey and Mumford examined the learning styles of individuals. This test found that entrepreneurs prefer to learn through action and experimentation, rather than through theory and reflection (Mumford and Honey 1992).

Jackson Personality Inventory (JPI). This test examines innovation, conformity, responsibility, and risk taking (Jackson 1976). Entrepreneurs (as compared to managers) were found to score low on conformity and high on measures of energy, risk-taking and autonomy.

Myers-Briggs Type Indicator (MBTI). This test measures on four dimensions: introversion-extroversion, intuition-sensation, thinking-feeling and judging-perception. Introversion-extroversion measures whether you are focused on your inner self, or on the outer world. Intuition-sensation measures whether you like to look for patterns and possibilities, or whether you require facts. Thinking-feeling measures whether you make decisions based on objective analysis, or on feelings or sympathy for others' views. Judging-perception measures whether you prefer to order and control life, or to flexibly respond to ever-changing opportunities (Myers and Briggs 1976).

Entrepreneurs tend to be more intuitive, thinking and perceptive than managers who tend to be more sensing, feeling and judging. Whereas the manager needs facts, is influenced by others, and seeks order and control, the entrepreneur tends to be alert to new possibilities, makes decisions with objectivity, and is willing to embrace change.

2.9 General Enterprising Tendency (GET) Test

Caird (1991a) developed and validated the Measure of General of Enterprising Tendency (GET) test using a multi-occupational sample of 262 respondents including small business owners, teachers, nurses, clerical staff, public service employees and university lecturers. The GET test evaluates a person's orientation on five key dimensions:

1. the need for achievement,
2. creativity,
3. the desire for autonomy,
4. risk taking capacity, and
5. an internal locus of control.

Compared with the other occupations, small business owners were found to score higher on all measures (Caird 1992). However, statistical tests of the difference in their scores found that people who owned and operated their own businesses were significantly more likely to score high on all five criteria than any of the other groups (Caird 1991b). The principal characteristics that define the entrepreneur tend to be a strong drive to achieve and a sense of competitiveness. They are creative and frequently open to new ideas and opportunities, but they also seek to do things quickly and can be impatient. Such people are often good initiators and have the ability to launch new ventures.

2.9.1 Need for Achievement

McClelland (1968) claimed that a need for achievement is linked to entrepreneurial potential, behaviour and economic growth. High levels of need for achievement are associated with self-awareness, planning ability, initiative, problem-solving, energy, innovation, determination and motivation (McClelland 1968). Need for achievement is aroused in situations involving competition and excellence. Entrepreneurs are often characterised by being self-starters and having a strong desire to compete and achieve challenging goals. It is important to focus on skills that help achievement. This can include the ability to set clear, measurable and realistic goals as well as the ability to self-assess and learn from mistakes. People who are high on achievement drive are less likely to be motivated strongly by the desire for power or status. While success in business might bring both power and status, it is less likely in the early years. Power and status are more likely to accrue to people in the professions or in government.

2.9.2 Creativity

Creative people are not just artistic, they can also think in an original way to generate new ideas or different ways of doing things. It was once thought that creativity was inherited, but it is now considered to be possible to teach creativity. Often creativity in ventures stems from the collective input of team members (Kuratko and Hodgetts 2004). Creativity is stimulated by an environment in which there is tolerance of failure and acceptance of diversity – or even a constant questioning of the *status quo* (Sonnenberg 1991). The Kirton adaption-innovation inventory has been used to measure the creative style of individuals. This measure looks specifically at whether their problem-solving style is adaptive or innovative. Adapters seek to improve within existing structures and innovators seek to change existing structures by taking risks (Caird 1993).

2.9.3 Desire for Autonomy

The desire for independence is considered a key driving force behind many contemporary entrepreneurs. Often the commitment to create something special along with frustration with rigid structures in corporate environments drives individuals to seek opportunities. The drive for autonomy does not prevent entrepreneurs from developing successful teams but makes them retain responsibility for critical decisions (Kuratko and Hodgetts 2004). Many small business owners, even though they work long hours and may earn little more than salaried employees, wish to retain their self-employed status on the grounds that they enjoy the freedom that it offers (Hankinson 2000).

2.9.4 Risk-Taking Orientation

Measures of risk-taking behaviour have been found to correlate significantly with entrepreneurial orientation (Caird 1993). It was John Stuart Mill (1848) who developed a definition of 'entrepreneur' that considered risk bearing to be the major difference between entrepreneurs and managers. However, Schumpeter (1934) did not emphasise risk as he acknowledged that both entrepreneurs and managers assume the risk of failure. Nevertheless, risk-taking propensity differs according to age, experience, gender, background, stage of business development, and type of business (Brockhaus 1987). McClelland (1961) found that a high need for achievement drove individuals to become entrepreneurs, and that those individuals with a high need for achievement tended to take moderate risks as a calculated function of skill.

Liles (1974) suggested that in new venture creation, risks born by the entrepreneur include financial, career opportunities, family relations and wellbeing. The decision to assume these risks depends upon the entrepreneur's perception of the level of risk involved in the venture (Liles 1974). McClelland identified three levels of risk preferences – low, intermediate/moderate and high – impacting an individual's decision to start a venture. Entrepreneurial risk can be further divided into three components:

1. the general risk-taking propensity of a potential entrepreneur;
2. the perceived probability of failure for a specific venture, and
3. the perceived consequences of failure (Brockhaus 1980).

In Brockhaus's (1980) study, risk-taking propensity did not distinguish entrepreneurs from managers; he found that both groups were moderate risk takers. (And therefore, the definition of entrepreneurs including risk-bearing does not have to be limited to ownership and can relate to entrepreneurial managers.)

2.9.5 Internal Locus of Control

Timmons (1999) has argued that drive and determination to pursue a goal, even when faced with difficulties, is one of the more important characteristics required of entrepreneurs. This ability to persist in the face of adversity is often found among people with a high internal locus of control, or among those that feel they alone make their own destiny. The ability to keep on going even when things look difficult can overcome many other short comings.

For example, … The typical small business start-up may involve increasing the mortgage on the house, taking a pay cut, losing some social status and power, and even reducing one's standard of living.

However, entrepreneurs are also able to calculate the risks that they are taking, and can back out or withdraw from a particular strategy quickly if they assess that there are better options elsewhere or if the risk is too great. In essence, the entrepreneurial mind is tenacious, disciplined, persistent, prepared for personal sacrifice, and totally committed to its goals.

2.10 Awakening the Entrepreneur: Application of the GET Test

The GET test has been examined by other researchers to evaluate its validity and reliability as a measure. Cromie and O'Donaghue (1992) conducted two studies using the GET test to evaluate the entrepreneurial tendencies of 194 managers and 661 undergraduate students. This study found that the GET test measure has criterion validity and was able to differentiate significant differences between the entrepreneur and the student populations, suggesting that the instrument has good validity. Further work was recommended on the GET scales to assess their discriminant and predictive validity and general psychometric properties when used with different samples.

Persons with entrepreneurial propensity were viewed as those with high creative tendency, above average need for autonomy, and high calculated risk-taking orientation. Such people may also have high need for achievement and internal locus of control, but potentially not be significantly different from others. Potential entrepreneurs were also more likely to have had a father who was self-employed or to have been self-employed at some stage in the past (Cromie et al. 1992). Stormer et al. (1999) also evaluated the GET test in order to assess its ability to predict small business success using a sample of 128 owner-managers. They found that the GET test has reliability in its use within research, but was poor at predicting success in small business. They recommended that the scale be revised to 'form more coherent, single aspects of personality' (p. 51).

Smith et al. (2014) also used the GET test to examine differences between social entrepreneurs and more traditional ones. They found that it provided a useful measure for differentiating the two groups, but that an alternative measure, such as the Bolton Thompson Entrepreneur Indicator (BTEI) (Bolton and Thompson 2003), might have offered better measure as it included a social dimension, which is absent from the GET test. However, Lyons et al. (2015) compared the GET test to a number of other entrepreneurial measures using a sample of students studying entrepreneurship at university level. They found problems with the scale reliability of the test, suffering from some internal consistency. Although it should be noted that they were seeking to make use of the GET test to provide a measure of entrepreneurial traits, which arguably the test is not originally designed to do.

It should be noted that the purpose of the GET test is not to determine the possible success as a business owner, or even to assess whether a person is, or has the potential to be an entrepreneur. The GET test is a measure of the enterprising tendencies that are inherent in all people and provides a guide for the individual manager to assess whether or not they have above average, average or below average scores on each of the five dimensions. Further, it does not provide an assessment of an individual's inherent entrepreneurial traits that remain permanent. Our experience with using the GET test has found that it is best used as a starting point for undertaking a self-assessment of a person's enterprise tendencies, then used as a reference point for a qualitative analysis of their personal and professional history. Rather than offering a robust psychometric measure of whether an individual is "entrepreneurial", the GET test provides a foundation against which a person can examine why they may have scored a given set of results, and the factors in their personal and professional life that may have led them to this world view. This is explained further in the following example.

In a study we undertook to demonstrate the application of the GET test, a comparison was made between 56 managers enrolled in an MBA program in entrepreneurship and 56 successful entrepreneurs (Mazzarol 2007). Each of the MBA student managers completed the GET test. They then interviewed a person who had been identified as a successful entrepreneur, and had them also take the GET test. The test results were then evaluated within the context of the individual's personal and professional lives in order to interpret the findings and to explain why they had profiled in that way. Table 2.1 outlines the results of this study.

In terms of the GET test scores, the entrepreneurs were found to score significantly higher than the MBA students on need for achievement, creativity and risk-taking. However, many of the student managers found that their scores were equal to or higher than the entrepreneurs they interviewed. When they reflected on their GET scores and compared them with those of the entrepreneurs, most of the MBA student managers were able to identify within their family or professional history explanations as to why they had these results, and more importantly why they had not followed an entrepreneurial career path.

For example, one female student manager aged 35, who was a registered nurse, scored an average of 22 out of 54 on the GET test which led her to proclaim,

Table 2.1 GET test scores – entrepreneurs vs. MBA students

GET test dimension	Entrepreneurs mean scores	MBA managers mean scores	GET test average (mean) scores
Achievement drive[a]	7.3	6.6	13.7
Autonomy	6.2	7.1	13.0
Creativity[a]	11.7	7.3	18.5
Risk taking propensity[a]	5.1	3.1	8.1
Locus of control	10.3	6.3	16.2
Total GET score			

Source: Mazzarol (2007)

[a]Entrepreneurs scored significantly higher than MBA students on these dimensions (as measured using a two-tailed t-test at the 0.05 level)

> The results of the GET test indicate that I have the entrepreneurial tendencies of an inanimate object!

Nevertheless, she felt she had several strengths, such as optimism and being forward thinking, self-sufficient and self-confident. In assessing her personal and professional background, she noted that all her working career had been spent in public hospitals. Her father had been an engineer who had established his own consulting engineering business by his mid-40s before tragically dying at the relatively young age of 51. In her view, the professional career that she had chosen was a key factor in influencing her GET test results. For example, as she concluded,

> In summary, I believe that my personal background – and especially the current context – impacts highly on my tendencies towards entrepreneurialism. While I did have a positive role model in my father in terms of new venture creation, my chosen profession is one that, in direct patient care, requires conformation to rules, with risk-taking (even moderate) and creativity being attributes that are not valued.

The entrepreneur she chose to interview was a 62-year-old Australian vascular surgeon who ran a highly successful medical practice which he had established 25 years earlier. His decision to enter private practice had been driven by 'an intense dislike' of being employed by hospitals where he worked long hours and became embroiled in their internal politics. At the relatively young age of 37, he took a personal loan from a bank and launched his own medical practice. The early years had been hard, and he had been forced to work within the hospital on a staff position in order to generate sufficient income to keep his home and business going.

The work pressures eventually cost him his first marriage, but by the mid-1980s he had established a privately-owned vascular ultrasound laboratory as a separate new business to compliment his surgery. This innovation was a breakthrough and positioned him as a market leader, allowing him to grow the laboratory to the point where it employed over 30 staff and operated at five separate locations. At the time of the interview, the entrepreneur had just sold the laboratory business to allow him more time to devote to his second wife, and to focus on a horse stud and wine import business that involved visits to France at least twice a year.

When analysing her interview and test scores, the nurse manager described the gap between her situation and that of the entrepreneurial surgeon as 'worlds apart'. However, she noted that the difference between her and the surgeon was that he had a clear vision of what he wanted to achieve and had taken calculated risks in order to achieve them. By comparison, she had a tendency toward 'safety' and that, as a nurse, this was part of her professional training and orientation.

An interesting conclusion to this case was that this student used the course to develop a business plan for her husband, a cardiac surgeon, to help him establish a new cardiac unit with another surgeon. In her words, the shift towards an entrepreneurial mindset was a challenge for her husband: 'My husband was often overwhelmed by the discussions that I would force him to participate in.'

Other student mangers had similar experiences after using the GET test to assess themselves and a successful entrepreneur, and then reflecting on their respective life histories to ascertain why they had taken the career paths they did. As one 32-year, old MBA student – who described himself as, 'the child of conservative baby-boomers' – remarked after comparing himself with a successful 64-year-old entrepreneur, any lack of enterprising activity was potentially due to his childhood. As he explained:

> I discovered through careful reflection that my low/moderate propensity for risk-taking and internal locus of control (believed to stem from a conservative upbringing) are potential barriers to any large-scale entrepreneurial pursuits. Having said that, I believe that, if I can build my confidence through a series of small successes (preferably with a partner), my risk-taking propensity will increase and perhaps one day I might be the person being interviewed. I would therefore define myself as a nascent entrepreneur.

This student manager noted that his GET scores were marginally better than the successful entrepreneur he had interviewed. He put his own lack of entrepreneurial activity down to his family background and to a lack of self-confidence.

These examples highlight an important factor about entrepreneurship. It is not something that you are born with; it is a choice that lies within the ability of every person. We all have the primary enterprising tendencies of achievement drive, creativity, desire for autonomy, risk-taking proclivity, and locus of control. These are not personality traits; rather, they are orientations that are shaped by our life history. As managers, it is important to understand that entrepreneurs are a product of both their social and family upbringing as well as their professional career history. While personality characteristics can shape a person's entrepreneurial orientation, anyone can be enterprising.

2.11 Entrepreneurial Orientation

While it may not be possible to transform all managers into entrepreneurs, it is possible for managers and their organisations to possess an entrepreneurial orientation, which has been defined as the processes, practices and decision-making style of an organisation that acts in an entrepreneurial way (Lumpkin and Dess 1996).

Figure 2.6 illustrates the concept of entrepreneurial orientation in which the characteristics of the firm's management team involve the key elements that define entrepreneurial behaviour. These are employed to configure the resources and competencies found within the firm to deal with the opportunities and threats found within the firm's task environment. This entrepreneurial approach to management can enhance the firm's overall performance in the market.

Of importance is the management team's ability to embrace innovation and manage risk in order to achieve strategic goals. Managers need to be pro-active and capable of working autonomously within competitive environments that might be complex, uncertain, dynamic and turbulent as they seek to enhance their firm's performance (Covin and Slevin 1989).

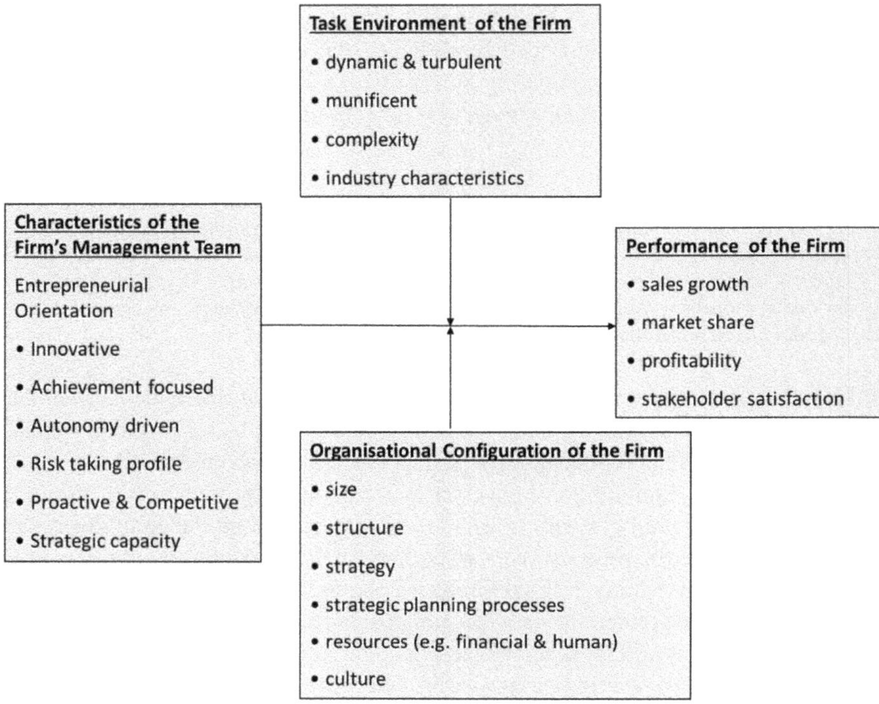

Fig. 2.6 Conceptual framework of entrepreneurial orientation. (Source: Lumpkin and Dess 1996)

2.11.1 Measuring Entrepreneurial Orientation

Academic research has attempted to develop measures for entrepreneurial orientation (Khandwalla 1977; Miller and Friesen 1982). Covin and Slevin (1989) proposed one of the first scales to measure entrepreneurial orientation (EO), using a study of small manufacturing firms. Their EO scale consisted of nine question items measuring innovativeness, pro-activity and risk-taking proclivity. In a study of 1067 SMEs in six countries, Kreiser et al. (2002) examined the EO scale and refined it into an eight-item measure that comprised the three factors of innovativeness, pro-activity and risk-taking proclivity. Figure 2.7 illustrates this model in which the eight items that measure each of the three key factors can be seen. Within this measure of entrepreneurial orientation, the eight measures used in the scale are:

1. *R&D Leadership* – whether the top management of the firm has a strong emphasis on R&D technological leadership and innovation.
2. *New product lines* – the number of new products or services that the firm has brought to market over the previous 3 years.
3. *Product changes* – whether changes in the products or services have been dramatic or minor in nature.

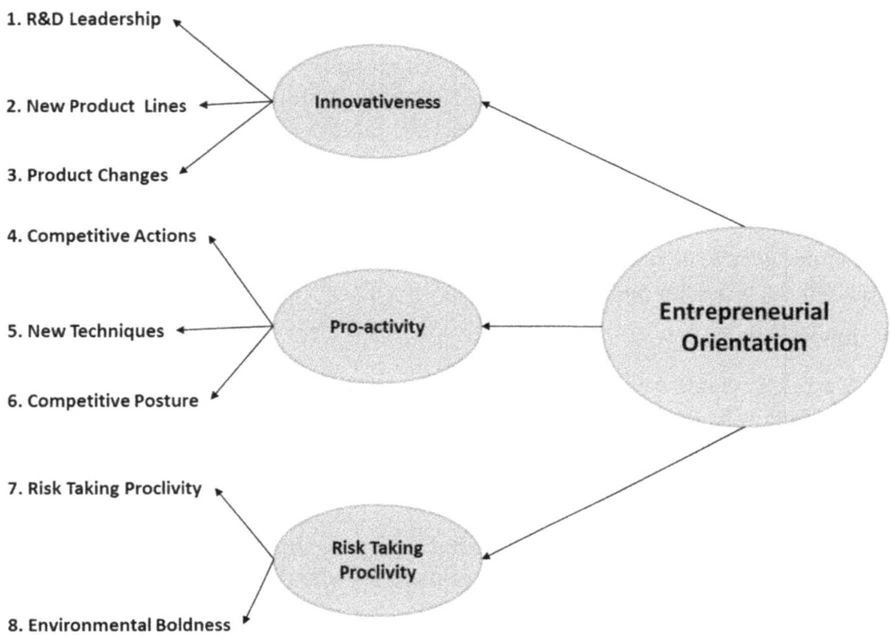

Fig. 2.7 Three factor measure of entrepreneurial orientation. (Source: Kreiser et al. (2002).

4. *Competitive actions* – whether the firm typically initiates actions to which competitors then respond, or is reactive to competitors.
5. *New technologies* – is the firm the first to introduce new products or services, administrative and operating techniques, or does it lag?
6. *Competitive posture* – does the firm adopt a very competitive 'undo the competitors' posture. or is it happy with a 'live and let live' posture?
7. *Risk-taking proclivity* – does the firm have a strong proclivity for high risk projects that offer very high returns, or is it satisfied with lower risk and return outcomes?
8. *Environmental boldness* – does the top management consider the environment requires bold, wide-ranging action to achieve its goals, or is a more cautious, incremental approach more appropriate?

2.11.2 Applying Entrepreneurial Orientation

Certo et al. (2009) have outlined a framework for how these entrepreneurial orientation elements might be applied by managers, entrepreneurs and individual employees in their daily work. They highlight how five of the EO attributes might be applied.

- Autonomy

Employees like a degree of autonomy within their work, and managers should allow their staff and work teams the freedom to champion new ideas. It is important for managers to monitor employee satisfaction, turnover and compensation in order to ensure that they are keeping pace with expectations. Entrepreneurs should seek to encourage and reward their employees to develop independent thinking that fosters innovation and to link compensation schemes to this behaviour. Individual employees should seek to develop independent thinking skills and should show initiative in highlighting problems and suggesting ways to enhance the firm's systems.

- Innovativeness

Managers should be willing to cannibalise existing products, services or processes within the business and seek new ways to do things. They should focus on monitoring such key measures as R&D to sales ratios, the number of new products/services launched per year, and the frequency of changes to products/services. Entrepreneurs should aim to identify new combinations of existing products and services so as to widen their market reach. Employees should suggest ideas for new product or process innovations to management, and should view themselves as part of the firm's innovation management system.

- Competitive Posture

Managers should be aggressive in the marketing of their products and services, and take steps to push for quality improvements and adding value in comparison to competitors. They should monitor their market share, price and quality in relation to competitors. Entrepreneurs should try to establish strategies for avoiding head-to-head competition with rivals, instead seeking unconventional tactics and filling niches not serviced by the major market incumbents. Employees should be aware that they can contribute to the firm's competitiveness by suggesting ways to enhance customer service and product quality.

- Proactivity

Managers should aim to influence market trends and create demand, rather than just playing follower-the-leader. They should monitor growth in new products and services to see how their customers are reacting to their strategies. Entrepreneurs should aim to seize the first mover advantage, or at least be a 'fast follower' to ensure that they are on the top of the wave and not left behind. Employees should try to think ahead and anticipate future needs within their organisation. They should actively participate in shaping the future of their firms.

- Risk-Taking

Managers should be prepared to commit significant resources to projects that they feel will generate high returns. They should monitor such key measures as debt-to-equity ratios and the percentages of resources invested in or committed to high risk projects. Entrepreneurs should be willing to incur financial debt and other risks in order to seize opportunities. Employees should seek out new responsibilities and make recommendations that might significantly enhance the business even if it might incur risk.

2.12 The Dark Side of Entrepreneurship

We should not conclude this chapter without a look at the less positive aspects of entrepreneurship, or what might be described as the *dark side* of entrepreneurship. Entrepreneurship involves risks and these are usually in the form of financial risk where the business venture established by the entrepreneur, should it fail, may leave the owner ruined. Although the total proportion of business bankruptcies is low it remains a problem for entrepreneurs (PSB 1999; OECD 2010c).

Not all business discontinuance results in bankruptcy, but entrepreneurs typically take on significant financial risk where they put a substantial portion of their savings or financial resources at stake, which will potentially be lost if the venture fails. Further problems can arise when the venture is growing as they may have to commit beyond their personal worth and take on excessive debt or sell equity to others with the risk of losing control.

Other risks facing entrepreneurs are those relating to their career, family and friends and psychological health. Many entrepreneurs, once they have worked for themselves for many years, find they either cannot or don't wish to go back to working for others. Well-educated and highly skilled people can often earn more working for others than working for themselves, particularly in the 1st years of founding their business. Career risk for entrepreneurs can occur if their venture fails. This is often a concern for persons already well-established in a secure, well-paid career. The entrepreneur is also at risk of becoming unemployable if their business fails and they have to seek paid work. Managerial positions are often closed to those who have been their own boss; and a failed business person is often viewed by recruiters as a risk.

The time taken to make a new business venture work can take the entrepreneur away from family and friends, placing pressure on their family and personal life. The long hours and total commitment required of the entrepreneur frequently means that they are drawn away from family and social relationships. This can expose weaknesses in family relationships and can lead to risks to marriage and friendships. It is most important that people who are seeking to launch a new business venture have the solid support of their partners and family. In Australia, the average full-time small business person works approximately 50 or 55 h per week as compared to their counterparts who are employees who work approximately 39.5 h per week (ABS 2005, 2010).

Stress from overwork is common among entrepreneurs who tend to be *Type A* individuals (e.g. people driven to rapid action and workaholic tendencies). Stress may come from loneliness, from obsession with the business, or from having to deal with people in difficult circumstances such as employees, customers, suppliers or partners. Even the need to achieve can push entrepreneurs to drive themselves too hard, leading to stress (Kuratko and Hodgetts 1998).

There is psychic risk, or that involving the wellbeing of the entrepreneur. For many people the psychological risk of failure may be too great to cope with, and a major business failure can lead to severe depression and suicide. However, the optimistic outlook and capacity for self-motivation and self-determination are important protections against such negative influences. Finally, if an entrepreneur experiences a major business failure, it can be devastating. The social stigma or 'loss of face' associated with this can lead some to mental breakdown or even suicide.

The motivation behind entrepreneurs wishing to start new business ventures or grow existing ones is complex. Ego plays a key role in this and can both keep the entrepreneur going through tough times and serve as a source of problems. According to Caird (1993), there is a risk that entrepreneurs may tend toward sociopathic behaviour. They can also become blinded by their desire to achieve and ignore warning signals, believing that they will succeed even when the odds are totally against them.

References

ABS. (2005). *Characteristics of small business in Australia* (Australian Bureau of Statistics Cat. No: 8127.0). Canberra: AGPS.

ABS. (2010). *Australian labour market statistics* (Australian Bureau of Statistics Cat. No: 6105.0). Canberra: AGPS.

Aldrich, H. (1980). Asian shopkeepers as a middleman minority: A study of small business in Wandsworth. In A. Evans & D. Eversley (Eds.), *The inner city: Employment and industry* (pp. 389–407). London: Heinemann.

Aldrich, H. (1990). Using an ecological perspective to study organizational founding rates. *Entrepreneurship Theory and Practice, 14*(3), 7–24.

Aldrich, H., & Waldinger, R. (1990). Ethnicity and entrepreneurship. *Annual Review of Sociology, 16*(1), 111–135.

Bhide, A. (1994). How entrepreneurs craft strategies that work. *Harvard Business Review, 74*(2), 150–161.

Bolton, W. K., & Thompson, J. L. (2003). *The entrepreneur in focus: Achieve your potential.* London: Thomson.

Brockhaus, R. H. (1980). Risk taking propensity of entrepreneurs. *Academy of Management Journal, 23*(3), 509–520.

Brockhaus, R. H. (1982). The psychology of the entrepreneur. In C. A. Kent, D. L. Sexton, & K. H. Vesper (Eds.), *Encyclopaedia of entrepreneurship* (pp. 39–56). Englewood Cliffs: Prentice Hall.

Brockhaus, R. (1987). Entrepreneurial folklore. *Journal of Small Business Management, 25*(1), 1–6.

Brockhaus, R., & Horwitz, P. (1985). The psychology of the entrepreneur. In D. Sexton & R. Smilor (Eds.), *The art and science of entrepreneurship* (pp. 25–48). Cambridge, MA: Ballinger.

Buttner, E. H., & Rosen, B. (1989). Funding new business ventures: Are decision makers biased against women entrepreneurs? *Journal of Business Venturing, 4*(4), 249–261.

Bygrave, W. D., & Hofer, C. (1991). Theorizing about entrepreneurship. *Entrepreneurship Theory & Practice, 16*(2), 13–22.

Caird, S. (1991a). Research note: The enterprising tendency of occupational groups. *International Small Business Journal, 9*(4), 75–181.
Caird, S. (1991b). Testing enterprising tendency in occupational groups. *British Journal of Management, 2*(4), 177–187.
Caird, S. (1992). Problems with the identification of enterprise competencies and the implications for assessment and development. *Management Education and Development, 23*(1), 6–17.
Caird, S. (1993). What do psychological tests suggest about entrepreneurs? *Journal of Managerial Psychology, 8*(6), 11–20.
Certo, S. T., Moss, T. W., & Short, J. C. (2009). Entrepreneurial orientation: An applied perspective. *Business Horizons, 52*(4), 319–324.
Collins, O. F., & Moore, D. G. (1964). *The enterprising man.* East Lansing: Michigan State University.
Cooper, A. C., Dunkleberg, W. C., Woo, C. Y. (1988). Survival and failure: A longitudinal study. In *Frontiers on entrepreneurship research* (pp. 222–237). Babson Park: Babson College.
Cope, J., & Watts, G. (2000). Learning by doing: An exploration of experience, critical incidents and reflection in entrepreneurial learning. *International Journal of Entrepreneurial Behaviour & Research, 6*(3), 104–124.
Covin, J. G., & Slevin, D. P. (1989). Strategic management of small firms in hostile and benign environments. *Strategic Management Journal, 10*(1), 75–87.
Cromie, S., & O'Donaghue, J. (1992). Research note: Assessing entrepreneurial inclinations. *International Small Business Journal, 10*(2), 66–74.
Cromie, S., Callaghan, I., & Jansen, M. (1992). The entrepreneurial tendencies of managers: A research note. *British Journal of Management, 3*(1), 1–5.
Cunningham, J. B., & Lishceron, J. (1991). Defining entrepreneurship. *Journal of Small Business Management, 29*(1), 45–61.
Deakin, M. (1996). European cities, planning systems and property markets. *Regional Studies, 30*(5), 539.
Gibb, A. (1988). The enterprise culture: Threat or opportunity? *Management Decision, 26*(4), 5–12.
Greenberger, D. B., & Sexton, D. L. (1988). An interactive model for new venture creation. *Journal of Small Business Management, 26*(3), 107–118.
Hankinson, A. (2000). The key factors in the profiles of small firm owner-managers that influence business performance. The south coast small firms survey, 1997-2000. *Industrial and Commercial Training, 32*(3), 94–98.
Hornaday, J. A. (1982). Research about living entrepreneurs. In C. A. Kent, D. L. Sexton, & K. H. Vespers (Eds.), *The Encyclopaedia of entrepreneurship.* Englewood Cliffs: Prentice Hall.
Hornaday, J. A., & Bunker, C. S. (1970). The nature of the entrepreneur. *Personnel Psychology, 23*(1), 47–54.
Jackson, D. (1976). *Personality inventory.* New York: Research Psychologists Press.
Kent, P. (1994). Management advisory services and the financial performance of clients. *International Small Business Journal, 12*(4), 45–58.
Khandwalla, P. N. (1977). Some top management styles, their context and performance. *Organization & Administrative Sciences, 7*(4), 21–51.
Kolvereid, L., Shane, S., & Westhead, P. (1993). Is it equally difficult for female entrepreneurs to start businesses in all countries. *Journal of Small Business Management, 31*(4), 42–51.
Kreiser, P. M., Marino, L. D., & Weaver, K. M. (2002). Assessing the psychometric properties of the entrepreneurial orientation scale: A multi-country analysis. *Entrepreneurship Theory & Practice, 26*(4), 71–94.
Kuratko, D., & Hodgetts, R. (1998). *Entrepreneurship: A contemporary approach* (4th ed.). Sydney: Harcourt and Brace.
Kuratko, D., & Hodgetts, R. (2004). *Entrepreneurship: Theory, process, practice* (6th ed.). Mason: Thomson South-Western.
Landström, H., Harirchi, G., & Åström, F. (2012). Entrepreneurship: Exploring the knowledge base. *Research Policy, 14*(7), 1154–1181.

Liles, P. (1974). Who are the entrepreneurs? *MSU Business Topics, 22*(1), 5–14.
Lumpkin, G. T., & Dess, G. G. (1996). Clarifying the entrepreneurial orientation construct and linking it to performance. *Academy of Management Review, 21*(1), 135–172.
Lyons, R., Lynn, T., & Bhaird, C. (2015). Individual level assessment in entrepreneurship education: An investigation of theories and techniques. *Journal of Entrepreneurship Education, 18*(1), 136–156.
Maslow, A. H. (1987). *Motivation and personality*. New York: Longman.
Matthews, C. H., & Moser, S. B. (1995). *The impact of family background and gender on interest in small firm ownership: A longitudinal study*. ICSB 40th World Conference, Sydney, 18–21 June. pp. 245–262.
Mazzarol, T. (2007). *Awakening the entrepreneur: An examination of entrepreneurial orientation among MBA students*. Paper presented at the EFMD 37th Entrepreneurship, Innovation & Small Business (EISB) Annual Conference, 13–14 September 2007, Ljubljana, Slovenia.
Mazzarol, T., Volery, T., Doss, D., & Thein, V. (1999). Factors influencing small business start-ups: A comparison with previous research. *International Journal of Entrepreneurial Behaviour & Research, 5*(2), 48–63.
Mazzarol, T., Volery, T., Doss, D., & Thein, V. (2001). Forces motivating small business start up among nascent entrepreneurs. *Small Enterprise Research: The Journal of SEAANZ, 9*(1), 3–18.
McClelland, D. C. (1961). *The achieving society*. Princeton: Van Nostrand.
McClelland, D. (1968). *The achieving society*. Van Nostrand, Princeton. (1961, 2nd Edition.)
Mill, J. S. (1848). *Principles of political economy*. London, England: John W. Parker.
Miller, D., & Friesen, P. H. (1982). Innovation in conservative and entrepreneurial firms: Two models of strategic momentum. *Strategic Management Journal, 3*(1), 1–25.
Morrison, A. (2000). Entrepreneurship: What triggers it? *International Journal of Entrepreneurial Behaviour & Research, 6*(6), 59–71.
Mumford, A., & Honey, P. (1992). Questions and answers on learning styles questionnaire. *Industrial and Commercial Training, 24*(7), 10–13.
Myers, I., & Briggs, K. (1976). *Myers-Briggs type indicator*. Palo Alto: Consulting Psychologists' Press.
Naffziger, D., Hornsby, J., & Kuratko, D. (1994). A proposed model of entrepreneurial motivation. *Entrepreneurship Theory & Practice, 18*(3), 29–33.
OECD. (2010a). *OECD economic outlook*. Paris: Organisation for Economic Co-operation and Development.
OECD. (2010b). *SMEs, entrepreneurship and innovation*. Paris: Organisation for Economic Co-operation and Development.
OECD. (2010c). *The OECD innovation strategy: Getting a head start on tomorrow*. Paris: Organisation for Economic Co-operation and Development.
Palmer, M. (1971). The application of psychological testing to entrepreneurial potential. *California Management Review, 13*(3), 32–38.
PSB. (1999). *Bankruptcies in Singapore*. Singapore: Productivity and Standards Board.
Rae, D. (2000). Understanding entrepreneurial learning: A question of how? *International Journal of Entrepreneurial Behaviour & Research, 6*(3), 145–159.
Rae, D., & Carswell, M. (2001). Toward a conceptual understanding of entrepreneurial learning. *Journal of Small Business and Enterprise Development, 8*(2), 150–158.
Reynolds, P. D. (1991). Sociology and entrepreneurship: Concepts and contributions. *Entrepreneurship Theory and Practice, 16*(2), 47–70.
Ronstadt, R. (1988). The corridor principle. *Journal of Small Business Venturing, 3*(1), 31–40.
Saracheck, B. (1978). American entrepreneurs and the Horatio Alger myth. *Journal of Economic History, 38*(2), 439–456.
Schere, J. (1982). *Tolerance of ambiguity as a discriminating variable between entrepreneurs and managers*. Proceeding of the Academy of Management Conference, New York, pp. 404–408.
Schumpeter, J. A. (1934). *The theory of economic development*. Cambridge, Mass: Harvard University Press.

Scott, M. G., & Twomey, D. F. (1988). The long-term supply of entrepreneurs: Students' career aspirations in relation to entrepreneurship. *Journal of Small Business Management, 26*(4), 5–13.

Sexton, D., & Seale, F. (1997). *Leading practices of fast growth entrepreneurs: Pathways for high performance*. Kansas City: National Centre for Entrepreneurship Research.

Shane, S. (2003). *A general theory of entrepreneurship: The individual-opportunity nexus*. Cheltenham: Edward Elgar Publishing.

Shane, S., Locke, E., & Collins, C. (2003). Entrepreneurial motivation. *Human Resource Management Review, 13*(2), 257–279.

Shapero, A. (1985). Why entrepreneurship? A worldwide perspective. *Journal of Small Business Management, 23*(4), 1–5.

Smith, R., Bell, R., & Watts, H. (2014). Personality trait differences between traditional and social entrepreneurs. *Social Enterprise Journal, 10*(3), 200–221.

Sonnenberg, F. K. (1991). Strategies for creativity. *The Journal of Business Strategy, 12*(1), 50–53.

Specht, P. H. (1993). Munificence and carrying capacity of the environment and organization formation. *Entrepreneurship Theory & Practice, 17*(2), 77–86.

Stanworth, J., Blythe, S., & Stanworth, C. (1989). Who becomes and entrepreneur? *International Small Business Journal, 8*(1), 11–22.

Stevenson, H., & Jarillo, J. (1990). A paradigm of entrepreneurship: Entrepreneurial management. *Strategic Management Journal., 11*.(Special Issue, 17–27.

Storey, D. J. (1982). *Entrepreneurship and the new firm*. London: Croom Helm.

Stormer, F., Kline, T., & Goldenberg, S. (1999). Measuring entrepreneurship with the general enterprising tendency (GET) test: Criterion related validity and reliability. *Human Systems Management, 18*(1), 47–52.

Timmons, J. (1999). *New venture creation: Entrepreneurship for the 21st century* (5th ed.). Singapore: McGraw-Hill International Editions.

Vernon-Wortzel, H., & Wortzel, L. (1987). The emergence of free market retailing in the People's Republic of China: Promises and consequences. *California Management Review, 29*(3), 59–76.

Volery, T., Mazzarol, T., Doss, N., & Thein, V. (1997). Triggers and barriers affecting entrepreneurial intentionality: The case of Western Australian nascent entrepreneurs. *Journal of Enterprising Culture, 5*(3), 273–291.

Weber, M. (1930). *The protestant ethic and the spirit of capitalism* (1904) (T. Parsons, Trans.). New York: Scribner.

3 The Entrepreneurial Process

3.1 Introduction

> Use your intuition because it never lies to you. Surround yourself with good quality people who are more experienced than you and learn from them, surrounding yourself with 'equals' is a waste of time. Build a network of positive people to support you. Think like a millionaire, don't be frightened to take risks and invest money, and believe in yourself.
>
> Source: Philippa Kerslake, owner of Pip's Cooking School.

This chapter examines creativity and its links to enterprise. This includes the three-stage process of entrepreneurship: opportunity screening; acquiring resources and building capability. Within this examination, the chapter reviews innovation and competitive advantage, financing ventures, team building and entrepreneurial growth. The process of entrepreneurship has been viewed as resting on four cornerstones. The first of these is the ability to impact your personal environment. Second is to possess a high degree of self-confidence. Next is the ability to create support networks that the entrepreneur can call upon for assistance, advice and resources. The final element is the ability to create a linkage from vision to action (Johannisson 1988). In this chapter, the role of creativity and the need to develop sound networks to support entrepreneurial activities are examined.

3.2 The Entrepreneurial Process

The entrepreneur is characterised by an ability to identify opportunities and then take action to explore and exploit them, typically taking risks and accepting the challenge of working within an ambiguous and uncertain task environment.

T. Mazzarol, S. Reboud, *Entrepreneurship and Innovation*, Springer Texts in Business and Economics, https://doi.org/10.1007/978-981-13-9412-6_3

Entrepreneurship requires that individuals hold different perceptions of their environment and the opportunities it affords. While all people possess some enterprising tendencies, not all are ready or willing to commit to entrepreneurial ventures due to their life stage or past history of family and professional career. The three principal components defining the entrepreneurial process are (Kourilsky 1995; Timmons 1999):

1. *Opportunity recognition* – identifying the business opportunity and developing sufficient passion to want to drive it forward to a reality that generates wealth.
2. *Marshalling of resources* – the entrepreneur is unable to achieve their goals alone. They must seek people, money, equipment and support in order to follow their vision. This capacity to marshal appropriate resources, usually in the face of risk, is an important feature of the entrepreneur. An important aspect of this is the entrepreneur's ability to develop networks of support.
3. *Developing capability* – the successful entrepreneur is able to marshal sufficient resources to start a business and then learn how to develop the new venture's capabilities to achieve prolonged sustainable growth.

While this three-step process seems simple, what is not clear is why some individuals take the plunge and decide to exploit their opportunities and while others do not? Shane and Venkataraman (2000) suggest that the reason some people discover opportunities and other don't is due in part to their possession of: (i) information that allows them to screen the opportunity, and (ii) the necessary cognitive properties to value it. Information is not distributed evenly across a population, and it is often the specialised skills or knowledge of the entrepreneur who is able to interpret the information that they receive and recognise it as an opportunity. The specific cognitive skills of the entrepreneur allow them to evaluate the opportunity and assess its merits as a potential course of action.

3.2.1 Opportunity Screening

Opportunity lies at the heart of the entrepreneurial process. However, a good idea does not necessarily make a good opportunity, with around 10% of ideas presented to investors meriting due diligence and 1% and 2% attracting funding. A key entrepreneurial skill is developing the ability to determine quickly whether serious potential exists for an idea.

A key issue for any future business opportunity is to determine whether there is a good level of demand for the products or services of this venture. According to Timmons (1999), several key questions should be asked. For example, Can the target market or customer be reached, and how long will it take to get customers to respond positively to the new venture?

Any business idea is only as good as its ability to diffuse into its target market. Many new innovative technologies fail to succeed commercially because they cannot be brought to customers due to the need for significant investment in distribution systems or enabling technologies. Distance can also be a challenge for many ventures.

The new venture opportunity should also offer good market growth potential, and this should be around a 20% annual rate of growth or better. Further, if the anticipated rate of growth is greater than 20%, the sustainability of the venture must be questioned (Timmons 1999). How achievable such growth rates are is likely to depend on the structure and overall size of the target market.

If the market is new and emerging, such as the personal computer market was in the 1980s, the growth potential will be good. However, if the market is fragmented or in decline, the opposite may be true. The overall market share potential for the venture should be considered to determine if there are any natural limits to growth. The existence of market entry barriers (e.g. regulations, patents, costs of infrastructure) should be examined, as should the erosion effect of there being no such barriers – allowing others to follow your lead and copy a good idea.

Timmons (1999) also suggests that an analysis of the profit margins that the new venture might generate can distinguish a potential opportunity from an idea. For example, will the venture seek to be a low-cost producer or a differentiator? If the aim is to offer low cost, the venture must be able to produce at less than its key competitors. Also, how much capital will be required to get the venture up and running and then sustain its growth?

Too many new ventures are launched without adequate capital and any growth can be fatal. Thus, a new venture's success is likely to depend on how quickly it reaches break-even. It may take 1 or 2 years to break even, but this will depend on the ability to keep overhead costs down and to ensure that the gross profit contribution from each sale are as high as can be achieved given operating costs and the price sensitivity of the market. Ventures with high overheads and low profit margins are vulnerable.

3.2.2 Marshalling Resources

A common misconception is that all resources must be in place initially to start a successful venture. Investment will follow good opportunities and entrepreneurial teams. There is a shortage of good entrepreneurs and opportunities, not a shortage of funds. Successful entrepreneurs are adept at marshalling and allocating scarce resources. The new venture should be kept lean and mean in its early years, with low overheads and as much 'sweat equity' that it can secure from family, friends and those who can share the passion for the venture. The term 'bootstrapping' has been used to describe this process. Bootstrapping can create significant competitive advantage; it creates a discipline of leanness and helps to maximise shareholder value.

The entrepreneur will need to beg, borrow and befriend as many people as they can to secure access to resources and skills that they don't currently possess. This is where the ability to build and use networks is most important. The ability of small firms to network has been found to be a major source of competitiveness (Ostgaard and Birley 1994). Small entrepreneurial ventures use strategic alliances to secure access to resources that they don't have themselves, as well as widening their access to new markets while seeking to protect their existing market share (Jarrett 1998).

3.2.3 Building the Capability of the Team

The entrepreneurial team is the key ingredient of higher potential ventures (Timmons 1999). Investors are drawn to excellent management teams, as building an effective team is seen as one of the greatest challenges of developing a successful venture. Strong teams are led by capable entrepreneurs with a good track record. Effective teams are characterised by a clear set of objectives and a willingness to work together to achieve them. Individual team members appreciate each other's capabilities and are tolerant of their limitations. Power is shared. Management of effective teams requires the skill of coaching members through the formative stages to a level of high performance (Koehler 1989).

Successful entrepreneurial ventures typically have a leadership that has strong entrepreneurial orientation and a management team that is composed of individuals with different functional backgrounds (Weinzimmer 1997). As the venture grows in size, it needs to take on more specialised skills and therefore more managers. However, it can also benefit from the formation of a strong, independent board of directors, drawn from a wide range of backgrounds, that can help to guide the strategic direction of the firm and give guidance to the entrepreneurial management team (Gabrielsson 2007).

3.3 The Theory of Effectuation

For the majority of entrepreneurs embarking on their first entrepreneurial venture, there are few sign posts and rules. Sarasvathy (2001) has sought to explain the entrepreneurial process through the theory of effectuation. This suggests that an individual seeking to launch a new venture will need to apply an effectuation process rather than a causation process.

In the causation process, there is a clear sense of the variables that need to be controlled in order to achieve a given outcome or end result. This implies cause-effect logic in which investment of time and resources in a project will lead to relatively predictable outcomes. This type of process is well suited to the exploitation of known markets and established knowledge. For example, a company might seek to increase market share in existing markets through competitive strategies aimed at enhancing their brand image, or the promotion of existing products and services. Causation processes work well in static, linear environments in which there is an underlying logic that, if the future can be predicted, it can be controlled.

By contrast the effectuation process is more suitable where the variables – and even the end state – are unknown or unpredictable. The focus is on the control of things that might assist in articulating through the process into an uncertain future. Effectuation assumes that the environment is dynamic, nonlinear and ecological in

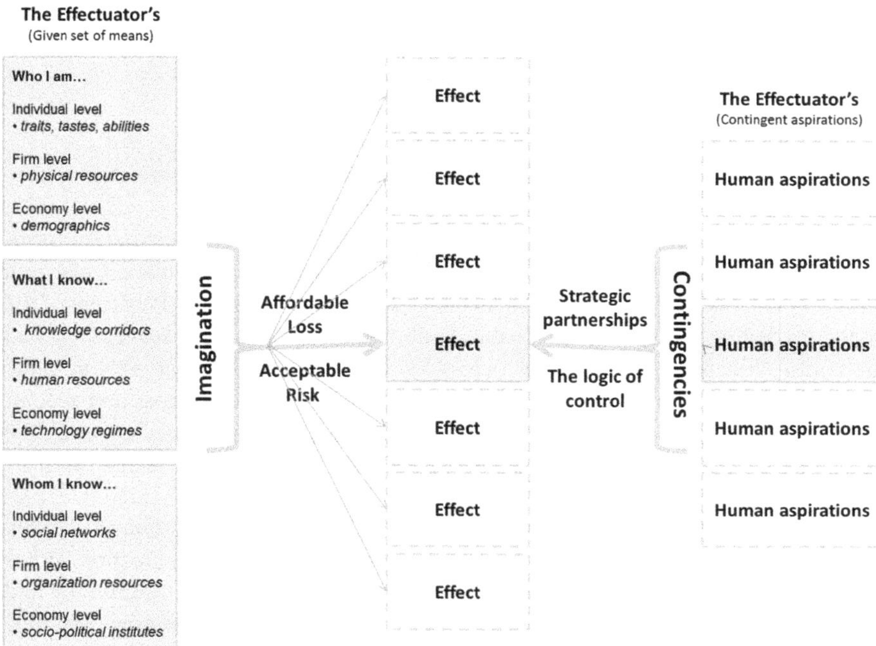

Fig. 3.1 The theory of effectuation. (Source: Sarasvathy 2001)

nature. It can be useful in the creation of new markets and products in which strategic alliances and collaborative strategies are important for success.

Figure 3.1 illustrates the conceptual framework of the theory of effectuation. As shown, the '*effectuator*', who is seeking to undertake an effectuation process begins not with certain knowledge of the end state they are seeking to achieve, but a given set of means that consist of who they are, what they know and whom they know. This occurs at the individual, firm and economy-wide level. The individual has their personality traits and enterprising tendencies. They are able to access information from a given set of 'knowledge corridors' and they will possess a given set of social and professional networks that contain people they can turn to for advice and support. Within the business venture there exists a given set of physical, human and organisational resources that the entrepreneur can apply to achieving their goals. Surrounding the venture is the economy or task environment that shapes the characteristics of the market into which they seek to trade.

Unlike causation, the effectuation process cannot focus on maximising potential returns through the selection of the best options. All that the *effectuator* can do is use their imagination and determine what they can afford to lose and what risks they can accept going forward. As they take action towards their objectives, they shape their aspirations using their imagination and the effects that they receive from what is an iterative process of continuous learning involving strategic partnering with others – including customers.

Sarasvathy (2001) suggests four principles of effectuation theory:

1. *Affordable loss*, rather than expected returns;
2. *Strategic alliances*, rather than competitive analyses;
3. *Exploitation of contingencies*, rather than pre-existing knowledge; and
4. *Control of an unpredictable future*, rather than prediction of an uncertain one.

She suggests that successful new ventures are best served by focusing on forming alliances and partnerships than on undertaking sophisticated market research and competitive analyses. Marketing in the effectuation process involves 'seat of the pants' marketing and selling via alliances rather than well-designed surveys and test marketing. Financial management is less likely to be based on net present value (NPV) analysis and more on short-term assessments of affordable loss and acceptable risk. It is also suggested that *effectuators* are more likely to fail, but would be able to manage failure more effectively and eventually build more successful firms over the longer term.

Since its emergence, the theory of effectuation has emerged as one of the key theoretical frameworks to help explain the process of new venture creation. It has been applied to innovation and new market creation in technology (Sarasvathy and Dew 2005). Its usefulness to managers lies in its recognition that new ventures, particularly those that involve disruptive technological innovations, are often unpredictable in terms of their future strategic directions. The notion that such ventures are well served by a formal approach to business planning and strategy may be false. Of more value is the entrepreneur's ability to network and control risk.

3.4 The Entrepreneurial Process Model

Timmons (1999) examined the principles that result in entrepreneurial success. His analysis suggests that a successful entrepreneurial process can be viewed as a balance between opportunity, resources and the team seeking to manage the venture. Figure 3.2 illustrates the dynamics at work in this process. The entrepreneurial process involves keeping the opportunity, resources and team requirements in balance throughout the development cycle. Key to this is the trio of elements of creativity, leadership and communications. Each of these works to support the process. For example, creativity links the opportunity to the team's effort and ensures enhanced outcomes.

Leadership is critical to matching the team effort to the available resources, while the assembling and coordination of the right resources to exploit the opportunity is contingent on effective communications. Forces that must be overcome are ambiguity and uncertainty, external market forces, and the financial sector's sentiment toward new business ventures. As shown in Fig. 3.2 these elements are coordinated via a business plan that seeks to fit the resources and team effort to fill gaps and develop the opportunity.

Fig. 3.2 The entrepreneurial process model. (Source: Timmons 1999)

The fundamental driving force of the entrepreneurial process, accounting for greater success among higher potential ventures, is that it is opportunity driven rather than necessity driven. There is usually a lead entrepreneur who is supported by an entrepreneurial team. Resources are generally limited, but creativity is usually high. Management of entrepreneurial ventures is holistic and integrated. Altering the balance of these driving forces can ultimately change the risk-reward ratio. These forces are the focus of due diligence by investors and founders in terms of what can be changed to improve the odds of success. The role of the entrepreneur is to take responsibility for and to manage the 'risk-reward' or 'success' eq.

3.5 3M Analysis for Opportunity Screening

A simple tool for screening future business opportunities is the employ a **3M analysis**. This focuses on the three M's – that is, the market, money and management requirements for the new venture. It offers a useful checklist for managers and entrepreneurs by addressing the following issues.

3.5.1 Market

- What Is the Customer Need?

Of importance, here is the ability to clearly identify that there is a need for the new product or service in the market and customers willing to buy it. This requires undertaking some market research and ideally talking to prospective customers or end users to determine what their needs are. Customers have three types of needs:

- *Basic* – what the customer assumes the new product will do;
- *Spoken needs* – what they say they want the new product to do;
- *Unspoken needs* – things that might delight them if provided.

It is important to spend time finding out about all three types of need, and to then configure your new product or service to best fit their needs profile.

- What Is the Product or Service?

Once you have identified the customers' needs, an assessment must be made of the product or service to ensure that it offers the features and benefits that match those needs. It is important that the new product or service satisfies the customer's or end-user's needs, and that is makes a clear customer value proposition.

- What Is the Size, Structure, Growth Rate and Demand Capacity of the Market?

There is little point in launching a new venture unless there is sufficient size and growth potential in the market to justify the investment. Some research should be undertaken to examine the size and structure of the target market, and to try to profile the target customers in terms of how they might segment along demographic and psychographic lines.[1]

- What Market Share Is Attainable?

In addition to knowing how large a target market is, it is also necessary to examine what potential share of that market might be secured by the new venture. This can be difficult to estimate, but realistic assessments with high and low estimates can be valuable in order to plan future sales forecasts that are essential for subsequent financial modelling.

- What Are the Barriers to Market Entry?

Not all markets are easily accessed, and the potential market share that might be obtained can be limited by natural or artificial barriers to entry. Barriers to entry may include economies of scale, switching costs, access to market distribution channels, controls over IP rights (e.g. patents and licences), government policies, brand equity, the market presence of existing market incumbents, and the cost of capital.

3.5.2 Money

- What Is the Investment Requirement?

Of importance, here is the estimation of how much money is required to fully commercialise the new product or process innovation that is to be delivered by the new venture. Start-up costs for new businesses can be much higher than anticipated.

[1] Psychographic refers to the values, attitudes and lifestyles of the customers.

How Much Money Is Needed? – VC Rule of Thumb
When asked how much money is typically required by ventures seeking to commercialise new innovations, an experienced venture financier remarked:

For every dollar, the entrepreneur says he or she needs to bring their new product technically to a stage where they can take it to market, they will probably require another 8 dollars. Five of these dollars will need to be spent on marketing and market development. The remaining three dollars will go on legal costs and the administration of the company.

- What Are the Fixed and Variable Costs?

Any financial analysis of the business venture needs to identify the fixed and variable costs. In general, the fixed costs relate to overhead expenses such as salaries, rents and long-term debt repayments. Ideally, a new venture should try to keep such costs to a minimum as they make it much harder for the business to reach break-even. Variable costs – or what are commonly called the 'costs of goods sold' or COGS – are things like sales commissions, third party licence fees, and freight and handling charges. The firm's gross profit will be enhanced by keeping variable costs under control.

- What Is the Gross Profit Margin?

Gross profit is the amount left over after variable costs are deducted from sales revenues. Dividing gross profit into sales produces a gross profit percentage or gross profit margin figure. The gross profit margin is one of the most important financial indicators for a new business venture. High gross margins allow the firm to reach break-even much faster than low gross margins. This is because they work like the gears on a bicycle. A large gross profit margin means that the amount of sales turnover required to generate the same amount of available money is much lower than if the gross profit margin were smaller.

- What Is the Profit After Tax?

Once fixed costs or overheads are deducted from the gross profit and taxes are deducted, the business is left with its net profit. The net profit is what the venture generates as retained earnings, and this is important for several reasons. First, net profit can be used to buy more assets to allow the venture to do more things and grow. Second, net profit can be used to pay down debt if the business has had to borrow money to get established. Third, net profit can be used to pay dividends to shareholders, which may be important if the venture has had to take in equity from others to help fund its capital requirements.

- What Is the Time to Break-Even?

After gross profit margin, the break-even point is another of the most important financial indicators in a new business venture. Break-even is where fixed and variable costs equal the sales revenues coming into the business. Business that have high fixed costs will have high break-even points and will require large sums of working capital (e.g. cash and other liquid assets) to allow them to keep trading. Many excellent businesses with wonderful products and services have failed due to being unable to reach and maintain break-even. Ideally, break-even should be kept as low as possible in the early years.

- What Are the Cash Flow Dynamics?

Linked to break-even is the ability of the business venture to take in and use cash. A business needs cash to pay wages and meet short term liabilities such as creditors (e.g. suppliers, rent and taxes). It is important not only to know how much profit is being made, but how quickly the firm debtors (e.g. customers) can pay their accounts and the business put that money into the bank.

- What Are the ROI and IRR Capital Requirements?

For some complex ventures that are seeking venture capital financing, it is also important to calculate the expected return on investment (ROI) and internal rate of return (IRR) for the venture or its products. Calculating this may be difficult where the new venture has insufficient information or market benchmarks to use. However, an entrepreneurial venture should pay the investors above average returns in order to justify the time and capital costs associated with it. Formal venture capital investors are likely to want to see such estimates and to seek investments that will generate ROI levels well above what they can get from investing in the stock market.

3.5.3 Management

- Is There Potential for Value-Adding?

The capacity to build market share and growth the business requires that there be an ability to keep on innovating and enhancing the products or services that are initially offered. Value-adding can be achieved by product or process improvements or by marketing and brand development.

- How Much Control Is There Over Resources?

The key to developing any new business venture is the entrepreneur's ability to marshal the necessary resources. In many cases these resources may not be within their direct control. For example, does the venture require access to IP rights that it does not own, or assets that it needs to borrow from others?

- What Is the Timing?

A key issue for many new entrepreneurial ventures is time to market. To capture the first mover advantage requires the business to achieve new product development cycles that allow it to gain early market access before the windows of opportunity close. Also important is how long it will take for the business to reach break-even and repay any investment capital.

- What Is the Room for Error?

Within any business venture there will be risk, failures and unforeseen delays. A risk assessment should be made to assess the impact of worse case scenarios and potential failures of supply or technology, or loss of key people or assets.

- Is There an Exit Strategy?

A critical issue for venture capital investors will be their exit strategy from the venture. They will want to know how quickly they can expect to get their money out and the conditions under which this exit can take place. Entrepreneurs also need to think in this way. New ventures are risky and a back-out plan in the case of things not working as forecast should be prepared. The entrepreneur should also consider whether they wish to exit from the venture within a given time period and what this exit might involve.

- Who Will Comprise the Team?

As discussed above, a key success factor for entrepreneurial ventures is their ability to assemble a high-quality management team with complementary skills. For example, within a new technology-based firm, the team should consist of people with technical, marketing, financial and strategic management skills (Edwards 2002).

- Is There a Suitable Fit?

Finally, the team that is to lead the new venture must be compatible. There is an old saying that 'the fish rots from the head'. Too often the best firms with the best products fail due to a lack of agreement between the key business partners. There needs to be trust, respect, empathy and a mutual benevolence between the key managers of the business. They also need to have complementary skills and a capacity to communicate effectively with each other to resolve differences.

3.6 The New Venture Creation Process

As illustrated in Fig. 3.3, the key elements of the start-up process involve the entrepreneur's initial motivation to found a new business venture. This frequently emerges as a raw idea that may exist within the nascent entrepreneur's consciousness for periods of years prior to a determined commitment to launching the business. The idea must first be validated through the entrepreneur testing their concept against the hard reality of the market place. Many nascent entrepreneurs cannot move beyond this first stage, as they find it too hard to bring all the necessary elements together to see how their new venture will be created. Business start-up support agencies are often focused on the development of a formal business plan as a first step in the creation of a new enterprise. However, most successful enterprise start-ups do not involve formal plan preparation. In fact, forcing entrepreneurs to prepare formal written business plans prior to start-up may only impede progress.

Once the venture is launched, the entrepreneur will need to identify and marshal resources. If money or staff are involved, the entrepreneur may be required to

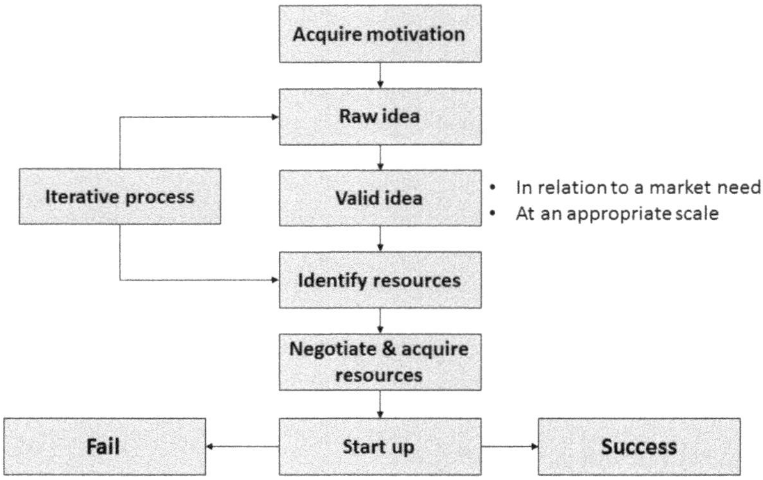

Fig. 3.3 A new venture start-up process model

prepare a formal business plan. The key issues for consideration by anyone launching a new business venture for their idea are:

- Does the entrepreneur have the required capability or experience to launch the business?
- Why should anyone buy the product or service?
- What might increase the chance of success and what gives the new venture a competitive edge (unique selling proposition)?
- Can the entrepreneur run the venture alone or do they need assistance?
- Is there sufficient capital for sustained growth?
- Will the venture yield an acceptable return?
- Is this really the venture the entrepreneur wants to run?
- Does the venture have a future?

3.7 A Study of the Process of Enterprise Formation

Volery et al. (1997) examined the triggers and barriers influencing new venture creation. Their model of enterprise formation presents a schematic overview of the start-up process and focuses on the assumption that the triggers and barriers influence the intention – and ultimately the decision – to launch the business (i.e. where triggers prevail over barriers) or to give up the idea (i.e. where barriers prevail over triggers). Figure 3.4 illustrates this process. It can be seen that a combination of personal and environmental influences affects the intentionality of the enterprise formation process.

The study selected 93 people who had attended small business start-up courses run by government and small business support centres. The sample was divided

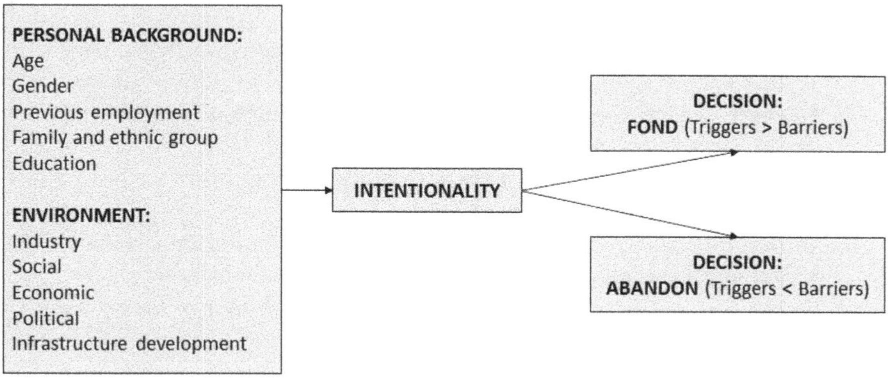

Fig. 3.4 A model of enterprise formation. (Source: Volery et al. 1997)

evenly into *novice entrepreneurs* who had commenced trading in their ventures within the 2 years prior to the interview, and *nascent entrepreneurs* who were yet to start or had abandoned their idea. A total of 48 novices and 45 nascent entrepreneurs were recruited. Each individual was interviewed face-to-face using semi-structured interviews that initially explored their motivations for starting or not starting their venture, and also had them complete a detailed questionnaire that offered a '360° scanning' of their personality and their perception of the environment.

3.7.1 Actions Taken Prior to Launch or Abandonment

Although some differences appeared among the actions taken, almost all these nascent and novice entrepreneurs had taken similar steps towards the planning of the launch of their business venture. In general, both groups:

- Gathered some information on business start-up from various government agencies and small business support and start-up services, or their family and friends;
- Prepared a business plan;
- Looked for facilities or equipment; and
- Were saving money to set up their business.

3.7.2 Triggers and Barriers to New Venture Creation

Respondents were asked how important various issues were to their decision to start or not-start their business. Twenty 'triggers' and 18 'barriers' were identified as being important to new enterprise creation. Following statistical analysis, a final list of six trigger factors and three barrier factors were identified.[2]

[2] This involved a principal component factor analysis.

Triggers for new venture creation:

1. *Creativity* – a measure of the desire to take advantage of personal talents, to have an interesting job, to create something new and to realise a dream.
2. *Autonomy* – a measure of the desire to work at a location of choice, to set your own working hours and to be your own boss.
3. *Money* – a measure of the desire to keep a larger proportion of the proceeds of your work and to earn more money.
4. *Market opportunity* – a measure of the identification of an opportunity in the market and a feeling that there were positive economic indicators.
5. *Investment* – a measure of the need to invest personal savings, for a job due to unemployment, to receive a salary based on merit, and to invest superannuation or redundancy pay-outs.
6. *Status* – a measure of the desire to follow the example of a person you admire, to increase your status and prestige, and to maintain a family tradition by setting up a business.

Barriers for new venture creation:

1. *Hard reality* – a measure of the perception that the risks are greater than expected, the task is more difficult than expected, there is too much uncertainty about the future, and a fear of failure.
2. *Lack of resources* – a measure of the person's lack of skills in marketing, finance or management, a lack of information on how to start a new business, plus difficulty in obtaining finance and in finding suitable premises for the business.
3. *Compliance costs* – a measure of the difficulty in finding suitable employees, the costs of taxes and start-up expenses, the complexity of government regulations, and the absence of anyone to turn to for help.

Analysis of these nine factors found that the most important for both the nascent and novice entrepreneurs was creativity. Of secondary importance were autonomy and money. In third place were hard reality and market opportunity, and in fourth place were investment, lack of resources and compliance costs. The least important factor was status. The relative importance placed on these factors was the same both for those who started and for those who did not start their venture. This suggests that both groups considered their ability to use their talents, to have an interesting job, and to create something or realise their dreams as the most important potential motivation to small business formation. The equal importance placed on autonomy and money suggests that these two factors are likely to relate to each other in terms of a trade-off of one for the other. The motivation to found a business in the light of a perceived market opportunity must be weighed against the risks and difficulties involved. The relatively low importance given to status suggests that the desire to emulate others or follow family tradition is not a particularly strong motivation for nascent entrepreneurs.

3.7.3 Implications of the Study

These findings highlight the relative importance of the entrepreneurial attributes of creativity and desire for autonomy as triggers for new venture creation. While many other factors may play a role, it is likely that entrepreneurial behaviour will be fostered by focusing on assisting people to pursue their dreams and use their creativity to seek and achieve the independence that entrepreneurship can give.

While the external environment cannot be discounted, the findings from the study suggest that the personality of the entrepreneur may play a key role in the start-up process. Those who effectively set up a new business venture were also those who had an overriding drive to create.

Both starters and non-starters appeared to face similar types of barriers. Some non-starters even did all the right things to successfully launch a new business venture (e.g. they saved money, they drafted a business plan, they sought the advice of government agencies), but they abandoned the idea to start because they lacked the passion to carry out their entrepreneurial dream. Nurturing the creativity and passion of nascent entrepreneurs could therefore sustain the process of entrepreneurship, hence inducing a boost in business start-ups.

This finding has important implications for small business assistance bureaus, industry policy-making and the entrepreneurs' community. Indeed, a lot of government resources have been directed toward nascent entrepreneurs in terms of financial aid or advice. Most of these resources have been successfully used in building so called 'hard skills' such as financial and business planning. However, it appears from this research that 'soft skills' such as networking and mentoring would be of great use to nascent entrepreneurs to make their dream become a reality (Mazzarol et al. 1998).

3.8 The Importance of Creativity Management

As Low and MacMillan (1988) remarked, opportunities are created as a product of ongoing networks of relationships and exchanges. Opportunities come most frequently to people located at advantageous positions within networks. Furthermore, exploiting an opportunity requires certain resources (capital, information and advice). Nascent entrepreneurs are therefore advised to evaluate and map their current networks. However, a key factor motivating entrepreneurs is likely to be their creative drive, which is also a critical element in the development of innovation.

The process of entrepreneurship and innovation is more than just having a good idea; it is about understanding and managing the creative thinking process that generates ideas, and the tenacity to see an idea through to implementation (Kuratko and Hodgetts 1998). An individual's approach to problem-solving may be 'adaptive' (e.g. a methodical approach, solving focus, refine existing practices, means oriented, detailed work, sensitive to group cohesion) or 'innovative' (unusual approaches, discovers problems, questions basic assumptions, interested in ends, little tolerance for routine, little need for consensus) (Kirton 1976). Different people, given the same problem, frequently adopt quite different solutions, and this creativity is what can form the basis of improvements to products and processes. However, creativity alone is not enough within a business environment. Highly creative environments – e.g. artistic communities – can be capable of producing some exceptional work, but can easily fail to generate anything of commercial value. Creativity, thus, must be linked to practical applications and the needs of the marketplace in order to be commercially valuable (Levitt 2002).

3.8.1 The Creative Thinking Process

Kuratko and Hodgetts (2004) outline a process model of creative thinking shown in Fig. 3.5. This comprises four elements that are discussed in the following sub-sections.

- Knowledge Accumulation

Innovation is usually preceded by information gathering through the absorption of information relating to the problem from a variety of different sources. Reading around the specific area under investigation is also useful, developing a range of perspectives on the problem. An information search process can also be useful. This can involve reading in a variety of fields, joining professional groups, attending meetings and seminars, travelling to new places, talking to different people, scanning publications, developing a subject library, carrying a notebook, and devoting time to pursuing natural curiosities.

- Incubation Phase

Allow your subconscious to mull over information gathered and the problem. It is suggested that you might engage in mindless activities such as exercising or playing, thinking about the problem before falling asleep, or meditating or relaxing.

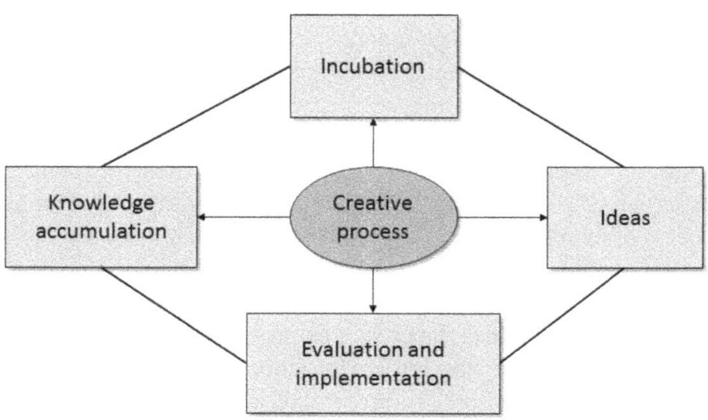

Fig. 3.5 The creative thinking process. (Source: Kuratko and Hodgetts 1998)

Freeing the mind from the mundane distractions can serve to enhance creativity. This may explain why some people get creative thoughts after sleep or during such things as routine walks, exercise or even showering.

- Ideas

If sufficient incubation has been undertaken, the discovery of a solution can appear suddenly or incrementally. The famous stories of Newton's moment of inspiration with the apple in the orchard, or that of Archimedes 'eureka' moment in his bath, are possible examples.

- Evaluation and Implementation

Identification of workable ideas that can be implemented requires the individual to be in good health and understand the business planning process. It is recommended that you should test ideas with experts, take note of intuition, and develop management skills. Learning how to sell and how organisations work is desirable. Seek advice early and view problems encountered as challenges that can be overcome.

According to McFadzean (1998) creative thinking within organisations can be enhanced where creative problem-solving satisfies one of these criteria. First, the idea or product generated should be novel and have value. Second, the thinking should be unconventional, challenging existing ideas and paradigms. Third, the thinking requires motivation and persistence taking place over time or at high intensity. Any creative thinking that is to have commercial value must be capable of being implemented. Creative thinking can be encouraged or developed by following some of the following strategies (Kuratko and Hodgetts 1998):

1. *Adopt a habit of thinking creatively;* this can be through the use of thinking exercises such as cryptic crosswords, word games and group storytelling.
2. *Identify habits and perceptions that prevent you from thinking creatively*, such as stock phrases that you use outwardly or inwardly to inhibit the progress of a new idea.
3. *Start to look at the complementary and appositional relationships between people and objects* – creative thinkers understand how people and things relate to one another.
4. *When considering relationships between people and things*, look at how they complement you in your attempts to satisfy your own needs.

3.8.2 Encouraging Creativity in the Workplace

Amabile (1998) suggests that creativity in the workplace is frequently killed by the everyday organisational structures and functions designed to maximise business effectiveness, efficiency and control. A balance needs to be found between those things that promote productivity and those that encourage creativity. More focus should be placed on enhancing creative skills among employees, and on motivating them to try new things and be creative.

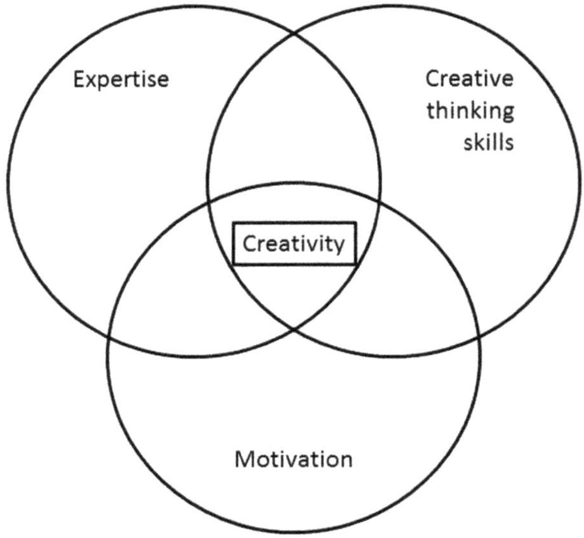

Fig. 3.6 The components of creativity. (Source: Amabile 1998)

The components that comprise creativity are thought to include expertise, the skills of creative thinking, and motivation. Figure 3.6 shows this structure. These three components can be influenced by work environment and managers. The details of these elements are explained by Amabile (1998) in the following ways:

- *Expertise:* This deals with the issue of technological, procedural and intellectual knowledge. Everything an individual knows – their intellectual space – is used to seek solutions to problems. It is therefore important to ensure that organisations recognise the importance of human expertise and seek to retain it.
- *Creative thinking skills:* These determine the flexibility and level of imagination individuals use when approaching a problem. Skills in creative thinking are related to the personality of an individual and their approach to problems. Work style also influences creativity, as the ability to put a problem aside and return with a fresh perspective helps to develop creative solutions.
- *Motivation:* The passion to derive solutions from a problem leads to more creative solutions than motivation by external rewards. Intrinsic motivation can be influenced by the work environment. Motivation determines what an individual will do. Intrinsic motivation has a greater influence on creativity than extrinsic motivation. Extrinsic motivation (rewards or threats) pushes individuals to seek a solution – but not necessarily a creative one. Passion and interest in the problem at hand sparks engagement in a task because of challenge and enjoyment.

Expertise and the development of creative thinking skills are long-term strategies; however, creating an environment of intrinsic motivation can be achieved by small changes within an organisation (Amabile 1998). Management practices that can affect creativity are:

- *Challenge:* Matching the right people with the right assignment stretches individuals without overwhelming them, but this also requires keeping good employee records and information about the assignments being given to people. It is important to avoid the 'shotgun wedding' scenario in which a task is given to someone without warning or adequate matching.
- *Freedom:* Freedom should be given to determine the means not the needs, with clear strategies and goals to enhance creativity. It is often difficult to work creatively towards a moving target. Giving people freedom over the process that they wish to follow in solving a problem allows them to approach a problem in a way that utilises their expertise and creative thinking skills.
- *Resources:* It is important to allow appropriate time allocation and not set too tight deadlines that can create distrust or burnout. Time should be allowed for the exploration and incubation of ideas.
- *Work-group features:* Another valuable strategy is to establish mutually supportive teams with diverse perspectives and backgrounds, and to enhance the intellectual space for creative thinking. Team members must share excitement over the team goal and be willing to help team mates. However, individuals must recognise the unique knowledge and experience of other members. Managers must also know enough about their staff to put together a good team.
- *Encouragement:* To sustain passion for creative work, people need to feel that their work is valuable. Managers should recognise creative work before the commercial impact is known. A culture of evaluation leads to a focus on external rewards and punishments rather than creativity. There is a need for managers to be aware of the value of failure of an idea.
- *Organisational support:* Finally, leaders within teams and organisations can support creativity by mandating collaboration and reducing politics to create a sense of mutual purpose and excitement.

3.9 The Effects of Time Pressure on Creativity

Fostering creativity within an organisation is also likely to be adversely affected by the amount of time given to employees to do their work and solve problems. The high-pressure work environment common to most organisations today reduces the opportunities for creativity by crowding out the time people have to free their minds and allow their thoughts to explore different ideas. Amabile et al. (2002) suggest that time pressure can be managed so as to encourage creativity. Figure 3.7 illustrates their time-pressure/creativity matrix.

Creativity does not always naturally flow just because time pressure is low. In many cases the employees simply go on autopilot, and even though they have free time they do not generate new ideas because creativity is not encouraged by management. There is usually little collaboration between people, and if this does occur it is often within group situations. When time pressure is high, the common situation is for people to feel as if they are on a treadmill. Here, they are too busy doing

		Time pressure	
		Low	High
Likelihood of creative thinking	High	**On an expedition** Creative thinking focuses on: • generation of ideas not seeking problems • Individual collaboration	**On a mission** Creative thinking focuses on: • One or a few activities • Concentration of human effort • Identifying problems and exploring new ideas
	Low	**On autopilot** Creative thinking is: • Not encouraged by management • Undertaken via group collaboration	**On a treadmill** Creative thinking is: • Difficult due to lack of focus • Little concentration of effort • Too much fragmentation of time

Fig. 3.7 The time-pressure/creativity matrix. (Source: Amabile et al. 2002)

tasks that are fragmented and unfocused on new issues, and are focused on getting on with the *status quo*. There is also little concentration of effort between people who are too busy to talk.

Encouraging creativity, whether time pressure is high or low, depends on how people are managed and focused. When time pressure is low but people are encouraged to think of new ideas, they feel as if they are on an expedition, searching for new ways of doing things or solving problems. Collaboration is often at an individual rather than a group level, and creative ideas are allowed to flourish. If time pressure is high but management focuses people's attention on solving a specific problem or set of problems, there is the feeling that everyone is on a mission. This encourages creativity, and a sense of importance about the work is a major motivator.

It is important for managers to recognise that individuals have different thinking styles: e.g. analytical, intuitive, conceptual, experiential, social, independent, logical and values driven. Organisations should be designed to encompass a broad range of approaches and let people approach tasks in a way that best suits them (Leonard and Straus 1997). Setting ground rules for team work to garner respect among diverse members is important. Managers can encourage creative behaviour through a process of understanding themselves (e.g. using self-assessment tools) and being aware of their leadership style.

According to McFadzean (1998), managers seeking to develop a creative climate within their organisation should ensure that employees feel secure when trying new things or suggesting new ideas. An organisational climate that tolerates failure in the pursuit of innovation is important to this process as argued by Farson and Keyes (2002). According to them, typical failure tolerant leaders should demonstrate six behaviours:

1. They engage at a personal level with the people they lead.
2. They avoid giving either praise or criticism, preferring to take a nonjudgmental, analytical posture as they interact with staff.
3. They openly admit their own mistakes rather than covering them up or shifting the blame.
4. They try to root out the destructive competitiveness built into most organizations.
5. First and foremost, though, failure-tolerant leaders push people to see beyond simplistic, traditional definitions of failure.
6. They know that as long as someone views failure as the opposite of success rather than its complement, that person will never be able to take the risks necessary for innovation.

Employees should also be encouraged to envisage future opportunities and to think about the future, rather than just focusing on the present. This should involve challenging assumptions and questioning the *status quo*. People should be allowed to spend time on their special 'pet projects' that can lead to new innovation. For example, the 3M Corporation provided employees with 15% of their time free to work on special projects.

Creativity should also be supported strongly and demonstrably by senior management so that everyone can see how important innovation is to the organisation. Finally, there should be a climate within the organisation of human fun and enjoyment at work, with some time allowed for play and quiet contemplation.

3.10 Creating Rich Pictures

One approach to fostering creativity is the development of rich pictures (McFadzean, 1998). The process of rich pictures allows the group to understand each other's perception of the problem and how they would like to see the future; pictures show patterns and relationships of the problem features. There are several stages to this process:

1. Group members write a brief statement of the problem.
2. Each member of the group draws two pictures. The first illustrates the way the situation should be in the future; the second shows how the situation is at present.
3. Members take turns to explain their pictures, starting with the present and then moving to the future. Each of the objects in the pictures should be described, explaining the reasons they are drawn that way and the relationships that are thought to exist between them.
4. A 'round robin' is held with each member putting forth priority functions and features to the group without evaluation or criticism.

5. The groups then rank the functions and features in order of importance.
6. Groups prepare a composite strategy that explains how to shift from the present situation to the preferred future.

The benefit of rich pictures is that they can quickly assemble a large amount of information and ideas, and enable a fast sharing of perspectives and thoughts. However, some people find it uncomfortable drawing and sharing their drawings in public. Many alternative techniques may be used that help participants to decontextualize the problem that has been submitted. Techniques like analogies, connection matrices, visual elicitation, help to think out of the box and find new perspective on a problem.

3.11 Applying Creativity Tools to Systems Thinking

The succession of these stages refers to Wallas (1926) seminal contribution. According to Wallas, humans go through four different stages when trying to solve a problem: preparation, incubation, illumination (i.e., insight), and verification. This has given many comparable models analysing the creative process, popularised among managers and consultants by Osborne as the Creative Solving Process (CPS) (Osborne 1953). This particular model encompasses six steps as described in Fig. 3.8. What is important to remember is that only a succession of divergent

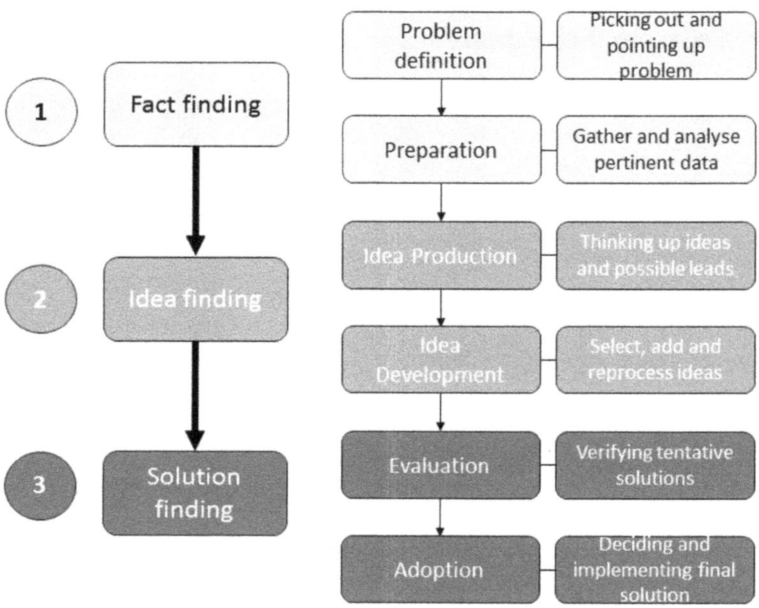

Fig. 3.8 Creative problem-solving model. (Source: Osborne 1953)

thinking then convergent thinking makes creativity possible at each step, as it enables to postpone judgement, thus facilitates the generation of ideas.

Research into applied creative undertaken by Basadur (1979, 1982, 1992) identified four similar stages through which an innovation process must move. These stages are:

1. *Generating*. This stage involves the generation of options in the form of new possibilities, new problems that might be solved, and new opportunities that might be capitalised upon.
2. *Conceptualising*. This stage involves creating options in the form of alternative ways to understand and define a problem or opportunity, and good ideas that can help to solve it.
3. *Optimising*. This stage involves creating options in the form of ways to get an idea to work in practice, and to uncover all the factors that go into a successful plan for its implementation.
4. *Implementing*. This stage involves creating options in the form of actions that get results and gain acceptance for the implementation of change or new ideas.

These four primary stages form what (Basadur 2004) describes as the SIMPLEX process of applied creativity. This is a tool that has been used with success in a number of organisations and environments (Basadur and Gelade 2003).

The SIMPLEX process can be divided into a total of eight stages that need to be worked through in order for an innovation project to be fully implemented (Basadur et al. 2000). These eight stages are illustrated in Fig. 3.9 and explained in more

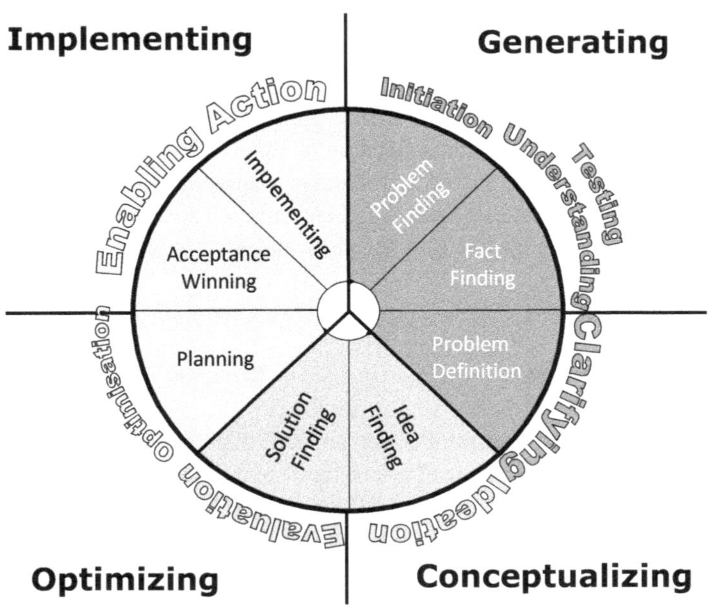

Fig. 3.9 The SIMPLEX applied creativity process. (Source: Basadur and Gelade 2003)

detail in subsequent sections. It should be noted that jumping between these stages can result in a loss of process quality, and may introduce or escalate the risk of failure. Each of these eight stages is associated with a specific work style, and it should be noted that each individual has their own preferred style (one of four styles), as discussed in the following sub-sections.

3.11.1 Generators

These people are attracted to new problems and challenges, and like to view the world from different perspectives. They like to think in a divergent way and to identify creative new options. Generators enjoy ambiguity and like to keep all their options open. These individuals are best engaged within the first two stages of the SIMPLEX process.

3.11.2 Conceptualisers

These people have a preference for abstract thinking and the creation of new insights. However, they also like to define problems and develop a clear understanding of the situation or problem they are seeking to solve. They are highly sensitive to and have an appreciation for new ideas and are not concerned with moving directly to action. Conceptualisers are well placed to engage within the third and fourth stages of the SIMPLEX process.

3.11.3 Optimisers

These people dislike ambiguity and have a preference for analytical thinking and finding practical solutions to well-defined problems. It is their preference to find the few critical factors that are causing a problem or needing attention. They are evaluative with their thinking rather than divergent, and see little value in 'dreaming'. Optimisers are best engaged within the fifth and sixth stages of the SIMPLEX process.

3.11.4 Implementers

These people have a preference for action and feel that understanding is not necessary. They adapt well to changing circumstances, and are enthusiastic but impatient with the ability to bring others on board. However, they dislike apathy. Implementers are best engaged in the final two stages of the SIMPLEX process.

3.11.5 Stage 1 Initiation: Problem Finding

This first stage is where the problem is initially analysed, identified and initiated. It is a most important step as it ensures that you are tackling the right problem. Albert Einstein once said that if he only had 1 h to save the world, he would spend the first 55 min defining the problem and then the last 5 min solving it (Basadur et al. 2000). During this stage the problem is a 'fuzzy situation' and should be approached with an open mind, not preconceived ideas.

3.11.6 Stage 2 Testing Understanding: Fact Finding

In this stage the challenge is to undertake a process of fact finding in order to collect sufficient information or data to fully understand the problem and help clarify the 'fuzzy situation'. You are essentially testing your understanding of the assumptions about what the problem you are trying to solve is, and the reality you feel existing in the organisational environment surrounding this project.

Key Fact-Finding Behaviours
Divergently search for possibly relevant facts.
Encourage several viewpoints.
Beware of assumptions.
Avoid a negative attitude towards problems.
Share information.
Say what you think.
Look for the truth, not ways to boost egos.

In working through these first two stages, it is important that you use divergent rather than convergent thinking. The most common response to a problem by a manager or their team is to rush in with a solution in order to fix the problem. This is using convergent thinking, which is a form of implementation thinking. However, innovation is about finding creative solutions to complex problems, and this requires a divergent thinking which explores a wide range of options.

Key Fact-Finding Questions
What do you know, or think you know, about this fuzzy situation?
What do you not know about this fuzzy situation (but you'd like to know)?
Why is this a problem for you and why can't you make it go away?
What have you already thought of or tried?
If this problem were to be resolved, what would you have that you don't have now?
What might you be assuming that you don't have to assume?

Table 3.1 Innovative results system

Diverge	→	Converge
Ideation	Options	Evaluate
	Points of view	
No judgment	Possibilities	Yes judgment
No logic	Facts	Yes logic
	Opinions	
Relax	Items	Clarify meanings
Quantity	Ideas	Use relevant criteria
Stream of options	Things	Focus of a few things
Radical options	Problems	Consider risky options
Think in pictures	Solutions	Modify and refine
Build onto fragments	Actions	Move toward action

Source: Basadur et al. (2000)

These two forces can be illustrated in Table 3.1, where it can be seen that the process needs to start with a divergent approach in which ideas are generated in an environment of no pre-determined judgments or logic. It is important in this stage to allow creativity to rule, and not a desire to jump in with a solution. Work towards convergence by moving through the process in the middle of the table to a point where a judgment and logic-based mindset can be used.

3.11.7 Stage 3 Clarifying: Problem Definition

In this stage the aim is to ensure that problems will be addressed in a way that is not too narrow but not too wide. The problem needs to be defined and the problem definition used as the foundation upon which future new creative ideas can be formulated. It is a good idea to write down a problem statement that seeks to concisely define the problem from the perspective of the underlying causes, based upon the fact finding and options generated in the previous stages.

Too often we rush into devising solutions without developing a good problem statement. What is important in this step is to use creativity to define our problem in an innovative way. Our problem definition becomes the way we choose to view our problem, or the direction we select. State the problem in a challenge form. People who shy away from negative problems often welcome positive opportunities and challenges. If we want to become more creative, adaptive individuals, then we need to say 'I can't because…' less frequently and ask 'how might I…?' instead.

Learn to broaden and narrow the view of the problem. Don't stop at a 'reasonable' preliminary problem definition. Defer convergence, and continue diverging and converging through the use of the 'why-what's stopping' analysis. This technique often yields the most surprising and fruitful ways to formulate a problem. This approach is based on two simple questions. Asking 'why?' of the challenge and then restating the answer into a new challenge broadens our problem definition.

We see more forest and fewer trees. By asking 'what's stopping me?' and subsequently restating our challenge, we narrow the problem definition, that is, we distinguish individual trees from the forest.

Look for more than one good answer. Ask repeatedly: 'why?' and 'what's stopping me?' (Why else? What else is stopping me?) You can transform each answer into at least one new 'How might I…?' challenge. By the way, this broadening and narrowing does not necessarily produce better problem definitions. The process simply gives you additional views of the problem statement. The best challenge statement might well turn out to be your original one.

The person who first asks the right question or restates the problem in an exciting, insightful way is invaluable. Skilled problem-definers use few key facts to create many different challenges. They can break large problems into smaller components, and see the bigger picture into which smaller components fit. By deferring convergence, they can continue to reformulate the problem to develop a clearly superior 'angle', which then stimulates creative solutions.

Guidelines for Effective Ideation

No evaluative or logical thinking permitted.
Relax your brain and don't worry about being right.
Quantity of options is all important.
Strive to maintain an uninterrupted stream of options.
Reach for radical, impossible options.
Think in pictures and use all five senses where you can.
In each new picture, pick 'option fragments' you like best and then add new fragments to form more options.
Deliberately transform options.

3.11.8 Stage 4 Ideation: Idea Finding

In the fourth stage you should move towards a process of brainstorming, using the data capture in the second stage and the problem definition of the third stage to generate as many ideas as possible that can work towards a solution of the problem but without judgment or evaluation.

In working through this stage, you will need to ensure that you maintain a divergent mindset. To do this you will need to defer your judgment and avoid jumping forward to the solutions and implementation. Some of the specific skills you will need to employ to help you defer judgment, especially in the conceptualisation phase, are (Basadur et al. 2000):

- Avoid making premature, negative judgments of fledgling thoughts (both when working alone and with others).
- Visibly value, appreciate and welcome other points of view as opportunities to strengthen thinking rather than as a threat to your ego.

- Patiently maintain an awareness that some facts are more difficult to perceive (more invisible) than others.
- Question assumptions for validity and search out hidden, unconscious assumptions which may be unwarranted.
- Tackle problems with an optimistic 'can do' attitude rather than prematurely concluding that it 'cannot be done' because 'I can't see how'.
- Tend not to jump prematurely to a conclusion as to what the 'real problem is' in a situation.
- Avoid attaching negative connotations to problems, as such prejudgment may bias fact finding efforts.
- Visibly stay open-minded to others' versions of the facts.
- Often pause deliberately to try an unusual approach to define a problem instead of automatically relying on an old approach.
- React positively to new radical thoughts as opportunities to build fresh new thinking.

3.11.9 Active Divergence

Some of the specific skills for *active divergence* within the conceptualisation phase are (Basadur et al. 2000):

- Search out many different facts and points of view before attempting to define a problem.
- Define problems in multiple and novel ways to get a variety of insights.
- Clarify problems by breaking them down into smaller, more specific sub-problems and also by opening them up into broader, less limiting challenges.
- Deliberately extend effort to create additional and unusual thought-provoking potential ways of defining a problem.
- Give credit for divergent thinking to others, praise others for alternative viewpoints, and try to build upon and strengthen such alternatives to increase the variety of choice.
- Turn premature, negative evaluations of ideas into positive challenges to keep the creative process flowing; that is, change negative 'We can't because …' thoughts into positive 'How might we …?' thoughts.
- Share information and ideas freely with other people and departments, hoping to build understanding of problems.
- Get teams to formulate problems in ways which transcend individual and departmental considerations.

In terms of techniques, this is typically the stage where a "detour" is needed and can be brought by pictures, metaphors, analogies, crushing methods (e.g. the SCAMPER method, where you can substitute, combine, adapt, modify, put to another use, eliminate, reverse elements of the problem), can be useful.

3.11.10 Active Convergence

Convergence is often underestimated, and less associated with creativity. It is a mistake, as converging is as important as diverging. Some of the specific skills for *active convergence*, especially in the conceptualisation phase, are (Basadur et al. 2000):

- Take the time to select, clarify and focus upon the most significant facts available prior to attempting to define a problem.
- Recognise and accept the critical few best problem definition options in terms of 'broadness vs. narrowness' of focus and in terms of insight provided.
- Open-mindedly develop and use multiple, unbiased criteria for selecting from among problem formulation options, rather than letting preconceptions or hidden motives sway decisions.
- Accept the risk of failing, or being criticised for being different, for selecting novel problem definitions.
- Be willing to accept and participate in consensus decisions about problem formulation, and move on decisively in the problem-solving process.
- Do not wait for the 'perfect' option to emerge; instead, take reasonable risks to finish the problem formulation stage.

It is also difficult to keep the richness of what has been produced during the divergent phase. Criteria for converging on best ideas include:

1. Targeted on solving your 'How might…' challenge – remember, you are trying to solve the challenge(s) converged on in Stage 3, Clarifying – problem definition.
2. Has an element of 'newness' – don't automatically revert to 'safe' choices you've known or experienced before.
3. Concrete – be able to visualise what this idea will look like when completed.
4. Easy to understand – an innocent, unknowing bystander should be able to read the idea and know what it means.
5. An easy next step is obvious – the wording of the idea suggests a next step that might be taken to implement it.

3.11.11 Stage 5 Evaluation: Solution Finding

In this stage you take the many promising ideas that you have generated in the previous four stages and begin to evaluate them. You should set criteria for success and employ decision-making techniques in order to evaluate, refine and select the most promising solutions.

The criteria grid (e.g. Table 3.2) is an organised approach to evaluating and selecting one or more good ideas from several 'top contender' ideas for solutions:

Table 3.2 The criteria grid

Rating Scale: 3 = Excellent 2 = Good 1 = Fair 0 = Poor	CRITERIA						
Weighting Factors:							
Idea #1:							
Idea #2:							
Idea #3:							
Idea #4:							

Source: Basadur (2004)

Guidelines for Effective Evaluation

Surface preconceived options and treat them the same as others on the list.

Focus on a few options to consider further and clarify to develop their meaning.

Generate relevant criteria for judging and consider what is most important.

Give serious consideration to superior but risky options and don't discard them prematurely.

Modify and refine incomplete but potentially good options.

Move good options forward and don't wait for a perfect answer.

1. Generate a list of possible criteria. Select the key criteria. Word them carefully.
2. Select a scale (e.g. 0–3). Fill in the chart carefully.
3. Proceed down the ideas with one criterion, in turn.
4. Examine possible weighting opportunities after filling in the chart.

Once you have completed the chart, you can converge onto a solution. The chart does not tell you what choice you make, but it will help you understand the strengths and weaknesses of each idea. Consider fine tuning one idea you liked, but scored less favourably. Sometimes ideas can be blended creatively.

3.11.12 Stage 6 Optimisation: Planning

In this stage the process of implementation commences with you drawing up an action plan that identifies who, what, when, where, why and how you will make the solution work. This is generally familiar territory for most managers and can be part of the business plan for the new venture, the commercialisation plan for the new product, or the strategic plan for a larger organisation.

3.11.13 Stage 7 Enabling Action: Acceptance Winning

During this stage your task is to sell the idea to your team and within your organisation. This stage addresses the complex issues that arise in the process of selling the solution to those in charge. For entrepreneurs the challenge is to sell their new idea or product into the market, or pitch a business case to potential investors. For managers within larger firms, this is often the stage in which the innovative project meets some of its toughest hurdles, as it needs to be sold actively to the senior management. However, if the first six stages have been done well, the plan will be more robust and have potentially more chances of being accepted.

3.11.14 Stage 8 Enabling Action: Implementing

Finally, in this stage the plan is put into action and the results of its implementation are monitored and assessed. The entrepreneur will take their signals from the market and how quickly customers accept the new product or service. Within large organisations, the implementation stage can involve significant project management responsibilities. Managers are usually good at implementing well-prepared plans; however, for entrepreneurial projects with high levels of innovation the implementation is more likely to follow an effectuation process than a causation one.

References

Amabile, T. M. (1998). How to kill creativity. *Harvard Business Review, 76*(5), 76–87.

Amabile, T. M., Hadley, C. N., & Kramer, S. J. (2002). Creativity under the gun. *Harvard Business Review, 80*(8), 52–61.

Basadur, M. (1979). *Training in creative problem solving: Effects on deferred judgment and problem finding and solving in an industrial research organization.* Doctoral dissertation, University of Cincinnati, Ohio.

Basadur, M. (1982). *Research in creative problem solving training in business and industry.* Paper presented at the Creativity Week 4, Greensboro, N.C., Centre for Creative Leadership.

Basadur, M. (1992). Managing creativity: A Japanese model. *Academy of Management Perspectives, 6*(2), 29–42.

Basadur, M. (2004). Leading others to think innovatively together: Creative leadership. *The Leadership Quarterly, 15*(1), 103–121.

Basadur, M., & Gelade, G. (2003). Using the creative problem solving profile (CPSP) for diagnosing and solving real-world problems. *Emergence, 5*(3), 22–47.
Basadur, M., Pringle, P., Speranzini, G., & Bacot, M. (2000). Collaborative problem solving through creativity in problem definition: Expanding the pie. *Creativity and Innovation Management, 9*(1), 54–76.
Edwards, L. (2002). *Building a winning team.* Canberra: AusIndustry, Department of Industry, Tourism and Resources, Commonwealth of Australia.
Farson, R., & Keyes, R. (2002). The failure-tolerant leader. *Harvard Business Review, 80*(8), 64–71.
Gabrielsson, J. (2007). Boards of directors and entrepreneurial posture in medium-size companies: Putting the board demography approach to a test. *International Small Business Journal, 25*(5), 511–537.
Jarrett, D. (1998). A strategic classification of business alliances: A qualitative perspective built from a study of small and medium-sized enterprises. *Qualitative Market Research, 1*(1), 39–49.
Johannisson, B. (1988). Business formation – a network approach. *Scandinavian Journal of Management, 4*(3), 83–99.
Kirton, M. (1976). Adaptors and innovators: A description and measure. *Journal of Applied Psychology, 61*(5), 622.
Koehler, K. (1989). Effective team management. *Small Business Reports, 14*(7), 14–16.
Kourilsky, M. L. (1995). Entrepreneurship education: Opportunity in search of curriculum. *Business Education Forum, Kaufman Center for Entrepreneurial Leadership* (October).
Kuratko, D. F., & Hodgetts, R. (1998). *Entrepreneurship: A contemporary approach* (4th ed.). Sydney: Harcourt and Brace.
Kuratko, D., & Hodgetts, R. (2004). *Entrepreneurship: Theory, process, practice* (6th ed.). Thomson South-Western: Mason Ohio.
Leonard, D., & Straus, S. (1997). Putting your company's whole brain to work. *Harvard Business Review, 75*, 110–122.
Levitt, T. (2002). Creativity is not enough. *Harvard Business Review, 80*, 137–144.
Low, M. B., & MacMillan, I. C. (1988). Entrepreneurship: Past research and future challenges. *Journal of Management, 14*(2), 139–161.
Mazzarol, T., Volery, T., Doss, N., & Thein, V. (1998). *Creativity drives the dream: An empirical analysis of the factors motivating business startups.* Paper presented at the ICSB Conference, June, Singapore.
McFadzean, E. (1998). Enhancing creative thinking within organisations. *Management Decision, 36*(5), 309–315.
Osborne, A. F. (1953). *Applied imagination: Principles and procedures of creative problem solving*. New York: Charles Scribener's Sons.
Ostgaard, T., & Birley, S. (1994). Personal networks and firm competitive strategy – a strategic or coincidental match? *Journal of Business Venturing, 9*(4), 281–306.
Sarasvathy, S. D. (2001). Causation and effectuation: Toward a theoretical shift from economic inevitability to entrepreneurial contingency. *Academy of Management Review, 26*(2), 243–263.
Sarasvathy, S. D., & Dew, N. (2005). New market creation through transformation. *Journal of Evolutionary Economics, 15*(5), 533–565.
Shane, S., & Venkataraman, S. (2000). The promise of entrepreneurship as a field of research. *The Academy of Management Review, 25*(1), 217–226.
Timmons, J. A. (1999). *New venture creation: Entrepreneurship for the 21st century* (5th ed.). McGraw-Hill International Editions.
Volery, T., Mazzarol, T., Doss, N., & Thein, V. (1997). Triggers and barriers affecting entrepreneurial intentionality: The case of Western Australian Nascente entrepreneurs. *Journal of Enterprising Culture, 5*(3), 273–291.
Wallas, G. (1926). *The art of thought.* New York: Harcourt, Brace.
Weinzimmer, L. G. (1997). Top management team correlates of organizational growth in a small business context: A comparative study. *Journal of Small Business Management, 35*(3), 1.

Entrepreneurship and Innovation in Large Firms

4

4.1 Introduction

> Don't for a moment think that change on this scale is easy; you've got to be very opportunistic. If you don't know where you are going, you will not see the opportunities as they waft passed your window; you have got to get your hand out there and grab them. Give them a good shake and decide if they are what you are trying to do. If they are, don't take no for an answer.
>
> Source: Dr. Penny Flett, CEO Brightwater Group.

This chapter examines: new venture creation in established organisations, the intrapreneurial process, the middle manager as an entrepreneur, the roles of sponsors, and climate makers. The infusion of entrepreneurial thinking into large corporate organisational structures has emerged as a key area of management attention since the 1990s. As levels of competition have accelerated, the creative and innovative nature of entrepreneurship has come to be seen as a way of enhancing the competitiveness of organisations and encouraging employees to view themselves as owners. This has seen organisations attempting to encourage employees to tap into their creative and innovative talents, and seeking to promote innovation.

4.2 The Entrepreneurial Manager

The word 'intrapreneur'is commonly used to describe entrepreneurs within large organisations. The word 'intrapreneurship'refers to entrepreneurs inside the corporation or agency who implement new ideas within the established organisation and who – although employed in a corporate position – are nevertheless given the

T. Mazzarol, S. Reboud, *Entrepreneurship and Innovation*, Springer Texts in Business and Economics, https://doi.org/10.1007/978-981-13-9412-6_4

freedom to create and market their own ideas. The intrapreneur demonstrates a set of enterprising attributes in a wide variety of situations. They make things happen.

Intrapreneurship

The purposeful and supported attempt to develop more entrepreneurial behaviour within a company to improve market performance. Intrapreneurship encompasses:

- activities that receive organisational sanction and resources to achieve innovative outcomes;
- the creation of an entrepreneurial spirit within an organisation, allowing an innovation culture to prosper;
- The generation, development and implementation of new ideas or behaviours;
- a focus on re-energising and enhancing a firm's ability to acquire innovative skills and capabilities; and
- the creation, by intrapreneurial individuals within an organisation, of:
- strategic renewal,
- innovation (introducing something new to the marketplace), and
- corporate venturing (creation of new business organisations).

Source: Kurakto and Hodgetts (2004).

For intrapreneurship to operate effectively in practice, the organisational climate must be right for the intrapreneur. It must foster creativity and innovation, tolerate failure and encourage enterprising behaviour. If successful, internal corporate venturing offers substantial opportunities for new products and ideas. However, it needs to be controlled and channelled or it can be harmful to the organisation. Many successful internal corporate ventures have resulted in spin-off companies that emerge as entrepreneurial small firms with financial backing from their parent firm which may also offer them marketing support. How the organisation is structured can influence the process of intrapreneurship. For example, rigid bureaucracy and poor communication flows within the firm will stifle it.

Rationalisation and outsourcing can also serve to harm intrapreneurship as ideas are lost to the organisation, and little incentive is created among sub-contractors to share innovations with the parent firm. On the other hand, spin-off opportunities from the encouragement of intrapreneurship can provide positive outcomes. *Intrapreneuring* can lead to a recharging of the business, making it more customer-focused or market-driven, with benefits for both the business and its customers. Managers who are offered opportunities for internal corporate venturing can develop new skills and abilities, and those with enterprising tendencies can find an avenue for such energy.

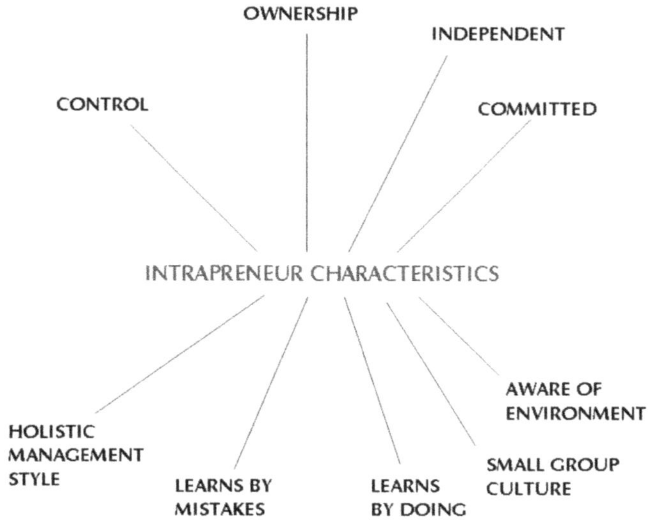

Fig. 4.1 A model of the entrepreneurial manager

As shown in Fig. 4.1, the entrepreneurial manager adopts a holistic view of their organisation, seeking to understand how their role contributes to the overall strategy of the entire firm. Unfortunately, many managers fear making mistakes and pride themselves on being expert professionals. By contrast, intrapreneurs are able to learn from their mistakes and have a reasonable tolerance of failure as a normal process of learning. This type of manager is usually found working in a small group culture as a team leader, but with a highly-developed sense of the key issues surrounding them in their environment and providing strategic insights.

Of high importance is the ability of the organisation within which the intrapreneur works to allow them control, ownership and independence, from which a strong sense of commitment can emerge. Providing control to a manager means allowing him or her to lead sub-units and to have full responsibility for the financial and other management of this entity. To offer ownership over the venture, an organisation must look to its remuneration and equity structure. Providing managers with financial incentives based on their performance, or offering share capital within the venture, are ways of achieving this. Independence comes from giving the manager control and ownership.

Fostering intrapreneurship among managers requires a focus on four key issues. First, the organisational structure should encompass a strong level of senior management support for entrepreneurial activity and innovation. Employees should be provided with a high degree of autonomy and discretion over their work. This should be linked to the reward systems, and there should be a recognition that time must be provided to foster creativity. Second, the organisation should have fuzzy boundaries that allow networking between employees and alliance partners from other firms. Third, the human resource strategies adopted by the organisation should seek to attract and retain achievement-oriented people with the ability to set their own goals and value independence, while having the creativity and risk-taking orientation to try new ideas.

It is also important for the organisation's reward structure to be goal-oriented and to offer strong feedback to employees. The system should allow individual responsibility, but there should be reward for effort. Finally, the senior management of the organisation should be tolerant of failure and risk, but also have the expectation that middle managers will lead innovation as a core part of their job. However, these managers must be provided with appropriate resources including time and money.

The rapid change taking place in many industries and throughout the global economy has presented substantial challenges for organisations. The need to adapt to the dynamic nature of contemporary industries has required firms to restructure and select new strategies designed to enhance competitiveness through innovation.

For organisations seeking to follow an intrapreneurial strategy, it is important for the senior management – and particularly the CEO – to fully support the initiative and to make frequent statements about the importance of innovation. Creativity and innovation should be given priority in reward and remuneration systems, recognising that creative people are driven by the need to create and are not solely motivated by money. Creative people can be difficult to hire, develop and manage, so a strategic commitment is required with appropriate human resource policies (Duncan et al. 1988).

Burgleman (1984) recommended bringing corporate strategy into alignment with the strategies of new venture development (NVD) and the venture or group leaders seeking to implement entrepreneurial programs. Achieving this requires linking the various levels of management, as well as putting into the senior ranks a CEO with some past experience of intrapreneurship. There should be reward and recognition systems in place to encourage junior levels of management, and the provision of adequate resources for middle level managers tasked with NVD. The level of entrepreneurial orientation within an organisation can be determined by their level of innovativeness, pro-activity and risk-taking proclivity. These are the key elements that will allow for enhanced intrapreneuring by managers. Firms that place high importance on R&D leadership, new product development, continuous improvements and constantly challenging the *status quo* in the market generally provide supportive environments for intrapreneurs.

4.3 Large Corporations as Successful Innovators

Large organisations that have succeeded in using intrapreneurship to foster a process of innovation among their staff generally have an atmosphere and vision that is focused clearly on enterprise and innovation. Such organisations are also strongly focused on the market and their customers. They seek to provide their customers with the best possible products or services. Many of these organisations adopt structures that are flat and built around semi-autonomous teams or sub-units that are relatively small (Quinn 1985).

These organisations encourage and support multiple approaches to fostering innovation. They may have several projects under development at any one time, recognising that some will succeed and some will fail. Learning and investigation among employees are valued within such organisations, and there is a high degree of interactive or mutual learning among people. Some organisations have achieved enhanced innovation by creating sub-units that have a high degree of autonomy without the traditional authority and bureaucracy of the larger firm. These 'skunk works' have proven to achieve rapid turnaround of new products and technologies, as well as higher levels of loyalty and identity among employees (Kuratko and Hodgetts 2004).

The impact of intrapreneurship on large corporations is a change in the way management is viewed and performed. According to Gerber (1998), most managers are motivated by two forces – fear and greed. Their fear is that they will lose their job and with it the nice salary, car, office and other benefits that it offers. Their desire to be a manager in the first place is frequently associated with these tangible benefits, and this is the association with greed. Gerber also argues that too many managers have little awareness of the real cost or benefit they bring to their jobs. They frequently deal in what he calls 'funny money'. As cost centre managers they have budgets and look at accounts, but may not actually relate such sums of money to the complete operation of the business. Also, the larger their company and its accounts, the less reality is often associated with their finances.

Breaking out of this mindset can be achieved by intrapreneurship. It offers firms the chance to subcontract non-essential work to smaller, more entrepreneurial firms, and to concentrate on core competencies. Creating smaller sub-units, within larger firms, that have responsibility for their own management and budgets can lead their managers to become closer to the customer. It can also lead to financial reward for good performance. Managers of entrepreneurial sub-units will need to develop the same holistic view of the business as entrepreneurs who operate their own small firms. This will result in flatter organisational structures. Also, the downsizing to more entrepreneurial sub-units will require managers to become more focused on strategic thinking rather than on corporate planning. Their careers will be linked to how well they manage their units, and such managers will be forced to adopt more multi-disciplined, multi-skilled roles. This will weaken the power of the financial controllers within larger firms as 'ownership' will be with managers and employees. Such organisations will need to be tolerant of failure' and must recognise that jobs for life are a thing of the past.

4.4 A Model of Corporate Intrapreneuring

Hornsby et al. (1993) outlined a model of corporate intrapreneuring as illustrated in Fig. 4.2. It can be seen that there must be a balance between organisational characteristics designed to support entrepreneurial activity and the individual characteristics associated with enterprise behaviour. Key organisational characteristics include appropriate senior management support for innovation and enterprise as well as

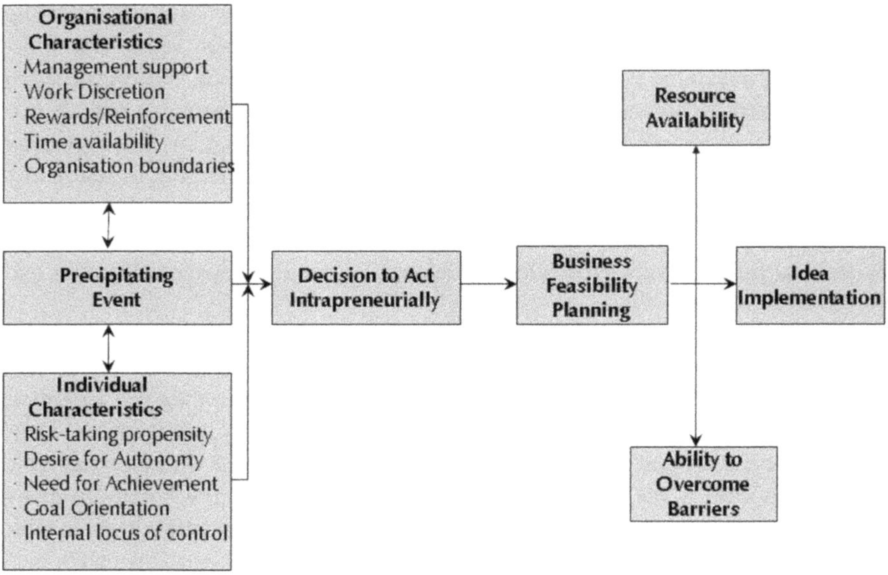

Fig. 4.2 A model of corporate intrapreneuring. (Source: Hornsby et al. 1993)

sufficient autonomy or work discretion for staff. Remuneration and reward systems should seek to recognise innovation and not be designed to treat all employees as the same regardless of effort. There should also be sufficient time made available for new ventures to get launched, and a recognition that the firm's organisation boundaries are not necessarily fixed, allowing for networking, joint venturing and alliances.

For intrapreneuring to commence, there should also be a culture that encourages or attracts individuals with the key enterprise tendencies; and these tendencies should be facilitated through the culture and structure (Kuratko and Montagno 1989). New ideas need to be screened before implementation, and resources must be provided to managers to enable them to overcome barriers and obstacles. The 'precipitating event' that serves to trigger a new enterprise or innovation can come from inside or outside the organisation. Ideally, this will not be a situation in which the organisation finds itself in adverse circumstances such as declining market share or falling stock price, seeking to start innovative and entrepreneurial programs under situations of crisis and financial stress can be most difficult.

Once the firm makes a decision to act in an entrepreneurial manner, the concept for the new product, process or business venture needs to be subjected to feasibility planning. If sufficient financial or other hurdles can be met, the new innovation is supported and resources (e.g. funding, people and/or equipment) are made available to ensure that the idea can be turned into a reality. This process of opportunity screening is important, and should be a well-developed system that allows a fair and objective assessment of the merits of new innovations or ventures. It is common for such screening to involve financial benchmarks such as return on investment, pay back periods, and gross profit contribution margins.

As the project moves forward, the new venture creation team or individual intrapreneur is likely to face a series of barriers to future success. These may be financial, technological, cultural or managerial. Whatever their nature, the successful intrapreneur will persist in the face of such difficulties and seek to overcome them. However, if the parent corporation has screened and approved the venture, it should serve as a venture capital investor to the new venture team. In doing so, it should provide funding and other resources (e.g. employees and/or facilities) against a well-developed business plan and clearly defined targets.

4.5 Challenges for Senior Management

Kuratko and Hodgetts (2004) suggest that organisations can 're-engineer their corporate thinking' to encourage intrapreneurship by focusing on things such as the setting of explicit, mutually-agreed goals that allow employees to share the vision and align their work with the broader corporate strategy. They also need to create a system of feedback and positive reinforcement that is accepted by the majority of employees and encourages them with rewards. It is important for such organisations to emphasise individual responsibility among employees, while also providing them with rewards based on results. These are major challenges to senior management, who need to develop a capacity for accepting failure as a necessary part of innovation and enterprise, and who need to learn to recognise the value that an internal corporate venturing process can deliver.

4.6 Failure Tolerant Leadership

Failure is a prerequisite to invention, and organisations need to encourage risk-taking and learning from mistakes. Senior management should seek to tolerate failure as a natural process of learning. Farson and Keyes (2002) advocate failure tolerant leadership in order to encourage innovation. This requires projects to have clear exit strategies built into them to allow an opportunity to limit the risk. New ideas for products or services should be subject to extensive market testing prior to a full-scale investment. It may also be appropriate for large organisations to launch two projects with the same goals to run in parallel in order to determine which one will produce the dominant design. This can create additional competition between the two internal corporate venture teams, thereby enhancing their efforts.

According to Farson and Keyes (2002), an excessive focus on personal failure and the stigma attached to it can sap the creative energy within an organisation. Executives have a key role to play in developing a failure tolerant culture by helping employees overcome their fear of failure. Failure tolerant leaders engage people and set good examples. They are prepared to admit their own mistakes and are non-judgemental, while being analytical – neither praising nor penalising. While healthy competition is a positive force, it is important for senior managers to take steps to remove any negative destructive competitiveness in organisations. This might involve removing rewards that focus only on winning and not on collaboration. It is important that reward systems seek to build communities that practice idea sharing and mutual trust and safety.

4.7 Unleashing the Intrapreneurs

Intrapreneurs are not always obedient and usually wish to steer their own internal course, set their own standards, and do what they see as necessary (Stein and Pinchot 1998). From a narrow perspective, the intrapreneur is little more than a middle level employee within an existing organisation who initiates and creates a new venture or significant initiative such as a new product or process. However, there is a broader view of intrapreneuring that seeks to use it to foster organisation-wide innovation and enterprise. It can also encompass those individuals who perform in an entrepreneurial manner to develop administrative or process innovations and who champion the development of new products.

The intrapreneur serves the role of a zealous volunteer champion who will quickly bring an innovation to the marketplace. If technical people have a high need for achievement, then the organisation needs to create an appropriate environment for intrapreneurship to emerge. This was the policy followed within the 3M Corporation whereby technical employees were given permission to allocate 15% of their time to new 'pet projects'.

Systematic approaches to internal corporate venturing have seen the appointment of dedicated *venture managers*. In many organisations intrapreneurs appear spontaneously, whereas venture managers are part of a preconceived corporate process responding to an opportunity. Intrapreneurs tend to be self-motivated, and their presence is more likely to lead to venture success. When a product concept has been accepted, the focus shifts to the venture manager resolving technical problems (David 1994).

Intrapreneurship is not confined only to middle level managers and a few creative individuals. It is also open to all organisations, not just large for-profit firms such as 3M. The fostering of innovation and entrepreneurial behaviour can be undertaken in all organisations including government and not-for-profit agencies. It is a mind-set in which the creative talents of the individual employees are linked to the dual purposes of achieving organisational and personal objectives.

4.8 Ten Principles of Intrapreneuring

Sholl (1998) has outlined ten principles for the successful management of an intrapreneurial new venture team within a large organisation:

1. Intrapreneurial team members must share a common dynamic vision that continually evolves.
2. The new venture team must be organised and must act like intrapreneurs. Independently-minded intrapreneurs should be placed under a corporate advisory board with clear lines of reporting to avoid conflicts.
3. Senior management must be kept well-informed by the new venture team, with frequent updates of how the project is going.
4. A healthy dose of the venture leader's personal time and attention must be devoted to managing the interaction with the larger corporation.
5. The venture management team and the corporation must enter into mutual agreements that allow the venture the required freedom to act.
6. Launching an intrapreneurial venture is not for the faint hearted. It is both risky and uncertain as to how it will turn out.
7. The relationship between the venture and corporation requires both parties to maintain open and effective communication channels.
8. The entire venture team must be encouraged to participate in planning the business' direction.
9. If a team lacks a 'passion' for the business and each other, it rapidly comes apart.
10. Venture team members become 'owners' of the business when compensation is directly linked to venture success in ways they never would if they were on a conventional compensation plan.

4.9 The Process of Internal Corporate Venturing

According to Burgleman (1984), the process of internal corporate venturing (ICV) offers large organisations an opportunity to diversify into new market and product combinations. It can take an average of 8 years for a new venture to reach its profitability, and 10–12 years before it produces a return on investment equal to that of the mainstream business. However, the process of growth in large corporations usually requires some diversification due to the saturation of existing markets. Burgleman (1984) identified four key problems with ICV activity, which are discussed in the following sub-sections.

4.9.1 Vicious Circles in the Definition Process

Problems can emerge where the organisation is initially unable to identify the merits of the new venture and therefore reluctant to provide adequate resources for it to proceed. Intrapreneurs seeking to pursue their ICV project will typically have to argue their case for resources and bootleg resources. Project champions and senior mentors willing to back the new idea are critical to its early survival. There will be problems defining the territorial boundaries of the ICV within the parent organisation. In order to overcome this problem, the organisation should seek to facilitate the process of defining the role and place of the ICV to assist its integration into the wider organisation. This can include a process of defining the way R&D will be conducted within the organisation and how new innovations are commercialised. It is the role of senior management to provide mentoring and coaching for ICV product champions and to facilitate 'give and take' between groups.

4.9.2 Managerial Dilemmas in Impetus Process

Once the project receives official venture status, its future development is likely to depend on its ability to achieve fast growth (e.g. typically \$50–\$100 million in 5–10 years). There may also be friction between maximising growth and building functional capabilities within the organisation. It is not uncommon for the ICV team to become isolated within the parent organisation. Senior managers of the ICV must continue to be strategic in their outlook to maintain growth; however, the ICV team also needs to have operational-level managers with the ability to serve as organisational builders, putting in place systems that will enable the venture to survive over the longer term.

4.9.3 Indeterminateness of Strategic Context of ICV Development

Many ICV projects are adversely influenced by the short-term strategic horizons of many senior managers. It is not uncommon for senior managers to have time horizons of little more than 3–5 years, while the time needed for the ICV project to reach its potential may be 5–10 years. The ICV team may therefore find itself being pressured by the parent organisation to deliver within unrealistic time periods or compared unfairly against more mature ventures. To address this challenge, the strategic context of the ICV should be clearly articulated to avoid any misunderstanding. The parent organisation should have a corporate development strategy that seeks to groom new ventures and do so as part of its longer-term commitment to innovation and growth. It should not view ICV projects as simple insurance against mainstream business activities.

4.9.4 Perverse Selective Pressures Exerted by Structural Context on ICV Development

The ICV also needs to have a structure that is appropriate to the strategic direction it is seeking to follow. There is a danger that the structure of the ICV project team can be forced upon it by the pressures of fast growth rather than that more appropriate to its needs. The organisation should adopt a tolerance for more flexibility in how it allows ICV projects to structure themselves, and this should be focused on the needs of new venture development.

4.10 Advice for Intrapreneurs

Successful entrepreneurs chose challenges that they perceive to be moderately difficult or risky. According to Pinchot and Pellman (1999), after committing to the pursuit of an opportunity an intrapreneur will do everything possible to reduce their risk, asking themselves the key question: 'If it were my money, would I risk it?' Reputation buys the freedom to innovate, and intrapreneurs rely on past successes to develop a strong reputation (Pinchot and Pellman 1999).

Learning by experience is critical in any innovation initiative. Successful intrapreneurial teams seek to learn at the lowest cost and keep their options open by avoiding investment in expensive equipment and experiments. Innovation requires a committed team, and intrapreneurs should seek to recruit willing volunteers who understand and support the vision and strategic intent of the team. It is important for the intrapreneurial manager to create within their team a sense of shared responsibility for creating the team vision and ensuring that all team members agree on goals, targets and responsibilities (Pinchot and Pellman 1999).

Pinchot (1987) has suggested that it is critical to recognise the difference between promoters and intrapreneurs. Promoters are poor executers of ideas and initiatives. They are often driven by power and status, and are willing to take unnecessary risks to advance their own interests. Promoters can be dishonest in their dealings, and can be little more than a 'flash in the pan'. By contrast, the intrapreneur is driven by a vision and takes calculated risks, persisting in the achievement of the goals, and usually dealing with people in an honest manner. These differences are summarised in Table 4.1.

Innovations require high-level sponsors who have the power to keep the project alive. Potential sponsors need to see commitment and the ability to follow through. The intrapreneurial manager should cultivate senior mentors, seeking to establish from them a pattern of small contributions and gradually building up to asking for larger commitment (Pinchot and Pellman 1999). With such support secured, the intrapreneur needs to build an aggressive plan that they can share with the ICV team, while at the same time allowing for strategic flexibility. It is suggested that the manager seeking to lead innovation: discovers a pattern that works, debriefs and analyses failures and successes, and seeks to understand where others are coming from when they criticise plans. It is important not to proceed with blind faith but to seek advice and feedback, embracing barriers as challenging opportunities.

Table 4.1 Intrapreneurs vs. promoters

The intrapreneur	The promoter
Is driven by vision	Is driven by power and status
Is a moderate risk taker	Is a high-risk taker
Is analytical and intuitive	Is analytical or intuitive
Is honest	Is often dishonest
Is persistent	Is a 'flash in the pan'
Is credible	Lacks a good track record

Source: Filion (1996, 2000)

In developing a clear strategic vision, the intrapreneurial manager should set targets that require a tenfold improvement in specific areas – on average companies achieve nearly 75% of goals when seeking to achieve ten times market enhancements. Goals can be created using a participative approach within the ICV team and the parent organisation. Key questions that should be discussed are:

- How do we contribute to overall success?
- Who are our customers?
- What are their needs? (Pinchot and Pellman 1999)

Intrapreneurial managers will need to span boundaries by creating visions that inspire people in other parts of the company. It is important for the ICV project to be viewed in the same way that a venture capitalist might view any stand-alone venture. The composition of the ICV team should be designed to satisfy the needs of balance and effectiveness in its commitment and mix of talents. It is important to ask whether the team has the intrapreneurial spirit and ability to work together as a high-performance team, the skills and experience for the job, and the ability to win against odds (Pinchot and Pellman 1999).

Finally, the intrapreneurial manager should learn to behave like a peer rather than a figure of power; otherwise, the ICV team may lose control and stop taking responsibility for decisions. Ways to lower power status are to sit physically lower than the team, speak softly, show uncertainty and show respect for the teams' opinions. Also, spending some casual time with the team to develop a greater understanding of the project and being willing as the team leader to ask for help with preparation for meetings will also help (Pinchot and Pellman 1999). This process of people management is highly important to the success of new ventures.

4.11 Developing HR Frameworks for Intrapreneuring

Savery and Mazzarol (2000) identify the key elements required within the larger firm to encourage corporate intrapreneuring. These are illustrated in Fig. 4.3. The first of these is an appropriate *reward structure*. Reward systems need to be tailored to encourage innovation and risk-taking. To be effective, they need to consider such things as: goal setting, feedback, individual responsibility, and reward for effort. Adequate reward systems need to reinforce and enhance innovative, creative behaviour. Firms must be characterised by: providing rewards contingent on performance, providing challenge, increasing responsibility, and making the ideas of innovative people known to others in the organisational hierarchy.

There must also be adequate management support. Both middle and senior management needs to be encouraged to accept the challenge of new innovative ideas. Managers and employees must be encouraged to believe that innovation is part of their role within the firm. It is important to have systems in place to quickly adopt

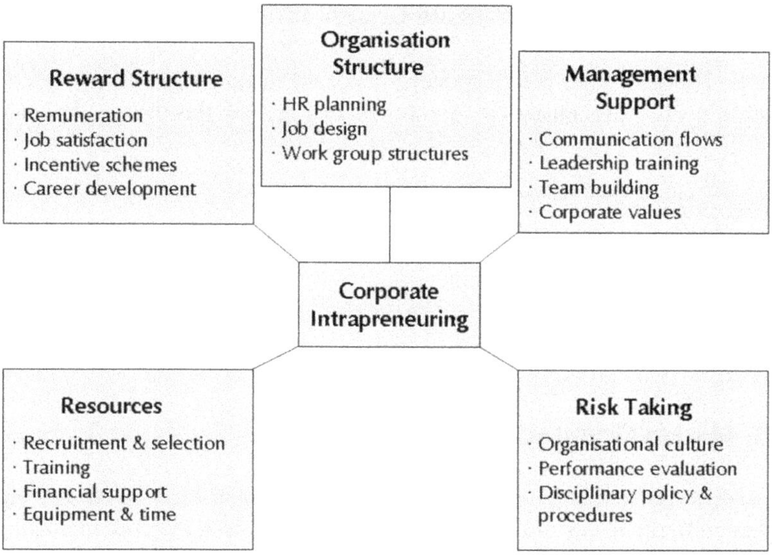

Fig. 4.3 An HR framework for corporate intrapreneuring. (Source: Savery and Mazzarol 2000)

new ideas and to recognise those who contribute such ideas. Support mechanisms for small experimental projects need to be put in place with appropriate seed capital to help get innovate ideas off the ground. Resource allocation within the firm must also be examined. Allocation of scarce resources to competing projects with different levels of risk and return is a major task for an organisation seeking to encourage corporate intrapreneuring. Employees must be encouraged to make best use of scarce resources, and learn to adapt and improvise. The fostering of new and innovative ideas requires that individuals have time to incubate these ideas. Firms must moderate the workload of people, avoid putting time constraints on all aspects of a person's job, and allow people to work with others on long-term problem-solving.

The firm's structure should seek to reduce bureaucracy and enhance the flow of resources, management support and rewards. Employees should be encouraged to look at problems from outside their own narrow job perspective. Firms should avoid having standard operating procedures for all major parts of jobs and should reduce the dependence on narrow job descriptions and rigid standards of performance. It is essential for any successful intrapreneuring process to create an environment that encourages risk-taking by managers and employees. Achieving a balance between controlled risk-taking to achieve innovative success and harmful excessive risk-taking is a major challenge. The creation of an organisational culture that is tolerant of controlled risk-taking is an essential step. This needs to be supported by structures that permit managers to undertake risk-taking within prescribed limits.

4.12 Creating the Innovative Organisation

Mazzarol (2004) has provided a framework for the development of entrepreneurial innovation within organisations. As shown in Fig. 4.4 this framework has five elements:

1. market orientation;
2. innovative leadership;
3. non-linear strategic planning;
4. ambidextrous structure; and
5. innovation focused culture.

4.12.1 Market Orientation

The possession of a strong market orientation that enables a firm to closely monitor and respond to the needs of customers has been recognised as a key element in the successful development of innovation (Quinn 1985). Successful innovators establish strategic partnerships within their industry supply chain, developing close relationships with lead customers and key suppliers as well as third-party resource

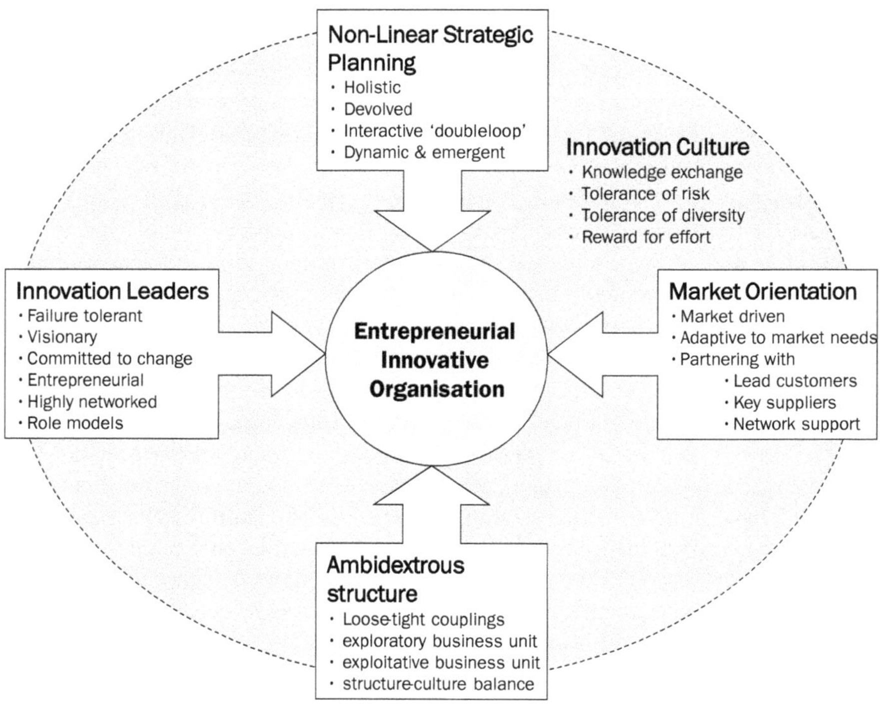

Fig. 4.4 A model of entrepreneurial innovative organisations. (Source: Mazzarol 2004)

network partners such as banks, venture capital suppliers and providers of new technology (Holmlund and Tornroos 1997).

While all customers are important, the *lead customer* is the most significant. Lead customers are defined as those that are dominant in their industry and generally have above average levels of competitiveness. Such customers are frequently demanding and push their suppliers to enhanced levels of performance. Lead customers assist the innovation process by demanding high standards and continuous improvements in both product differentiation and cost reduction via process enhancements. They also keep the innovator firm informed of new market trends and frequently serve as development partners, generating ideas for innovations and assisting in their eventual implementation. A similar relationship can be developed with key suppliers or those suppliers that provide a critical level of components to the firm.

Miller (2001) argues in favour of closely engaging with customers and suppliers to examine needs and possibilities in what has been described as a fourth generation (4G) spiral process for innovation (Miller and Morris 1999). Within business networks, the interaction between the supplier firm and its lead customers can lead to this type of innovation and diffusion process. Collaboration over identifying new products or processes can be achieved if such customer-supplier relationships are carefully leveraged.

4.12.2 Innovative Leadership

Innovation is a process rather than a destination. This process involves the full chain of actors who comprise the firm's value chain and industry supply chain, ranging from the customers throughout the firm and on to the supplier. Management, particularly senior managers, play a crucial role in the innovation process. Managing innovation within an organisation requires leadership to set strategic directions, to motivate and empower employees, and to guide activity in desired directions. At least four key management problems have been identified in the innovation management process (VanDenVen, 1986).

The first of these is dealing with human capital, specifically capturing people's attention and focusing their efforts on innovation. By nature, people tend to focus on maintaining the *status quo* and harvesting established strategies or technologies rather than seeking new solutions. Further, the more successful an organisation is, the more complacent its people can become. The second problem is related to process, specifically how to get innovative ideas from people's heads and into action. Some large service firms in Europe have now established innovation departments that focus purely on capturing good ideas and examining their feasibility. A third problem is associated with organisational structure. Here the manager must find a way to integrate a variety of functional responsibilities and intellectual or professional disciplines together to achieve optimal outcomes. This places pressure on the structure and culture within the firm. Finally, there is the problem of strategy. Innovations lead to dynamic change within the firm and within industries. Because change is frequently risky and difficult for organisations, there must be strong institutional leadership to guide change and to find ways to transform the structure and culture of the firm (Stringer 2000).

Research into the factors likely to influence innovative behaviour among employees highlights the importance of leadership and role modelling by senior managers. The expectations that managers were seen to have toward innovative behaviour was of significant importance. When employees understood that managers expected them to behave in an innovative way, they were more likely to respond. Supporting this was the overall quality of the relationship between the manager and the employee, and how that exchange served to reinforce the manager's commitment to innovation within the organisation. What this study highlights are the critical importance of leadership within organisations that are seeking to become more innovative. Only where managers serve as role models, and communicate their desire for innovation and how such innovation may be achieved, will employees respond with strong innovative behaviour (Scott and Bruce 1994).

4.12.3 Non-linear Strategic Planning

Organisations seeking to enhance their innovation need to possess a strategic planning process that is non-linear in nature, which implies flexibility and a capacity for entrepreneurial flair (Quinn 1980, 1985). This latter point refers to the ability of the planning process to remain flexible and permit all functional areas of an enterprise to contribute to the process (Takeuchi and Nonaka 1986).

Innovation management should be viewed as a strategic process with a formal strategic innovation plan developed by senior management to spell out the organisation's goals in relation to new product or venture creation. Managers should commence by setting clear goals for innovation within the firm. They should consider what specific areas are to be targeted by innovation and what is the current capacity within the firm for innovation (e.g. core competencies). Once these issues are addressed, the manager can determine the future actions required to implement changes (Foster and Prior 1986).

Attention should be given to using innovation as a means of enhancing return on investment, expanding new product development opportunities, or lowering cost. Managers seeking to achieve this can speed up the adoption of new technologies to assist in the improvement of products and processes. The shortening of development and implementation cycles for new products or ventures and the creation within the firm of a culture of innovation are also part of the innovation management process. Thus, managers also need to learn how to identify barriers to innovation within the firm. Such barriers may include a culture adverse to risk-taking, or a lack of reward or incentive for new ideas (Foster and Prior 1986).

Strategic planning is frequently logical, systematic and prescriptive in nature, while strategic thinking is more intuitive, fluid, creative and divergent (Graetz 2002). Strategy has been likened to a 'double-loop' process (iterative and continuous), while planning has been viewed as a 'single-loop' process (Heracleous 1998).

Formal, linear planning is inconsistent with the dynamic strategic approach adopted by entrepreneurs, which involves a process of the continuous screening of opportunities, the weeding out of less promising options selection, and prompt exploitation – usually with only limited analysis (Bhide 1994). Whereas large firms consider options carefully and invest against clearly defined financial benchmarks, entrepreneurs act more intuitively, taking calculated risks and using creative vision and market opportunity as their guide. Sequential or linear strategic planning involves the identification of an opportunity, an evaluation of its strategic value, the formulation of strategy, the commitment of resources, the transfer of responsibility to an implementation team, and the implementation of the strategy. This process is generally risky in nature and involves a fairly lengthy time from conception to market acceptance. By contrast, the non-linear or simultaneous process of strategic planning sees opportunity identification, opportunity screening, resource allocation and implementation taking place concurrently and with shorter cycle times (Feurer et al. 1995).

To create such non-linear strategic planning processes requires the combination of the other four key elements described so far. Close partnering with lead customers offers organisations the opportunity to develop new products and services and to bring them to market quickly, confident of ready acceptance and eventual diffusion. Innovative leadership by senior managers of employees who are supported by an innovative culture and ambidextrous structure is more likely to embrace the dynamic and challenging requirements of non-linear strategic planning. Effective strategies must be market or customer focused, with the ability to be continuously fine-tuned in the face of external change while also maintaining a clear focus on the core competencies that underwrite the firm's competitive advantage. Such strategies should also be clearly communicated to all key stakeholders including customers, suppliers, employees and the resource network (Nohria et al. 2003).

4.12.4 Ambidextrous Structure

For large organisations seeking to encourage high levels of innovation, a common impediment is their own organisational structure. By its nature innovation involved new combinations of skills, resources and technologies. In its most radical form it carries higher than average risks, and is frequently enhanced by placing the responsibility for the new product or process into the hands of a cross-functional team with the ability to see the project through from start to finish (Pinchot 1987). Such requirements can place pressure on existing organisational structures in which people – and resources – are already committed to the status quo and may either resist new change or lose sight of the whole innovation effort (VanDenVen 1986).

Organisational structures that are better suited to radical innovations usually have a smaller, flatter management structure and cross-functional teams that operate with greater autonomy than is usual for the larger organisation. However, they remain linked to the parent organisation with the ability to leverage its strength in resources and implementation skills (e.g. marketing and production). According to

O'Reilly and Tushman (2004), the ambidextrous organisation needs to develop two distinct organisational forms. First are the exploratory businesses that are focused on innovation and growth. They are adaptable and entrepreneurial, with relatively loose rules and regulations and a greater capacity to take risks and exploit new opportunities in an entrepreneurial manner. The second are exploitative businesses that are focused on cost and profit. Their strength lies in being highly efficient in operational implementation and in keeping costs down through well-designed systems and routine procedures. However, such firms are also more rigid in their cultures and less flexible or open to creativity and risk-taking.

This 'ambidextrous structure' is reflective of the need for large, more exploitative organisations to establish smaller, more exploratory sub-units that might eventually spin-out from their parent firm. Internal corporate ventures (ICV) are often formed as separate business units so as to enter different markets and develop new product or process innovations faster and with less bureaucratic interference. Such ICV structures usually have autonomy in marketing and R&D functions, and have venture managers with sound relationships with senior management through a venture sponsor or mentor based in the parent firm (David 1994).

4.12.5 Innovation Culture

Entrepreneurial orientation within small firms is usually the responsibility of the entrepreneur who sets the strategic direction of the company and typically leads its innovation. In larger organisations the challenge has been to foster entrepreneurial spirit among employees via a process of internal corporate venturing that may promote innovation (Burgelman 1984). This has been seen as achievable via the empowerment of middle management (Kanter 1982), or via the formation of 'innovation management task forces' that can motivate employees and implement strategies (Foster and Pryor 1986).

Innovative behaviour among employees has been found to be positively associated with the level of support for innovation engendered within the organisation's culture. This is more important than the availability of resources for undertaking innovative activities (Scott and Bruce 1994). Organisational cultures that foster creativity are likely to be more conducive to innovation (Sonnenberg 1991). Senior management within such enterprises will also need to be more tolerant of failure (Farson and Keyes 2002), and encourage subordinate staff to be more autonomous and willing to take calculated risks (Pearson 1988). Such initiatives may be increasingly more important within industries where product and process technologies have reached the limits of further development. Under such conditions, investment in human resources via training and skill development can become a source of competitive advantage (Pfeffer 1994).

In seeking to generate a suitable climate for innovation, organisations must look to their strategic human resources management policies. First, they need to examine their reward structure to ensure that employees are suitably recognised and rewarded for innovation and risk-taking. This needs to consider goal setting feedback, individual responsibility and reward for effort. Adequate reward systems need to reinforce and enhance innovative, creative behaviour. Firms must be characterised by providing rewards contingent on performance, providing challenges, increasing responsibility, and making the ideas of innovative people known to others in the organisational hierarchy. Middle managers and employees must be encouraged to believe that innovation is part of their role within the firm. Resource allocation within the firm must also be examined. Allocation of scare resources to competing projects with different levels of risk and return is a major task of an organisation seeking to encourage innovation. Time and workloads must be reviewed to ensure that teams have the capacity to pursue new ideas. There must also be a tolerance of risk-taking within the organisation, and a flexibility of structure to adapt and change as required (Savery and Mazzarol 2000).

4.13 Balancing Culture and Structure

Gresov (1984) suggests that the dilemma facing many managers seeking to enhance the innovation within their firms is the tension between structure and culture, implementation and innovation issues. As shown in Fig. 4.5 an organisation that has a highly centralised structure will be strong in terms of its capacity for implementation but weak in terms of innovation. By contrast, the more 'complex' (organic) a firm is, the more likely it will be good at innovation but weak at implementation. In terms of culture, the firm with a homogeneous culture is likely to be good at implementation but weak at innovation. Firms with highly heterogeneous cultures are likely to have good capacity for innovation but less for implementation.

		Capacity for	
		Innovation	Implementation
Organisation's Structure is	Centralised	NO	YES
	Complex	YES	NO
Organisation's Culture is	Homogeneous	NO	YES
	Heterogeneous	YES	NO

Fig. 4.5 Organisational culture and innovation. (Source: Gresov 1984)

This dilemma is what faces many managers seeking to encourage innovation within their firms. Firms which centralise authority structures too rigidly and tolerate little homogeneity in their culture are unlikely to be effective innovators, even if they are competent implementers. The same is true of firms that have high levels of heterogeneity in culture and complexity in structure. While innovation may be high, they are frequently unable to capitalise on such ideas and effectively bring them to market.

Restructuring the firm to encourage innovation (e.g. shifting from a centralised to complex structure) may not be sufficient if the culture remains unchanged. Because culture is frequently highly resistant to change, structures may move well before the culture does (if at all). In a similar manner, attempting to generate innovation by absorbing other entities, hiring new employees or creating new spin-offs may create shifts in culture (e.g. from homogeneous to heterogeneous), but will not truly supply innovation if the structure of the firm remains too centralised.

According to Gresov (1984), a possible solution to this dilemma is for firms to develop a 'hybrid' organisation-culture format. This seeks a structure that is either both homogenous in culture and complex in structure, or centralised in structure and heterogeneous in culture. As shown in Fig. 4.6, the four combinations of culture and structure are:

- *Centralised structure (homogenous culture).* This structure is likely to be weak in innovation but strong in implementation. It is suitable for firms that have relatively low levels of technology within their industries and are more concerned with the effective implementation of established technologies via efficient production and distribution.
- *Centralised structure (heterogeneous culture).* This combination has the potential to be strong in both innovation and implementation. Such firms may be difficult to control given the likely tensions between the culture and structure.
- *Complex structure (homogeneous culture).* This combination is likely to be strong in both innovation and implementation. However, it will need to be careful not to allow the homogeneity of its culture to overwhelm the need for innovation and diversity.

		Organisation's Structure is	
		Centralised	Complex
Organisation's Culture is	Homogeneous	Weak in innovation Strong in implementation	Strong in both
	Heterogeneous	Strong in both	Strong in innovation Weak in implementation

Fig. 4.6 Balancing organisational culture and structure. (Source: Gresov 1984)

- *Complex structure (heterogeneous culture).* This combination is likely to be strong in innovation but weak in implementation.

Managers seeking to enhance innovation or implementation levels within their firms must consider the dual impacts of both culture and structure. They can adjust either one or both depending on the current nature of their existing organisation. For example, a manager within a complex-heterogeneous firm might seek to enhance the implementation capacity by leaving the structure (complex) alone and working on the culture via training or cross-functional education-awareness campaigns.

4.14 Open Innovation and Absorptive Capacity

The success of large firms engaging in innovation, in particular new product development (NPD) and commercialisation, needs to rely not just on the development of their culture and structure, but also their ability to open up to new knowledge and greater sharing of ideas with outsiders. This requires attention to two concepts, *open innovation* and *absorptive capacity*, which are discussed below.

4.14.1 Open Innovation

The concept of *open innovation* was introduced by Chesbrough (2003) who examined case studies of how large U.S. companies (e.g. Xerox, IBM) historically managed their R&D and NPD processes in a largely closed manner. In this *closed innovation* model, there was a reluctance to share proprietary knowledge, and a preference to hold all R&D centrally within specialised research centres or laboratories. However, over time this led to erosion of competitiveness due to a separation of research from development, which slowed down the commercialisation process, and detached the researchers from the marketing teams.

While the closed innovation model had served most large firms well during much of the last century, things began to change as the pace of technological change accelerated during the 1980s and 1990s. Digital technologies such as computers, information and communications systems and other electronic automation, was transforming the nature of industries in what has been identified as the 3rd Industrial Revolution (1969–2010) (Kagerman et al. 2013; WEF 2017). Innovation, in particular R&D focused commercialisation, was shifting away from the larger firms and into universities and small companies. In fact, many of the latter had been founded by former engineers from the larger firms who had been champion intrapreneurs, but found their ambitions stymied by the culture and structure of the closed innovation environment.

In response, many large firms began to open up their R&D systems to outsiders, often from universities, research centres and smaller firms. This helped to speed up the rate of commercialisation and helped IBM transform itself in the 1990s from a closed to an open innovation model. A transition that was driven by its ‘near-death experience' in the early 1990s (Chesbrough 2003). This transformation within IBM took place during the revolution of micro-computing, along with information and communications technologies (ICTs), that swept through the world in the 1990s and early 2000s. This saw the rise of many technology-based firms (e.g. Intel, Apple, Google) that adopted an open innovation paradigm as a foundation for their approach to R&D. Reflecting the view that successful innovation requires opening up the organisation's boundaries to a free flow of ideas and knowledge (Chesbrough 2006).

The New Rationale for Internal R&D

In a bountiful knowledge landscape, a company organizes its internal R&D for the following reasons:

- To identify, understand, select from, and connect to the wealth of available external knowledge;
- To fill in the missing pieces of knowledge not being externally developed;
- To integrate internal and external knowledge to form more complex combinations of knowledge, to create new systems and architectures;
- To generate additional revenues and profits from selling research outputs to other firms for use in their own systems

The company will also need technologies that its internal research organization will not create. Research takes a long time to deliver useful outcomes, and company strategies change at a far faster rate than the rhythm of basic research. In the new paradigm, the company's businesses cannot (and should not) wait for the internal technologies to arrive; instead, they should access what they need, as soon as they need it—either from inside the company's own research labs or from the knowledge created in someone else's lab.

Source: Chesbrough (2003), 53.

Greco et al. (2016) conducted a study into the benefits of open innovation on firm performance within the EU. They found that it had positive benefits, particularly where the innovation being developed was radical rather than incremental in nature. A collaborative and/or networked strategy was likely to have the most benefits in these cases. They recommended that a firm seeking to use open innovation for a radical innovation project.

> **Firms seeking to engage in open innovation,** …should enter into collaborative agreements with a few knowledge-intensive partners, ensuring frequent interactions that may favour the transfer of knowledge across organizational boundaries (Greco et al. 2016, 514).

However, where the innovation is of an incremental nature, the most appropriate strategy is to maintain more informal relationships with a wide-range of outside network partners and put the task to a more “crowd sourced” model. It was noted that in both cases there is a process of diminishing marginal returns to any strategy. These findings are similar to those of a study of open innovation within firms in Switzerland, which suggested that the search and engagement strategy a firm might follow is likely to depend on the type of innovation being considered (e.g. radical or incremental) (Garriga et al. 2013).

4.14.2 Absorptive Capacity

An important ingredient in the application of open innovation is the ability of the organisation to effectively manage flows of information and knowledge that flow between it and its network partners within the external environment. This requires the firm to acquire knowledge from a range of external network actors (e.g. customers, suppliers, competitors and R&D partners). It must also be able to appropriate this knowledge via formal and informal means, and then it must have the ability to integrate this knowledge into its commercialisation systems (Huang and Rice 2009). This requires the firm to possess what Cohen and Levinthal (1990) refer to as *absorptive capacity,* which involves the ability of the firm to leverage existing stocks of knowledge, to acquire, absorb and then make effective use of new knowledge.

For an organisation to have effective absorptive capacity, it must first possess a culture and structure that encourages and facilitates its employees to possess the necessary mindsets and competencies to acquire, assimilate, transform and exploit knowledge, and do so rapidly (Zahra and George 2002). This requires not only the firm’s ability to effectively connect and communicate with external actors in the exchange of knowledge, but to also connect and communicate with internal actors in this knowledge exchange process (Cohen and Levinthal 1990). For example,

> Absorptive capacity refers not only to the acquisition or assimilation of information by an organization but also to the organization’s ability to exploit it. Therefore, an organization’s absorptive capacity does not simply depend on the organization’s direct interface with the external environment. It also depends on transfers of knowledge across and within subunits that may be quite removed from the original point of entry. Thus, to understand the sources of a firm’s absorptive capacity, we focus on the structure of communication between the external environment and the organization, as well as among the subunits of the organization, and also on the character and distribution of expertise within the organization (Cohen and Levinthal 1990, 131–132).

Absorptive capacity has been found to have mixed influences on enhancing a firm’s ability to collaborate with external actors in the acquisition of knowledge. However, it appears to play an important role in enhancing the firm’s ability to benefit from such acquisition and this has benefits to both financial performance and innovativeness (West and Bogers 2014).

4.14.3 Managing Open Innovation

Despite its benefits, open innovation has been largely concentrated within the realm of R&D management and has not been given much attention within the broader disciplines of management and economics (West et al. 2014). A key issue for the management of open innovation is the control over intellectual property (IP) rights (Gambardella and Panico 2014). According to Chesbrough (2003), the mindset managers need to adopt in relation to IP rights when pursuing open innovation, is to assume that there is a 'bountiful supply of potentially useful ideas outside the firm' (p. 155). In so doing, the manager should approach IP rights not as a protector of their firm's patents, but as a trader in the rights of IP use. This can encompass the licensing of IP rights to other firms, even competitors, to maximise the value capture from the firm's intangible assets.

Carayannis and Meissener (2017) examined case studies of organisations that had made use of open innovation as a corporate strategy. They found that such firms had to become less 'dogmatic', with many firms making use of 'cover collaboration agreements' that enabled their R&D partners to have equal rights to IP when engaged in joint developments. However, this requires dedicated staff training in the management of IP rights, and well-designed protocols to protect intangible assets and the dissemination of research findings.

In addition to the issue of IP rights, open innovation management requires organisations to address their human resource management (HRM) systems. According to Carayannis and Meissener (2017), all employees need to understand that "open innovation is considered 'everybody's job' without separate incentives or measures in scorecards (p. 246)." This can be supported by education and training of personnel, as well as careful selection of new employees. Here the emphasis is on knowledge sharing and collaboration, as well as providing a clear understanding of the company's commitment to open innovation, as well as what that means and how it works. Engineers and other staff employed in innovation projects, are rewarded for their ability to develop and maintain commercially valuable collaborations and networks with outsiders.

Finally, it is important that any organisation seeking to embrace the open innovation paradigm approach this in a strategic manner, and adopt what Lichtenthaler (2008) describes as an *integrated technology commercialisation roadmap*. This should be developed from the firm's business strategy and offers an integrated, multiyear business plan that links all technology and applications together, with reference to how R&D and NPD project development roadmaps will integrate with both internal and external actors as the commercialisation process is undertaken.

Figure 4.7 illustrates a technology commercialisation roadmap for a large chemicals company. It is designed to link together the R&D, engineering and marketing activities within the firm with the roadmap for the internal process of commercialisation shown in the upper segment, and the links to any external relationships that involves an exchange or collaboration with outsiders, shown in the lower segment. In the middle, are the specific technologies that are being managed both inside and

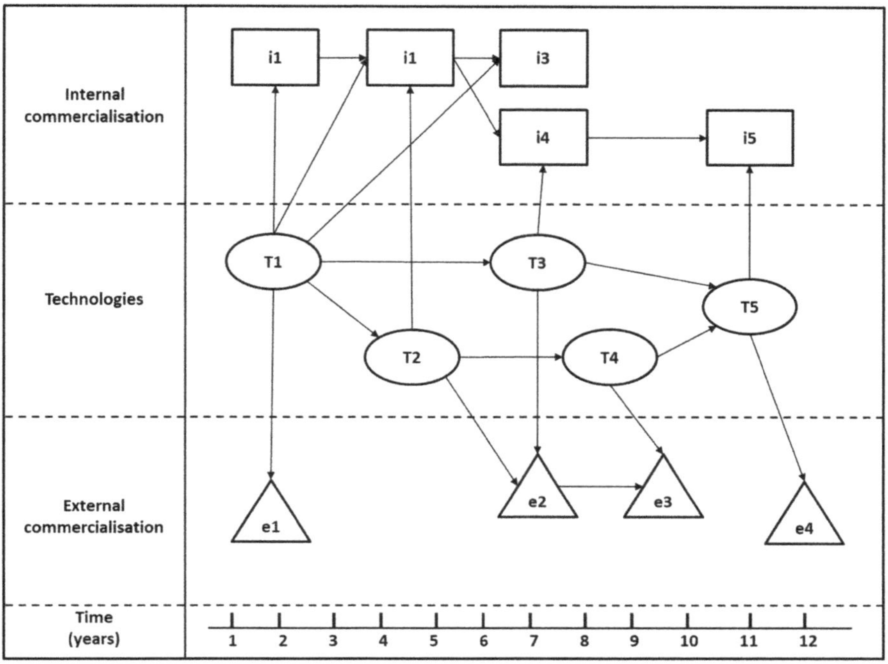

Fig. 4.7 Integrated technology commercialisation roadmap for a large organisation. (Source: Lichtenthaler 2008)

externally by the company. These range from single licencing agreements (e1), to more collaborative and strategic alliances (e2 and e3).

4.15 Innovation in Public Sector Organisations

The government and non-profit sectors are faced with increasing pressures to adopt commercial orientations and competitive market responses. Managers within such organisations must lead innovation in the creation of new products, services and processes in order to survive. However, innovation is the offspring of creative, entrepreneurial minds with the willingness to take risks and commit to sustained persistent efforts. Managers within government and non-profit organisations are frequently challenged in achieving such innovation by structural impediments and 'sticky' organisational cultures.

4.15.1 Key Challenges Facing Public and Non-profit Sectors

Over recent decades there has been a sea change in the managerial environment facing organisations within the government and non-profit sectors. The overall level of complexity associated with the operation of such organisations has increased dramatically, along with greater demands for accountability and responsiveness to community needs. For many government agencies, their role as regulators and planners is paramount. This traditional role has led to them becoming bureaucratic, centralised and technically specialised – but frequently obsessed with structure.

The rapid pace of social and technological change is a challenge to the traditional role of regulatory government. Formerly bureaucratic agencies have found themselves facing significant obstacles from environmental lobby groups, community pressure groups, political parties and business. The complexity and cost of government has risen, while local, state and federal governments have begun to demand greater levels of accountability. There is a need for greater managerial skills and a reorganisation of the internal structures within public sector and non-profit agencies to achieve greater economies, better reporting and enhanced performance measurements. Public organisations must become more innovative and flexible as well as responsive to their community's needs. This requires enhanced mechanisms for researching the needs of the community as well as developing 'customer focused' service provision (Baker 1994).

Public sector managers have been caught within the dual forces of public policy pressures for their organisations to become more commercial while simultaneously needing to find increasing resources from tight budgets to offer high quality services to an ever more demanding public. Government and non-for-profit organisations must now be market- or client-oriented, and be led by highly professional management teams with the skills to be innovative. As many organisations are service providers, the demand for innovation and strategic flexibility is even more pronounced. Innovation in service organisations is frequently more intense than in other types of business, and requires continuous interaction between the organisation's management and staff and its customers (Sundbo 2001).

4.15.2 The Role Orientations of Public Agencies

How the twenty-first century public organisation manager responds to these challenges is addressed via the model illustrated in Fig. 4.8, which suggests that public sector organisations have four role orientations that they can adopt (Baker 1995).

The first orientation, which is the more traditional role, is that of the bureaucratic regulator (Flynn 1998). As shown in quadrant one (bottom left), this is defined by an inward-looking organisation focused on planning and the regulated distribution of services. Such agencies are frequently self-absorbed with their bureaucratic systems and internal structures. The second orientation quadrant (top left) is more responsive to market forces but remains inwardly focused, seeking increasing internal efficiencies rather than benefits to clients. Such an organisation is likely to be intrapreneurial (Pinchot 1987), but may still lack a strong focus on the customer or client's requirements.

The shift to quadrant three (top right) sees the agency becoming outward looking and market oriented. Such an orientation is more appropriate to a private sector

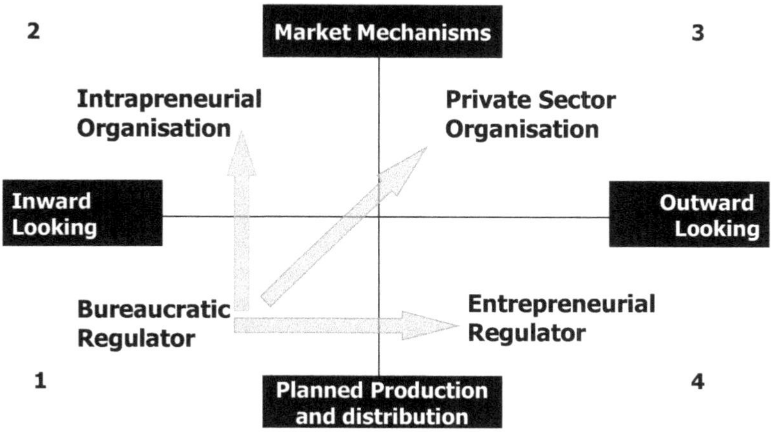

Fig. 4.8 What is the role of government? (Source: Baker 1995)

entity. Whatever its merits, this position is likely to suffer from problems in dealing effectively with 'public good' issues where market forces cannot apply. Finally, there is the orientation of quadrant 4 (bottom right). Here the public sector agency can look outward toward the community but without losing sight of their important role as regulator and planner. They must be responsive to the community while maintaining accountability. This orientation is that of the entrepreneurial regulator.

In practice the public organisation will not sit entirely in any particular quadrant, but can shift its focus, as the task requires. In some circumstances there may be a need to move closer to the private sector model; while in other situations may call for a bureaucratic regulator. Of importance is the ability of the organisation to be innovative and flexible.

4.15.3 Fostering Innovation in Public Organisations

A study undertaken in the US with state and local government senior managers focused on the role of innovation and how this might operate in practice (Zegans 1992). When asked to define the concept of innovation for public sector management, the following key ideas were identified:

- Innovation is a tool for improving agency performance, not an end in itself.
- Innovation is the process of implementing an idea or enacting a technology that is novel to a given situation.
- Successful innovation depends more on implementation skills and political savvy than on creative thinking.
- Innovation is an intrinsic part of the public manager's job.

The purpose of innovation, according to these managers, was to improve productivity, increase proficiency and advance policy. They drew a distinction between 'policy' and 'innovation'. The former was the responsibility of politicians and involved establishing broad purposes. The later was more the domain of the public sector manager. This involved developing the means to achieve the purposes identified by the policy makers.

It was acknowledged that high levels of innovation were possible within public sector management. To achieve this there must be discretion granted to managers to adopt new innovations. In healthy public sector agencies, employees innovate as part of their normal practices without subverting routine or regulations. In dysfunctional agencies, employees showed little initiative and those who attempted to be innovative were generally isolated and forced to 'go around the system' to see through their ideas.

Healthy vs. Dysfunctional Public Sector Organisations
In a healthy public sector organisation:

- employees seek to innovate as a normal part of their job routine, and
- new ideas are encouraged and supported.

In a dysfunctional public sector organisation:

- employees show little initiative, and
- isolated innovators find it difficult to gain support and must 'go around' the system.

Source: Zegans (1992).

The role of senior management in public sector agencies was viewed as critical to the successful encouragement of innovation. To achieve this, senior managers need to find ways to create a climate and culture within their organisation where employees feel 'comfortable' in coming forward with new ideas; they also need to be able to point out when things go wrong. The key challenges for senior managers appear to be:

1. *Overcoming complacency.* The tendency for public organisations to become complacent must be overcome. To achieve this, they must foster problem-solving attitudes among their staff and direct attention outside the organisation to community needs. Employees should also be made accountable for their actions, and the organisation should become more customer or client focused.
2. *Empowering employees.* To empower employees, the senior manager must first overcome the fear of reprisals that frequently infects the staff of public

organisations who seek to show initiative. Training and support for new venture or new project teams is one way of achieving this.

3. *Communicate.* Opening up the lines of communication to allow good ideas to surface is critical. This involves role modelling for junior staff, and signalling intentions clearly. There should be a full and timely disclosure of relevant information. Employees should be encouraged to do likewise.

4.15.4 Measuring Innovation in Public Organisations

Another important issue for managers of public sector organisations is how to measure innovation. Without reliable measures, the management of innovation becomes problematic. Traditionally, measurement of innovation within public sector organisations was undertaken via interviews and case studies, which usually reported best practice examples. However, more quantitative measures to provide reliable performance benchmarks have proven difficult. The use of internal surveys to assess innovation within public sector organisations only commenced in the 2000s. Although there was still a lack of reliable, international benchmarks for innovation. To address this issue, attention turned to the use of the *Oslo Manual*, which provides guidelines for the measurement of scientific and technological activities (OECD 2001; OECD/Eurostat 2018). The Oslo Manual was launched in 2001, but had been regularly updated since that time and used, along with other measures, to examine innovation within the public sector (Arundel 2014). Arundel et al. (2019), have proposed that the latest Oslo Manual offers a useful framework for measuring innovation in public sector organisations.

Arundel et al. (2019) note that measuring innovation within public sector organisations is different from measuring it within conventional service firms. Table 4.2 provides a summary from their research that outlines the comparability and differences between the measures used in the Oslo Manual and those likely to be encountered in public sector organisations. It can be seen that while most measures offer moderate to high levels of comparability, two areas that pose some problems are 'innovation expenditure' and 'obstacles'.

Arundel et al. (2019) suggest that the key factors that influence innovation within public sector organisations are:

1. *The role of governance in shaping innovation*: Public sector organisations face pressures from elected representatives in government, and from the public service bureaucracy. Politicians typically seek innovations that are large-scale, linked to public policy objectives, and likely to have relatively short deadlines. By comparison, innovations generated from within the public service are more operational and procedural in nature.
2. *The sources of ideas for innovation*: Due to the internal and external stakeholder environment that most public sector organisations face, the sources of ideas for innovation are likely to come from both a 'top-down' and a 'bottom-up' direction.

Table 4.2 Comparability between Oslo Manual topics for innovation measurement and data collection requirements for the public sector

Oslo manual topic	Public sector compatibility	Comments
Innovation definitions	Moderate	Workable general definition of innovation available for both the business and public sectors, but public sector includes innovation types (conceptual and policy innovations) that are difficult to fit within the Oslo Manual typology.
Innovation activities	Moderate	Some of the activities covered in the Oslo Manual (R&D, acquisition of external knowledge such as intellectual property, engineering) are less commonly used in the public sector, while other activities (training and purchases of equipment) are frequently undertaken in the public sector
Innovation expenditures	Low	Difficult to obtain expenditure data for innovation in the public sector because internal investments focus on staff, with measurement in terms of personnel numbers or person-months for innovation
Knowledge sources	High	Good comparability, but public sector surveys need more details on government sources
Collaboration	High	Good comparability, but public sector surveys need more details on government sources
Drivers	Moderate	Common drivers for the business sector (profit and competitiveness) are less relevant for the public sector, but both share consumer demand as a driver of service innovations
Objectives/ outcomes	Moderate	The public sector lacks a sales measure for services, but shares qualitative outcomes such as quality, lower costs, speed of delivery, etc.
Obstacles	Low	Similar interests in insufficient resources, but the public sector potentially faces many internal obstacles that are not discussed in the Oslo manual, such as staff resistance, a negative innovation culture and risk aversion

Source: Arundel et al. (2019)

The first is from government ministers seeking to have their policies implemented. The second is likely to come from rank-and-file public servants who see ways to improve service delivery.

3. *The innovation culture of the public sector organization*: As discussed earlier, innovation is facilitated or impeded by organisational culture and how it deals with risk and failure.
4. *The capabilities and tools available to managers to support innovation*: It is also important that any examination of innovation within the public sector include a review of any training, education, and/or supporting tools that might be deployed to help enhance employee engagement.
5. *Objectives, outcomes, drivers and obstacles*: Finally, there is a need to have well-developed objectives, with reference to costs/savings, outcomes, time invested and consideration of factors motivating or impeding success.

4.15.5 Lessons from Innovation Within Public Organisations

Borins (2001), in a review of innovation practices within the public sector, identified several characteristics of successful innovative government:

1. *The use of a systems approach.* After planning to innovate, it is important to map out the steps to implement the plan.
2. *The use of information technologies.* There is a trend towards an e-government model that is collaborative, with information sharing behaviours as important both within and outside of the organisation for formal and informal networks.
3. *Process improvement.* This extends to the involvement of private or voluntary sectors in consultative and collaborative processes.
4. *Empowerment of communities, citizens and staff.* Research indicates that front-line employees and middle managers are the most frequent indicators of public sector management innovations.

In conclusion, we can make reference to several lessons that we have learnt from being involved in innovation and change programs within government agencies and non-profit sector organisations over recent years.

- Lesson 1: Be Willing to Change

The organisation, and specifically its leadership and employees, must be willing to change and adapt. It should not resist new ideas, or succumb to pressures from outside. Use external change agents if required to assist the process. Innovation is a process of change, and continuous innovation requires continuous change. For most people, change can be unsettling, and constant significant change can lead to change fatigue setting in, where employees become resistant to new ideas and initiatives. The change process requires the unfreezing of existing frames of reference and behaviours, the implementation of the change, and then the refreezing of the culture (Lewin 1946).

- Lesson 2: Build on Firm Foundations

Base any future change process on sound research and facts, not on opinions and hearsay. You should also commission independent studies to identify problems and evaluate options or ideas. The possession of well-supported facts offers the change management team a solid base from which to tackle opposition or resistance. Change programs built on solid theory and good research are more likely to succeed, and they can be more readily sold to key stakeholders both within and outside the organisation.

- Lesson 3: Have a Clear Strategic Vision

The senior leadership of the organisation and their boards or ministers must be focused on the same goals and share the same sense of purpose. This is likely to be the most difficult process for many organisations. Shared vision emerges via a strategic dialogue that takes place among the organisation's senior leadership during which they share perceptions and beliefs about such key issues as the market environment, political forces, the competition, and the internal organisational climate and culture. It is critical for senior managers to 'make their beliefs visible' to each other (Lorsch 1986). Only after such a strategic dialogue has been held can the management team fully understand each other's perspectives and develop a unified vision for the future.

- Lesson 4: Shift Mindsets

Be politically savvy and devote time to winning over employees and key stakeholders by selling the need for change using the foundations of facts gathered in point two. According to Quinn (1980), the manager seeking to achieve strategic change needs to first create awareness and commitment for the need to change. This can be achieved by sensing the needs of people or by developing supporting networks of like-minded people willing to assist the change process.

Further, the manager should seek to amplify understanding and awareness by communication and consensus building, rather than employing the usual managerial process of 'satisficing' (in which almost nobody is totally happy). Managers also need to take care when introducing new ideas not to 'step on the toes' of those who have been responsible for past strategies. Taking such care can assist in legitimising new viewpoints.

In seeking to implement strategic change, the manager needs to engage in a trial and error process that is likely to involve tactical shifts and partial solutions as they seek to massage the firm towards achieving their visionary goals (Quinn 1980). This may be particularly important if the change has to deal with entrenched cultures that might be resistant. As a change agent, the manager needs to recognise the value of winning support for the change across a wide cross-section of areas within the firm.

To achieve this, they need to broaden political support through committees, task forces and strategic retreats. If faced with opposition (more common in normal or good times than during a crisis), the manager may need to both seek out zones of indifference where the new ideas will not meet resistance, and also find 'no lose' situations where various stakeholders can embrace the change without fear of loss. Managers may also need to create resource 'buffers' or 'slacks' into their planning to ensure that there is flexibility as the change process moves forward. Also, key will be the existence of 'activists' who are ready to serve as champions and leaders of change. Patience and willingness to trial new concepts are also important in this process.

- Lesson 5: Encourage Innovation

Finally, encourage, reward and reinforce a commitment to innovation among all employees. As noted earlier in this chapter, the likelihood of employees displaying innovative behaviour is contingent on the creation of a climate of innovation within the organisation. While the inherent creativity and enterprise of individual employees is important, the key appears to be the capacity of the managerial leader to communicate their expectation of innovative behaviour among employees, and to reinforce this through ongoing communication. Further, once the senior management of the organisation have made a commitment to innovation, they need to support this in tangible ways through the reward and remuneration systems and the organisational structure.

References

Arundel, A., (2014). *Final report of the OECD cognitive testing results for innovation in the public sector*. Mimeo.

Arundel, A., Bloch, C., & Ferguson, B. (2019). Advancing innovation in the public sector: Aligning innovation measurement with policy goals. *Research Policy, 48*(3), 789–798.

Baker, W. (1994). The paradox of empowerment. *Chief Executive, 93*, 62–65.

Baker, F. P. (1995). Marketing in a local authority. *Journal of Marketing Practice: Applied Marketing Science, 1*(4), 73–84.

Bhide, A. (1994). How entrepreneurs craft strategies that work. *Harvard Business Review, 74*(2), 150–161.

Borins, S. (2001). *The challenge of innovating in government*. Toronto: The Price Waterhouse Coopers Endowment for The Business of Government.

Burgelman, R. A. (1984). Managing the internal corporate venturing process. *Sloan Management Review, 25*(2), 33–48.

Carayannis, E. G., & Meissner, D. (2017). Glocal targeted open innovation: Challenges, opportunities and implications for theory, policy and practice. *Journal of Technology Transfer, 42*(2), 236–252.

Chesbrough, H. W. (2003). *Open innovation: The new imperative for creating and profiting from technology*. Boston: Harvard Business School Press.

Chesbrough, H. W. (2006). Open innovation: A new paradigm for understanding industrial innovation. In H. Chesbrough, W. Vanhaverbeke, & J. West (Eds.), *Open innovation: Researching a new paradigm* (pp. 1–12). Oxford: Oxford University Press.

Cohen, W., & Levinthal, D. (1990). Absorptive capacity: A new perspective on learning and innovation. *Administrative Science Quarterly, 35*(1), 128–152.

David, B. L. (1994). How internal venture groups innovate. *Research Technology Management, 37*(2), 38–42.

Duncan, W. J., Ginter, P., Rucks, A., & Jacobs, T. D. (1988). Intrapreneurship and the reinvention of the corporation. *Business Horizons, 31*(3), 16–21.

Farson, R., & Keyes, R. (2002). The failure tolerant leader. *Harvard Business Review, 80*(8), 64–72.

Feurer, R., Chaharbaghi, K., & Distel, M. (1995). Dynamic strategic ownership. *Management Decision, 33*(4), 12–21.

Filion, L.-J. (1996). Différences dans les systèmes de gestion des propriétaires-dirigeants, entrepreneurs et opérateurs de PME. *Canadian Journal of Administrative Sciences/Revue Canadienne des Sciences de l'Administration, 13*(4), 306–320.

Filion, L.-J. (2000). Six types de propriétaires-dirigeants de PME. *Organisations & Territoires, 9*(1), 5–16.

Flynn, D. (1998). Plan ahead for your company's survival. *World Wastes, 41*(8), 44–48.

Foster, W. K., & Pryor, A. K. (1986). The strategic management of innovation. *The Journal of Business Strategy, 7*(1), 38–42.

Gambardella, A., & Panico, C. (2014). On the management of open innovation. *Research Policy, 43*(5), 903–913.

Garriga, H., Von Krogh, G., & Spaeth, S. (2013). How constraints and knowledge impact open innovation. *Strategic Management Journal, 34*(9), 1134–1144.

Gerber, M. (1998). *The E-myth manager: Why management doesn't work and what to do about it*. New York: Harper Business.

Graetz, F. (2002). Strategic thinking versus strategic planning: Towards understanding the complementarities. *Management Decision, 40*(5/6), 456–462.
Greco, M., Grimaldi, M., & Livio, C. (2016). An analysis of the open innovation effect on firm performance. *European Management Journal, 34*(5), 501–516.
Gresov, C. (1984). Designing organizations to innovate and implement: Using two dilemmas to create a solution. *Columbia Journal of World Business, 19*(4), 63–67.
Heracleous, L. (1998). Strategic thinking or strategic planning? *Long Range Planning, 31*(3), 481–487.
Holmlund, M., & Tornroos, J.-A. (1997). What are relationships in business networks? *Management Decision, 35*(4), 304–309.
Hornsby, J., Naffziger, D., Kuratko, D., & Montagno, R. (1993). An interactive model of the corporate entrepreneurship process. *Entrepreneurship: Theory and Practice, 17*(2), 29–37.
Huang, F., & Rice, J. (2009). The role of absorptive capacity in facilitating "open innovation" outcomes: A study of Australian SMEs in the manufacturing sector. *International Journal of Innovation Management, 13*(2), 201–220.
Kagermann, H., Wahlster, W., & Helbig, J. (2013). *Recommendations for implementing the strategic initiative INDUSTRIE 4.0*. Berlin: Industrie 4.0 Working Group of Acatech.
Kanter, R. M. (1982). The middle manager as innovator. *Harvard Business Review, 60*(4), 374–386.
Kuratko, D., & Hodgetts, R. (2004). *Entrepreneurship: Theory, process, practice* (6th ed.). Mason: Thomson South-Western.
Kuratko, D., & Montagno, R. (1989). The Intrapreneurial Spirit. *Training and Development Journal, 43*(10), 83–85.
Lewin, K. (1946). Action research and minority problems. *Journal of Social Issues, 2*(4), 34–46.
Lichtenthaler, U. (2008). Integrated roadmaps for open innovation. *Research Technology Management, 51*(3), 45–49.
Lorsch, J. W. (1986). Managing culture: The invisible barrier to strategic change. *California Management Review, 28*(2), 95–109.
Mazzarol, T.W. (2004). *Creating the innovative organisation, CEMI Discussion Paper 0306*. www.cemi.com.au Centre for Entrepreneurial Management and Innovation (CEMI).
Miller, W. (2001). Innovation for business growth. *Research Technology Management, 44*(5), 26–41.
Miller, W. L., & Morris, L. (1999). *4th Generation R&D: Managing knowledge, technology, and innovation*. New York: John Wiley & Sons.
Nohria, N., Joyce, W., & Robertson, B. (2003). What really works. *Harvard Business Review, 81*(7), 43–52.
O'Reilly, C. A., & Tushman, M. L. (2004). The ambidextrous organisation. *Harvard Business Review, 82*(4), 74–81.
OECD. (2001). *Oslo manual: The measurement of scientific and technological activities: Proposed guidelines for collecting and interpreting technological innovation data*. Oslo: Organisation of Economic Co-operation and Development, European Union, Eurostat.
OECD/Eurostat. (2018). *Oslo manual 2018: Guidelines for collecting, reporting and using data on innovation, 4th edition, the measurement of scientific, technological and innovation activities*. Paris: OECD Publishing.
Pearson, A. E. (1988). Tough-minded ways to get innovative. *Harvard Business Review, 66*(3), 99–106.
Pfeffer, J. (1994). Competitive advantage through people. *California Management Review, 36*(2), 9–28.
Pinchot, G. (1987). Innovation through intrapreneuring. *Research Management, 30*(2), 14–19.
Pinchot, G., & Pellman, R. (1999). *Intrapreneuring in action: A handbook for business innovation* (Part 3 – Chapters 9–11). San Francisco: Berrett-Koehler Publishers.
Quinn, J. B. (1980). Managing strategic change. *Sloan Management Review, 21*(4), 3–2.
Quinn, J. B. (1985). Managing innovation: Controlled chaos. *Harvard Business Review, 63*(3), 73–84.

Savery, L., & Mazzarol, T. (2000). Intrapreneuring – An HRM success strategy for the next millennium. In T. Travaglione & V. Marshall (Eds.), *Human resource strategies: An applied approach* (pp. 159–180). Sydney: McGraw-Hill.

Scott, S. G., & Bruce, R. A. (1994). Determinants of innovative behavior: A path model of individual innovation in the workplace. *Academy of Management Journal, 37*(3), 580.

Sholl, J. (1998). Ten principles of intrapreneuring. *Executive Excellence, 15*(1), 17–18.

Sonnenberg, F. K. (1991). Strategies for creativity. *The Journal of Business Strategy, 12*(1), 50–53.

Stein, R., & Pinchot, G. (1998). Are you innovative? *Association Management, 50*(2), 74–77.

Stringer, R. (2000). How to manage radical innovation. *California Management Review, 42*(4), 70–88.

Sundbo, J. (2001). *The strategic management of innovation: A sociological and economic theory*. Cheltenham/Northampton: Edward Elgar.

Takeuchi, H., & Nonaka, I. (1986). The new product development game. *Harvard Business Review, 64*(1), 137–146.

VanDenVen, A. (1986). Central problems in the management of innovation. *Management Science, 32*(5), 590–607.

WEF (2017). *Digital transformative initiative: Mining and metals industry*. www.reports.weforum.org, World Economic Forum.

West, J., & Bogers, M. (2014). Leveraging external sources of innovation: A review of research on open innovation. *Journal of Product Innovation Management, 31*(4), 814–831.

West, J., Salter, A., Vanhaverbeke, W., & Chesbrough, H. (2014). Open innovation: The next decade. *Research Policy, 43*(5), 805–811.

Zahra, S., & George, G. (2002). Absorptive capacity: A review, re-conceptualization and extension. *Academy of Management Review, 27*(2), 185–203.

Zegans, M. D. (1992). Innovation in the well-functioning public agency. *Public Productivity & Management Review, 16*(2), 141–152.

Innovation in Small Firms

5

5.1 Introduction

> Run yourself like a large business, even if you are a small one; the systems discipline is essential for future growth.
>
> Source: Garth Humphries, CEO Biota Environmental Consultants.

This chapter examines the small business sector and the differences that exist between entrepreneurs and small business owner-managers. The "myth" of small business innovation and the entrepreneurial growth cycle of small firms are also explored along with the need for small firms to establish collaborative support networks. The importance of small business entrepreneurs being able to develop strategic thinking skills is highlighted along with the need for them to learn how to balance strategy, structure and resources.

Small to medium-sized enterprises (SMEs) comprise the majority of all businesses in most economies and are a major contributor to job creation and value adding (OECD 2010b). Within the field of entrepreneurship, a lot of attention has been given to the process of new venture creation and psychology and the behaviour of nascent and novice entrepreneurs (Shane and Venkataraman 2000). However, as defined in that chapter, the entrepreneur must be distinguished from the small business owner-manager by their greater focus on profit and growth, plus their use of strategic management practices in their business (Carland et al. 1984).

SMEs remain an important element within the economy, and policy makers have sought to encourage the small business sector in difficult economic times ever since Birch (1987) reported his findings that firms with fewer than 20 employees generated around 88% of all employment growth in the United States over the period 1981–1985 (Birch 1987). Subsequent examination of the actual contribution of SMEs to job creation has suggested that their role may be less than was initially

T. Mazzarol, S. Reboud, *Entrepreneurship and Innovation*, Springer Texts in Business and Economics, https://doi.org/10.1007/978-981-13-9412-6_5

predicted (Storey 1994). Nevertheless, the small business sector continues to remain a major provider of employment and self-employment for people throughout the world, and is a major contributor to the national economies of most countries (ABS 2005; APEC 2003; OECD 2010b).

It is worth noting that, within the 21 countries that comprise the APEC forum, SMEs represent 95% of all enterprises, with 74% being micro-firms with fewer than five employees (APEC 2002). These SMEs are responsible for 69% of all employment across the region. In Australia 99% of all firms are SMEs, and micro-firms comprise around 96% of all enterprises, with 63% employing only the owner-manager (OECD 2010b).

5.2 Definition of Small Firms

The definition of what constitutes a *small firm* is a surprisingly complex and difficult area for academic research (Headd and Saade 2008). Throughout the world countries use a wide range of different definitions (Kushnir et al. 2010), and there is no single, universally accepted definition of a small business (Storey 1994; Tonge 2001). In a review of the academic literature relating to entrepreneurship and small business research, no consistent approach was found, and as many as 31% of papers (in even the most highly ranked journals) failed to provide any definition at all (Reboud et al. 2014a).

However, good definition is important, not only because poor or absent definition undermines scientific credibility, but because definitions impact on how SMEs are dealt with in relation to regulation, taxation and support (Keefe et al. 2005). This is a problem throughout the world where a *small business* is defined differently by different government agencies with differing impacts in relation to regulation. For example, in Australia, the definition of what a *small business* is varies across government statutes and agencies, with quite significant variations and types of measure. This includes the number of employees, the size of annual turnover, size of payroll, size of assets or size of business debt (ASIC 2015; Productivity Commission 2013). This complexity and diversity in the definition of a small business is also found in the United States where federal and state statutes define a small business in a range of ways using turnover, employment and assets. This has direct influence on workplace relations, environmental and economic regulations and programs that offer support to SMEs (Keefe et al. 2005).

Academics seeking to define the term *small to medium enterprises* (SMEs) when undertaking research tend to rely on official classification systems used by governments (Al-Qirim 2005; Audretsch 2002). The most usual criteria for such definitions include the number of employees, annual turnover or assets under management (APEC 2002; OECD 2004). A review of how SMEs are defined across 75 countries within the Asia-Pacific region found that there were 60 different definitions used (Zhang 2013).

Table 5.1 OECD and EU definition of small firms

	Employees	Annual turnover	Assets
Micro-enterprise	1–9	<€2 million	<€2 million
Small enterprise	10–49	<€10 million	<€10 million
Medium-sized enterprise	50–249	<€50 million	<€43 million
Large enterprise	>250	>€50 million	>€43 million

Source: OECD (2004)

Table 5.2 IFC definition of small firms

	Employees	Annual turnover	Assets
Micro-enterprise	1–9	<US $100,000	<US $100,000
Small enterprise	10–49	<US $3 million	<US $3 million
Medium-sized enterprise	50–299	<US $15 million	<US $15 million
Large enterprise	>300	>US $15 million	>US $15 million

Source: IFC (2012)

Many different definitions exist for SMEs depending on whether they are used for statistical, legal or administrative definitions. Distinctions are also made in some countries on the basis of whether a business is engaged in manufacturing, services and retailing. Whether the firm is independently owned and managed may also form part of a country's definition of an SME, as well as the level of investment.

This plethora of definitions is unsatisfactory when attempting to study SMEs or develop international comparisons. To address this problem, the European Union (EU) undertook a program of developing a standardised definition for SMEs for use across the EU group of countries. This was first issued in 2003, and is outlined in Table 5.1.

The OECD/EU definition of an SME is now the most commonly used definition, and a study of 132 economies found that around a third of all countries used the figure of 250 employees as a cut-off for differentiating SMEs from large firms (Kushnir et al. 2010). Nevertheless, the OECD/EU definition has recently been challenged by the International Finance Corporation (IFC) with an alternative definition outlined in Table 5.2.

The comparison with Germany and their dynamic *Mittelstand* led France to identify an intermediary category between SMEs and GEs: the ETIs (for Entreprise de Taille Intermédiaire: intermediary sized firm), between 250 and 5000 employees), supposed to be more likely to grow and to be profitable. Research has started to analysed their potential specificities (Chabaud and Messeghem 2014), in terms of business models and dynamic capabilities (Claveau et al. 2014), in terms of growth path (Grandclaude et al. 2014) and identified a series of common factors among the group of French ETIs. Their main characteristic is their capacity to grow and this is likely to lead policy makers to try to better support them. They seem to have survived the GFC better than the bigger firms.

As mentioned above, quantitative definitions tend to be the most common. Government agencies usually require definitions that are measurable and not easily open to subjective interpretation. This is particularly important for regulation and enforcement around taxation or financial assistance programs. However, such definitions do not always provide the level of flexibility and subtly that accurately represents the actual diversity of SMEs, as a firm's identity is not influenced only by a few quantitative measures such as employment size or turnover. Such measures are also context dependent and differ across industries and national jurisdictions.

5.3 Characteristics of Small Firms

In a classic paper titled "*A small business is not a little big business*", published in the *Harvard Business Review*, Welsh and White (1981) addressed the challenges facing managers from small firms. Their analysis highlighted the "*resource poverty*" that distinguishes small firms from their larger counterparts. This lack of resources in areas such as finance, capital assets, physical facilities, workforce, expertise and time, requires the owners and managers of small firms to operate quite differently to their counterparts in larger companies. Small businesses are characterised not only by the size of their payrolls, but also by their managerial structure and environment. For example, small firms usually have an independent ownership structure and operations that involve close control by owner-managers. Such people typically contribute the majority – and in some cases perhaps all – of the working capital required by the business, and are responsible for making most – if not all – of the decisions relating to the firm's operations.

In a study of small business owners in the United Kingdom, Hankinson (2000) interviewed 90 owners and investigated their characteristics and management behaviour. Although this was a British study, the profiles of these owner-managers are relevant for SME owners throughout the world. Most of these small business operators were middle aged, and had completed high school diplomas or technical certificates as their most advanced level of education. They typically worked between 47 and 65 h per week. One of their main problems was managing time, with 93% of their time spent working operationally in the business. Of this time, over half (55%) of their time was involved with internal staff-level meetings, 38% in telephone calls, and 7% travelling. Most lacked skills in marketing, financial management, HRM and leadership. These small business owner-managers were also found to be weak on delegation, and made little use of outside consultants. Most had at least one frontline manager, but this person was a technical specialist with limited management responsibilities.

An examination of small business owners in Australia (ABS 2013) showed that most (67%) were men who had operated their business for more than 10 years, with 24% having operated the firm for more than 20 years. Most of these full-time owner-managers worked over 40 h per week, with 32% reporting they worked more than 49 h per week. Male owner-managers tended to work longer hours than their female counterparts. Other characteristics of Australia's small business operators were that individual weekly incomes were generally lower than their counterparts who were not self-employed. The majority (70%) of these small business operators were born in Australia.

Another feature of small firms is their use of computers and the internet, which has been increasing but remains an area that continues to warrant further attention, in particular their use of e-commerce, e-marketing and e-business (Mazzarol 2015) For example, a study of SMEs in Australia around 98% of small firms owned a computer and 80% of owner-managers have a smartphone. Also, 93% of small firms were connected to the internet, with 87% having broadband access. However, while 61% had a website and had engaged in e-marketing, only 54% of these firms are engaged in e-commerce and a mere 22% of such websites had a transaction functionality (Sensis 2017).

5.4 The "Myth" of Innovation in Small Firms

Small firms have traditionally been viewed as the engine room of innovation within a nation's economy. For example, during the 1980s the United States Small Business Administration (SBA) reported that their research suggested SMEs were likely to generate twice as many innovations per employee as large firms, and that these small firms spent double the proportion of their R&D budgets on fundamental research than their larger counterparts (SBA 1986). This was a time when the small business sector was identified as the primary generator of new job creation within the US economy (Birch 1987).

Government interest in small business as a key source of both innovation and employment can be traced back to at least the early 1950s, but it became of particular interest in the 1970s and 1980s. From a policy perspective, this took the form of programs and agencies established to help create and grow SMEs. With a gradual shift from *small business policy* – focusing primarily on regulation, advisory services, training and financing – to *entrepreneurship policy* – focusing on fostering entrepreneurial culture, innovation, technology and globalisation (Mazzarol and Clark 2016).

This has attracted a lot of interest from academics, students, the media and the wider community in entrepreneurship. However, the reality of the small firm as a key driver of innovation and job creation needs qualifying. Analysis of small firm data shows that the majority of SMEs are not growth oriented and engage in only modest innovation activities (Hendrickson et al. 2015). The small firms that do make a significant contribution to employment generation are those that actively seek to grow, and such firms are usually innovative because without innovation they could not hope to grow. These firms were identified by Birch (1987) and labelled *gazelles* due to the fact that they demonstrated explosive growth from start-up.

Research undertaken across a number of countries suggests that innovation and job creation is primarily due to a small number of *gazelle* firms (Clayton et al. 2013; EDSE 2016; OECD 2002). The *gazelle* firm is defined by the OECD (2010a) as a business that is younger than 5 years old, employs at least ten people, and has experience an annualised average growth rate of more than 20% over a 3-year period.

Such growth is extremely difficult to sustain and can be highly risky. In any given economy, the total number of *gazelles* is estimated to be less than 1% of all firms by employment and 2% by annual turnover (OECD 2010a).

Although the impact of high-growth firms and *gazelles* can be significant, it is also difficult to predict. The rapid growth and relatively immaturity of *gazelles* makes them inherently risky businesses. More recently, the emergence of high profile globally expanding start-up ventures like Uber and Airbnb, has triggered an interest in the application of public policy to help generate similar firms known as *Unicorns*, which are defined as firms aged less than 10 years old, but with an asset value of over $1 billion. Such firms are even more rare and unpredictable than *gazelles* (Reboud et al. 2016).

Some researchers are now raising concerns over the emphasis being placed on the role of entrepreneurship and small firms in the economy, and the fostering of new start-ups (Davila et al. 2015; Nightingale and Coad 2014; Shane 2009; Welter et al. 2017). The risk and uncertainty associated with the successful launch and growth of a *Gazelle* or *Unicorn* firm has led to a rethink of entrepreneurship and small business policy, with less emphasis on start-up and more attention to scale-up once the business has survived its often-turbulent early years (Davila et al. 2015; Welter et al. 2017).

The original research undertaken by Birch (1987) has been subject to challenge, primarily for its methodology (Davis et al. 1994). However, while there is subsequent research to support the job creation role of small firms (Neumark et al. 2011), more job growth seems to be generated by older high-growth firms than the younger *gazelles* (Clayton et al. 2013).

In addition to their role in job generation, small firms as innovators is another area that requires some scrutiny. A longitudinal analysis of people who launched new business start-ups found that most did so merely to replace an existing job, and that most were financially worse off than they would have been remaining in employment. Further, this was the case for both high-tech and ordinary firms (Acs et al. 2016). Australian research has found that most SMEs don't innovate or grow, but that the few *gazelles* that do (approx. 3%), can be found in all industries not just the "high-tech" fields (Hendrickson et al. 2015). So, there is something of "myth" about innovation, growth and job creation within small firms, particularly start-ups, leading some researchers to suggest that too much focus has been given to new venture creation.

> **For example,** … Few new firms enter to innovate, and very few entrepreneurs hire anyone except themselves and have no interest or ability to expand after creating a job for themselves. In conclusion, supporting people to become entrepreneurs would mostly support one-man, me-too shops in low-growth, low-margin industries where there is little or no innovation undertaken. (Acs et al. (2016) p. 16)

However, in considering this rather dismal view it should be acknowledged that SMEs comprise the vast majority of all firms in the economy. They also provide employment for more than half the workforce and contribute a significant amount of value added (DIISR 2011; OECD 2010b). Innovation within small firms can be fostered and there is evidence that it can be found within both low and high-tech sectors successfully generating sustainable growth (Hirsch-Kreinsen et al. 2005; Reboud et al. 2014b).

5.5 Advantages and Disadvantages of Small Firms

Ownership of a small firm has many advantages but also several disadvantages. For many people, their own small business can be a source of independence. Many people are motivated by the desire to be their own boss, set their own hours of operation, and make full use of their talents and creativity. Self-employment within a small business can also offer the opportunity to earn more money and build wealth for the future or a legacy for their family. The prospect of making more money and generating wealth is often a key motivator for many owner-managers, although many don't actually focus on this as the primary goal (Mazzarol et al. 2001). Self-employment can also be an opportunity for many to create a career option for their children or other family members. Despite its risks, self-employment can offer greater job security as they are not subject to unforeseen job redundancies that may take place regardless of how long or hard, they have worked.

The motivation for many small business owners is to follow a dream, a passion or a market opportunity, and to prove their worth to the wider community via their success. However, small business ownership has its risks. There can be periods of irregular sales, and this can place pressure on cash flow and the ability of the owner to draw earnings. In worst case situations, the owner can lose the business and potentially their home, as this is often used to provide the investment capital for the venture.

Once a small firm is established, the business owner must deal with the stress and unpredictability of the market and the long hours of hard work as well as the need to pay taxes, fees and other compliance costs. For many small business owners, the ability to find skilled and capable employees is a major challenge, as is dealing with customers and learning how to market. Furthermore, it is common for small business owners to have to work very long hours to find themselves with less time for family and friends than they would like (Hankinson 2000).

Research undertaken by the OECD (2009) indicates that most small business start-ups are terminated within their first year of trading. The turnover of such firms is also much higher within services sectors than manufacturing. This is due to the higher start-up costs associated with manufacturing businesses, and therefore they are likely to be of a larger size when founded and possibly better planned. However, if they do fail, they do so on a larger scale. Also found was that, while the 'ease of doing' business was generally viewed in a positive way by small firms around the world, compliance costs associated with new venture formation were generally still viewed as overly complex and bureaucratic.

5.6 SMEs vs. Large Firms

The increased levels of global competition and the impact of ICT have forced significant change upon large corporations, requiring them to seek enhanced innovation via the creation of entrepreneurial cultures and intrapreneuring (Duncan et al. 1988). Firms in the large corporate sector often ask themselves how they can achieve the flexibility and responsiveness to market changes that they view as common within the small business sector. However, due to their lack of resources and their idiosyncratic management, small businesses are not just 'downsized' versions of large firms. On one side, the small firm is typically defined by informality, loose job definitions and open communication flow. On the other side, the large firm is usually more rigid and formal, with highly-structured communication systems. Ironically, while large corporations are often found to be striving to be more like small entrepreneurial firms, small businesses often need to move more towards the systems-driven stability of their larger counterparts and away from the idiosyncratic management practices that usually typify them.

An example of the differences between large and small firms can be seen in marketing. Large corporations have substantial resources to devote to marketing and frequently have many levels of marketing management with responsibilities for national and regional operations or for different product lines (Webster 1992). A feature of the large corporation is its use of formal planning processes to guide its marketing activities (McColl-Kennedy et al. 1990). By contrast, most small business proprietors find the marketing of their businesses a complex and difficult task. Unlike larger firms, small businesses usually lack both resources and expertise (DITR 1987).

While large corporations can afford a dedicated team of trained marketing or other specialists, the small business proprietor is forced to carry the burden of being responsible for sales, marketing, personnel, publicity, production and financial matters. In most cases, these duties are performed by the proprietor without any formal training. Marketing knowledge and skill among small business proprietors is generally low, and many consider marketing to be little more than selling or advertising (Gold 1993).

Small firms also lack the systems that allow strategic planning, human resource management and financial control to take place in the same way as it does in large firms. Entrepreneurial SMEs are therefore characterised by informality and lack of systems. They can be highly flexible in the face of external environmental challenges or opportunities; however, they remain dependent to a much greater degree on their entrepreneurial leaders or owners.

5.7 Less Formality in Small Firms

Compared with their larger counterparts, small firms tend to have more female owners and senior managers, and the managers tend to have fewer formal qualifications. Overall, formalisation is generally much lower among small firms as SMEs are less likely to have formal business planning processes, quality assurance systems and human resource management practices than their larger counterparts (Julien 1990; Torrès and Julien 2005). The majority of small firms are non-unionised and are less likely to export or obtain venture financing.

A distinction must be made between high growth *gazelle* firms and their ordinary counterparts in the mainstream SME community. The *gazelle* firm has an average annual growth rate of more than 20% over a 3-year period, with growth in both turnover and employees (OECD 2010a). Such firms – comprising only a minority of all SMEs – are more likely to have formal systems and to embrace innovation. In the United States during the 1990s, such *gazelle* firms were responsible for 55% of the innovations in 362 different industries and for 95% of all radical innovations. *Gazelle* businesses produced twice as many product innovations per employee compared with larger firms, and obtained more patents per sales dollar (Kuratko and Hodgetts 1998).

For a small firm to compete with its larger counterparts, it must concentrate on its core competencies that offer a distinctive edge and its ability to provide world class products and services. Small businesses must be as efficient as the best in their industries and need to find market niches that allow them to hold a dominant position against their larger and better-resourced competitors. This efficiency and positioning are likely to be enhanced by the adoption of new technology and by being well-networked – both locally and globally.

5.8 The Entrepreneur and the Owner-Manager

An important issue when considering small business activity is the distinction between the entrepreneur and the owner-manager of a small firm. While the act of establishing and/or purchasing a small business venture is in many respects an example of entrepreneurial behaviour, it is not correct to assume that the majority of small business owners are entrepreneurs. As shown in Fig. 5.1, the two concepts occur at either end of a continuum, defined to a large extent by the owner's orientation toward growth and profit maximisation at the expense of lifestyle and their ability to control the venture in a direct way.

As previously discussed, the entrepreneur can be defined as an individual who establishes a business venture for the specific purpose of maximising profit and seeking growth. Innovation is a key element of their behaviour which is aimed at securing market access and differentiating the venture and its products from competitors; if they use management skills, they will do so in a strategic manner to guide the venture's growth. By contrast the small business owner-manager launches a new venture to pursue personal goals. The business is usually their sole source of income and requires all their time to manage successfully – at least in the early years. The owner-manager will often view the venture as an extension of themselves and their personal needs (Carland et al. 1984).

While the entrepreneur is focused on growth and the maximisation of profit, the majority of small business owners are focused on lifestyle. For many small business

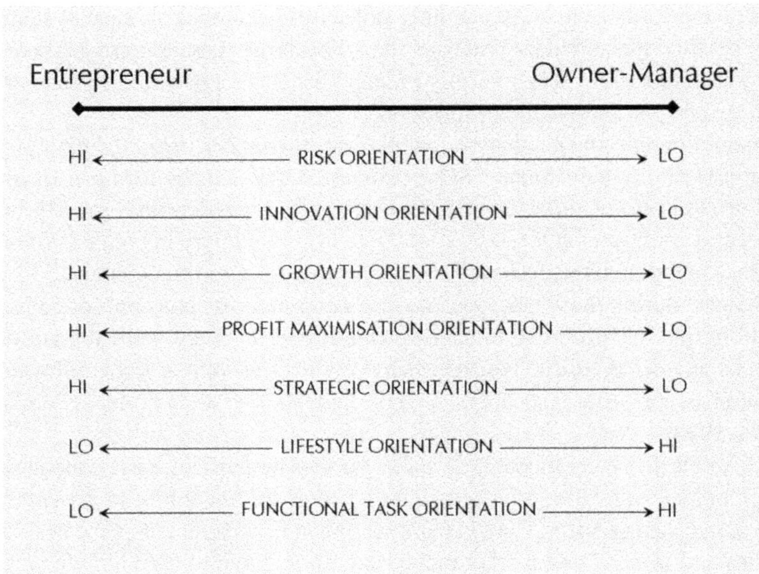

Fig. 5.1 A model of the entrepreneurial manager. (Source: Mazzarol 2005)

proprietors, the desire to work for themselves and control their own future is more important than the merits of their venture (Mazzarol et al. 2001). It is not uncommon for small business owner-managers to make a decision to deliberately place a cap or limit on the growth of their business in order to enjoy a better lifestyle (McMahon 1998). There is evidence from the United States that the most common points at which small business owners choose to 'cap' the future growth of their business is either while it has fewer than 10 employees and an annual turnover below US$0.5 million, or when it has around 25 employees and annual turnover of about US$2 million (Hanks et al. 1993). This decision to restrict the future growth of their venture is often due to the desire to maintain a lifestyle at the expense of future profits, but with reduced risk or stress.

The small business owner-manager is therefore someone who is frequently found to be working alone, with limited resources and high levels of uncertainty. They are often forced to depend on others external to their firm for assistance due to the absence of sufficient resources to bring such capacity 'in-house'. On the positive side, the owner-manager of a small firm is usually very close to customers and has the ability to see the venture in a holistic manner, encompassing all aspects of its activities. They can make changes quickly in the face of external threats or the desire to pursue opportunities. Less positive is their relative isolation and excessive workloads due to the necessity of having to deal with all responsibilities. It is important for small business owners to develop a strong network of support that should include professionals such as accountants, bankers and lawyers as well as a peer group of other small business proprietors. A small firm is usually totally dependent on the owner-manager for its survival and will adopt a culture that is reflective of the personality of the founder.

5.9 Theories of Small Business Management

Tan et al. (2009) note that small businesses have played a key role in entrepreneurship research over the past 20 years. They have done so due to their accessibility and their ability to offer a micro-environment for researchers. However, the diversity of SMEs has also meant that there is some difficulty in generating clear theory for the small firm. Problems associated with academic research into small business are due to differing definitions around the world as to what an SME is, a lack of longitudinal studies, inconsistent use of measures, and weaknesses in the validity of research designs (Bouckenooghe et al. 2007; Kraus et al. 2005).

This relative absence of theory in relation to small business management is surprising given their importance within the world's economies. D'Amboise and Muldowney (1988) sought to address this gap in the theory of small business management. They suggested that to understand the operation of a small firm requires attention to be given to three primary areas:

1. *Task Environment.* The small firm's task environment comprises the customers, suppliers, competitors and government agencies that the small business must deal with in its daily operations.
2. *Organisational Configuration.* The organisational configuration of the small firm encompasses the formal and informal structure of the business, including how many administrative levels it has, whether it is owned by a single person or multiple individuals, and if it has single or multiple sites or divisions.
3. *Managerial Characteristics.* The characteristics of the firm's top management team include such things as their age, gender, education and professional background. It also encompasses whether or not they are entrepreneurial.

Their analysis pointed to three organisational types in relationship to small firms, described as, (i) craft, (ii) promotion, and (iii) administrative. The 'craft' type firm is characterised as having a focus on comfort and survival, with a leadership that is traditional and a 'craftsman' or technical specialist who is able to provide a product or service using conventional methods of production. Such a firm is generally not growth focused, and operates best in a stable or benign task environment. A 'promotion' type firm is focused around the personal ambitions of a leader who is entrepreneurial and makes strong use of innovation to seek growth and the exploitation of market opportunities. This type of firm operates well in a dynamic, uncertain task environment. Finally, the 'administrative' type organisation is one that has its main focus on adaptation to market conditions and on the development of an established product or service portfolio. Such a firm is usually led by a professional team of managers and may have a hierarchical structure. A key feature of this type of firm is its ability to manage risk.

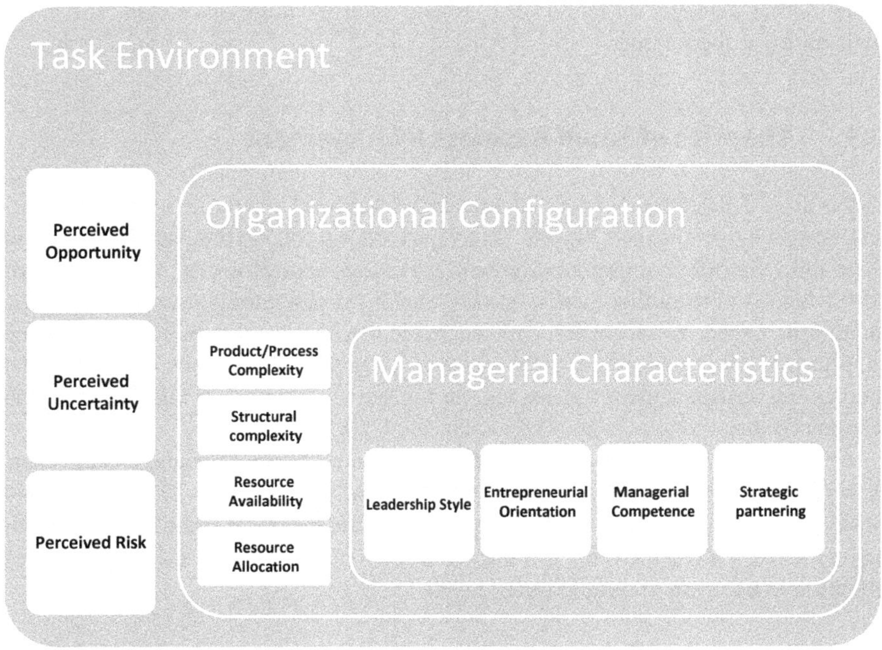

Fig. 5.2 The behaviour of small firms, key units of analysis. (Source: Mazzarol and Reboud 2009)

In order to understand the behaviour of small firms, several units of analysis should be examined. These are illustrated in Fig. 5.2. As shown, there are the three primary elements already described, and within each main area are several sub-units. For example, within the task environment, attention needs to be given to the perceived opportunity, uncertainty and risk as seen from the perspective of the firm's top management team. The ability to identify an opportunity and manage the process of exploiting it while dealing with uncertainty and risk is a critical part of the entrepreneurial process. Whether or not a small firm is the growth-seeking 'promotion' type or a non-growth focused 'craft' type may depend on how these elements are perceived.

Research suggests that managers with high entrepreneurial orientation will be more likely to perceive risk as benign or controllable (Sitkin and Pablo 1992). According to some researchers (see, Brockhaus 1980; Perry 1990) managers who have a high entrepreneurial orientation don't necessarily have a greater proclivity for taking risks; they simply perceive risk differently (Reboud and Séville 2016). Entrepreneurs have been found to have a more optimistic view of their chances to control or manage risk, and use biases and heuristics to confirm their positive view that the risk is manageable and the opportunity attractive (Busenitz 1999).

The key points of focus in relation to the firm's organisational configuration are fourfold. First, how much complexity is there in the production of the firm's product or process technologies and systems? Where a firm has a fairly simple product or process technology, the level of capital investment is likely to be less, as is the sophistication of the firm's organisational and managerial competencies. Second, the complexity of the firm's structure, as measured by the number of departments or sub-units, can impact on the number of managers required and their functional specialisation. In a micro-firm, there may only be a single owner-manager who is responsible for all duties. However, in a small or medium-sized firm there can be multiple managers with different roles.

The third and fourth elements within the organisational configuration are related to the way in which the firm's resources are allocated and how many resources are available. A key problem for small firms is that their resources are few, and how the management team configures the resources can be a vital part of their ability to exploit market opportunities and secure a competitive advantage (Alvarez and Barney 2005; Alvarez and Busenitz 2001).

At the level of the firm's managerial characteristics are the leadership style, entrepreneurial orientation, managerial competence and capacity for strategic partnering within the firm's top management team. These elements interact to drive and shape the strategic behaviour of the small firm, which is typically heavily dependent on the abilities of its founders to make effective strategic decisions and manage innovation successfully.

Leadership styles can take the form of transformational or transactional behaviours (Bass and Avolio 1994). Managers with transformational styles are likely to be visionary and have a capacity to lead change. A transformation leadership style is likely to be required if a small firm is to engage in innovation (Jung et al. 2008). By contrast, a transactional leadership style is focused on the successful completion of tasks to a given performance level. Managers with transactional styles are likely to focus on meeting deadlines, and also on aligning the individual team members' various personal needs and wants with these organisational objectives.

The managerial competence of the owner-manager or the top management team of the small firm and their willingness to form strategic alliances are also important areas that need to be examined. In addition to specific functional skills in their 'craft', the owner-manager of a small firm also needs competencies in financial management (McMahon 2001) and skills in problem-solving (Pareek and Rao 1995) and business planning (Woods and Joyce 2003).

There is evidence that small firms benefit from strategic partnerships and alliances (Watson 2007). However, the personal and professional background of the entrepreneur who runs the business, the task environment, and the nature of the firm will play a role in determining how and if they choose to form such networks (Street and Cameron 2007).

As Welsh and White (1981) correctly observed in their paper '*A small business is not a little big business*', it is a unique management environment. And, while many of the practices, processes and theories of managing large organisations can apply to the small firm, care needs to be taken.

For example, … Owner-management of a small business is a distinct discipline characterized by severe constraints on financial resources, a lack of trained personnel, and a

> short-range management perspective imposed by a volatile competitive environment. Liquidity must be a prime objective. The analytical models applicable to big business are of limited use in this arena. (Welsh and White (1981) p. 32)

5.10 Causes of Small Business Failure and Success

The failure of a small business is a complex issue. It is usually identified as a halt in the firm's operations. Williams (1987) found that newly-founded small businesses have around an 82% chance of surviving beyond the first 6-months. After approximately 2 years, this survival rate falls to around 52%. The probability of survival beyond 3 years is as low as 39%. A study of business bankruptcies in Australia found that the most common reasons given were, (i) poor economic conditions (33%); (ii) personal reasons such as ill health (13%); lack of business ability (12%); and excessive drawings (10%) (ABS 2007).

There are many possible causes of failure in a small business. Poor economic conditions such as a severe recession can certainly impact on small business survival, these external factors are difficult for an owner-manager to control. However, as outlined above, the causes of failure are often due to the way the business is managed. Some of the most common are outlined in the following sub-sections.

- Underestimation of the Start-Up Time

Too often the founders of a new venture fail to appreciate the time it will take to get the business up and running. The requirements of developing the new products and arranging the logistics, staffing and sales effort are all likely to take much longer than originally envisaged.

- Undercapitalisation

A particularly common problem among small firms is a lack of start-up capital. While most are launched with little more than their owner's savings, the capital requirement for sustained growth can place intolerable strain on the fledgling company. It is perhaps fortunate than many owner-managers choose not to grow their business as to do so without adequate capital would risk failure.

- Overestimation of the Market Size

It is also common for the owner-manager of a start-up venture to overestimate the size of the market share that they can secure in the initial years. They will often become convinced that their product or service will be a success because they have such faith in it. They may also become blind to the likelihood that competitors will fight to retain their existing customers and thereby restrict the market entry of a new rival.

- Lack of Expertise by Management

Inadequate managerial skills – particularly in financial control and budgeting – are a common cause of failure among small firms. It is important for owner-managers to take steps to improve their management expertise by undertaking courses in specific skills and by seeking help from third party specialists such as accountants and business advisors.

- Lack of Working Capital

The working capital within a business refers to the liquid assets – particularly cash – that the firm needs to maintain its short-term operating requirements. A well-run business will seek to reduce its working capital requirements, but growth on any scale is likely to place increased demands on working capital to pay creditors and employees. If the firm does not have sufficient cash flows and profitability to cover its working capital needs, it is most likely that it will have to borrow such funds – if it can – via either an overdraft facility or by imposing itself on its suppliers through late payments, thus risking creating a poor image that may not be tolerated over the longer term. Many small firms with excellent products have found themselves in similar positions where they are running out of cash and unable to pay their wages and short-term liabilities.

- Confusion of Cash-Flow over Profit

The amount and timing of cash flow is often critical to the survival of a small business. However, the amount of sales turnover a business makes is not as important as the amount of gross profit generated from each dollar of sales. For example, a small business with an annual turnover of $2 million but a gross profit margin of 5% is less attractive than a business with an annual turnover of only $500,000 but a gross profit margin of 50%. The first will produce a gross profit of $100,000, while the second will generate $250,000 in gross profit. It is important for the owner-manager to maximise gross profit and also to keep overhead costs low in order to reach breakeven as early as possible.

- Wrong Location of the Business

For many small firms, the location of the business can be a critical factor in their success. Retailers and many service firms, e.g. restaurants, hairdressers, and professional agencies, may succeed or fail depending on the location chosen for the business premises. Most small business owners select their location based on its proximity to their own home rather than its merits as a suitable site for servicing their customers (Mazzarol and Choo 2003).

- No Unique Selling Point

Very few small firms can compete purely on price due to a lack of economies of scale and scope. It is therefore necessary for these firms to find a point of differentiation for their products or services. Many small firms fail to find a unique selling point and therefore compete only on price, eventually suffering very low profit margins and subsequent financial problems.

- Recruitment of the Wrong People to Staff It

One of the most critical factors in the success of a new venture is the development of a strong team who can make it work. Most small firms lack the financial strength to hire the best staff they would like or need. In fact, the majority of small business proprietors seek to operate without any staff at all. However, once the firm begins to move beyond the size where it can be operated by a single individual or couple, it must start to hire. This is where many owners make the mistake of selecting people on the basis of inadequate screening, with the result that they provide a weak and poorly structured team.

- Failure to Monitor the Business Performance

Even if the owner is able to address the issues discussed above, they will need to develop key performance indicators that allow them to regularly monitor their firm's progress. Too often the small business owner will rely on annual financial accounting to determine their business performance, or ignore the need to monitor wastage or productivity levels within the venture. Each business and industry may require different types of performance measures, but most small firms will require regular monitoring to ensure that working capital levels are adequate to meet obligations.

- Failure to Retain Profits in the Business to Fund Growth

Finally, the owner-manager who is experiencing success and rapid growth can fall victim to their own hubris. Too many owners pay themselves too much or quickly run down the firm's equity to fund lifestyle. Spending the company profits on a beach home or luxury car may be a nice reward for hard work, but if the business is to grow, this money should be retained to fund future business activity.

In contrast to these causes of failure the main causes of small business success are the competencies of the owner-managers and their skills in the financial, marketing, production and human resource areas as well as in strategic planning. As discussed earlier, the small firm should have a clearly identified unique selling point that can provide a niche in the market from which it can secure above-average pricing and profit margins. The quality of products or services will therefore be critical to success, and this is likely to involve a degree of innovation in their design and development. The owner-manager needs to be willing to seek external advice and have the ability to secure adequate credit and sources of capital to fund growth. Cultivating a good relationship with the bank is therefore sensible. Finally, the firm should employ good business systems such as computer-based accounting and marketing tools.

5.11 The Growth Cycle of Small Firms

Research into the growth cycle of small firms has indicated that small businesses move through a number of defined stages as they grow. In 1980s a number of stage-theory models of business growth were proposed, most of which had between three to five stages (Barnes and Hershon 1976; Churchill and Lewis 1983; Scott and Bruce 1987; Steinmetz 1969). While the actual growth cycle of a small business may not be as neatly linear as suggested in these models, they remain a useful framework for understanding the process of growth within SMEs.

Figure 5.3 illustrates the model developed by Scott and Bruce (1987). In this start up stage the business is conceived and established. During this period, it is entirely the creation of its entrepreneur founder(s). All attention is given to finding customers and maintaining adequate cash flows to survive. The owner is the most important asset of the business, providing all its managerial skills, direction and capital.

If it survives, the business will pass into a survival stage. During this period the business is financially viable and may even hire additional staff. The owner-manager usually remains in control of the business and usually undertakes only minimal formal planning (Churchill and Lewis 1983). Many small firms continue to operate in this stage for long periods of time, with a single or limited product line and any growth being driven by natural market expansion (Scott and Bruce 1987).

From the perspective of growth, it is the third stage that may be most critical. Churchill and Lewis (1983) identify two sub-stages in this growth or success period. The first of these is that of 'success-disengagement'. Here the business is economically strong and has sufficient size and market penetration enabling it to sustain its current position. Its size is such as to require professional managers. In this sub-stage the owner-manager makes a decision to either grow or not. The business is usually profitable and can continue in its present form or is even sold at a profit (Scott and Bruce 1987).

If the owner-manager decides to opt for growth, the business will enter the 'success-growth' sub-stage during which the owner-manager frequently places the business under risk to finance growth. The need for professional managers may also increase along with the need for systems and enhanced planning. As noted by Scott and Bruce (1987), the most likely crises facing the business during its growth are the

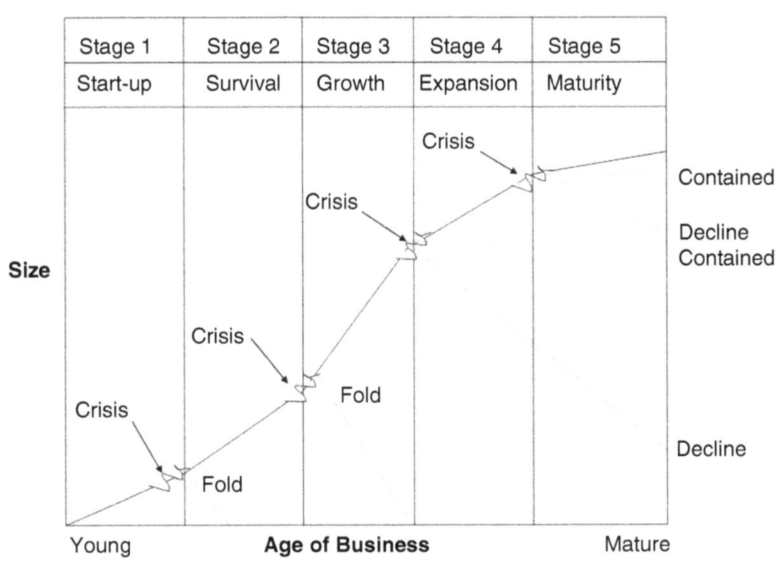

Fig. 5.3 A model of the entrepreneurial growth cycle. (Source: Scott and Bruce 1987)

threats posed by larger competitors and the demands placed on its resources as it seeks to develop new products and/or markets.

A successful growth strategy will then take the business into the fourth stage of take-off or expansion. This stage can also be identified as involving a process of team building and delegation. The owner-manager must develop a management team capable of taking over the increasingly complex tasks associated with running the business. If the owner-manager cannot learn to delegate their responsibilities, they will have trouble achieving effective growth. Furthermore, as the business moves into the resource mature stage it will require greater team-based development. Failure to achieve an effective management team effort will impede its efficiency.

In this critical stage, the businesses will either succeed and develop into a large business, or not. As it grows, the business will become more formalised in its accounting, management and other systems. The needs for greater quantities of capital are likely to lead the business towards equity finance. This may pose difficulties as the business seeks to secure long-term debt against its assets. Major crises facing the business during this stage are frequently those associated with the distancing of the original entrepreneur-owner from the day-to-day running of the firm as expansion requires the introduction of more professional managers.

> **For example,** … Professional managers will not have the commitment to the business that those who were the with the business from the early stages had and are unlikely to be prepared to make the same sacrifices 'for the sake of the business.' This situation is potentially dangerous and can cause a crisis. (Scott and Bruce (1987), pp. 50–51)

The fifth and final stage of maturity or resource maturity sees the business with sufficient resources to conduct formal strategic planning. Its management structure is likely to be decentralised, and there is a greater separation between the owner and the business in terms of financial and operational matters. Many entrepreneurs have trouble with pressure from shareholders over strategic directions. Large-scale investment in marketing and production facilities during this stage may result in additional equity financing.

5.12 What Strategic Options Do Small Firms Have?

While growth can be a challenging process for the owner-manager of a small firm, it is not the only strategic choice that they can adopt. The owner-manager essentially has three primary strategic options, (1) growth, (2) exit, and (3) stasis. Each of these three strategic options requires the owner-manager to adopt a particular planning approach. In the following sub-sections, we examine each option and the nature of the planning required to achieve success at this strategy (Mazzarol and Reboud 2009).

- Option 1: Growth

Growth is the strategic option that has garnered the most attention both in academic research and in wider public interest (Tonge 2001). As discussed above, the fast-growing *gazelle* firm is a major source of innovation and employment growth. However, it is not a strategic option chosen by the majority of small business owners. The growth option needs visionary leadership, entrepreneurial orientation and strategic thinking within the firm's top management team (Filion 2000). In her analysis of the theory of economic growth of the firm, Penrose (1959) drew a distinction between what she described as 'entrepreneurial competence' as opposed to 'managerial competence'. The first is associated with entrepreneurial behaviour, of risk taking and the maximisation of profits through the pursuit of opportunity; the second is associated with a focus on efficiency and the maintenance of the *status quo*. Owner-managers who consciously choose the option of growth are what Pleitner (1989) describes as 'true entrepreneurs' compared to 'would be entrepreneurs.'

- Option 2: Exit

The exit option can take at least two forms. The first is the abandonment and closure of the firm, while the second is the transfer of ownership to a new management and/or ownership team. Failure in the small firm is commonly associated with bankruptcy, but the reality is more complex. Watson and Everett (1996) suggest that the notion of 'failure' in the small firm is poorly defined and understood. Cochran (1981), in a review of the literature relating to small business failure, identified bankruptcy as only one form of failure. Other failures involved termination with losses to creditors, termination to avoid losses, failure as an opportunity cost while the owner seeks more lucrative employment options, and simple discontinuance by the owner-manager.

Longitudinal analysis of small business failures over a 15-year time period suggests that simple discontinuance is the most common form of small business exit, and one that substantially exceeds the rate of insolvencies and bankruptcies (Everett and Watson 1998). These results suggest that many businesses are sold or cease trading voluntarily, and that their proprietors are able to time their exits to best take advantage of prevailing economic conditions. Thus, depending on the definition of failure adopted, a positive economic outlook may be associated with an increase in the rate of small business failure (Everett and Watson 1998).

Exit via abandonment through voluntary discontinuance is therefore a very common strategic option employed by owner-managers in small firms. Their decision to exit the business is often the result of simply being 'unable to make a go of it' (Cochran 1981). However, this may not be associated in the mind of the owner-manager as a failure. While a bankruptcy or insolvency is a major problem for the small business, voluntary discontinuance may be a rational decision by an owner-manager. Operating a small business is difficult and can create high levels of stress. Abandoning the venture in favour of salaried employment may be a more beneficial option. An exit strategy of this kind is therefore common, and failure in the small firm needs to be approached with more caution and careful definition (Watson and Everett 1996, 1999).

Succession as an exit strategy involves a different dynamic and more considered planning. For example, within the family owned business only three out of ten firms survive into a second generation (Kuratko and Hodgetts 1998). Even these odds fall dramatically as the firm enters a third generation, with survival rates of only 14–16% (Hisrich and Peters 1998). Succession planning requires attention to be given to the distribution of equity, the drafting of legal buy-sell agreements, debt retirement, estate planning, risk management via insurances, and the restructuring of managerial functions (Flynn 1998) This is the case regardless of whether the business is to transfer ownership and control within the family or to non-family members (Ellentuck and Resnick 1994).

- Option 3: Stasis

For the small firm to achieve stasis seems relatively straightforward. However, if the objective of the owner-manager is to secure a comfortable and secure lifestyle with relatively little stress, they will need to ensure that their firm is well-organised and managed. The task environment of the firm will need to be benign and the firm will need to be configured in such a way that the business is profitable, controllable and efficient. Owner-managers who aspire to enhanced lifestyle will not only need to ensure that their firm is profitable; they will also need to delegate operational responsibility to a team who have the competence to alleviate the daily workload of the owner.

Filion (2000) has characterised this type of small firm as the 'classical SME'. The owner-manager of such a firm is focused strategically on survival, and looks to consistency rather than innovation. Their attention is devoted to daily activities with routine, repetition and stability in their task environment. The organisational configuration is simple and its resources are generally limited. This type of owner-manager often finds delegation of their authority difficult. The values of such a firm are based on the quality of the relationship between the owner-manager and their employees.

5.13 The Importance of Strategic Thinking

One of the key points of difference between the entrepreneur and the small business owner-manager is the ability of the former to think and act strategically. As discussed earlier, the growth of a firm is contingent on the entrepreneurial orientation and competence of its top management team. Most small business owners are more interested in maintaining a steady, profitable business that helps to sustain their lifestyle. They are not strategic in their thinking and suffer from *strategic myopia* (Mazzarol and Reboud 2009), which is the lack of long-term vision about where they want their business to go. This can be linked to a proximity bias identified by Torrès as part of the microcosm effect making what is near in time of much more importance that what is remote (Torrès 2003)

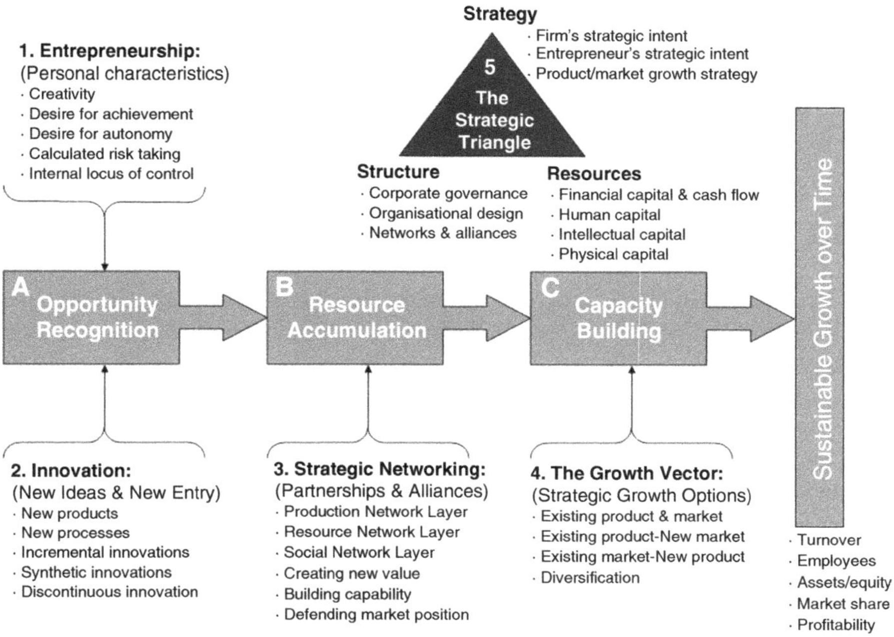

Fig. 5.4 Strategic management of entrepreneurial ventures framework. (Source: Mazzarol 2005)

> **For example,** … Strategic myopia is the affliction of short sightedness in which there is no long-range vision or consideration over what the future might hold. Change in business is a constant; owner-managers who wish to meet such change must lengthen their strategic horizon and develop the capacity for strategic thought and action. (Mazzarol and Reboud (2009), p. 148)

Figure 5.4 outlines a framework for the strategic management of entrepreneurial ventures (Mazzarol 2005). This diagram examines the interrelationship between the basic entrepreneurial processes, e.g. opportunity recognition, resource accumulation and capacity building, and five key elements considered to be important in the successful development of an entrepreneurial venture, namely, entrepreneurship, innovation, strategic networking, the growth vector and the strategic triangle.

5.13.1 Entrepreneurship

The first of these elements is the role of the entrepreneur within the business venture. As noted earlier, the difference between the owner-manager of a small firm and the entrepreneur of a dynamic growing business is their strategic orientation and their capacity to seek growth and the maximisation of profit. It is important to look at the characteristics of the venture management team and to see how well they profile in terms of the entrepreneurial qualities of creativity, achievement drive, desire for autonomy, calculated risk taking and internal locus of control (Caird 1993). In essence, the mental attitude of the owners of the venture can determine how well the venture is likely to perform in the future.

5.13.2 Innovation

The second element that is important within the framework is the ability of the venture to employ innovation to secure a clear point of differentiation within its chosen markets. Any business that does not continuously seek a competitive edge through value-adding to products, services or processes is unlikely to achieve much sustainable growth. Such innovation can be radical and leading edge, as is common with high technology firms. However, many small firms succeed in maintaining a lead within their selected markets by continuously innovating in a more incremental manner. It is also common for small firms to adapt ideas and technologies from other industries or markets into hybrid or synthetic innovations that can provide a unique solution to a particular problem and thereby secure a market lead (Tushman and Nadler 1986).

A study by Khan and Manopichetwattana (1989) of 50 small manufacturing firms in the United States found that small businesses typically clustered into five different types made up of innovators and non-innovators. The innovators grouped into what were called 'young Turks' and 'blue chips.' The first group of 'young Turks' was generally younger with more product differentiation and investment in R&D. These firms were more likely to be risk-oriented and proactive in trying new innovations in the market. The second group of 'blue chips' was characterised by better educated senior managers, more sophisticated market and environmental scanning, and strategic decision-making controls and analysis. Compared to their counterparts in the young Turks group, the blue chips were more likely to have professional management teams and make use of professional management systems.

Three sub-groups were identified among the non-innovator firms entitled, 'the silver spoons', 'the striving stoics' and 'the kismets' (Khan and Manopichetwattana 1989). The 'silver spoons' group was the worst performing of all and represented almost the reverse of the 'blue chips', with poor planning and control systems, and limited analysis and strategic orientation. Management of such firms tended to be complacent and reliant on well-developed strategies. By comparison, the 'striving stoics' were characterised by hard-working and committed managers who tried to achieve innovative outcomes but with only limited success. Finally, the 'kismets' were firms with managers who did poorly on all characteristics but who possessed a high external locus of control, suggesting that they trusted luck rather than good management to get them through. This study by Khan and Manopichetwattana (1989) highlights the links between the characteristics of the entrepreneur and the innovation performance of the firm. Key differences found between these innovative and non-innovative firms were due to the attitudes and behaviour of the senior managers who ran them.

In a study of almost 600 SMEs in a French Region, Reboud et al. (2016, 2018) found different innovation propensity depending on the specific strategic situation of the small firm. Using a taxonomic approach, they identified seven types of SMEs, with different management styles, innovation propensity and strategic thinking (Table 5.3).

Table 5.3 Detailed classification of the taxonomy

Class	Type (example)	Description	Sample firms	% from total
Class 1	Reactive SMEs	Non-innovative, non-exporting	51	8.6%
		Market expectations mostly focused on price and lead time		
		Owner-manager only shareholder		
		Short term perspective, no competitive advantage		
		Customised product/service		
Class 2	Operationally focused SMEs	Rather big (sales), rather old (25 years)	66	11.1%
		Over 60% employees are workers		
		Market expectations mostly focused on reliability and lead time		
		Mainly men in the board		
		Short term perspective		
		Importance of processes		
		Manufacturing and industry, specialised, expertise oriented		
Class 3	Ad Hoc SMEs	Not well organised, no procedure manual	81	13.64%
		Small (less that 1 M€), young firms (less than 8 years)		
		Do not trade with big firms		
		Don't innovate because perceive difficulties		
		Don't succeed in analysing their competitors		
		Short term perspective		
		Perceive a strong dependency from lead customer		
		Their competitive advantage is the price		
		The owner-manager decides for everything		
Class 4	Established SMEs	Development based on quality (product), customer oriented	131	22%
		Manufacturers (60%), structured		
		Market expectations: product quality		
		1–5 M€, more than 25 years		
		Subsidiaries		
		Stagnation		

(continued)

Table 5.3 (continued)

Class	Type (example)	Description	Sample firms	% from total
Class 5	Entrepreneurial SMEs	Entrepreneurial, growing	101	17%
		Market is growing, niche market		
		Rather in service industries (30%), like computing and communication		
		Young and small		
		Innovation drives the strategy		
		Customize their offer		
		Are interested in international (scan the market)		
Class 6	Anti SMEs	Internationalised	80	13.47%
		Big SMEs (5–10 M€ sales)		
		Women in their board		
		Have an R&D activity, file patents		
		Structured, long term perspective		
		Have a board and shareholders		
		Manufacturing		
Class 7	Participative SMEs	High level of empowerment	84	14.1%
		CSR and HRM matter		
		Plan, have brands and trademarks		
		Are autonomous (84%)		
		Not international		

Source: Reboud et al. (2016)

5.13.3 Strategic Networking

The third element of the framework relates to strategic networking. Because small firms lack the resources needed to undertake all the work, they need to do to achieve their goals, it is necessary for them to form strategic alliances with other organisations. Such alliances are most commonly with leading customers who may even agree to co-invest in the development of new products, or with key suppliers that can help the firm lower input costs or maintain quality. However, there may also be alliances with firms that lie outside the 'production network' into what is termed the 'resource network', including providers of finance such as banks or venture capital firms, or professional groups such as accountants and lawyers. Such networks are usually held together by social contacts between the entrepreneur and the managers of these other organisations (Holmlund and Tornroos 1997). Most of these alliances are either designed to provide the small firm with access to resources and markets, or to assist with the defence of an existing market position (Jarrett 1998). The small firm and its owner-manager or entrepreneur is engaged in a web of important

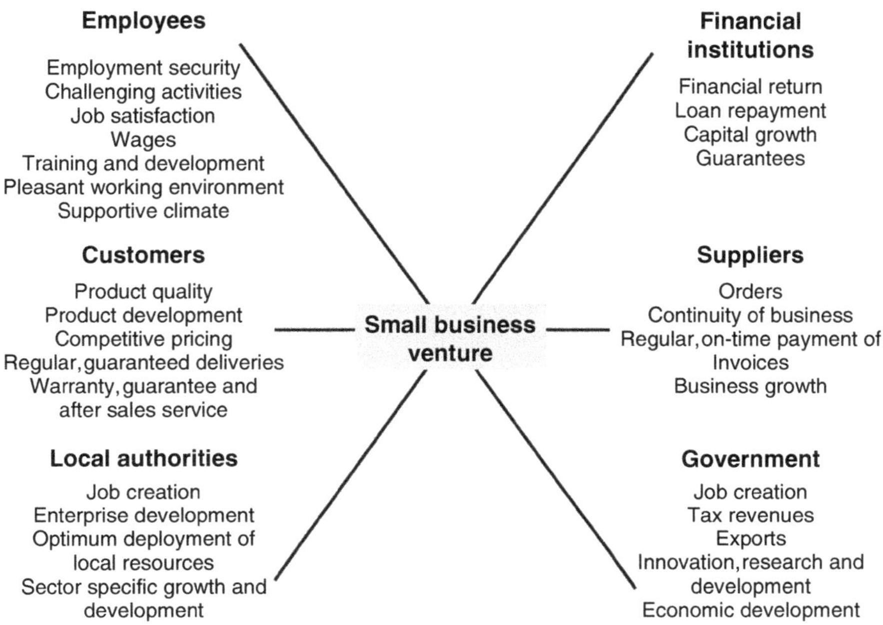

Fig. 5.5 Stakeholder web of the small firm. (Source: Jennings and Beaver 1997)

stakeholders with whom the firm must interact in order to secure its future. Jennings and Beaver (1997) suggest that the small firm operates within a network or 'stakeholder web' comprising both internal and external actors. Figure 5.5 illustrates this web of stakeholders.

Within the firm are the employees, who seek a variety of benefits or outcomes from the owner-manager including their job security, job satisfaction, career development and overall day-to-day satisfaction with their working environment. To establish and grow, a successful firm requires the hiring, retention and development of a competent and dynamic team of employees. Also, surrounding the firm is a range of other stakeholders including, financial institutions, customers, suppliers, local government authorities and government. Each of these places demands and expectations on the small firm and its owner-manager.

The range of pressures that might be placed on the small business owner-manager by this stakeholder web can be quite diverse. However, the successful entrepreneur can also leverage this network to secure support, finance, and market access and market intelligence. Partnering with customers, employees, suppliers, financial institutions and government agencies is the hallmark of successful small firms. This partnering involves developing mutually beneficial relationships that can enable the small firm to leverage resources and improve its competitiveness (Hall 1992).

5.13.4 The Growth Vector

The fourth element within the framework is the 'growth vector' initially identified by Ansoff (1965). This suggests that growth is achieved by a combination of matching products to markets. To achieve growth requires offering new products into established markets, taking existing products to new markets or diversifying into new product-market combinations. While diversification is a common – and necessary – strategy among large corporations seeking growth, most small firms will find diversification overly risky and a potential overstretch of their resources.

As shown in Fig. 5.6, the opportunity to grow is contingent on the firm being able to find product and market combinations that will allow sufficient sales to fund the business and to allow expansion. Most firms commence trading within a given market segment with a specific product or service.

Future growth within this existing product market space (e.g. quadrant 1) will depend on how large this segment is. If the segment is mature, then the business will need to consider one of three options, (i) market share growth; (ii) new product development, and (iii) diversification.

- Market Share Growth

This involves taking the existing products or services to new markets, which may involve opening new outlets, selling interstate or even exporting. This option involves a risk factor that may be four times that of the existing product market combination. The level of risk is proportionate to the experience of the firm in each of these new markets.

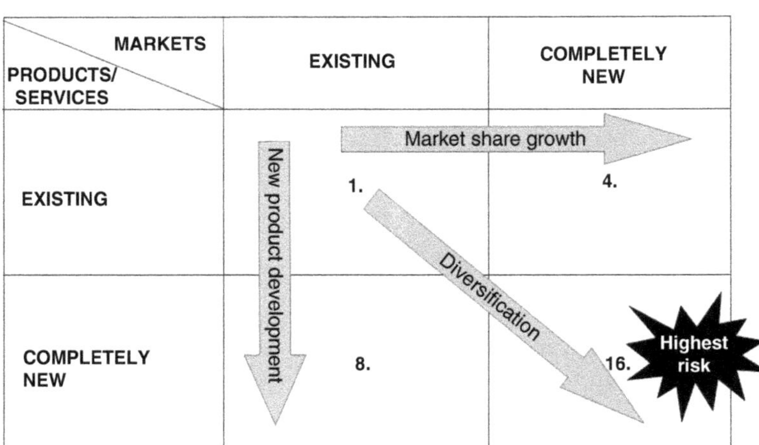

Fig. 5.6 The growth vector framework. (Source: Ansoff 1965)

- New Product Development

This option involves the firm developing new products or services that can be offered to the same customers or market segment. To follow this growth strategy, the business will need to have a good level of innovation capability and invest in new product development and R&D. The risk level associated with new products is typically eight times that of the existing product-market combinations.

- Diversification

The combination of new products and new markets involves a diversification strategy that may see the business moving outside its experience base. For this reason, the risk factor associated with diversification could be as much as 16 times that of the existing *status quo*. Small firms should consider diversification strategies with care, as they will face a situation in which their experience in both product and market is weak.

In considering which option to follow within the growth vector, the small business owner-manager should consider their base potential across the key areas of resources, experience, control, ideas and leadership as defined by Gibb and Davies (1992). It is particularly important to review the overall business model that is to be used as the growth vehicle.

As shown in Fig. 5.7, the ability of the small firm to successfully develop this vehicle for growth will depend on the base potential that the business has for growth (e.g. its resources, skills and capabilities), the degree of change required to move in

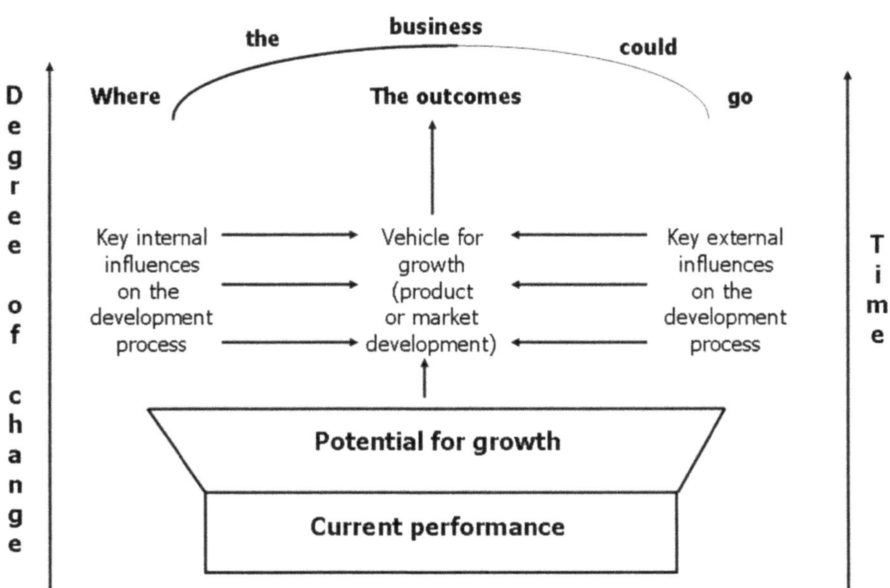

Fig. 5.7 A model of growth in small firms. (Source: Gibb and Davies 1992)

the new direction, the internal and external factors enhancing or impeding the process, and the time available to achieve the goals.

Gibb and Davies (1992) suggest that the key elements which should be examined in reviewing the base potential of a small firm that is considering future growth include:

1. *How good has the firm's performance been over recent years?* Consideration should be given to the firm's market penetration and market share. How efficient is its production and overall financial performance? Is it profitable on all product/market segments?
2. *How strong is the firm's base potential for growth?* The base potential refers to the resources, i.e. money, people, equipment and time, that are available to allocate to future growth. There is little point in trying to grow a small business if the firm's entire resources are already fully committed to maintaining its existing operations.
3. *Assess the experience base.* Of importance, here is whether the owner-manager of the small firm has sufficient expertise to fully exploit new product or market opportunities. For example, a small firm that decides to commence exporting will find that foreign markets require the development of new knowledge and skills that are not easily learned. Finding a joint venture partner or local agent from the target market who can provide expertise in dealing in that country may be necessary to achieve success.
4. *Assess the leadership base.* The growth of the firm into new markets or products is likely to require the recruitment of new people, and this expansion of the venture team will place added demands on the owner-manager's leadership skills.
5. *Assess the control base.* Expansion of the business into new product lines or new markets that may be geographically dispersed will require the firm to have enhanced control systems that allow the owner-manager to monitor performance. This control base is likely to include both financial and managerial systems that can deliver a set of key performance indicators (KPI) measuring the firm's behaviour against established benchmarks or targets.
6. *Assess the ideas base.* The growth in new product-market combinations is also likely to require the firm to embrace innovation in the development of new products or marketing strategies to achieve points of differentiation and market advantage. There must be attention given to R&D, new product development and commercialisation.
7. *How sound is the business model?* Any future growth strategy is going to require a well-considered and sound business model. 'Soundness' is a vague concept. However, before going forward, the small business owner-manager should ensure that they assess the risks and returns of the new venture. Will they require external financing? What is the 'opportunity cost', i.e. the potential lost opportunity, associated with directing their energies and resources to this new project rather than something else?

5.13.5 The Strategic Triangle

Finally, the framework includes a strategic management triangle which comprises the three elements of, strategy, structure and resources. This strategic triangle recognises that the process of strategic management requires the harmonisation of three key elements:

1. strategic direction;
2. organisational structure; and
3. the allocation of resources.

The balance between strategy and structure is recognised as being of critical importance to effective sustained growth (Chandler 1962). Any change to the strategy of a firm must be associated with a change in the firm's structure. If these two elements are not in harmony, then the implementation of any strategy will be difficult. The inclusion of the third element of resources is of key importance as small firms are characterised by resource scarcity. Managing the small firm requires the entrepreneur to keep both strategy and structure in harmony with the firm's resources. Resource allocation is of key importance in identification of core competencies that may be configured to achieve competitive advantage (Penrose 1959).

Figure 5.8 illustrates the strategic triangle. It suggests that the owner's attention should focus on keeping a balance between the three elements. Strategy requires the owner-manager to clearly define the future vision they have for both the firm and for themselves. Their strategic intent and the product-market growth vector they feel needs to be followed should be determined. In doing so, they need to ensure that they have undertaken adequate market research and prepared a business case.

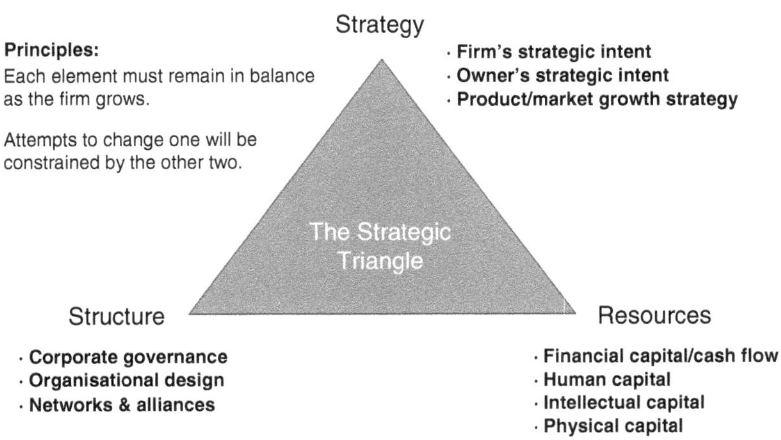

Fig. 5.8 The strategic triangle. (Source: Mazzarol 2005)

Once the strategy is clear, the owner-manager needs to review their structure and determine if they have an appropriate organisational design to allow them to pursue the strategy they have chosen. The managerial governance of the business should be considered. As Hofer and Charan (1984) have shown, the owner-manager may need to work through the seven stages of professional managerial development, eventually appointing a board of directors to assist them in managing the business. For many small firms the lack of internal resources is likely to require them to form strategic alliances to allow them to access management and operational skills and resources that they cannot afford to own directly.

References

ABS. (2005). *Characteristics of small business in Australia*. Australian Bureau of Statistics Cat. No: 8127.0. Retrieved from AGPS Canberra

ABS. (2007). *Australian capital territory in focus*. Australian Bureau of Statistics Cat. No, 1307.8. Retrieved from AGPS Canberra: www.abs.gov.au

ABS. (2013). *Counts of Australian business operators 2011–2012*. Australian Bureau of Statistics Cat. No, 8175.0. Retrieved from Canberra: www.abs.gov.au

Acs, Z. J., Åstebro, T., Audretsch, D., & Robinson, D. T. (2016). Public policy to promote entrepreneurship: A call to arms. *Small Business Economics, 47*(1), 35–51.

Al-Qirim, N. (2005). An empirical investigation of an e-commerce adoption-capability model in small businesses in New Zealand. *Electronic Markets, 15*(4), 418–437.

Alvarez, S. A., & Barney, J. B. (2005). How do entrepreneurs organise firms under conditions of uncertainty? *Journal of Management, 31*(5), 776.

Alvarez, S. A., & Busenitz, L. W. (2001). The entrepreneurship of resource-based theory. *Journal of Management, 27*(6), 755–775.

Ansoff, H. I. (1965). *Corporate strategy*. New York: McGraw-Hill.

APEC. (2002). *Profile of SMEs and SME issues in APEC 1990–2000*. Singapore: APEC Secretariat, World Scientific Publishing.

APEC. (2003). *Small business and trade in APEC: A report highlighting the contribution of medium, small and micro enterprises to the Asia Pacific region*. Singapore: Asia Pacific Economic Cooperation (APEC).

ASIC. (2015). *Small business what is small business*. Australian Securities & Investments Commission, Australian Government. Retrieved from www.asic.gov.au

Audretsch, D. B. (2002). The dynamic role of small firms: Evidence from the U.S. *Small Business Economics, 18*(1–3), 13–40.

Barnes, L. B., & Hershon, S. A. (1976). Transferring power in the family business. *Harvard Business Review, 54*(4), 105–115.

Bass, B. M., & Avolio, B. J. (1994). *Improving organizational effectiveness through managerial applications* (3rd ed.). New York: Free Press.

Birch, D. L. (1987). *Job generation in America: How our small companies put the most people to work*. New York: The Free Press.

Bouckenooghe, D., Clercq, D. D., Willem, A., & Buelens, M. (2007). An assessment of validity in entrepreneurship research. *Journal of Entrepreneurship, 16*(2), 147–171.

Brockhaus, R. H. (1980). Risk taking propensity of entrepreneurs. *Academy of Management Journal, 23*(3), 457–460.

Busenitz, L. W. (1999). Entrepreneurial risk and strategic decision making: It's a matter of perspective. *The Journal of Applied Behavioral Science, 35*(3), 325–340.

Caird, S. (1993). What do psychological tests suggest about entrepreneurs? *Journal of Managerial Psychology, 8*(6), 11–20.

Carland, J. W., Hoy, F., Boulton, W. R., & Carland, J. A. C. (1984). Differentiating entrepreneurs from small business owners: A conceptualization. *Academy of Management Review, 9*(2), 354–359.

Chabaud, D., & Messeghem, K. (2014). Les ETI. Un nouvel objet de recherche. *Revue Française de Gestion, 244*(7), 95–110.

Chandler, A. D. (1962). *Strategy and structure: Chapters in the history of the industrial enteprise*. Cambridge MA: MIT Press.

Churchill, N., & Lewis, V. (1983). Business growth the five stages of small business growth. *Harvard Business Review, 61*(3), 30–50.

Claveau, N., Séville, M., Prim-Allaz, I., & Ambroise, L. (2014). Les logiques de développement des entreprises de taille intermédiaire. Une approche par leurs Business Models. *Revue Française de Gestion, 244*(7), 111–132.

Clayton, R. L., Sadeghi, A., Spletzer, J. R., & Talan, D. M. (2013). High-employment-growth firms: Defining and counting them. *Monthly Labour Review, 136*(6), 3–13.

Cochran, A. B. (1981). Small business mortality rates: A review of the literature. *Journal of Small Business Management, 19*(4), 56–59.

D'Amboise, G., & Muldowney, M. (1988). Management theory for small business: Attempts and requirements. *Academy of Management Review, 13*(2), 226–240.

Davila, A., Foster, G., He, X., & Shimizu, C. (2015). The rise and fall of startups: Creation and destruction of revenue and jobs by young companies. *Australian Journal of Management, 40*(1), 6–35.

Davis, S. J., Haltiwanger, J., & Schuh, S. (1994). Small business and job creation: Dissecting the myth and reassessing the facts. *Business Economics, 29*(3), 13–21.

DIISR. (2011). *Key statistics: Australian small business*. Canberra: AGPS Canberra, Department of Innovation, Industry, Science and Research.

DITR. (1987). *The major determinants of small business growth* (Vol. 1–4). Melbourne: Department of Industry, Technology and Resources, Jean Gordon Government Printer.

Duncan, W. J., Ginter, P., Rucks, A., & Jacobs, T. D. (1988). Intrapreneurship and the reinvention of the corporation. *Business Horizons, 31*(3), 16–21.

EDSE. (2016). *Employment and social developments in Europe 2015*. European Commission. Retrieved from www.ec.europa.eu

Ellentuck, A., & Resnick, T. (1994). Preparing for a shift in ownership. *Nation's Business, 82*(1), 44–47.

Everett, J., & Watson, J. (1998). Small business failure and external risk factors. *Small Business Economics, 11*(4), 371–390.

Filion, L.-J. (2000). Six types de propriétaires-dirigeants de PME. *Organisations & Territoires, 9*(1), 5–16.

Flynn, D. (1998). Plan ahead for your company's survival. *World Wastes, 41*(8), 44–48.

Gibb, A. A., & Davies, L. (1992). Methodological problems in the development of a growth model of business enterprise. *The Journal of Entrepreneurship, 1*(1), 3–35.

Gold, A. (1993). The how-to of small business marketing. *Australian Professional Marketing, 2*(4), 18–20.

Grandclaude, D., Nobre, T., & Zawadzki, C. (2014). L'entrepreneuriat est-il soluble dans l'ETI? *Revue Française de Gestion, 244*(7), 133–148.

Hall, D. (1992). *The hallmarks for successful business: Survival-change-growth*. London: Mercury Books.

Hankinson, A. (2000). The key factors in the profiles of small firm owner-managers that influence business performance. The south coast small firms survey, 1997–2000. *Industrial and Commercial Training, 32*(3), 94–98.

Hanks, S. H., Watson, C. J., Jansen, E., & Chandler, G. N. (1993). Tightening the life-cycle construct: A taxonomic study of growth stage configurations in high-technology organizations. *Entrepreneurship Theory and Practice, 18*(2), 5–29.

Headd, B., & Saade, R. (2008). *Do business definition decisions distort small business research results?* Available at SSRN: http://ssrn.com/abstract=1228536, 34 p.

Hendrickson, L., Bucifal, S., Balaguer, A., & Hansell, D. (2015). *The employment dynamics of Australian entrepreneurship*. Office of the Chief Scientist, Department of Industry and Science, Australian Government. Retrieved from www.industry.gov.au/Office-of-the-Chief-Economist/Research-Papers/Documents

Hirsch-Kreinsen, H., Jacobson, D., & Robertson, P. L. (2005). *'Low-tech' industries: Innovativeness and development perspectives a summary of a European research project*. Pilot Consortium. Retrieved from Dortmund.

Hisrich, R. D., & Peters, M. P. (1998). *Entrepreneurship*. Boston: Irwin McGraw-Hill.

Hofer, C. W., & Charan, R. (1984). The transition to professional management: Mission impossible? *American Journal of Small Business, 9*(1), 1–11.

Holmlund, M., & Tornroos, J.-A. (1997). What are relationships in business networks? *Management Decision, 35*(4), 304–309.

IFC. (2012). *Interpretation note on small and medium enterprises and environmental and social risk management*. International Finance Corporation – World Bank Group. Retrieved from Washington, DC: www.ifc.org

Jarrett, D. (1998). A strategic classification of business alliances: A qualitative perspective built from a study of small and medium-sized enterprises. *Qualitative Market Research, 1*(1), 39–49.

Jennings, P., & Beaver, G. (1997). The performance and competitive advantage of small firms: A management perspective. *International Small Business Journal, 15*(2), 63–75.

Julien, P.-A. (1990). Vers une définition multicritère des PME. *Revue Internationale PME, 3*(3–4), 411–425.

Jung, D., Wu, A., & Chow, C. W. (2008). Towards understanding the direct and indirect effects of CEOs' transformational leadership on firm innovation. *The Leadership Quarterly, 19*(5), 582–594.

Keefe, R., Gates, S., & Talley, E. (2005). *Criteria used to define a small business in determining thresholds for the application of federal studies – Working Paper*. Kauffman-RAND Centre for the Study of Small Business and Regulation. Retrieved from http://www.rand.org/content/dam/rand/pubs/working_papers/2005/RAND_WR292.pdf

Khan, A. M., & Manopichetwattana, V. (1989). Innovative and non-Innovatitve small firms: Types and characteristics. *Management Science, 15*(5), 597–606.

Kraus, S., Schwarz, E. J., & Reschke, C. H. (2005). *Strategic planning as a prerequisite for growth and success in SMEs – Literature review and implications*. Paper presented at the DRUID Tenth Annual Summer Conference on Dynamics of Industry and Innovation: Organizations, Networks and Systems, Copenhagen, Denmark 27–29 June 2005.

Kuratko, D. F., & Hodgetts, R. (1998). *Entrepreneurship: A contemporary approach* (4th ed.). Sydney: Harcourt and Brace.

Kushnir, K., Mirmulstein, M. L., & Ramalho, R. (2010). *Micro, small, and medium enterprises around the world: how many are there, and what affects the count*. World Bank. Retrieved from Washington.

Mazzarol, T. (2005). A proposed framework for the strategic management of small entrepreneurial firms. *Small Enterprise Research: The Journal of SEAANZ, 13*(1), 37–53.

Mazzarol, T. (2015). SMEs engagement with e-commerce, e-business and e-marketing. *Small Enterprise Research, 22*(1), 79–90.

Mazzarol, T., & Choo, S. (2003). A study of the factors influencing the operating location decisions of small firms. *Property Management, 21*(2), 190–208.

Mazzarol, T., & Clark, D. (2016). The evolution of small business policy in Australia and New Zealand. *Small Enterprise Research, forthcoming*, 22 pages.

Mazzarol, T., & Reboud, S. (2009). *The strategy of small firms, strategic management and innovation in the small firm*. Cheltenham: Edward Elgar Publishing.

Mazzarol, T., Volery, T., Doss, D., & Thein, V. (2001). Forces motivating small business start up among nascent entrepreneurs. *Small Enterprise Research: The Journal of SEAANZ, 9*(1), 3–18.

McColl-Kennedy, J. R., Yau, O. H. M., & Keil, G. (1990). Marketing planning practices in Australia: A comparison across company types. *Marketing Intelligence and Planning, 8*(4), 21–29.

McMahon, R. G. P. (1998). Stage models of SME growth reconsidered. *Small Enterprise Research: The Journal of SEAANZ, 6*(2), 20–35.
McMahon, R. G. P. (2001). Deriving an empirical development taxonomy for manufacturing SMEs using data from Australia's business longitudinal survey. *Small Business Economics, 17*(3), 197–212.
Neumark, D., Wall, B., & Zhang, J. (2011). Do small businesses create more jobs? New evidence for the United States from the National Establishment Time Series. *The Review of Economics and Statistics, 93*(1), 16–29.
Nightingale, P., & Coad, A. (2014). Muppets and gazelles: Political and methodological biases in entrepreneurship research. *Industrial and Corporate Change, 23*(1), 113–143.
OECD. (2002). *High-growth SMEs and employment*. Organisation for Economic Co-operation and Development. Retrieved from Paris: http://www.oecd.org
OECD. (2004). *SME statistics: Towards a more systematic statistical measurement of SME behaviour.* Paper presented at the Promoting Entrepreneurship and Innovative SMEs in a Global Economy, Istanbul, 3–5 June.
OECD. (2009). *Measuring entrepreneurship, a collection of indicators*. OECD-Eurostat Entrepreneurship Indicators Programme. Retrieved from Paris: https://papers.ssrn.com/sol3/papers.cfm?abstract_id=1581491
OECD. (2010a). *High-growth enterprises – What governments can do to make a difference.* Retrieved from Paris.
OECD. (2010b). *SMEs, entrepreneurship and innovation*. Paris: OECD (Organisation for Economic Co-Operation Development).
Pareek, U., & Rao, T. V. (1995). Counselling and helping entrepreneurs. *The Journal of Entrepreneurship, 4*(1), 19–34.
Penrose, E. (1959). *The theory of the growth of the firm*. Oxford: Blackwell.
Perry, C. (1990). After further sightings of the Heffalump. *Journal of Managerial Psychology, 5*(2), 22–31.
Pleitner, H. J. (1989). Strategic behavior in small and medium-sized firms: Preliminary considerations. *Journal of Small Business Management, 27*(4), 70–76.
Productivity Commission. (2013). *Regulator engagement with small business*. Melbourne: Productivity Commission, Government of Australia. Retrieved from.
Reboud, S., & Séville, M. (2016). De la vulnérabilité à la résilience : développer une capacité stratégique à gérer les risques dans les PME. *Revue Internationale PME, 29*(3–4), 27–46.
Reboud, S., Mazzarol, T., Clark, D., & Mamouni Limnios, E. (2014a). *One more time: why it is important to define the small enterprise.* Paper presented at the 59th International Council for Small Business (ICSB) Conference, 11–14 June, Dublin.
Reboud, S., Mazzarol, T., & Soutar, G. (2014b). Low-tech vs high-tech entrepreneurship: A study in France and Australia. *Journal of Innovation Economics & Management, 14*(2), 121–141.
Reboud, S., Serboff, T., Goy, H., Mazzarol, T., & Clark, D. (2016). *Exploring the diversity of SMEs: A taxonomic approach in a French Region.* Paper presented at the 30th ANZAM Conference, Brisbane, Au, 6–9 December.
Reboud, S., Serboff, T., Goy, H., Mazzarol, T., & Clark, D. (2018). Les politiques publiques face à la diversité des PME, les apports d'une approche taxonomique en Rhône Alpes. *Revue Internationale PME, 31*(2), 27–56.
SBA. (1986). *Innovation in small firms*. US Small Business Administration Office of Advocacy. Retrieved from Washington D.C.
Scott, M., & Bruce, R. (1987). Five stages of growth in small business. *Long Range Planning, 20*(3), 45–52.
Sensis. (2017). *Sensis e-Business Report 2016: The online experience of small and medium enterprises*. Retrieved from www.sensis.com.au
Shane, S. (2009). Why encouraging more people to become entrepreneurs is bad public policy. *Small Business Economics, 33*(2), 141–149.
Shane, S., & Venkataraman, S. (2000). The promise of entrepreneurship as a field of research. *The Academy of Management Review, 25*(1), 217–226.

Sitkin, S. B., & Pablo, A. L. (1992). Reconceptualizing the determinants of risk behavior. *Academy of Management Review, 17*(1), 9–38.
Steinmetz, L. (1969). Critical stages of small business growth. *Business Horizons, 12*(1), 29–36.
Storey, D. J. (1994). *Understanding the small business sector*. London: Routledge.
Street, C. T., & Cameron, A. F. (2007). External relationships and the small business: A review of small business Alliance and network research. *Journal of Small Business Management, 45*(2), 239–266.
Tan, J., Fischer, E., Mitchell, R., & Phan, P. (2009). At the center of the action: Innovation and technology strategy research in the small business setting. *Journal of Small Business Management, 47*(3), 233–262.
Tonge, J. (2001). *A review of small business literature part 2: Birth, growth and death of the small business*. Centre for Corporate and Public Affairs, Manchester Metropolitan University Business School. Retrieved from Manchester.
Torrès, O. (2003). Petitesse des entreprises et grossissement des effets de proximité. *Revue Française de Gestion, 144*.(mai-juin 2003, 119–138.
Torrès, O., & Julien, P.-A. (2005). Specificity and denaturing of small business. *International Small Business Journal, 23*(4), 355–377.
Tushman, M., & Nadler, D. (1986). Organizing for innovation. *California Management Review, 28*(3), 74–92.
Watson, J. (2007). Modeling the relationship between networking and firm performance. *Journal of Business Venturing, 22*(6), 852–874.
Watson, J., & Everett, J. (1996). Small business failure rates: Choice of definition and the size effect. *Journal of Entrepreneurial & Small Business Finance, 5*(3), 271–285.
Watson, J., & Everett, J. (1999). Small business failure rates: Choice of definition and industry effects. *International Small Business Journal, 17*(2), 31–47.
Webster, F. E. (1992). The changing role of marketing in the corporation. *Journal of Marketing, 56*(4), 1–17.
Welsh, J. A., & White, J. F. (1981). A small business is not a little big business. *Harvard Business Review, 59*(4), 18–32.
Welter, F., Baker, T., Audretsch, D. B., & Gartner, W. B. (2017). Everyday entrepreneurship—a call for entrepreneurship research to embrace entrepreneurial diversity. *Entrepreneurship Theory and Practice, 41*(3), 311–321.
Williams, A. J. (1987). *The characteristics and performance of small business in Australia – 1973 to 1985*. Newcastle: University of Newcastle.
Woods, A., & Joyce, P. (2003). Owner-managers and the practice of strategic management. *International Small Business Journal, 21*(2), 181–195.
Zhang, Y.-B. (2013). SMEs in the APEC region. In *APEC policy support unit - Asia-Pacific economic cooperation*. Retrieved from http://publications.apec.org.

6 Adoption and Diffusion of Innovation

6.1 Introduction

> We were technically far superior, but we were so engrossed in it – that is, developing the software – that we didn't see what was happening around the corner.
>
> Source: Peter Clifford, CEO MINEMAP.

This chapter examines theories of the adoption and diffusion of innovation. It explores the issue of whether innovation diffusion is a social or economic process, and the importance of initial customer selection. Also discussed are the need to identify clear pathways to market, the barriers to market entry, and substitution threats. The need for the formation of strategic alliances is also considered.

Within business, innovation should be focused on ways to enhance the competitiveness of the organisation by converting ideas, processes, technologies and alliances into commercially valuable outcomes. Innovation is recognised as important to the ability of most organisations to secure and retain a competitive advantage in commercial environments (Drucker 2002). There are many avenues through which innovation can be developed within an organisation. While the most common are product and service innovations, it is also possible to consider innovation in marketing and market development practices, innovation in process technologies, and even innovation in administration (North and Smallbone 2000). While the majority of innovations may be small and incremental in nature, it is the less common radical ones that capture the most attention. Such radical innovations require two necessary conditions: first, there must be a significant change to the 'core concept' of the product; second, there must be a major change to the *way* in which the core components of the product are configured (Henderson and Clark 1990).

T. Mazzarol, S. Reboud, *Entrepreneurship and Innovation*, Springer Texts in Business and Economics, https://doi.org/10.1007/978-981-13-9412-6_6

The conversion of innovative ideas into commercial outcomes is a complex and often difficult process, but generally sees the innovation providing a combination of newness and market value. A study undertaken by the Australian Manufacturing Council in the 1990s found that innovative firms trawled the market seeking solutions and created the need for new ideas by challenging existing processes. Such firms were also noted for their ability to maximise the skills of their people (AMC 1995). The study concluded that most firms could be innovative and that innovation was frequently stimulated by exporting – presumably because overseas markets demand greater quality and product differentiation. Innovation among Australian manufacturing firms was characterised by the following:

- Innovative firms adopted practices to put them in the most competitive markets and in contact with the most demanding customers.
- Innovative firms used their internal capacity to identify, gain access to and use the external environment for expertise and knowledge.
- The skills of employees within innovative firms were valued. Interaction between skilled workers with technical skills enhanced creative opportunities and the generation of new ideas.

6.2 Three Innovation Paradigms

The nature and origins of innovation within business have been examined by Sundbo (1998) who has argued that historically there have been three distinct paradigms of innovation. As shown in Fig. 6.1, the first was that of the creative genius or amateur inventor, the *Gründer*. This actor is driven by psychological motivation to follow a passion or dream drawn from their own creative imagination, or in response to a problem or market opportunity. During the eighteenth and nineteenth centuries, the majority of innovation was driven by this paradigm and saw individuals such as

	The Creative Genius	***Technology Push***	***Market Pull***
Explanation of innovation	Psychological	Technological	Sociological
Determinant of innovation	Entrepreneurship	Technological development	Market-oriented Strategy
Agent of Innovation	The Gründer ('Amateur')	Scientist/ Engineer	The professional Manager
Result	Economic Growth & Corporate Development		

Fig. 6.1 Three innovation paradigms. (Source: Sundbo 1998)

James Hargreaves and Samuel Crompton whose inventions of spinning and weaving machines in the 1760s stimulated the industrial revolution. Edmund Cartwright's first power loom of 1785 revolutionised textile manufacturing and expanded British industry although he was an amateur inventor and clergyman who had not even seen a working loom prior to starting his innovation (Warner et al. 1961). Today, this amateur inventor-innovator lives on in the many small business entrepreneurs who continue to follow a dream or creative problem-solving process producing successful innovations from small laboratories or backyard workshops.

The second paradigm is that of the professional technician, engineer or scientist. This technology-push paradigm is determined less by entrepreneurship than a predetermined plan to follow established research methodologies and formal patterns of new technology development. This paradigm was first evidenced in the work of Bell Laboratories and Thomas Edison's systematic approach to new technology research and development for commercial benefit. Along with the rise of the corporate manufacturing giants in the twentieth century was the heavy investment by national governments in state funded research centres. For example, Australia's Commonwealth Scientific and Industrial Research Organisation (CSIRO) was founded in 1920 as the Institute of Science and Industrial Technology. It sought to pursue planned research into key areas of need such as agriculture and then military technologies during the Second World War (Turner 1974). Innovation was focused on planned technologies and not commercially driven in response to market demand. The Centre National de la Recherche Scientifique (CNRS) in France has been founded in 1939 by the French President Albert Lebrun to develop science at the beginning of the Second World War, after years of heavy complaints by renowned scientists and policy makers about the difficulty to conduct scientific experiments in France (CNRS 2019).

Finally, the third paradigm is that of the professional manager. It is a paradigm in which market forces are dominant, and has emerged in the late twentieth century in response to increasing levels of competition in most industries throughout the world. The professional manager is focused on the satisfaction of customer or market demand and relatively fast returns to investment in any new innovation. Unlike the professional engineer or technical specialist, the manager is likely to be less concerned over the technological brilliance of the innovation as they are over the ease with which the innovation can be accepted by the market. All three paradigms are to be found in the current environment. It is still possible to find entrepreneurial *Gründer* within the small business sector, and publicly-funded research centres continue to focus on technology-push rather than market-pull orientations. Radical innovation is more likely to be generated by the technology-push than the market-pull paradigm, while the creative genius is capable of both disruptive and incremental innovations.

6.3 Generation and Diffusion of Innovation

Innovation is a specific function of entrepreneurship and is the means by which the entrepreneur creates new wealth-producing resources or endows existing resources with enhanced potential for creating wealth (Drucker 1985). It is the process by which entrepreneurs convert ideas into marketable opportunities. To be successful, innovation should offer both newness and market value. Novelty alone will not secure market acceptance or a satisfactory return on investment. Innovative firms are those that continuously seek new ways to do things and that challenge the status quo (Cobbenhagen 2000).

Innovation can be radical, synthetic or incremental in nature and can involve new products or services as well as administrative and technical processes (OECD 2005). Process innovations are defined as tools, devices and knowledge in throughput technology, mediating between inputs and outputs that are new to the industry. Product innovations are outputs or services that directly benefit the customer or client. Radical innovations produce fundamental changes in organisations or industries and a clear departure from existing practice; they increase uncertainty and result in transformation of the firm or the industry. Incremental innovations call for only a marginal departure from existing practices and often reinforce the existing capabilities of the organisation. Technical innovations include products, processes and technologies used to produce products or render services directly related to the activities of an organisation. Administrative innovations relate to organisational structure, administrative process and human resources; they are indirectly related to the basic work activity of the organisation and are more directly related to its management.

The OECD draws a distinction between technological product and process innovations, and the more incremental innovation associated with marketing and administrative enhancement. A technological product innovation must deliver new or improved benefits to the customer that can be objectively measured, while the technological process innovation involves a significant improvement in production or delivery methods (OECD 2005).

As illustrated in Fig. 6.2, each stage of the innovation generation process is devoted to removing uncertainty about the innovation. Idea generation to problem solving comprises activities that lead to an original combination of information about a need or want and the means by which the need or want may be met. Design, development and commercialisation phases focus on developing a product and commercially exploiting it after establishing its economic feasibility.

The commercialisation of an innovation requires the new product or process to be successfully taken from the idea – or 'ideation' – stage to full market acceptance. It has been likened to a process of bridging a gap and requires attention to be given to both the technology associated with the product or process and the acceptability of this innovation within the target market (ISR 2001). Bridging this gap between the initial creative idea and successful diffusion of the innovation into the market not only requires the creation of a viable product or process that can offer significant value, but also requires a business model or entrepreneurial vehicle that can carry the new innovation along the commercialisation pathway.

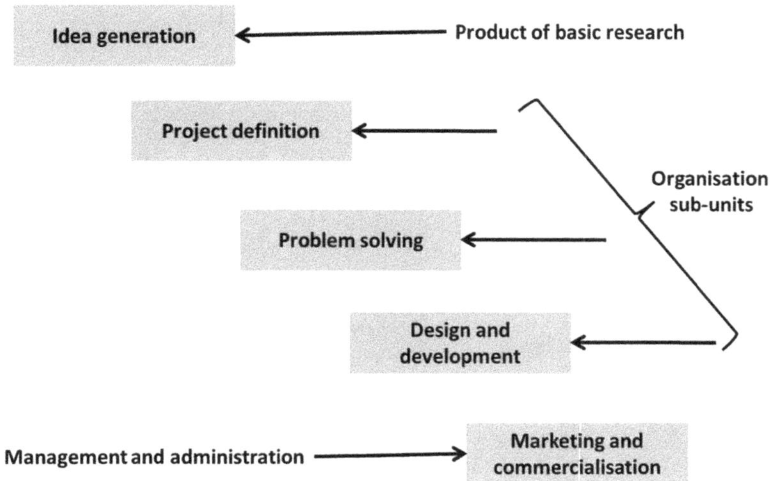

Fig. 6.2 Generating innovation

The adoption of new technology is frequently unable to move past the initial imitators or early adopters who readily take up the innovation but fail to influence the mainstream end-user group or wider community. As shown in Fig. 6.3, there is a chasm into which the innovation may fall. Many excellent ideas or products fail to take off despite superior apparent advantages. In many cases the failure of a new innovation to gain adoption is due to an inadequate understanding of the dynamics associated with the technological feasibility and the market demand for the technology. Innovation is a multi-dimensional concept that can involve product or process, technological or administrative and incremental or radical changes (Cooper 1998).

The fact that a new technology is feasible and may fill a particular need within the market does not mean that it will be readily accepted by the end-user if that party is unwilling to adopt it (Price 1996). Resistance to technology adoption can be attributed to factors inherent within an organisation, such as structural or systems issues impeding innovation and change. It can also be found within the individual and can involve psychological and emotional factors.

Generation of commercially-valuable innovations is therefore a process that can benefit from a systematic approach that seeks to tap the creativity and entrepreneurial capacities of people, search for the best new technologies, and match them to the needs of target markets. Kuratko and Hodgetts (1998) suggest that there are several major myths relating to innovation, which are discussed below.

Myth number 1: Innovation is planned and predictable

The idea that innovation is best left to the R&D department who can plan for new products or new technologies is a myth. This is spurious as many really successful innovations emerge from unrelated practices. While it is desirable for an organisation to adopt a systematic approach to the management of innovation and new

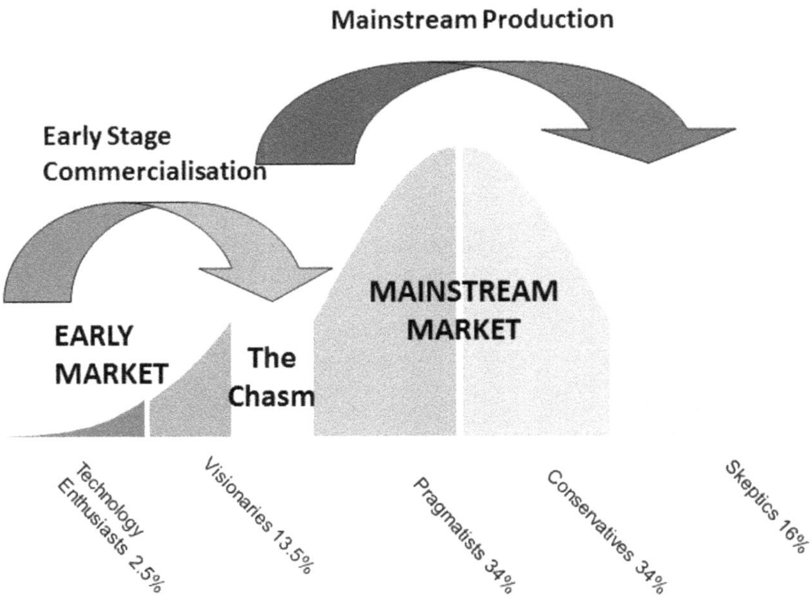

Fig. 6.3 Innovation diffusion model. (Source: Moore 2014)

product development, the 'technology-push' paradigm is not the only one that can achieve success.

Myth number 2: Technical specifications should be thoroughly prepared

Flexibility is important and not all details will be known until the new development process has commenced. A systematic approach to innovation management must be capable of adapting to unforeseen events and the need to modify the prototype should market feedback suggest that changes are required.

Myth number 3: Creativity relies on dreams and blue-sky ideas

Most business innovations are generated by practical people for practical outcomes. The role of creativity is important to the innovation generation process, but ideas that cannot find acceptance within the market by offering value to customers will not succeed.

Myth number 4: Big projects develop better innovations than smaller ones

Incremental innovation is usually more useful than radical change. While large scale radical innovation is exciting and able to attract public attention if it succeeds, the majority of innovations are incremental. They are often a response to customer feedback and involve adapting existing products or processes to better suit the needs of the market.

Myth number 5: Technology is the main driving force for innovation and success

While technology is important, it is not the only source of innovation. Marketing forces derived from the customer or from attempts to solve customer problems are often the most significant source of commercially-useful ideas.

6.4 Theories of Diffusion

Diffusion refers to the process by which an innovation is communicated through different channels over time among members of a social system. The effect of technological change on economic growth depends upon the degree of innovation diffusion. The diffusion of innovations such as new technologies within markets has been examined from both an individual and organisational perspective. Rogers' (1962, 1995) diffusion of innovation theory and Ajzen and Fishbein's (1980) theory of reasoned action are examples of individual adoption and diffusion models, as is the technology acceptance model of Davis et al. (1989).

According to Rogers (1962, 1995), the diffusion of innovation is contingent on five perceived attributes: relative advantage, complexity, compatibility, trial-ability and observability. In other words, does the innovation offer any significant relative advantage over existing technologies or processes? Is it of a complexity level that makes it difficult to use or employ? Is the new innovation compatible with existing technologies or processes, or will it force these to be replaced? (As noted previously, this can be the cause of conflicts.) Can the new innovation be subject to trial before adoption and is it something that can be observed in practice before adoption?

The adoption of any new technology is likely to be influenced by these five attributes, with end-users accepting or rejecting the innovation in terms of how well it satisfies these criteria in various combinations. By contrast, the technology acceptance model has only two perceived attributes: usefulness and ease of use (Davis et al. 1989). This draws upon the work of Ajzen and Fishbein's (1980) theory of reasoned action.

Figure 6.4 illustrates the theory of reasoned action (TRA) in which the best predictor of an individual's future action or behaviour is the stated behavioural intention (BI). This is itself mediated through the combination of their attitudes (Aact) toward the behaviour and the influence of third parties, as measured by the subjective norm (SN).

Of these, the attitude (Aact) toward the behaviour is a product of the individual's beliefs (b) about the merits of the behaviour and their evaluation (e) of this behaviour as an appropriate course of action. The subjective norm (SN) is determined by the normative beliefs (Nb) that the individual has in relation to the expectations or opinions of others in relation to the intended behaviour and their motivation to comply (mc) with such social pressure or expectation (Ajzen and Fishbein 1980).

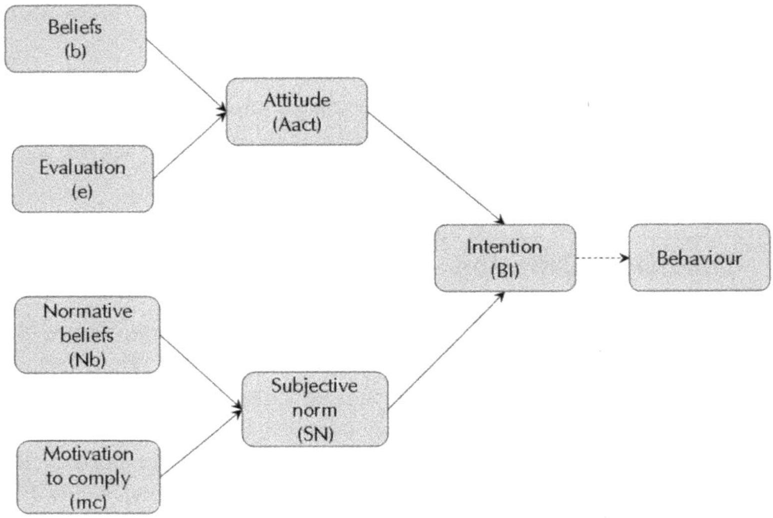

Fig. 6.4 Theory of reasoned action model (TRA). (Source: Ajzen and Fishbein 1980)

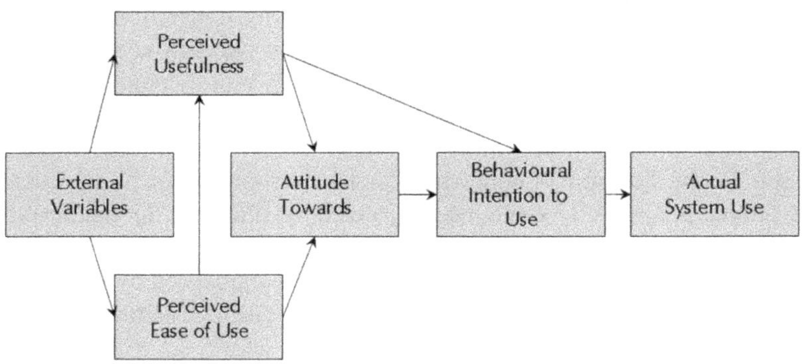

Fig. 6.5 Technology acceptance model (TAM). (Source: Davis et al. 1989)

The TRA framework was a foundation upon which the technology acceptance model (TAM) of Davis et al. (1989) was developed (Legris et al. 2003). As shown in Fig. 6.5, the TAM model draws upon the behavioural intention element of the TRA and seeks to explain technology adoption in terms of the antecedent attitudes and perceptions held by those who may choose to adopt the new innovation.

According to the TAM, whether or not a new technological innovation is adopted and therefore diffused into the target market is contingent upon the attitudes the adopters hold toward the innovation, and these in turn influence their behavioural intention to adopt or 'dis-adopt'. Influencing the adopter's attitudes are their perceptions of the ease with which the innovation will be used and also how useful the new technology is likely to be. Many new technologies fail to diffuse due to prejudice toward them by adopters either who feel they are too complex or difficult to

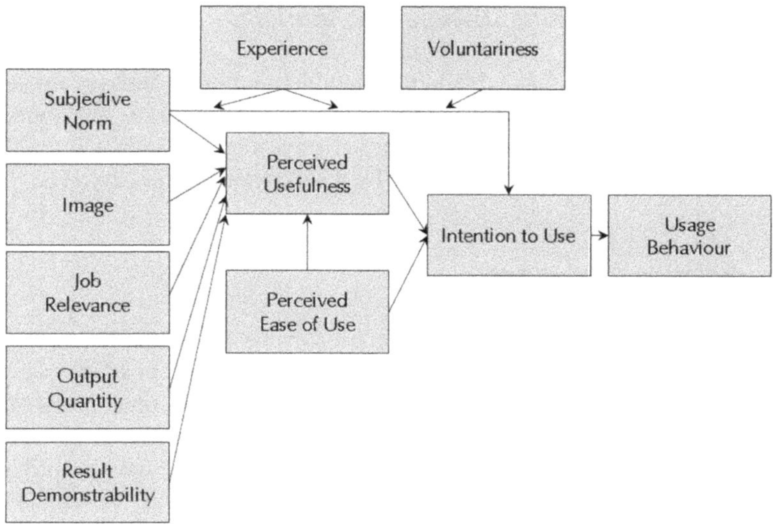

Fig. 6.6 Technology acceptance model 2 (TAM2). (Source: Legris et al. 2003)

implement, or who cannot see that they offer significant advantages over existing technologies. Determinants of perceptions of its effectiveness and complexity include external variables such as: the activities of competitor technologies, changes to the regulatory or technical environment, or feedback from others who have already adopted the innovation.

Legris et al. (2003) have sought to develop the basic TAM framework further with their TAM2 model. Figure 6.6 illustrates the TAM2 model where it can be seen that the basic TAM framework is further extended with five independent variables influencing the perceived usefulness of the technology comprising:

- the influences of third parties (subjective norm);
- how the innovation is viewed in terms of its usefulness (image);
- how strongly the innovation impacts on the adopter's own work environment (job relevance);
- whether the benefits of the innovation can be quantifiably measured (output quantity); and
- whether the results can be shown or demonstrated prior to adoption (result demonstrability).

This process is also affected by two mediating variables. The first is the depth of experience the adopters have had with technology or innovation acquisitions of this type; the second is the degree to which the adopter has discretion over whether or not they adopt, i.e. voluntariness.

6.5 Why Innovations Diffuse into Markets

The willingness of a customer to accept a new product or technology is likely to depend on several factors that determine the speed with which the innovation will diffuse into the market. As noted above, at least five key attributes will need to be satisfied before the innovation is accepted by most customers (Rogers 1962, 1995).

6.5.1 Relative Advantage

The first of these is the relative advantage offered by the new technology, product or service to the customer in comparison with those already being supplied by existing systems. Any new product or process must be able to demonstrate that it offers a significant advantage in relation to existing systems, or it is unlikely to be viewed as worth the cost and effort of switching. The benefits offered by the new product or process need to be important to the customer and may not always be related to the technologies associated with the innovation. Technical sophistication that is not able to offer measurable benefits to the customer is unlikely to be adopted. This suggests that the innovation's technical complexity may sometimes be a liability to the rate of market adoption.

6.5.2 Complexity

The second attribute that can determine how quickly an innovation is diffused into a market is its technical complexity. Products or processes that are overly complex can be too difficult for the customer to understand and use. The early market penetration of the computer and the internet were largely confined to academic, technical and business communities who had the necessary skills to operate the equipment. User-friendly software has been able to increase the market adoption rates for personal computers and the internet, which has assisted in the lowering of costs.

6.5.3 Compatibility

For many customers, the ability to have a new technology integrate with their existing systems is a major attraction. The third attribute that determines the adoption rate of a new product or process is how compatible it is with established systems. Where an innovation can integrate with the existing technologies operated by the customer, there is likely to be less cost and disruption. This means that new products or processes that are not compatible are likely to be viewed by the customer as inherently riskier. Customers have typically invested a good deal of money, time and even reputation in their existing technologies. Asking them to make sudden and costly changes is likely to be met with resistance.

6.5.4 Trial-Ability

The fourth attribute associated with the adoption of innovation is whether the customer can trial the new product or process prior to purchase or full adoption. As noted above, the adoption of any new technology carries with it some degree of risk. Customers like to test drive cars and try on shoes and clothing prior to purchase both to determine if they are going to be happy with the purchase and to experience first-hand the benefits offered. Apple Computers achieved this in the 1980s with the launch of their Macintosh system. They knew that the graphic user interface on the new product would be well-received by customers, but to get this point across they offered a free 'test drive' program allowing the computers to be taken home and used for a few days with a no obligation return policy if the purchaser did not want to proceed with the deal. The majority of customers bought the computer (McColl-Kennedy et al. 1990).

6.5.5 Observability

The fifth and final attribute is the ability for the customer to observe the innovation's benefits and to be able to measure them. Where the product or process can clearly demonstrate its value to the customer with measures of lowered costs, enhanced performance or ease-of-use, the chances of the technology being accepted will increase. For some process innovations and many services, the ability to observe benefits is not always possible.

6.5.6 Usefulness and Ease of Use

Additional factors that may influence the customer's decision to adopt a new technology are the perceived usefulness of the innovation and its overall ease-of-use (Davis et al. 1989). While this may seem self-evident, the innovator needs to fully explore these issues from the customer's perspective to ensure that the new product or process is perceived as useful to them in solving their problems or achieving their goals, and that it can be understood sufficiently to allow it to be used without excessive learning. A technology may be perceived as useful, but if it takes the customer too long to learn how to use it, the innovation is likely to be abandoned and its rate of diffusion within the chosen market will be slow or limited.

6.5.7 Subjective Influences

Where an innovation is disruptive (e.g. it does not integrate or is not compatible with existing systems), there is likely to be added resistance to market adoption. Customers will be unlikely to have any experience of the new product or process and may find it difficult to evaluate the relative advantage of the innovation. It should also be noted that customers are also influenced by the views of family, peer groups, professional associations and the media in their decisions. These influences can be highly subjective in nature, but can work to create either a positive or negative attitude toward the new technology – often determining in advance their intention to adopt or reject an innovation (Ajzen and Fishbein 1980).These influences have been also described as "translation" from one particular actor (a translator, able to explain and influence potential adopters) by French sociologists studying the diffusion of innovations on a sociological point of view (Akrich et al. 1988a, b). Their theory is built around the role of specific actors, able to influence a network. If these actors are interested in the innovation, they may be able to advertise it in their network and hence foster the diffusion.

6.6 The Critical Mass of Adoption

Baptista (1999) overviews the economic theories and empirical research associated with innovation diffusion. The recognition that innovation diffusion tends to define an 'S' shaped curve – or sigmoid curve – along the lines of that illustrated in Fig. 6.7 may arguably be simplistic, but remains a useful framework for understanding the basic principles. This is based essentially on a social model that assumes innovation is diffused through the process of communication from one innovation adopter to another.

The sigmoid curve model in Fig. 6.7 assumes that the rate of adoption of interactive innovations often reaches a critical mass when enough individuals have adopted to make further adoption self-sustaining. Interactive innovations such as email and facsimile have a degree of interdependence among adopters as the more that adopt, the more that adopters are able to communicate through that innovation. That is, the utility of the innovation increases as the number of adopters increases.

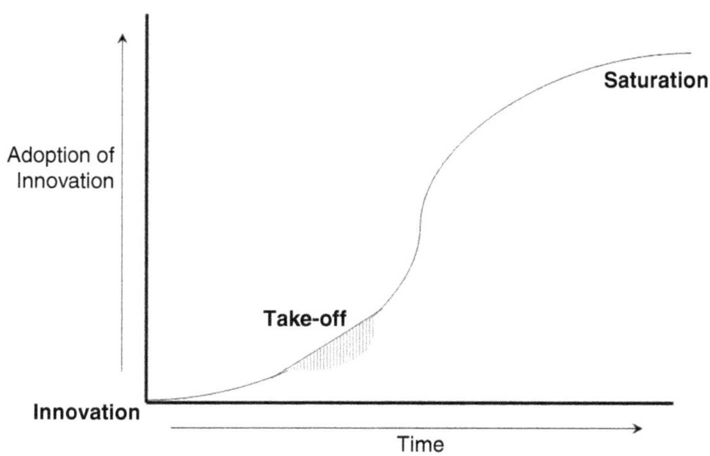

Fig. 6.7 Innovation diffusion model (sigmoid curve model)

Individuals adopt an innovation partly on the expectation of others adopting that innovation too (Rogers 1962, 1995). In this scenario, earlier adopters affect later adopters in the adoption decision, and later adopters affect earlier adopters in the dis-adoption of an innovation. Critical mass typically involves opinion leaders in a social system and operates at the aggregate or social system level. The threshold number of adopters before an individual adopts operates at the individual level and explains the S-shaped diffusion curve. Critical mass or take-off can occur in non-interactive innovations. Take-off usually occurs between 5% and 20% adoption – after this point, very little external promotion is required.

This S-shaped diffusion curve was identified as early as the nineteenth century by French sociologist Gabriel Tarde (1903) who recognised that social exchange was a critical element in the adoption of new ideas. Communications and the ability to leverage networks and geographic proximity of individuals and firms to achieve a more rapid diffusion is important (Baptista 1999; Kinnunen 1996; Michaelides and Theologou 2010). However, the novelty of an innovation generates an element of risk, as can the level of disruption that the new technology places on the adopter's existing practices or processes (Rogers 1962, 1995). Interpersonal communication and the ability to transfer knowledge of the innovation throughout the adopting community is therefore a key factor that can influence the rate and pattern of diffusion (Gatignon and Robertson 1985).

For Tarde (1903), the early imitators are critical because if they reject the innovation, it will die an early death. His nineteenth century perspective saw the upper classes as the most likely – and important – early imitators whose endorsement of a new invention was critical to its subsequent adoption and wider diffusion. This model is still applicable within the twenty-first century where new ideas or products become picked up by opinion leaders and then diffused across industries or communities.

The diffusion process is a social one because it involves a two-way communication exchange between imitators with opinion leaders influencing others within their social circle to adopt or not to adopt (Akrich et al. 1988a, b). Such innovation can either be cumulative, involving incremental additional steps to existing products and processes or substitutive, involving the replacement of existing processes or products with new ones. There is generally a low level of social conflict arising in the case of cumulative innovations but a higher level of social conflict in the case of substitutive innovations.

6.7 Diffusion of Innovation in Historical Context

An example of technology diffusion within a historical context is shown in Fig. 6.8 (Grubler 2000). Here, transport innovations within the United States are mapped on a timescale from 1800 to the present. As can be seen, each new transport technology follows an S-shaped curve as originally identified by Tarde (1903). The adoption of canals commenced in the late 1790s and became a dominant technology by the mid-1830s.

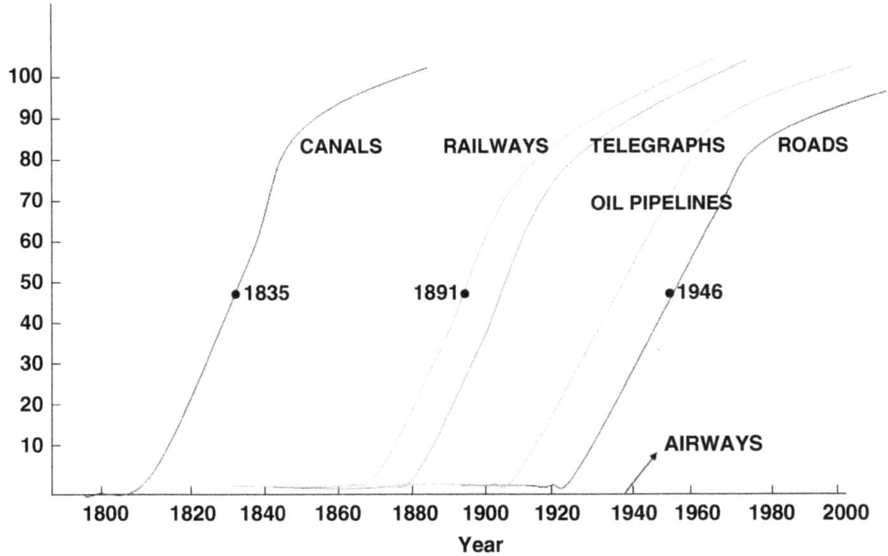

Fig. 6.8 Innovation diffusion patterns in United States. (Source: Grubler 2000)

The development of railways and telegraphs occurred almost simultaneously, commencing slowly over the period from the late 1830s and not really taking off until the 1860s. By the 1890s, the diffusion-adoption rate had reached critical mass and these technologies were being widely adopted, virtually changing the face of the United States. A similar pattern of development and diffusion took place with national highways and oil pipelines, commencing over the last decades of the nineteenth century and taking off into the early years of the twentieth century.

The adoption of such technologies was made possible by a combination of complementary technologies. For example, the adoption of hydraulic locks and control devices for the canals as well as internal combustion engines to power the barges. For the railways there was the development of the steam engine. The construction of rail lines aided the development of telegraph lines which could be run alongside the rails, assisting communications and control. Motor vehicles and petrol-powered engines were critical to the development of oil pipelines and highway systems. Technological innovations do not exist in isolation. They must be examined within their wider context. The successful diffusion of an innovation is likely to be determined by the complementary social, technological and economic forces existent in the environment into which the new invention is being launched.

6.8 Diffusion Adoption Patterns

Adoption usually follows a normal distribution as illustrated in Fig. 6.9, where it can be seen that a standard bell curve pattern is typically found among the market diffusion of an innovation. This pattern was recognised by Rogers (1962, 1995) who

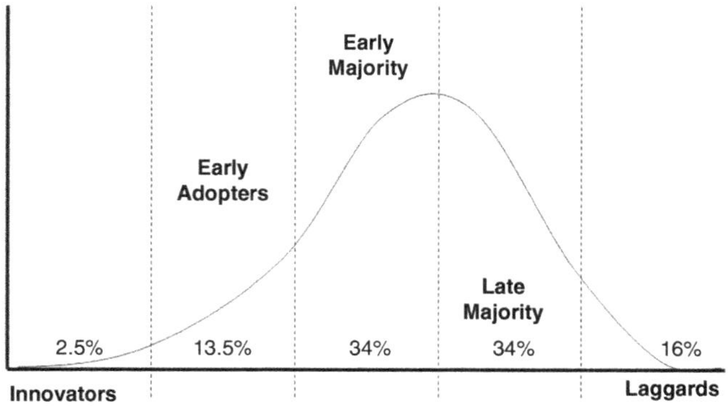

Fig. 6.9 Innovation diffusion-adoption patterns. (Source: Rogers 1962, 1995)

suggests that diffusion takes place through the activation of peer networks that increase the spread of knowledge about an innovation. The model tracks the diffusion process whereby the innovation is initially adopted by innovators and then early adopters who typically embrace new ideas first. Once these groups have adopted the new innovation, it can be accepted by the mainstream of adopters. As shown, the early stage adopters typically represent around 16% of the population.

As shown in Fig. 6.9, there are several categories of adopter depending on the timing of their take-up of the innovation. These are classified in five distinct groups described below.

6.8.1 Venturesome Innovators

This group demonstrates a keen interest in new ideas which leads these innovators to seek information about new ideas outside of their social circle and to form more cosmopolitan relationships. It is common for this group to possess substantial financial resources, to have the ability to understand complex technical knowledge, and to have a low risk aversion. While this group may not always command the respect of the majority, they serve to bring the innovation into the social system as 'gatekeepers.' In some new product development environments, this group can be highly useful as pioneers offering feedback on the performance of prototypes.

6.8.2 Respectable Early Adopters

This group has local social networks and the greatest degree of opinion leadership of any category. Change agents seek this group out because they serve as role models for the average member of the social system. After adoption of an innovation, the early adopter will communicate subjective evaluation of the innovation to peers through interpersonal networks. Such opinion leaders are often an important link in the diffusion chain.

6.8.3 The Deliberate Early Majority

This group adopts innovations just before the average member of the social system. They also have frequent contact with their peers, providing interconnectedness between early and late adopters. Their adoption process is longer than innovators and early adopters.

6.8.4 The Sceptical Late Majority

This group adopts innovations just after the average member of the social system. Adoption may be an economic necessity and may be due to increased pressure from peers. Social system norms favour the innovation before this group adopts, making the adoption easier and more socially acceptable.

6.8.5 Traditional Laggards

The last group to adopt, laggards have the most localised outlook and border on isolation. Decisions about innovations are often made with reference to what happened in the past. They are suspicious of change agents and innovations, and hold traditional values that result in a lengthy adoption process. Resistance may be rational as resources are scarce.

6.9 The Innovation Decision Process

Rogers (1962, 1995) conceptualises the individual adoption process in five stages of behaviour as illustrated in Fig. 6.10. In the first stage, knowledge, the innovation is brought to the attention of the adopter who begins to learn of its merits and characteristics. During the second stage, persuasion, the adopter forms an attitude toward the innovation that may be either favourable or unfavourable.

By the stage three, decision, the adopter either accepts or rejects the innovation. If the innovation is accepted, the fourth stage, implementation, occurs where the adopter puts the innovation to use. In the final stage, confirmation, the adopter seeks

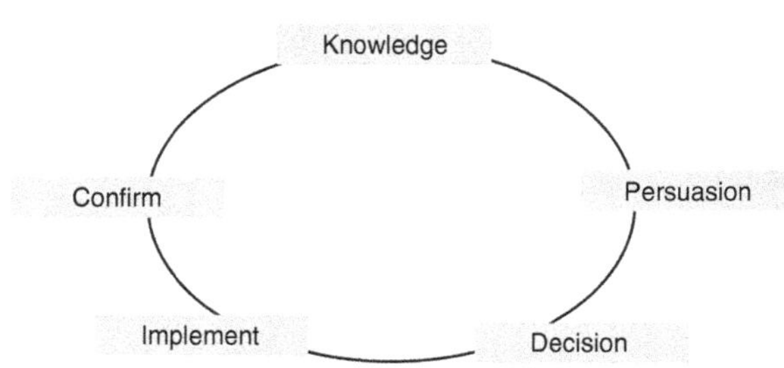

Fig. 6.10 Innovation decision cycle model. (Source: Rogers 1962, 1995)

reinforcement about the decision to accept or reject the innovation. This stage may result in the reversal of a previous decision on an innovation because of conflicting information about the innovation.

The process of adoption defined in the innovation decision cycle model is essentially one of strong interpersonal communications in which early adopters pass on their views to their colleagues within the industry or community, leading to a shaping of attitudes. Rogers' (1962, 1995) research was based on the adoption of innovation in agricultural communities where such communication and endorsement is common practice. Consumer behaviour in adopting new technologies may follow a similar pattern. However, this pattern is less applicable in large organisations.

6.10 Innovation Adoption in Organisations

Research into organisational adoption and diffusion of innovation has identified a two-stage process involving first a decision by the firm's management to adopt the technology, and then the implementation stage in which the end-users are engaged (Leonard-Barton and Deschamps 1988; Zaltman et al. 1973). This suggests that the attitudes and perceptions of adopters within organisational settings must be addressed at both the management and end-user levels. The extra level of adopter complexity makes diffusion of new technologies and other types of innovation into large organisations more difficult.

Gallivan (2001) suggests that the adoption of technological innovation within organisations needs to be examined in two distinct stages, commencing with the initial decision by senior management to adopt the innovation, i.e. the primary authority adoption decision, but moving to the level of how the innovation is then assimilated into the organisation, i.e. the secondary adoption and organisational assimilation process. Key elements of this process are discussed in the following sub-sections.

6.10.1 Managerial Intervention

Following the initial senior management decision to adopt the innovation, it becomes important whether there is sufficient support by management to assist the end-users to acquire and implement the new technology. If the decision is imposed upon the end-users rather than accepted willingly, this can influence the adoption process. The provision of training and support to the end-users may also prove to be of key importance in relation to how successful the innovation adoption process is.

6.10.2 Subjective Norms

As initially outlined in the TRA and TAM models, the influence of peers or co-workers and other sources of influence can affect how well the innovation is diffused into the organisation. Customers, senior management, professional networks and even subordinates can influence the adopters' attitudes towards the innovation in either a positive or negative manner, depending on the environment.

6.10.3 Facilitating Conditions

How easily the new innovation can be implemented and the compatibility of the new technology with existing technologies or processes can be important. What are also likely to influence the innovation adoption process are the attributes of the organisation and its employees. Organisational cultures that are open to new ideas and flexible in their ability to respond quickly to change may be more likely to adopt innovations than ones that are less open and less flexible. The general level of education and knowledge within the workforce can also impact upon the ease and speed of adoption.

6.10.4 Secondary (Individual) Adoption Process

The ability of the individual end-user within the organisation to adopt the innovation is dependent upon the factors discussed above. If conditions are right, they will adopt and the next stage will be reached.

6.10.5 Assimilation

At this stage the organisation will seek to bring the innovation 'on stream', putting it through several stages:

- *Initiation* – the innovation is launched;
- *Adoption* – the innovation is put into trial;
- adaptation – all end-users learn to deal with it and adapt work practices or systems;
- *Acceptance* – the innovation is accepted after trial;
- routinisation – the new technology is now mainstream; and
- *Infusion* – following regular use, the innovation may spur new opportunities or uses.

6.10.6 Consequences

If the adoption process proceeds to the assimilation stage, there will be outcomes or consequences for both the organisation and the end-users. If successful, the new innovation will be identified through the adoption and assimilation stages as being of benefit, and positive attitudes toward it are likely. However, if the innovation is found to be less useful or more difficult to implement, then the opposite is likely.

6.11 Rogers Innovation Adoption Model

Rogers (1962, 1995) provided a six-stage process model for the adoption of innovation in organisational contexts that provided a foundation for the Gallivan (2001) model described above. These stages are described below and illustrated in Fig. 6.11.

Stage 1: Agenda setting

In this stage the organisation begins to identify the need for an innovation through the definition of problems that the new technology or process might solve. It is common for a list of priorities to be developed and for organisations to actively search for innovations to solve priority problems. Agenda-setting is a continual process. Problem identification is defined as a performance gap that motivates or triggers an organisation to seek an innovation. Opportunistic surveillance of the environment for beneficial innovations is also undertaken.

Stage 2: Matching

In this stage the organisation seeks to match the innovation with the perceived problem or desired solution. This virtual evaluation and planning process will lead to adoption or rejection of an innovation depending on whether or not a match is found.

Stage 3: Decision

At this stage the organisation selects the solution to its priority problem and decides to adopt or not adopt a particular innovation.

Stage 4: Re-defining/restructuring

The adoption of an innovation is followed by a period of reinvention of the innovation to match the organisation's needs, or a restructuring of the organisation to fit with the innovation. This must occur before the innovation becomes a routine process in the organisation. A restructuring of the organisation is most likely to take the form of human capital changes, i.e. improved training or technical competence to

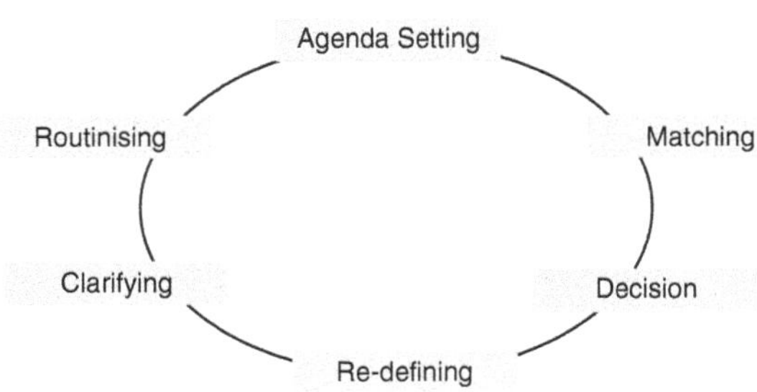

Fig. 6.11 Organisation innovation adoption model. (Source: Rogers 1962, 1995)

ensure that the innovation can be implemented. It is most common for the organisation to undergo a process of restructuring where the adoption of the new innovation demands such change due to the incompatibility of its existing structure.

Stage 5: Clarifying

This stage occurs as the innovation is put to widespread use, with the innovation becoming clearer to the members of the organisation. Questions regarding how the innovation will work and how it will affect members are asked at this stage and must be answered. The clarifying stage signifies a move towards a common understanding of the innovation within the organisation – this occurs through interpersonal communication. Key issues facing the acceptance of the innovation at this stage are its perceived usefulness and ease of use, the level of support for the innovation from both inside and outside of the organisation, and the behavioural intentions of the end-users, e.g. whether they were pre-disposed to adopt this or an alternative innovation.

Stage 6: Routinising

When the innovation is incorporated into the organisation and becomes routine, it is no longer a separate identity to the organisation and is no longer considered a new idea. It remains a core system or product until challenged and replaced by another new innovation. Dis-adoption of the innovation can and does occur at this stage, with the end-user community abandoning the technology for a variety of reasons.

6.12 Innovation Diffusion as a Social Process

As noted above, Tarde (1903) was among the first to identify the social nature of innovation diffusion. According to his 'theory of imitation' the human society adapts and evolves via imitation of one 'inventor' by one or more 'adopters'. The speed at which a new invention is diffused is likely to depend on the innovation's usefulness, its ease-of-use, and the other key issues identified by Rogers (1962, 1995). However, it is also strongly influenced by the social system in which it is being diffused.

> **For example,** … Diffusion occurs within the boundaries of the social system or market segment. The diffusion pattern at the social system level is an outcome of the distribution of individual adoption decisions. These individual adoption decisions are influenced by personal characteristics, perceived innovation characteristics, personal influence, and marketing and competitive actions. The latter also have an influence in defining the perceived innovation characteristics and affecting the personal influence process. (Gatignon and Robertson (1985) p. 850)

The process of diffusion involves a series of seven distinct elements that form together to create the overall system in which the innovation is diffused. These elements include: the item or innovation that is to be diffused, the time it takes to diffuse within a given community, the adopting units (e.g. individuals, groups, organisations), the social structure and culture found within the adopting community, the channels of communication through which the diffusion process is transmitted, and finally the acceptance of the innovation within the community (Katz et al. 1963). An examination of the research literature into innovation diffusion identified three major components critical to understanding the nature of the process (Wejnert 2002), which are discussed below.

6.12.1 Characteristics of the Innovation

An initial important consideration is whether the innovation has public or private consequences, as well as the costs and benefits associated with its adoption. For example, a new product such as the Apple iPad has largely private consequences, while the introduction of a national broadband network has public consequences. The innovation with a public consequence would involve large numbers of different stakeholders and would require a public debate.

6.12.2 Characteristics of the Innovator

Also, of importance is whether the innovator is a person, group or organisation, and also what their status or esteem is within the wider social network of future adopters. Writing in the late nineteenth century, Tarde (1903) noticed that the social status of an individual was important to whether others sought to imitate them. For example, the decision by Queen Charlotte to grant Josiah Wedgwood the right to declare his fine pottery the 'Queen's Ware' and to carry a 'by appointment to the royal household' title served to promote the company's products and build the market adoption of Wedgwood china.

6.12.3 Environmental Context in Which the Diffusion Is to Occur

How quickly an innovation diffuses is will also depend on the social and economic conditions into which it is entering, the geographic distance it has to travel, and the political support or opposition that it might encounter. For example, the diffusion of technological innovations slowed dramatically during the Great Depression as economic times restricted investment, but advanced rapidly during World War Two (Hamblin et al. 1979).

6.12.4 The Role of Word-of-Mouth Communication

Coughenour (1964) observed that the rate of adoption and diffusion can be influenced by the attitudes, knowledge and decision-making abilities and interpersonal competence of the adopting community. Also important are the social relationships of the people in these communities and the type of innovation being diffused. For example, when a new computer program is released, its adoption is likely to be more rapid within a 'tech-savvy' community. This is also what has been developed in the "Network-Actor Theory" by Akrich et al. (1988a, b).

Word-of-mouth communication between individuals can play a key role in the diffusion process. For example, when Westinghouse first launched its range of small air-conditioning systems for retro-fitting into houses in the early 1950s, much of the diffusion took place as a result of word of mouth. Upwardly mobile young professional couples in cities like Philadelphia who purchased them would tell their friends and invite them to dinner during summer in the comfort of their air-conditioned homes. The product quickly diffused across these neighbourhoods (Brooks 1957). A similar pattern was observed in the diffusion of hybrid corn seed in rural Iowa during the 1930s when farmers, who were early adopters of the new product, told their friends and neighbours about its performance, leading to its eventual diffusion to the wider community (Ryan and Gross 1943).

The social network theory of the diffusion of innovation has been demonstrated with the work of social geographers who have mapped the adoption of new technologies. According to this evidence, the network of social communications that facilitates the diffusion of an innovation can be mapped from person to person as the local level, then from community to community at the regional level, and finally across regions or nations at the international level (Brown 1969). Early research into the spread of rumours through university student populations and the populations of small towns found that the spread of such rumours moved rapidly from an initial point of introduction into a community, but faded quickly without their perpetuation via the mass media (Dodd 1952).

The advent of the internet has given firms the ability to engage consumers and early adopters of innovation in a two-way dialogue utilising the power of Web 2.0 technologies (Riegner 2007). Consumer reviews of new products and services posted on blogs offer an opportunity for timely dissemination of positive and negative market feedback, and serve as a form of opinion leadership or electronic WOM (Chen and Xie 2008). These global communications networks offer the potential for innovation diffusion to become far more rapid and to encompass a huge range of adopters around the world.

6.13 The Failure of Innovation Diffusion

Drucker (1985) suggests that the failure of an innovation to succeed is due in part to the inability of those seeking to commercialise the new technology or business concept to undertake a detailed analysis of the social, economic, technical or cultural factors required for diffusion. Typically, it is due to the need for concurrent development of additional innovation processes and products to enable the initial idea to succeed.

The Failure of British Innovations

Particularly instructive is the failure of the British to reap the harvest from their own knowledge-based innovations.

The British discovered and developed penicillin, but it was the Americans who took it over. The British scientists did a magnificent technical job. They came out with the right substances and the right uses. Yet they failed to identify the ability to manufacture the stuff as a critical knowledge factor. They could have developed the necessary knowledge of fermentation technology; they did not even try. As a result, a small American company, Pfizer, went to work on developing the knowledge of fermentation and became the world's foremost manufacturer of penicillin.

Similarly, the British conceived, designed and built the first passenger jet plane. But de Havilland, the British company, did not analyse what was needed and therefore did not identify two key factors. One was configuration, that is, the right size with the right payload for the routes on which the jet would give an airline the greatest advantage. The other was equally mundane: how to finance the purchase of such an expensive plane by the airlines. As a result of de Havilland's failure to do the analysis, two American companies, Boeing and Douglas took over the jet plane. And de Havilland has long since disappeared.

Such analysis would appear to be fairly obvious, yet it is rarely done by the scientific or technical innovator. Scientists and technologists are reluctant to make these analyses precisely because they think they already know. This explains why, in so many cases, the great knowledge-based innovations have had a layman rather than a scientist or a technologist for their father or at least their godfather.

Source: Drucker (1985), pp. 106–107.

According to Drucker (1985), the requirements needed to successfully commercialise knowledge-based technological innovations include the ability to conduct a proper analysis of all the factors needed to ensure that the innovation can become a commercial success rather than just a scientific or technical one. If such analysis has been completed, the innovator needs to develop a clearly-focused market entry strategy designed to ensure that the innovation can diffuse quickly and can secure a strong and defensible position in the market. This is the business model that will ensure the innovation is carried forward along its commercialisation pathway.

A successful business model must provide the entrepreneur with a means to diffuse the innovation into its target markets in such a way that the customers and suppliers are satisfied. This market focus is vitally important. The example of DuPont's diffusion of nylon in the 1940s is provided by Drucker (1985). To secure sufficient market diffusion, DuPont identified women's hosiery and underwear as a market niche and essentially created a new market for nylon products in this area. By doing so, DuPont secured a strong strategic position with a clear point of differentiation. According to Drucker (1985), the organisation that is seeking to implement successful commercialisation strategies for its innovations needs to embrace entrepreneurial management practices and orientation. This requires a focus that is market-oriented and customer-centred rather than overly focused on technical or scientific issues.

References

Ajzen, I., & Fishbein, M. (1980). *Understanding attitudes and predicting behaviour*. Englewood Cliffs: Prentice-Hall.
Akrich, M., Callon, M., & Latour, B. (1988a). A quoi tient le succès des innovations? 1: L'art de l'intéressement. *Gérer et comprendre, Annales des Mines, 1988*(11), 4–17.
Akrich, M., Callon, M., & Latour, B. (1988b). A quoi tient le succès des innovations? 2 : Le choix des porte-parole. *Gérer et comprendre, Annales des Mines, 1988*(12), 14–29.
AMC. (1995). *The innovation cycle: Practical tips from innovative firms*. Melbourne: Australian Manufacturing Council.
Baptista, R. (1999). The diffusion of process innovations: A selective review. *International Journal of the Economics of Business, 6*(1), 107–129.
Brooks, R. C. (1957). "word of mouth" advertising in selling new products. *Journal of Marketing, 22*(2), 154–161.
Brown, L. (1969). Diffusion of innovation: A macro view. *Economic Development and Cultural Change, 17*(2), 189–211.
Chen, Y., & Xie, J. (2008). Online consumer review: Word-of-mouth as a new element of marketing communication mix. *Management Science, 54*(3), 477–491.
CNRS. (2019). Aux Origines du CNRS. Retrieved from http://histoire.cnrs.fr/
Cobbenhagen, J. (2000). *Successful innovation: Towards a new theory for the management of small and medium-sized enterprises*. Cheltenham/Northampton: Edward Elgar Publishing.
Cooper, J. R. (1998). A multidimensional approach to the adoption of innovation. *Management Decision, 36*(8), 493–502.
Coughenour, C. M. (1964). The rate of technological diffusion among locality groups. *American Journal of Sociology, 69*(4), 325–339.
Davis, F. D., Bagozzi, R. P., & Warshaw, P. R. (1989). User acceptance of computer technology: A comparison of two theoretical models. *Management Science, 35*(8), 982–1003.
Dodd, S. C. (1952). Testing message diffusion from person to person. *The Public Opinion Quarterly, 16*(2), 247–262.
Drucker, P. F. (1985). *Innovation and entrepreneurship*. Oxford: Butterworth-Heinemann.
Drucker, P. F. (2002). The discipline of innovation. *Harvard Business Review, 80*(8), 95–106.
Gallivan, M. J. (2001). Organizational adoption and assimilation of complex technological innovations: Development and application of a new framework. *The Data Base for Advances in Information Systems, 32*(3), 51–85.
Gatignon, H., & Robertson, T. S. (1985). A propositional inventory for new diffusion research. *Journal of Consumer Research, 11*(4), 849–867.
Grubler, A. (2000). Time for a change: On the patterns of diffusion of innovation. *Journal of Regional Science Review, 125*, 19–42.
Hamblin, R. L., Miller, J. L. L., & Saxton, D. E. (1979). Modeling use diffusion. *Social Forces, 57*(3), 799–811.

Henderson, R. M., & Clark, K. B. (1990). Architectural innovation: The reconfiguration of existing product technologies and the failure of established firms. *Administrative Science Quarterly, 35*(1), 9–30.

ISR. (2001). *From invention to investment: Pathways to commercialisation for emerging technologies*. Competitive Australia, Industry Science and Resources. Retrieved from Canberra, ACT: https://www.industry.gov.au/

Katz, E., Levin, M. L., & Hamilton, H. (1963). Traditions of research on the diffusion of innovation. *American Sociological Review, 28*(2), 237–252.

Kinnunen, J. (1996). Gabriel Tarde as a founding father of innovation diffusion research. *Acta Sociologica, 39*(4), 431–442.

Kuratko, D. F., & Hodgetts, R. (1998). *Entrepreneurship: A contemporary approach* (4th ed.). Sydney: Harcourt and Brace.

Legris, P., Ingham, J., & Collerette, P. (2003). Why do people use information technology? A critical review of the technology acceptance model. *Information & Management, 40*(2), 191–204.

Leonard-Barton, D., & Deschamps, I. (1988). Managerial influence in the implementation of new technology. *Management Science, 34*(10), 1252–1265.

McColl-Kennedy, J. R., Yau, O. H. M., & Keil, G. (1990). Marketing planning practices in Australia: A comparison across company types. *Marketing Intelligence and Planning, 8*(4), 21–29.

Michaelides, P. G., & Theologou, K. (2010). Tarde's influence on Schumpeter: Technology and social evolution. *International Journal of Social Economics, 37*(5), 361–373.

Moore, G. A. (2014). *Crossing the chasm, 3rd edition: Marketing and selling disruptive products to mainstream customers*. New York: HarperBusiness Essentials.

North, D., & Smallbone, D. (2000). The innovativeness and growth of rural SMEs during the 1990s. *Regional Studies, 34*(2), 145–157.

OECD. (2005). *Oslo manual: Guidelines for collecting and interpreting technological innovation data* (3rd ed.). Oslo: Organisation of Economic Co-operation and Development, European Union, Eurostat.

Price, R. M. (1996). Technology and strategic advantage. *California Management Review, 38*(3), 38–56.

Riegner, C. (2007). Word of mouth on the web: The impact of Web 2.0 on consumer purchase decisions. *Journal of Advertising Research, 47*(4), 436–447.

Rogers, E. M. (1962). *Diffusion of innovations*. New York: The Free Press.

Rogers, E. M. (1995). *Diffusion of innovations* (4th ed.). New York: The Free Press.

Ryan, B., & Gross, N. C. (1943). The diffusion of hybrid seed corn in two Iowa communities. *Rural Sociology, 8*(1), 15.

Sundbo, J. (1998). *The theory of innovation: Entrepreneurs, technology and strategy*. Cheltenham: Edward Elgar.

Tarde, G. (1903). *The laws of imitation*. New York: Henry, Holt and Co. (translation and publication in 1962).

Turner, I. (1974). 1914–19. In F. K. Crowley (Ed.), *A new history of Australia* (pp. 312–356). Melbourne: William Heinemann.

Warner, G. T., Marten, C. H. K., & Muir, D. E. (1961). *The new groundwork of British history*. London: Blackie & Sons Ltd.

Wejnert, B. (2002). Integrating models of diffusion of innovations: A conceptual framework. *Annual Review of Sociology, 28*(1), 297–326.

Zaltman, G., Duncan, R., & Holbeck, J. (1973). *Innovations and organizations*. New York: Wiley.

Planning, Business Models and Strategy 7

7.1 Introduction

> If you always know where you are and where you want to be, you'll always get there.
>
> *Source: Kevin Inkster, inventor, founder and CEO of Arbortech.*

This chapter examines the relationship between the entrepreneur's vision and the need for strategic planning. It recognises that flexibility is critical in the development of entrepreneurial ventures and that the planning process must be non-linear in nature if it is to be responsive to the opportunities that market or product innovation offer. While the discipline of formal business planning is highly important to the development of a successful venture, the plan is only a manifestation of the business case or model that underlies the venture. The chapter explores the nature of planning and strategy, business model design and offers both a theoretical and applied view of these areas.

A business plan seeks to outline – in a formal manner – the overall 'blueprint' for the business, and to communicate to third parties what the entrepreneur is seeking to achieve with the venture (Ackelsberg and Arlow 1985). The business plan is popularly acknowledged to be a key component in the success or failure of a commercial venture – whether new or established. However, the possession of a business plan is not a guarantee of success and there is mixed evidence that firms with formal plans are any more profitable than firms without (Pearce et al. 1987). According to Timmons (1999), the business plan is largely obsolete the moment it leaves the printer. This is due to the rapid pace of change that occurs within most markets as well as the dynamic nature of technological change.

To keep pace with market opportunities, the process of planning within the entrepreneurial, innovative venture requires flexibility and recognition that the process is

T. Mazzarol, S. Reboud, *Entrepreneurship and Innovation*, Springer Texts in Business and Economics, https://doi.org/10.1007/978-981-13-9412-6_7

more important than the plan itself. The entrepreneur who is seeking to launch or grow a new business venture must be willing to adapt to new market opportunities or threats, and adjust the business plan to suit the conditions that they face as they move through the growth cycle. However, there is a difference between the business plan and the entrepreneurial vision.

7.2 The Value of the Business Plan

A formal written business plan is a communications tool designed to inform, guide and sometimes sell a business concept or case to a third party. If the entrepreneur is seeking to raise external capital and attract investors to their venture, the business plan becomes important. However, a plan can also be required when dealing with a bank to secure debt financing and sometimes when seeking to secure contracts from large customers or suppliers. Each of these applications of the business plan requires slightly different emphasis. For example, the venture financier is likely to want to see evidence that the plan allows for good financial returns and a clear exit strategy for investors. By contrast, the banker is more likely to be concerned over your capacity to repay debt and whether you have assets or loan guarantees.

One of the most useful applications of the business plan is simply to guide the management of the business venture. For very small firms, the need for a formal written business plan is probably less important than for their larger counterparts. This is not because small firms don't need a plan, but because they have fewer people to coordinate and communicate with. The discipline of writing down the entrepreneur's thoughts about the venture and its future directions into a coherent documented plan is highly beneficial. It requires attention to details and a systematic approach to the way the venture will operate.

7.3 Do Business Plans Really Matter?

The evidence that possession of a formal written business plan makes it more likely a business will succeed is inconclusive. Most small firms do not possess written business plans (Unni 1984), and many entrepreneurs lack business planning skills (Posner 1985). A review of past research studies undertaken into the benefits of strategic business planning within small firms found a positive relationship between formal strategic planning and performance, but the formality and amount of planning did not appear to make a significant difference, what was of more importance was the owner-manager to reconfigure their firms resources and business structure to adapt to the customer or market needs using their judgment rather than relying on formal planning processes (Mazzarol and Reboud 2009).

> **For example,** … More significant is the ability of the owner-manager to apply systematic analytical thinking to their management of the task environment. If formality in the planning process is to be used, it is likely to occur in response to a need to coordinate the

organisational structure of the firm, or to satisfy the needs of external stakeholders (Mazzarol and Reboud (2009) p. 99).

This view has been supported by other research that suggests formal business planning is beneficial, but that it is dependent on contextual factors such as the age of the venture and the organisational culture and climate the venture exists within. Entrepreneurial ventures in which there are high levels of environmental uncertainty may not benefit from excessive planning (Brinckmann et al. 2010). Under such conditions, the entrepreneur is better to maintain a more intuitive approach to planning involving continuous learning and '*sense-making*' (Weick 1988).

Despite these misgivings, small entrepreneurial firms can benefit from strategic planning, particularly if it involves long-range thinking and systematic screening of opportunities (Schwenk and Shrader 1993). Further studies that examined the nature of business planning activities undertaken by small firms suggest that a relationship exists between enhanced sales growth and the implementation of sophisticated business planning techniques (Berman et al. 1997).

A lack of formal business planning has also been identified as a potential source of failure among start-up ventures (Castrogiovanni 1996). Formal business planning may also be related to higher profitability among early stage ventures and superior market growth among established ones (Robinson et al. 1984). However, such studies have not been able to provide conclusive evidence that formal planning will result in enhanced performance, particularly profitability (Robinson and Pearce 1983, 1984).

In a study of 65 fast growth family-owned businesses, the majority of companies had formal business plans. These were found to be sufficiently detailed to allow the management to control management compensation against performance benchmarks. Such firms regularly shared information with their employees and linked their company performance to business goals. Such firms were more likely to seek differentiation and innovation in products or services, rather than simply competing on price (Upton et al. 2001).

Formal business planning among entrepreneurs is likely to reduce failure rates even if it does not significantly enhance profitability, and may be dependent on the level of strategic orientation of the entrepreneur (Sexton and Van Auken 1985). Whether or not an entrepreneur decides to engage in formal business planning activities is likely to depend on their background. Those with previous management experience within larger organisations or with formal management education are more likely to undertake business planning than those without such backgrounds (Olson and Bokor 1995).

A relationship exists between the size of the business venture and the level of formal planning activity that takes place. Not surprisingly, the larger an organisation becomes, the more likely it will engage in formal business planning. Larger firms tend to employ more professionally educated managers who may encourage the preparation of business plans. However, even though the entrepreneur may not possess a formal business plan, they are still likely to be engaged in informal or 'intuitive' business planning (Mazzarol 2001). As the venture grows in size or seeks to develop new markets or raise external funding, the necessity for a formal business plan and related planning process increases.

A longitudinal analysis of the planning behaviour of small Australian firms found that planning activity shifted from formal to informal at different points in time, perhaps in response to specific requirements or changes in their task environment. Other factors likely to influence planning behaviour include the size and complexity of the business, and the characteristics of the firm's senior management – particularly their level of formal education and past experience with business planning (Gibson and Cassar 2002).

Further research undertaken with nascent and novice entrepreneurs in Sweden found no positive relationship between the development of a formal business plan and successful survival, which was 'unrelated to business planning' (Honig and Karlsson 2004). It seems, therefore, that the merits of business planning, at least within the early start-up phase of a venture, are problematic. Many entrepreneurs will engage in business planning more out of a desire to imitate what they feel a successful firm does, or because they have been told to plan by external stakeholders such as government support agencies, accountants, universities or providers of finance.

7.4 What Is Business Planning?

As a document, the business plan can take a variety of forms depending on the purpose for which it was prepared and the nature of the industry or venture. In terms of length, it is generally accepted that business plans should be kept to within 40 pages and written in a clear and straightforward style that is easily understood by anyone, regardless of their knowledge of the particular industry or profession (Stevenson et al. 2000). It should be noted that the success of a new venture is not guaranteed by the business plan, and that a business plan ranks no higher than a two on a scale from one to ten as a predictor of how successful a venture will be.

It is also important to recognise that the business plan should not be viewed as little more than a complex financial analysis. While it is important to include into business plans financial information such as cash flow forecasts and profit projections, these numbers will often be little more than a rough guide to where the business may be headed in the future and what its likely future performance may be. This is particularly the case for start-up ventures and early stage businesses where there are numerous unknown factors that can influence the firm's performance.

> **For example,** … Most business plans waste too much ink on numbers and devote too little information that really matters to the intelligent investor…numbers should appear mainly in the form of a business model that shows the entrepreneurial team has thought through the key drivers of the venture's success or failure (Sahlman 1997).

In essence, the plan is important but the business model or underlying strategy that lies behind the venture is more important. We will examine the concept of the business model in more detail later, but first let us quickly review the three generic types of business plans.

7.5 Types of Business Plans

There are at least three common types of business plans:

1. an application for finance;
2. a supply chain driven plan; and
3. a plan for internal use.

The first of these comes in two derivatives. One financial application plan is targeted at the equity market and seeks to attract the potential investor. This type of plan requires attention to be placed on the key things that such an investor is likely to be interested in. These can include: the rate of potential return to the investment, sales growth and profitability, the ownership structure and share of equity being offered and the level of risk and control that an investor is likely to face. Also, of interest will be the exit strategy for the investor and how quickly they will be able to leave. The other financial application plan is targeted at the banker and seeks to raise debt financing. This plan will need to highlight: the capacity to repay debt, assets that can provide security for such debt, and a stable trading history and credit rating.

Definition of a Business Plan
A business plan is a written document that describes the current state and the presupposed future of an organisation.

Source: Honig and Karlsson (2004).

Plans that are driven by the supply chain are often triggered by a request from a larger customer or supplier who wishes to see a documented business plan before signing a contract. Customers may want to see evidence of how well the firm handles quality and continuity of supply, as well as cost and related issues. The supplier may be interested in the ability of the venture to grow a market and deal with distribution, warranty or service issues on their behalf. Finally, the plan that is developed for internal use is likely to be the most useful from the entrepreneur's perspective. It should be designed to communicate to the firm's staff how the vision of the entrepreneur will be implemented.

The business plan seeks to draw together the key elements of the opportunity – the resources needed to exploit the opportunity and the team that will make this happen. In short, it must communicate how entrepreneurial leadership will be used creatively to blend these three key elements together into a viable business model.

We will return to the elements of a business plan and outline some of the key issues that should be considered when preparing one. However, the plan is essentially a blueprint for how the underlying business model is to be implemented. This is a strategic issue and, as Sahlman (1997) noted, the business model is more important than the business plan.

7.6 Writing a Business Plan

A business plan should be viewed as a blueprint for the business model that underlies the venture. Designing a sound business model is similar to how an architect designs a new building. Initial sketches are converted into a detailed blueprint that shows those who will build the actual structure, what is to be constructed, and how it will be built. The business plan offers a common language for all those who will work within the venture team, setting out a clear vision and objectives that all stakeholders can understand and apply (Grupp and Maital 2001).

Table 7.1 lists the general layout and key elements of a business plan. However, plans can be much less detailed and should be developed in relation to what they are being tasked to do. Often the shorter they are the better.

According to Sahlman (1997), a good business plan should have at least four key elements: (i) the opportunity; (ii) the environmental context; (iii) the risk-reward, and (iv) the team. Each of these is discussed below.

- The Opportunity

The plan should make clear to the reader the business or market opportunity that the venture is seeking to follow. It should explain how the venture will create new value for both the customers and the shareholders, and how sustainable this can be. The products or services that are to be sold and the customers who will buy them should be clearly identified. The plan should also make it clear that the customer is well understood and should demonstrate when, how and why the customer will buy the products/services.

- The Environmental Context

The plan should also outline a sound understanding of the industry or market within which the venture is to operate and any key trends that might enhance or hinder its growth. A discussion should be provided that addresses any political, economic, social or technological factors that might affect the business – both the things that can be controlled and those that cannot need to be identified.

Table 7.1 General layout of a business plan

Section	Description
Executive summary	A short (<3 pages) summary of the key elements of the plan. Should outline the business model and if it is aimed at raising capital it should state how much money is required, how it will be used and what the anticipated return to the investor is. This is often the first and last section that will be read by investors.
Company overview	This section provides a description of the business and its trading history. It might include some brief information on the industry or market in which it operates. Information on the firm's ownership, management and governance structure should be provided. It is also worth highlighting any distinctive competencies the firm might possess.
Product or services	This section describes the firm's products and services so as to give the reader sufficient understanding of their nature and value. Past sales and market share data, patent ownership rights and other relevant information can be included. Additional information can be included in the appendices
Market opportunity	One of the most important sections. It should provide the reader with a clear understanding of the size and anticipated demand for the products and services. Also included are findings from market research, customer feedback and any testimonials
Competition and threats	This section provides an objective summary of the main competitors, including their products, pricing and marketing strategies, strengths and weaknesses. Other threats such as government regulations, customer switching behavior and potential substitutions should also be included if relevant.
Economics of the business	This section summarizes the key performance indicators (KPI) likely to be critical to the future success of the business. This should include gross profit margins, sales revenue required to cover fixed and variable costs, a break-even analysis, and cash flow forecast. Ideally this should be supported by graphs.
Marketing strategy	This section should outline a clear pathway to market or growth for the business. It should include pricing and sales strategies, plus any details of future marketing and promotional campaigns. It might also contain information on any distribution systems, third party agreements and post-sales warranty and service issues.
Operations	This section outlines how the products or services will be produced. It may cover any major plant and equipment requirements, facilities, employment and use of sub-contractors or outsourcing. How quality will be measured and controlled may also be relevant along with work health and safety, and environmental issues.
Management team	This section should provide a detailed explanation of the firm's organisational structure and the key managers working within the business. An organisation chart showing structure (both current and planned) with lines of reporting is also a good idea. Any significant outside advisors (e.g. accountants, lawyers) should also be mentioned.
Financial plan	This section should show any past financial reports (i.e. balance sheet, profit & loss), and also make forecasts of future growth. This is particularly important if the plan is designed to raise money from banks or investors. All assumptions relating to future cash flow and profit projections should be clearly stated.
Appendices	This section might contain product brochures, resumes of the management team, independent reports from auditors, market research firms, and letters of support from customers or suppliers.

Sources: Timmons (1999) and Golis (2002)

- The Risk-Reward

The plan should make a clear statement of the profitability of the proposed venture, and an objective assessment of how much cost and risk will be required to achieve this outcome. If a major investment is required, the forecasts should include calculations of the likely break-even and time to break-even, as well as the anticipated returns and payback period for investors. A realistic evaluation of the things that might go wrong – and how these will be managed – should also be explained.

- The Team

A key part of the plan is a description of the team that will manage the venture. A quality management team is more likely to succeed than one that is poorly balanced in terms of its skills or expertise. Access to third party expertise such as accountancy firms or lawyers and other advisors should be outlined. If the venture has a board of directors or an advisory board, it is important that their profiles are provided. The current and future employment or staffing formula for the venture should be outlined along with a human resource plan or strategy to acquire the right people while retaining existing ones.

7.7 Designing the Business Model

The business plan is only a blueprint for a well-considered business model that should have been thoroughly examined and discussed prior to the preparation of the actual planning document. The business model of an entrepreneurial venture is more generic than the financial or strategic design that is part of its structural configuration. It seeks to generate a mechanism that can deliver value to a target customer or market segment in a sustainable manner, and with an appropriate allocation of resources to achieve this outcome. While the concept of the 'business model' has become widely used in management circles, there is surprisingly little underlying theory relating to this concept.

What is a 'Business Model'?
A business model is a conceptual tool containing a set of objects, concepts and their relationships with the objective to express the business logic of a specific firm. It is a description of the value a company offers to one or several segments of customers and of the architecture of the firm and its network of partners for creating, marketing and delivering this value and relationship capital to generate profitable and sustainable revenue streams.

Source: Osterwalder et al. (2005).

Prior to the 1990s relatively little attention was given to business models in the academic research literature. During the period 1998–2010 a relatively small number of studies were published exploring the concept and its application to entrepreneurship and innovation (Trimi and Berbegal-Mirabent 2012). However, the emergence of technology-based businesses, in particular online or internet-based e-business models provided an impetus to this academic interest. Key areas of focus were the ability to understand how to capture value and increased revenue by configuring the business model to attract and retain suppliers and buyers (Mahadevan 2000). Attention was also given to how value was captured by firms engaged in the commercialisation of innovation, as illustrated by Chesbrough and Rosenbloom (2002) in the examination of the Xerox PARC R&D facility at Palo Alto, California.

With the emergence of interest in entrepreneurship and new venture creation in the first decade of the twenty-first century, a renewed focus on business models grew. However, even by the mid-2000s there was still no generally accepted definition of what a business model was, how it was constructed, or what its best configuration should comprise (Morris et al. 2005). The concept of the business mode remained poorly understood.

For example, … The concept of a business model has no established theoretical grounding in economics or in business studies (Teece 2010).

Academic research into business models began to move from the largely operational, into the realm of strategic management. It was recognised that the business model was a strategic rather than an operational tool for managers who had been trained to plan rather than implement (Hrebiniak 2006). The key elements of importance to the design and development of business models were gradually identified. A key issue was understanding how to design products and services that create and capture value for customers, while simultaneously generating profit for the business. The configuration of the firm's key resources and processes so as to deliver this value in a consistent and sustainable manner were also identified as key areas of focus (Johnson et al. 2008; Osterwalder et al. 2005).

In recent years, the process of business model analysis and design has become recognised as a key strategic tool for entrepreneurs and managers seeking to capture value and build successful, sustainable enterprise (Amit and Zott 2001; Amit et al. 2012; Teece 2010). It is a conceptual tool that can be applied to any industry and should be undertaken in conjunction with any business planning and strategy.

For example, … No matter what the sector, there are criteria that enable one to determine whether or not one has designed a good business model. A good business model yields value propositions that are compelling to customers, achieves advantageous cost and risk structures, and enables significant value capture by the business that generates and delivers products and services. 'Designing' a business correctly, and figuring out, then implementing e and then refining e commercially viable architectures for revenues and for costs are critical to enterprise success. It is essential when the enterprise is first created; but keeping the model viable is also likely to be a continuing task. Superior technology and products, excellent people, and good governance and leadership are unlikely to produce sustainable profitability if business model configuration is not properly adapted to the competitive environment (Teece (2010) p.174).

7.8 The 'Business Model Canvas' for Business Model Design

One of the most popular tools for analysing and designing business models is the "*Business Model Canvas*" for business model generation developed by Osterwalder and Pigneur (2010). This is a framework that comprises nine key areas or "building blocks" that need to be considered when designing business models. It is important to note that the *Business Model Canvas* is a strategic planning tool, and that the interrelationship between the nine areas of the framework can differ depending on the nature of the business or the industry in which it is seeking to operate. The notion of a "canvas" is to recognise that good design should start with a blank page or canvas upon which new ideas, assumptions and concepts can be drawn without the relative restrictions of conventional business planning. Time should be spent brain storming, visualising and testing new ideas with the *Business Model Canvas* tool. These should be tested within the market through customer engagement and discovery, then idea validation, before the final business model takes shape (Blank and Dorf 2012; Osterwalder and Pigneur 2010).

Figure 7.1 illustrates the *Business Model Canvas* with a list of questions that we have added into each of the nine boxes. As can be seen, the centre of the canvas has the *value proposition* that the business model seeks to make to the customer. This is a central pillar for any business model design. On far right is another key pillar that addresses the *customer segments* that the business model is being designed for. Over

Strategic Partners	Key Activities	Value Proposition	Customer Relations	Customer Segments
Do you need to work with others or can you proceed alone? If you need others who are the: • Lead customers? • Key suppliers? • Resource network actors?	Operations management CRM systems Financial control systems HRM Systems Rules, policies, metrics	How does the product or service help the customer: • Save money • Save time • Add value • Increase profits	What are the customers': • Acquisition costs? • Retention costs? • Switching costs? • Life time value?	Who is the customer? What are their main problems or needs? What goals do they have? Demographics? Psychographics?
	Key Resources Core competencies ? Team structure? Physical resources? Financial resources?		**Channels** How do you reach your customers? How can you deliver value to them? Can you do this directly or do you need to work via others?	
Cost structure (how much it cost?) What are the main over head (fixed) costs? What are the anticipated variable costs? What is the anticipated gross profit margin? When will the business break even?		**Revenue Stream (Monetizing)** How much is the customer willing to pay? How many customers will pay? How frequently will they pay? Cash cycle & cost-profit-volume analysis		

Fig. 7.1 Elements of the business model. (Source: Adapted from Osterwalder and Pigneur 2010)

on the far left is a third major pillar relating to the *strategic partnerships* that need to be considered within the business model. Linking these three key pillars are four additional building blocks relating to *customer relations*, *channels*, *key activities* and *key resources*. The bottom of the canvas has two additional areas relating to the *revenue stream (monetising),* and *cost structure how much it costs).*

In the *Business Model Canvas*, the *value proposition* pillar can be understood as representing the logic of *"What"* the business model needs to generate in order to over value to target customers. The *customer segments* pillar addresses the logic of *"Who"* the end user or target customer is. Once these pillars are explained the two linking blocks of *customer relations* and *channels* deal with the logic of *"How"* the business model can deliver value to the customer. These four areas relate largely to external market-oriented issues.

On left hand side of the canvas the *strategic partners* pillar addresses the logic of *"What & Who*" might be required to ensure that the business model can deliver the *value proposition*. It is linked to the central pillar via the *key activities* and *key resources* blocks, which address in turn the "*What & How*" and "*Who & What*". The elements on this side of the *Business Model Canvas* are largely focused on internal resources and capabilities.

Finally, the *revenue stream* area also looks at "How" the business model will be able to generate sufficient income to make the model workable and sustainable. The analysis emerging from the four building blocks on the top right-hand side of the canvas should feed into this area. In turn, the *cost structure* block on the bottom left hand side addresses the issue of "*What?*" it will cost to build the business model. Here the analysis of the cost of activities and resources required to deliver the *value proposition* need to flow into the *cost structure*. Where the firm cannot find these resources or capabilities alone it will need to consider *strategic partners*, and any costs arising from these relationships need to be identified. Each of the nine building blocks of the *Business Model Canvas* are discussed in the following sub-sections. However, Grupp and Maital (2001) suggest several considerations need to be made before the development of the business model commences. These issues are discussed in the context of the *Business Model Canvas* elements.

7.8.1 Customer Segments and Market Segmentation

Before the *value proposition* can be fully addressed it is first necessary to get an in-depth understanding of the customer, who they are. Of importance are the key tasks of understanding what their main problems or needs are, and what goals they have. Osterwalder et al. (2015) have proposed a complementary canvas, named the *Value Proposition Canvas*, to guide the analysis of customer needs and difficulties. This tool relies on the principle of empathy maps (Ferreira et al. 2015) and lists the elements that should be observed when trying to understand the potential customer: their jobs, their pains and their gains. This leads to design the value proposition and its features and elements, including pain killers and value creators (see Fig. 7.2).

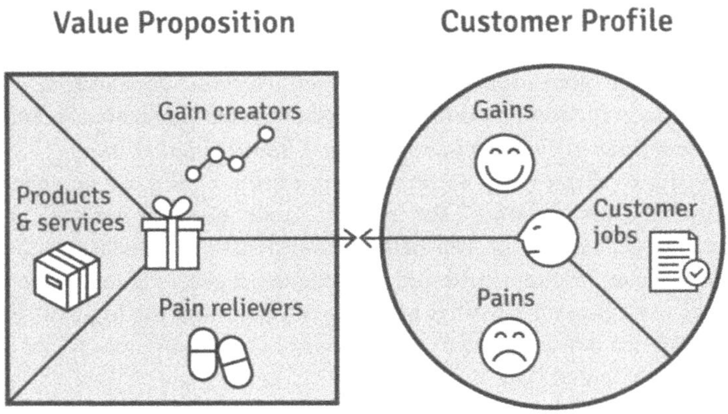

Fig. 7.2 The Value Proposition Canvas. (Source: Osterwalder et al. 2015)

- Basic Assumptions

According to Grupp and Maital (2001) it is important to start with an examination of the market, and seek to gain a comprehensive understanding of the customer's perspective of the situation. Are there any demographic (i.e. age, income, education, marital status, occupation, gender, location), or psychographic (i.e. values, attitudes, lifestyles) trends that suggest the market place is changing fundamentally? There should be a clear understanding of why and how prospective customers buy the products or services that are being planned, and whether or not there are any needs that are not being met by existing suppliers. Once the overall customer and market environment is understood, the next most critical element to understand is the way profit is driven within the market. Will the new venture or product offer sufficient opportunity to generate substantial profit margins, or will prices be too low due to customer reluctance to pay premium prices? Threats from new entrants or substitutes should also be considered.

- What Are the Target Market Segments?

Every market needs to be segmented in order to ensure that the product or service can be adapted to meet the needs of the end user. Not all customers will want or need the same things, and it is unlikely that any single product can satisfy all customers. Segmentation strategies can be undertaken using a variety of measures including the customers' demographics and psychographics. The size and potential responsiveness of each target segment needs to be carefully considered.

- What Do the Targeted Customers Want?

Customers within each market segment will have different expectations and past experience of the product or service that is being offered. Research of customer expectations and behaviours should be undertaken when developing the business model. Customers have three types of need: (1) basic, (2) spoken, and (3) unspoken. While the first deals with what they expect the product to do and the second with what they say they want it to do, the third is often the most important to identify. Satisfying an unspoken need will allow you to delight the customer by offering them a benefit that they had not expected or even thought of. This type of need cannot be identified by simply asking the customer what they want. It requires you to research how they currently use existing products and services. It then involves looking for ways to enhance the customer experience or reduce their time or cost of using such things.

7.8.2 The Customer Value Proposition (CVP)

The primary focus for any business model is its product or service offering to the customer and its ability to make a proposition of value. Teece (2010) suggests that the key questions that should be asked about a business model are:

- What is the specific customer value proposition that the business is to offer?
- What is the best mechanism to assemble the organisation's resources to deliver this?
- How might imitators be held at bay?

The key considerations within the product area of the business model are related to the customer or target market and getting an understanding of the customer's perspective about the new product or service. Whatever the product or service that is being offered, a primary consideration should be to understand how the product or service helps the customer secure value. This is typically achieved by saving them money or time, adding value or increasing their profitability.

- What Is the Overall Customer Value Proposition?

The customer value proposition (CVP) is focused on taking the answers emerging from the questions raised in the *customer segments* area, and using them to generate a product or service solution for the target customer that solves a specific need or problem and makes an offer that satisfies or fulfils this need (Johnson et al. 2008). Research into customer perception of value suggests that it is a complex trade-off between what price is to be paid and what benefits are to be obtained. The price paid or the cost of the product or service is weighed against the perceived quality of the product, service and technical service issues. These can be influenced by brand image, the image of the supplier, and the perception of risk associated with the purchase (Sweeney and Soutar 2001).

- Customer Selection

An important first question for any new venture is to decide on which customers the business is to serve (Grupp and Maital 2001). This is less easily dealt with than might first appear to be the case. Frequently a new innovative venture will identify a wide range of potential market opportunities and yet it will not be able to easily decide which of these it should target. The selection of the *first* customer can be a critical issue, as this decision can determine the speed with which a new innovation is diffused within a target market. For many small entrepreneurial ventures, the role of leading customers is to assist the business with ideas, funding and market access. It is of some importance then that the initial customer base is selected. Customers who might readily partner with the venture are highly valuable. Customers that can be retained and who will be loyal over time are also highly valuable.

7.8.3 Customer Relationships

Once the customer segment has been selected, there needs to be consideration of how this market niche can be better served by the new venture than by existing competitors. It is most important for the new venture to identify what the existing standards or benchmarks are in the industry and then to seek ways to provide *customer delight* (Hall 1992). The process of delighting the customer is to exceed the current levels of cost, service or quality being offered in the market and to use innovation to maintain such an advantage. Within industrial markets, attention should be given to identifying and understanding the nature of the customer's customer. By ensuring that the product or service assists the customer to service *their* customers better, the new venture can secure a position of strength in its selected market space.

Over time, the profitability of any particular market segment is likely to determine the sustainability and growth potential for the venture. Attention should be given to whether or not leading customers will be willing to pay premium prices for the product/service offering, and how easily the venture will be able to reach such customers on a regular basis. At the end of the analysis, the most important issue will usually be whether or not the price that can be secured in the chosen market is sufficient to generate a profit margin that will sustain the business.

In terms of *customer relations,* the cost of winning and retaining a customer needs to be considered. Some customers are likely to be easier to acquire than others, but they may be only loyal for a short time. The costs incurred by a customer in switching from one supplier to another is also of importance. This can be measured in both direct and indirect costs.

For example, a customer who has a long-term investment in a particular technology, and knows how it works may consider that the cost of switching to an alternative is more than just the purchase price, but also the cost of re-learning the new system. The lifetime value of the customer is also important because once a customer is won, the aim should be to keep them loyal.

- What Key Customer Relationships Must Exist?

The ability to deliver value to the customer will depend not only on the quality of the product but also on the quality of the service experience and the ease and convenience of delivering it to them. It is a good idea to draw up a list of the various types of customer relationships or points of contact with each market segment, and determine how to build them into relationships that can offer a competitive edge.

For example, the development of the *iTunes* website offered a competitive point of customer relationship for Apple as it rolled out its *iPod* MP3 player. It has continued to evolve this business model via the 'App Store' for its *iPhone* and *iPad* devices. The *iTunes* software and website offers Apple a dedicated point of customer contact and an opportunity to obtain data on customer purchasing behaviour, as well as offering the customer product updates and cross-selling to other products. It also serves as an isolating mechanism that can potentially lock out the competition that might otherwise erode Apple's relationship with its customers.

7.8.4 Channels – Your Go to Market Mechanism

Once the customer is fully understood the challenge of how to reach the target customer and deliver value to them needs to be addressed. Can the business do this alone and without outside help, or does it need to work via a distribution system or network? The "*go to market mechanism*" is an area that is often overlooked in developing the business model (Grupp and Maital 2001). For example, will there be a process of direct selling by the principals, or will it employ a sales force?

If a sales force or agency system is used, consideration will need to be given to commissions and reward structures. Franchising has become a popular mechanism for this but can involve significant legal and administrative costs. Perhaps the ideal model is to go directly to the customer and to establish control and a reputation via a face-to-face process. For example, the decision by Dell Computers to use the internet for direct selling was an example of a strategic *go to market mechanism* that succeeded.

- Differentiation

Any new business venture is going to struggle in the market if it fails to offer a clear point of differentiation over the competition. It is therefore important for the firm's basis of differentiation to be identified and a unique value proposition to be developed that allows a clear reason for the customer to do business with you. Knowing who the key competitors are and what they currently offer as their main points of differentiation is an essential starting point. Competitors will hardly stay static in the face of direct competition, so consideration will need to be given to what they are or are likely to do over the foreseeable future – e.g. 1–5 years. The final offering to the market must be capable of convincing the customer that the new venture offers a better deal than the competition.

7.8.5 Revenue Stream – Capturing Value

The analysis from these customer-focused areas of the business model should allow an assessment of the *revenue streams* likely to be drawn in from the target market. This is where the real value of the business model can be captured. Important considerations are how price sensitive the market is and how much the customer is willing to pay. Also, of importance are how many customers will be captured in a given time, and how frequently they will purchase. Answers to these questions will allow a full assessment of the likely cash flow cycle and cost-profit-volume dynamics of the business model.

- Value Capture

An important consideration in any new business model is how it will capture the value that it has created for the customer. Many dot.com start-ups failed because they did not find how to acquire a sufficient income stream from the value they had created through their online websites. Will the customer pay you directly or via a third party? Using agents or intermediaries to collect your revenues can pose problems for cash flow and control.

Given the nature of the customer and their purchasing behaviour, it is necessary to determine how frequent or irregular any income might be, as this can affect cash flows and many new businesses that have had excellent products or services as well as good margins have starved due to the lack of a regular cash flow. The number of customers likely to be repeat purchasers is also important. As it usually takes less time to get an existing customer to purchase from you than it does to secure a brand-new customer, a business that can rely on a base of regular customers is preferred.

In addition to determining how the business venture will capture value from the customer, attention should also be given to how the shareholders will be rewarded. As has been noted earlier, the shareholder should be offered a clear exit strategy, and clear policies need to be developed over the payment of dividends versus the reinvestment of profits back into the venture.

- Financial Analysis of Operations

The financial dynamics of the venture should be carefully assessed as the business model is being refined. Once price is known, the variable and fixed costs associated with the production, distribution and sale of the product/service should be examined. Where possible, the level of fixed costs or overheads should be kept to a minimum, i.e. 'keep the team lean'.

Fixed costs raise the break-even point for the venture and make it riskier to launch the venture. By contrast, variable costs are more dynamic and allow the venture to ride out periods where income is slow. The level of fixed or variable costs within the business model can be determined by decisions to sub-contract or outsource key functions rather than carry these within the fixed costs of the venture. Several important questions that need answering are discussed below.

- What Is the Revenue for Each Product/Market Area?

Once the key target market segments have been identified, attention should be given to estimating what anticipated annual revenue might be obtained from each one. If there is past experience from previous years of sales, this data should be examined. It is important to identify which target segments are likely to grow and what market share could be obtained within a given time period.

- What Is the Cost Structure?

An important consideration in any business model is the cost associated with establishing the venture or bringing the new product to market. Overhead costs need to be examined to see if these can be reduced in order to allow the venture to reach break-even a quickly as possible. Also of importance are any variable costs that will impact on the firm's gross profit.

- What Is the Profit Margin?

The gross and net profit margins are important when determining the overall profitability of the venture. Each target market segment needs to be examined in order to evaluate potential profit margins. For example, some target segments will be more price sensitive and will not allow you to command the same price point as another less sensitive segment. If costs of production and delivery are the same for both segments, one will generate superior profit margins over the other.

As a general rule, the higher the profit margin the better. Furthermore, the most important figure to consider is gross profit margin rather than net profit margin. This is the more dynamic figure and it is common to find different products or segments of the market having different gross profit margins due to differing variable costs.

- What Are the Financial Measures?

Against each product and market area you should consider such things as the time it takes to recover money from customers and how long it might take to reach break-even. The time it takes to receive payment from customers can be vital to the survival of a small business start-up that needs regular cash flow to maintain its solvency. It is also important to work out the time to break-even, as this will impact on the amount of up-front capital needed to sustain the business in its early years.

7.8.6 Key Resources

The opportunities identified in the previous areas of the *Business Model Canvas* now need to be examined in terms of the key resources that will be required to deliver the CVP. *Key resources* refer to the people, equipment and other assets that the venture needs in order to fulfil the mission and deliver the CVP. It can encompass "core" or *distinctive competencies*, which are the skills and knowledge that are required to compete at the required level (Prahalad and Hamel 1990). It can also encompass the firm's organisational structure, governance and team composition, plus the physical facilities that will be needed to house the operations. Another important part of the resource set is the partnerships and strategic alliances that are going to be needed for the entity to fulfil its purpose.

- What Core Competencies Are Required?

It is useful here to list the skills, abilities and other resources that are likely to be needed to allow the venture to deliver its CVP in a consistent way to the target customers. Any gaps that are identified within the firm's own resources should be filled via alliances where possible. Moreover, it can be useful to understand which of the key resources and competence make the firm legitimate as perceived by the target customers to offer this particular value proposition.

- The Management Team

Each member of the management team should be examined to ensure that they fully understand the new venture's products or services and have a working knowledge of the market, production processes and the financial structure. If the team has not previously worked together, attention should be given to personalities and getting to know each other. Who the managers are and what specific skills they bring to the company should also be considered? Of particular importance is the overall integrity of these people. Background checks can be useful to ensure that they are who they say they are, and extreme care should be taken in recruitment, selection and appointments.

- What Is the Best Way to Structure Teams?

The team or teams of people who are to make the business model work and deliver the CVP need to be designed, and attention should be given to how large they should be and to their composition. It is important to build teams that have the right combination of skills and abilities, as well as the right leadership.

- Organisational Configuration

As discussed elsewhere in this chapter, the best organisational structure needs to be found to complement the proposed strategy and available resources. How centralised or devolved the new venture will be and whether managers are to be grown organically or recruited externally are important issues. Corporate governance in the form of the executive management team and board of directors should be carefully clarified. Attention should also be given to setting up a structure that promotes a good communication flow and allows for organisational learning.

- What Physical Facilities Will Be Needed?

The business model must also consider the physical facilities that will be required. It is useful to make a list of the things that might be required, such as websites, ICT systems, buildings, plant and equipment. Each will have a cost.

- Capital Intensity

Consideration should also be given to the level of capital intensity required by the new venture. As noted above, the need to acquire high cost capital items can significantly increase the fixed costs of the business and force up the break-even point. However, the use of automated systems may assist in reducing labour costs over time and may thus justify higher initial set-up costs. Another consideration is whether the venture needs to possess state-of-the-art technology and systems, or whether it can make do with less sophisticated equipment in the early years.

Capital items can often be acquired second hand at a much lower cost than a new purchase, and are frequently able to perform well despite their level of financial depreciation.

7.8.7 Key Activities

In addition to the resources required it is also important to consider the *key activities* that will need to be undertaken to ensure that these resources are appropriately used to deliver value to the customer and the firm. These activities can include a wide range of things depending on the nature of the business. Typical areas related to customer relationships management (CRM) systems, financial management and control systems, operations management practices and HRM systems, plus any related polices, rules and metrics. Consideration should be given to the overall scope of business operations; the purchasing systems and how future R&D and new product development is to be managed.

- Scope of Operations

Once the customer has been fully examined, the next area to be addressed is the operational management of the venture. Key questions that need to be answered include:

- What products are to be sold?
- Which activities should be retained?
- Which should be outsourced?

In terms of the type of products that are to be sold, the longer-term issue of product-market growth should be examined to see if the product can form the basis for a range of new product lines with the potential for exploitation of alternative markets.

Most new technologies have the capacity to be employed within a range of market segments, with each new market posing a different set of entry requirements and product-service configurations that can impact the way the venture structures its operations. For example, a business that has sold into the civilian market may see an opportunity to secure contracts in the defence sector, but they may lack the competencies and contacts to fully exploit this due to differences in tendering and procurement processes.

For many firms, there will need to be a decision made as to what operations are to be undertaken in-house and which are to be outsourced. Sub-contracting work is popular with many businesses due to the fact that it reduces the level of direct investment required into the company and moves some of the costs of capital and human resources off the balance sheet. However, sub-contracting can also prove dangerous if strategic-level assets or capabilities are allowed to leak out of the firm to sub-contractors (Quinn and Hilmer 1994).

- Purchasing Systems

For many firms, suppliers play a most important role in providing critical inputs without which the business will not operate. Key suppliers can also be a source of value adding through the transmission of ideas, knowledge and the transfer of technologies. As part of the development of the business model, it is important to consider how supply chain relationships will be handled. Will suppliers be retained on short- or longer-term contracts and will ecommerce be employed to provide a lower cost of transaction? Inventory control and logistics management systems employing computer management linked to suppliers can be a major source of competitive advantage and cost reduction. Suppliers should be viewed as potential partners who offer value and who form part of a team. Where suppliers are kept at arm's length and treated as little more than cost burdens, the opportunities for innovation and strategic networking can be lost (Jarillo 1988).

- R&D and New Product Development

Innovation through ongoing research and development (R&D) and new product development is often essential to the success of the new venture over the long term. However, the entrepreneur needs to consider whether the R&D function is to be retained within the venture or outsourced. It may be useful to form a separate venture to focus on R&D, thus allowing production and implementation work to be carried out by another business.

When developing an innovation strategy, some of the key considerations include: how much should be spent on R&D? and how can the R&D function be linked closely with the work of the marketing, production, financial and other functions in the venture? R&D teams can also tend to become too focused on the research, and need to be provided with systems to ensure that they keep to strict timetables for the completion of projects.

- What Is the Best Configuration of Key Systems?

Attention must also be given to the way in which the various systems relating to human resources, operations, culture, policies and various other key performance indicators (KPI) are to be configured so as to keep track of the ability of the business to deliver value.

7.8.8 Strategic Partners

Once the issues examined in the previous sections have been addressed it will be important to identify whether the business model can be managed alone or if it requires collaboration with others. This can involve lead customers willing to work with the firm to *co-create* a new product or service. Key suppliers can also be a valuable partner assisting with technology transfer and knowledge. Third party firms that provide resources (i.e. banks, venture financiers, university research centres) can also assist, playing the role *resource network actors* (Holmlund and Törnroos 1997).

The development of new and existing market segments often requires the formation of strategic alliances with customers, suppliers and third-party complementary firms that can assist in providing competencies that are not available within the venture. This is particularly the case for small firms and start-up ventures that lack resources.

- The Support Network

In addition to the management team that will control the new venture, some consideration should be given to the formation of a wider network of supporting specialists and organisations to which the venture can turn when needed. This can include the services of a legal team, an accounting professional and a marketing agency. The new venture will benefit from having a high-quality advisory board or formal board of directors. These people should be recruited from a range of backgrounds and skill sets, and should have the ability to network the venture to a wider set of industries or markets if possible.

7.9 The Role of Vision

Of more importance than the products or services that are to be sold are the management team and the vision they have for the business and how it will work in the market place (Hamel and Prahalad 1989; Kantabutra and Avery 2010). Before launching into a comprehensive business planning activity, it is most important to first ask whether the venture has any real innovation or if it is merely a 'me too' business. If intellectual property is the foundation of the business venture, this should be carefully assessed and steps taken to protect it. If the business is likely to need external investors, it is most important to identify how they will make their money back, and how and when they can exit the investment.

7.9.1 A Vision to Align and Motivate

A clear vision of the future of a venture is important, but its ability to be achieved will depend on the financial viability of the business model. As discussed earlier, you need to know how the cash flow cycle will work through the business, and particularly the time it will take for payment to be received from customers and timelines for paying suppliers. Projected sales forecasts should be based on realistic and well researched data with attention given to the time needed to identify new customers and get them to pay.

As noted earlier, the gross profit margin that can be generated from each sale will determine the amount of cash flow available to the venture. Excessive fixed costs such as salaries and lease or mortgage payments will raise the break-even point for the venture and place pressure on the firm's profitability. Too many new ventures fail to allow for the amount of working capital required for their operations. Working capital refers to the liquidity levels needed – e.g. cash and liquid assets – to pay suppliers, salaries and wages and the variable costs associated with the day-to-day operations. These pragmatic considerations can make or break a grand vision.

While many entrepreneurs launch highly successful business ventures with little or no formal planning, the process of preparing a well-considered business plan is a good discipline that can assist in identifying any weaknesses in the business model. Entrepreneurial vision and the planning ethos are not mutually exclusive. Without a clear vision of the future, the planning process is left unfocused and lacking in direction. Business plans that lack vision can be short sighted and often fail to excite. Equally, a strong entrepreneurial vision that lacks the discipline of the formal business planning process risks becoming unfocused and can fall victim to problems of implementation.

7.9.2 Don't Confuse Planning for Clear Vision

The development of a well-written business plan is no guarantee of success, and an entrepreneur should not assume that just because they like an idea it will be successful. It is suggested that once the business plan has been written, the document should be given to one or two third party individuals who can read it and provide unbiased, constructive feedback (Golis 2002). It should be remembered that, if the plan seeks to raise venture capital, most professional investors see thousands of business plans each year and such people will see through any gaps in the document and are likely to view 'great ideas' as little more than hype.

A study by Ernst and Young (2004) of 135 winners of the Australian Entrepreneur of the Year Award found that the majority (72%) considered that their greatest contribution to their business venture was the ability to provide vision and focus. The most common motivation for these entrepreneurs in launching their venture was to create a business that would fulfil their vision of the future.

For example, … A strong vision is an essential part of entrepreneurship, but successful entrepreneurs also have the ability to plan the journey towards achieving their vision. The Entrepreneurs' Barometer found that 46 percent of successful entrepreneurs nominated effective strategy as the key factor in the success of their business (Ernst and Young 2004).

The majority (85%) of entrepreneurs surveyed by Ernst and Young (2004) were still engaged in active day-to-day management of their ventures, and were largely optimistic about the future outlook for their firms. While only 36% were involved in export markets, at least half were seeking to move into global markets over the short to medium term, e.g. 2–3 year). The majority (60%) were seeking to raise external financial capital to assist with their business growth, but most were planning to use this funding to invest in the organic growth of their existing business model rather than to acquire other businesses. This suggests that these entrepreneurs had confidence in their own business models.

7.10 How Entrepreneurs Craft Strategy

The business plan is a manifestation of the strategic thinking generated by the entrepreneur who lies behind the venture. Bhide (1994) provides an overview of the way entrepreneurs 'craft' strategy based on his analysis of 100 successful cases from the United States. As noted earlier, formal planning is not a strong characteristic of many entrepreneurs and a rigid adherence to a business plan can be a negative in the early years of a new venture. Of more importance is the ability to screen opportunities quickly and to quickly identify a few things that can get the process started. Flexibility and the capacity to act quickly to follow up or exploit new opportunities is a key feature of the successful entrepreneur.

Ideas for new business ventures are sourced by entrepreneurs from a wide range of areas, but the majority have been found to stem from interaction with the market rather than from systematic research or development. When new opportunities emerge, it is common for the entrepreneur to quickly screen out those options they consider to be less desirable. The process is therefore one of screening ideas out rather than selecting the 'best' option.

Factors Influencing the Value of Planning

Task environment:

- Environmental turbulence surrounding the firm
- Uncertainty in knowledge relating to new products
- Uncertainty in knowledge relating to markets
- Perceived risks associated with future investment decisions
- Environmental munificence in future target markets

Organisational configuration:

- The age and maturity of the firm resulting in stability in its processes
- The complexity of the firm as it grows larger in scale and scope
- The size of the firm's financial resources available for future investments
- The size and complexity of the firm's human resource needs

Managerial characteristics:

- The level of entrepreneurial orientation of the management team
- The level of industry competency of the management team
- The level of planning competency of the management team

Source: Mazzarol and Reboud (2009)

Once an idea is chosen for further action, the entrepreneur needs to determine its future objectives and attract suitable resources, e.g. money, customers and employees. Many of the most successful ideas are not radical or industry-disrupting in nature but simply incremental innovations that offer greater value or superior performance. According to Bhide (1994), only 28% of the successful entrepreneurs whom he studied had prepared a full-blown business plan prior to the launch of their new venture. Forty-one percent had not prepared any formal plan at all and 26% had only a rudimentary 'back of the envelope' plan.

For many of the entrepreneurs who Bhide (1994) studied, the market opportunity that they exploited was found in new emerging industries rather than more mature established ones. This is not surprising as these new industries offer a better chance for a new entrant to get started and leverage changes in technologies or market dynamics. Such new industries are also more likely to have only limited competition in comparison with the more mature sectors that are generally dominated by well established businesses.

The basis of competition used by the successful entrepreneur is also interesting. In many of the cases examined by Bhide (1994), the possession of proprietary assets such as patents, locations and brand names were not the basis of success. Of more importance was the ability of the entrepreneur to 'hustle' using their selling skills and communications ability to secure strong market positions in industries where possession of proprietary assets was not the main basis of competition.

7.11 Developing Entrepreneurial Strategy

As discussed, the vision an entrepreneur has for their business is very important – and often more important than the business plan. Strategy and planning are not the same. Strategy is a continuous process, as illustrated in Fig. 7.3. It involves undertaking a strategic analysis of the various opportunities and threats facing the firm and how best to apply the firm's resources to build on strengths while also addressing weaknesses. A strategic choice must then be made from a range of options, and

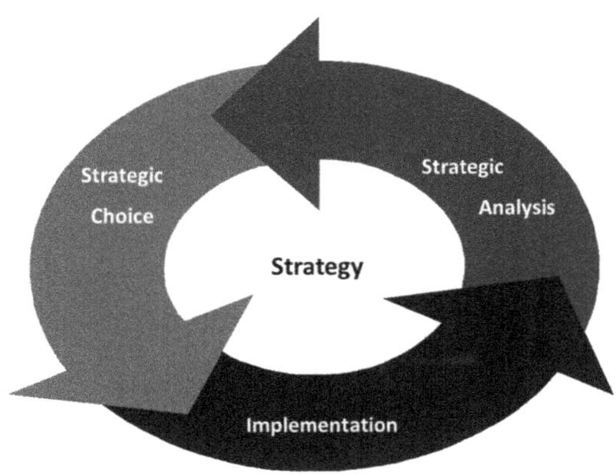

Fig. 7.3 Strategy as a continuous process

the strategy implemented. The success of this strategy is then monitored as part of an ongoing process of strategic analysis. Strategy has been likened to a 'double-loop' process due to its continuous cycle, while planning has been likened to a 'single-loop' process as it typically has a defined end-point where the objectives are achieved and the plan is complete (Heracleous 1998).

At the individual level, there needs to be a holistic understanding of the firm and how it sits within its task environment. The vision and creative drive of the entrepreneur can play a key role in helping shape future strategic plans. At the firm level, there needs to be an on-going 'strategic dialogue' within the firm's top management team as well as with employees, leading customers and key suppliers. The ingenuity and creativity of all employees needs to be harnessed in order to assist the business to implement strategic plans and fulfil its mission and vision.

7.12 The Strategy Development Framework

The process of developing strategy can be complex, and numerous texts have been written on the topic. The *Strategy Development Framework* (SDF) (Mazzarol 2015), shown in Fig. 7.4 offers a way to simplify the process. The SDF draws together a range of existing concepts used in strategy formulation and represents them as an integrated framework. This is designed to provide an overview of the main areas

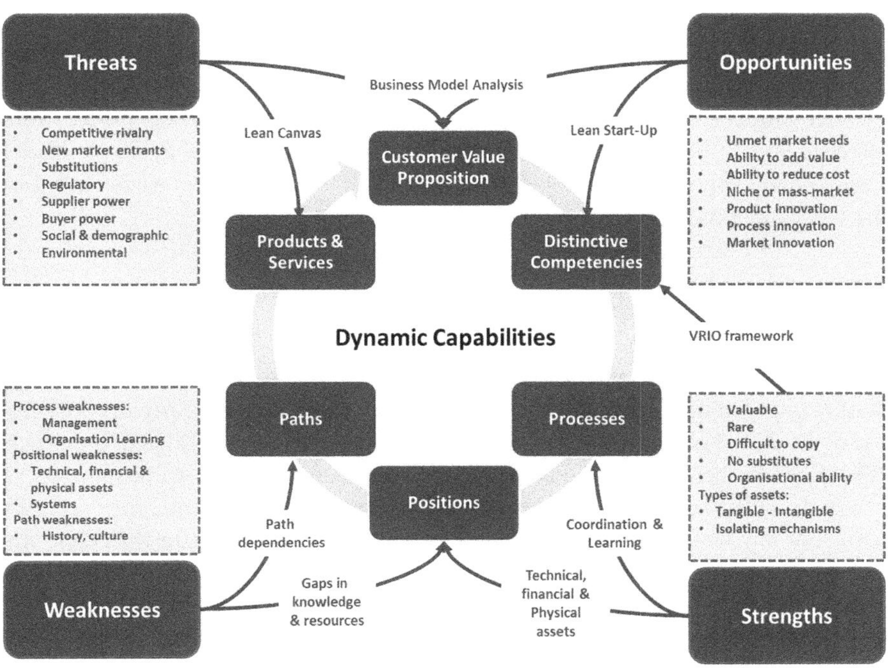

Fig. 7.4 Strategy Development Framework. (Source: Mazzarol 2015)

that should be considered when developing strategy. It provides managers with an easy reference point for strategic planning. The main elements of the SDF are discussed below.

7.12.1 TOWS Matrix Analysis

On the four corners of the framework are the core elements of the SWOT analysis (Mintzberg 1990), with the model placed in reverse showing as Threats, Opportunities, Weaknesses and Strengths (SWOT). This approach to the SWOT analysis enables a more systematic approach to be undertaken focuses on the firm's external task environment first providing a TOWS Matrix (Proctor 1997). All items above the middle of the SDF diagram relate primarily to issues external to the organisation. Those at the bottom relate primarily to issue internal to the organisation. The items listed adjacent to each of the four elements of the TOWS Matrix are important areas for consideration in the planning phase.

7.12.2 Assessing Competitive Threats

An initial starting point for using the SDF is to undertake an assessment of the likely threats facing the implementation of the business model. Here it is useful to employ a "*5-Forces Analysis*" assessing: i) the overall level of competitive rivalry found within the target market; ii) the ease of entry to new businesses; iii) potential substitution threats; iv) supplier bargaining power; and v) buyer bargaining power (Porter 1979, 1980, 2008). Attention should also be given to any regulatory, social and demographic, or environmental factors likely to impact the business model. This analysis should be undertaken concurrently with the use of the *Business Model Canvas* and overall design and development of the business model as discussed in the preceding sections.

7.12.3 Assessing Market Opportunities

Following on from the assessment of threats is an assessment of the anticipated market opportunities. As noted above, this can be undertaken concurrently with the use of the *Business Model Canvas* as the business model is being designed. Important considerations here are related matching the customer to the product or service.

On the customer side, it is important to explore what the customer may need, in particular any unmet needs. An example is the success of Nintendo with their *Wii* gaming platform. Unable to compete directly with Sony's *PlayStation* or Microsoft's *X-Box*, Nintendo identified a segment of the market that was not being targeted by those incumbent products. The core target customers for the *PlayStation* and *X-Box* were men, who wanted high definition, realistic game play requiring relatively high levels of skill. Nintendo positioned the *Wii* at the women and children market segment, offering a quality product that was fun and easy to use.

It is important that the analysis finds ways to offer a CVP that the customer will want. This can be based on a *differentiation strategy* that seeks to add new value, or a *cost-leader strategy* that can help to lower costs (Porter 1996, 2008). Considerations should also be given to whether the targeted customers are found in mass or niche market (Murray 1988).

Once the customer analysis is complete attention should be given to the nature of the innovation that needs to be developed and commercialised in order to satisfy this anticipated need. Managing the innovation requires consideration of the nature of the product, process and even market innovations required. The interaction between four elements need to be understood. The first is the type of innovation (i.e. incremental or radical). The second is the nature of the market environment (i.e. uncertain, complex). Also important is the configuration of the business structure and processes that might be relevant to the innovation. Finally, there is the ability of the innovation to deliver enhanced performance (i.e. growth, market share) (Tidd 2001).

7.12.4 Assessing Resource Weaknesses

As shown in Fig. 7.4, the SDF involves an examination of the firm's available resources that can be used to meet threats and exploit opportunities. Attention should be given to assessing the *key activities* and *key resources* identified within the business model with a view to assessing process weaknesses in management or organisational learning. *Positional weaknesses* in relation to technical, financial and physical assets should also be identified, which is usually fairly easily done as these resources are generally tangible. However, less easily identified are *path weaknesses*, which involve the history and culture of the organisation that might serve to impact on how readily the firm adapts, innovates and pivots. Any major weaknesses in these areas can feed into the *path dependencies* and *gaps in the knowledge and resources* that will impact the firm's *paths* and *positions* thereby affecting how well it can configure its resources and achieve success through *dynamic capabilities* (Teece et al. 1997).

7.12.5 Assessing Resource Strengths

Counter to the assessment of the firm's resource weaknesses is the need to fully assess the strengths it has in its resources that can provide a foundation for the development of a competitive strategy. The ability to possess resources that are valuable, rare, difficult to copy and with no readily available substitutes offers a firm the basis of a sustainable competitive advantage (Barney 1991). In particular, if the firm can develop an organisational ability to "bundle" or reconfigure assets, both intangible and tangible, so as to create *isolating mechanisms* (i.e. patents, proprietary knowledge) it can develop *distinctive competencies* that provide a competitive advantage. This is what Barney (2011) and Barney and Clark (2007) refers to as the VRIO framework (value, rare, imitability, organisation).

The SDF describes the process of assessing market threats and opportunities, matching them to internal resource weaknesses and strengths, and applying *dynamic capabilities* to the continuous generation of new products and services to deliver a CVP. It also recognises the need to make use of a range of tools such as business model analysis and the *Business Model Canvas*. However, it also recognises the value of integrating the *Lean Start-Up* process (see Chap. 9), particularly in the identification of *distinctive competencies*.

7.12.6 Dynamic Capabilities

The items in the centre relating to what Teece et al. 1997 refer to as *Dynamic Capabilities* are also important. However, these relate more to the implementation of the strategy. As can be seen from Fig. 7.4, these elements are related in an iterative loop, which reflects the dynamic nature of strategy formulation and implementation. Strategy is non-linear in nature as opposed to planning. Plans are the implementation tool of strategy.

A strategy typically looks out over anywhere from 3 to 5 years or more. It seeks to achieve a large or major vision or goal for the entire organisation. It is often not clear how a strategy will be fully implemented as there is usually insufficient information to know what is going to happen. By contrast, plans operate on shorter lifecycles with 6–12 months being the most likely timeframe for any workable plan. However, much depends on the nature of the organisation, its industry and how dynamic the task environment is within which it is trying to operate.

Within the SDF there are several arrows connecting the four elements of the TOWS Matrix to the elements within the *Dynamic Capabilities* loop. These related to a range of strategy tools and concepts that can be applied by managers when developing strategic plans or assessing strategy options and assessing business model designs.

The findings from the TOWS Matrix and *Business Model Canvas* analysis should be used to define the CVP. However, the *Distinctive Competencies* assessment should aim to link the assumptions, or hypotheses about what constitutes customer value and future growth options, with the VRIO framework. Of importance is need for managers to recognize that just possessing resources is not sufficient to achieve competitive success. The defining skill of entrepreneurial firms is their ability to apply organisational learning, creative thinking to "re-bundle" existing assets (both tangible and intangible) into new innovative products or services (Alvarez and Busenitz 2001).

This ability to apply effective coordination and learning into *processes* that can both create and apply these resource bundles to deliver value to the customer is critical (Teece et al. 1997). Of particular importance is the firm's ability to adapt and change.

For example, … Change is costly and so firms must develop processes to minimise low pay-off change. The ability to calibrate the requirements for change and to effectuate the necessary adjustments would appear to depend on the ability to scan the environment, to evaluate markets and competitors, and to quickly accomplish reconfiguration and transformation ahead of competition (Teece et al. (1997) p. 521).

Also important are the decisions the firm makes in relation to the *positions* it takes in relation to the deployment of its resources. This includes the technical, physical, financial, human and knowledge assets it possesses. For many firms, particularly small firms, all the necessary resources for success will not be available. This requires consideration of forming strategic alliances to help fill in any identified resource or knowledge gaps.

Over time the firm should develop its ability and capacity to successfully implement its strategy and operate its business model. This experience generates a *path dependency* that can provide a source of strength if conditions remain static and the firm's *competencies*, *processes* and *positions* continue to be suitably configured. However, if the task environment changes this "history" may serve as a constraint to innovation and change (Teece et al. 1997). This highlights the need for the firm to be open to new ideas and willing to learn.

For example, … To be successful for any length of time a firm must innovate…Since innovation requires a certain amount of pre-existing capabilities…, firms need to be able to learn. In order for firms to innovate the skills and resources to sustain innovation must be present (Alvarez and Busenitz 2001).

7.13 Strategic Planning Responses

The development of strategy within a business can be explained in terms of the response its management makes to the level of uncertainty in the task environment and to the level of complexity within its organisational configuration (Tidd 2001). Mazzarol and Reboud (2009) suggest that there are four generic strategic planning types that are appropriate responses for a given set of conditions. These are illustrated in Fig. 7.5.

Each of the four strategic planning types is a response to the level of uncertainty found within the task environment and the level of complexity found within the firm's organisational configuration. These conditions also determine and are determined by the characteristics of the firm's management, with a focus on either operational or strategic issues as a priority. The four types – the shopkeeper, the salesman, the administrator and the CEO – are described below.

7.13.1 The Shopkeeper

Where the task environment is certain and the organisational structure is simple, the appropriate planning response is that of an informal or unstructured planning

Fig. 7.5 Four strategic planning types. (Source: Mazzarol and Reboud 2009)

process. The focus in this situation should be more operational than strategic – or 'fine tuning the businesses. This planning response has been referred to as 'The shopkeeper'. Some of the key areas of focus for this type of planning are to improve the flow of management information to assist financial control and reporting, or the operational systems associated with information technologies and process capabilities. A 'shopkeeper' planning response is appropriate where there is a steady market, few competitors, established customers or long-term contracts, a standard product technology, and guaranteed suppliers.

7.13.2 The Salesman

Where the task environment is uncertain but the organisational structure or product/process technologies are simple, the appropriate planning response is that of an intuitive strategic planning process. This planning response is that of the 'salesman' and the focus is primarily on market development. 'Salesman' strategy involves a high emphasis on marketing and networking. The key areas for attention are marketing and sales activities, developing customer delight programs, and building up the level of strategic networks and alliances. Most of these are designed to help the firm access new markets or widen its existing market share. A 'salesman' planning response is appropriate where there are well-organised markets with some competitors, and where customer behaviour is uncertain with fluctuations in orders. Suppliers may not be guaranteed, although product technology is largely routine and not radical.

7.13.3 The Administrator

Where the task environment is certain but the organisational structure or product/process technologies are complex, the appropriate planning response is that of a structured operational process. Here, the emphasis is on operational efficiency and cost control. This planning response is that of 'the administrator' with a primarily internal rather than external focus. The primary focus for this planning response is on quality and operational control. An 'administrator' planning response is appropriate where the product or process technology is complex but with a predicable pathway to market. Also, where there is limited competition within diversified markets, this type of planning is appropriate.

7.13.4 The CEO

Where the task environment is uncertain and the organisational configuration or product/process technologies are complex, the appropriate planning response is structured and strategic in nature. This response type is the 'CEO', and the focus is on strategic transformation. It typically involves taking new product technologies into new markets, and needs a systematic approach to planning within R&D, new product development (NPD), and operational controls. High levels of innovation and technological complexity combined with uncertain markets are the domain of the 'CEO'.

7.14 Use Your Common Sense

As can be seen from the previous discussion, the business plan can be very detailed and complex. However, remember that the business plan is really just a communications or sales device designed to get across a clear sense of what the business venture is trying to do and how it might work. If the plan is for external venture capital investors it may need to be detailed and may need to encompass the things described above. If it is for internal purposes, you should design it to be user friendly.

Many business plans get written and never used because they are too long and complex for everyday practical use. For this reason, a simple plan can be better than a complex one. Quite often the only part of the business plan that is really read by investors is the executive summary. From this you can deduce that *less is more* when it comes to writing business plans.

Some advocates suggest that a business plan be distilled into a single page that outlines the firm's vision, mission, objectives and general strategies, with brief action plan summaries. Whatever you choose to do, make sure that the plan is shaped to meet your needs and the needs of the audience for whom you are writing it. And, use your common sense.

The preparation of a business plan should also follow, or be undertaken at the same time, as the development of a business model analysis and formulation of a business strategy. Once the business model analysis and strategic level issues are addressed and choice of strategic direction resolved, you can develop a set of objectives for the business. Objectives need careful attention. It is essential that each objective has four elements:

1. A clear statement of what must be done;
2. Performance benchmarks as to how it must be done;
3. A deadline for when it must be completed; and
4. A nominated owner (person or group) who are responsible to make sure the objective is achieved.

When the objectives have been developed, the plan's implementation can commence. It is here that process management becomes critical. Major strategy involves multiple projects and a high level of change. People within the firm and outside will need to be consulted and their participation enlisted to help its implementation proceed. The plan will need to be monitored to make sure that performance benchmarks and deadlines are achieved.

You should never underestimate the difficulties of getting strategy implemented. It will require adjustments to the firm's structure and a re-allocation of resources. Employees, customers, suppliers, shareholders and a myriad of other stakeholders will need to be engaged with in order to get the plan completed. In environments where the level of uncertainty is low and the level of complexity in the organisational configuration is also low, little strategic planning may be required as it is 'business as usual'. Yet, in highly uncertain environments and highly complex organisational structures, the opposite will be true.

References

Ackelsberg, R., & Arlow, P. (1985). Small businesses do plan and it pays off. *Long Range Planning, 18*(5), 61–67.

Alvarez, S. A., & Busenitz, L. W. (2001). The entrepreneurship of resource-based theory. *Journal of Management, 27*(6), 755–775.

Amit, R., & Zott, C. (2001). Value creation in E-business. *Strategic Management Journal, 22*(6–7), 493–520.

Amit, R., Zott, C., & Pearson, A. (2012). Creating value through business model innovation. *MIT Sloan Management Review, 53*, 1–15.

Barney, J. B. (1991). Firm resources and sustained competitive advantage. *Journal of Management, 17*(1), 99–120.

Barney, J. B. (2011). *Gaining and sustaining competitive advantage* (4th ed.). Harlow: Pearson.
Barney, J. B., & Clark, D. N. (2007). *Resource-based theory: creating and sustaining competitive advantage*. Oxford: Oxford University Press.
Berman, J. A., Gordon, D. D., & Sussman, G. (1997). A study to determine the benefits small business firms derive from sophisticated planning versus less sophisticated types of planning. *Journal of Business and Economics Studies, 3*(3), 1–11.
Bhide, A. (1994). How entrepreneurs craft strategies that work. *Harvard Business Review, 74*(2), 150–161.
Blank, S., & Dorf, B. (2012). *The startup owner's manual: The step-by-step guide for building a great company*. BookBaby.
Brinckmann, J., Grichnik, D., & Kapsa, D. (2010). Should entrepreneurs plan or just storm the castle? A meta-analysis on contextual factors impacting the business planning–performance relationship in small firms. *Journal of Business Venturing, 25*(1), 24–40.
Castrogiovanni, G. J. (1996). Pre-startup planning and the survival of new small businesses: Theoretical linkages. *Journal of Management, 22*(6), 801–822.
Chesbrough, H., & Rosenbloom, R. S. (2002). The role of the business model in capturing value from innovation: Evidence from Xerox Corporation's technology spin-off companies. *Industrial and Corporate Change, 11*(3), 529–555.
Ernst, & Young. (2004). *Entrepreneurs' Barometer 2003–2004*. Ernst & Young Australia.
Ferreira, B., Silva, W., Oliveira Jr, E. A., & Conte, T. (2015). *Designing personas with empathy map*. Paper presented at the SEKE.
Gibson, B., & Cassar, G. (2002). Planning behavior variables in small firms. *Journal of Small Business Management, 40*(3), 171–186.
Golis, C. (2002). *Enterprise and venture capital: A business builder's and investor's handbook* (4th ed.). Sydney: Allen & Unwin.
Grupp, H., & Maital, S. (2001). *Managing new product development and innovation: A microeconomic toolbox*. Cheltenham/Northampton: Edward Elgar.
Hall, D. (1992). *The hallmarks for successful business: Survival-change-growth*. Oxfordshiire: Mercury Books.
Hamel, G., & Prahalad, C. K. (1989). Strategic intent. *Harvard Business Review*, 63–76.
Heracleous, L. (1998). Strategic thinking or strategic planning? *Long Range Planning, 31*(3), 481–487.
Holmlund, M., & Törnroos, J.-A. (1997). What are relationships in business networks? *Management Decision, 35*(4), 304–309.
Honig, B., & Karlsson, T. (2004). Institutional forces and the written business plan. *Journal of Management, 30*(1), 29–48.
Hrebiniak, L. G. (2006). Obstacles to effective strategy implementation. *Organizational Dynamics, 35*(1), 12–31.
Jarillo, J. C. (1988). On strategic networks. *Strategic Management Journal, 9*(1), 31–41.
Johnson, M. W., Christensen, C. C., & Kagermann, H. (2008). Reinventing your business model. *Harvard Business Review, 86*(12), 50–59.
Kantabutra, S., & Avery, G. C. (2010). The power of vision: Statements that resonate. *Journal of Business Strategy, 31*(1), 37–45.
Mahadevan, B. (2000). Business models for internet-based E-commerce: An anatomy. *California Management Review, 42*(4), 55–69.
Mazzarol, T. (2001). Do formal business plans really matter? – A survey of small business owners in Australia. *Small Enterprise Research: The Journal of SEAANZ, 9*(1), 32–45.
Mazzarol, T. (2015). *Strategic thinking and action* (UWA Business School Executive Education). Perth: Advanced Management Program, AIM WA.
Mazzarol, T., & Reboud, S. (2009). *The strategy of small firms, strategic management and innovation in the small firm*. Cheltenham: Edward Elgar Publishing.
Mintzberg, H. (1990). The design school: Reconsidering the basic premises of strategic management. *Strategic Management Journal, 11*(3), 171–195.

Morris, M., Schindehutte, M., & Allen, J. (2005). The entrepreneur's business model: Toward a unified perspective. *Journal of Business Research, 58*(6), 726–735.

Murray, A. (1988). A contingency view of Porter's generic strategies. *Academy of Management Review, 13*(3), 390–400.

Olson, P. D., & Bokor, D. W. (1995). Strategy process-content interaction: Effects on growth performance in small, start-up firms. *Journal of Small Business Management, 33*(1), 34–43.

Osterwalder, A., & Pigneur, Y. (2010). *Business model generation: A handbook for visionaries, game changers, and challengers*. Wiley.

Osterwalder, A., Pigneur, Y., & Tucci, C. L. (2005). *Clarifying business models: Origins, present, and future of the concept.* Paper presented at the Communications of AIS, May 2005.

Osterwalder, A., Pigneur, Y., Bernarda, G., & Smith, A. (2015). *Value proposition design: How to create products and services customers want.* New York: Wiley.

Pearce, J. A., Freeman, E. B., & Robinson, R. B. (1987). The tenuous link between formal strategic planning and financial performance. *Academy of Management Review, 12*(4), 658–675.

Porter, M. E. (1979). *How competitive forces shape strategy* (pp. 102–117). Readings: Strategic Planning.

Porter, M. E. (1980). *Competitive strategy: Techniques for analyzing industries and competitors.* Boston: The Free Press.

Porter, M. E. (1996). What is strategy? *Harvard Business Review, 74*(6), 61–78.

Porter, M. E. (2008). *Competitive advantage: Creating and sustaining superior performance.* New York: Free Press.

Posner, B. G. (1985). Real entrepreneurs don't plan. *INC, 7*(11), 129–132.

Prahalad, C. K., & Hamel, G. (1990). The Core competence of the corporation. *Harvard Business Review, 68*(3), 79–91.

Proctor, T. (1997). Establishing a strategic direction: A review. *Management Decision, 35*(2), 143–154.

Quinn, J. B., & Hilmer, F. G. (1994). Strategic outsourcing. *Sloan Management Review*, 43–55.

Robinson, R. B., & Pearce, J. A. (1983). The impact of formalized strategic planning on financial performance in small organizations. *Strategic Management Journal, 4*(3), 197–207.

Robinson, R. B., & Pearce, J. A. (1984). Research thrusts in small firm, strategic planning. *Academy of Management Review, 9*(1), 128–137.

Robinson, R. B., Pearce, J. A., Vozikis, G. S., & Mescon, T. S. (1984). The relationship between stage of development and small firm planning and performance. *Journal of Small Business Management, 22*(2), 45–52.

Sahlman, W. A. (1997). How to write a great business plan. *Harvard Business Review, 75*(4), 98–108.

Schwenk, C. B., & Shrader, C. B. (1993). Effects of formal strategic planning on financial performance in small firms: A meta-analysis. *Entrepreneurship: Theory & Practice, 17*(3), 53–64.

Sexton, D., & Van Auken, P. (1985). A longitudinal study of small business strategic planning. *Journal of Small Business Management, 23*(1), 7–16.

Stevenson, H., Grousbeck, H., Roberts, M., & Bhide, A. (2000). *New business ventures and the entrepreneur*. Boston: Irwin McGraw-Hill.

Sweeney, J. C., & Soutar, G. N. (2001). Consumer perceived value: The development of a multiple item scale. *Journal of Retailing, 77*(2), 203–220.

Teece, D. J. (2010). Business models, business strategy and innovation. *Long Range Planning, 43*, 172–194.

Teece, D. J., Pisano, G., & Shuen, A. (1997). Dynamic capabilities and strategic management. *Strategic Management Journal, 18*(7), 509–533.

Tidd, J. (2001). Innovation management in context: Environment, organization and performance. *International Journal of Management Reviews, 3*(3), 169–183.

Timmons, J. A. (1999). *New venture creation: Entrepreneurship for the 21st century* (5th ed.). Boston: McGraw-Hill International Editions.

Trimi, S., & Berbegal-Mirabent, J. (2012). Business model innovation in entrepreneurship. *International Entrepreneurship and Management Journal, 8*(4), 449–465.

Unni, V. K. (1984). An analysis of entrepreneurial planning. *Managerial Planning, 33*(1), 51–54.

Upton, N., Teal, E. J., & Felan, J. T. (2001). Strategic and business planning practices of fast growth family firms. *Journal of Small Business Management, 39*(1), 60–72.

Weick, K. E. (1988). Enacted sensemaking in crisis situations. *Journal of Management Studies, 25*(4), 305–317.

Risk Management in Innovation

8

8.1 Introduction

> Sometimes you just have to believe in the impossible…and you've got to have faith to breakthrough.
>
> Source: Peter, CEO software development company.

This chapter examines the issue of how to manage risk in the process of innovation. By its very nature, innovation is inherently risky. The more radical and disruptive the innovation, the more uncertainty and potential risk is created. However, the management of risk remains an important issue for any manager or organisation seeking to engage in the commercialisation of innovation. Risk management, or *enterprise risk management* (Brustbauer 2016; Reboud and Séville 2016), is viewed as a major concern for managers today and the number of large companies having a risk manager is growing. However, within the context of new entrepreneurial ventures the dynamics are different, because such businesses are particularly risky, and face greater uncertainty. This is particularly the case in innovation where structured, systematic approaches are necessary.

8.2 Risk Management

Since the 1990s the field of *Risk Management* has emerged as a specialized field of management that even has its own dedicated academic journals (Smith and Fischbacher 2009). While the area of risk management originally focused on operational areas (e.g. work health and safety, project risk), it has now evolved into a strategic-level activity, *Enterprise Risk Management* (ERM) (Arena et al. 2010). Around the world large companies use ERM as a core element in their strategic

T. Mazzarol, S. Reboud, *Entrepreneurship and Innovation*, Springer Texts in Business and Economics, https://doi.org/10.1007/978-981-13-9412-6_8

planning, project management and budgeting, with full-time risk management executives employed within the senior management team (Aon Analytics 2010).

A global study undertaken within the financial services sector found that 63% of 131 large firms had a formal risk management ERM strategy within their corporate governance model (Deloitte 2010). The majority (85%) of these firms sent regular reports to their board of directors who reviewed them against the ERM framework. An equally large proportion (86%) employed a Chief Risk Officer (CRO), and this pattern of behaviour relating to risk management was viewed as a growing trend.

The *Global Financial Crisis* (GFC) of 2007–2009 accelerated the level of interest in risk management within large firms, particularly those in the financial services sector. In the immediate aftermath of the GFC it was estimated that between 80% and 90% of businesses with more than $1 billion in annual turnover were engaged in implementing ERM systems, with 25% already using it as a standard management framework (Lam 2010).

8.3 Risk Management in Entrepreneurial Ventures

Although risk management is now embraced by most large businesses, it remains less appreciated by small firms. This is a concern because the ability to manage risk is a critical element in young and small firms, particularly those engaged in growth driven strategies involving innovation and the commercialisation of new products and services. Risk management in new ventures is often addressed by the entrepreneur and is carried out tacitly, without any specific tools (Jayathilake 2012). It is not necessarily subject to a specific investment and its impact on performance remains difficult to demonstrate, so risk management in new ventures has so far not been considered either as a source of specific cost, or as a source of significant value creation. Moreover, risk management has long been restricted to the financial dimensions of the organization, which is considered the major source of risk because it can lead to its failure (Reboud and Séville 2016).

8.3.1 Proximity Effects

One of the main characteristics of a new venture's strategy and management is the strong influence of what can be grouped under the name of *proximity effects,* resulting in filters of perception and action (Mazzarol et al. 2015; Torrès 2003). The concept of *proximity* implies that individuals are attracted to, and give more importance and attention to, those people, physical surroundings and events that are physically close to them and familiar (Moles and Rohmer 1978). This is what Thorndike (1907) defined as the *law of proximity*.

Small business owner-managers and entrepreneurs in young, fast growing companies are likely to be impacted by a *microcosm effect* (Mahé de Boislandelle 1996; Torrès 2003). This typically results in them focusing on the views of a relatively few people (i.e. existing lead customers, employees, other directors), with decisions made on relatively limited data (*small number effect*), and their own sense of what they believe should happen (*ego effect*). The emotional intensity and sense of urgency that is common within such firms, and the lack of formal risk management systems, places small business owner-managers and entrepreneurs at greater risk of making poor decisions.

8.3.2 Informality

As noted above, a common feature of small firms and new business ventures is their lack of formalisation of processes, relationships and strategy (Julien 1990; Torrès and Julien 2005). The frequent recourse to intuition, or what may be called *the law of small numbers*, reinforces the perception of a lack of resources and the absence of benefit to formalise procedures. In relation to the management of innovation, this has the consequence of generating a chronic underestimation of the value of intellectual property (IP) issues by small and new firms (Reboud et al. 2014). Indeed, besides the perception of the cost of IP by the entrepreneurs, it seems that the relationships of trust that they feel they have built with their clients, often leads them to overestimate the reliability of such relationships when they develop innovations (Kitching and Blackburn 2003).

Further, this informality in the management of innovation creates an ad hoc approach to strategic decision-making including activities such as new product development (NPD) and commercialisation. This was shown in a study of 567 SMEs across 11 OECD countries, investigating the management practices of these firms in relation to NPD and commercialisation. The majority did not have a formal NPD process, nor had they undertaken a formal risk assessment, fully assessed their competition, customer or supplier reactions, impact of government regulations, or threats of substitute technologies. Only a few reported having a formal, written business plan for their innovation or having completed a comprehensive financial model of the innovation (Mazzarol and Reboud 2011).

8.3.3 Resource Scarcity

Another key issue facing small and young firms engaged in innovation is their lack of resources. From a risk management perspective this is problematic because any minor event or anomaly can become a source of crisis by the effects of cascading risks (Reboud and Séville 2016). Due to the small size of new ventures, any event likely to interrupt their functioning (e.g. absenteeism, breakdown of machines), and any changes to market conditions (i.e. reluctance of the customer to buy, variation of the price of the raw materials), can cause operational or even human risks (Everett and Watson 1998; Islam and Tedford 2012; Thun et al. 2011). The consequences of these events are also amplified in small ventures by what Torrès (2003) calls the *proportion effect*.

The specificities often attributed to small firms – a certain strategic myopia, a lack of tools and limited resources – are traditionally identified as a source of organisational vulnerability. They are supposed to negatively influence their ability to anticipate and confront all undesirable events or shocks and even more, to rapidly implement solutions (St-Pierre and El Fadil 2017). Such vulnerability could contribute to the low survival rate of firms beyond their third or fourth year of operation (Clusel 2012).

This may occur at a stage in their lifecycle when their organizational vulnerability increases because of the development of multiple vulnerabilities. These can include financial vulnerability, due to the difficulties in securing seed funding, but also a strategic vulnerability, due to difficulties in finding new sources of growth. It may also be associated with the psychosocial risks and the sources of professional stress that can affect the employees but even more the entrepreneur (Lechat and Torrès 2016; Reboud and Séville 2016).

The study of 567 SMEs mentioned earlier also found that the many did not have a management advisory board to provide guidance, and also felt that they lacked the necessary physical resources, and the full range of technical and business competencies, needed to commercialise their innovation. Most also reported a lack of staff and financial resources to fully develop their innovation alone (Mazzarol and Reboud 2011).

8.4 Planning and Entrepreneurial Risk Perception

As discussed in Chap. 2, a key attribute of entrepreneurs is their ability to deal with risk. A major reason why entrepreneurs engage in formal planning and the development of formal systems in the management of innovation is to mitigate risk, or at least the perception of risk. Planning, which includes the development of business models, strategy and NPD *road maps*, is a process involving the making of assumptions, then gathering information, and then using it to test the assumptions. This feedback loop is then used to systematically assess opportunities and threats facing the business venture. Through the planning process, the entrepreneur can reduce the perceived risk by demonstrating that conditions associated with the market, financials and management of the business have been considered. To understand why planning is or is not undertaken and how much formality is involved, let us briefly examine the notion of entrepreneurial risk perception.

8.4.1 The Notion of Risk

As a concept, risk is a perception of the variation in future outcomes of an action plus their likelihood of occurring and subjective value (March and Shapira 1987). Risk can be measured quantitatively by estimating the likely cost or loss that can arise where an event takes place. Any situation in which the probability of an event occurring increases and the size of the potential loss also increases leads to a rise in the level of risk. The formula for this is:

$$\textbf{Risk} = (\textbf{Probability of an event}) \times (\textbf{Possible losses})$$

It is important to distinguish risk from uncertainty. Risk is something that can be measured in a quantitative manner and assessed. However, uncertainty is not so readily quantitatively measured (Knight 1921). Uncertainty is a condition caused by having insufficient information or knowledge to make accurate predictions about the likely outcome or future state of an action or event. In other words, if you can determine the odds of something happening, you can assess the risk of gain or loss and make a rational choice. However, where uncertainty exists you cannot assess the risk so clearly. In this case you can take a blind risk, or you can engage in a process of information gathering to help increase your knowledge and to allow you to better assess the odds.

The *entrepreneurial orientation* (EO) theory suggests that people with high EO have a greater proclivity towards taking risks. However, this view has been challenged by those who argue that entrepreneurs don't have any greater risk-taking proclivity than the average person. What they do have is a propensity to perceive risk differently to others (Brockhaus 1980). Rather than perceive the risk as high and proceed with caution, people with high EO are prone to using *biases* and *heuristics* to convince themselves that the risk is less than it might otherwise be (Busenitz 1999).

The *effectuation theory* also suggests that entrepreneurs adopt a different approach to risk. Following that theory, successful entrepreneurs are more likely to assess their own *affordable losses* than their expectations of returns, leading them to assess risk taking with a different scale (Sarasvathy 2001).

8.4.2 Entrepreneurial Risk Perception

When an entrepreneur assesses a future investment in a new venture or innovation, they are dealing with several variables. First, they have to consider the uncertainty of the outcome. Second, they consider the expected outcome if the investment is successful. Third, they consider the potential of the outcome to return high profits or losses, e.g. *How bad can it get?* (Sitkin and Pablo 1992). For example, the higher the level of perceived risk, the stronger the association between risk propensity and risk behaviour, except that for risk-seeking decision-makers this effect will reach a limit defined by their propensity (Sitkin and Pablo 1992).

Experiments involving entrepreneurs and non-entrepreneurs have found that people with lower risk perception will take greater risks (Sitkin and Weingart 1995).

Entrepreneurs appear to deal with risk by trying to manage it, and to *expand the problem space* by actually investing more so as to maximise their returns. Entrepreneurs, appear to accept risk as a given and focus on controlling outcomes at any given level of risk; they also frame their problem spaces with personal values and consequently assume greater personal responsibility for influencing outcomes (Sarasvathy et al. 1998).

Many entrepreneurs make use of only limited information. As noted earlier this is described as the *law of small numbers*, i.e. taking feedback from only one or two key customers or relying on the support of friends and family, to help them decide whether to invest (Keh et al. 2002). They also rely heavily on past experience to convince themselves that they can succeed in future ventures, and blame past failures on factors external to them (Forlani and Mullins 2000).

The entrepreneur's decision to invest time and money into a future opportunity is therefore tempered by their perception of the level of risk they face. However, they employ cognitive biases and heuristics, such as their illusion of future control or their overconfidence, to influence how risky they feel these investment decisions are. Impacting on their cognitive biases are the forces of social capital such as the ties they have with family, friends and potential customers, the trust they have in the market's willingness to adopt their innovation, and the other influences that provide positive reinforcement to their investment decision (De Carolis and Saparito 2006).

8.4.3 The Impact on Planning Behaviour

Many entrepreneurs and small business owner-managers don't engage in formal planning and only do so when required to generate business plans by outsiders. To understand this behaviour, we need to reflect on the issues associated with entrepreneurial risk perception. This process can be explained with reference to the interplay between the firm's task environment and the characteristics of the firm's top management team (Mazzarol and Reboud 2009). Figure 8.1 illustrates this dynamic. It can be seen that the perceived risk is reduced by the level of information that is available. Increasing levels of information reduce uncertainty and perceived risk. Business planning and formalisation is a mechanism to provide information that can assist in reducing the level of perceived risk to a point at which it is acceptable to proceed with future investment.

In Fig. 8.1 the vertical axis measures the level of perceived uncertainty and risk within the task environment, while the horizontal axis measures the level of knowledge and competence within the owner-manager or entrepreneur. Where the perceived uncertainty and risk within the task environment is high and the entrepreneur's knowledge and competence is low, there is a greater likelihood that they will see value in planning and therefore their propensity for planning will increase. By contrast, where risk and uncertainty are high but the entrepreneur feels that they have the knowledge and competence to manage through, the opposite is likely. In this situation, planning behaviour is a response to both the perceived risk and

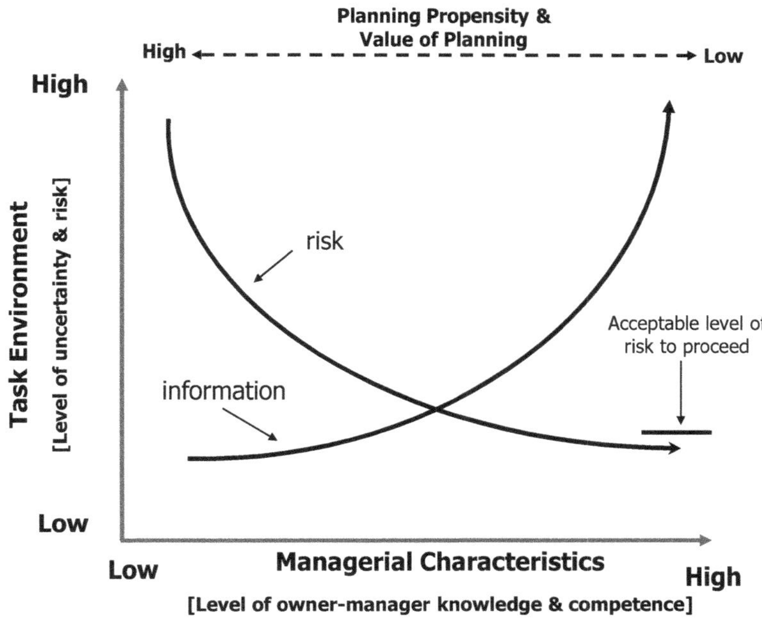

Fig. 8.1 Managerial characteristics and task environment. (Source: Mazzarol and Reboud 2009)

uncertainty in the task environment and to the perceived level of confidence and competence within the entrepreneur.

The fact that so many entrepreneurs do not engage in formal business planning until required to do so may be due to their perception of being in control. The *biases* and *heuristics* – or simple overconfidence – that is a common feature of many entrepreneurial personalities is likely to account for this lack of planning. It follows that a person with high entrepreneurial orientation (EO) will be inclined to see the level of risk as being lower than a person with low EO. Figure 8.2 illustrates this relationship. It can be seen that, if actual risk and the optimal level of necessary information (or planning) is found at RP0 = PR0, a person with high EO will perceive risk at RP1 and only seek information (or plan) to point PR1. By contrast, the person with low EO will perceive risk to be at RP2 and will seek information (or plan) to point PR2.

The net effect of this risk perception (RP) and planning response (PR) behaviour is that the low-EO person will wait to get more information before proceeding to exploit a market opportunity (if they do so at all), while the high-EO person will launch their venture or investment activity early. This helps to explain why the entrepreneur is frequently the first mover in a new market niche, and jumps into the implementation of their business without much formal planning.

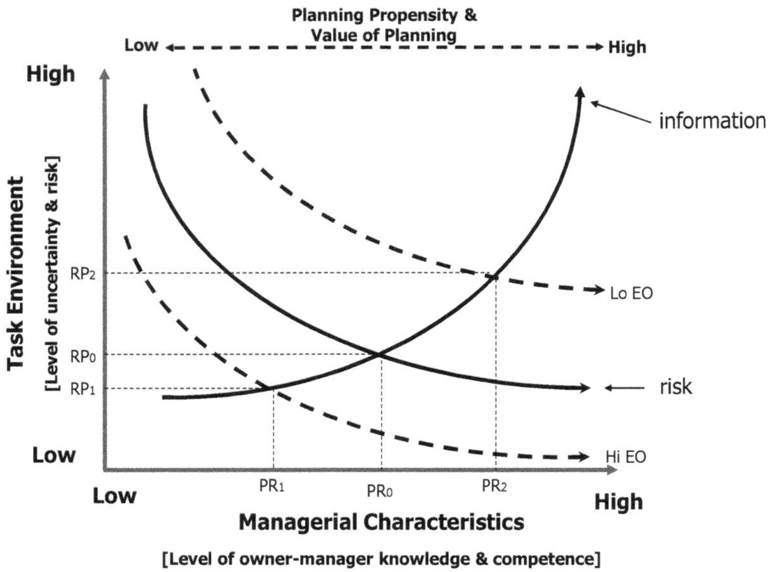

Fig. 8.2 The effect of external risk perception on planning response. (Source: Mazzarol and Reboud 2009)

These theoretical concepts relating to the reasons why entrepreneurs do or don't plan, at least in a formal way, are important in order to understand what we need to look for when seeking to determine how much planning is needed. There are several factors at work within the firm's task environment, organisational configuration and managerial characteristics that can determine if – and to what level of formality – business planning will take place. Included in these factors are: how much uncertainty and turbulence exists within the task environment; how established, large and complex the firm is; and the experience, competence and level of EO of the firm's top management team.

8.5 Plan or Just Storm the Castle?

The issue of how much formal planning should be undertaken in entrepreneurial ventures remains a contentious issue. A major review of the academic literature relating to the nature and value of formal planning within small firms found that while there was evidence that such planning was beneficial, it was difficult to ascertain precisely what the benefits were (Mazzarol and Reboud 2009).

> **For example,** ... Based on the evidence so far, we can conclude that while small firms appear to gain benefits from planning, the value of this planning is contingent on the nature of the interplay between the firm's task environment, organisational configuration and managerial characteristics. Firms that are faced with stable or munificent task environments are less likely to find value in planning that those where the task environment is more turbulent.

> The complexity of the organisational configuration (for example manufacturers versus service firms) may also play a role in determining the value of planning, and whether this value comes from more operational or strategic planning. Finally, the value of planning seems to hinge upon the capability of the firm's owner-manager or senior management team to effectively undertake the planning response (for example quality not quantity). (Mazzarol and Reboud (2009) p. 73)

The pattern emerging from this review of the literature suggests that the value of formal planning within the small firm was contingent on the ability of the owner-manager or entrepreneur, to "*apply systematic analytical thinking to their management of the task environment*" (Mazzarol and Reboud (2009) p 99). The level of formality is likely to increase along with the size and complexity of the business. This is usually due to the need for the organisation's management team to coordinate an increasing number of people and related systems. However, the benefits of planning can be obtained if the owner-manager is able to adopt systematic, if not necessarily formal, approaches to assessing risk and controlling uncertainty.

Brinckmann et al. (2010) conducted a meta-analysis of 47 empirical studies that examined the process of planning and performance in small firms. Their paper titled: *Should Entrepreneurs Plan or Just Storm the Castle?* found that the benefits of formal planning were moderated by at least three factors. The first of these is the relative age of the business, with new or early-stage firms getting less benefit than established ones. A second influencing factor is the level of tolerance for or avoidance of uncertainty by the managers who owned and operated the firm. A third factor is the formality or sophistication of the planning process.

In relation to the first factor, firm age, while a significant and positive relationship was found between formal planning and success in start-up ventures, it was much weaker than the effect such planning appears to have within established firms.

> **For example,** … Entrepreneurship literature hypothesizes that planning should yield greater returns for new firms than for established firms due to positive motivational effects of self-set goals in new firms versus relative performance goals of established firms and due to shorter planning-outcome feedback cycles…Our findings suggest, however, that the contrary is the case. Business planning promises greater returns for the average small firm than for the new small firm. Established small firms have information from their prior operations as well as routines and processes in place, which support planning. By contrast, new small firms generally have to carry out business planning without prior information while missing structures and procedures that support planning". (Brinckmann et al. 2010, p. 36)

The second factor, uncertainty avoidance, was considered to be a cultural issue. Brinckmann et al. (2010), point to some countries where the prevailing national culture is more likely to orient towards uncertainty avoidance (e.g. Germany), and this sees managers engaging in formal planning in order to help reduce uncertainty. Of importance here is the ability of the owner-manager or entrepreneur to learn and adapt as they seek to implement their plans.

As regards the third factor, their analysis found that formality (i.e. the possession of a formal, written business plan) was little guarantee of the value of planning. Of more importance was the ability of the management team to systematically implement the plan and apply adaptive learning as noted above (Brinckmann et al. 2010).

What these reviews of the research literature suggest is that the value of planning to a small, entrepreneurial firm is likely to depend level of perceived uncertainty facing the owner-manager or entrepreneur with the firm's task environment, as well as their capacity to deal with this uncertainty. Planning becomes more valuable when the level of uncertainty is reduced. As such, the planning process should aim to enhance the level of information and knowledge available to the entrepreneur or owner-manager. This can occur via a simple "*learning by doing*" or "*trial and error*", but it is relatively high-risk way to gain knowledge.

8.6 Absorptive Capacity and the Management of Risk

Shepherd and Patzelt (2017) note that while innovation is a key component of entrepreneurship, these two areas have tended to be examined separately within the academic literature. They point to the importance of understanding the intersection of two "cornerstones"; *absorptive capacity* and the systematic approach to managing innovation known as *Stage-Gate®* (Cooper and Edgett 2005; Cooper and Kleinschmidt 1993, 1995). They also suggest that the entrepreneurial process associated with NPD and commercialisation can be addressed through what they describe as "*operational entrepreneurship*".

> **For example,** … Operations management refers to the 'the selection and management of transformation processes that create value for society'… With this definition as a foundation, *operational entrepreneurship* can be defined as 'the selection and management of transformation processes for recognizing, evaluating, and exploiting opportunities for potential value creation'. (Shepherd and Patzelt 2017 p. 122)

While academic researchers may have examined entrepreneurship and innovation separately, the reality facing managers, particularly those operating within small, entrepreneurial firms engaged in NPD and commercialisation, is quite different (Cobbenhagen 2000). For these managers there is a need to pursue opportunities, allocate resources, assess and take calculated risks, and make strategic decisions that have the potential to make or break their businesses. What such managers need is a systematic approach to assessing risk in the management of innovation that can emulate the theoretical notion of *operational entrepreneurship* as proposed by Shepherd and Patzelt (2017).

Building on Cohen and Levinthal (1990) and Zahra and George (2002) suggest that firm's ability to acquire, assimilate, transform and exploit information and knowledge represents an *absorptive capacity* that can form the basis of a *dynamic organizational capability* (Teece et al. 1997). This ability to rapidly acquire and use knowledge to generate innovative new products, processes and services is a hallmark of success, particularly in commercialisation.

The relationship between a firm's *absorptive capacity* (ACAP), and its ability to achieve success through *dynamic capability* is a function of how well the

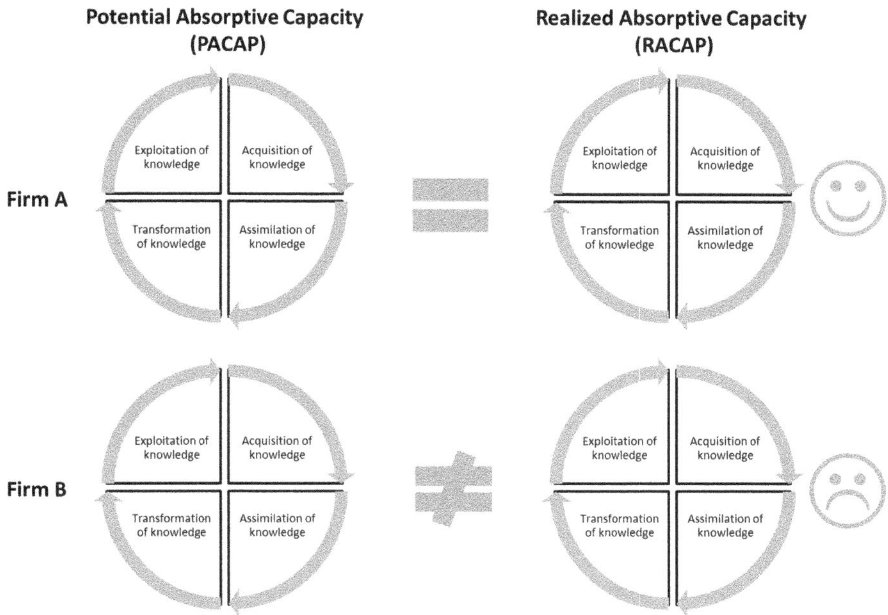

Fig. 8.3 The key elements of absorptive capacity

management and their staff can allocate resources and use tacit and explicit knowledge to help them generate value through the bundling of resources (some of which they may not own directly) into new combinations for commercial exploitation (Gray 2006).

For small firms engaged in innovation there are generally limited resources to work with, and what is important is the ability of the firm to translate its *potential absorptive capacity* (PACAP) in to a successful *realized absorptive capacity* (RACAP). As shown in Fig. 8.3, *Firm A* can successfully realise its potential absorptive capacity to acquire, assimilate, transform and exploit knowledge, while *Firm B* cannot.

This may be due to many factors. This might include how well it keeps its resources, capabilities and routines up to date. It might also be influenced by the entrepreneurial and managerial competencies of the owner-manager or entrepreneur in control of the business. Other issues that might play a role are the firm's ability to access reliable and quality information from inside and outside sources, as well as its ability to understand and utilise this information. Also, of importance may be the firm's ability to use creativity to generate innovative outcomes (Gray 2006). The firm's ability to translate its *potential absorptive capacity* into *realized absorptive capacity* (e.g. where PACAP = RACAP) is an ideal situation. This should provide the firm with a solid foundation for not only developing a competitive advantage through dynamic capabilities, but also assisting it to more effectively manage risk.

As noted above, the process of managing risk is characterised by the acquisition of information to reduce uncertainty. Where a firm can rapidly acquire, assimilate, transform and exploit information, and where such information is reliable, it can more effectively reduce uncertainty and thereby manage risk. In the process of managing innovation this has been enhanced by the adoption of systematic approaches to NPD and commercialisation such as the *Stage-Gate®* (Cooper and Edgett 2005) or *Lean Start-Up* (Ries 2011) (see Chap. 9 for more detail).

8.7 Commercialisation and the Systematic Management of Risk

For entrepreneurial firms, the issue of risk management looms largest in relation to the commercialisation of new products and services. Commercialisation defines the process of taking an innovation from the initial idea stage to eventual market diffusion. It has been likened to a process of *crossing the chasm* from the initial invention and prototype development, through the securing of patents and investors, to the eventual creation of a successful company (ISR 2001).

Commercialisation is one of the most important elements in the management of innovation. However, it is also one of the least understood areas (Adams et al. 2006). Herdman (1995) defined commercialisation in the following terms:

> **Commercialisation is,** …the attempt to profit from innovation through the sale or use of new products, processes, and services. More than invention or innovation, commercialization is driven by the firm's expectation that it can gain a competitive advantage in the marketplace for a particular product, process, or service (p. 2).

Successful commercialisation is generally associated with the ability to find a ready market for a product or service innovation and this requires a realistic market assessment with evidence of real customers willing to buy sufficient quantities to justify the investment. There should be a clear market pathway, and opportunities for growth and returns on investment that are superior to alternative investment choices. In addition to a sound market assessment, there should also be evidence of a unique IP asset base that can be commercially protected as well as the existence of a management team for the venture that works well together and shares a common vision (Atkins and Anderson 1999).

A critical first step in the commercialisation process is the creation of new products and services. This process of *new product development* (NPD), is a separate, but closely related area of innovation management. Investment in R&D, and the NPD process, is inherently risky and many new products fail (Biyalogorsky et al. 2006; Hlavaceck et al. 2009; Millson 2013).

8.7.1 Fuzzy Front-End

The cycle through which an innovation moves as it forms into a new product idea, is developed and then commercialised is illustrated in Fig. 8.4. As shown, the initial starting point is a *fuzzy front end* (FFE), which is an environment characterised by a high degree of uncertainty. Firms seeking to develop new products need to learn how to operate in this often chaotic and unpredictable environment. For most projects the initial stage requires some exploration, experimentation, testing of concepts and theories, and *bootstrapping* with limited resources. This is all designed to help reduce uncertainty and risk (Koen et al. 2002).

However, once this initial FFE stage is completed a more disciplined and goal-focused approach to the project can take place. There will still be a high level of uncertainty and therefore risk, but if a systematic approach is taken to the NPD process, with stages and milestones that can allow "GO/KILL" decisions or *pivots* to take place, the risks can be controlled and managed. In this phase the NPD process should be less about customer discovery and more about product feasibility, with attention given to budgets and targets (Ozer 2004). Keeping good metrics, particularly from any initial sales, is important.

Once the product has moved through all the necessary stages of the NPD process – which might be relatively few taking only weeks or months, or much longer – the commercialisation phase can commence. Here the product and its target market should have been validated through the first two phases. At this stage the firm can start to make more formal plans with attention to marketing and sales targets, anticipated revenue and profit forecasts, and operational plans for full scale production and scalability.

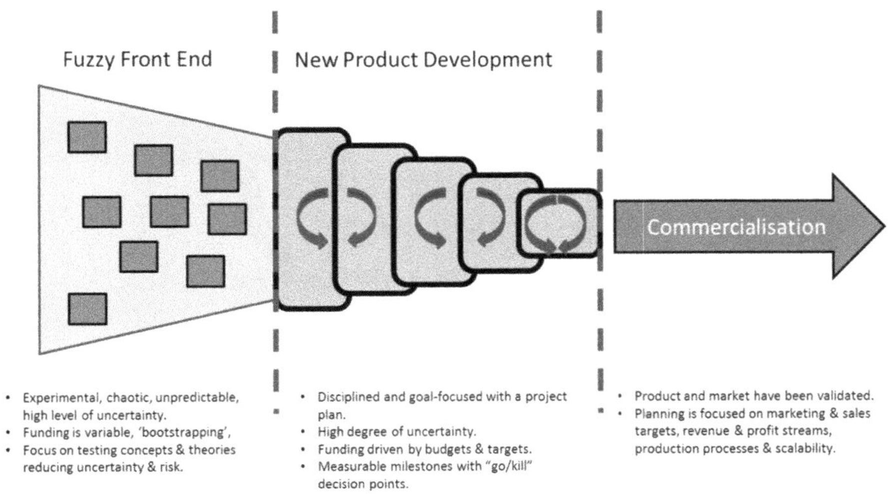

Fig. 8.4 The process of discovery, NPD and commercialisation. (Source: Adapted from Koen et al. 2002)

8.7.2 New Concept Development

In order to address the challenges of the *fuzzy front end* and mitigate risk, Koen et al. (2002). propose working through a systematic approach that is illustrated in Fig. 8.5. As shown, it consists of a series of five interlocking stages that an NPD project team should work through. At the heart of the process is the *engine*, which contains the senior leadership team of the company undertaking the commercialisation, as well as the organisational culture and business strategy. Any NPD project must be driven and supported by this engine, and the project team must ensure that their activities are congruent with these company-level attributes. Senior management must view innovation as a strategic priority and encourage all employees to engage actively in the process. The firm's culture and structure also must remove any internal barriers between different parts of the company (e.g. R&D, production, finance, marketing and sales), so as to allow multi-disciplinary project teams and collaboration to take place.

The five interconnected stages comprise: (i) *opportunity identification*; (ii) *opportunity analysis*; (iii) *idea generation & enrichment*; (iv) *idea selection*; and (v) *concept definition*. It should be noted that these stages are not linear, but iterative in nature and reflect the need for the team to work around each stage multiple times so as to ensure that they have a product concept fully understood and validated before proceeding further. This reflects the learning process described above in relation to the process of *absorptive capacity*. The model also reflects the fact that this iterative

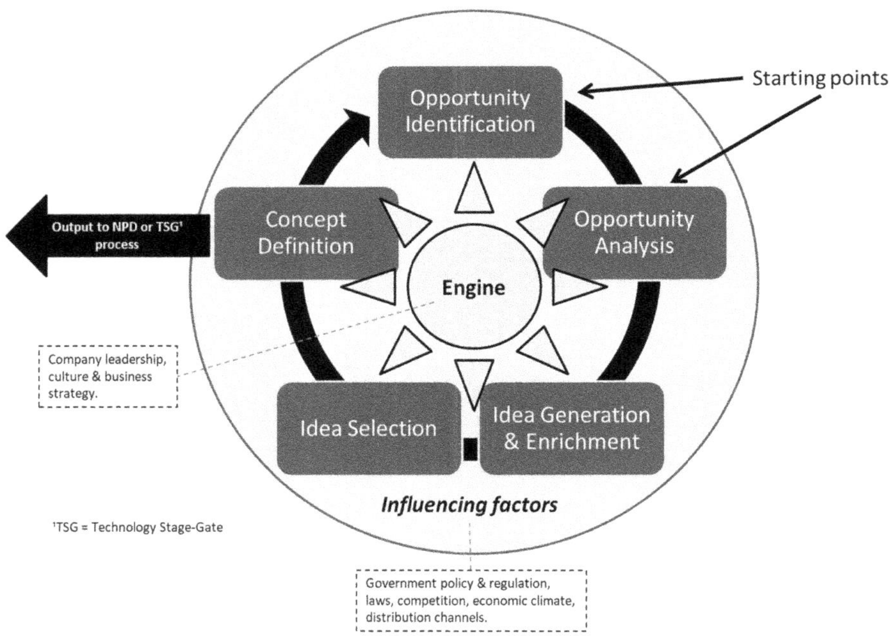

Fig. 8.5 The new concept development model. (Source: Adapted from Koen et al. 2002)

process through the five stages takes place within the context of external environmental *influencing factors* such as government policy, regulation and laws, market competition and macro-economic impacts. The project team must keep these factors in mind when developing the product concept.

Although it is an iterative process, the most likely starting points within the inner five stages are *opportunity identification* and *opportunity analysis*. The first of these relates to the firm's ability to systematically encourage innovation within its employees, as well as maintaining close contact with customers, suppliers and other third-party actors within its market and industry context. When opportunities are identified, they should be examined and through a robust process of *opportunity analysis* assessment to identify how it can benefit the firm's innovation agenda and existing product-technology road-mapping. If it passes this stage, it moves to the *idea generation & enrichment* stage, where the opportunity is mapped against the firm's existing product-technology road-map, and subjected to formal assessments of its benefits, costs and technical and market risks.

Depending on the outcomes from the previous stages the *idea selection* stage involves the selection of those innovations that might be taken forward into the final *concept definition* stage. The *idea selection* stage should involve a rigorous screening process that places each idea or emerging technology within the context of the firm's overall product-technology mix, and draws upon customer feedback, market research, technology trend analysis, competitive market intelligence, technology road-mapping, and other strategic business issues, to ascertain why and how the innovation should be incorporated into new products or services. If it is accepted, it can be taken into the final *concept definition* stage, where the elements of a new innovation application can be refined and worked into a project concept brief for deployment within the NPD team's existing project work, or placed within the firm's *technology Stage-Gate®* commercialisation process (see Chap. 9).

8.8 Assessing the Technical and Market Risk

Assessing the technical and market risk of an NPD project may be done to determine if a single project should be launched, continued or perhaps aborted, but may also done in the context of managing a portfolio of NPD projects where the focus is not on a single project, but on the selection of the most promising set of projects for an organisation to pursue. At a conceptual stage, the risk of a new product is often visualised by placing it into a matrix of technical and market risk (see Fig. 8.6). This allows making comparisons and gaining intelligence from both successful as well as unsuccessful new products in related markets and technology fields.

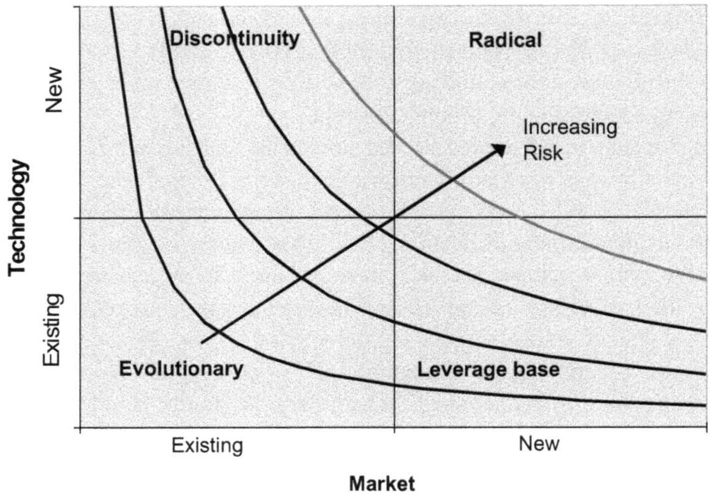

Fig. 8.6 Mapping technical risk vs. market risk. (Source: Schnepple 2005)

8.9 Managing Risk, General Principles and Techniques

In addition to the NPD and commercialisation systems described above, managers and entrepreneurs can employ a range of risk management tools that assist in the mitigation of technical and financial risk. A formal approach to managing risk can be found in the Australian standard (AS 4360) 'Risk Management'. This provides a generic and very broad framework for risk management containing six key elements:

1. *Establish the context.* Are you managing the risk of a project affecting the whole company, or perhaps just the technical risk of an R&D effort being successful?
2. *Identify the risks.* What can happen and how can it happen?
3. *Analyse the risks.* Analyse the likelihoods, consequences, controls and level of risk.
4. *Evaluate the risks.* Evaluate and rank risks, then decide if risk can be accepted or must be treated.
5. *Treat the risks.* Reduce the likelihood of future risks; reduce the consequences of risk, transfer the risk (e.g. via insurance), or avoid the risk.
6. *Monitoring risks.* Regularly check for new or changed risks.

This framework is intuitive and easy to understand, and can be applied to any industry where risk management is required, e.g. in the insurance, banking, resources or construction industries.

8.9.1 Technology Project Risk Model

While the AS 4360 risk management model is intuitive and easy to understand, it is very generic and is not particularly helpful in identifying cause and effect relationships. The technology project risk model developed by Merritt and Smith (2004) that is shown in Fig. 8.7 attempts to address these shortcomings. This model does not replace the risk management process as proposed in AS 4360, but it significantly enhances the steps of analysing and evaluating the risks for technology projects.

Separating the risk event from its impact clarifies cause and effect. Quantifying risk probabilities is never an easy task, and is usually directed to experienced experts. Clearly identifying cause and effect relationships is a significant help – both in quantifying risk as well as in defining appropriate countermeasures. This makes it also easier to communicate the outcomes of risk analyses to higher levels of management as well as to potential investors (see Table 8.1).

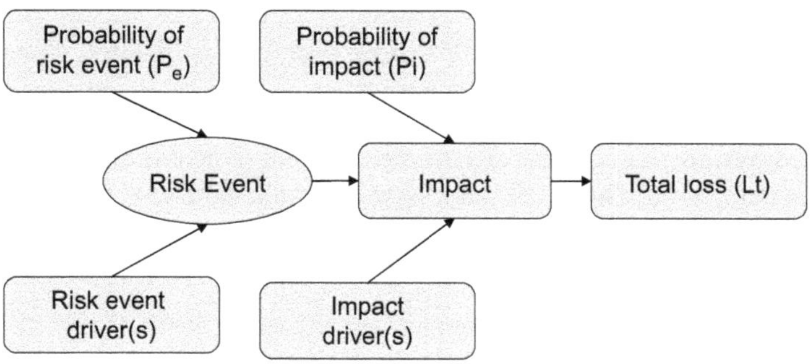

Fig. 8.7 Technology project risk model. (Source: Merritt and Smith 2004)

Table 8.1 Example of risk management

Context	Protecting your home	
Identify the risk	Burglary	
Analyse the risk	Likelihood	1/20 chance per annum of being burgled
	Consequences	Loss of items of value, including laptop containing valuable confidential data
Evaluate risk	Not acceptable	
Treat risk	Reduce likelihood	Install burglar alarm, install safe to store laptop
	Reduce consequences	Maintain regular laptop backup
	Transfer	Take out home contents insurance
Monitor risk		Is remote alarm enough?
		Upgrade to monitored alarm?

Source: Schnepple (2005)

8.9.2 Quantifying Risks

Quantifying risks is almost always a difficult task. Some approaches documented in the literature are as follows:

1. Simplify risk quantification to 'low', 'medium' and 'high'.
2. Use expert opinion to assign risk probability on a scale (0…1 or 0...100%).
3. Use anchored scales to assign risk probability on a discrete scale (e.g. 0...5).

The first approach is suggested by Davis (2002) on the basis that it is unproductive to even attempt to quantify risk probability to any accuracy. This puts more emphasis on understanding cause and effect relationships, and avoids unproductive discussions about the precision of estimates. The second approach is perhaps the most widely used, but the precision of estimates even by experienced experts if often far from satisfactory.

The third approach attempts to generate more objective risk estimates by providing a set of descriptions (= anchored scales) for a number of discrete risk values. This reduces the spread of risk estimates by different individuals. However, the anchored scales are usually written for assessing a certain kind of risk (e.g. technical or market risk from a generic point of view) which makes it difficult to use them when more specific risks are assessed. Another aspect of quantifying risk lies in the dimension being used. The Technology project risk model above asks to quantify a 'total loss'. This could be expressed as a monetary value, a time delay, or the reduced quality or performance of the product.

8.9.3 Failure Mode and Effects Analysis (FMEA)

Failure mode and effects analysis (FMEA) is a methodology normally used for assessing technical risk early in the product development cycle. While the FMEA is primarily an engineering tool to enhance product reliability and safety, its impact on managing the commercialisation risk of the venture should not be underestimated. In many markets, either regulatory requirements or industry standards require formal methods of technical risk analysis. For example, ISO 14971 specifies the risk analysis for medical devices, and QS9000/SAE J1739 (superseded by ISO/TS 16949) specifies FMEA for suppliers to the automotive industry.

Even in the absence of formal requirements for a risk analysis or a FMEA, having prepared a thorough FMEA (or risk analysis) will be highly beneficial should there be any future product liability litigation. Future venture capital investors or alliance partners will also demand to see a formal risk assessment during the due diligence process, at which point the absence of any form of technical risk assessment would be seen as a major concern. There are several types of FMEA, of which design FMEA and process FMEA are the most common ones, focussing on the design of a system or component and a manufacturing process respectively.

The FMEA process begins with identifying all the functions of the product or process and identifying all possible failure modes. This is followed by identifying the effects of a potential failure mode, and rating its severity (SEV column) on a scale from 1 to 10. Next comes the identification of causes for the failure, along with a rating of the likelihood of its occurrence (OCC column). Detection is a rating corresponding to the likelihood that the detection methods or current controls will detect the potential failure mode before the product design is released for production (design FMEA), or before it leaves the production facility (process FMEA). Table 8.2 outlines this process in relation to a car airbag system. The risk priority number (RPN) is a mathematical product of the numerical severity, probability and detection ratings, and is used to prioritise items than require additional quality planning or action.

$$\mathbf{RPN} = (\mathbf{Severity}) \times (\mathbf{Probability}) \times (\mathbf{Detection})$$

Design improvements and reliability/validation tests are typical controls in design FMEA, while inspection and statistical process control are typical controls in process FMEA. The scales for severity (SEV), occurrence (OCC) and detection (DET) are very much an example of *anchored scales*. Standards such as SAE J1739 include suggested scales that suit automotive applications but may not be appropriate in other areas, e.g. an occurrence rating of 2 equates to a failure rate of 1/150,000 which may be an inappropriate scale for a low volume product. Additional columns for severity, occurrence, detection and risk priority number are usually added to the right, with data reflecting the expected outcome once the recommended corrective actions have been implemented.

8.9.4 Anchored Scales

One research effort to develop a method to determine a project's probability of success has been made by the Industrial Research Institute (IRD) (Davis et al. 2001). Their goal was to develop a method that would ensure that different people assessing the same project arrive at similar answers that can be compared across projects. Anchored scales form the basis of their method for assessing five areas of technical and six areas of commercial (i.e. market) risk.

An example of one such scale is shown in Table 8.3. As can be seen, the scale is designed to measure the firm's competencies and skills in relation to technical issues. The rating scale from 1 to 5 has anchor points that provide a clear description of what each score represents. Assuming that these scale items are a reliable measure and that all members of the team understand them, the scale can provide a useful way to measure this aspect of the firm's performance.

Table 8.2 FMEA worksheet for automotive airbag system

Product function or purpose	Failure mode	Effect(s) of failure	SEV	Mechanism(s) and causes(s) of failure	OCC	Controls/fault detection	DET	RPN	Recommended corrective action(s)
Inflate airbag	Bag does not open on impact	Injure passenger	8	Sensor is not functioning properly	2	Light to notify that system is malfunctioning	6	96	Add redundant sensor to monitor impact
Restrain passenger	Occupant unable to withstand inflation force	Injure lightweight passenger	8	Passenger not wearing seatbelt	4	None	10	320	1. Install switch to deactivate system if seatbelt is not worn
		Bruise passenger in crash	3	Force regulator not working	2	Repeatability tests in lab	3	18	2. Consumer education of air bag system potential failures

Source: Schnepple (2005)

Table 8.3 Example – Anchored scale

Anchor point	Anchor point description
5	We are experts and have done (implemented) this before
4	It is a good fit with our core competencies, but we have not done a project like this before
3	This is not new to us, but it is not one of our present competencies
2	This is new to us, but not new to the world
1	This has never been done before

Anchored scale for competencies/skills – determines the probability that available technical resources have the required competencies to successfully undertake the research project
Source: Schnepple (2005)

Table 8.4 Technical success factors

Technical success factor	Weight (W = 0…1)	Rating (R = 1…5)	Score (= W × R)
Proprietary position	.3	2.3	0.69
Competencies and skills	.5	3.5	1.75
Complexity	.1	3.5	0.35
Access to external technology	0	n/a	0
Manufacturing capability	.1	4	.4
Total	100%		1.66

Source: Davis et al. (2001)

Equivalent anchor point descriptions can be used for all of the technical and commercial success factors relevant to a project. Table 8.4 shows weights and ratings given for a particular project in relation to technical success factors. It can be seen that the firm's manufacturing capability is viewed as the strongest area and that access to external technology the least important. Each item is then given a final score that combines the weightings and ratings and this is totalled to provide a final overall score.

By comparison, Table 8.5 assesses the firm's commercial success factors. As can be seen from Tables 8.3 and 8.4, it is clear that the firm's confidence in their commercial success factors is much lower than in their technical success factors. A discussion of the data will quickly identify the lack of access to distribution channels as the key reason for the low overall score for commercial success factors (see Table 8.5). Not as strong, but still significant, would be the poor rating for the proprietary position on the technical success factors (see Table 8.5). Many users of this system will find that some of the success factors are not applicable to their business, and this example reflects this by assigning a weight of 0 to the importance of those factors.

Table 8.5 Commercial success factors

Commercial success factor	Weight (W = 0…1)	Rating (R = 1…5)	Score (= W × R)
Customer/market need	.2	2.3	0.46
Market/brand recognition	.2	1.5	0.3
Distribution channels	.6	1.5	0.9
Customer strength	0	n/a	0
Raw materials supply	0	n/a	0
Environment, health and safety	0	n/a	0
Total	100%		1.66

Source: Davis et al. (2001)

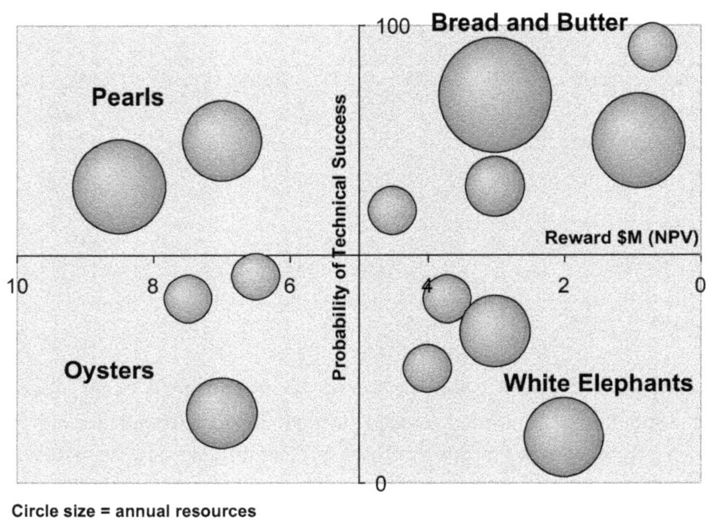

Fig. 8.8 Risk vs. reward and resource requirement chart. (Source: Cooper et al. 2001)

8.10 Portfolio Management Approach

It may be helpful to understand the portfolio point of view that a venture capital (VC), or alliance partner will have when considering investing in or partnering with a business. The insights gained from looking at the business as just one component of the VC or alliance partners portfolio will help in selecting the right partners, and once found, will also help in designing the business model so as to maximise its attractiveness to the other party. Evaluating a NPD project from a portfolio management point of view is also very much about focusing on developing the right product(s), not just developing a product right.

There are a number of tools useful in evaluating a portfolio of projects. The bubble chart shown in Fig. 8.8 displays a number of projects against monetary reward (x-axis), probability of technical success (y-axis), while the bubble sizes represent the annual resource requirement for each project. This is just an example of how a portfolio of projects may be evaluated. There are four common denominators across businesses when it comes to portfolio management: four macro or high-level goals. The goal you wish to emphasize most will in turn influence your choice of portfolio methods. These four broad or macro goals are discussed below.

8.10.1 Value Maximisation

Here the goal is to allocate resources so as to maximize the value of your portfolio. That is, you select projects so as to maximize sum of the values or commercial worth's of all active projects in your pipeline in terms of some business objective (such as long-term profitability, economic value added, return-on-investment, likelihood of success, or some other strategic objectives) (Cooper et al. 2001).

8.10.2 Balance

Here the principal concern is to develop a balanced portfolio – to achieve a desired balance of projects in terms of a number of parameters; for example, the right balance in terms of long-term projects versus short ones; or high risk versus lower risk projects; and across various markets, technologies, product categories, and project types (e.g., new products, improvements, cost reductions, maintenance and fixes, and fundamental research).

8.10.3 Strategic Direction

The main goal here is to ensure that, regardless of all other considerations, the final portfolio of projects truly reflects the business's strategy – that the breakdown of spending across projects, areas, markets, etc., is directly tied to the business strategy (e.g., to areas of strategic focus that management has previously delineated); and that all projects are "on strategy".

8.10.4 Right Number of Projects

Most companies have too many projects underway for the limited resources available. The result is pipeline gridlock: projects end up in a queue; they take longer and longer to get to market; and key activities within projects – for example, doing the up-front homework – are omitted because of a lack of people and time. Thus, an over-riding goal is to ensure a balance between resources required for the "GO" projects and resources available (Cooper et al. 2001).

8.11 Real Options Reasoning and Decision Tree Analysis

A final tool for management of risk in innovation is *Real Options Reasoning*, which is an approach whereby the decision maker invests in an option that grants them the right, but not the obligation to make future investments (Shepherd and Patzelt 2017). It is a method that is suited to investment environments in which there is a high degree of uncertainty and therefore the greater risk of failure.

The formal valuation of IP assets can be complex and requires having access to data that may not be available in many early-stage ventures. The uncertainty and lack of market-based information makes conventional *net present value* (NPV) calculations problematic. Even *Real Options*, which seeks to take risk and uncertainty into consideration, is limited as it does not help to quantify the risk of the venture (Steffens and Douglas 2004). Potentially more useful approaches to risk assessment can be found in decision tree analysis, which is derived from the *First Chicago Method.*

8.11.1 The First Chicago Method

This method typically considers three outcome scenarios for the venture: a best guess, a best case, and a worst case. Further, the possibility of aborting the venture due to R&D being unsuccessful is also included. Probabilities are assigned to the different scenarios. The decision tree illustrated in Fig. 8.9 is evaluated from right to left. The three outcomes at T = 5 are multiplied with their probabilities to obtain an expected value of \$120 m at T = 5. This terminal value is discounted @20% by 1 year, and the commercialisation investment of \$70 m is subtracted, giving a NPV of \$30 m at T = 4. Discounting this value further to T = 0 gives \$14.47 m. The overall NPV of the project is shown at the bottom of the graph. In this method, the

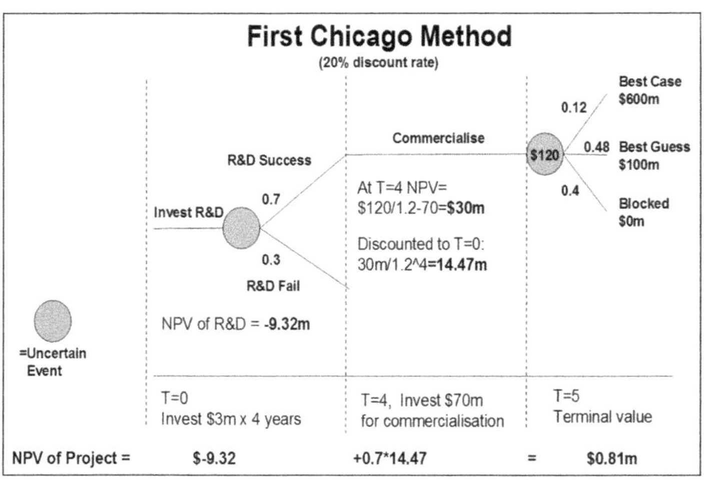

Discount Rate	Valuation ($m)
15%	\$3.90
20%	\$0.81
25%	-\$1.40
30%	-\$2.98
40%	-\$4.90
50%	-\$5.84

Fig. 8.9 First Chicago Method. (Source: Schnepple 2005)

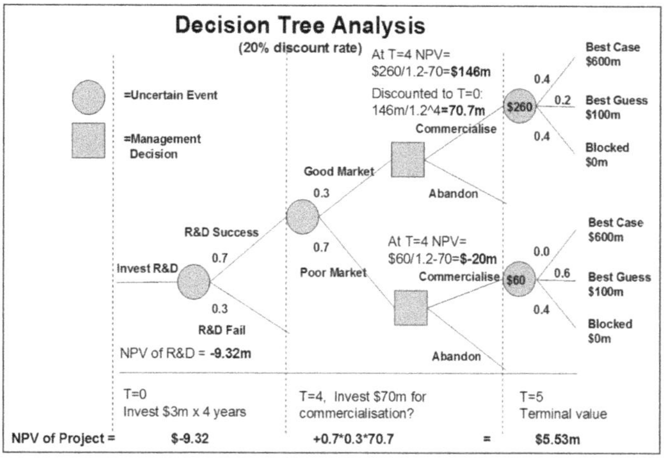

	Valuation Decision Tree ($m)	Valuation First Chicago ($m)
15%	$8.89	$3.90
20%	$5.53	$0.81
25%	$3.01	-$1.40
30%	$1.10	-$2.98
40%	-$1.44	-$4.90
50%	-$2.94	-$5.84

Fig. 8.10 Decision tree analysis. (Source: Schnepple 2005)

riskiness is reflected in the probabilities shown in the decision tree rather than by the discount rate chosen. This way, different phases in time are penalised with the appropriate risk factor, rather than having to apply a single *penalty discount rate* for the whole project.

8.11.2 Decision Tree Analysis

Decision tree analysis extends the methodology of the *First Chicago Method* by adding in management decision points, at which management can make a choice about future action. The previous example (see: Fig. 8.9) is extended in Fig. 8.10 by reassessing the market conditions at the start of year 4. New terminal values for best case, worst case and best guess are set for both good and poor market conditions. Again, the decision tree is evaluated from right to left. Under poor market conditions, the NPV at T = 4 is in the red by 20 m, and hence the management decision would be to abandon the project. Comparing the valuations between the First Chicago method and the decision tree shows that the 'option' to discontinue the project at T = 4 is of significant value. The terminal value of the decision tree, when weighted by the good/poor market probabilities, gives an expected value at T = 5 of $120 m – which is identical to the previous example.

8.12 Assessing the Risk-Return for an Innovation: Innovation Rent

Prior to the launch of a new product or process innovation attention needs to be given to the potential return likely to accrue from the investment and this will require a systematic approach to screening new opportunities. Traditional financial models (e.g. Net Present Value, Real Options and Decision Tree Analysis) can offer a guide to the potential attractiveness of an innovation, but these have limitations in terms of their ability to fully assess the true risk-return associated with the project. To address this problem a risk-return model has been developed to provide a quick screening tool for small firms (Reboud and Mazzarol 2006). This draws on a model of *Innovation Rent* from a future innovation that is a function of three variables:

1. *Volume* – as measured by the volume of sales over a year;
2. *Rate* – the profit margin likely to be generated from the innovation; and
3. *Length* – the duration of the lifecycle of the innovation (Santi et al. 2003).

This can be illustrated in the following model:

$$\mathbf{RENT = VOLUME \times RATE \times LENGTH}$$

This process is illustrated in Fig. 8.11 that shows the potential returns are influenced by the volume of sales generated from the innovation, its profitability and the length of time that the innovation can be maintained in the market before its competitiveness is eroded by competitors or substitutions. Profitability is a critical issue and is determined by the price-cost relationship of the innovation.

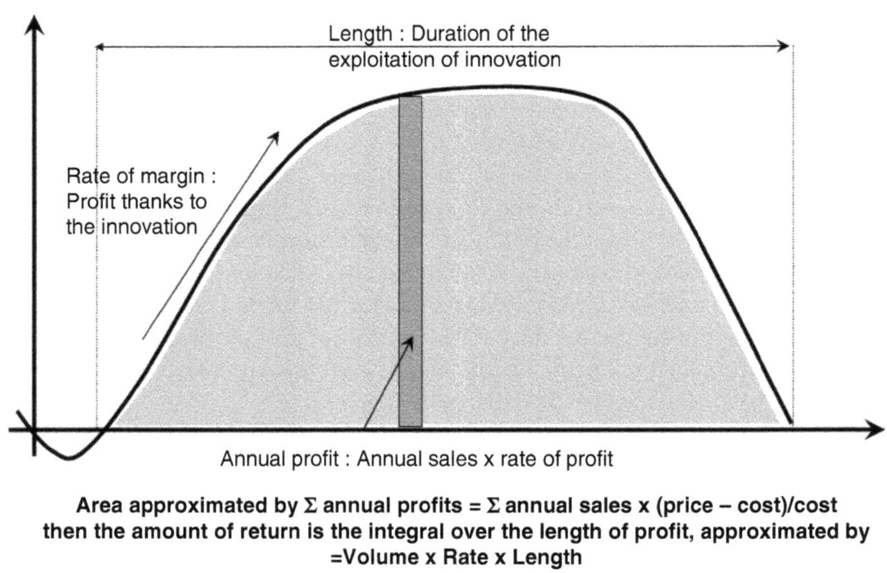

Fig. 8.11 Components of RENT. Area approximated by Σ annual profits = Σ annual sales × (price – cost)/cost then the amount of return is the integral over the length of profit, approximated by = Volume × Rate × Length. (Source: Reboud and Mazzarol 2006; Santi et al. 2003)

A key indicator of the potential *Volume* to be achieved by a particular innovation is the size of the industry or market sector being targeted by the new product. Also important is the size of any end-user market if the product is to be on-sold beyond the immediate customer. The size of any future sales volume may also be determined by the geographic diffusion potential of the product; this is particularly the case in terms of its ability to be exported or developed for a global market Finally, the volume may be influenced by the presence of prior patents (held by others) that might restrict its capacity to be exported.

The profit *Rate* that can be generated by the innovation may be influenced by the type of innovation process involved or the innovation itself. Highly complex technical products or processes are often easier to secure against competitors and this can allow a limited monopoly to be created with the opportunity for maximisation of profits. Protection of the IP inherent in the innovation is thereby critical.

The *Length* of time over which the innovation can be held in the market may depend on the technological base of the innovation (e.g. whether it is complex or easy to copy). The level of the innovation intensity of the firm that uses the innovation may also impact this, as highly innovative industries frequently turnover such innovations as they seek continuous advantages. Legal protection of the IP associated with the innovation is also a key means of protecting the length of time over which it can be held in the market. However, eventually all innovations will be eroded and replaced. These issues are illustrated in Table 8.6.

8.12.1 The Theory of Innovation Rents

The concept of *Innovation Rent* is derived from the concept of *economic rent* that has its antecedents in economics, where the scarcity of resources or assets (either tangible or intangible) can enable the owner to extract above average rents from those who wish to use or acquire them (Schoemaker 1990). The *economic rent* concept is an important foundation of *resource-based theory* (Barney 1986) within strategic management, that suggests a firm's ability to secure a sustained competitive

Table 8.6 Measures of potential RENT

Components of RENT	Indicators
Volume (potential annual sales)	Size of industry or market sector
	Geographic diffusion potential
	Size of end-user markets
	Limits due to prior patents
Rate (potential profit margin)	Type of innovation process involved
	Type of innovation involved
	Level of prior protection for intellectual property
Length (potential lifecycle of innovation)	Technological basis of innovation
	Innovation intensity of the user centre
	Legal and technical protection of intellectual property

Source: Santi et al. (2003)

advantage is contingent on the ability to own and control strategic assets or resources that offer value, but cannot be easily substituted or replicated (Barney 1991; Mosakowski 1998).

There at least two distinct types of *economic rents* relevant to strategic management of innovation. The first is *Ricardian rent*, which draws on the work of economist David Ricardo (1772–1823) who postulated the *Law of Rent*, which suggests that the rent of an asset is equal to the economic advantage that might be gained by using this same asset for the same purpose directly. In other words, the owner might use the asset for generating wealth or rent it out for a return from someone else's use of the asset.

The second type of *economic rent* is *Schumpeterian rent*, named after the economist Joseph Schumpeter (1883–1950), who has been associated with entrepreneurship as a change agent or "creative destroyer "within the economy. *Ricardian rent* is broadly consistent with the *resource-based theory* or *resource-based view* (RBV) suggesting that the firm's competitiveness can be built on owning and controlling valuable and rare assets that cannot be easily substituted or copied (Barney 2001; Penrose 1959; Wernerfelt 1984). By contrast *Schumpeterian rent* places its focus on the firm's ability to use its resources and assets in an innovative way to create value through the process of bundling existing resources (Makadok 2001). In this way, *Schumpeterian rent* is more consistent with the strategic management theory of *dynamic capabilities* (Amit and Schoemaker 1993; Teece et al. 1997).

Schumpeterian rent is important for firms engaged in the management of innovation and the commercialisation of new products and services. Where a firm has strong control over specific assets in a relatively stable market environment it is more likely to use *Ricardian rent* (Lim et al. 2013). However, for firms in dynamic or turbulent market environments engaged in the commercialisation of potentially disruptive innovations, the *Schumpeterian rent* is more appropriate (Do et al. 2014).

In Chap. 13 we outline the role played by intellectual property rights (IP rights) to generate *isolating mechanisms* that would assist a firm to secure a competitive advantage. In particular, these *isolating mechanisms* allow a small firm stronger bargaining power when seeking to negotiate with others (i.e. customers, suppliers, investors, joint venture partners). IP rights offer firms the ability to secure control over assets and use them to build a competitive edge. They also offer a way to take *Schumpeterian rents* and convert them into *Ricardian rents* as the formalization of the ideas behind the innovation, and their legal registration and protection (i.e. patents, design registrations), gives them a tangible quality that allows them to be traded and licensed.

8.12.2 Typology of Innovation Rents

As the combination of these three variable components, an *Innovation Rent* can be characterised by its extreme profile: (i) large/small volume; (ii) high/low rate of margin and (iii) short/long life cycle. With two possibilities for each variable a total of eight combinations can be identified. These are illustrated in Fig. 8.12, where the

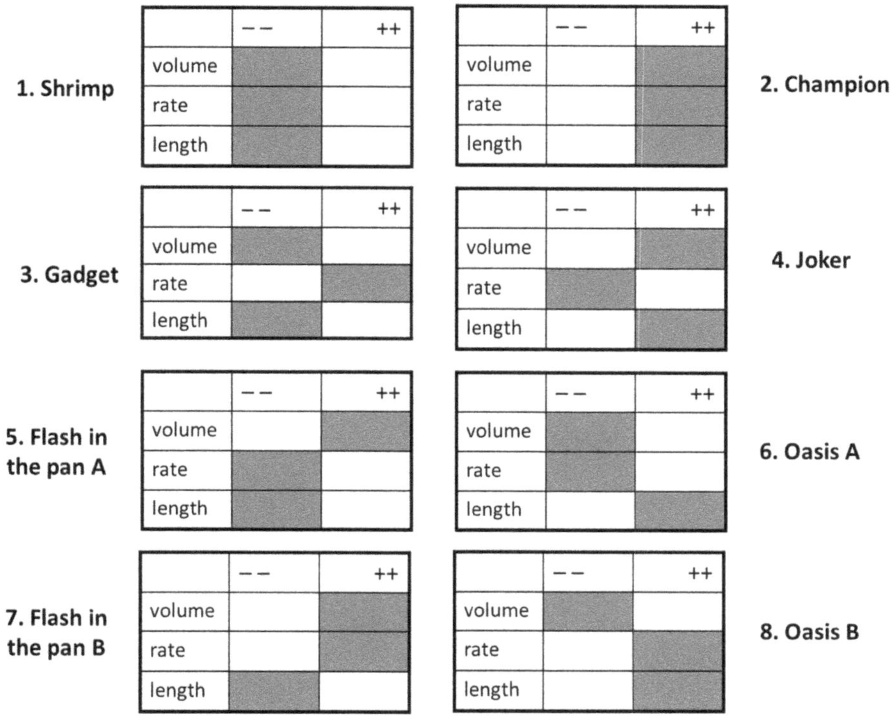

Fig. 8.12 Typology of configurations of anticipated innovation RENT. (Source: Mazzarol and Reboud 2009)

options are shown with their various trade-offs of volume, rate and length within the rent equation. Each configuration involves different levels of volume, rate and length thereby determining the anticipated rent to be derived from the innovation. These *Innovation Rent* configurations are described in the following sub-sections.

- Shrimp

The *Shrimp* type of innovation offers a low or modest volume of sales, perhaps within a niche market, plus a modest or low rate of profit and has a short lifecycle. It may not be of particular interest to high growth-oriented firms, but can represent a good opportunity for firms that have low to medium levels of technology and need to maintain a competitive edge with continuous incremental innovation. Many process innovations can be *Shrimp*. A positive attribute of the *Shrimp* is that it can usually be commercialised without the need for outside help.

- Champion

The *Champion* innovation is potentially able to offer high levels of sales volume, probably from national or global markets. It also has the potential for above average profits and has a long lifecycle. This type of innovation is most likely to be associated with radical, disruptive technological innovations that can be securely protected by formal patents or trademarks. While superficially this may seem a highly attractive innovation, the *Champion* requires a substantial investment in both product and market development in order to secure the anticipated returns. For many small firms the *Champion* may be high risk and need resources that they don't possess.

- Gadget

The *Gadget* innovation at first appears unattractive as it offers only a relatively short production run with modest sales. However, it has the potential to generate above average profits and for some types of firm this may be a worthwhile investment. To get the most out of *Gadget* innovation a firm will need to employ a first mover advantage and seek to appropriate rents quickly. Some examples of *Gadget* innovations are the software applications or *Apps* that are now commonly found for products like the Apple iPhone or iPad.

- Joker

A *Joker* innovation offers a long lifecycle and large sales volumes, but its rate of profit is modest. For some firms this may be unattractive, but there can be value in the *Joker*. Firms in industry sectors where radical innovation is not possible, and where cost leadership rather than differentiation strategies can be followed might secure benefit from the *Joker*. In many cases the *Joker* is a process innovation rather than a product innovation. The process innovation may not generate high profits, but it will make steady profits over the long term within a large market.

- Flash-in-the-Pan (Type A)

The *Flash-in-the-pan* innovation has two types. The *Type A* has the ability to generate high sales volume, but with only modest rates of profit over a short lifecycle. Such an innovation may be a poor option, particularly as it can require significant investment in production and marketing in order to service the future market demand, but without the profitability or lifecycle to recover this initial outlay.

- Flash-in-the-Pan (Type B)

By comparison the *Flash-in-the-pan Type*-B is the high profit cousin of the *Type A*. The high rates of profit and high sales volumes may make this innovation attractive. However, the short lifecycle means that the firm seeking to commercialise such an innovation must secure a first mover advantage and focus on market development as a high priority. For firms that cannot be sure of their ability to quickly secure market accesses this innovation may pose an undesirable risk.

- Oasis (Type A)

The *Oasis-Type*-A innovation offers a long lifecycle but with only modest sales volume and rate of profit. For firms interested in fast growth opportunities this type of innovation is unattractive. It may be attractive to other firms that have modest production capacity and that are content with low to moderate rates of profit over a long lifecycle. It is also common in process innovations that fit into small, niche markets with modest rates of profit, but long lifecycles. Licencing agreements over this type of innovation can be attractive to some firms.

- Oasis (Type B)

The *Oasis-Type*-B innovation is the high profit counterpart to the *Oasis-Type*-A. Its high rate of profit and long lifecycle make it potentially attractive, however, it only has a small potential sales volume making it a niche differentiation strategy option. Such an innovation may be a good option for small firms with modest production capacity.

8.12.3 The RENT Configuration and Planning

Tidd (2001) suggests that to understand the process of innovation within the firm requires attention to the interplay between environmental uncertainty and organisational complexity. This view was shared by Mazzarol and Reboud (2009) who in reviewing the strategic planning behaviour of small firms drew similar conclusions and proposed a contingency framework consisting of the two dimensions of complexity and uncertainty as proposed by Tidd (2001), suggesting that planning responses should be contingent on the task environment's uncertainty and the complexity of the firm's organisational configuration. In Chap. 7 we introduced the four generic strategic planning types: *The Shopkeeper*, *The Salesman*, *The Administrator* and *The CEO* (Mazzarol and Reboud 2009).

As illustrated in Fig. 8.13 the four different planning responses suggested by Mazzarol and Reboud (2009) can be correlated with the eight RENT configurations that have been discussed throughout this book. For example, the *Champion* innovation requires the structured strategic planning response of *The CEO* and therefore greater levels of formality. Without such formal, systematic planning it is less likely that the *Champion* innovation will gain traction in a national or global market, secure its profit potential and sustain a long lifecycle. The *Flash-in-the-Pan Type–B* innovation is also best dealt with by *The CEO* planning response due to its need to reach a large market and maintain a high profit margin. This requires premium pricing and product differentiation strategies.

By contrast the *Shrimp* innovation is appropriately dealt with via the more informal, ad hoc approach of *The Shopkeeper* as it is typically less complex and sells into a smaller market albeit with modest profit and short lifecycle. The *Oasis-Type-A* innovation has similar dynamics which has a long lifecycle, but the same market and profit characteristics of the *Shrimp*. The *Joker* innovation with its long lifecycle and high sales but modest profit margin requires careful management and close attention to operational costs to ensure that the limited margins are able to generate a profit. For this reason, the most appropriate planning response is that of *The Administrator*. This is also likely to be the case for the *Flash-in-the-Pan-Type-A* due to its low rate but high sales volume.

Finally, the *Gadget* and *Oasis-Type-B* innovations are likely to be best served by the planning response of *The Salesman*. These innovations target niche markets but

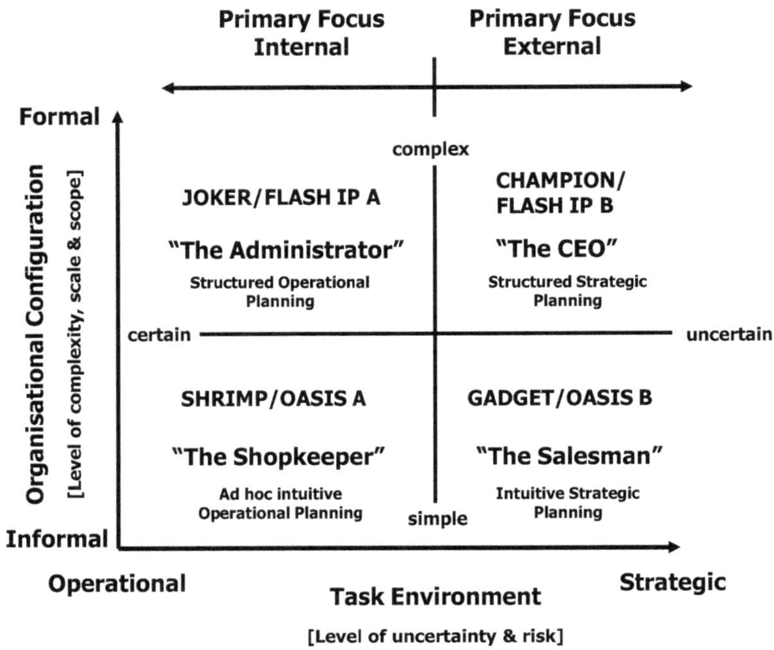

Fig. 8.13 Planning response contingency matric for the *Innovation Rent*. (Source: Mazzarol and Reboud 2009)

offer good profit margins. The *Gadget* has a short lifecycle and needs to be commercialised quickly, while the niche market long lifecycle characteristics of the *Oasis-Type-B* require careful targeting of customers who can remain loyal to the product over the longer term. The intuitive style of *The Salesman* planning approach is not particularly formal, but it is strategic in nature.

8.13 The Risk-Return of Commercialisation Pathways

The *Innovation Rent* typology described above assumes that the firm's management can make an initial assessment of the *potential rent* that they might secure from their innovation. This *potential rent* has also been described as *entrepreneurial rent*, and is rents generated under conditions of uncertainty (Alvarez 2007; Alvarez and Barney 2004). As shown in Fig. 8.14, it is an initial screening by the firm's management to consider the options it has for future commercialisation and the strategic implications that this entails. The firm will need to assess the characteristics of the innovation (i.e. size of market, ability to generate strong isolating mechanisms), as well as the competitive environment into which it is to seek commercialisation. Key

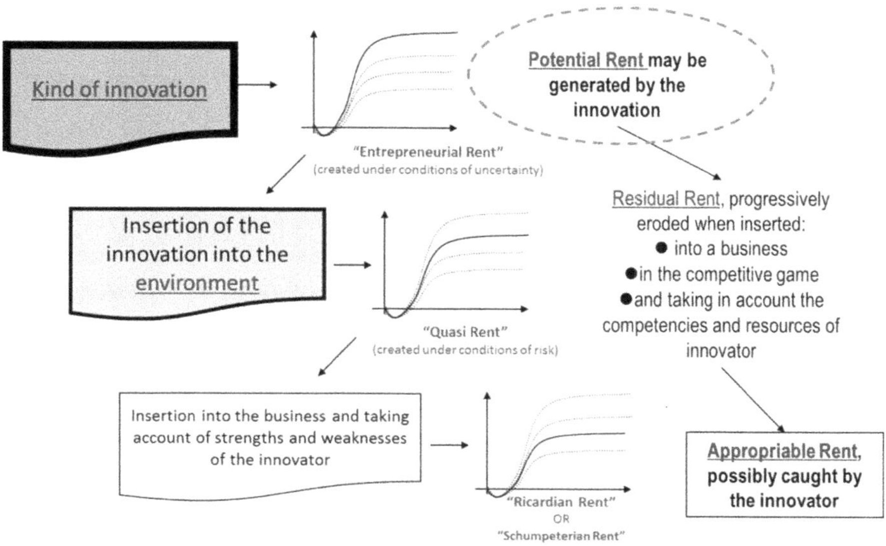

Fig. 8.14 Generation and appropriation of economic rents. (Source: Mazzarol et al. 2017)

issues here are the nature of competitive rivalry, barriers to entry, the bargaining power of suppliers and customers, and risks of substitution (Duhamel et al. 2014).

Once the innovation has been taken to market (i.e. initial pilot testing of a minimum viable product), it will be possible for the firm's management to use the market feedback to reassess the future value of the innovation and from this it can generate a *residual rent* also known as a *quasi-rent*. This type of *innovation rent* is created under conditions of risk rather than uncertainty (Alvarez 2007). In many cases the original *potential rent* assessment will be diminished at this stage in the light of market feedback. As noted above, the *Fuzzy Front End* (FFE) of the commercialisation process is very important an if the firm is to secure the full benefit from their innovation, they will need to successfully turn their PACAP into RACAP. This ability to learn and adapt, reconfigure the innovation and *pivot* the business model will all determine how successful the final outcomes are.

In reviewing the information and knowledge that comes back from this initial market testing, the firm's management will need to review its resources and make a judgment as to whether it can proceed with the commercialisation and capture sufficient value in the final *appropriable rent* that can be secured. The final nature of this *appropriable rent* is likely to depend on the firm's ability to generate strong *isolating mechanisms* (i.e. patents), and whether it has the resources and capabilities to proceed alone, or whether it needs to form strategic partnerships (Do 2014; Do et al. 2014; Duhamel et al. 2014).

References

Adams, R., Bessant, J., & Phelps, R. (2006). Innovation management measurement: A review. *International Journal of Management Reviews, 8*(1), 21–47.

Alvarez, S. A. (2007). Entrepreneurial rents and the theory of the firm. *Journal of Business Venturing, 22*(3), 427–442.

Alvarez, S. A., & Barney, J. B. (2004). Organizing rent generation and appropriation: Toward a theory of the entrepreneurial firm. *Journal of Business Venturing, 19*(5), 621–635.

Amit, R., & Schoemaker, P. J. H. (1993). Strategic assets and organizational rent. *Strategic Management Journal, 14*(1), 33–46.

Aon Analytics. (2010). *Global enterprise risk management survey 2010.* Chicago: Aon Corporation.

Arena, M., Arnaboldi, M., & Azzone, G. (2010). The organizational dynamics of enterprise risk management. *Accounting, Organizations and Society, 35*(7), 659–675.

Atkins, M., & Anderson, A. (1999). Risk, uncertainty and the entrepreneurial vision. *Risk Management, 1*(2), 35–48.

Barney, J. B. (1986). Types of competition and the theory of strategy: Toward an integrative framework. *Academy of Management Review, 11*(4), 791–800.

Barney, J. B. (1991). Firm resources and sustained competitive advantage. *Journal of Management, 17*(1), 99–120.

Barney, J. B. (2001). Resource-based theories of competitive advantage: A ten-year retrospective on the resource-based view. *Journal of Management, 27*(6), 643–650.

Biyalogorsky, E., Boulding, W., & Staelin, R. (2006). Stuck in the past: Why managers persist with new product failures. *Journal of Marketing, 70*(2), 108–121.

Brinckmann, J., Grichnik, D., & Kapsa, D. (2010). Should entrepreneurs plan or just storm the castle? A meta-analysis on contextual factors impacting the business planning–performance relationship in small firms. *Journal of Business Venturing, 25*(1), 24–40.

Brockhaus, R. H. (1980). Risk taking propensity of entrepreneurs. *Academy of Management Journal, 23*(3), 457–460.

Brustbauer, J. (2016). Enterprise risk management in SMEs: Towards a structural model. *International Small Business Journal, 34*(1), 70–85.

Busenitz, L. W. (1999). Entrepreneurial risk and strategic decision making: It's a matter of perspective. *The Journal of Applied Behavioral Science, 35*(3), 325–340.

Clusel, S. (2012). *Définition d'une démarche de réduction des vulnérabilités des TPE/PME fondée sur le cycle de vie.* Thèse de Doctorat en Sciences et Génie des Activités à Risques, Ecole Nationale Supérieure des Mines de Paris, Paris.

Cobbenhagen, J. (2000). *Successful innovation: Towards a new theory for the management of small and medium-sized enterprises.* Cheltenham: Edward Elgar Publishing.

Cohen, W. M., & Levinthal, D. A. (1990). Absorptive capacity: A new perspective on learning and innovation. *Administrative Science Quarterly, 35*(1) (Special Issue: Technology, Organizations, and Innovation), 128–152.

Cooper, R. G., & Edgett, S. J. (2005). *Lean, rapid, and profitable new product development.* Ancaster: Product development institute.

Cooper, R. G., & Kleinschmidt, E. J. (1993). Screening new products for potential winners. *Long Range Planning, 26*(6), 74–81.

Cooper, R. G., & Kleinschmidt, E. J. (1995). Benchmarking the Firm's critical success factors in new product development. *Journal of Product Innovation Management, 12*(5), 374–391.

Cooper, R., Edgett, S., & Kleinschmidt, E. (2001). Portfolio management for new product development: Results of an industry practices study. *R&D Management, 31*(4), 361–380.

Davis, C. R. (2002). Calculated risk: A framework for evaluating product development. *MIT Sloan Management Review, 43*(4), 71–78.

Davis, J., Fusfeld, A., Scriven, E., & Tritle, G. (2001). Determining a project's probability of success. *Research-Technology Management, 44*(3), 51–57.

De Carolis, D. M., & Saparito, P. (2006). Social capital, cognition, and entrepreneurial opportunities: A theoretical framework. *Entrepreneurship Theory and Practice, 30*(1), 41–56.

Deloitte (2010). Global risk management survey, 7th Edition, Navigating in a changed world: Deloitte Touche Tohmatsu Ltd.

Do, T. H. (2014). Determinants of innovation commercialization management and anticipated returns: An exploratory typology of SMEs. *International Journal of Innovation and Technology Management, 11*(06), 1450042.

Do, T. H., Mazzarol, T., Volery, T., & Reboud, S. (2014). Predicting anticipated rent from innovation commercialisation in SMEs. *European Journal of Innovation Management, 17*(2), 183–208.

Duhamel, F., Reboud, S., & Santi, M. (2014). Capturing value from innovations: The importance of rent configurations. *Management Decision, 52*(1), 7–7.

Everett, J., & Watson, J. (1998). Small business failure and external risk factors. *Small Business Economics, 11*(4), 371–390.

Forlani, D., & Mullins, J. W. (2000). Perceived risks and choices in entrepreneurs' new venture decisions. *Journal of Business Venturing, 15*(4), 305–322.

Gray, C. (2006). Absorptive capacity, knowledge management and innovation in entrepreneurial small firms. *International Journal of Entrepreneurial Behavior & Research, 12*(6), 345–360.

Herdman, R. C. (1995). Innovation and Commercialization of Emerging Technologies: Printing Office of Technology Assessment, USA.

Hlavaceck, J. D., Maxwell, C., & Williams, J., Jr. (2009). Learn from new product failures. *Research-Technology Management, 52*(4), 31–39.

Islam, A., & Tedford, D. (2012). Risk determinants of small and medium-sized manufacturing enterprises (SMEs) – an exploratory study in New Zealand. *Journal of Industrial Engineering International, 8*(1), 1–13.

ISR. (2001). *From invention to investment: Pathways to commercialisation for emerging technologies.* Competitive Australia, Industry Science and Resources. Retrieved from Canberra, ACT: https://www.industry.gov.au/

Jayathilake, P. M. B. (2012). Risk management practices in small and medium enterprises: Evidence from Sri Lanka. *Zenith International Journal of Multidisciplinary Research, 2*(7), 226–234.

Julien, P.-A. (1990). Vers une définition multicritère des PME. *Revue Internationale PME, 3*(3–4), 411–425.

Keh, H. T., Der Foo, M., & Lim, B. C. (2002). Opportunity evaluation under risky conditions: The cognitive processes of entrepreneurs. *Entrepreneurship Theory and Practice, 27*(2), 125–148.

Kitching, J., & Blackburn, R. A. (2003). Innovation, intellectual property and informality. In R. A. Blackburn (Ed.), *Intellectual property and innovation management in small firms* (pp. 19–40). London: Routledge.

Knight, F. H. (1921). *Risk, uncertainty and profit.* Boston: Houghton Mifflin Company.

Koen, P. A., Ajamian, G. M., Boyce, S., Clamen, A., Fisher, E., Fountoulakis, S., . . . Seibert, R. (2002). Fuzzy front end: Effective methods, tools, and techniques. In P. Belliveau, A. Griffin, & S. Somermeyer (Eds.), *The PDMA tool book 1 for new product development.* New York: Wiley.

Lam, J. (2010). Enterprise risk-enterprise risk management: Bark to the future-the promise of ERM will remain unfulfilled if critical challenges are not addressed. *RMA Journal, 92*(9), 16.

Lechat, T., & Torrès, O. (2016). Les risques psychosociaux du dirigeant de PME: Typologie et échelle de mesure des stresseurs professionnels. *Revue Internationale PME, 29*(3–4), 135–160. forthcoming.

Lim, D. S. K., Celly, N., Morse, E. A., & Rowe, W. G. (2013). Rethinking the effectiveness of asset and cost retrenchment: The contingency effects of a firm's rent creation mechanism. *Strategic Management Journal, 34*(1), 42–61.

Mahé de Boislandelle, H. (1996). *L'effet de grossissement chez le dirigeant de PME : ses incidences sur le plan du management des hommes et de la GRH.* Paper presented at the 3ème Congrès International Francophone PME (CIFPME), Trois Rivières, Québec.

Makadok, R. (2001). Toward a synthesis of the resource-based and dynamic-capability views of rent creation. *Strategic Management Journal, 22*(5), 387–401.
March, J. G., & Shapira, Z. (1987). Managerial perspectives on risk and risk taking. *Management Science, 33*(11), 1404–1418.
Mazzarol, T., & Reboud, S. (2009). *The strategy of small firms, strategic management and innovation in the small firm*. Cheltenham: Edward Elgar Publishing.
Mazzarol, T., & Reboud, S. (Eds.). (2011). *Strategic innovation in small firms, an international analysis of innovation and strategic decision making in small to medium enterprises*. Cheltenham: Edward Elgar Publishing Ltd.
Mazzarol, T., Reboud, S., & Clark, D. (2015). *Proximity effects in SMEs: Up close and personal but strategically myopic*. Paper presented at the 29th ANZAM Conference, 2–4th December, Queenstown, NZ.
Mazzarol, T., Malone, P., & Reboud, S. (2017). Scanalyse – A case study of the role of social capital, strategic networking, and word of mouth communication in the diffusion of an innovation. In N. Pfeffermann & J. Gould (Eds.), *Strategy and communication for innovation: Integrative perspectives on innovation in the digital economy* (pp. 147–174). Cham: Springer International Publishing.
Merritt, G. M., & Smith, P. G. (2004). Techniques for managing project risk. In D. I. Cleland (Ed.), *Field guide to project management* (2nd ed., pp. 202–218). New York: Wiley.
Millson, M. R. (2013). Refining the NPD/innovation path to product market success with partial least squares path analysis. *International Journal of Innovation Management, 17*(02), 1350001.
Moles, A., & Rohmer, E. (1978). *Psychologie de l'espace, 2ème édition*. Paris: Editions Casterman.
Mosakowski, E. (1998). Managerial prescriptions under the resource-based view of strategy: The example of motivational techniques. *Strategic Management Journal, 19*(12), 1169–1182.
Ozer, M. (2004). Managing the selection process for new product ideas. *Research Technology Management, 47*(4), 10–11.
Penrose, E. (1959). *The theory of the growth of the firm*. Oxford: Blackwell.
Reboud, S., & Mazzarol, T. (2006). Évaluation du risque lié à une innovation pour les PME: proposition d'un outil. *Revue Internationale PME, 19*(2), 133–161.
Reboud, S., & Séville, M. (2016). De la vulnérabilité à la résilience: développer une capacité stratégique à gérer les risques dans les PME. *Revue Internationale PME, 29*(3–4), 27–46.
Reboud, S., Santi, M., & Mazzarol, T. (2014). Pourquoi devrais-je protéger mon innovation ? Gestion stratégique de la PI dans les PME. In G. Lecointre (Ed.), *Le Grand Livre de l'Économie PME, 3ème édition* (pp. 335–359). Paris: Éditions Gualino.
Ries, E. (2011). *The lean startup: How today's entrepreneurs use continuous innovation to create radically successful businesses*. New York: Random House LLC.
Santi, M., Reboud, S., Gasiglia, H., & Sabouret, A. (2003). *Modèle de valorisation et de protection intellectuelle des innovations des PEI*. HEC-INPI Research Report. Retrieved from Paris:
Sarasvathy, S. D. (2001). Causation and effectuation: Toward a theoretical shift from economic inevitability to entrepreneurial contingency. *Academy of Management Review, 26*(2), 243–263.
Sarasvathy, D. K., Simon, H. A., & Lave, L. (1998). Perceiving and managing business risks: Differences between entrepreneurs and bankers. *Journal of Economic Behavior & Organization, 33*(2), 207–225.
Schnepple, T. (2005). Managing commercialisation risk. University of Western Australia: Innovation Excellence Program, Centre for Entrepreneurial Management and Innovation.
Schoemaker, P. J. H. (1990). Strategy, complexity, and economic rent. *Management Science, 36*(10), 1178–1192.
Shepherd, D. A., & Patzelt, H. (2017). *Trailblazing in entrepreneurship: Creating new paths for understanding the field*: Springer.
Sitkin, S. B., & Pablo, A. L. (1992). Reconceptualizing the determinants of risk behavior. *Academy of Management Review, 17*(1), 9–38.
Sitkin, S. B., & Weingart, L. R. (1995). Determinants of risky decision-making behavior: A test of the mediating role of risk perceptions and propensity. *Academy of Management Journal, 38*(6), 1573–1592.

Smith, D., & Fischbacher, M. (2009). The changing nature of risk and risk management: The challenge of borders, uncertainty and resilience. *Risk Management, 11*(1), 1–12.

Steffens, P., & Douglas, E. (2004). *Use real options but not real options analysis when valuing new technological ventures.* Paper presented at the 17th Annual SEAANZ Conference – Entrepreneurship the Way of the Future, 26–29 Brisbane.

St-Pierre, J., & El Fadil, J. (2017). Gestion de l'incertitude et du risque: Une capacité stratégique à développer. In J. St-Pierre & F. Labelle (Eds.), *Les PME : d'hier à demain*. Québec: Presses de l'Université du Québec, à paraitre.

Teece, D. J., Pisano, G., & Shuen, A. (1997). Dynamic capabilities and strategic management. *Strategic Management Journal, 18*(7), 509–533.

Thorndike, E. L. (1907). *The elements of psychology*. New York: Seiler.

Thun, J.-H., Drüke, M., & Hoenig, D. (2011). Managing uncertainty – An empirical analysis of supply chain risk management in small and medium-sized enterprises. *International Journal of Production Research, 49*(18), 5511–5525.

Tidd, J. (2001). Innovation management in context: Environment, organization and performance. *International Journal of Management Reviews, 3*(3), 169–183.

Torrès, O. (2003). Petitesse des entreprises et grossissement des effets de proximité. *Revue Française de Gestion, 144*.(mai-juin 2003, 119–138.

Torrès, O., & Julien, P.-A. (2005). Specificity and denaturing of small business. *International Small Business Journal, 23*(4), 355–377.

Wernerfelt, B. (1984). A resource-based view of the firm. *Strategic Management Journal, 5*(2), 171–180.

Zahra, S. A., & George, G. (2002). Absorptive capacity: A review, reconceptualization, and extension. *Academy of Management Review, 27*(2), 185–203.

Disruptive Innovation and the Commercialisation of Technology

9

9.1 Introduction

> Innovation is a prerequisite for sustained growth. No other path to profitable growth can be sustained over time. Without continual innovation, markets stagnate, products become commodities and margins shrink.
>
> Chairman, Proctor & Gamble.

This chapter examines the role of innovation as a key economic driver and the nature of radical or disruptive innovations as a major source of new technological products and processes. It examines the theory and practice of strategic management of innovation, and the generation of *innovation value* through the adoption of a *Blue Ocean* strategy. The chapter also provides an overview of new product development processes such as *Stage-Gate*® and *Lean Start-Up*, plus the process of assessing *innovation rent*.

9.2 Innovation as a Key Economic Driver

Technology has been one of the main driving forces within human society, enhancing productivity and enabling ever increasing levels of wealth.

> **For example,** … It has been found that, as patenting activity rises with the Australian economy, so too does the level of labour productivity and overall economic growth. (Crosby 2000, p. 262)

This suggests that investment in new technological innovation is highly beneficial to national economic development. Innovation can be associated with either product or process, as well as be radical or incremental in nature. The radical or

T. Mazzarol, S. Reboud, *Entrepreneurship and Innovation*, Springer Texts in Business and Economics, https://doi.org/10.1007/978-981-13-9412-6_9

disruptive innovations are those that produce *fundamental changes* in the activities of an organisation or an industry, and represent clear departures from existing practices. Such innovations usually lead to increasing uncertainty within industries, and serve to transform either the firm or the industry itself (Gopalakrishnan and Damanpour 1997). Technological innovations typically include products, processes and technologies that are used for further production activities or result in the delivery of services.

The relationship between innovation and economic growth is well-recognised by governments around the world. For this reason, many countries invest significantly into R&D via government funding to supplement money being invested by private industry. As illustrated in Fig. 9.1, there is a positive correlation between the level of government funding of business R&D and the relative R&D intensity within the business sector. South Korea (KOR) and Germany (DEU), both have relatively high R&D intensities within their business sectors, in relation to the level of government support to R&D. By contrast, France (FRA), Hungary (HUN) and Russia (RUS), have relatively high levels of government support in relation to their industries R&D intensity. Some countries provide R&D tax incentives designed to stimulate business investment in R&D, but the benefits of these policies remain open to some debate (OECD 2015).

In global terms the United States remains the world's most significant generator of R&D driven innovation and this reflects the substantial amount of investment that is made by government and industry into R&D by that country. The total expenditure on R&D in the United States in 2013 was around US $433 billion, which exceeded similar investments made by China (the second largest investor) by more than one-third. Figure 9.2 illustrates this, showing a number of OECD and other

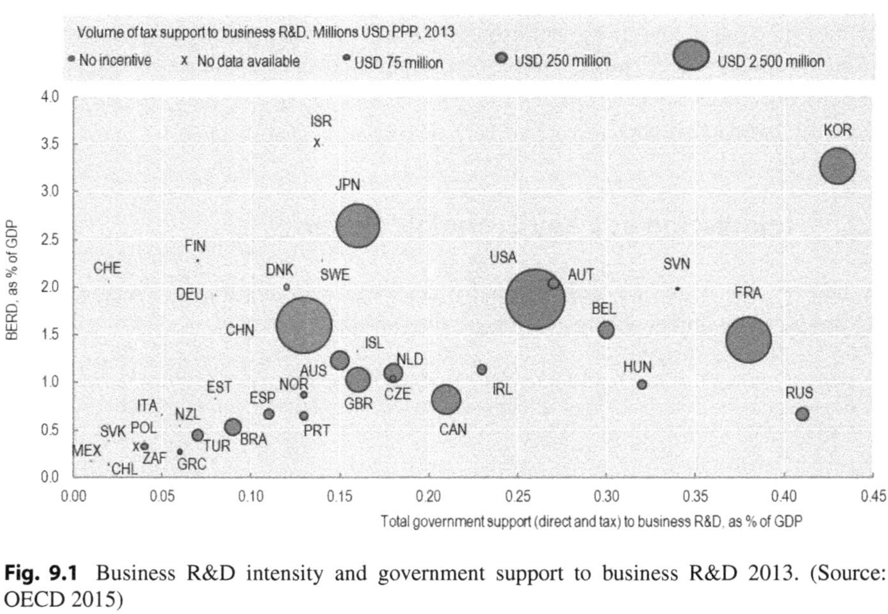

Fig. 9.1 Business R&D intensity and government support to business R&D 2013. (Source: OECD 2015)

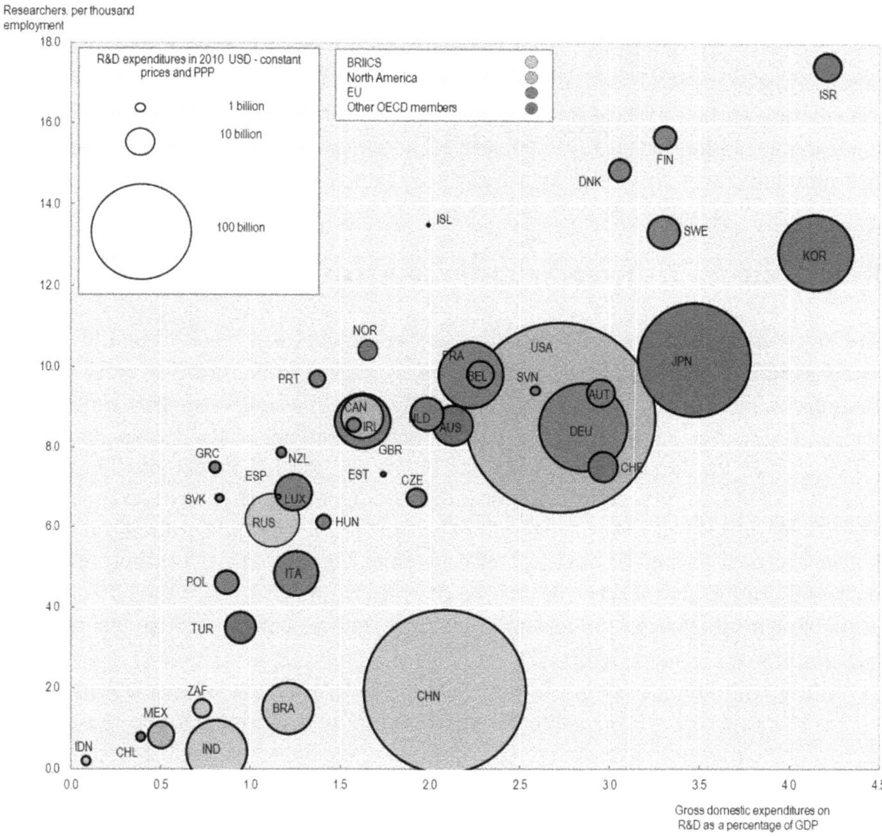

Fig. 9.2 R&D in OECD and key partner countries 2013. (Source: OECD 2015)

countries in terms of the size of their overall R&D expenditure (size of the bubble), R&D expenditure as a proportion of GDP (horizontal axis), and number of researchers per thousand employees (vertical axis) (OECD 2015).

It can be seen from Fig. 9.2 that Israel (ISR) and South Korea (KOR) have the highest R&D expenditures as a proportion of GDP, and Israel has the highest concentration of researchers per thousand employed. Most of the OECD group of countries have similar R&D/GDP and researchers/employed ratios to the United States. For example, Austria (AUT) Australia (AUS), Belgium (BEL), France (FRA), Germany (DEU), Japan (JPN), and Switzerland (CHE). However, their respective gross expenditures on R&D (GERD) vary considerably. By comparison, the newly developing BRICS economies, Brazil (BRA), Russia (RUS), India (IND), China (CHN) and South Africa (ZAF), have relatively lower R&D/GDP and researcher/employed ratios.

According to the OECD (2017) businesses make the largest contribution to investment in R&D, with the majority of countries within its membership getting 60% or more of the total business expenditure on R&D (BERD) sourced from the business sector. This pattern of expenditure has remained fairly constant over the period 2005–2015, but in China and Turkey, the level of BERD has grown significantly. Most of the R&D activity is still found within large firms although SMEs are contributing around 35% of this activity, and such firms also receive about 60% of government funding for R&D, which reflects policy decisions to help foster SME innovation and growth.

9.2.1 Patents, Trademarks and Productivity

Two key measures of innovation are the number of patents located within the *triadic patent families'* database, as a per capita measure, and the number of cross-border trademarks per capita. Triadic patent families are those patents that have been applied for within the three major patents office systems of the European Patent Office (EPO), the Japanese Patent Office (JPO) and the US Patent and Trademark Office (USPTO) to protect the same invention. The global diffusion of an innovation requires IP rights protection in each jurisdiction. The triadic patent family database is a measure of global IP diffusion (Dernis and Khan 2004). Cross-border trademarks offer a further measure of the rate of innovation diffusion at the global level. Unlike patents they serve to measure marketing innovations rather than just technological ones.

A study of triadic patent families and cross-border trademarks undertaken by the OECD shows a clear relationship between economic development and these measures. For example, Switzerland (CHE) has one of the highest scores on both indicators, while India (IND) and Indonesia (IDN) have some of the lowest scores. The OECD group of advanced industrial economies all have high scores in relation to triadic patent families and cross-border trademarks. By comparison the developing economies all have scores that are below the world average (OECD 2010). Figure 9.3 shows these results.

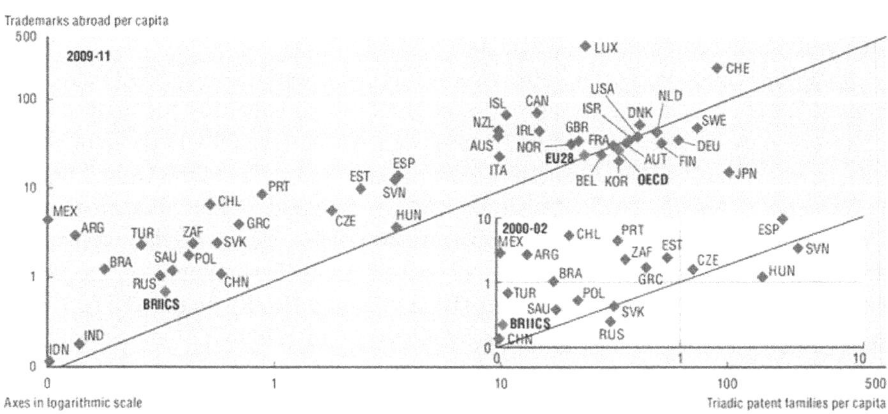

Fig. 9.3 Patents and trademarks per capita, 2002 and 2011 (Average number per million population, OECD and G20 countries). (Source: OECD 2014)

However, it should be noted that many of the patents and trademarks registered internationally are owned by foreign companies who in turn operate via proxy states where they receive more favourable taxation arrangements.

> **For example,** …More than 80% of the technological and product innovations protected in Europe and the United States by top-global R&D investors headquartered in Hong Kong, China, Bermuda, Ireland and the Cayman Islands, are generated by foreign affiliates. The United States and China stand out as the dominant locations of these affiliates. In general, while top-R&D performers rely differently on innovators located abroad, the location of innovative affiliates generating technological, product and service innovations in the United States and Europe are often the same: The United States is the top location, followed by Germany, China and France. (OECD 2015, p. 75)

A study investigating the geographic distribution and activity of the world's leading investors in R&D found that that 65% of these leading companies had their head offices in just four countries, namely the United States, Japan, Germany and the United Kingdom. A further 15% were based in China or Chinese Taipei (Daiko et al. 2017). The most common industries that represent the leading investors in R&D were in information and communications technologies (ICT), followed by pharmaceuticals, machinery, transport equipment and chemicals (Daiko et al. 2017).

9.2.2 Global Collaboration Is Critical

Scientific R&D and technological innovation also involves a high level of international collaboration. For example, nanotechnology or *nanoscience* has emerged as a new multi-disciplinary field involving physics and chemistry. An analysis of scientific publications of jointly authored papers from authors located in different disciplines and geographical locations highlights this. Key *hot research clusters* that were identified in 2008 included particle physics and cosmology, post-genome research, plant science research, research into infectious diseases and immunology, obesity research and nanoscience (OECD 2010).

The United States continues to dominate the global research landscape with the largest number of scientific articles authored or co-authored by researchers from that country. However, other countries are rapidly emerging to challenge this dominance. China is the most significant of these. While China was a small player in the global scientific and R&D community in 1998 with a profile similar to that of Canada or Australia, by 2008 it had grown to be more significant than any other country other than the United States. In fact, there has a been a major shift towards a much greater level of international collaboration and openness in scientific research since the 1990s, and this has grown to include countries such as China and Russia as a result of the ending of the Cold War, and the opening up of greater cultural, scientific and economic exchanges between nations (OECD 2015).

Figure 9.4 shows the network of scientific collaboration that has emerged at a global level over the period from 1996 to 2013. This network represents the flow of scientific research knowledge and collaboration as measured by co-authored

Fig. 9.4 International citation network in science and technology 1996–2013. (Source: OECD 2015)

citations in scientific journals with authors from different countries. It can be seen that the United States remains at the centre of this global network, and this reflects its leadership in many fields of science, as well as the substantial investment that is made by that country in research within universities and other research centres.

As noted by the OECD (2015) in relation to Fig. 9.4,

> **For example,** …The United States is firmly placed at the centre of the international citation network, with a larger number of works in any country citing publications with US-based corresponding authors than vice versa. Citation networks are closely linked to scientific collaboration and mobility networks but the citation network exhibits a more skewed pattern. For example, many China or Germany-based corresponding authors cite US-based authors, whereas few US-based authors cite authors based in China or Germany. This network shows that China has a much smaller size in terms of citations received from abroad than would be implied by its overall publication volume. (OECD 2015, p. 67)

What this OECD data shows is the globalisation of innovation, particularly scientific and technological innovation, as well as the inter-connectivity between countries and research teams. This is important because entrepreneurs or organisations seeking to commercialise radical innovations are going to have to deal directly with a global market from the outset. This will require not only the need to secure access to global markets, but to protect IP rights in multiple jurisdictions and benchmark any new inventions and technology against international best practice. It is an increasingly interconnected world with new players.

9.3 Defining Technological Innovation

The OECD distinguishes conventional innovations from technological innovations. According to this analysis, technological product and process innovation (TPPI) is associated with substantially and objectively measurable new or improved benefits to the customer or associated work methods (OECD 2001). As defined by the OECD:

> A **technological product innovation** is the implementation/commercialisation of a product with improved performance characteristics such as to deliver objectively new or improved services to the consumer.
>
> A **technological process innovation** is the implementation/adoption of new or significantly improved production or delivery methods. It may involve changes in equipment, human resources, working methods, or a combination of these (OECD 2005).

9.4 Evolution of Strategic Technology Management

In an analysis of the evolution of strategic technology management written in the 1980s Ansoff (1987) mapped a transition from a process focused to a strategic focused paradigm. He suggested that the twentieth Century saw a trend from entrepreneurial industry founders – such as Henry Ford (the Ford Motor Company) who were focused on process innovations – to entrepreneurial 'technologist-entrepreneurs' (*technopreneurs*) – such as Bill Gates (Microsoft), Steve Jobs (Apple), Jeff Bezos (Amazon) or Mark Zuckerberg (Facebook).

In the 1900s many of the great firms of the twentieth Century were already in existence, led by their founder entrepreneurs who revolutionised industries through the application of efficient production and distribution systems. The case of Ford Motor Company is a good example. For 60 years, the key focus for such firms was the efficient production of standardised products. Mass production was accelerated during the two world wars as were many advances in technology (e.g. aircraft, pharmaceuticals and radio). These firms were the product of the second Industrial Revolution, which was built on standardisation of products, and mass production efficiencies from the harnessing of electrical power and the internal combustion engine to routine factory labour (Schwab 2016).

However, by the 1960s, the pace of technology was accelerating but so was the level of competition within industries. Firms at this time could be divided into two broadly separate types:

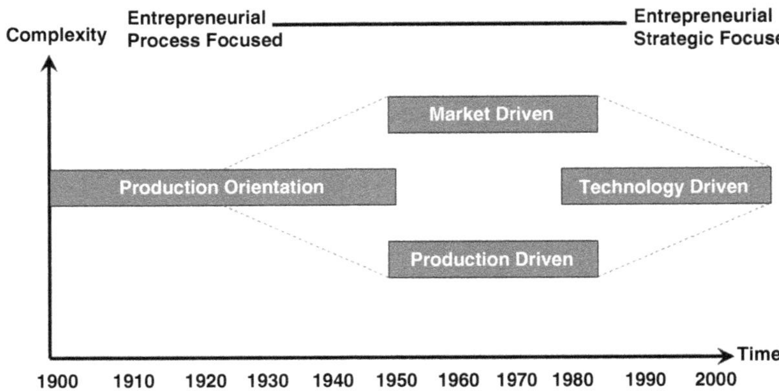

Fig. 9.5 Framework of organisational innovation adoption. (Source: Ansoff 1987)

- *Production driven* – with a key focus on efficiency and cost reduction; and
- *Market driven* – with the primary focus on differentiation of products.

In the first type of firm, production was dominant over marketing, while in the latter this situation was reversed. During the 1980s, the focus shifted to the *technologist-entrepreneur* with technology-driven firms such as CISCO, Microsoft, Intel and Dell emerging (see Fig. 9.5). Even well-established firms were required to focus their resources more on finding technology-driven strategies to maintain their competitive advantage. This was the result of the emergence of the 3rd Industrial Revolution, one driven by electronics, computing and ICTs to drive productivity (Schwab 2016, 2018).

What emerged Ansoff (1987) suggested was a shift from a 'single-function orientation' to a 'multi-function orientation' or *strategic orientation.*

> **For example,** … the influence of a single dominant function is replaced by a balance of functional influences. The power centre shifts from the dominant function to the general management, and the key decision criterion is no longer optimisation of a key function's performance but optimisation of the return on the firm's investment in the marketplace. (Ansoff 1987)

Ansoff (1987) examined the development of industries over the course of the twentieth Century and observed that three types of technology levels exist within most industries. The first type were *low technology* industries, which were characterised by technology that lasted throughout the demand life cycle and where there were relatively low levels of product or technology substitution. The second type were *medium technology* industries, where the basic technology remained unchanged, but products proliferated with numerous incremental differentials designed to achieve competitive advantage. Finally, there were *high technology* industries, in which both the technology was subject to frequent substitution threats and the product proliferation levels were high (Hirsch-Kreinsen et al. 2006).

Firms in the low technology industries usually had little difficulty with the management of technology, but this was not generally the case with their counterparts in the medium and high technology areas. The two main issues that managers must deal with were: (i) product proliferation; and (ii) technology substitution.

In dealing with the first of these, the firm needed to recognise that, products proliferate as new technologies advance, and more success could be obtained by focusing on the needs of the customer or the market, rather than on the technological strengths of the competing product. Customers frequently wanted a pause in the advance of technologies and a consolidation of products to ensure that they offer superior benefits to the market. Firms that continued to pursue new technologies for their own sake risked finding themselves unable to sustain long term market share and profits.

In dealing with the problem of technology substitution, managers were advised to commit to making a continuous search for the sources of new technologies and assess how likely they are to have a significant impact on the firm. As each new technology begins to emerge, the manager should evaluate its usefulness and seek to either acquire it or withdraw from that market in an orderly manner. If the decision is to acquire and remain in the market, investment in the new technology must become a prime concern.

9.5 The Impact of the Fourth Industrial Revolution

Since Ansoff (1987) outlined his ideas about organisational innovation, the world's economy has shifted into what has been identified as a fourth Industrial Revolution or *Industry 4.0* (Kagermann et al. 2013; Schwab 2016, 2018; Liao et al. 2017). This is driven by the convergence of a range of digital technologies based on *Cyber-Physical Systems* (CPS), which comprise physical equipment that is enhanced with computing and ICT to create 'Smart Machines' that can operate within a networked environment. This includes digital connectivity via the *Internet of Things* (IoT), with *artificial intelligence* (AI), *machine learning*, *cloud computing* and *big data* providing support (Xu et al. 2018).

This digital transformation has been forecast to disrupt and transform every industry and most organisation over the course of the next 20 years (Schwab 2016, 2018; WEF 2017). Its impact will be significant on how production systems operate, but also on labour markets and the future of the workforce (Liao et al. 2017). It will also have a profound impact on the nature of commercialisation by disrupting business models, creating new opportunities for innovation, and accelerating the pace of new product development (NPD) and commercialisation (Kagermann et al. 2013; Pereira and Romero 2017).

Some of the likely impacts of this *Industry 4.0* include a disruption to existing business models, with concurrent effects on organisational structure. For example, in manufacturing, it is anticipated that this new technological revolution will lead to much greater geographic decentralisation and dispersal of production facilities, with greater levels of autonomous control by CPS systems able to make predictions and respond more rapidly to externally driven changes in supply or demand conditions than has previously been the case. The nature of products is also likely to change. This will include greater individual customisation rather than mass-produced standardisation. Products will also become more modular and able to be adapted to suit different end user needs, plus they are likely to possess embedded systems that will allow them to be monitored, tracked and then supported in use. Business models will also be impacted, with the potential for much greater integration of customers and suppliers in the value chain. On the positive side this will provide significant levels of productivity, reduced wastage, less work health and safety problems, and value creation for customers. However, on the negative side it will also lead to a significant loss of existing jobs, and require a substantial transformation of the workforce and the organisations that employ them (Pereira and Romero 2017; WEF 2017; Deloitte 2018; Liao et al. 2017).

There is a need for organisations and their managers and employees to understand how the process of commercialisation is changing, and the key drivers of success and failure. This will require investigation in a range of different industry and organisational contexts, and across organisations of varying sizes and complexity. The very nature of how competitiveness is defined, understood and measured are likely to change as a result of the impact of the fourth IR (Liu 2017).

9.6 The Strategic Management of Technology

According to Ansoff (1987), the capability profile required for strategic management of technology is for the CEO of the firm to be an entrepreneur – or at least to possess entrepreneurial tendencies. As such they must be visionary and creative, with the ability to adopt new ideas and take calculated risks. The success model most likely to apply to such firms is to position the business in new opportunity niches where innovations in product or process technologies can secure superior profits and strong market share growth.

Key Elements of Innovation Management

- *Inputs* – people, physical and financial resources, tools.
- *Knowledge management* – idea generation, knowledge repository, and information flows.
- *Innovation strategy* – strategic orientation and leadership.
- *Organisation and culture* – culture and structure.
- *Portfolio management* – risk/return balance, optimisation tool use.
- *Project management* – project efficiency tools, communications and collaboration.
- *Commercialisation* – market research, market testing, marketing and sales.

Source: Adams et al. (2006).

The power within such firms is likely to be concentrated within the general management team surrounding the CEO, but with strong attention being given to market development. This will strengthen the role of marketing and related areas within the firm in relation to production. Rewards in such firms are allocated to those innovations that lead to the development of future profit potential.

Planning is usually the responsibility of the entrepreneur in small firms, but in larger firms the responsibility for strategic planning should be devolved to the managers of individual strategic business units (SBU). Ansoff (1987) suggests the need in medium to larger firms for a "strategic planning system" capable of embracing all elements within the firm. Use of the Kaplan and Norton (1993) balanced scorecard model with adequate links between objectives and measures and budgetary outcomes can assist this process. This seeks to tie together the financial, marketing, HRM, production and innovation objectives in a balanced set of key performance indicators (KPIs) that can be used to guide the activities of the firm.

The key to successful technology management in technology-driven firms is good project management. According to Ansoff (1987), medium and high-technology firms are generally good at project management due to their R&D expertise. They have systems in place to guide the implementation of strategic decisions. Finally, such firms need flexible organisational structures that can respond to dynamic environments and deal with change as a regular part of their activities.

Cooper and Schendel (1976) examined the experience of firms facing threats from new technology. They found that the introduction of new technology did not always totally extinguish existing technologies, and did not always lead to immediate financial returns for those firms that introduced them. Further, firms engaged in more traditional industries that attempted to embrace the new technologies did not generally succeed. Also, of importance was the level of commitment that the firm's senior managers were willing to make to the new technologies.

Autio and Lumme (1998) conducted a study of 392 new technology-based firms (NTBF) in Finland, and found four generic types:

1. *Technology innovators* – those that introduce new generic technologies into existing markets;
2. *Application innovators* – those that apply existing technology in established markets;
3. *Market innovators* – those that develop new product concepts by combining them into existing markets; and
4. *Paradigm innovators* – those that produce new product concepts with completely new technology.

Figure 9.6 illustrates these types. The analysis found that application innovators and technology innovators were the oldest and largest among these four groups of firms. On the other hand, the largest potential for growth was found among market innovators and paradigm innovators. The analysis also suggests that the contention of the market-based approach to research on new, technology-based firms applies particularly well both to application innovators and to market innovators. The trend

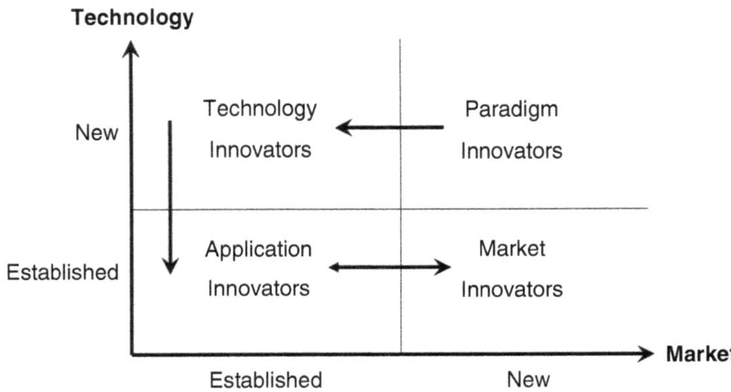

Fig. 9.6 Innovator types for new technology-based firms. (Source: Autio and Lumme 1998)

in technology diffusion between these four generic types of NTBF was found to flow from the paradigm innovators to the technology innovators, then down to the application innovators. Market innovators' ideas also flowed toward the application innovators. Whether a firm is a NTBF or a well-established one, it must recognise product proliferation or technology substitution threats and develop appropriate responses.

9.7 Commercialisation of Disruptive Technologies

While innovation is still relatively unexplored from an academic perspective, the area of commercialisation is even less well understood, but essentially relates to the process of taking an innovation from initial idea to market. It has been likened to the crossing of a gap in which the idea is developed into a prototype or format that can be tested and evaluated by potential investors and customers (ISR 2001). However, the features associated with disruptive technologies and their contexts are worth noting.

According to Christensen et al. (2002), at least six issues are important here. First, the pace of technological change in most industries outstrips the customers' ability to make use of improved versions of a product. Second, higher profit margins can be secured by moving products from lower yield markets to upmarket customer segments that are willing to pay premiums for enhanced innovation. Third, the notion of providing incremental innovations to keep established markets satisfied with established technologies is not a disruptive process, but rather a sustaining one. Fourth, established market players are likely to win if they choose to compete vigorously against new entrants – even if the new entrants launch new technologies. This is due to the stronger level of resources usually available to the established firms. Fifth, disruptive technologies are often attractive to customers that are not themselves attractive to the established market players. This allows the new entrant firm to secure a niche. Sixth, the opportunity for new growth can be found in disruptive technologies due to the lack of interest that is often shown by established firms towards such innovations.

9.7.1 Consider the Readiness of the Market

While the need to consider the customers' views, is frequently the most important issue for a successful commercialisation process, this is not always the case. Where the market is relatively educated to the use of existing technologies and the new product or process is a largely incremental innovation, the adoption and diffusion process is likely to be enhanced through customer feedback. However, where the innovation is highly disruptive or radical in nature, the role of the customer may be quite different. Bower and Christensen (1995) highlight this in their example of the computer hard disk drive industry in the 1980s and 1990s. They point to the lack of interest by established firms in many new, radical innovations because these innovations are initially unattractive and don't meet the direct needs of customers.

Where a new product or process can be readily integrated into the customer's existing systems the adoption rate is likely to be higher than where such compatibility is absent. An innovation that compliments or integrates into the existing technological or market paradigm is referred to as a "Sustaining Technology", while one that challenges the existing status quo is a "Disruptive Technology" (Christensen et al. 2002). For firms seeking to commercialise a disruptive technology there are often significant market entry barriers to overcome. These include the perceived risk and cost of replacing existing systems with the new one, and the opposition that is likely to be mounted by competitor firms who own the existing technologies and who have built up market reputation.

9.7.2 Consider the End User

While the process of selling a new product or service to an organisational buyer is complex enough, the overall success of the adoption and diffusion process may ultimately rest with the individual end user. Companies that adopt a new technology will do so based on the premise that it will benefit either their employees or customers or both. This highlights the need for close attention to be given during the market assessment process of how the end user behaves and how the new technology can benefit them. Ease of use and perceived benefits from the use of the technology need to be considered.

Within large organisations employees should be provided with adequate training and support to ensure that they don't abandon the new technology because they find it too difficult to use. The innovator firm that is selling their new product or process to an organisational buyer needs to research the way the end user will use the new system and ensure that it is configured to make adoption easy, and that there are no peer group prejudices likely to work against adoption. Trade Unions have often served as blocks to the adoption of new technologies out of concern over loss of jobs, or erosion of conditions. However, if the new technology is found to be too complex to learn or operate the end user is likely to reject it regardless of any benefits it might otherwise offer.

9.7.3 Beware Existing Market Players

Innovator firms with disruptive technologies should be cautioned that their pathway may be blocked by established market players who will react negatively to the introduction of the new product or process. This opposition can come from the suppliers of the rival products, as well as those firms that supply to them, and even third-party actors that may have a vested interest in maintaining the status quo. A small innovator firm seeking to penetrate the market will normally fail against a well-established market player if the latter decides to defend its market share (Christensen et al. 2002).

9.7.4 Look for Market Gaps

The innovator firm seeking to promote its disruptive technology should avoid taking on well entrenched competitors on their own ground. For small firms a toe-to-toe battle on these conditions is likely to have only one outcome; the destruction of the smaller player. A better strategy is to look for market gaps where the new technology can find a niche and gain a foothold. As Christensen et al. (2002) point out: "disruptive technologies are often attractive to customers that are not themselves attractive to the established market players". This allows the new entrant to secure a niche with these customers that are not being well served by the status quo. Further, if the existing market players are not interested in chasing such customers, it is possible for the smaller firm to build a strong beachhead in the market by targeting these customer segments.

To illustrate the ability to look for market gaps we can take the case of soft drink manufacturer 'Red Bull'. It would have had little chance to compete directly with Coca Cola or Pepsi for dominance in the soft drinks market had it simply played by the same rules as these market giants. However, by finding a niche entry point and offering a solution that filled a market gap, Red Bull was able to exploit an opportunity. Even its early marketing strategy was innovative and avoided taking on the major incumbents on equal terms which would have not been feasible for the company at that early stage.

Case Study – How Red Bull Built Its Brand

The new wave soft drink manufacturer Red Bull illustrates the way a new product can enter a niche in the market and secure a foothold in the face of well entrenched competition. Although the soft drinks market is dominated by the likes of Coca Cola and Pepsi the up-start Red Bull was able to secure a significant market share by targeting customer segments not well served by the established players.

Launched in Europe in 1987, Red Bull was the brainchild of Dietrich Mateschitz an Austrian businessman who first identified the product in Thailand. The key target customer for Red Bull in its early years were sports people who found the energy drink gave them a useful boost to assist their training. They also targeted fire fighters and construction workers, but the real breakthrough was in the trendy night club scene. Young urban workers who go to night clubs found the non-alcoholic Red Bull a good substitute for traditional drinks. Red Bull's mix of caffeine (80 mgs per can), B vitamins and taurine, plus its sweet lemony taste, were a welcome substitute for coffee and the ubiquitous Coke or Pepsi. For young trendy consumers the cola drinks were viewed as lacking the necessary image of "cool" and were too easily associated with the mainstream.

In targeting this younger demographic Red Bull has sought to build an image around its product of being "cool" and different. Its smaller sized cans sell at a premium price but reflect a more sophisticated image. The company launched into the U.S. market in 1997 targeting the San Francisco Bay Area, which is noted for its willingness to adopt new ideas and experiment with them. A process of "viral" marketing was used in which company representatives targeted trendy clubs and sports centres, sold to local opinion leaders and left them to promote the product word of mouth. In recent years Red Bull has sponsored extreme sports to reinforce its image. In 2001 the Red Bull company had 70% of the US energy drinks market with annuals sales of around US $140 million.

Source: Noonan (2001).

9.8 Steps to Developing Disruptive Technologies

According to Bower and Christensen (1995), the process of spotting and cultivating disruptive technologies involves five distinct steps. The first is the ability to screen the disruptive technologies from among the field of emerging new ideas. They suggest that the engineering or technical people within a large organisation are more likely to spot the next wave of technologies than the finance or marketing staff. The second step is to adequately define the significance of the disruptive technology.

Figure 9.7 illustrates how this process can work. It commences with a review of the expected performance curve of existing technologies and the trend in customer expectations over such performance growth. The new technology is then assessed in

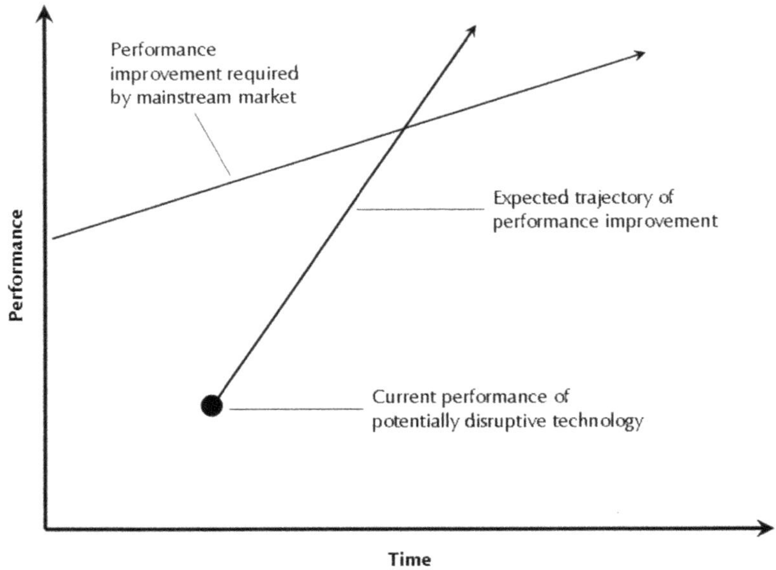

Fig. 9.7 How to assess disruptive technologies. (Source: Bower and Christensen 1995)

terms of its anticipated trajectory; if it is likely to move faster than the market's expectations, it may be worthy of consideration. What is important is not that the new innovation is currently superior to that of existing technologies, but that its capacity for future improvement is likely to be greater. Once again, this is more likely to be determined by the technologist than the marketer or financier.

Having decided that the new technology has the potential for disruption, the third stage outlined by Bower and Christensen (1995) is to find a market that can adopt the innovation. Once again, the traditional marketing approaches are not thought to be much use. This is because customers don't really know how to respond to the new opportunity, and when asked to comment on a new radical innovation they find it difficult to know how to evaluate it. This may require the company to undertake a process of creating new markets (Kim and Mauborgne 1999). While easy to acknowledge, this is often a much harder process to achieve – unless there is an equally radical and innovative marketing strategy associated with the new technology.

The next step in the development process is to locate the responsibility for the new innovation in a small, independent organisation (Bower and Christensen 1995). This need to establish a new 'spin out' firm to champion the disruptive technology is driven by the recognition that radical ideas that target new markets may be treated by the established organisation as too unimportant or unusual to warrant support from managers.

According to Bower and Christensen (1995), the need to keep new disruptive technology in the hands of small, independent teams rather than those of larger and more bureaucratic organisations is important to the development process. As they state in their paper,

> … The key to prospering at points of disruptive change is not simply to take more risks, invest for the long term or fight bureaucracy. The key is to manage strategically important disruptive technologies in an organisational context where small orders create energy, where fast low-cost forays into ill-defined markets are possible, and where overhead is low enough to permit profit even in emerging markets. (Bower and Christensen 1995)

An example of this need to create a spin-out and keep the innovation within a small, entrepreneurial team when seeking to develop disruptive technology in large organisations can be illustrated by the case of Japan's NTT DoCoMo and the development of the G3 telecommunications network.

9.9 How NTT DoCoMo Created Japan's G3 Network

When Japanese telecommunications giant NTT-DoCoMo needed to develop its new third generation mobile telephone system, it created an entirely new organisation GBD and gave it responsibility for developing the new product (Kodama 2002).

As shown in Fig. 9.8, the parent firm NTT-DoCoMo was an organisation of 10,625 employees with a culture focused on deliberate strategy and incremental

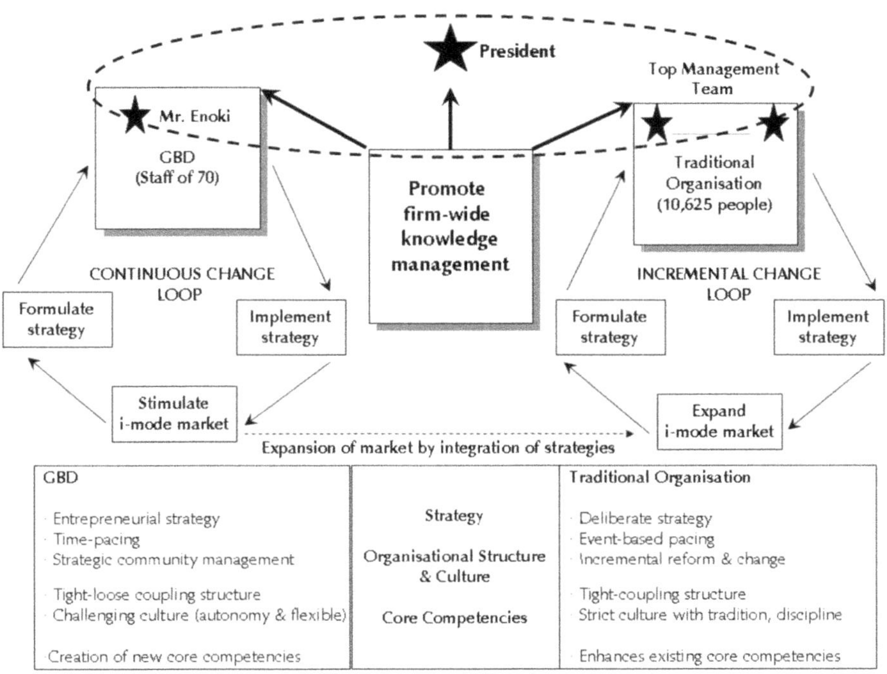

Fig. 9.8 How NTT-DoCoMo developed GBD. (Source: Kodama 2002)

change. It had quite formal systems, and was driven by efficiency and slow change. By contrast, GBD was a small unit of only 70 people and was led by a dynamic and entrepreneurial manager, Mr. Enoki. This business was tasked with creating the new I-Mode system. It adopted a fast-paced, innovation intensive culture that was concerned with the future. Importantly, GBD was strongly supported by the top management of the parent company, and was able to leverage the resources of that organisation (Kodama 2002).

The parent firm NTT DoCoMo was a traditional organisation that followed deliberate strategy and an 'event-based' system of production with incremental reforms and changes. Its culture was one of continuous improvement of the existing technology. This had the strengths of good discipline, excellent implementation skills and strong core competencies in traditional or established fields. However, it was less able to engage in rapid development of radical new technologies and technology platforms.

By contrast the spin-out firm GBD was nimble and entrepreneurial in its approach to strategy. It followed a time-paced production process and was engaged in what has been described as 'continuous loop' R&D where the ideas for a new design are introduced, evaluated and market feedback received, tested and a new prototype or design produced before commencing the cycle again.

While NTT DoCoMo was committed to the development and enhancement of existing core competencies, GBD was committed to the creation of entirely new competencies. Its objective was to design the future 3G, I-Mode system and essentially the entire 3G market for Japan.

One of the tasks GBD had to undertake was to build a strong network of links – both within its parent organisation and with key groups outside in areas critical to development of the new technology. As shown in Fig. 9.9, at least four key

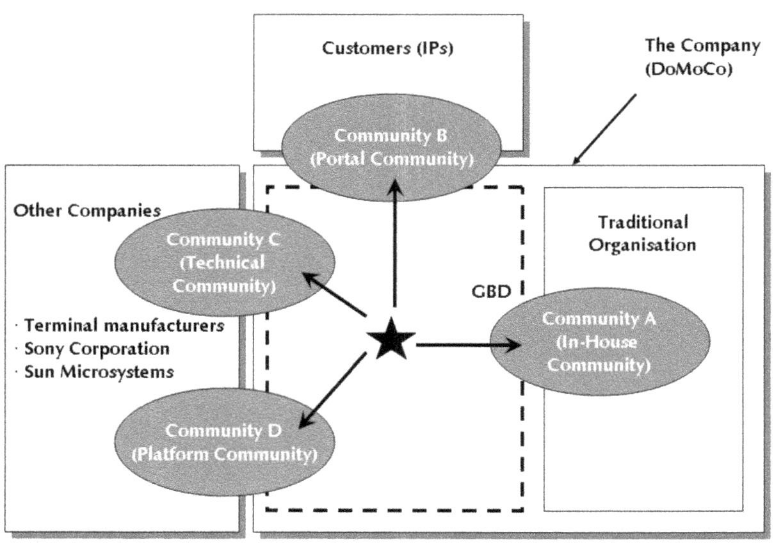

Fig. 9.9 How GBD developed I-Mode. (Source: Kodama 2002)

communities of practice were created by GBD in this development process: (i) an in-house community within the parent company; (ii) a portal community among the ISPs; (iii) a technical community, within the manufacturers and designers in hardware and software; and (iv) a platform community within the manufacturers of computer terminals such as Sony Corporation and Sun Microsystems.

Each community offered GBD and NTT-DoCoMo resources, complementary skills, technologies and ideas (Kodama 2002). What this case study illustrates is not only the value of creating a flexible, ambidextrous organisational structure, but the need to use strategic alliances and partnerships to successfully develop a radical innovation. The creation of a new, more flexible and innovative organisation is therefore a potentially useful means of commercialising a disruptive technology.

9.10 Strategies for Disruptive Technologies

Christensen et al. (2002) suggest that strategies that disrupt by creating new market opportunities for new customers should meet three critical tests:

1. Do the innovation target customers who in the past haven't been able to do it themselves' for lack of money or skills?
2. Is the innovation aimed at customers who will welcome a simple product?
3. Will the innovation help customers do, more easily and effectively, what they are already trying to do?

They point to examples of how firms that have attempted to launch new radical technologies have failed to pass all or some of these tests. It is important to find the market niche where customers have had a problem working within the established industry paradigm. Offering solutions that customers can quickly adopt using the new technology is important to facilitate diffusion into the market. It is to avoid excessive complexity that simplicity is maintained in the new product during its early market entry. Innovation adoption and diffusion can be adversely influenced by such complexity, making the technology too difficult to use or evaluate by prospective customers (Rogers 1995).

In seeking to develop strategies for disruptive technologies, it is considered important to screen them using two additional tests. The first relates to whether or not existing products are good enough, and whether the disruptive technology is substantially better. If existing technologies can continue to be improved and customers will continue to pay a premium to established market players for new incremental improvements, the opportunities for disruptive technologies are likely to be low.

The second test of strategy relates to whether or not it is possible for a new business model to be developed. This is often achieved by offering attractive new products or services at the lower end of the market. However, the success of such a strategy is likely to depend on the ability to develop a new business model that allows good profit margin to be secured while offering customers lower costs or enhanced value for the same price (Christensen et al. 2002).

9.11 Market Adoption of Technological Innovation

The ability for any new technology to be brought to market quickly is likely to be contingent on the process of innovation adoption and diffusion (Rogers 1995). The process of innovation adoption and diffusion is fraught with many problems for new products or services seeking to gain access to markets. For the disruptive or radical technologies, the ease of market acceptance is more complex because customers are generally not able to evaluate new innovation and have little or no experience to draw upon or compare against when examining such technologies.

An analysis by Frambach and Schillewaert (2002) has suggested two interconnected frameworks that seek to explain the organisational and individual level processes associated with the adoption of innovation. Figure 9.10 illustrates the framework as it applies to the organisational adoption process. As this diagram shows, the factors likely to influence the readiness of an organisation to adopt a new innovation are the lobbying or marketing effects of the supplier organisation, and the role of both social and environmental influences that might include the social networking of senior managers or the adoption by competitors of similar or competitive technologies. Such influencing factors do not directly determine whether or not a new innovation is adopted. These are frequently filtered through the organisation's considerations of the innovation in terms of the main criteria associated with the adoption of innovation that were originally identified by Rogers (1995). What is also likely to impact the adoption decision are characteristics of the adopter organisation that relate to its size and industry dynamics.

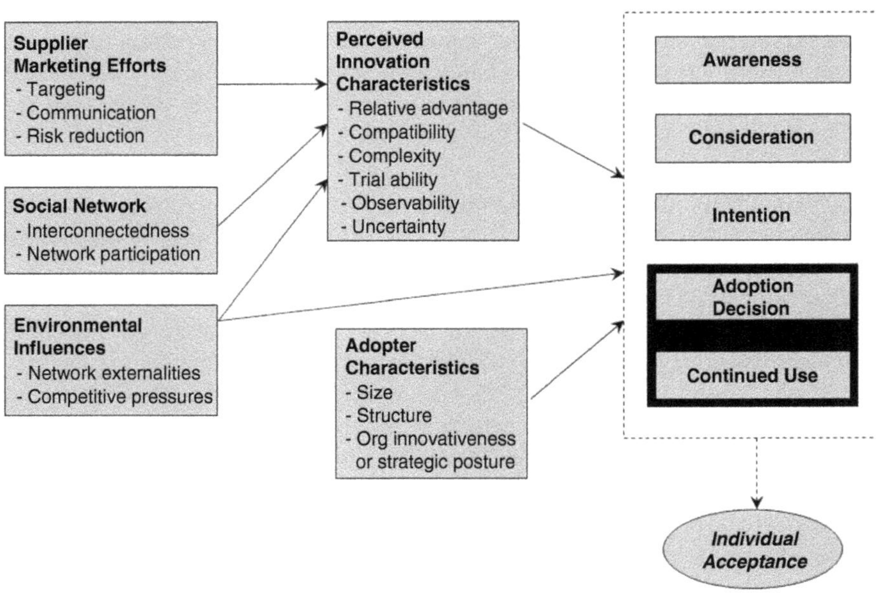

Fig. 9.10 Framework of organisational innovation adoption. (Source: Frambach and Schillewaert 2002)

The actual adoption process is passed through a process of initial awareness of the innovation, consideration of its merits, an intention to adopt, the adoption decision process, and usage behaviour over time. Individual acceptance within the organisation is a secondary outcome, as the employees or customers associated with the organisation are usually the last group to make a decision relating to the technology.

For individual adoption behaviour, the process is slightly different according to Frambach and Schillewaert (2002). As shown in Fig. 9.11, the individual is often influenced by organisational facilitators or internal marketing efforts designed to promote the innovation among the organisation's staff. Also, likely to have an influence on individual adoption behaviour are the personal characteristics of the people who are to adopt the innovation. If individuals have a predisposition to accept new innovations or social milieu that support the adoption of new technologies, they are likely to more readily accept the new innovation than if this is not the case.

All these influences – whether organisational or individual in nature – are important to the issue of technology acceptance and adoption. For any technology such influences are important, but for disruptive technologies these factors may play an even more critical role. By their nature, disruptive or radical technologies are often difficult to evaluate as a customer and may carry with them a higher level of risk due to their newness. They are not necessarily highly complex in nature, but are generally not compatible with the existing technologies in use by the market. As such they may not be able to readily meet the perceived innovation characteristics that are typically considered important for adoption (Rogers 1995).

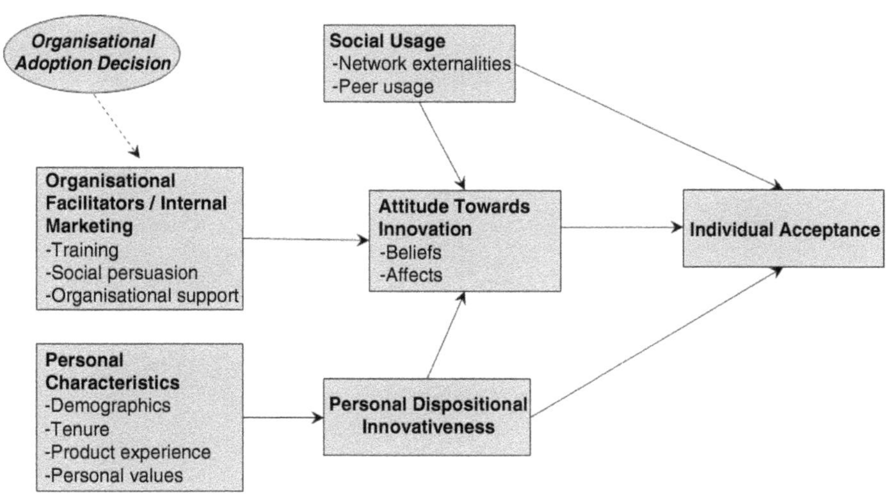

Fig. 9.11 A framework of individual innovation acceptance in organisations. (Source: Frambach and Schillewaert 2002)

9.12 Creating New Market Space

Disruptive technologies, by nature, are unlikely to respond to traditional marketing approaches. Where no pre-existing market can be found for a new product or service, the challenge for marketing is to create the market using selective strategies designed to gain the most cost-effective market diffusion pathway. Kim and Mauborgne (1999) discuss the process of creating new market space, and use a variety of illustrations from retail hardware to make their case.

According to Kim and Mauborgne (1999), the process of creating new market value is to analyse the existing market structure and ask a series of key questions. Figure 9.12 illustrates their suggested approach. Four criteria need to be considered relating to what should be *raised*, reduced, created and eliminated. The issue of what should be raised relates to the gaps that are currently to be found within the existing product/market offerings and what the company might offer that would raise value for customers. The issue of *reducing* below industry standards reflects the tendency for many product or service offerings to be overly-complex and expensive when first introduced.

9.12.1 Blue Ocean Versus Red Ocean Strategy

Kim and Mauborgne (2004, 2005) have described this strategy of seeking to create new value as a *Blue Ocean Strategy*, as opposed to the *Red Ocean Strategy* where firms are competing directly one with another. However, as outlined in Table 9.1, this head-to-head competition is not necessary.

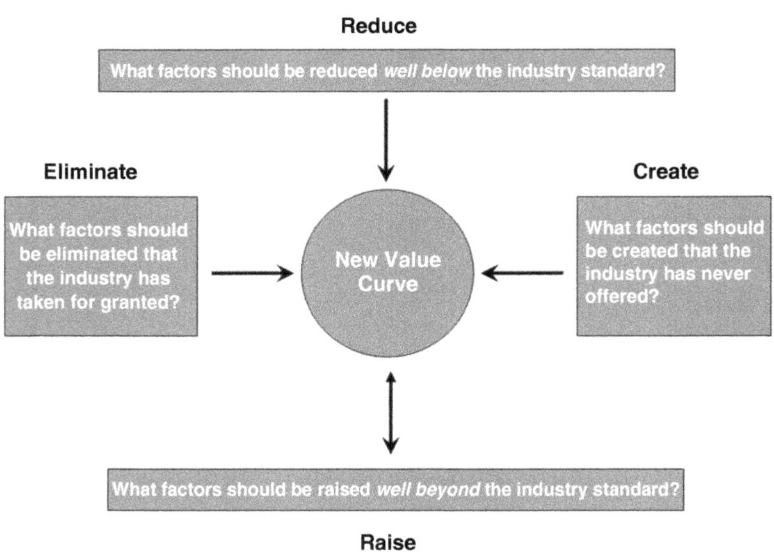

Fig. 9.12 Creating new market value. (Source: Kim and Mauborgne 1999)

Table 9.1 Red Ocean versus Blue Ocean strategy

Red Ocean strategy	Blue Ocean strategy
Compete in existing market space	Create uncontested market space
Beat the competition	Make competition irrelevant
Exploit existing demand	Create and capture new demand
Make the value/cost trade-off	Break the value/cost trade-off
Align the whole system of a company's activities with its strategic choice of differentiation *or* low cost	Align the whole system of a company's activities in pursuit of differentiation *and* low cost

Source: Kim and Mauborgne (2004)

The foundation principle of *Blue Ocean* strategy is to think differently to where the incumbent market and competition is operating within the target industry. Rather than the binary trade-off of *differentiation or cost leadership* as strategic positioning options, and use disruptive innovation to launch new business models that can offer both *differentiation and cost leadership.*

> **For example,** … Quicken accounting software's primary substitution threat was not alternative software for accountants, but the humble pencil. Quicken found a way to raise the speed and accuracy of their product above that of the pencil while lowering the complexity of the accounting software along with the cost, and thereby offering customers a better value option.

9.12.2 Value Innovation

Creation and elimination of features relates to the need for a new product or service offering to consider what can be trimmed out of the business model to lower cost and shift the offering to a new area not being addressed by the existing business paradigm. According to Kim and Mauborgne (2004) the *Blue Ocean* opportunity lies in the common space between the decrease of costs and the enhancement of the buyer's value. This is illustrated in Fig. 9.13.

The creation of *value innovation* requires the development of strategies for the creation of new market space that examines opportunities across six key areas (Kim and Mauborgne 1999):

1. *The industry*, in which the firm is operating;
2. *The strategic group*, from within the firm (assuming a large company);
3. *The buyer group*, or customers of the firm;
4. *The scope of product/service offerings*, with a view to creating a strong customer value proposition;
5. *The 'functional-emotional' issues at work within the industry*, or how the industry culture and practices operate – the "rules of the game"; and
6. *Time*, or what is the anticipated market window of opportunity?

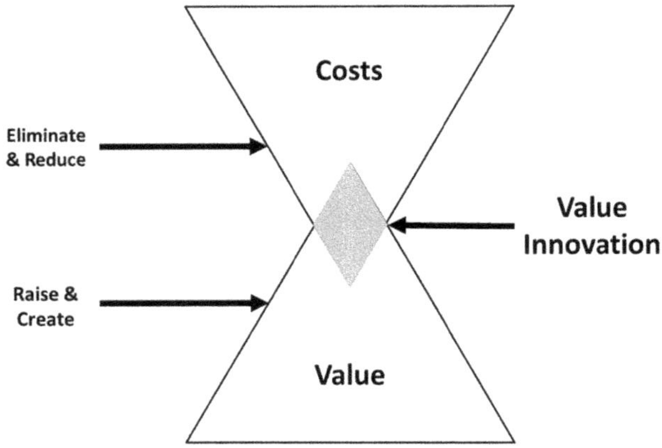

Fig. 9.13 Value innovation in a *Blue Ocean* strategy. (Source: Kim and Mauborgne 2004)

9.12.3 Creating New Market Space

These six areas are outlined in Fig. 9.14 along with a comparison of the factors important to shifting from *Red Ocean* head-to-head competition to *Blue Ocean* creation of new market space with value innovation.

- Industry

Conventional head-to-head competition focuses on taking competitors on directly within these six areas – more or less within the established paradigms set by

The conventional boundaries of competition	Head to Head Competition		Creating new market space
Industry	Focuses on rivalry within its industry	→	Looks across substitute industries
Strategic group	Focuses on competitive position within strategic group	→	Looks across strategic groups within its industry
Buyer group	Focuses on better serving the buyer group	→	Redefines the buyer group of the industry
Scope of product & service offerings	Focuses on maximizing the value of product and service offerings within the bounds of its industry	→	Looks across to complimentary product and service offerings that go beyond the bounds of its industry
Functional emotional orientation of an industry	Focuses on improving price – performance in line with the functional – emotional orientation of its industry	→	Rethinks the functional – emotional orientation of its industry
Time	Focuses on adapting to external trends as they occur.	→	Participates in shaping external trends over time.

Fig. 9.14 Strategies for creating new market value. (Source: Kim and Mauborgne 1999)

the industry. By contrast, the new market creation approach is more innovative. This seeks to look at industry structure with a view to finding ways to substitute rather than compete directly.

For example, … Low cost airfares are not a direct competitor to existing airline services, but rather are a substitute for driving your own car or taking a train.

- Strategic Groups

Shifting competition *across* strategic groups is a reference to the tendency of most industries to generate a small number of firms that compete directly with each other along almost identical lines. Banking is a good example. All the major banks in Australia (there are essentially four) look and act the same. A financial service provider that can offer banking services (e.g. competitive loans and access to credit) via a different business model would succeed if it were prepared to break out of the established banking paradigm.

- Buyers

The process of redefining the buyers within the market refers to the desire to look closely at the marketing channel and to decide who the end-user is and where the final decision-making power is to be found. Direct selling over the internet by Dell to the end-user rather than via a wholesaler or retailer was a major – and successful – rethinking of that business paradigm.

- Scope of Products and Services

Complementary products and services are those that offer the ability to be used in conjunction with those of your own business and which provide synergies (Brandenburger and Nalebuff 1995). Finding ways to link your product or service to another industry sector or enabling technology can significantly assist the diffusion of the new innovation.

- Functional Emotional Orientation of Industry

Also important is the ability to understand the functional-emotional orientation of the industry. This refers to the ability to tap into the psyche of the market and build a brand image around the product that is less concerned with practical or functional issues and more focused on style and image. For example, Starbucks and their ability to transform coffee from a commodity into a lifestyle issue.

- Time

Finally, there is the issue of time and the ability of the firm to adapt to the market's readiness to adopt an innovation and leading the market by shaping the pace of technology. This was illustrated by the case of NTT DoCoMo in building the I-Mode G3 mobile telecommunications system in Japan. GBD was driven by a 'time-paced' strategy. Thornke and von Hippel (2002) suggest that the process of developing new product/market combinations can be secured by getting customers to collaborate in the new product development process. Their suggested process involves the creation of user-friendly 'tool kits' that allow the customer to adapt the product to suit their specific needs, and to join with the supplier firm in the innovation process associated with the product's development. This requires a high level of flexibility in the production process of the innovator firm and the careful selection of the firm's customers. Such customers need to be prepared to partner with the innovator firm and to provide the necessary feedback required to undertake the new product development. This is supported by research into the relationship between innovation and the performance of small firms has highlighted the need for a systematic approach to be taken that is more than just investment in R&D, but also considers the need for management and marketing strategies and the need for establishing strategic alliances with other firms that can assist in the commercialisation process (Kemp et al. 2003).

9.13 New Product Development and Commercialisation

The process of bringing an innovative idea to market involves working through a new product development (NPD) process. This can take a variety of forms, but typically new product development moves through a variety of stages, as shown in Fig. 9.15.

The new product development (NPD) process involves three distinct phases. Phase 1 commences with an initial idea generation and screening of the concept prior to any future development. In phase 2, the process begins to take two separate but mutual supporting pathways – one technical in nature and the other focusing on

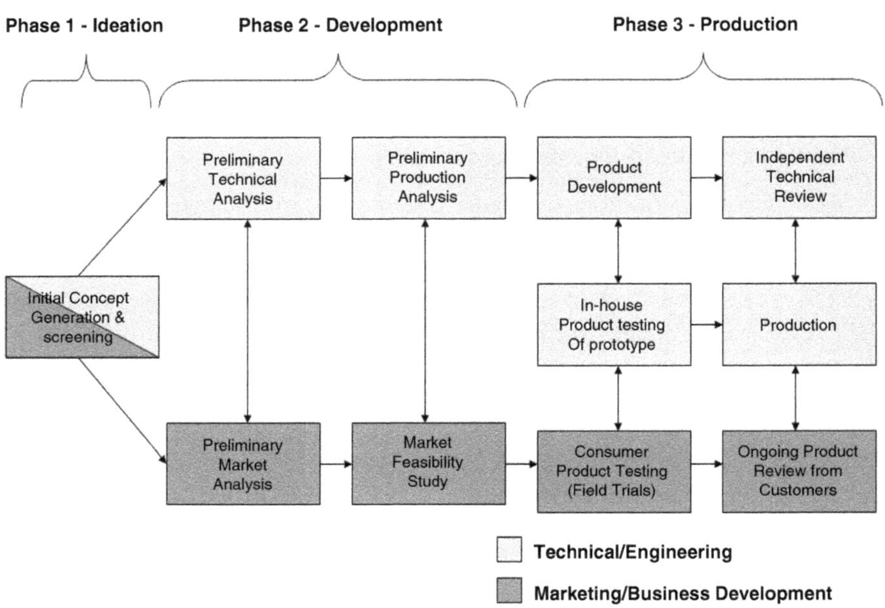

Fig. 9.15 New product development process model

marketing and business development. Looking at the technical pathway, the key stages include a preliminary technical analysis to determine if the innovation will work, and a preliminary assessment of the production costs associated with the new idea. These two stages can typically be undertaken simultaneously.

Parallel with this technical development is the market development process. As the initial technical and production analysis is being undertaken, it is necessary to also conduct a market analysis and feasibility study. This examines the likely adoption of the new innovation by the market, and what pricing and competitor issues are likely to be faced. If the market assessment suggests that the innovation is unlikely to return satisfactory market growth or profitability, the product will need to be questioned regardless of its technical development.

Phase 3 involves the production of the new product and its eventual market development process. If the technical and production feasibility assessments suggest that the product is worthy of future development, the process can move to the next stage of product development with prototypes being produced. These will need to be independently tested prior to full scale production. Simultaneously, the new product should be tested in the market via field trials and ongoing customer reviews designed to evaluate the merits of early stage prototypes.

Research studies suggest that Australian small firms are generally very good at the creation of new ideas and the preliminary technical assessments and production analysis required in the development phase. If the product is moved to the third phase, small firms can also deal with in-house product development processes. However, it is in the area of market analysis and feasibility studies and market testing during the production phase that most small firms face problems. These same firms are also generally poor at handling pre-commercialisation financial analysis. Performance in terms of successful commercialisation outcomes was also associated with both technical and market development processes and the presence of a formal system of new product development (Huang et al. 2002).

The process of new product development is therefore a holistic one that requires attention to both the market and technical development issues. Determining which innovations are selected for future development requires a systematic screening process that is flexible, able to consider the market environment, and its readiness to adopt the new innovation. Market testing and evaluation should also be an ongoing or continuous process that sees the firm closely engaged with its leading customers to ensure that the final product package is tailored to their needs. There should be a high degree of openness within the firm in its selection or rejection of new product ideas, regardless of the time it may have taken to generate the prototypes. A strong focus should also be put on learning and implementation to ensure that the lessons of unsuccessful product initiatives are not lost and to allow for adequate planning and preparation of the more complex phase of market development. Finally, the system used to screen and select a new product should be developed into a system and taught to all members of the team (Ozer 2004).

9.14 The Stage-Gate® Process

Numerous research efforts have been undertaken to examine and understand the factors that make new product development successful. What has emerged from this research is the *Stage-Gate®* process of NPD (Cooper and Edgett 2005). This is a systematic *step-wise* approach to the management of NPD, but also of the risk associated with commercialisation of an innovation. At its foundation is a recognition of the importance of *absorptive capacity* and the need for the firm to learn as quickly as possible how to identify customer or market needs, generate prototypes and develop them for successful commercialisation. The *Stage-Gate®* process emerged from academic research undertaken in the 1970s and 1980s by Robert Cooper, Scott Edgett and Elko Kleinschmidt. This examined the NPD and commercialisation practices of hundreds of large firms and then developed best practice benchmarks (Cooper et al. 2004a, b, c).

There are seven foundation principles of *Stage-Gate®*, which are illustrated in Fig. 9.16.

1. *Customer Focused;* The NPD process must be focused on the needs of the customer with the ability to offer a *value proposition.*
2. *Front-end loaded;* Attention must be given in the initial stages to understanding the needs of the customer and the market, investigating and discovering unmet

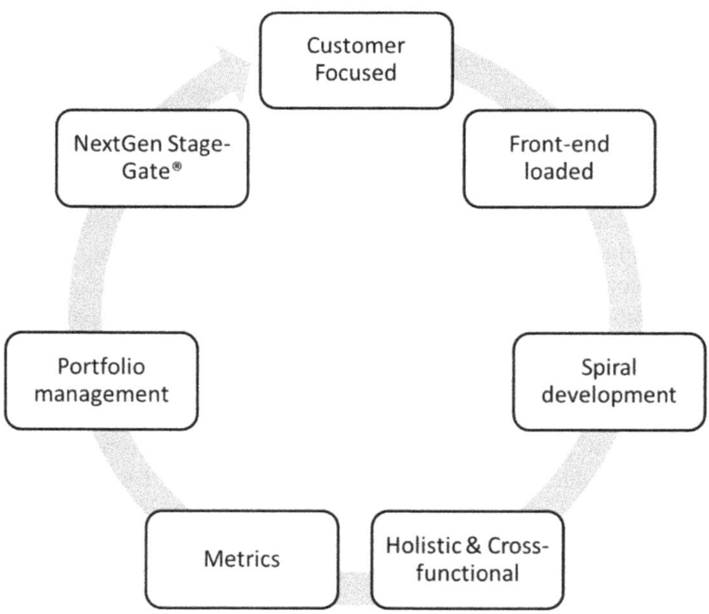

Fig. 9.16 The 7 principles of lean, rapid and profitable NPD. (Source: adapted from Cooper and Edgett 2005)

needs, problems, gaps and areas for opportunity. This equates to the *Fuzzy Front End* (FFE) concept outlined above.
3. *Spiral Development;* The feedback from the customer or market must be developed into prototypes or initial product offers that can be tested and evaluated. It is a process of iterative loops or *spiral loops* that may continue until a winning solution is generated or the project is killed.
4. *Holistic and cross-functional teams;* The most successful approach to NPD and commercialisation is to integrate all aspects of the business (i.e. marketing, sales, R&D, operations, finance etc.) so that there is strong engagement in the project by all parts of the company. This is generally common in small firms, but requires careful management in larger ones.
5. *Metrics;* As the process unfolds it is essential that good data is kept and used to help make decisions. This can include market research, sales, adoption and retention rates, product performance, production costs and returns to investment at all stages of the cycle. The data should allow the management team to make "GO/KILL" decisions and adjustments as the project develops.
6. *Portfolio management:* Firms that are strongly committed to innovation, particularly large companies, will have a number of NPD projects taking place at any time. Each project must be examined to ensure that it is making the desired progress through the system. As resources will always be finite and scarce, decisions will need to be made over which projects to invest in, which to suspend and which to kill.
7. *Stage-Gate® process:* The operational system to help implement these principles is a *"lean, scalable and adaptable process"*, which has emerged as *Stage-Gate®*. However, as we will show later, there are other systems that offer similar approaches such as *Lean Start-Up* (Ries 2011).

9.14.1 Spiral Development Via Stages and Gates

As shown in Fig. 9.17, the *Stage-Gate®* process involves the movement of the innovation through a series of *stages* and *gates* where "GO/KILL" decisions are made once the initial FFE stage is completed. The number of stages and gates is dependent on the type of project being commercialised and the complexity of the underlying technology. However, in broad terms the process involves a series of iterations or loops (pivots), that follow the process of *build-test-obtain feedback-revise* (Cooper 2006). These stages are briefly discussed below, but it is important to note that this process is essentially the application of the *absorptive capacity* process described earlier.

> **For example,** … The innovation process can be visualized as a series of stages, with each stage comprised of a set of required or recommended best-practice activities needed to progress the project to the next gate or decision point…Each stage is designed to gather information to reduce key project uncertainties and risks; the information requirements thus define the purpose of each of the stages in the process. (Cooper 2008, p. 3)

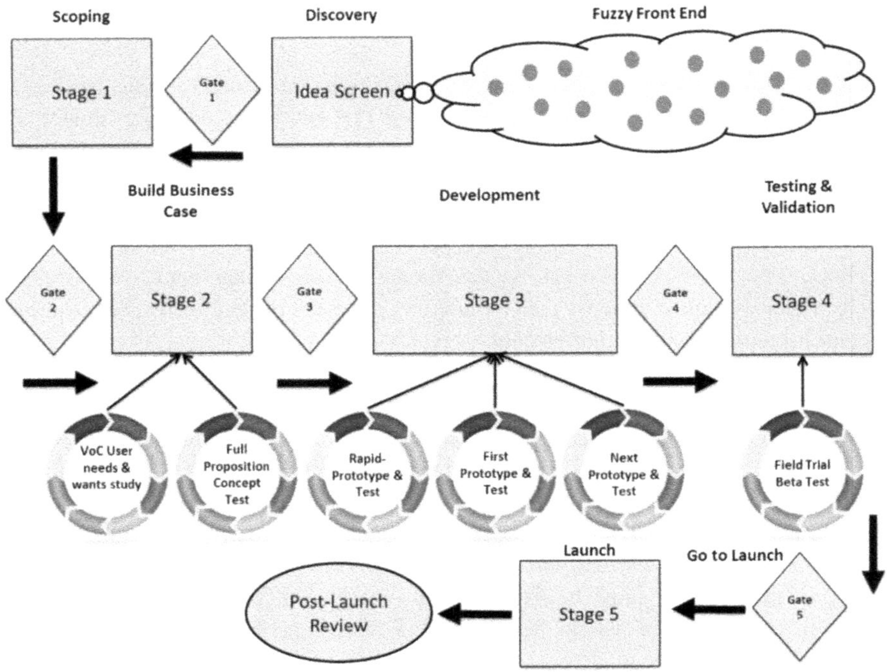

Fig. 9.17 The *Stage-Gate*® process of spiral development. (Source: adapted from Cooper and Edgett 2005)

- Stage 1: Project Scoping

The outcome from the initial *Fuzzy Front End* (FFE) *discovery* process should result in the generation of sufficient information to undertake an assessment of the project and whether it is ready to move forward. This should involve a preliminary market, technical and financial analysis to assess the viability of the business model. Recommendations for future action (i.e. "GO/KILL/HOLD/RECYCLE") can then be made.

- Stage 2: Build the Business Case

One of the most important stages is the *building of the business case*, which usually involves the ability to *listen to the voice of the customer* (VOC), and obtain solid market information and an understanding of customer needs and wants. This enables the development of a clear early *product definition*, which can be further developed into a full proposition and concept for testing. Key issues that should be considered here are the development of a product definition that helps to build clear business model for the innovation. This should clarify what is to be developed as well as making a case for why this project should receive further investment. It should also generate an action plan or *product roadmap* that outlines how the NPD and commercialisation process is likely to unfold.

- Stages 3, 4 and 5: Development, Testing and Validation and Launch

The *Stage-Gate®* process typically has five stages (although this can be modified). In addition to the first two stages described above, the final three stages involve product development, product testing and validation, and product launch. Each stage moves the project through a series of development cycles with gates that can result in "GO/KILL/HOLD/RECYCLE" outcomes depending on the key performance indicates (KPI) or progress hurdles that the management team has set (Cooper and Kleinschmidt 1993). These should progress all the way to launch and post-launch review.

9.14.2 Criticism of Stage-Gate®

The criticism of *Stage-Gate®* is that it is too rigid and may see potentially valuable, but highly innovative and entrepreneurial projects killed before they have been fully assessed (Shepherd and Patzelt 2017). Concern has also been expressed that *Stage-Gate®* serves as a restriction on learning and is therefore an impediment to *absorptive capacity* (Sethi and Iqbal 2008). However, Cooper (2006) argues that *Stage-Gate®* is significantly more flexible and adaptable with much greater recognition of the needs facing smaller companies.

> **For example,** ... Don't confuse Stage-Gate of the twenty-first century with the traditional "phased review" process of the 1960s–80s...By contrast, today's Stage-Gate system is built for speed. The stages are cross-functional, and not dominated by a single functional area: This is a business process, not an R&D or Marketing process. (Cooper 2008, p. 4)

According to Cooper (2008) *Stage-Gate®* is not a functional, phased review process, a rigid "lock-step" process, a linear system, nor a project control mechanism. It is also not stagnant, bureaucratic or totally data-driven. He suggests that the process of gatekeeping is one of the critical areas for attention. Projects should not be allowed to bypass gates, but there should be engagement from project owners and gatekeepers at any meetings, with decisions to "GO/KILL/HOLD/RECYCLE" based on valid, objective data, *"facts, not emotion and gut feel!"* (Cooper 2008 p. 8).

Since its introduction in the 1980s *Stage-Gate®* has become widely accepted by many companies. It has also been developed and adapted into different configurations. These include *NextGen Stage-Gate®; Stage-Gate XPress®* (for rapid development); *Stage-Gate Lite®* (for small projects), and *Stage-Gate TD®* (for technology development projects). This evolution of the *Stage-Gate®* process is illustrated in Fig. 9.18. According to Cooper (2019) the process and the number of stages that the project is put through, depends on the context within which the NPD project team is working. For example, the full 5-stage process of the original *Stage-Gate®* process is more appropriate for a new, potentially complex and high-risk project where a lot of care needs to be taken in progressing from the initial idea screening phase to the

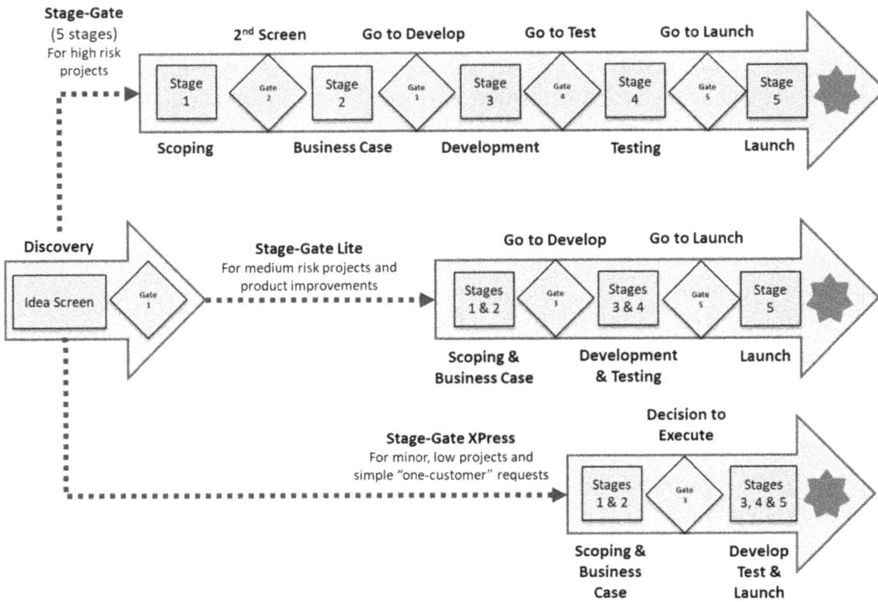

Fig. 9.18 The *Stage-Gate*® process evolved. (Source: adapted from Cooper 2019)

product launch into the market. By contrast, projects of lesser risk can be moved more rapidly through *Stage-Gate Lite* or *Stage-Gate Xpress*, which have fewer steps.

9.15 The Lean Start-Up Process

As noted above, there are now a number of systems that have been offered as potential solutions to the reduction of risk in the NPD and commercialisation process. One of these is the *Lean Start-Up* method as developed by Ries (2011). It has become popular within the entrepreneurship start-up community and some academic programs. It has its antecedents in a number of previous approaches to new product development (NPD), in particular the *Plan-Do-Check-Act* cycle of continuous improvement originally developed by W. Edwards Deming in the 1950s (Trimi and Berbegal-Mirabent 2012). In *Lean Start-Up* this process is described as *Adapt-Innovate-Batch-Grow* (Ries 2011).

The basic structure of the *Lean Start-Up* process is illustrated in Fig. 9.19 where it can be seen that the entire process is an iterative learning-loop that works through six primary components. In this regard it is also conceptually an *absorptive capacity* approach, and one that has a similar dynamic to *Stage-Gate*® whereby it is focused on discovery of customer needs, development of products able to offer value, and the capturing of data and its assimilation, transformation and exploitation in a rapid and cost-efficient manner.

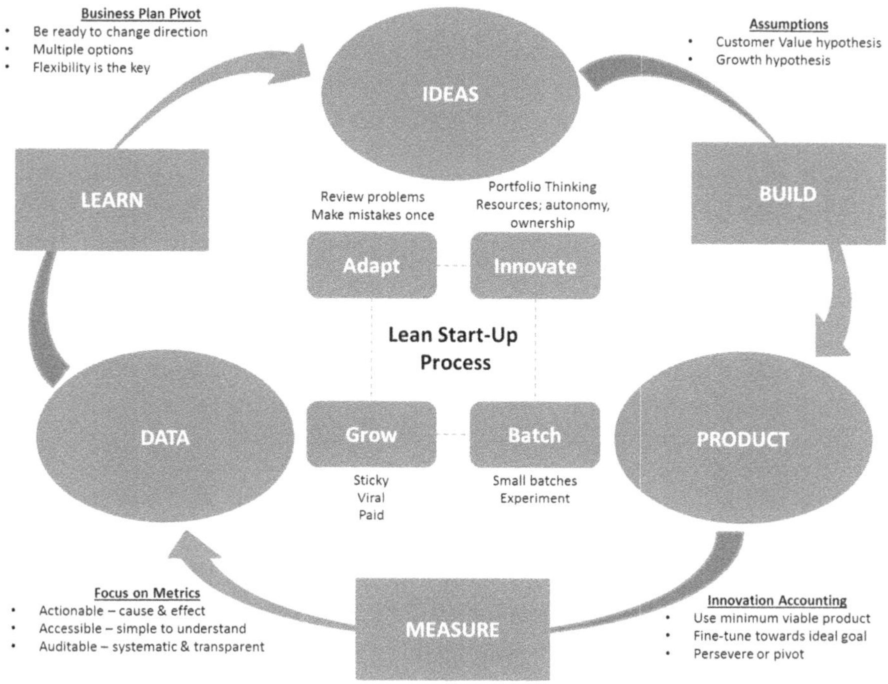

Fig. 9.19 The lean start-up process. (Source: adapted from Ries 2011)

This enables the generation and testing of not only products and services but business models. The notion of "Lean", as expressed by Ries (2011) owes its origins to the principles of *lean manufacturing*, with its antecedents in *Quality Function Deployment* (QFD) as practiced by Japanese companies such as Toyota and Mitsubishi (Akao and Mazur 2003). This aimed to improve quality and reduce cost and risk in NPD through the application of a systematic process. The focus on "Lean" was the recognition that a good system would reduce waste and improve efficiency.

9.15.1 Principles of Lean Start-Up

Ries (2011) had experienced failure in his own business start-ups and wanted to avoid the risk and cost of making mistakes. The *Lean Start-Up* process emerged from this and focuses around five basic principles:

1. *Entrepreneurs are everywhere;* The initial principle is that entrepreneurs don't have to be special or unique people. Anyone can engage in the launch of a new business venture, or innovative project. They can be self-employed entrepreneurs, or *intrapreneurs* working within large firms.

2. *Entrepreneurship is management;* This principle suggests that the process of entrepreneurship is not focused on a single product, or the special gifts of talented people. Instead it is a managerial process that can be taught and learnt, and is about the development of business model not a product.
3. *Validated learning;* In this principle, the aim of a new start-up business should be not just to make products and money, or deliver services. Its purpose should be to learn how to build a sustainable business model using information and knowledge (e.g. via ACAP) to experiment and test assumptions and validate them in the market.
4. *Build measure learn;* Related to the previous principle is the notion that a fundamental activity of any start-up venture is the need to apply ACAP and learn how to acquire, assimilate, transform and exploit knowledge. The faster the start-up team can move through this cycle and the stronger their PACAP = RACAP ratio, the more likely their success. This cycle is referred to as a *Pivot* by Ries (2011).
5. *Innovation accounting;* The final principle is the need to record, analyse and then use data to help make decisions about future investments in the business. In this sense, as well as the iterative process of NPD, the principles of *Lean Start-Up* and *Stage-Gate®* are similar.

9.15.2 The Lean Start-Up Framework

The different elements of the *Lean Start-Up* process are illustrated in Fig. 9.18. Each of these elements is briefly discussed in the following sub-sections.

- Ideas and Assumptions

The first phase of the *Lean Start-Up* process involves generating ideas and making assumptions that can be tested. The generation of ideas for future products or services should be developed with reference to the issues, discussed above, relating to exploring the customer's needs and wants. Ries (2011) suggests the development of *Customer Archetypes* that help to identify and define the target customer. A series of initial assumptions will need to be made about what might be the customer's response to the CVP that is to be offered. This is a *Customer Value Hypothesis* that will need to be tested, much as a scientist might test a scientific theory. There should also be a *Growth Hypothesis* that emerges from the business model analysis and makes some forecasts as to likely market adoption and sales generated.

- Build a Minimum Viable Product

The next phase in the *Lean Start-Up* process is to build a *Minimum Viable Product* (MVP), which is a prototype that is just sufficient to enable an early adopter, or lead customer, to trial it and provide feedback. In some cases, this might be an initial product or service that is offered to the market as an experiment to test the hypotheses described above. The development of the product can take some time and so the MVP should be viewed as an experimental device. It may be possible to launch the MVP into a real market to test the hypotheses. However, in other circumstances (i.e. biotechnology), any testing of products will need to take place under strict controls.

- Innovation Accounting: Focus on Metrics

In the fourth phase the data collected from the initial market tests of the MVP are evaluated. The collection of reliable data that can be used to reliably evaluate the product's performance in the market is critical. According to Ries (2011) there should be three "*learning milestones*" that form the basis of *Innovation Accounting*. The first is the use of an MVP to collect data from the customer. Second, as the data is received it is important to "*tune the engine from the baseline to the ideal*". This involves making small changes to the product or service to identify whether it is worth further investment. Third, a decision whether to continue or not should be made.

Rapid prototyping and other techniques aimed at quickly creating and then revising the product are important in this process. However, the process must be viewed as experimental in nature with a recognition that the MVP may not be fully accepted by the target customers. Here it is important that the management team be willing to persevere if market feedback is positive, or to *pivot* and change if not. It is important that good, reliable data be collected. This should have three essential properties:

- *Actionable* – the data should show a clear cause-effect relationship;
- *Accessible* – the data should be simple to understand;
- *Auditable* – the data should be both systematic and transparent. This is much the same as the approach taken by scientists when conducting experiments and then reporting their findings.

- Learning to Pivot

The final phase of the *Lean Start-Up* process is the ability to undertake a business plan pivot if required. A *pivot* is a change of product or business strategy, or even business model design based on the lessons learnt from analysis of the data collected in the previous phases. It aims to test assumptions about the product, business model or growth strategy. There are multiple options for pivots as listed in Table 9.2.

9.16 Best Practice in NPD

A study undertaken into successful NPD practices of 800 firms found a series of common patterns of behaviour (Akgun et al. 2004). Seven types of practice were found:

1. *Project visioning;* Successful projects were marked by having a clear vision for their design and implementation, with clearly defined target markets and with technical and financial goals that all levels of the firm agreed with. Such goals remained fairly stable over the life of the project.

Table 9.2 Pivots

Pivot type	Description
Zoom-in pivot	What was once thought to be a single feature of a product becomes the whole product
Zoom-out pivot	What was previously considered to be the whole product becomes a single feature of a much larger product
Customer segment pivot	Product solves a real problem for customers but not the type of customers originally targeted
Customer need pivot	Recognition that the problem you thought you were solving is not very important to the target customers, thus requiring product redesign
Platform pivot	Shifts the product from a component within a wider platform to the actual platform, or vice versa
Business architecture pivot	Shift from high margin low volume (complex systems model) to low margin high volume (volume operations model) or vice versa
Value capture pivot	Changes to the way a product captures value using different revenue models
Engine of growth pivot	Change to the nature of the growth engine underlying the business model
Channel pivot	Change to the channel structure used by the company to reach its customers
Technology pivot	Change to the way that solutions are delivered using different technology

Source: Ries (2011)

2. *Management support;* Successful projects were marked by having a clear vision for their design and implementation, with clearly defined target markets and with technical and financial goals that all levels of the firm agreed with. Such goals remained fairly stable over the life of the project.
3. *NPD process proficiency;* The processes followed by successful NPD teams were more proficient, and involved a clear, well-defined road map with measurable milestones. There were also established methods for idea screening, evaluation, testing, development and launch. Systems were also in place to track the progress of the project and to control or stage-gate its costs.
4. *Team processes;* Successful NPD teams were notable for their cohesion and capacity to resolve conflict in a constructive manner. There was a high level of diversity in the team, with the free flow of ideas and knowledge sharing. Members demonstrated mutual respect for each other as well as demonstrating both interest and enthusiasm for the project. A common vision and sense of purpose was to be found within the team. Project teams were generally comprised of a core of experienced people, with new members making up the balance. Turn over within the team was low, and team leaders had a previous track record of success in the same field.
5. *Documentation systems;* The NPD teams maintained meticulous records of everything from laboratory trials and testing to customer or market surveys. Record keeping was undertaken in a manner that allowed the project team to access information and to undertake analysis readily, with computer-based data

capture and management systems used extensively. Data capture was systematic and was designed to preserve the knowledge developed within the project team.

6. *Communication;* Formal and informal communications activities were of a higher quality among the successful NPD teams, with greater depth and richness. Formal communications involved memos, emails, reports and staff meetings. Informal communications involved coffee chats and social exchanges or lunchroom discussions that focused on the project. Monthly meetings were held with other project teams to compare notes, and monthly memos or progress reports were generated. Also, the social network of people from one project team usually included members from other project teams.
7. *Establishing project deadlines;* The final element found within successful NPD teams was the ability to set clear project deadlines and to work toward these systematically. By setting realistic but tight deadlines, the team members were pushed to work effectively and efficiently toward their project timelines.

9.17 The Innovation Diamond

Cooper and Edgett (2009) suggest that there are four common denominators of best practice in NPD, which are illustrated in Fig. 9.20 as the *Innovation Diamond.* The first element in the NPD *Innovation Diamond* is the ability of the firm to build a

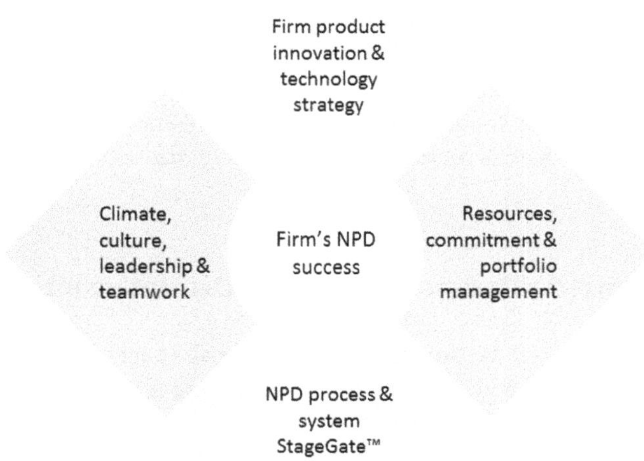

Fig. 9.20 The innovation diamond – four common denominators of best practice in NPD. (Source: Cooper and Edgett 2009)

coherent strategy for their innovation and its pathway to market. It is important that the firm's top management makes a strategic commitment to innovation, NPD and commercialisation as a primary focus for achieving competitive advantage. This will impact on the allocation of scarce resources as well as focusing the firm's key people and employees on NPD as a core process.

As an outcome of this strategic focus, the firm should then allocate sufficient resources to R&D, NPD and commercialisation, to allow company to succeed. Attention should be given to at least six areas: (i) fostering ideas for innovation and new products and processes; (ii) management of knowledge and expertise within the project team; (iii) NPD strategy and its relationship to corporate strategy; (iv) portfolio management; (v) project management and (vi) commercialisation (Adams et al. 2006). Of these, the management of scarce resources in relation to risk associated with NPD portfolios is important as it enables the management team to assess the risk and return of projects and make more effective decisions over resource allocations (Cooper and Edgett 2009).

The organisational climate and culture, plus the ability of the firm's management to provide effective leadership are also critically important to successful NPD and commercialisation (Adams et al. 2006). Senior managers are responsible for fostering a strong focus on innovation and encouraging their teams to generate new ways to add value and create new products and services (Cooper and Edgett 2009).

It is also important that firms engaging in NPD and commercialisation processes adopt formal or at least systematic approaches. As discussed above, systems such as *Stage-Gate*® and *Lean Start-Up* are now available to help entrepreneurs and managers in both large and small firms, manage risk through a systematic process of testing and validating their ideas before making significant and expensive commitments. There are several that have become popular in recent years. One of these is *Stage-Gate*® developed by Cooper and Edgett (2005), another is *Lean Start-Up* (Ries 2011). Both of these are briefly discussed below. However, what such systems do is provide managers with frameworks that can help them make decisions about whether to "Go" or "Kill" a project and by doing so assist with the management of risk.

9.18 Commercialisation Pathways for Disruptive Innovation

In Chap. 8 we examined the process of managing risk in innovation and commercialisation. There it was noted that the main issue facing firms engaged in commercialisation of new products or services is the uncertainty that accompanies the innovation process. This level of uncertainty rises where the innovation is more radical or disruptive in nature. As discussed above, systems such as *Stage-Gate*® or *Lean Start-Up* are designed to help alleviate uncertainty and mitigate risk by following step-wise approaches. The concept of *innovation rent* and the relationship this has with the firm's strategic management of innovation, in particular the *resource-based view* (RBV) (Barney 1991; Mosakowski 1998), and *dynamic capabilities* theories (Amit and Schoemaker 1993; Teece et al. 1997) were also discussed in Chap. 7. These concepts become important to managers seeking to commercialise their innovations, and select the most appropriate pathway for this to occur.

There are five broad commercialisation pathway options for a firm to take. These are illustrated in Fig. 9.21, where it can be seen that they encompass *autonomous development*, *develop in partnership*, *delegate development*, *transfer development* and *withdraw*. As shown, each has different levels of potential risk and return, with *withdraw*, or the abandonment of the project as the lowest risk option, and *autonomous development* the highest risk.

The decision as to which of the five commercialisation pathways to follow will depend on several factors. The first is the nature of the innovation (i.e. whether it is radical or incremental). The *Innovation Rent Typology* highlights eight rent configurations that might define the type of innovation. A second factor is whether the innovation is *isolated* or *systemic*. An *isolated* innovation is one that has the ability to stand alone without any need to be integrated into existing technical or commercial systems. By comparison, a *systemic* innovation is one that integrates into a system. Where the firm can fully commercialise the innovation alone it won't need to look for outside support. However, a further factor is whether the firm has all the resources it needs. If not, it will have to choose either: *development in partnership*, *delegate development* or *transfer development*.

Each of these three pathway options involve different levels of strategic engagement with third parties. The *develop in partnership* option typically results in a joint venture with one or more third parties. If the firm is small, it will need to possess strong *isolating mechanisms*, such as patents or other proprietary IP rights, that it can use to strengthen its bargaining position. The *delegate development* option will also require the firm to have strong IP rights so that it can negotiate a good outcome over licensing. Finally, the *transfer development* option will also benefit from the

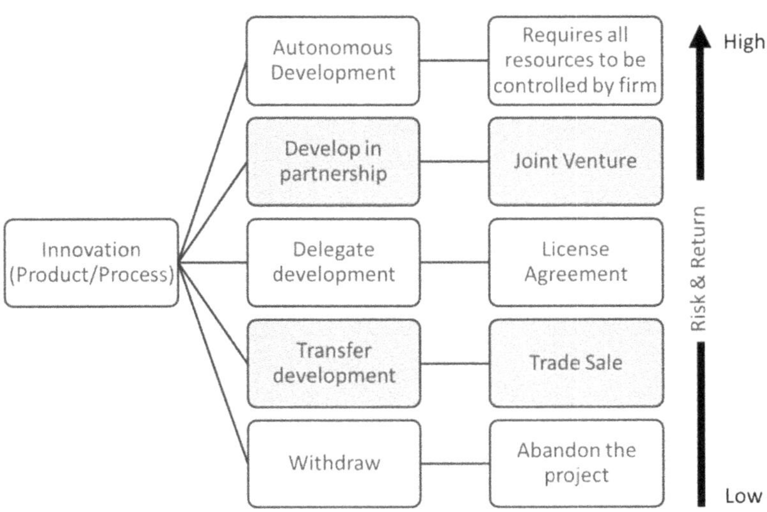

Fig. 9.21 Commercialisation pathways

firm's ability to show that the innovation has sufficient tangibility that it can be sold for a good return to the original inventor. This too, will require strong IP rights or other assets that a potential buyer might value.

9.18.1 Commercialisation Pathways and Innovation Rent Analysis

The eight *innovation rent* configurations outlined in Chap. 9 can be used to help managers make decisions over commercialisation pathway options. Figure 9.22 illustrates the *process and general model of innovation rent analysis* (Santi et al. 2003). This draws together the *Innovation Rent Typology* with the three stages of the commercialisation cycle (i.e. innovation, market insertion and firm insertion), and applies them to the commercialisation pathways.

Each of the eight *innovation rent* configurations outlined in Chap. 8 have different potential commercialisation pathways as we will discuss below. However, as noted above, the key factors of innovation type, *isolated* or *systemic*, and available resources will play an important role.

- Commercialisation of the Shrimp

It will be recalled that *The Shrimp* configuration is an innovation with low rates of anticipated sales volume, rates of profit and length of lifecycle. When considering a *Shrimp* innovation, it is important to determine whether it is *isolated* or

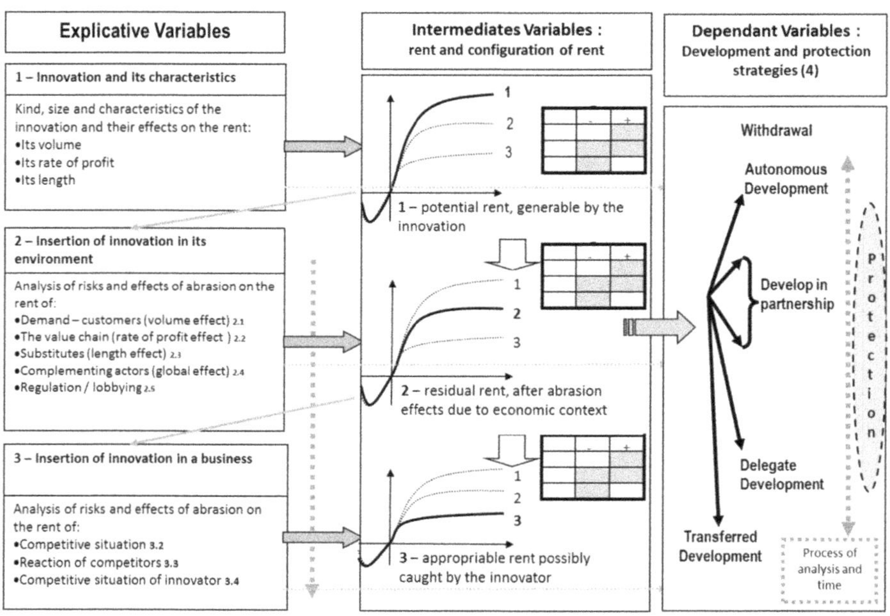

Fig. 9.22 Process and general model of *innovation rent* analysis. (Source: Santi et al. 2003)

systemic. In the case of an *isolated Shrimp* the firm is likely to be able to progress the commercialisation alone so long as the returns to future investment are sufficiently attractive. However, if the *Shrimp* innovation is *systemic* the firm will need to assess whether the commercialisation pathway is focused on an existing market or the creation of a new one.

In the case of an existing market the firm, particularly if it is a small firm, will need to see if it can negotiate with the major firms within the system to adopt the new innovation. This is common in the case of many software Apps that are written to plug into established software platforms as productivity enhancers or tools. In the case of a new market that the firm might have to create alone, the potential rent from the *Shrimp* is unlikely to warrant full commercialisation.

- Commercialisation of the Champion

The *Champion* has the potential for high volume of sales, high rates of profit, and a long length of lifecycle. It is usually a radical or disruptive innovation. Where the *Champion* is *isolated* the firm will also need to consider whether the innovation is targeting an existing market or needs to create an entirely new one. In the case of an *isolated Champion* seeking to enter an existing market the firm will need to assess whether it has sufficient resources to progress to full commercialisation. It will need very strong *isolating mechanisms* and the resources to not only protect its IP rights in competitive global markets, but also exploit them via international marketing efforts.

Small firms may need to seek partnerships in the form of joint ventures, or look to licencing deals. Where the market needs to be created the firm should start alone or in partnership to prove the concept. It can then consider licensing or trade sale. Once again, this will require strong IP rights protections across a wide geographic area. If the innovation is a *systemic Champion* seeking to enter an existing market the firm will need to consider if it has sufficiently strong *isolating mechanisms* in place and also whether it can secure partnerships with a major firm to integrate its innovation into existing systems. The options of joint venture, licensing or trade sale will be determined by the firms IP rights position, resources and capacity to negotiate. However, where a *systemic Champion* needs to create a completely new market, the small firm may struggle. If it can form a joint venture or alliance to prove the concept it can then chose to delegate through licensing, or transfer ownership via trade sale.

- Commercialisation of the Gadget

The *Gadget* innovation has low volume and length with a potential for high rates of profit. However, it is important to determine if the rate of profit can be sustained at a high level and this won't always be possible once the innovation is inserted into the market. Where the *Gadget* is *isolated* the firm might proceed with a rapid commercialisation so long as it has the resources to this alone. If not, it might seek a partnership such as a joint venture. However, the short lifecycle and modest sale volume anticipated for the innovation will necessitate a rapid commercialisation. It might also make the creation of strong *isolating mechanisms* challenging as the cost of patents and related formal IP rights may be unjustified. In this case a firm might use trade secrets and a strategy of continuous new product development instead. Where the *Gadget* is a *systemic* innovation the need to commercialise rapidly within a small or even niche market may prove challenging. If the firm has to negotiate with a wide network to achieve this, it may be very difficult. Also, the relatively short lifecycle of the *Gadget* means that it may not be worthwhile investing too much in formal IP rights protection. Instead the focus should be on trade secrets and branding with a desire to offer cross licensing agreements that will help to quickly diffuse the innovation into its target markets.

- Commercialisation of the Joker

The *Joker* is an innovation with high potential volume of sales and a long lifecycle length. However, it also has only a low or modest anticipated rate of profit. In this case the *Joker* that is *isolated* and aimed at an existing market should be carefully assessed. If the IP rights are strong and there is a firm platform of identifiable assets that can be used as a negotiating position, there may be an opportunity for joint venture, licensing or trade sale. Yet if this is not the case the best option might be to abandon, or at least shelve any future development until things change. Where the innovation is an *isolated Joker* that needs a new market to be created, the firm should consider stating alone, or in partnership to prove up the concept. Then it might be able to licence or trade sale the innovation. However, where the firm lacks these options it should consider a trade sale or withdrawal.

A *systemic Joker* innovation that is targeted at an existing market may pose significant challenges for a small firm. Although it offers large potential sales and a long lifecycle, the modest rates of potential profit may create problems in relation to the firm's ability to finance the commercialisation. This might require the firm to delegate via licensing, or transfer via trade sale the innovation to a larger firm that might value it for its ability to complement their existing systems. This is often the case for process innovations and can result in licencing agreements that offer modest but steady returns to inventor. Finally, a *systemic Joker* that is targeted at the creation of a completely new market will most likely require a small firm to form a partnership (i.e. joint venture) at the beginning. This will allow it to develop the innovation and prove the concept. It may then enable a licencing or trade sale to take place. In some cases, the joint venture partner may acquire the innovation from the smaller firm, or even acquire the smaller firm!

- Commercialisation of the Flash in the Pan

The *Flash-in-the-Pan* innovation has high potential volume, but a relatively short lifecycle, and can have either a low rate of profit (*Type A*) or a high rate of profit (*Type B*). It is important for the firm to first determine which of these two types the *Flash-in-the-Pan* is. Where the *Flash-in-the-Pan* is, *isolated* and aimed at an existing market, the short lifecycle may create undue risks. However, these risks will be potentially greater for *Type A* than *Type B* because the lower rate of profit may cause financial problems as the firm seeks to exploit a large market space. By contrast the

Type B offers less risk as the greater rate of profit will generate more financial returns for each product sold.

If the innovation has to create an entirely new market the firm should consider rapid commercialisation alone as the short lifecycle will mean that the market window of opportunity will also be short. However, this option will only work if the firm has sufficient resources to proceed alone. If not, it may have to find a partner to assist with the co-development of the innovation, and then consider licensing or trade sale. The high profit rate of the *Flash-in-the-Pan Type B* will make such activities potentially easier.

In the case of a *systemic Flash in the Pan* any targeting into an existing market may be highly problematic due to the short lifecycle. This would apply particularly to the low profit *Type A*. The firm will need to seek licencing or trade sale deals with complementary firms and the *Type B Flash-in-the-Pan* is more likely to prove attractive than its low profit *Type A* counterpart. Where a new market is to be created, the firm might need to find joint venture partners, particularly with larger firms that can help it to co-create the market and then delegate or transfer via trade sale. Once again, the high profit *Type B Flash-in-the-Pan* is a more attractive option. If the firm lacks the ability to find partners it may have to withdraw.

- Commercialisation of the Oasis

The *Oasis* innovation has low potential volume of sales and a long lifecycle. It also has two types, an *Oasis Type A* with low rates of profit, and an *Oasis Type B* with high rates of profit. A firm that finds it has an *Oasis* innovation should first ascertain which type it has and how sustainable this profitability will be.

Where the innovation is an *isolated Oasis* and the firm has the resources to proceed to commercialise alone it should do so. This is particularly the case for an *Oasis Type B* as this can offer good profits over a long period of time. For small firms the modest sales where profits are good, is potentially attractive as it would not unduly strain the firm's productive resources. Over time the firm might seek a partnership to assist it to maintain the length of the product lifecycle. Once again, the high profit *Oasis Type B* may be beneficial because the higher rate can carry a broader distribution of profit share amongst partners.

In the case of a *systemic Oasis* the most desirable option is likely to be a partnership. Where the firm may be able to take a leadership role in the industry network or system, it should do so, on the condition that it is not highly dependent on other network actors. It will need strong IP rights protections and may need to secure cross licensing agreements and the maintenance of patents and other formal IP rights over time. The higher profit *Oasis Type B* will be a more attractive option due to its ability to generate stronger cash flows and retained earnings.

- Market and Firm Insertion Are the Final Arbiters

It should be acknowledged that the *Innovation Rent Typology* is a first step on the longer pathway of commercialisation. It offers an initial view of the *potential rent* and once the innovation has been developed into a minimum viable product or prototype and inserted into the market its true value will not be known. Even when the market feedback is received the firm will have to assess its resources and capabilities to determine if it can proceed alone to commercialise or seek partnerships. What the final *appropriable rent* from the innovation is will be contingent on the outcome of these interactions between the innovation, the market, the firm's resources and any partners it may need to work with. The more disruptive the innovation the more challenging these issues become. NPD processes and systems such as *Stage-Gate®* and *Lean Start-Up* offer a systematic approach to assessing these interactions and determining which of the commercialisation pathways is optimal for the firm.

References

Adams, R., Bessant, J., & Phelps, R. (2006). Innovation management measurement: A review. *International Journal of Management Reviews, 8*(1), 21–47.

Akao, Y., & Mazur, G. H. (2003). The leading edge in QFD: Past, present and future. *The International Journal of Quality & Reliability Management, 20*(1), 20–35.

Akgun, A. E., Lynn, G. S., & Byrne, J. C. (2004). Taking the guess work out of new product development: How successful high-tech companies get that way. *Journal of Business Strategy, 25*(4), 41–46.

Amit, R., & Schoemaker, P. J. H. (1993). Strategic assets and organisational rent. *Strategic Management Journal, 14*(1), 33–46.

Ansoff, H. I. (1987). Strategic management of technology. *The Journal of Business Strategy., 7*, 28–39.

Autio, E., & Lumme, A. (1998). Does the innovator role affect the perceived potential for growth? Analysis of four types of new, technology-based firms. *Technology Analysis & Strategic Management, 10*(1), 41–45.

Barney, J. B. (1991). Firm resources and sustained competitive advantage. *Journal of Management, 17*(1), 99–120.

Bower, J. L., & Christensen, C. M. (1995). Disruptive technologies: Catching the wave. *Harvard Business Review, 73*(1), 43–54.

Brandenburger, A., & Nalebuff, B. (1995). The right game: Use game theory to shape strategy. *Harvard Business Review, 73*(4), 57–71.

Christensen, C. M., Johnson, M. W., & Rigby, D. K. (2002). Foundations for growth. *MIT Sloan Management Review, 43*(3), 22–31.

Cooper, R. G. (2006). Formula for success in new product development. *Marketing Management, 15*(2), 18–24.

Cooper, R. G. (2008). The stage-gate idea-to-launch process update, what's new and NextGen systems. *Journal of Product Innovation Management, 25*(3), 213–232.

Cooper, R. G., & Edgett, S. J. (2005). *Lean, rapid and profitable new product development*. Ancaster: Product Development Institute Inc.

Cooper, R. G., & Edgett, S. J. (2009). *Product innovation and technology strategy*. Hamilton: Product Development Institute Inc.

Cooper, R. G., & Kleinschmidt, E. J. (1993). Screening new products for potential winners. *Long Range Planning, 26*(6), 74–81.

Cooper, A. C., & Schendel, D. (1976). Strategic responses to technological threats. *Business Horizons, 19*(1), 61–69.

Cooper, R. G., Edgett, S. J., & Kleinschmidt, E. J. (2004a). Benchmarking best NPD practices – I. *Research Technology Management, 47*(1), 31–43.

Cooper, R. G., Edgett, S. J., & Kleinschmidt, E. J. (2004b). Benchmarking best NPD practices – II. *Research Technology Management, 47*(3), 50–59.

Cooper, R. G., Edgett, S. J., & Kleinschmidt, E. J. (2004c). Benchmarking best NPD practices – III. *Research Technology Management, 47*(6), 43–55.
Crosby, M. (2000). Patents, innovation and growth. *Economic Record, 76*(234), 255–262.
Deloitte. (2018). *The future of mining in Africa: Navigating a revolution.* www2.deloitte.com Deloitte Touche Tohmatsu.
Dernis, H., & Khan, M. (2004). *Triadic patent families methodology* (OECD Science and Technology Working Papers 2004/2). Paris: OECD Publishing.
Frambach, R. T., & Schillewaert, N. (2002). Organisational innovation adoption: A multi-level framework of determinants and opportunities for future research. *Journal of Business Research, 55*(2), 163–176.
Gopalakrishnan, S., & Damanpour, F. (1997). A review of innovation research in economics, sociology and technology management. *Omega International Journal of Management Science, 25*(1), 15–28.
Hirsch-Kreinsen, H., Jacobson, D., & Robertson, P. L. (2006). 'Low-tech' industries: Innovativeness and development perspectives—a summary of a European research project. *Prometheus, 24*(1), 3–21.
Huang, X., Soutar, G. N., & Brown, A. (2002). New product development processes in small- to medium-sized enterprises: Some Australian evidence. *Journal of Small Business Management, 40*(1), 27–42.
ISR. (2001). *From invention to investment: Pathways to commercialisation for emerging technologies*. Canberra: Competitive Australia, Industry Science and Resources.
Kagermann, H., Wahlster, W., & Helbig, J. (2013). *Recommendations for implementing the strategic initiative INDUSTRIE 4.0.* Berlin, Industrie 4.0 Working Group of Acatech.
Kaplan, R., & Norton, D. (1993). Putting the balanced scorecard to work. *Harvard Business Review, 71*(5), 134–142.
Kemp, R. G. M., Folkeringa M., de Jong, J. P. J., & Wubben, E. F. M. (2003). *Innovation and firm performance*. Zoetermeer, Netherlands, EIM Research Report H200207 SCALES Scientific Analysis of Entrepreneurship and SME.
Kim, W. C., & Mauborgne, R. (1999). Creating new market space. *Harvard Business Review, 77*(1), 83–94.
Kim, W. C., & Mauborgne, R. (2004). Blue Ocean strategy. *Harvard Business Review, 82*(10), 71–79.
Kim, W. C., & Mauborgne, R. (2005). Value innovation: A leap into the blue ocean. *Journal of Business Strategy, 26*(4), 22–28.
Kodama, M. (2002). Transforming an old economy company into a new economy success: The case of NTT DoCoMo. *Leadership & Organisation Development Journal, 23*(1), 26–39.
Liao, Y., Deschamps, F., Loures, E., & Ramos, L. (2017). Past, present and future of industry 4.0 – a systematic literature review and research agenda proposal. *International Journal of Production Research, 55*(12), 3609–3629.
Liu, C. (2017). International competitiveness and the fourth industrial revolution. *Entrepreneurial Business and Economics Review, 5*(4), 111–133.
Noonan, D. (2001). Red bull's good buzz. *Newsweek Online*, May 14, 2001.
OECD. (2001). *Oslo manual: The measurement of scientific and technological activities: Proposed guidelines for collecting and interpreting technological innovation data.* Oslo: Organisation of Economic Co-operation and Development, European Union, Eurostat.
OECD. (2010). *Measuring innovation: A new perspective.* Paris: Organisation for Economic Co-operation and Development.
OECD. (2014). *OECD science, technology and innovation outlook 2014.* Paris: Organisation for Economic Cooperation and Development.
OECD. (2015). *OECD science, technology and industry scoreboard 2015: Innovation for growth and society*. Paris: Organisation for Economic Cooperation and Development.
OECD. (2017). *OECD science, technology and innovation outlook 2017.* Paris: Organisation for Economic Cooperation and Development.

Ozer, M. (2004). Managing the selection process for new product ideas. *Research Technology Management, 47*(4), 10–11.

Pereira, A. C., & Romero, F. (2017). A review of the meanings and the implications of the industry 4.0 concept. *Procedia Manufacturing, 13*(1), 1206–1214.

Rogers, E. M. (1995). *Diffusion of innovations*. New York: The Free Press.

Santi, M., Reboud, S., Gasiglia, H. & Sabouret, A. (2003). *Modèle de valorisation et de protection intellectuelle des innovations des PEI*. July, HEC/INP: 63.

Schwab, K. (2016). *The fourth industrial revolution*. London: Portfolio Penguin.

Schwab, K. (2018). *Shaping the fourth industrial revolution*. Geneva. www.weforum.org: World Economic Forum.

Sethi, R., & Iqbal, Z. (2008). Stage-gate controls, learning failure, and adverse effect on novel new products. *Journal of Marketing, 72*(1), 118–134.

Shepherd, D., & Patzelt, H. (2017). *Trailblazing in entrepreneurship: Creating new paths for understanding the field*. Cham: Palgrave Macmillan.

Teece, D. J., Pisano, G., & Shuen, A. (1997). Dynamic capabilities and strategic management. *Strategic Management Journal, 18*(7), 509–533.

Trimi, S., & Berbegal-Mirabent, J. (2012). Business model innovation in entrepreneurship. *International Entrepreneurship and Management Journal, 8*(4), 449–465.

WEF. (2017). *Digital transformative initiative: Mining and metals industry*. www.reports.weforum.org, World Economic Forum.

Xu, L. D., Xu, E. L., & Li, L. (2018). Industry 4.0: State of the art and future trends. *International Journal of Production Research, 56*(8), 2941–2962.

Screening Opportunities and Assessing Markets

10

10.1 Introduction

> The value of the voice of the customer is well known to product innovators. By now, nearly everyone is also familiar with the *crowdsourcing* models of firms such as Threadless, in which customers design and select new t-shirt designs, and Innocentive, which runs technical crowdsourcing efforts for large business-to-business (B2B) and business to consumer (B2C) companies including pharmaceutical and consumer packaged goods companies.
>
> Source: Schirr (2013, p. 231).

This chapter examines the process of screening opportunities for new product development (NPD), and the importance of undertaking detailed market assessments of the customers' needs and wants. It discusses the use of a range techniques and associated concepts including voice of customer, quality function deployment (QFD), Kano analysis, CAGE modelling, customer archetyping, product concept development, and product-technology road mapping. The chapter also provides an overview of how this screening and market assessment process can be undertaken with reference to many of the concepts covered in Chaps. 7, 8, and 9.

Any investment in the commercialisation of a new product or service should involve an in-depth assessment of the customers' needs and how the features and attributes of the proposed product will offer perceived value (Griffin 2013). There should be a close integration of the R&D and NPD process with the marketing and market development activities within the business (Hansen et al. 2008). In most small to medium enterprises (SMEs), this closely integrated relationship is common, because the size of the firm ensures that the senior managers, usually the owner-managers, enjoy close proximity with their customers (Gibb and Scott 1985). When such firms actively engage in preliminary market analysis, customer product

T. Mazzarol, S. Reboud, *Entrepreneurship and Innovation*, Springer Texts in Business and Economics, https://doi.org/10.1007/978-981-13-9412-6_10

testing and test marketing, the overall success rate of their NPD and commercialisation processes is likely to be greater (Huang et al. 2002).

However, regardless of their size, firms seeking to successfully commercialise an innovation, must engage with the customer to develop a deep understanding of their needs, and how the firm might configure its technological and organisational resources within the business model to satisfy those needs (Teece 2018). In the case of the small firm, the relative absence of resources typically means that they cannot satisfy all potential customers and may have to focus on niche market segments where they can build a competitive advantage. Yet, in the case of large firms, even where they have the necessary resources, there may be bureaucratic, organisational and cultural factors that make it difficult for R&D and NPD teams to work closely with marketing and sales teams within the firm, and for the firm to develop an *open innovation* approach to engagement with customers and other outsiders (Griffin and Hauser 1996; West and Bogers 2014). In general, successful commercialisation is often less about the size of the firm than how well it can configure its resources and competencies to rapidly respond to meeting customer needs.

> **For example,** … Large firms are more likely to possess the relevant specialized and cospecialized assets within their boundaries at the time of new product introduction. They can therefore do a better job of milking their technology, however, meagre, to maximum advantage. Small domestic firms are less likely to have the relevant specialized and cospecialized assets within their boundaries and so will either have to incur the expense of trying to build them, or of trying to develop coalitions with competitors/owners of the specialized assets. (Teece 1986, p. 301)

10.2 Causes of Innovation Failure

Deschamps (2017) highlights a number of what he calls "classic root causes of innovation failures." These relate to: (i) failure to anticipate and act with sufficient speed to changes in the external market and industry environment; (ii) failure to develop appropriate product development road maps and project management systems; (iii) failure to develop coherent business models; (iv) failure to secure technology leadership; (v) failure to secure product leadership; and (vi) failure to gain access to the market. We discuss each of these issues in the following sub-sections as they provide a useful starting point for understanding why some firms fail to adequately screen opportunities and assess markets.

10.2.1 Neglected Strategy and Market Assessment

The first failure in the process of managing innovation and commercialisation is the ability of the firm to maintain a clear understanding of what their customers need and want, and the changes that are taking place within the external task environment. Some of these environmental conditions might include: (i) changes to industry structure and regulations; (ii) the convergence of existing market segments or even industries; (iii) changes to customer behaviours, needs, demographics and psychographics; (iv) changes to incumbent business models; and (v) the impact of new technologies and market entrants.

As we discussed in Chap. 9, the emergence of new digital technologies such as *cyber-physical systems* and the effects of a 4th industrial revolution will challenge many, if not most, existing industries and the business models of firms within them (Schwab 2016, 2018). According to Deschamps (2017), a root cause of this failure to keep abreast of environmental and market changes is an 'inward-looking' attitude and mindset within the firm's senior management. Alternatively, this can be caused by a second root cause, which is the managers obsession and 'love' of their firm's incumbent technology and products.

For example, IBM was the dominant market leader in the computer industry, and even pioneered the micro or personal computer (PC) in the 1980s, but was blind to the disruptive potential that this new technology would have on its incumbent main frame computing business. It nearly fell into bankruptcy by the early 1990s (Heller 1994). Nokia was the world's leading mobile phone business by 2006, but failed to react to the emergence of the 'smart phone' in the form of Apple's iPhone in 2007 leading to its gradual decline as a market leader and sale of its mobile phone business to Microsoft at a bargain price of $7.2 billion in 2013 (Kuittinen 2013).

10.2.2 Neglected Execution and Product-Technology Road Mapping

Another problem experienced by firms seeking to commercialise is the lack of ability and perhaps experience with the NPD process and other systematic approaches to commercialisation. Deschamps (2017) argues that one of the most common causes of this failure to properly manage commercialisation is the lack of awareness of the importance of *product-technology road mapping*. The concept of a product-technology roadmap is discussed in more detail later in this chapter, but it offers a systematic approach to linking marketing, R&D, production, financing and intellectual property (IP) rights management together.

> **For example,** … A good process map recognizes the peculiarities of the creative "fuzzy front-end", with its unavoidable uncertainties, iterations and loops, and those of the more predictable "speedy back-end," which requires a lot of discipline. A good process map should provide elements of structure and solidarity while maintaining adaptive flexibility. (Deschamps 2017, p. 44)

A 'root cause' of this failure is the lack of understanding of the role and importance of developing an integrated product-technology road map that helps to link the market assessment with the NPD process, and then connect both into the business model and overall business strategy. However, this problem is compounded by a lack of adequate product specification and design, which is typically caused by ineffective collaboration between the R&D, NPD project team on the one side, and the marketing team on the other. As noted above, this is often not a major concern within SMEs, where these functional areas are often shared across a small project team. Yet, it is a problem in larger organisations where the "siloing" of functional areas, and a lack of cross-functional team structures, generate undesirable internal barriers (Deschamps 2017).

10.2.3 Not Recognising What It Takes to Succeed

The commercialisation process is often a long and challenging one, which requires success in at least three critical areas: (i) technology leadership; (ii) product leadership; (iii) market leadership. Deschamps (2017) cites the work of Ad Huijser, former Chief Technology Officer (CTO) and research President of Phillips, who developed the *Huijser innovation success formula* illustrated in Fig. 10.1. As shown, this suggests that the probability of successful commercialisation within a target market, is a function of how well the innovation project team can secure and assemble the necessary co-specialised assets across the areas of R&D, NPD and marketing, to secure leadership in each area. This is a fundamental principle of *dynamic capabilities* which suggests that a sustainable competitive advantage can be secured by combining physical, human and IP assets into winning combinations that deliver value to the market (Teece et al. 1997).

Success in the market is conditional upon how well the firm's original technological assets are structured, and the relative strength if its platform IP and related portfolio of propriety technologies that can be applied to the development of a new product. In turn, these assets must be designed into the new product, which must then be able to be produced at a competitive price for quality, and supported by related process technologies that allow the firm to sustain this competitive edge. The use of sub-contractors and outsourcing is often a feature of many firm's both large and small. However, care must be taken to ensure that such outsourcing doesn't

Fig. 10.1 The Huijser innovation success formula. (Source: adapted from Deschamps 2017 originally sourced from Huijser)

result in either a loss of valuable competencies, or the loss of quality within the firm's value chain leading to negative impacts on its market reputation (Spiller and Barilla 2014). Finally, the firm must be able capture sufficient market share, and this will require it to have: (i) an in-depth understanding and knowledge of the target market, and the end-user customer: (ii) access to reliable and effective distribution channels, and (iii) a strong company brand equity that can allow it to secure credibility from the start (Deschamps 2017).

An example of how this process works can be seen in the case of Apple's successful market entry into the lucrative mobile telecommunications sector with the iPhone (see case study *Nokia Sells Out* in the work book (Mazzarol 2013). The convergence of multimedia technologies into portable hand-held smart phones was both a major opportunity for Apple, and potential risk to its existing iPod market. Once the MP3 digital audio enabled smart phone technology diffused into the market, the iPod was likely to be seriously challenged. While existing mobile phone market leaders such as Nokia were aware of the potential of the multimedia smart phone (Nokia 2004), they were less agile than Apple at seizing the market opportunity. Apple's success was enabled by its existing software and hardware technology platforms, that enabled it to rapidly "put an aerial in an iPod", and bring to market a leading product design in the iPhone. In addition, Apple had an existing global market of loyal customers who owned iPods and Apple iTunes accounts. Therefore, the company's brand equity was readily transferrable from the iPod to the iPhone as Apple entered the mobile telecommunications market. This ability to rapidly assemble its proprietary specialised and co-specialised assets, to pursue this market opportunity was the key to Apple's competitive advantage.

10.3 The Customer Development Process

In their *Startup Owner's Manual*, Blank and Dorf (2012) devote several chapters to the process of customer development. Figure 10.2 illustrates this *customer development process*, commencing with an initial *search* phase in which there is a two-step *customer discovery* and *customer validation* process. This is followed by an *execution* phase, which also has a two-step *customer creation* and *company building* process. During the initial search phase, it is important to build the business model (see Chap. 7) around the information that is obtained from a close engagement with customers or potential customers.

As shown in Fig. 10.2, there is likely to be an iterative process involving the generation of a set of assumptions about the future market acceptance of a new product or service, but until those assumptions are tested and a *minimum viable product* (MVP) introduced to the customer for validation, no full-scale commercialisation can take place. This is a similar approach to the *fuzzy front end* (FFE) concept within NPD management that was discussed in Chap. 8, and it is also consistent with the principles of *Lean Start-Up* (Ries 2011), that were discussed in Chap. 9. In the following sub-sections, we briefly discuss the key elements of this customer discovery and validation processes.

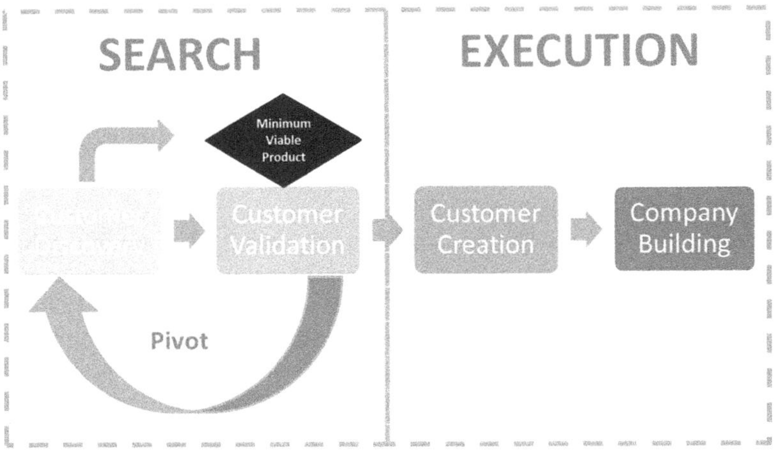

Fig. 10.2 Customer development process. (Source: adapted from Blank and Dorf 2012)

Table 10.1 Customer discovery process

Phase	Actions
Develop theory	State hypotheses about product/market potential
	Draw up a business model canvas
	Prepare one-page briefs of each hypothesis with tests or experiments required to prove/disprove each one
Test theory	Test the problem hypotheses
	Test most elements of business model (e.g. CVP, pricing, channels)
	Get facts and develop new hypotheses
Go to market	Test the solution
	Present MVP to customers
	Use "pass/fail" goals to measure progress
Validate/refute theory	Verify or pivot
	Get full understanding of customers' problems, passions or needs
	Confirm value proposition solves problems, passions or needs
	Ensure market size is viable and pricing works
	Ensure that revenue will generate profits

Source: developed from Blank and Dorf (2012)

10.3.1 Customer Discovery

The process of customer discovery has at least four phases as outlined in Table 10.1. The first, is the need to "develop theory" or hypotheses/assumptions about the likely needs that a target customer group might need and the potential for a new product or service to meet those needs. Ideally this should be built on the start-up team's experience and observations, plus as much secondary data that can be obtained about the target market. With these hypotheses developed, the start-up project team should then build a business model using the *Lean Canvas* for a business model framework (see Chap. 7). As part of this process Blank and Dorf (2012) recommend the preparation of a series of one-page briefs for each of the hypotheses, with a proposal for how these will be tested via market research or experimentation in order to help generate sufficient information to prove or disprove each one.

As we discussed in Chap. 9, in relation to the use of the *Lean Start-Up* framework, the first step in the development of a viable business model should be the generation of ideas and assumptions and then their validation and testing. This is consistent with the second phase of the customer discovery process in which the theory and hypotheses developed in the first phase are tested. The tests or experiments developed in the first phase, should be undertaken and this should involve testing all elements of the business model, e.g. customer value proposition (CVP), pricing and marketing or distribution channels.

To achieve this theory testing, it will be necessary to make direct contact with customers or potential customers, via the third "go to market" phase. Here the project team will have a prototype or *minimum viable product* (MVP) to offer to customers in order to collect first-hand buyer feedback. This might be done via market research, or the sale of a limited range of batch production products to early adopters. In some cases, this can be undertaken with existing *lead customers* that are willing to collaborate with the project team in the co-creation of the new product. During this third phase it is important to have clear "pass/fail" goals to assess the progress of the commercialisation and use these to decide if the business model and MVP are on track.

This is a similar process to the *Stage-Gate®* system of NPD that was outlined in Chap. 9. There, it will be recalled, the development process involves moving through a series of defined stages with "GO/KILL/HOLD" decision points at each stage (Cooper and Edgett 2005, 2009; Cooper 2006, 2008). In this third phase of testing the theory and hypotheses through market insertion, it is important to focus on the collection of data that is reliable. As explained in the previous chapter, this is what Ries (2011) refers to as *innovation accounting*, and notes that any data collected should be: (i) *actionable* – able to show clear cause-effect relationships; (ii) *accessible* – simple to interpret and understand; and (iii) *auditable* – be both systematic and transparent.

The Customer Development Manifesto

- *Rule 1:* There are no facts inside your building, so get outside.
- *Rule 2:* Pair customer development with agile development.
- *Rule 3:* Failure is an integral part of the search.
- *Rule 4:* Make continuous iterations and Pivots.
- *Rule 5:* No business plan survives first contact with the customers so use a Business Model Canvas.
- *Rule 6:* Design experiments and test to validate your hypotheses.
- *Rule 7:* Agree on market type – it changes everything.
- *Rule 8:* Start-up metrics differ from those in existing companies.

(continued)

- *Rule 9:* Fast decision-making, cycle time, speed and tempo.
- *Rule 10:* It's all about passion.
- *Rule 11:* Start-up jobs are very different from that of a large company.
- *Rule 12:* Preserve all cash until needed then spend.
- *Rule 13:* Communicate and share learning.
- *Rule 14:* Customer development success begins with buy-in.

Source: Blank and Dorf (2012).

In the final phase of the customer discovery process, the project development team should examine their findings from the first three phases and make a decision to persevere with their business model and product or service idea, or make a change in design of one or both through what Ries (2011) describes as a *Pivot*. There are many options for business pivots and those have been outlined in Table 9.2 in the previous chapter. If the data collected in this initial process does not support the hypotheses developed in the initial theory the project team should go back to the start and revisit their assumptions.

10.3.2 Customer Validation

Assuming that the initial response from the target customers is positive, the start-up project team then needs to progress to the customer validation stage. This also has four phases, which are outlined in Table 10.2. The first of these is to commence making early sales, and this is likely to require a review of the business model, building on the information gathered from the test-market research that was obtained in the previous stage. It is important here to develop a sales team and a sales management process. Blank and Dorf (2012) recommend hiring a 'sales closer', someone who is capable of winning new business and generating the revenue. However, they also emphasize that it is important for the founders of the company to be closely involved in the customer validation process and therefore the sales activities. They also suggest that a market distribution "channel plan" and "sales roadmap" should be developed, and an "advisory board" consisting of experts who can assist in guiding the company through its early development phase.

The ability to secure as many sales as possible in the early stage of a new business start-up is critical in order to both validate the customer's interest in the product, and to generate sufficient cash flow to sustain the company. Blank and Dorf (2012) recommend targeted early adopters, or what they refer to as "Early-Vangelists". However, it is important to select the right early customers, particularly in business-to-business (B2B) sales environments. Consideration in such an environment should be given to addressing the following questions originally posed by Rogers (1995):

Table 10.2 Customer validation process

Phase	Actions
Get ready to sell	Determine the product positioning strategy
	Prepare the sales/marketing message strategy
	Hire a “sales closer”
	Create a distribution channel plan
	Prepare a sales roadmap
	Create an advisory board
Sell to early-Vangelists	Target early adopters
	Seek feedback and critical assessments
	Use prototypes, models, brochures or presentations
	Validate the sales road map
	Prove predictability of the sales funnel
	Validate the business model via real world tests
Develop positioning	Take customer feedback and refine product
	Position the company and its product offer
Pivot or proceed	Undertake detailed “pivot or proceed” analysis
	Verify that customer validation is complete
	Can the company scale up?
	Is the business model worth pursuing?
	Will it generate sufficient revenues and profits?
	Can the company implement it?

Source: Blank and Dorf (2012)

- *Relative advantage.* How much better is the new product versus the product that customers currently use?
- *Compatibility.* Can the customer use the product without changing its organization and infrastructure?
- *Complexity.* How easily and fast can the customer deploy the new product without too much training?
- *Triability*. Can the new product be tried easily and at no or low cost?
- *Observability*. Where can one see the new product being used?

For those selling into a business to consumer (B2C) market Deschamps (2017, p. 59) recommends that attention be given to addressing the following questions on what he calls the “5-A” checklist:

1. *Awareness*. Are customers aware of the existence of the new product?
2. *Attractiveness*. How will customers appreciate the benefits of the new product?
3. *Affordability*. Will customers be able to afford the product without too much sacrifice?
4. *Availability*. Where will the new product be available?
5. *Accessibility*. How easily accessible will the new product be for each type of adopter?

The careful selection of early adopter *lead customers*, particularly in B2B markets, is very important as it is common for these customers to be willing to help co-create the product. Within industrial sales teams this is referred to *key account management* (KAM), and involves the development of a long-term, trusted relationship between the supplying firm and the customer. This focuses on tailoring the product, process and ongoing contractual arrangements to create a best-fit for both the customer and supplier (Millman and Wilson 1995).

This requires a *relationship selling* approach that is built on trust between the two parties, and a capacity for openness and a willingness to collaborate to secure a win-win outcome for both sides (Foster and Cadogan 2000). It is essential to the customer validation process as customer feedback will need to be taken onboard and use to help refine and develop the product and the firm's overall market positioning strategy. A systematic approach is needed that sets specific targets for sales revenue and builds on realistic *sales and marketing metrics* that forecast the number of new sales leads required to generate sufficient prospects that can be converted into paying customers within a given time period (Plaskoff 2003). Each new product and market may have different response and conversion rates, but maintaining a set of metrics to monitor pre and post-sale activities within the target market sales and distribution channels is the key to obtaining reliable and valid data to assess whether the project in on track to procced, or wither it needs to pivot again (Ambler 2000).

10.3.3 Developing Customer Archetypes and the Customer Analysis Process

As noted in Chap. 9, a key principle of the *Lean Start-Up* process is the development of what Ries (2011) refers to as the *Customer Archetype*. This is a summary of all the key features, attributes, behaviours, needs and wants that can be determined about the "typical" customer or end-user for a new product or service. It is the foundation data that is collected from market research and used to formulate the hypotheses that will be used to shape the theory development and testing taking place in the customer discovery stage. The process for developing a *Customer Archetype* should follow at least seven key steps:

1. Segment the target market.
2. Define the customer problem.
3. Define the customer type.
4. Identify the customer's wants and needs?
5. Assess how the customer can benefit from the product?
6. If an organisational buyer, prepare organisational and customer influence maps.
7. Review the Business Model Canvas (Blank and Dorf 2012).

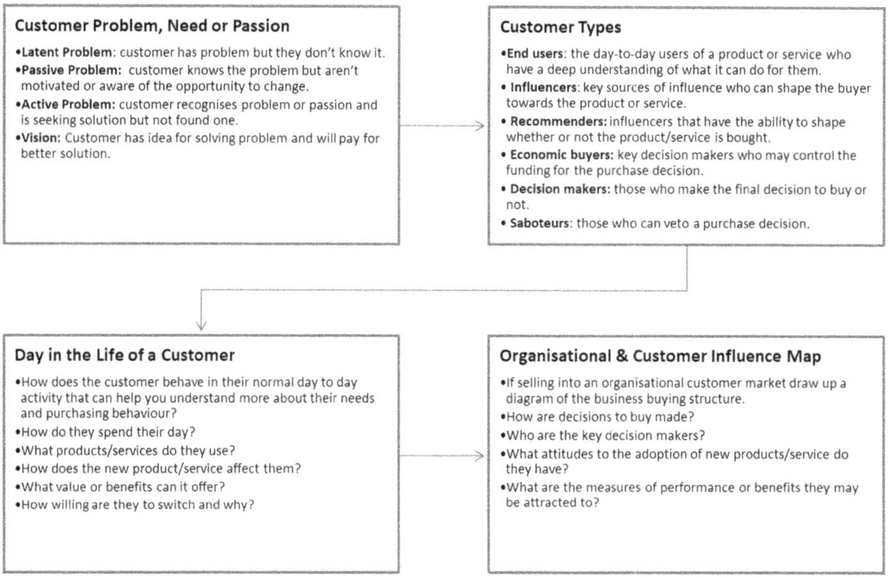

Fig. 10.3 Customer analysis process. (Source: adapted from Blank and Dorf 2012)

According to Blank and Dorf (2012), the customer analysis process that helps to validate the customer should comprise four interrelated elements, which are illustrated in Fig. 10.3. First, the key problems, needs or wants that the target customer has should be identified. These might be *latent*, *passive* or *active* in nature and discussions with the customers or other market research activity should be used to ascertain whether the customer has already developed a *vision* or idea of what their ideal solution to their problem might be. Once this is known, the target market should be classified into a series of customer types e.g. *end-users, influencers, recommenders, economic buyers, decision makers* and *saboteurs*. Each can play a potential role in facilitating or impeding the product's commercialisation.

The market research process should then gather as much data as possible on the why that a typical customer might spend their day. This can be undertaken in B2C and B2B environments, and might follow a range of different techniques ranging from surveys, interviews, focus groups, consumer diaries and direct observation. Once this data has been gathered and analysed, an *influence map* should be drawn up of both the target organisation, in the case of a B2B market, or the target customer/end-user, in the case of a B2C market. Here the aim is to how they might make decisions to purchase a new product or service, and the performance assessments that they might use to assess it. The list of questions for addressing B2B and B2C markets listed in the previous sub-section are a useful framework for this process.

10.4 Customer Value Proposition and Erosion Effects

As discussed in Chap. 7, the primary focus of a business model is the *customer value proposition* (CVP), which sets out the specific value (e.g. features, attributes, benefits) that the new product or service is to offer. It should also consider the best way for the firm to bundle its resources to deliver this, and also how to ensure that any initial competitive advantage that it might secure, can be sustained over the longer term and not be eroded by competitors (Teece 2010). Any CVP must therefore bring significant benefit and perceived value to the customer, and that should be readily identifiable and meet or exceed their expectations. In this regard the CVP is often a trade-off between the benefits that can be offered and the cost and risk of adoption. The following formula expresses this:

CVP = perceived benefits – perceived sacrifices

The business model and CVP design must also consider the *erosion effects* that might emerge once the product or service is launched. These can take the form of imitation and substitution threats from competitors, or just the customer growing tired or bored with the product/service. Strategies to protect against this can include the building of *isolating mechanisms*, such as patents, design registrations and trademarks, that secure proprietary rights to the technology. However, these will face erosion effects (e.g. patents have only 20 life).

10.4.1 NPD and CVP Analysis

In the development of new products, there must be a close relationship between the NPD process and the CVP analysis. The 'value' that a new product might offer is only relevant from the customer's perspective and not from the perspective of the producer. A customers' perception of value is a complex process that typically involves a trade-off of a range of factors that include perceptions of quality and price, as well as social and emotional values (Sweeney and Soutar 2001).

> **Customer perceived value** … is the result of the customer's evaluation of all the benefits and all the costs of an offering as compared to that customer's perceived alternatives. It's the basis on which customers decide to buy things. (Miller and Swaddling 2012, p. 89)

According to Miller and Swaddling (2012), the intersection between the NPD process and the customer's perception of value within the CVP should be structured around the process illustrated in Fig. 10.4. As shown, the NPD process and the CVP development process should be undertaken in conjunction with each other in a mutually reinforcing manner.

The first stage of this process involves matching the evolving product idea as it emerges within the *fuzzy front end* against market research and customer feedback

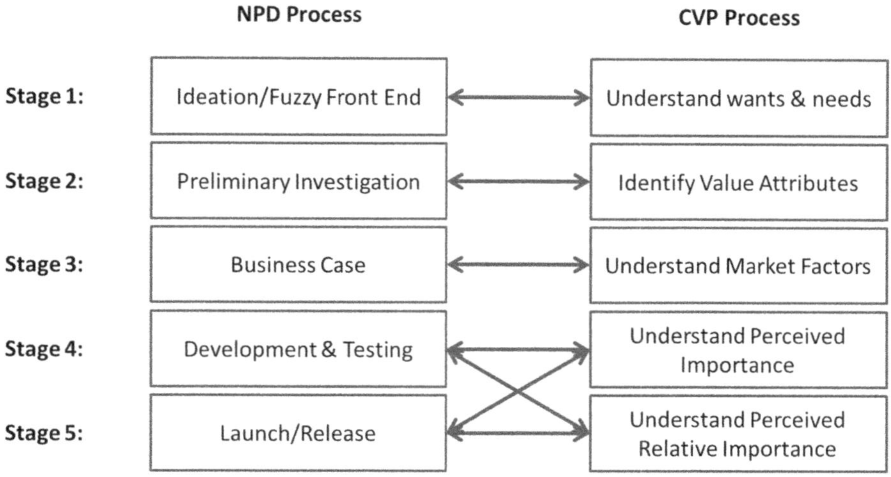

Fig. 10.4 New product development (NPD) and customer value proposition (CVP) research process. (Source: adapted from Miller and Swaddling 2012)

that helps to gain an in-depth understanding of customer/end-user needs and wants. This is followed in stage 2 by a preliminary investigation of the features and attributes that might be configured within the product concept to best satisfy the key attributes that the target customer is likely to perceive as offering value. With these first two steps completed, the project team then develops a business case for the new product, and in doing so, pays close attention to the main factors that are operating to shape potential adoption within the target market. As previously discussed, the success of the new product is likely to be contingent on the ability of NPD project team to configure the necessary specialised and co-specialised assets to secure both technology and product leadership and gain market access (see Fig. 10.1).

The final two steps involve the product development and testing and ultimate launch and release being undertaken simultaneously with ongoing engagement between the R&D and marketing teams, to fully understand the customer's perception of the importance of the various attributes that the new product is offering. These perceptions should involve not only the customer's perception of the overall importance of an attribute or feature, but the relative importance of these. Later we will discuss how this can be undertaken using specific tools. It should be noted that there is a high degree of interconnection between the last two stages of both the NPD and CVP processes.

Achieving a satisfactory outcome, with a new product that can be produced by the firm at an acceptable cost-price-volume equation, and that also a satisfied customer who perceives value in the product requires trade-off of costs and benefits. As illustrated in Fig. 10.5, this is a balancing act that requires a careful matching of attributes, benefits and costs, to the target customer's perception of value. As noted, the perception of value is complicated and relative to alternatives and substitutions available in the market. Further, as Miller and Swaddling (2012) suggest, the

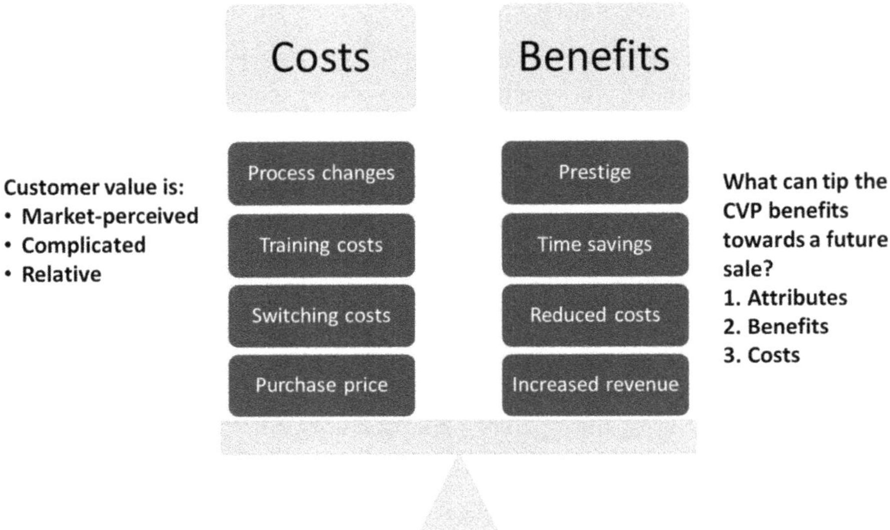

Fig. 10.5 CVP balance scale. (Source: adapted from Miller and Swaddling 2012)

customer's perception of value is 'dynamic' and frequently subject to change as their sense of what relative importance to place on features and benefits found within the product. As a result, managers who wish to maintain their competitiveness must continuously monitor their customers' perceptions of value, and be prepared to innovate in a timely manner to generate new products and services that make a compelling CVP.

10.4.2 CVP and Erosion Effects on the Innovation Rent

In Chap. 8 we introduced the concept of *Innovation Rent* and a *typology of innovation rent configurations* (see Fig. 8.11). This typology was based on a formula comprising the trade-off between high or low *volume* of sales, *rate* of profit, and *length* of lifecycle for a specific innovation. For managers seeking to commercialise innovations with the expectation of yielding above average rent returns for any investment, consideration must be given to the factors that can erode any perceived rate of either volume, rate or length. In the following sub-sections, we discuss the CVP and potential erosion effects on the innovation rent.

- CVP and Erosion Effects on the Volume of Sales

As discussed above, the customer's perception of value is a trade-off between perceived benefits that a new product or service might offer, and the perceived sacrifices that they might have to make in acquiring and adopting it. Figure 10.6 illustrates the potential trade-offs that a customer may see, and the effects that these have on the future commercialisation of the innovation. The model identifies a typology of four possible scenarios defined by high or low perceived benefits or sacrifices.

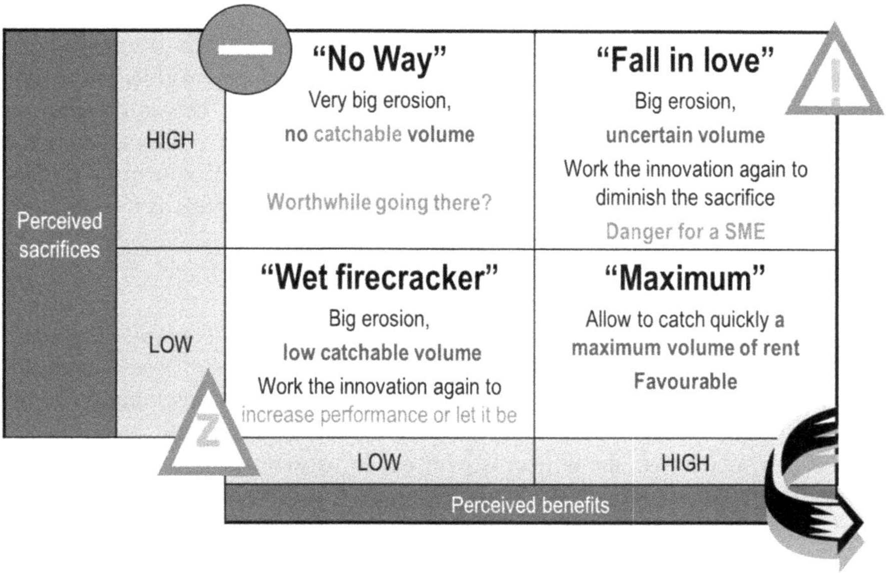

Fig. 10.6 CVP and erosion effects on volume of sales. (Source: with permission from Santi et al. 2003)

The *Maximum* represents the optimal condition where the customer perceives the innovation offers high benefits but low sacrifices. This should allow the innovation to secure good sales and market penetration, and to generate a high rate of rent if conditions relating to the rate of profit are also favourable. By contrast where perceived benefits are low, but perceived sacrifices are high, the outcome is a *No Way*, which places a significant erosion risk on the innovation. The chances of securing significant sales and market share are low and it may not be worthwhile pursuing the project.

By contrast the *Fall in love* option sees the customer perceive high benefits, but at a high level of sacrifice. This should not necessarily kill the innovation project. If the factors that have generated high perceived sacrifices can be reduced through either a redesign of the product, or a reconfiguration of the marketing and sales process, it might allow the firm to proceed. However, for the customer to adopt the innovation under these conditions they would indeed really have to 'fall in love' with the product. An example of this is the initial high cost of new aircraft for airlines, or smart phones for consumers. The provision of leasing arrangements for airlines, or payment plans for the smart phone buyers can significantly reduce the perceive sacrifices. Such strategies are not uncommon for large firms to employ, but it can be a danger for SMEs, where heavy discounts, deferred payment, or major product redesigns, and erode profit margins and place the business at risk.

Finally, the *Wet firecracker* option sees both low perceived sacrifices and benefits. It is essentially not a difficult product or service to adopt, but it offers little incentive for the customer to switch over and buy it. In this case the project team should decide whether to abandon the innovation, or invest in ways to redesign it to offer enhanced features that might boost its perceived benefits. A *Wet firecracker* scenario can emerge when the incumbent product technologies within competitor offerings are enhanced through the normal process of NPD. This is common in highly competitive and crowded markets. An example is motor vehicles, where the differences in brands, product range and models are very close. Competition is often based as much on pricing deals and after sales servicing warranties as it is on product technology and design attributes.

- CVP and Erosion Effects on the Rate of Profit

The rate of profit that can be generated from an innovation is contingent on many factors, such as the cost of production, distribution and sales. These factors are inherent in the firm's value chain and affected by the relative bargaining power of suppliers and customers. In assessing the potential erosion effects on the profitability of a new innovation, the project team needs to consider this bargaining power. Figure 10.7 illustrates a typology for assessing the CVP and its relationship in generating erosion effects on the rate of profit. As shown, the model is a trade-off between the relative bargaining power of the business seeking to commercialise their innovation and their suppliers and customers.

Where the business enjoys a strong position relative to both its suppliers and customers it can most likely enjoy high rates of profit margin and little fear over having this eroded. This can occur where the firm has a unique but valuable technology to sell, or where it has many alternative suppliers for its major inputs. However,

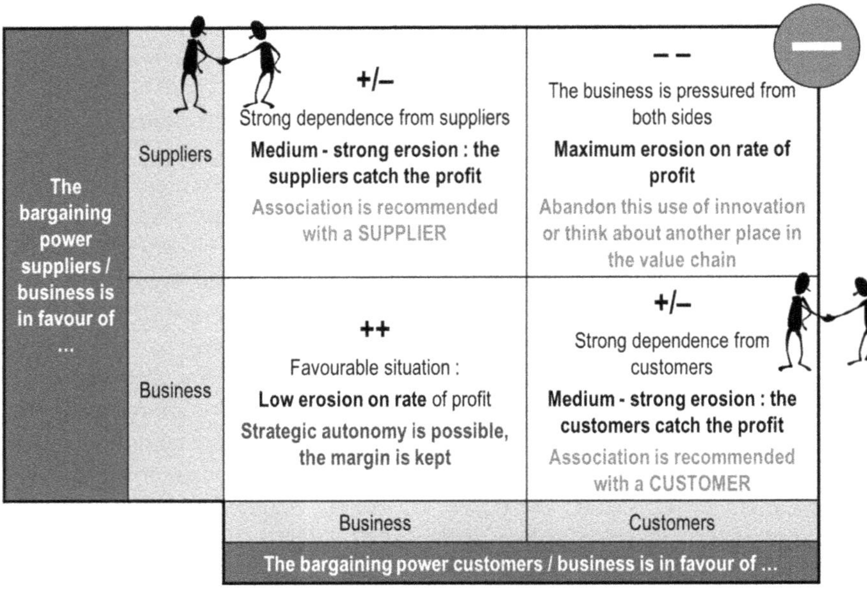

Fig. 10.7 CVP and erosion effects on rate of profit. (Source: with permission from Santi et al. 2003)

where the bargaining power is equally strong for both its customers and suppliers, the business will face significant pressure on its profit margins and it may even be prudent to withdraw from this particular market and place in the value chain, and consider moving into a new market segment or position in the value chain.

In circumstances where the business faces customers with strong bargaining power it can still compete, but it may be forced to accept lower margins through being squeezed on price. The same can occur with suppliers that might possess strong bargaining power. Unless the business can find alternative customers and suppliers its best option is likely to be for it to try to forge a strong strategic alliance or association with the customer or supplier an negotiate reasonable terms. For SMEs this can be challenging.

10.4.3 CVP and Erosion Effects on the Length of the Lifecycle

The ability to maintain a long lifecycle for a particular innovation is usually dependent on the impact of technological and commercial risk. The importance of assessing technical and market risk within the NPD process was discussed in Chap. 8. Figure 10.8 illustrates a model showing the trade-off between high and low commercial (market) and technological (technical) risk. It can be seen that the best option is to have an innovation that has both low commercial and technological risk. In this case the risk that market entry and adoption will be difficult is low, and the risk that there will be major problems in getting the underlying technology accepted and adopted are also low. As a result, this will have very low risk of erosion and should enable the product lifecycle to be quite long.

Substitution risk and erosion effects		**Technological risk:** width and maturity of technological alternatives	
		LOW	HIGH
Commercial risk: customers propensity towards adoption of innovations	HIGH	Low technological risk but high market adoption risk + Requires strong marketing effort difficult for SME	Very high risks and erosion effects − − STOP
	LOW	Very low risks and erosion effects ++	High technological risk but low market adoption risk − Requires strong technical effort difficult for SME

Fig. 10.8 CVP and erosion effects on length of lifecycle. (Source: with permission from Santi et al. 2003)

Where the commercial and technological risks are both high, the likelihood that customers may seek substitutes or switch to new products, and that such alternatives will be entering the market, means that the innovation lifecycle is going to be short. In this case the prospect that the innovation will enjoy sufficient time in the market to provide a good return on investment remains low. Alternatively, where commercial risk is low but technological risk is high, the commercialisation project team will need to ensure that the can invest sufficiently into R&D to enable them to achieve leadership in both technology and product. However, this is likely to be very difficult for most SMEs who lack the necessary resources and the depth of specialised and co-specialised proprietary assets. In this case the SME is either forced to seek collaboration with other organisations (e.g. larger customers, universities) to assist with the commercialisation process, or abandon the project. In a similar manner, if the commercial risk is high and the technological risk is low, the project team will need to invest more into marketing. Once again, this is likely to be difficult for SMEs due to their lack of resources, brand equity, sales and market distribution networks. They will either have to forge strategic alliances with large lead customers, or abandon the project.

An example of this strategy can be seen in the case of *Research in Motion* (RIM) during the commercialisation of the BlackBerry digital, mobile email messaging device during the 1990s. As a small, Canadian company, RIM's ability to overcome technological and commercial (market) risks, in what was a rapidly changing and highly competitive market, was highly challenging. However, RIM secured strong strategic alliances with a number of larger firms, such as U.S. telecommunications giant BellSouth, and the American Mobile Satellite Corporation (AMSC). These strategic alliances provided RIM access to technical and marketing resources that helped to reduce the risk levels on both fronts and enable the BlackBerry to secure a dominant market position for a number of years (Carayannopoulos 2005).

10.5 Listening to the Voice of the Customer

As noted above, the success or failure of a commercialisation process is often contingent on how well the project team understands the customer's needs and wants, as well as the context in which the customers/end-users will be using the product or service in their personal and professional lives. Only by integrating information gathered from a process of listening to the *voice of the customer* (VOC), will it be possible to determine if the new innovation is going to meet the customer/end-user needs and requirements and therefore offer an attractive CVP (Cleland 2004). In the following sub-sections, we examine a number of different approaches to securing VOC insights in the NPD commercialisation process.

10.5.1 Quality Function Deployment

The concept of gaining an in-depth understanding of customers' needs and wants as part of a commercialisation process is not new, and has been closely linked to a range of quality management systems since at least the 1980s (Sarazen 1990). Its origins can be traced back to the foundations of the *total quality management* (TQM) systems that were championed by Deming (1982, 1986, 1993), Juran (1951, 1954, 1967), and Feigenbaum (1961), who brought the concepts to Japan in the late 1940s and early 1950s as part of the post-war reconstruction of that country. This helped to transform the mindset and practices of Japanese management, who readily adopted the TQM principles. The global success of Japan's large manufacturing *Keiretsu* enterprises led these concepts to be brought back to the United States and adopted worldwide during the 1980s and 1990s in both large and small firms (Haksever 1996). The adoption of TQM and the associated International Standards Organisation (ISO) quality management systems ISO 9001 and now ISO 900 (McAdam and McKeown 1999; ISO 2015).

The Eight Key Elements of "Voice of Customer" in Quality Function Deployment

- *Customer Perceptions* – how does the customer perceive the problem that the new product or service might be targeted at solving? This should be based on direct feedback from end users within the target market.
- *Customer Needs* – do all target customers have similar needs? How do they segment into end users with different needs?
- *Basic, Spoken & Unspoken* – what are the essential 'must have' (e.g. *basic*) product attributes? What additional new features can the customers identify (e.g. *spoken*)? What product attributes can be identified that the customer might want that they have not identified (e.g. *unspoken*)?
- *Importance Rankings of needs* – what is the relative importance of these attributes to the customers?
- *Design Attributes* – what attributes and features can the new product be equipped with that would meet or exceed these customer needs?
- *Relationship between Customer Needs & Design Attributes* – what is the match between existing products and customer needs and how might value be designed into the new product?
- Costs & Feasibility – what is the cost of developing a new product that contains all the features desired by the customer? Can these design attributes be feasibly built into the new product given existing technologies?
- *Engineering Measures* – what are the existing performance standards that competing products offer to the customer against these design attributes? How might these performance standards be met or exceeded within the new product design?
- *Trade Offs* – what are the trade-offs that need to be made between the customers' desired product attributes and the actual technical, cost and engineering attributes that the company can build into the new product?

Sources: Akao and Mazur (2003); Griffin and Hauser (1993).

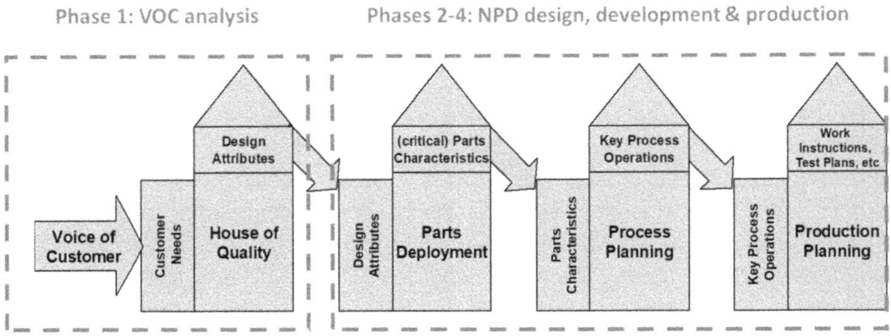

Fig. 10.9 The four houses of the Quality Function Deployment (QFD). (Source: Schnepple 2005)

Within this package of TQM systems is the *Qualify Function Deployment* (QFD) or *hinshitsu tenkai* process that was pioneered in Japan in the 1960s by Mizuno and Akao (1978). This is a product or service development process that focuses on the integration of multi-functional teams across areas such as R&D, engineering, manufacturing and marketing. It was pioneered in Mitsubishi's Kobe shipyards in the early 1970s, and then adopted by Toyota in the late 1970s. The benefits of QFD were substantial savings in the time and cost of product design and development (Griffin and Hauser 1993). A key principle of QFD is the need to listen to the *voice of the customer* (VOC), via a systematic and hierarchical set of customer needs assessment (see text box).

The QFD process encapsulates a comprehensive process of building the VOC input into a pipeline of new product development described as taking place within "four houses of QFD". Figure 10.9 illustrates these four houses of which the first is the "House of Quality", within which the customer's needs, wants and anticipated specifications are interpreted against the technical design attributes that might be designed into the product. From here, the new product design is moved to the second house where the design attributes are matched to the critical parts of the new product. In turn, the prototype is moved to the third house, where the prototype is examined in terms of how it might be further developed to ensure that it is optimised for full-scale production. Finally, the project moves to the fourth house where the planning is undertaken for full production. Throughout the entire NPD process, the starting point is the data captured from the VOC.

10.5.2 House of Quality Analysis

An important role played by the QFD process is to ensure that the internal divisions within the company, such as R&D, production, marketing and sales, are all actively involved in integrating VOC with the NPD process (Farrell 1994). The initial stage of the *House of Quality* is perhaps the most critical. As illustrated in Fig. 10.10, the key elements of the 'house' are the customer needs (basic, spoken and unspoken), design attributes, costs and feasibility, engineering measures and customer

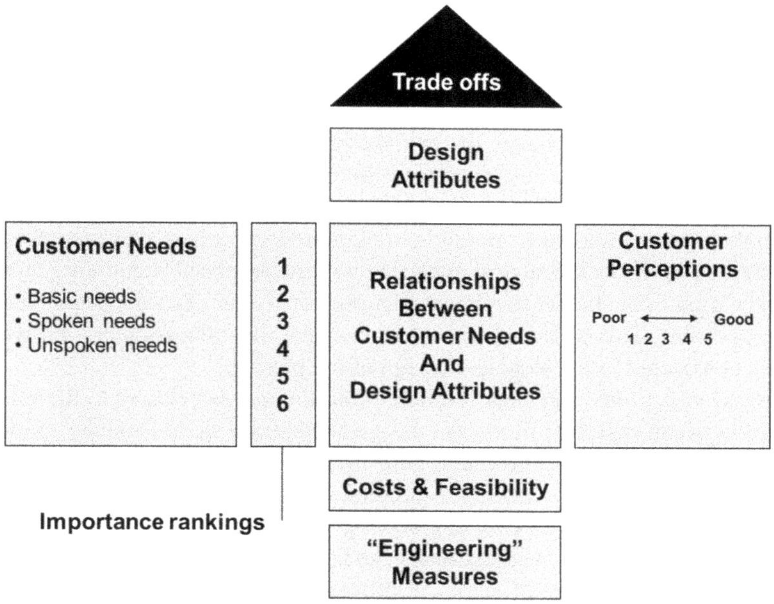

Fig. 10.10 House of quality in QFD. (Source: Griffin and Hauser 1993)

perceptions. These are cross-matched within the 'house' framework in order to generate the most optimal product design.

The House of Quality is essentially a matrix linking the design of the product to the needs of the customer integrating the technical and market development processes. Eight key elements make up the House of Quality:

1. *Customer Perceptions* – market research should be gathered to provide a picture of customers' perceptions of the relative performance of existing products currently in the market. If no rival product currently exists this research should examine customers' perceptions of how they now fulfil their needs. It is important to identify which current products are perceived to satisfy which needs best and to note where any gaps exist.
2. *Customer Needs* – this element contains the findings from market research and seeks to list the key spoken and unspoken needs of the customer. The focus should be on identifying at least three types of customer needs: (i) basic needs (what the customer assumes the product will do); (ii) articulated or spoken needs (what a customer says they want a product to do); and exciting or unspoken needs (those needs that will delight the customer if they were fulfilled). These can be identified using *Affinity Diagrams* (White et al. 2002). These can be used in a focus group or other qualitative research methodology to better understand the way that consumers see a problem. Where the total number of needs is greater than 20–30 items these should be placed into a hierarchy with primary, secondary and tertiary needs identified.

3. *Importance Rankings* – customers will usually place greater importance on some needs than others. Market research can examine the relative importance of customer needs and provide a statistically measurable hierarchy that can be used to guide the NPD process.
4. *Design Attributes* – these are the engineering measures of product performance that seek to address the customer needs in technical performance terms.
5. *Relationships between Customer Needs and Design Attributes* – as data is entered into the matrix it should be possible to map the areas where customer needs are addressed by the technical design attributes of the proposed technology. Symbols can be used in the model to represent strong positive or negative relationships or average ones. This process is designed to check that all customers' needs have been considered in the technical design of the product.
6. *Costs & Feasibility* – as data is entered into the matrix relating to the relationships between customer needs and design attributes it should also be possible to determine whether it is feasible or cost effective to develop the product to meet all these requirements. Seeking to produce the perfect product may slow down the NPD process and risk over engineering the solution.
7. *Engineering Measures* – assessments can be made by the technical design team to determine the degree of technical difficulty involved in meeting each of the customers' needs and how the proposed new product parameters compare to those of any existing product currently in the market. It is recommended that competitor or existing technology be acquired and examined to determine industry benchmarks and to capture data on current performance standards. Additional market relevant information such as warranty or service fault frequency and costs might also be examined.
8. *Trade Offs* – as all data is entered into the house of quality matrix the "roof matrix" combines the various technical design attributes to specify the engineering relationships among the design attributes. This is illustrated in Fig. 10.11 where it can be seen that symbols can be used to map the strength of these interactions.

The House of Quality stage in QFD provide better design outcomes, improved customer satisfaction, better cross-functional communication and collaboration within large organisations, and reduced product development cycle time (Cristiano et al. 2000). Figure 10.11 illustrates the layout of a House of Quality framework set up in an EXCEL spreadsheet. The example used here is that of a new refrigerator. I can be seen that the traditionally 'roof shaped' trade-off matrix has been replaced by a "stairway" which facilitates implementation with an EXCEL spreadsheet at the cost of being somewhat less intuitive than a "roof-matrix".

Customer requirements obtained from market research are used to assess customer needs and these are listed in the rows below "customer needs". It can be seen that these consist of: low energy consumption, quietness, good storage space, reliability and low service costs. The overall importance of these attributes, as

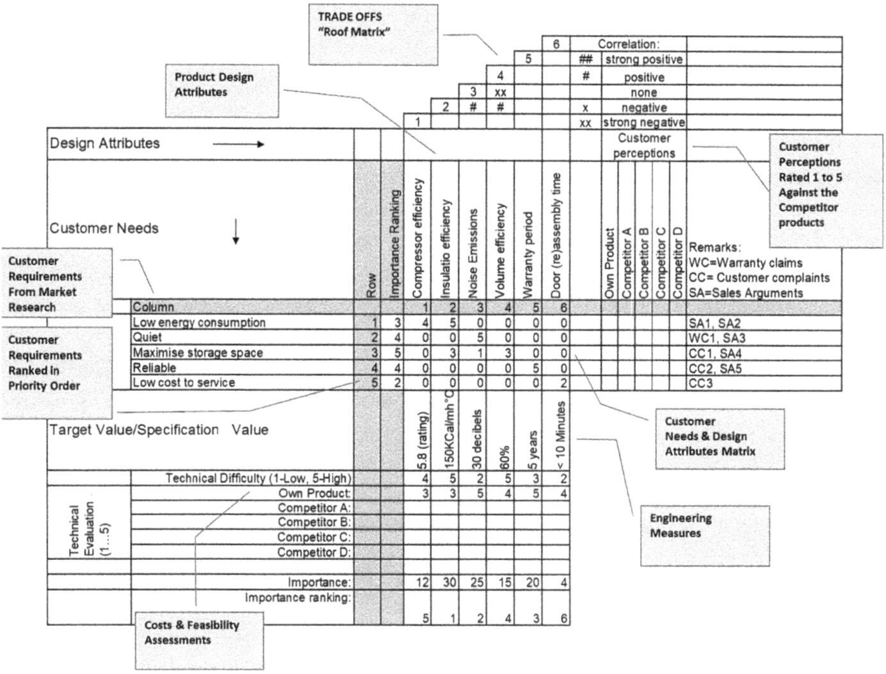

Fig. 10.11 House of quality applied. (Source: Schnepple 2005)

perceived by the customers (from market research), are entered into the spreadsheet. Here it can be seen that storage space was the most important attribute, followed by quietness of operation and reliability, which were of equal importance. The product design attributes that would need to be considered in order to meet the customers' requirements are listed in the columns along the top of the model, and include compressor and insulation efficiency, noise emissions, volume efficiency, the warranty period.

The House of Quality Summary

- A tool to "negotiate" product specification between marketing and technical staff.
- Marketing staff get insights into technical trade-offs.
- Technical staff get insights into the voice of the customer.
- Helps to identify the right priorities.
- Achieve better designs.
- Improve customer satisfaction.
- Reduce product cycle time (get it right first time).
- Concept is very intuitive, hence easy to understand.

Also shown in Fig. 10.11 are the engineering measures, cost and feasibility assessments and the customer perceptions of competitor products (as identified in market research). This information is entered into the spreadsheet and used to assess the trade-offs that will need to be made to help optimise a new product design. It should be noted that the spreadsheet shown here should be seen as a starting point only. Extra information can be added when appropriate. For example, additional rows can be added that list the technical specifications of competitor products, an extra column could be added to give a target rating to be achieved for customer perceptions plus another column to rate the development effort required to achieve such a rating. The remarks column above lists abbreviations that of course must be documented outside the matrix.

A number of checks can be applied to the relationship matrix to ensure customer needs are properly translated into design attributes. *An empty row* – meaning a customer need is not related to any of the design attributes – suggests the list of design attributes is incomplete. *An empty column* – meaning a design attribute is not related to any of the customer needs – suggests the design attribute is not really needed (feature creep?), or perhaps is not a feature of the product itself. *Rows that repeat identical relationships* – check for duplicate customer needs. Duplication of needs does inflate the importance calculation and should be avoided.

10.5.3 Kano Model Analysis

Another useful tool that can be used in the QFD, NPD process is the Kano model analysis, which draws on the work of Noriaki Kano, a Professor quality management at Tokyo University. As shown in Fig. 10.12, the Kano model employs a matrix that trades off lo to high performance of a product's technical features, against lo to high satisfaction with those features from the customer. In the bottom right hand quadrant are the *must-be (basic) attributes*, which are the features that a product or service must have in order to satisfy the customer. These attributes or features are usually so common in products or services that the customer expects them, and adding them will not make the customer any more satisfied. However, if they are absent, the customer will be very dissatisfied.

An example, is an air-conditioner in a car today. The first car air-conditioners were installed in America in 1939 by the Packard company. By the 1950s, in response to a growing after-market business of car air-conditioner installations, General Motors began to offer car air-conditioners on their prestige cars as an optional extra from the factory. By the 1980s virtually all cars were being sold with air-conditioners as standard. So, what was once an optional extra to help delight the customer, is now a *must-be (basic) attribute* that will cause dissatisfaction if it is absent.

The next element within the Kano model are the *one-dimensional attributes* that satisfy the customer when they are present, but cause dissatisfaction when they are missing. They are different from the *must-be (basic) attributes* in that those don't

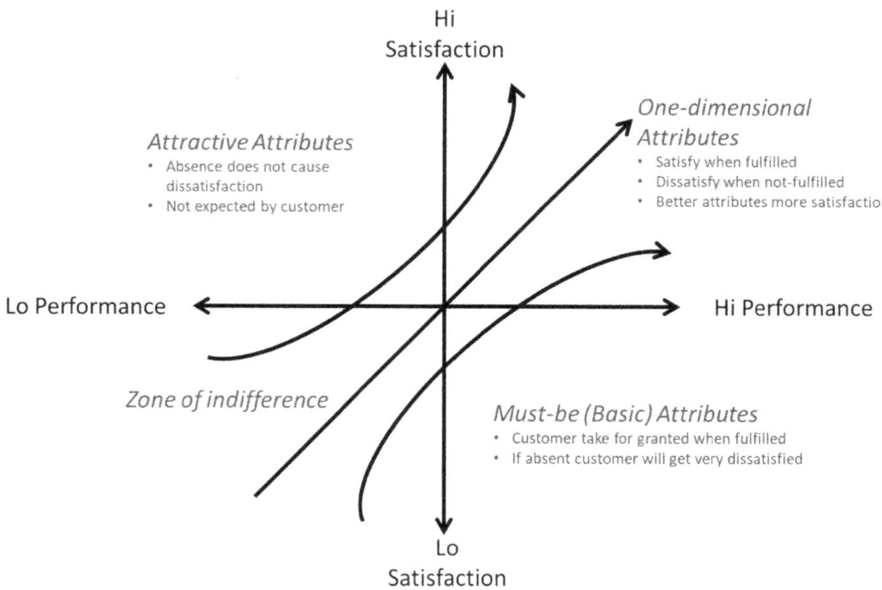

Fig. 10.12 Kano model analysis. (Source: adapted from Tan and Shen 2000)

satisfy the customer – because they are expected – and only dissatisfy them when they are not present. An example of a *one-dimensional attribute* is the length of the service warranty on a new car. The manufacturers' warranties on new cars can vary between 1 and 3 years, and may be based on age (years since purchase), or mileage (distance travelled). These warranties cover a range of repair and maintenance issues related to the vehicle and typically provide a guarantee that the parts or maintenance required within the terms of the agreement will be covered low or no cost to the consumer (subject to conditions). Car manufacturers have gradually extended their warranty terms without additional cost to the point where a standard new car warranty has grown from 3 to 5 years. For customers who once viewed the 3-year warranty attractive when compared to only 1 year, the more generous 5-year warranty is now the new benchmark of satisfaction.

Finally, there is the third element of the *attractive attributes*. These are the features or attributes that will not be expected by the customer because they are not known or common. To not offer them will not incur any dissatisfaction from the customer, but if they are offered, the customer will be delighted. An example, is the inclusion of leather seats or satellite navigation in cars at no extra cost. When Japanese car manufacturers began to expand globally during the 1970s and 1980s, they packaged their vehicles to include such features as radio, cassette tape players, air-conditioners, carpets and automatic transmissions and extended warranties as standard. This made them very attractive to customers and forced the competitor manufacturers in the United States and Europe, to respond in-kind.

Kano Performance Requirements

- You must start by offering the "must have" attributes in your product or service.
- Focus on the "one-dimensional" attributes to offer superior performance but ensure that you keep these at or above best practice.
- Look for ways to offer "attractive attributes" that the customer has not expected (customer delight) but remember that once offered the customer will begin to expect these and no longer see them as attractive.
- Any new "attractive attributes" will also risk being copied or imitated by your competitors unless "isolating mechanisms" can be put in place.
- Look for the "zone of indifference" where the customer is not interested in an attribute.
- Look for "reverse requirements" that decrease satisfaction when present and increase satisfaction when missing.

Source: Kano et al. (1984).

10.5.4 VOC CAGE Model

In addition to the Kano model, another useful tool for NPD project teams is the CAGE model, illustrated in Fig. 10.13. This comprises three overlapping elements represented by the circle, the rectangle and the oval shapes. These are interpreted by looking at the areas where there are overlaps and where they are not overlapped. The oval shape represents the data collected from the VOC market research and customer feedback about their needs, problems and potential requirements for a

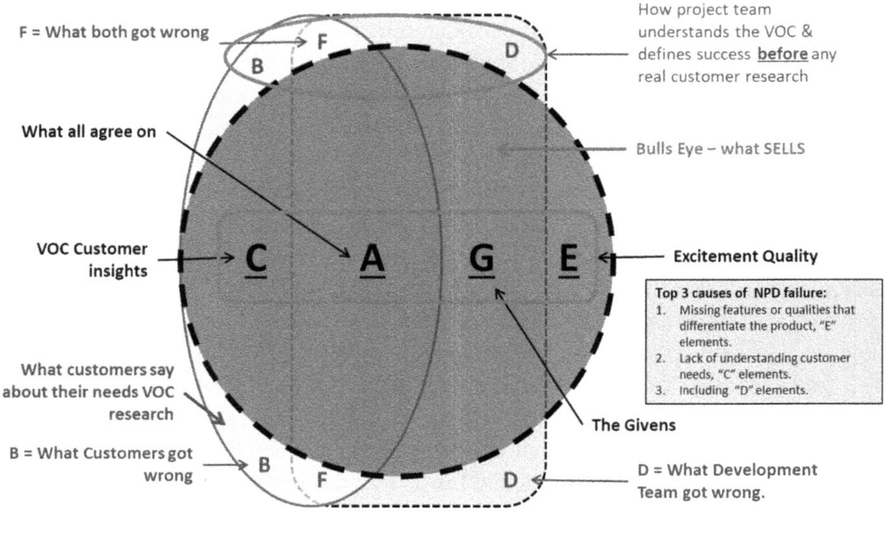

Fig. 10.13 Voice of the customer CAGE model. (Source: adapted from C2C Solutions 2015)

product or service. The rectangle represents the things that the NPD project team understands or thinks about the product requirements before they have undertaken any VOC related research. The circle is the application of the CAGE model "bulls-eye" and defines what is likely to sell.

The bold letters C.A.G.E represent areas where there are potential opportunities for consideration in the design of a new product concept:

- *C* – represents the things that the VOC research indicated the customers might wish to see or might want in a new product.
- *A* – represents the things that both the NDP project team and the VOC customer research agree on.
- *G* – represents the 'givens' or the things that are the *must-be* attributes any new product will need to provide.
- *E* – represents the things that offer a potential excitement quality by delivering new and attractive attributes to the customer.

Other important elements in the model are represented by capital letters. These include:

- "B" – what the customers got wrong or missed about the attributes that the new product could offer;
- "D" – what the NPD project got wrong or missed, and
- "F" – what both the customers and the NPD project team got wrong.

Amongst the most common causes of failure in NPD commercialisation are: (i) missing features or qualities that differentiate a new product (e.g. the "E" elements); (ii) a lack of understanding about customer needs (e.g. "C" elements); and including into a new product attributes from within the "D" element that are of no real interest to the customer.

10.5.5 Techniques for VOC Research

The process of gathering data to identify customer needs can involve a range of market research techniques comprising both qualitative and quantitative methodologies. Table 10.3 lists some of these.

One of the most popular methods is the *focus group* of 8–12 people who are guided by a facilitator through a discussion lasting around 1–2 h. This technique has been in use since the late 1940s and is useful for circumstances where it is desirable to have people share their opinions or views on a subject, as this often helps to elicit information less likely to emerge in one on one interviews (Hines 2000). An advantage of focus groups is their ability to draw together a relatively large number of customers in a single meeting and capture a large amount of data fairly quickly. The focus group is often found to stimulate participants thinking and can elicit

Table 10.3 Voice of customer research methods

VOC method and example	Description
Focus groups to define big problems with solutions iterations	Run focus group sessions on customers to identify problems, issues & points of pain. Observe or film the meetings and brainstorm solutions to problems, then take back to focus group. Customers then vote on solutions or suggest improvements (iterative process)
Brainstorming event with customers	Invite customers for an innovation day that includes a set of inverse and regular brainstorming sessions designed to find creative ways to destroy the product. Identify three major weaknesses and look for new solutions
In-depth interviews via customer visits	Select cross-functional interview teams, visit key customers and conduct in-depth interviews with customer groups. Use an interview guide with direct and indirect questions to help customers articulate needs, likes, dislikes and desires. Allow customers to engage with the product
"Camping out" via ethnographic research	Identify customer sites and spend time there (e.g. full day). Watch them use a product, discover how they spend their day and use the technology or services
Working with lead or innovative customers	Find early adopters (EarlyVangelists) and work with them to create new ideas or solutions. Run a workshop and invite them to participate in the co-creation of the new product
Crowdsourcing	Using in online media get customers to suggest ideas, create content and co-design products. Select the best and share with other customers for evaluation

information that could otherwise be missed in surveys or one-to-one interviews. However, the focus group needs to be facilitated by an experienced researcher to get the best outcomes (Threlfall 1999). Care also needs to be taken in the selection of participants as the point of the *focus group* is to concentrate people who are willing to share their experiences, thoughts and ideas with others and provide rich information. The environment is therefore not suitable for situations where someone might feel threatened or intimidated by sharing their views with others. The focus group is also a largely exploratory research design (Garson 2014).

Another group-based research method is *brainstorming* in which the members of a group (e.g. customers), individually write down their ideas and then post them up for all to share and participate in a group discussion about the merits of each idea. This can be undertaken with customers or members of the NPD project team, and is often able to generate better outcomes if it is facilitated by someone who is experienced in the technique (Githens 2002). An alternative is to conduct one-to-one interviews with customers. This is more time consuming and therefore expensive, but can be just as revealing and evidence suggests two interviews can yield as much information on customer needs as one focus group, and that 20–30 interviews can generally produce around 90–95% of the customer needs information required for an NPD project (Griffin and Hauser 1993).

Techniques for Focus Groups and Interviews

- Ensure that the objectives of the study are clearly outlined and understood.
- Work from a prepared discussion or interview guide that maintains the overall structure of the questions and avoids things being side tracked.
- Ask open ended questions that evoke responses that allow the customer to talk about the things that they like or dislike about the status quo and avoid "Yes" or "No" answers.
- Do not allow interviewer opinions or biases to dominate or influence customer responses.
- Have interviews or focus groups facilitated by trained or experienced market researchers and who are not directly associated with the NPD process.
- Ensure interviews or discussions are recorded, ideally using audio and/or video.

A less commonly used, but potentially very powerful, research method to obtain insights into customer behaviour and attitudes is the *ethnography*. The concept of ethnographic research comes from anthropology and has been designed to study human behaviour, in particular, the cultures and sub-cultures that comprise it. The ethnographic method typically involves the researcher spending time with a group of people, who may or may not know the researcher's purpose, and obtaining in-depth information and understanding of their social system. This can be undertaken at a macro-level across a broad group, or at a micro-level within specific targeted groups (Garson 2013). Data collection can also involve giving customers diaries to complete, or being asked to make short videos, or capture photos of their daily life. More recently, the ability to collect data by monitoring consumers' online activity via social media or web browsing has provided additional ethnographic research data.

The opportunity to leverage the experiences of existing lead customers and use their goodwill to help generate ideas for new products and services, or to improve existing ones is also a potentially valuable research method. This can take the form or focus groups or any of the other techniques described above. However, the lead customer, particularly in B2B marketing channels, is often a valuable way to co-create future innovative ideas. Finally, there is the benefit of running online *crowd-sourcing* campaigns. This has become an effective tool for many, particularly large firms, to engage in *open innovation* programs and invite people to assist with identifying solutions to technical problems, and to do so at a lower cost than might have otherwise been possible (Yu 2017).

10.5.6 Affinity Diagrams

Once data has been captured from a focus group or set of customer interviews it needs to be carefully analysed to identify patterns and trends. A useful technique in undertaking this analysis is to develop an *Affinity Diagram*. This allows the organisation of a large amount of qualitative data (such as transcriptions of taped focus group discussions or interviews) to allow a better understanding of the problem. The development of an affinity diagram involves at least seven stages commencing with the assembly of a study team comprising at least two people who will cross-check and validate each other's findings. It is expected that any focus group or interview data will already have been gathered and the research problem or question(s) will already have been identified. This might be something like: "What is it about products currently in use in this target market that dissatisfies customers" (White et al. 2002). In undertaking this analysis, the study team will usually read through the data from the transcripts and look for customer comments that indicate views critical of existing products. These should be sorted and arranged into groups to identify common categories and also to de-duplicate multiple responses.

Steps for Developing an Affinity Diagram

- *Step 1*: Assemble your research team
- *Step 2*: Prepare the research question(s)
- *Step 3*: Brainstorm answers to the question(s) omitting any duplicate answers
- *Step 4*: Post answers on a whiteboard or spreadsheet
- *Step 5*: Sort into related groups – each team member does this independently
- *Step 6*: Develop Header Cards – using descriptive sentence to define the card's grouping
- *Step 7*: Draw the Affinity Diagram

Source: White et al. (2002).

Figure 10.14 illustrates the process of developing an *affinity diagram*. Sorting large amounts of qualitative data can be highly time consuming and is facilitated by using Post-it notes on a board or wall, or a whiteboard that can be erased. In the initial stage all participants suggest their ideas, which are written onto the Post-it notes and placed randomly. Then each idea is discussed and they are sorted and grouped, placed under headings. Once completed the final structure can be captured as an *affinity diagram*. It is recommended that two or more members of the team work independently of each other in reviewing and sorting the data to allow some degree of cross-checking and internal validity control. A consensus should then be reached on the groupings which are then placed onto "header cards" containing a brief sentence describing and defining the group of customer comments or product

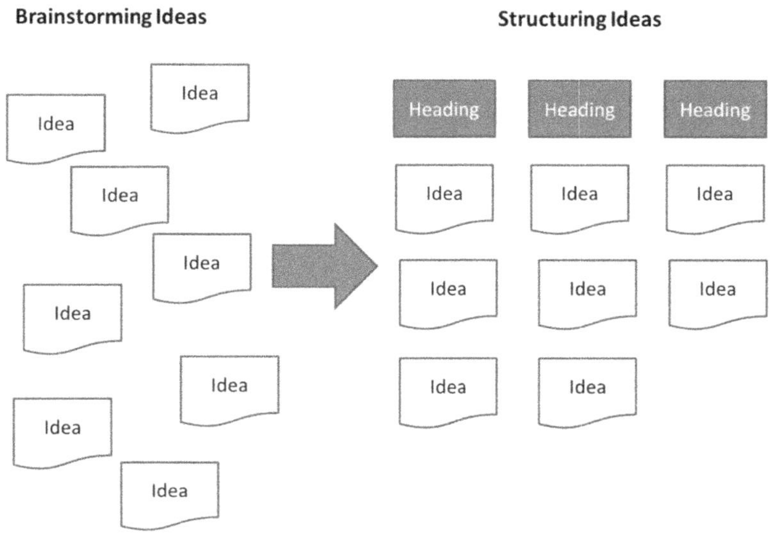

Fig. 10.14 The product development and definition

attributes. The aim is to finish with only a few groupings. When evaluating a particular product or service separate diagrams should be created for positive and negative customer comments. The data from the affinity diagram can be fed directly into the House of Quality in the "customer needs" and "customer perceptions" sections.

A spreadsheet program (e.g. EXCEL) can be used to sort comments and then quickly arrange them into groups. The spreadsheet also allows quantitative coding to be applied and used for statistical analysis. More sophisticated software for qualitative data analysis is also available, such as NVivo (Bazeley and Jackson 2013) and Leximancer (2018). NVivo is a specialised software for analysis of large amounts of qualitative data such as text, audio and video. It requires the analyst to have an expertise in qualitative data analysis and coding (Sladaña 2016). Leximancer is a text analytic software that uses algorithms to structure large amounts of text into concept maps. It offers a faster way to quickly sort data and identify concepts and relationships between them, and provides greater reliability as it is not as dependent on analyst judgment (Sotiriadou et al. 2014).

10.6 Outcomes Based Market Research

While emphasising the benefits of listening to customers, there are also pitfalls of listening too much to them. Customers only know what they have experienced. They cannot imagine what they don't know about emerging technologies, new materials and the like (Ulwick 2002). They should therefore not be trusted to come up with solutions. Rather, customers should only be asked for outcomes, what they want a new product or service do for them. Customers themselves would never have come up with ideas for innovations such as Velcro or Post-it-notes. Solutions proposed by lead users must also be evaluated carefully to make sure they actually appeal to the wider market. To help assess the market opportunity of a new product, it is useful to ask the users to rate the importance of each identified outcome, along with a satisfaction rating as to how well it is currently met.

The Lead User Process

Step1: Start of the Lead User Process:

- Building an interdisciplinary team
- Defining the target market
- Defining the goals of the lead user involvement

Step 2: Identification of Needs and Trends:

- Interviews with experts (market/technology).
- Scanning of literature, internet, databanks.
- Selection of most attractive trends (market, technology and anticipated benefits).
- Step 3: Identification of Lead Users.
- Networking based search for lead users.
- Investigation of analogous markets.
- Screening of first ideas and solutions generated by lead users.

Step 4: Concept Design:

- Workshop with lead users to generate or improve product concepts.
- Evaluation and documentation of the concepts (e.g. by projecting concepts onto general market).

Source: Lüthje and Herstatt (2004).

10.6.1 Probe and Learn

Conventional market research methods, including the voice of the customer techniques, may not be sufficient in new and turbulent sectors. Product and market development in such turbulent sectors are often an emergent process in which the premium is on learning and rapid incorporation of that learning into subsequent products and services (Cole 2001). Such a *Probe and Learn* methodology encourages the successive generation of error, early and often, as part of the learning process. A great deal of the valuable learning in the product development cycle comes at the point of new product introduction. Every time a company introduces a new product into the marketplace, it receives a rush of feedback that is unavailable to competitors. Customers provide feedback on the new product, but they may also 'invent' new ways of using the product in ways never intended before, thus creating new market opportunities. The more often a company introduces new products, the more it learns about the dynamics of its marketplace (Miller and Morris 1999). Deciding to pursue a *probe and learn* approach must usually be made by senior management due to the increased costs in having many small instead of a few large product iterations. 'Probe and Learn' should be seen as a strategic choice rather than just as a design optimisation tool.

10.7 From Discovery to Development

Once the customer discovery and VOC analysis has taken place, the NPD project team can start to define and develop the final product concept. Following a systematic approach to this is important to the ultimate success of the commercialisation process (Akgun et al. 2004). Speed to market is now becoming increasingly important with closer customer/end-user interaction along all stages of the NPD commercialisation process from ideation to launch (Cooper 2019). According to Cooper (2011) the success or failure of any NPD project is to *get rid of the fuzziness* as quickly as possible. This is achieved by investing in a "solid front end" that allows the project team as complete an understanding of the target customer or end-user needs and requirements. The VOC analysis plus clear and early product definition are critical.

The overall process for the discovery stage of the NPD process is illustrated in Fig. 10.15, where it can be seen that the initial *front-end work process* of the *Stage Gate*® (shown at the bottom) moves through the stages of discovery (ideas), project scoping, business case and development, with Go/Kill stage-gates at each transition point. This initial discovery phase takes place within the wider strategic context of broader company business strategy. The NPD project team must be aware of this strategic context, which includes both industry and company level analysis, and how their project contributes to corporate strategy. The NPD process will be influenced by the iterations of communication between the team and other parts of the company such as marketing and sales, production, corporate legal, strategic planning and finance. It will also need to engaged with a wider number of groups outside the firm in the *open innovation* network.

Following the initial discovery stage, the *project scoping* stage seeks to undertake a quick assessment of the project to determine if it is worthwhile moving to stage two and developing the business case. Within the *project scoping* stage, there are three primary actions that must be undertaken (Cooper 2011):

1. *Preliminary market assessment,* – this is a quick scoping of the market to assess the likelihood that the new product will be accepted. It should not be too exhaustive and can be informed from existing VOC market research.

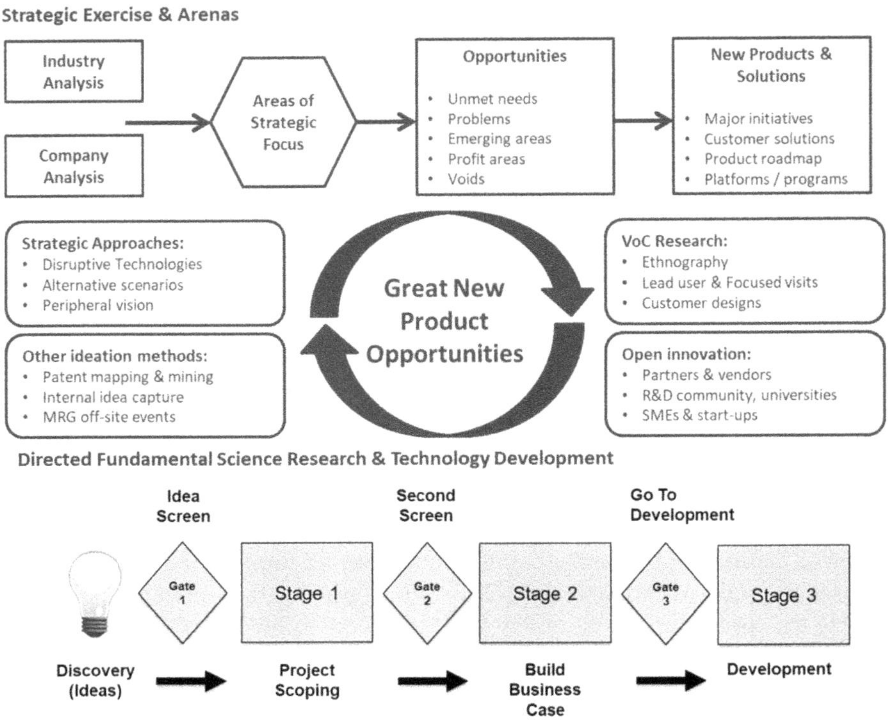

Fig. 10.15 The discovery stage for NPD. (Source: adapted from Cooper 2011; Cooper and Edgett 2005)

2. *Preliminary technical assessment,* – this involves a conceptual assessment of the technical feasibility of the new product, so as to identify any technical risks, review the firm's ability to produce it, and whether there are any IP rights issues, or the need for strategic partnerships with other firms.
3. *Preliminary business and financial assessment,* –an assessment is undertaken of the commercial risks likely to emerge in any future commercialisation, and the need for additional financial resources.
4. *Recommendations and action plan for Stage 2* – here the final Go/Kill recommendation is made along with an action plan if the project is to proceed.

During the second stage of *building the business case* at least three additional activities should be completed. The first of these is the development of a *project definition*, which addresses the question of what specific product will be developed. This will require attention being given to the target market, how the product concept will meet customer and end-user requirements, the positioning of the product, the technical attributes, features and specifications, and how they combined to create a powerful CVP. The next action is to *justify the project*. This will require a business case to be prepared that comprises an objective assessment of the financial, technical and market risks and returns. Finally, the *action plan* for future development will be generated. This should detail all the stages and activities that will have to take place to bring the product from initial market testing to full scale production and distribution (Cooper 2011). In the following sub-sections, we discuss two key elements, product definition and product-technology road-mapping.

10.7.1 Defining the Product

An important stage of NPD is the development of a clearly defined conceptualisation of the new product. This is illustrated in Fig. 10.16 where it can be seen that the *product definition* is the sum of a number of related elements that address the project scope, target market, project concept, pricing and positioning issues, CVP, identified benefits that the new product can offer, the technical features, attributes and requirements needed within the design to produce the desire outcome, and the high-level specifications that must be included versus those that can be optional. Information for addressing these eight elements and their associated questions, will be obtained from the VOC customer discovery and market research processes discussed above.

Cooper and Edgett (2005) suggest that a feature of highly successful NPD commercialisation is for the project teams to keep moving forward without becoming stuck in the early stages of the process. Instead they recommend *simultaneous execution*, which is employed by the Toyota corporation, to allow NPD project teams to make progress on new product design and development, without having to wait for all data to become available. However, rather than the R&D, NPD project team working in isolation, they are in continuous communication and data sharing with

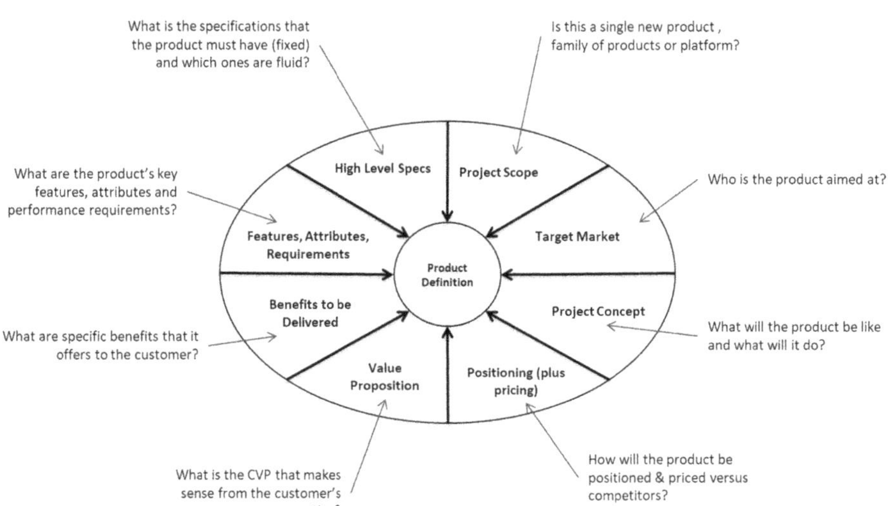

Fig. 10.16 The integrated product definition. (Source: adapted from Cooper and Edgett 2005)

other parts of the company such as production, marketing and sales. The most important thing is to evolve the NPD commercialisation process rapidly but with structure and continuous learning.

> **For example,** … The fundamental principle is this: Undertake only enough homework to yield data that is essential for the key decisions you must make. Examples of key decisions in these earlier stages are design decisions (the product definition) and Go/Kill decisions on the project. The rule is simple: It's alright to move forward without complete information. That is, the project team can begin the next activity within a stage with partial information. (Cooper and Edgett 2005, p. 56)

10.7.2 Product-Technology Road-Mapping

Once the product definition process has been completed and the NPD project is moving into the development stage, it will be important to coordinate all activity within the *action plan* and a useful tool to assist with this is the *product-technology roadmap*. The process of technology road-mapping has been widely adopted throughout industry as a mechanism to assist firms with technology management (McMillan 2003). This requires attention to be given to a number of levels of activity in relation to the firm's strategy, technology and general operations development. At the strategy level this involves consideration of the corporate strategy for any new product being generated, and how this new product will fit within the firm's overall market positioning as a cost leader or differentiator (Albright and Kappel 2003). For example, the decision by Toyota to enter the prestige brand market segment led the company to developing not only a more up-market range of vehicles, but also a new *Lexus* brand with its own marketing and distribution channels. This highlights the need for the NPD project to be considered within the context of how it adds value to the overall portfolio of existing products and services being produced, as well as to the generation of a clear CVP within its target market. Once these issues have been addressed the project team will need to ensure that their activities are undertaken with consideration of marketing, production, distribution and IP management strategies (Phaal et al. 2004).

There are many approaches to the development and use of a product-technology roadmap, although the simplest use a structure as illustrated in Fig. 10.17. As shown the roadmap is drawn up with the key activities listed on the vertical axis and the timeline for the development on the horizontal axis. The activities that a project team places into the roadmap will depend on the complexity of the project. In this case the key areas being considered are the development of the firm's R&D/IP rights portfolio to take into account such things as the securing of patents, design registrations or licencing of third-party IP for the project. Next is the technology development process, followed by the product development and then the market development. The resources required to have this roadmap implemented are listed on the bottom of the model, with reference to capital investment requirements, logistics for supply-chain management and the upgrading of factory facilities also mapped.

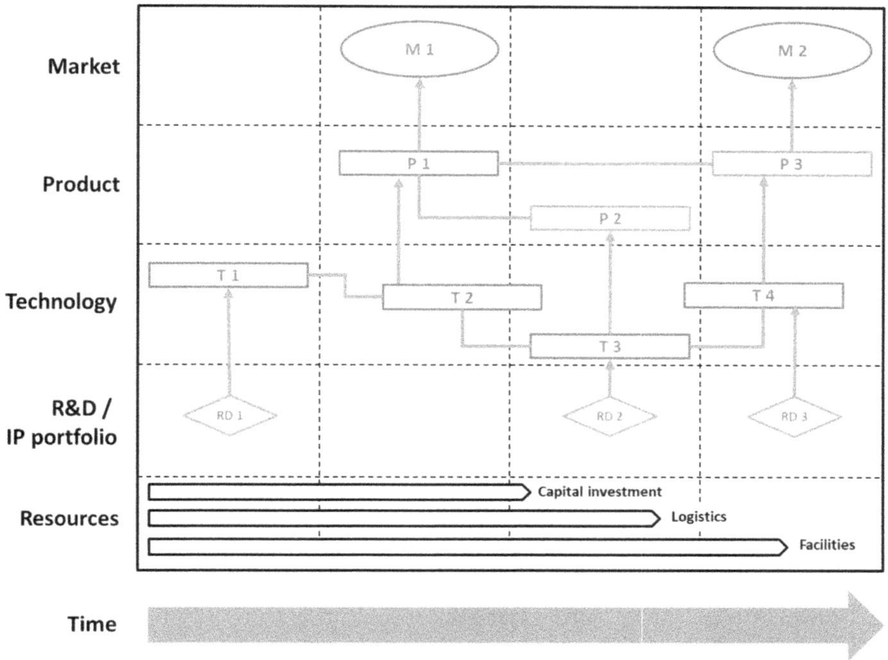

Fig. 10.17 Product-technology roadmap

What is important in this roadmap development is to ensure that it provides a clear picture of the key things that the project team will need to do, or consider, during the anticipated project timeline (Vatananan and Gerdsri 2012). The depth and complexity into which a product-technology roadmap can be developed is significant, with many large companies developing company-wide models and using them to coordinate the activities of a diverse range of project participants and ensure that they are all focusing on achieving a common outcome (Albright 2002). This ensures that the project team addresses the critical issues as listed in Table 10.4.

Simple product-technology roadmaps can be set-up in EXCEL spreadsheets, or more sophisticated software products designed to facilitate project team activities. These should have a Gantt chart function and the ability to exchange documents, emails and other information within the project team and third parties. A range of such software tools are already on the market, and these include:

- *Microsoft Project*, a proprietary project management software sold by Microsoft that has Gantt chart, tasking, tracking and other functions including budgeting and workload analysis. It runs in Microsoft Windows.
- *Smartsheet*, a cloud-based software designed for project management and collaboration developed and marketed by Smartsheet Inc. It has a Gantt chart, document sharing, email messaging, calendars and task assignment functions.

Table 10.4 Product-technology roadmap common framework

Key questions:	Actions
"Know-why" definition and scope	Understand applications and/or markets
	Target key segments
	Identify competitors, complementors and partners
	Set strategic direction
"Know-what" direction	Define architecture
	What characteristics/features are most important?
	Link application drivers to specific challenges and evolution
	Set multi-year targets
"Know-how" technology roadmap	What technologies are most important?
	Link drivers to technologies and evolution
	Identify multi-generation technology investments to maintain competitiveness
"To-do" action plan and investment strategy	What resources and investments are needed?
	Plan projects with the highest priorities.
	Are technology investments in the most important areas?
	Identify and track risk areas
"Know-when" time	What are the key milestones for each activity to be completed?

Source: Albright (2003)

Released in 2006 it is compatible with Microsoft Windows, Apple IOS and Android. It is also available in a range of languages.

- *Gantt Project*, a GPL-licensed Java project management software that is compatible with Microsoft Windows, Linux and Mac OS X operating systems and released in 2018.
- *OpenProj*, an open-source project management software written in Java and released in 2008.

10.8 Integrating the Customer Discovery and NPD Processes

This chapter has provided an overview of the main approaches to the screening of opportunities and assessment of markets. It has reviewed the *customer development and discovery* (CD) approach of Blank and Dorf (2012), the *Fuzzy Front-End* (FFE) analysis of Koen et al. (2002), and the VOC *Stage-Gate*® NPD process championed by Cooper and Edgett (2005, 2009). Each of these approaches offer different pathways to the same general goal of ascertaining what the configuration of features and attributes of a new product or service should look like in order to meet the needs and requirements of customers/end-users in a target market. These different approaches have their relative strengths and weaknesses and project teams should consider using them where and when they are most appropriate.

To conclude this chapter, we draw on the work of York and Danes (2014) who examined the current field of literature relating to these three approaches. Their analysis is summarised in Table 10.5, where it can be seen that the *Stage-Gate*®

Table 10.5 Difference between NPD, FFE and CD

Key issues	New product development (NPD)	Fuzzy front-end (FFE)	Customer development (CD)
Nature of work	Disciplined and goal oriented with a project plan	Experimental, often chaotic. "Eureka" moment. Can schedule work, but not invention	Iterative, with continual influx of new information processing hypotheses
Commercialisation	High degree of certainty at conclusion	Unpredictable or uncertain	Higher degree of certainty after completion of CD process
Funding date	Budgeted	Variable – in the beginning phases many projects may be "bootlegged," while others will need funding to proceed	Only for minimum viable product until business and sales model developed
Revenue expectations	Predictable, with increasing certainty, analysis, and documentation as the product release date gets closer	Often uncertain, with a great deal of speculation	Must know sales and pricing model for first stage introduction
Activity	Multifunction product and/or process development team	Individuals and team conducting research to minimize risk and optimise potential	All members involved in extensive "outside of the building" largely 1:1 customer contact
Measure of milestone achievement	Progress	Strengthened concept	Minimum viable product, product/market fit
Expenses	Increase with each stage	Increase with each stage	Revenue can begin after MVP identified
Decision process	Go/no go/kill stages	Indeterminate	Pivots to new directions

Source: York and Danes (2014)

NPD process is more formal and structured than the other two. As discussed in Chap. 9, the *Stage-Gate®* system was developed from observations of how large manufacturing companies undertake their NPD and commercialisation projects.

Stage-Gate® has been criticised for being too linear and inflexible, although this has been disputed by Cooper (2019), who has suggested that the process has now adapted to include a number of new approaches: e.g. *NextGen Stage-Gate®; Stage-Gate XPress®* (for rapid development); *Stage-Gate Lite®* (for small projects), and *Stage-Gate TD®* (for technology development projects). For NPD project teams who are operating within established businesses that have multiple product lines and more divisional organisational structure, the *Stage-Gate®* NPD process is likely to be the most appropriate system as it offers better structure and is well-placed to draw upon a range of techniques and tools that assist in the product development and project management.

For smaller firms, and start-up project teams, the FFE and CD approaches may offer a more appropriate model. The CD approach championed by Blank and Dorf (2012) has its origins in the *Lean Start-Up* concepts developed by Ries (2011) (see Chap. 9). In this type of environment, the project team is not just developing a new product, they are also developing a completely new business model and business venture. This accounts for the small-team focus of the CD approach, with all project team members, including the senior managers, engaging directly with the target customers and end-users. It essentially follows the *Lean Star-Up* process, which Blank (2013) has argued is a major game changer in how new business ventures are established.

The FFE approach is less of a completely separate system for NPD project management and more a useful framework for dealing with the early stages of the product development process. As York and Danes (2014) note, it is an "experimental" approach and is potentially valuable in helping project teams investigate unknown and complex task environments characterised by high levels of uncertainty. It may be employed as an initial stage before moving into the more structure *Stage-Gate®* NPD process.

References

Akao, Y., & Mazur, G. H. (2003). The leading edge in QFD: Past, present and future. *The International Journal of Quality & Reliability Management, 20*(1), 20–35.

Akgun, A. E., Lynn, G. S., & Byrne, J. C. (2004). Taking the guess work out of new product development: How successful high-tech companies get that way. *Journal of Business Strategy, 25*(4), 41–46.

Albright, R. E. (2002). How to use road mapping for global platform products. *PDMA Visions, 26*(4), 19–22.

Albright, R. E. (2003). A unifying architecture for roadmaps frames a value scorecard. *IEEE International Engineering Management Conference*. 2–4 November, Albany N.Y.

Albright, R. E., & Kappel, T. A. (2003). Road mapping in the corporation. *Research Technology Management, 46*(2), 31–40.

Ambler, T. (2000). Marketing metrics. *Business Strategy Review, 11*(2), 59–66.

Bazeley, P., & Jackson, K. (2013). *Qualitative data analysis with NVivo, second edition*. London: Sage.

Blank, S. (2013). Why the lean start-up changes everything. *Harvard Business Review, 91*(5), 65–72.

Blank, S., & Dorf, B. (2012). *The startup owner's manual: The step-by-step guide for building a great company*. Pescadero: K&S Ranch Publishing.

C2C Solutions. (2015). VOC CAGE model. www.c2csolutions.com

Carayannopoulos, S. (2005). Research in motion: A small firm commercializing a new technology. *Entrepreneurship Theory & Practice, 29*(2), 219–232.

Cleland, D. I. (2004). *Field guide to project management*. New York: Wiley.

Cole, R. E. (2001). *From continuous improvement to continuous innovation*. Milwaukee: American Society for Quality.

Cooper, R. G. (2006). Formula for success in new product development. *Marketing Management, 15*(2), 18–24.

Cooper, R. G. (2008). The stage-gate idea-to-launch process update, what's new and NextGen systems. *Journal of Product Innovation Management, 25*(3), 213–232.

Cooper, R. G. (2011). *Winning at new products: Creating value through innovation*. New York: Basic Books.

Cooper, R. G. (2019). The drivers of success in new-product development. *Industrial Marketing Management, 76*(1), 36–47.

Cooper, R. G., & Edgett, S. J. (2005). *Lean, rapid and profitable new product development*. Ancaster: Product Development Institute Inc.

Cooper, R. G., & Edgett, S. J. (2009). *Product innovation and technology strategy*. Hamilton: Product Development Institute Inc.

Cristiano, J. J., Liker, J. K., & White, C. C. (2000). Customer-driven product development through quality function deployment in the U.S. and Japan. *Journal of Product Innovation Management, 17*(4), 286–308.

Deming, W. E. (1982). *Quality, productivity, and competitive position*. Cambridge, MA: Massachusetts Institute of Technology.

Deming, W. E. (1986). *Out of the crisis*. Cambridge, MA: Massachusetts Institute of Technology.

Deming, W. E. (1993). *The new economics for industry, government, and education*. Boston: MIT Press.

Deschamps, J.-P. (2017). Classic root causes of innovation failures – things we all know but sometimes forget. In N. Pfeffermann & J. Gould (Eds.), *Strategy and communication for innovation: Integrative perspectives on innovation in the digital economy* (3rd ed., pp. 41–60). Cham: Springer.

Farrell, R. (1994). Quality function deployment: Helping business identify and integrate the voice of the customer. *Industrial Engineering, 26*(10), 45–45.

Feigenbaum, A. V. (1961). *Total quality control*. New York: McGraw-Hill.

Foster, B. D., & Cadogan, J. W. (2000). Relationship selling and customer loyalty: An empirical investigation. *Marketing Intelligence & Planning, 18*(4), 185–199.

Garson, G. D. (2013). *Ethnographic research*. Asheboro: Statistical Publishing Associates.

Garson, G. D. (2014). *Focus group research*. Asheboro: Statistical Publishing Associates.

Gibb, A., & Scott, M. (1985). Strategic awareness, personal commitment and the process of planning in the small business. *The Journal of Management Studies, 22*(6), 597–632.

Githens, G. D. (2002). How to assess and manage risk in NPD programs: A team-based risk approach. In P. Belliveau, A. Griffin, & S. Somermeyer (Eds.), *The PDMA tool book 1 for new product development*. New York: Wiley. chapter 8.

Griffin, A. (2013). Obtaining customer needs for product development. In K. B. Khan (Ed.), *The PDMA handbook of new product development* (pp. 213–229). Hoboken: Wiley.

Griffin, A., & Hauser, J. R. (1993). The voice of the customer. *Marketing Science, 12*(1), 1–27.

Griffin, A., & Hauser, J. R. (1996). Integrating R&D and marketing: A review and analysis of the literature. *Journal of Product Innovation Management, 13*(3), 191–215.

Haksever, C. (1996). Total quality management in the small business environment. *Business Horizons, 39*(2), 33–40.

Hansen, H., Samuelsen, B., & Silseth, P. (2008). Customer perceived value in B-t-B service relationships: Investigating the importance of corporate reputation. *Industrial Marketing Management, 37*(2), 206–217.

Heller, R. (1994). *The fate of IBM*. London: Little Brown & Co.

Hines, T. (2000). An evaluation of two qualitative methods (focus group interviews and cognitive maps) for conducting research into entrepreneurial decision making. *Qualitative Market Research, 3*(1), 7–16.

Huang, X., Soutar, G. N., & Brown, A. (2002). New product development processes in small to medium-sized enterprises: Some Australian evidence. *Journal of Small Business Management, 40*(1), 27–42.

ISO. (2015). *Quality management principles*. Geneva: International Standards Organization (ISO).
Juran, J. M. (1951). *Quality control handbook*. New York: McGraw-Hill.
Juran, J. M. (1954). Universals in management planning and control. *Management Review, 43*(11), 748–761.
Juran, J. M. (1967). The QC circle phenomenon. *Industrial Quality Control, 23*(7), 25–34.
Kano, N., Seraku, N., Takahashi, F., & Tsuji, S. (1984). Attractive quality and must-be quality. *Hinshitsu (Quality, The Journal of Japanese Society for Quality Control), 14*(2), 39–48.
Koen, P. A., Ajamian, G. M., Boyce, S., Clamen, A., Fisher, E., Fountoulakis, S., Johnson, A., Puri, P., & Seibert, R. (2002). Fuzzy front end: Effective methods, tools and techniques. In P. Belliveau, A. Griffin, & S. Somermeyer (Eds.), *The PDMA tool book 1 for new product development*. New York: Wiley. chapter 1.
Kuittinen, T. (2013, February 9). Nokia sells handset business to Microsoft at a shockingly low price. *Forbes*. www.forbes.com
Leximancer (2018). *Leximancer user guide release 4.5.* www.leximancer.com Leximancer Pty Ltd.
Lüthje, C., & Herstatt, C. (2004). *The lead user method: An outline of empirical findings and issues for future research, user innovation MIT EDU*. www.userinnovation.mit.edu
Mazzarol, T. (2013). *Nokia sells out – Case study*. Perth: UWA Business School.
McAdam, R., & McKeown, M. (1999). Life after ISO 9000: An analysis of the impact of ISO 9000 and total quality management on small businesses in Northern Ireland. *Total Quality Management, 10*(2), 229–241.
McMillan, A. (2003). Road mapping – Agent of change. *Research Technology Management, 46*(2), 40–47.
Miller, W. L., & Morris, L. (1999). *Fourth generation R&D*. New York: Wiley.
Miller, C., & Swaddling, D. C. (2012). Focusing NPD research on customer-perceived value. In P. Belliveau, A. Griffin, & S. Somermeyer (Eds.), *The PDMA tool book 1 for new product development* (pp. 87–114). New York: Wiley.
Millman, T., & Wilson, K. (1995). From key account selling to key account management. *Journal of Marketing Practice: Applied Marketing Science, 1*(1), 9–21.
Mizuno, S., & Akao, Y. (1978). *Quality function deployment: A company-wide quality approach*. Tokyo: JUSE Press.
Nokia. (2004). *The mobile device market*. Nokia Corporation Vision and Strategy. www.nokia.com
Phaal, R., Farrukh, C. J. P., & Probert, D. R. (2004). Technology road mapping – A planning framework for evolution and revolution. *Technological Forecasting and Social Change, 71*(1), 5–26.
Plaskoff, M. (2003). Sales and marketing metrics. *Professional Builder, 68*(7), 75–76.
Ries, E. (2011). *The lean startup: How constant innovation creates radically successful businesses*. London: Portfolio Penguin Books.
Rogers, E. M. (1995). *Diffusion of innovations*. New York: The Free Press.
Saldaña, J. (2016). *The coding manual for qualitative researchers* (3rd ed.). Los Angeles/London/New Delhi/Singapore/Washington, DC: SAGE.
Santi, M., Reboud, S., Gasiglia, H., Sabouret, A., (2003, July). *Modèle de valorisation et de protection intellectuelle des innovations des PEI*. HEC/INPI.
Sarazen, J. S. (1990). Voice of the customer: The competitive imperative of the '90s: A management education perspective. *Manage*, July, 28–36.
Schnepple, T. (2005). *Managing commercialisation risk* (Innovation Excellence Program). Perth: University of Western Australia, Centre for Entrepreneurial Management and Innovation (CEMI).
Schwab, K. (2016). *The fourth industrial revolution*. London: Penguin.
Schwab, K. (2018). *Shaping the fourth industrial revolution*. Geneva: World Economic Forum. www.weforum.org
Shirr, G. R. (2013). User research for product innovation: Qualitative methods. In K. B. Khan (Ed.), *The PDMA handbook of new product development* (pp. 231–243). Hoboken: Wiley.
Sotiriadou, P., Brouwers, J., & Le, T.-A. (2014). Choosing a qualitative data analysis tool: A comparison of NVivo and Leximancer. *Annals of Leisure Research, 17*(2), 218–234.

Spiller, P., & Barilla, D. (2014). New role for the CPO: Orchestrating the end-to-end value chain. *Supply Chain Management Review, 18*(4), 27–33.
Sweeney, J. C., & Soutar, G. N. (2001). Consumer perceived value: The development of a multiple item scale. *Journal of Retailing, 77*(1), 203–220.
Tan, K. C., & Shen, X. X. (2000). Integrating Kano's model in the planning matrix of quality function deployment. *Total Quality Management, 11*(8), 1141–1151.
Teece, D. J. (1986). Profiting from technological innovation: Implications for integration, collaboration, licensing and public policy. *Research Policy, 15*(6), 285–305.
Teece, D. J. (2010). Business models, business strategy and innovation. *Long Range Planning, 43*(2/3), 172–194.
Teece, D. J. (2018). Business models and dynamic capabilities. *Long Range Planning, 51*(2018), 40–49.
Teece, D. J., Pisano, G., & Shuen, A. (1997). Dynamic capabilities and strategic management. *Strategic Management Journal, 18*(7), 509–533.
Threlfall, K. D. (1999). Using focus groups as a consumer research tool. *Journal of Marketing Practice: Applied Marketing Science, 5*(4), 102–105.
Ulwick, A. W. (2002). Turn customer input into innovation. *Harvard Business Review, 80*(1), 91–97.
Vatananan, R., & Gerdsri, N. (2012). The current state of technology road mapping (TRM) research and practice. *International Journal of Innovation & Technology Management, 9*(4), 1–20.
West, J., & Bogers, M. (2014). Leveraging external sources of innovation: A review of research on open innovation. *Journal of Product Innovation Management, 31*(4), 814–831.
White, E., Behara, R., & Babbar, S. (2002). Mine customer experiences. *Quality Progress, 35*(7), 63–67.
York, J., & Danes, J. (2014). Customer development, innovation and decision-making biases in the lean start up. *Journal of Small Business Strategy, 24*(2), 21–39.
Yu, H. H. (2017). When business model meets open innovation. In N. Pfeffermann & J. Gould (Eds.), *Strategy and communication for innovation: Integrative perspectives on innovation in the digital economy* (3rd ed., pp. 29–40). Cham: Springer.

Team Building, Company Leadership and Strategic Alliances

11

11.1 Introduction

> How accepting you are of the input of your staff is a key determinate of the business's growth…A strong board who constructively challenge you as CEO is critical to the growth of the company.
>
> Source: Ned Montarello, CEO Thinksmart.

This chapter examines the nature of corporate structure and governance for high-growth firms as well as the process of team building both in early stage and in more mature ventures. The importance of getting the right team and the need to ensure that the team is balanced and effective are also considered. It also examines some of the issues associated with the management of strategic partnering through joint ventures and alliances.

11.2 Leadership in Entrepreneurial Companies

Business has been likened to a team sport in which the collaboration and contribution from several people is more valuable than the activities of a single person. This chapter focuses on the importance of developing both the *corporate* leadership structure within the entrepreneurial venture and the *team* environment that can make it work successfully. Dingee et al. (1995) emphasise the importance of having a good team involved in an entrepreneurial venture. They point to the desire by venture capitalists to see a well-balanced team with the right combination of skills that can represent the seven management functions. These functions are outlined in Table 11.1.

T. Mazzarol, S. Reboud, *Entrepreneurship and Innovation*, Springer Texts in Business and Economics, https://doi.org/10.1007/978-981-13-9412-6_11

Table 11.1 Key areas of skill for the management of an entrepreneurial firm

Marketing and sales	General management
Operations management	Personnel management
Research and development	Legal and taxation
Financial management	

Source: Dingee et al. (1995)

For the smaller firm, it is usually impossible to assemble all these various management competencies in the three to four key people who will comprise the executive management team. It is probably best to focus on the sales and marketing, financial control and operations management areas as a priority, with general administration, human resource management, and legal and tax management issues being sub-contracted. A well-designed board of directors that brings in specialists from outside the firm can be one means of accessing strategic management and specialist legal or accounting advice, research and new product development is often integral to the venture from its inception – particularly among the more technology intensive firms.

11.2.1 Leading Practices of Fast Growth Entrepreneurs

A study of the practices of 906 winners of the *Ernst & Young Entrepreneur of the Year* awards in the United States found that successful entrepreneurs focused strongly on good management and team building within their companies (Sexton and Seale 1997). According to the findings from this study of successful entrepreneurs, the size of the top management team was typically from three to six people, each with the capacity to become the CEO if required. Entrepreneurial fast growth firms had only three to four levels of management, with a matrix of three to six top managers and three to four managerial levels being viewed as optimal. It was also considered important to ensure that the top management team had strong competencies in the functional areas of finance, marketing and operations.

Leading Practices of Fast Growth Entrepreneurs

The fast growth CEO must create dynamic management structures and teams fully capable of responding to the issues of growth, while recognising that the responsibilities of individual members will expand in a short period of time. Structuring and selecting the top management team can be one of the most difficult challenges facing the CEO who plans to grow the organisation at a rapid pace. Traditional organisational development tools and resources are typically not available.

Source: Sexton and Seale (1997).

At the board level, the typical fast growth entrepreneurial firm had a management board comprising three or more directors. There was an equal balance in the membership of these boards between directors who were *internal* and directors who were *external* to the firm. In most cases the board was comprised of the key directors of the company who had executive functions and an equal number of external directors. For family-owned companies, the ratio of family to non-family members on the board was 20% family and 80% non-family. This suggests that the successful family-owned firms were ensuring that non-family members were engaged in decision-making within the company. Among the fast growth entrepreneurial firms, the board of directors held meetings on at least a quarterly basis with monthly meetings also being common. These boards also participated in approximately 80% of decisions made by the firms, with a high level of involvement in the monitoring of the company's performance, the monitoring of the performance of the CEO, and the approval of formal business plans (Sexton and Seale 1997).

Key Lessons from Fast Growth Entrepreneurial Firms

A fast growth entrepreneur is often characterised as a lone ranger who adopts a ready-shoot-aim approach as a management style. As this study shows, fast growth CEOs make their decisions with the concurrence of top management teams and consistently utilise their boards in making strategic decisions. They also balance the number of management levels to the number of top managers. Finally, they tend to prioritise developing the functional areas of finance, marketing and operations.

Source: Sexton and Seale (1997).

11.2.2 Building an Awesome Organisation

As shown in the study of successful US entrepreneurs, the importance of assembling a well-balanced team to provide the management for a fast-growing entrepreneurial venture is significant. In new technology-based ventures there is a need for the management team to include a cross-section of skill sets, including technologists, marketing and sales people, and those with financial and executive skills. These roles have been depicted as the 'T-shirts' (inventors), 'turtlenecks' (marketing & sales) and 'ties' (financiers) (Edwards 2002). Research into the experiences of successful entrepreneurs suggests that leadership and team building are among the most crucial factors determining success.

For example, … A study by the Kauffman Centre (1999) highlighted the importance of teamwork in the success of entrepreneurial organisations.

In a series of focus group workshops that brought together some of America's most successful entrepreneurs, the Kauffman Centre study emphasised the need to bring into the management team a person whose role was team building. Rewards and incentives for good work and a willingness of the senior managers to get 'hands on' with the employees were all viewed as desirable. Also common was the identification of clear company values followed by an attempt to recruit and develop staff that conformed to these values. It was also noted that a major effort was put into trying to align the employees' goals to those of the company, and to create a culture that respected each individual's personal and family life.

Creating the Awesome Organisation

The best thing I've done for creating an awesome organisation is hiring people that are smarter than me in a lot of areas but have been stifled in other companies. We've been able to give them an opportunity to grow and expand within their fields of expertise. It's like taking a plant that's root bound, cutting off the old roots and giving it room to grow. A lot of it involves having them set their goals and making sure their core goals coincide with company goals. (Quotation from a successful entrepreneur).

Source: Kauffman Centre (1999).

Additional studies of a similar nature undertaken by the Kauffman Centre (1997, 1998) that focused on attracting and retaining the best possible staff for high performance ventures noted that *good fit* needs to be found between the firm and the employee. The type of person being sought is frequently as enterprising and capable as the original entrepreneurial founders of the company. For small firms the challenge is to attract and retain high calibre people when budgets preclude paying high salaries and when the size and market profile of the firm is low.

Among the many challenges facing entrepreneurs who are seeking to attract and retain high calibre people include the need to make the company look different from other companies in the same industry, and then actually finding good applicants during periods of low unemployment. Good people are often aware of their talents and selective about the organisations for which they work.

For small firms, there is the problem that high performers might feel that the company will not really challenge them enough. Also, common to small, fast growing firms is the difficulty in clearly identifying the role of the employee. Most small firms require the management team to be cross-functional and willing to be flexible in a job role. In some industries, there is high mobility, with technical staff showing more loyalty to the project than the firm; and younger employees are becoming more concerned with life-work balance than those of an earlier generation might have been (Kauffman Centre 1997, 1998).

Offering bonuses and equity deals to compensate for lower base salaries and designing the job to suit the person are among the *solution strategies* followed by successful entrepreneurs seeking to build a well-balanced, dynamic team. The need to highlight an applicant's ability to be a good team member over their previous industry experience or any technical or academic skills they might have is also an important consideration.

For example, … One entrepreneur hired a former sportsman with no prior industry experience due to his strong team orientation. (Kauffman Centre 1997)

Hiring Awesome People: Worst Interviewing Mistakes

According to successful entrepreneurs, these are among the worst mistakes made during their interviewing of new employees:

- Making an emotional judgment;
- Lack of preparation;
- Failing to check references;
- Having preconceived notions based on others who have already interviewed the applicant;
- Wandering onto subjects that have nothing to do with the goal of the interview; and
- Overlooking 'must haves' because other skills were strong.

Source: Kauffman Centre (1997).

11.3 Developing Effective Management Boards

For senior management levels, particularly for the board of directors and senior business advisor functions, the major challenge is finding ways to get the best people when the budget cannot stretch to the remuneration levels they are expecting. Small firms seeking to attract such high-level people may be able to appeal to them on a different level – such as offering them the opportunity to play the role of mentor. Offering such people equity is another strategy that can be used, although care needs to be taken not to create a confusing share register that might prove detrimental in subsequent capital raising activities (Kauffman Centre 1998).

At the senior management level, the development of a board of directors to assist the CEO and executive management team is important, but good working relationships also need to exist between the executive and the board. Kaufman (2002) highlights problems that can arise due to a dysfunctional board. She highlights five typical 'renegade' types of board member:

1. *Retired and looking for work* – This type of board member is often a retired former CEO who still hankers after the challenge of running a company. It is not uncommon for such individuals to demand a lot of time from the executive officers and staff, with requests for a lot of detailed information. They may also slow down the decision making at the board by wanting to discuss issues in depth and by wanting to gain control over the decision-making process. It is suggested that such people be kept busy running committees established by the board that address specific issues, thereby making use of their specialist skills in a productive way.

2. *The knowledge expert* – This type of board member is often a functional specialist such as an accountant or lawyer. They are prone to becoming passionate about areas within their professional field of expertise. For example, a CPA accountant on a board could take an intense interest in the firm's day-to-day accounting activities and give the chief financial officer a real headache. To keep such board members in check, the CEO should try to task these experts to undertake special work – perhaps via the board's committees – that is an outlet for their skills. A dialogue should also be established with them to explain the difference between the strategic, policy level role of the board and the daily activities of the executive team.
3. *The 'C' performer* – This person is usually poorly prepared for each board meeting and can waste everyone's time asking basic questions they should have noted in the pre-reading. Such people may also be prone to arriving late and requesting the chairman to bring them up to speed. They may also miss meetings due to conflicting appointments. To manage such 'C' performers, the chairman or CEO should advise them of the need to attend meetings, to be on time and to read the materials in advance. It may be necessary to develop board policies that penalise tardy or absent members, thereby indirectly forcing them to resign.
4. *Special interest flag bearer* – This refers to the person who joins a board to follow a personal, political or social agenda. Such individuals may be difficult to deal with as they often have strong political skills and may speak well and enjoy community support. People that have strong views on technology, social or environmental and political causes can be a major problem. Such individuals should be counselled in a diplomatic manner so that they better understand the way in which their behaviour impacts on the good functioning of the board. Allowing them to join a committee that offers them an outlet for their passions may also offer a means of settling them down. Boards might also develop a code of conduct to help alleviate some of the more extreme behaviour.
5. *New board member* – A newly-appointed member of the board can also become a renegade if they are captured by a factional group within the board in order to secure their vote. Setting up an induction program for the board can help alleviate this problem. It may also be useful to appoint a mentor to the new board member from among one of the more experienced and impartial members.

According to Kaufman (2002), the successful management of boards can be achieved if the recruitment process for selecting new board members is managed systematically. Selection should be based on the ability of board members to provide the company with particular skills or expertise, and not because of mate-ship, personal references or personality. The board should have a common sense of vision and purpose, and policies and codes of practice need to be formally set and agreed. Getting the board to meet regularly and to participate in regular retreats and induction programs is also important. Setting the ground rules for how the board's business is to be managed is also critical. The need for preparation prior to meetings, the order of business and the role of questions are all areas of detail that should be effectively managed. The CEO and chairperson should work closely together to ensure that these issues are dealt with in the most efficient way. It is important for there to be a strong level of communication both *with* the board to keep them informed of what is taking place within the company and *within* the board to allow members to better understand each other's views.

11.4 Blueprinting the Senior Company Leadership

In conjunction with the establishment of a board of directors, the firm also needs to develop a clear blueprint for how the senior management will function. One of the most critical roles is that of the CEO – who may or may not be the original founder-entrepreneur and principal shareholder. Small businesses are owned and managed by the same person or persons. As such the process of corporate governance is found to vest largely in the owner-manager(s).

However, for fast growth entrepreneurial firms the CEO function usually needs to be reserved for an individual with the capacity to design and implement strategic plans and to devote time to external boundary spanning. It is the role of the CEO to seek growth opportunities in new markets or with new products and via strategic alliances or acquisitions. At the same time the CEO needs to ensure that the firm's internal organisational structure and team environment is conducive to successful implementation of these new growth opportunities (Goodale 2001).

In addition to the CEO there needs to be a chief operating officer who has the role of maintaining the *internal* efficiency of the company, thereby allowing the CEO to focus on the *external* environment. According to Goodale (2001), the general manager for operations is something of a 'traffic cop' who has the role of allocating workloads to the team and ensuring that things are flowing smoothly.

While there may be a series of teams, each with a team leader, the role of the chief operating officer is to be the team leaders' team leader. At the team level, the team leaders are responsible for their individual team members, and each team member reports to the team leader. It is important to give team leaders the authority to make their own decisions, but they also need to maintain an effective dialogue with other team leaders. Figure 11.1 illustrates this suggested structure.

According to Edwards (2002), the major traps that teams can fall into are group thinking, poor individual performances and *siloing*. The first of these occurs when the entire team conforms to a similar viewpoint and fails to critically assess the merits of its decisions. This can lead to self-deception and a tendency to overlook both sides of an argument. A well-balanced team with a diversity of views is less likely to suffer from group think. Having a board of directors or advisory board comprised of a balance of people who are both internal and external to the firm can also help protect against group think.

In a study of 429 employees from 23 small manufacturing firms Chandler et al. (2000) found that supervisory support and reward systems were positive drivers for innovation. Smaller firms with less formalisation in their human resource management systems were more likely to be innovative than larger, more formalised companies. A further study by Mazzarol (2002) of 137 entrepreneurs from small firms

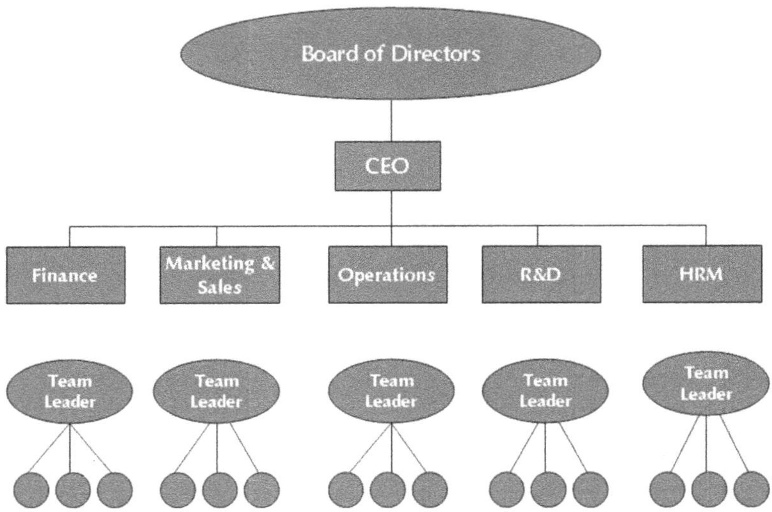

Fig. 11.1 Organisational structure of the typical entrepreneurial firm

in Australia found that innovativeness within the venture was influenced by at least five antecedents – mostly focusing around the entrepreneurial leader. These were:

1. *Business values* – This relates to the personal values that the owner-manager or entrepreneur holds for their business and how they communicate these to their employees to encourage innovation.
2. *Defining quality* – This relates to the firm's understanding of what quality is and how it should be achieved. It is important for the firm's owner-manager or CEO to explain to the team what they understand by quality, both in terms of service and of product development. Formal quality assurance is important, but by itself it does not encourage a team to really seek to provide quality and added value.
3. *ASA/ISO 9000* – This relates to the formal quality assurance process used by the firm to achieve benchmarked performance. As a quality management system, formal ASA/ISO accreditation will help a business avoid errors and assist it to develop systems. However, this remains a base line benchmark that needs to be built upon for enhanced innovation in product or service development.
4. *Changing beliefs and attitudes* – This relates to the ability of the owner-manager to lead change in the firm and to assist employees within the company team to understand the need for change.
5. *Staff partnerships* – This relates to the relationship between the employees, the business and the owner. Innovation in a small firm is often led by the owner-manager or entrepreneur, but can also be the responsibility of the employees. New product or service ideas or new process innovations require strong team commitment, and this can be enhanced where the employees feel a partnership relationship exists with the firm.

For the small firm seeking to create a culture of innovation, the lessons from this research are that the owner-manager or entrepreneur needs to have a clear sense of their own business values and how they translate into the type of innovative company they are endeavouring to build. Benchmarking quality through formal assurance systems is likely to be important when trying to ensure that the company achieves and maintains a competitive standard within its industry. However, the senior management of the firm needs to make it clear to the workforce what they understand by quality and innovation, while also encouraging this. The willingness of the owner-manager to get directly involved in change management and to lead the process of change that is usually instrumental to innovation will be vital. Finally, if the owner-manager has a sound, partnership-like relationship with his or her employees, it is more likely that the company will respond to these other factors (Mazzarol 2002).

11.5 Creating Entrepreneurial Teams

The development of an effective team can be constrained by a lack of support from senior management and by insufficient clarity and focus in the firm's strategic vision and capacity for goal setting. Support for team building is critical, and the organisation must ensure there is sufficient time allocated to team members to perform their roles and that team members receive adequate training and rewards if successful. Complex tasks often take time, and an impatient senior management looking for fast results can often impact negatively on a team's performance. What is also likely to have a negative impact is political meddling and the excessive centralisation of power and authority away from the team, denying them sufficient autonomy (Drew and Coulson-Thomas 1996).

Drew and Coulson-Thomas (1996) conducted a study of 100 firms and their approaches to team building and teamwork. They argue that the future of many industries will demand greater teamwork within organisations of all sizes. Further, the competitive success of firms may depend on their ability to develop new organisational structures that take advantage of teamwork and bring together networks or clusters of teams and firms spanning many traditional functions. The challenge for managers will be to implement adequate training and team development processes to take advantage of the opportunities.

Figure 11.2 shows their conceptualisation of the framework required to develop a high-energy team. As shown, it commences with a clear vision and goal setting, moves into the selection of the team and their training and skills development. The organisation that seeks to make best use of the team must also ensure that it provides adequate resources and empowerment to team members. It will be important for the firm to have a culture that is highly supportive of teamwork and management systems that facilitate such work. The challenge for the entrepreneurial leader is to create fit and balance of the key drivers of success. This approach can be used by the founder to identify and evaluate future scenarios and the challenges generated by venture growth.

Fig. 11.2 Developing teamwork. (Source: Drew and Coulson-Thomas 1996)

While the team is important, no team is going to perform well if individual members are not contributing *their* best. This requires not only the recruitment and selection of the best people, and also the monitoring both of individuals' performance and that of the team. Finally, the creation of teams within an organisation can lead to the emergence of *silos* of competing power, culture and influence. *Siloing* can divide a company and is largely dysfunctional in nature. It is important to ensure that teams are able to connect with other teams and that communication flows run horizontally as well as vertically. Flexibility and the ability to quickly break up a team or link it with another should also be highlighted (Edwards 2002).

As shown in Fig. 11.3, the requirements for a well-balanced team in an entrepreneurial company comprise three primary elements (Edwards 2002):

- *Intelligence* – This relates to the tacit and explicit knowledge found within the intellectual capital of the business. It can be developed into company systems and procedures, and forms the basis of future intellectual property (IP) that might be protected with copyright, patents or trade secrecy.
- *Emotional intelligence* – This relates to the culture and human capital operating within the firm. The ability of all people to understand each other and to make teamwork a priority is a feature of this type of intelligence. How flexible people are and their ability to adapt to change is also important.
- *Implementation intelligence* – This type of intelligence is associated with the ability of the company to implement plans and produce results. It is focused on project management and operational systems design and implementation.

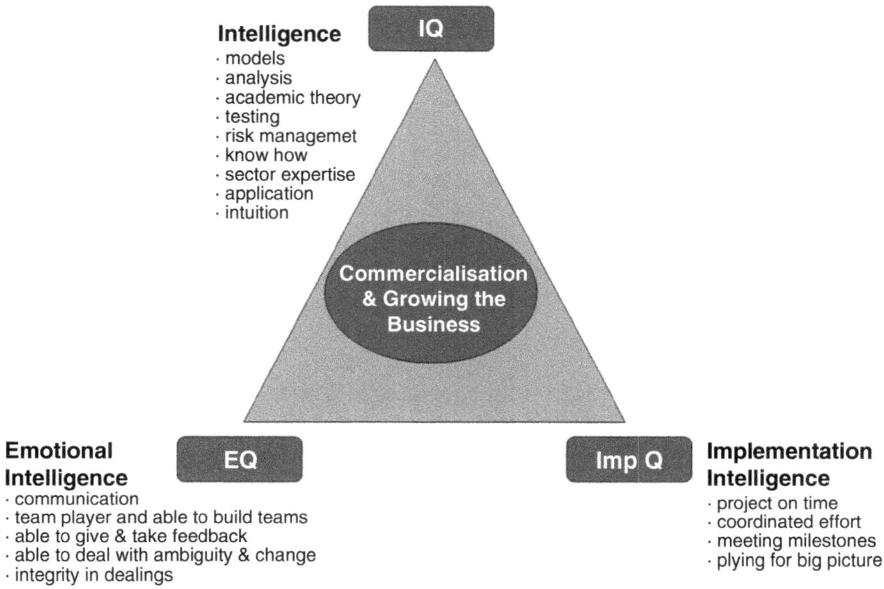

Fig. 11.3 Requirements for high performance teams. (Source: Edwards 2002)

The need for each individual to make their own contribution to the team effort raises the need for organisations to focus on the process of developing individual employees as a part of the overall development of the organisation. As shown in Fig. 11.4, this involves combining managerial knowledge with what Harvey and Butcher (1998) refer to as *meta-abilities* that have the potential to enhance the *influencing skills* of individual team members. These meta-abilities serve to complement the more technical or functional managerial skills, and might be viewed simply as good judgement or common sense. According to Harvey and Butcher (1998):

> **Meta-abilities are** … personal, acquired abilities which underpin and determine how and when knowledge and skills will be used.

Harvey and Butcher (1998) identify four types of meta-ability:

1. *Cognitive skills* – These relate to intellectual capacity and involve the ability of the individual to process and analyse complex information and to think creatively and flexibly about problems. What is also important here is the individual's ability to hold a long-term vision while also focusing on immediate details, and to maintaining an ability to remain aware of changes taking place in their immediate environment.
2. *Self-knowledge* – This relates to the ability a person has to see both sides of the problem and to understand how others might view them. The ability to know yourself and to have the capacity to realistically see how you are perceived by others – while also understanding how the other person feels and thinks – is an important ability.

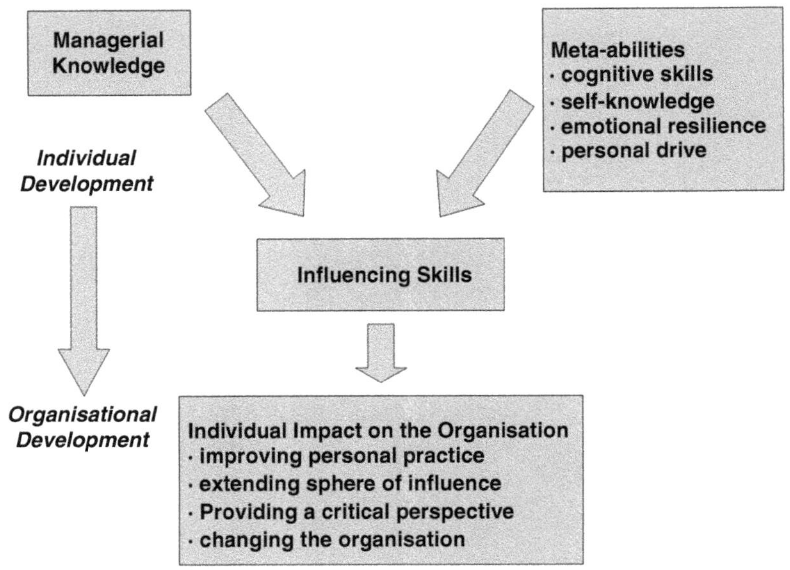

Fig. 11.4 Individual development as organisational development. (Source: Harvey and Butcher 1998s)

3. *Emotional resilience* – A person with strong emotional resilience has the capacity for self-control and self-discipline. When placed under pressure or facing setbacks, they can cope well and will 'bounce back' to try again. They can see a way forward while also noting the challenges they face.
4. *Personal drive* – this refers to the individual's achievement drive and ambition. People with high personal drive are likely to be self-motivated and to possess the ability to motivate others and take on new challenges and risks to fulfil their goals.

These meta-abilities are important qualities to identify and develop within the management team of any organisation. They are not particularly easy to measure or evaluate prior to appointment, but they will have a strong impact on the success of the firm. It suggests that a good *all-round* manager should have not only sound intellect, achievement drive and technical competency, but also the maturity for self-reflection, empathy toward others, emotional self-control and self-discipline.

11.6 Leadership in Innovation

A key role of entrepreneurs seeking to build high growth business ventures and commercialise new innovations is to provide effective leadership of their company it its project teams. Contemporary leadership theory sees the leader's management style comprising of two primary directions. The first of these is *transformational leadership* (Bass 1990) while the second is *transactional leadership* (Bass and

Avolio 1994). Let us examine each of these two leadership styles in more detail and how they relate to innovation.

11.6.1 Transactional Leadership

A *transactional leadership style* is one in which the manager focuses their team members on the completion of tasks to expected performance levels. They focus on meeting deadlines, achieving goals and also aligning the individual team members' various personal needs and wants with these organisational objectives. Transactional leadership is comprised of three key components identified by Bass and Avolio (1994):

- *Contingent Reward* – to get followers motivated to accomplish tasks the leader needs to employ a process of contingent reward. This involves provision of support, resources (e.g. time, equipment etc.), and rewards in exchange for the followers' efforts. They also need to be able to clearly communicate what goals they hope to achieve and allocate work tasks to their team. When the team performs as planned the leader offers appropriate recognition. They are also focus on making sure that the team follows the best work standards.
- *Active Management-by-Exception* – active MBE is where the leader is focused on the identification and correction of mistakes or deviations from agreed performance standards. They can take action to correct these errors and impose penalties or punishments for any followers who fail to comply. A strict adherence to work standards is common.
- *Passive Management-by-Exception* – passive MBE involves a negative style of leadership in which the focus is on only taking action when problems become chronic. This style seeks to avoid conflict with others and therefore does not intervene. Management behaviour is mainly reactive and there is a tendency towards supporting the status quo and resisting change out of concern that it will create problems.

Transactional leadership is important when the tasks are routine and the focus is on the implementation of a plan and/or the maintenance of quality standards. Entrepreneurs will need to possess good transactional leadership skills if they want to build capability and maintain control over quality and the more routine operational aspects of the business. It is important to strike a balance between the excessive 'micro-management' associated with *Active MBE* and the hands-off approach of *Passive MBE*.

11.6.2 Transformational Leadership

While transactional leadership is a necessary requirement for routine operations, it does not deal effectively with change. For this to occur the manager must display a *transformational leadership style* in which they lead change. Avolio and Bass (2011) have identified four key elements that make up the transformational leadership style. These are the so called *Four Is*:

1. *Idealized influence* – transformational leaders often serve as role models for their followers by displaying positive or attractive behaviours. This includes their ability to communicate a set of personal values and beliefs, and to behave in a manner that is consistent with these. They also express a strong sense of purpose or mission for the followers to work towards a common set of goals. Their focus is on collective rather than individual benefit, and they are strong promoters of teamwork, while also engendering trust between all members.
2. *Inspiration* – an important characteristic of transformational leadership style is the ability to inspire and motivate followers. They encourage their followers to believe that they have the ability to succeed at a task and support them during the process. They also remain optimistic about the future and maintain a realistic vision for the team's ultimate success. When faced with challenges, the transformational leader will demonstrate a resilience and commitment to overcome such obstacles. Finally, they make their vision and mission clear to followers and thereby provide a context into which the team's activities can be focused.
3. *Intellectual stimulation* – because transformational leadership is mostly about change to the status quo, it is important for such leaders to encourage their followers to think differently. They question the status quo and promote creativity and innovation in order to find ways to improve. Their approach to problem solving is a combination of emotional and rational thinking, and they manage risk effective by generating solutions that can be readily understood by followers.
4. *Individualised consideration* – another important element of the transformational leadership style is their consideration of the individual's needs for achievement and growth. They are tolerant of individual differences and take time to get to know their followers so as to understand their motivations. In designing the team's tasks, the transformational leader will provide challenges for each member and try to create opportunities for learning and growth. This may include delegating responsibility to individuals in order to help them learn and grow. They are often more attentive to follower's concerns.

Transformational leadership qualities are very important for innovation as they offer the right capacity for leading change and encouraging new ways of problem solving. Transformational leaders can identify the vision for future products, innovation and change, and then motivate their followers to move towards the achievement of these goals.

11.6.3 Management and Situational Leadership

While transactional and transformational leadership styles are important the entrepreneurial manager seeking to lead their team within a small firm or an innovation project must also understand the role of situational leadership. *Situational*

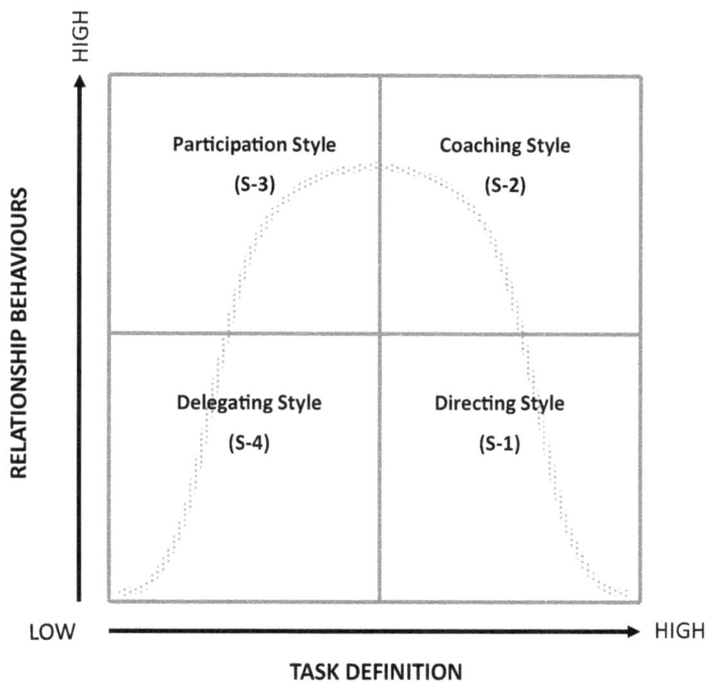

Fig. 11.5 Situational Leadership Model. (Source: Hersey and Blanchard 1982)

Leadership is a contingency model that recognises the leader exists within a given context or organisational situation. Hersey and Blanchard (1982) proposed a situational leadership model as illustrated in Fig. 11.5. This suggests at least four distinct types of leadership style that are appropriate for a given situation.

The first of these (S1) is a *Directing Style* of leadership in which the focus is on giving subordinates clear instructions for how they are to act and keeping a close eye on their performance. This has been called *Telling*. The second type (S2) is a *Coaching Style* of leadership in which the leader explains what needs to be done and why, with scope for more feedback and clarification of what is expected from the team members. This style has also been called *Selling*. The third style (S3) is a *Participation Style* of leadership in which the leader and their team share ideas and reach decisions via mutual agreement. Finally, the fourth style (S4) is a *Delegating Style* of leadership where the leader delegates authority to their team for all decisions and implementation.

11.6.4 Follower Versus Leader Directed Behaviour

An important issue within the situational leadership model is the degree to which the followers or team members are ready to take on their own responsibility for self-management. Where the team members are, unable or unwilling to accept the responsibility for their own management, or feel insecure or where they are willing but unable to do so due to lack of experience or skills, the leader must take responsibility. In these instances, the most appropriate leadership style is coaching or directing. Where followers are able and willing to assume self-management, or where they are able but unwilling or lacking confidence, the delegating and participating leadership styles are more appropriate. The leader-manager should therefore assess both the willingness and the ability of their team members before deciding which leadership style to employ. Where team members are both willing and able it can be possible to delegate more responsibility. However, where they are unwilling but able a more participatory style is required. In a situation where team members are willing but unable, the manager should employ coaching, and where the team is unwilling and unable, they will be forced to engage in a directing style.

11.7 Managing Growing Entrepreneurial Ventures

When a business is small the entrepreneur can employ a directing style of leadership and perhaps focus on *active MBE* to ensure that tasks are carried out correctly. However, as the business grows, the entrepreneur must learn how to transfer knowledge from themselves to their employees. This requires the shift towards a coaching style of leadership as the team is developed and trained to take on the tasks that were previously undertaken by the original business owner.

In the early years following start up, it is to be expected that the entrepreneur will be critical to the success of the venture. Without their involvement in the business, there is no business. As such, the concentration of knowledge lies mainly with the business founder across all key areas of management. However, as the business gets larger and the scale and scope of its operations widens, the entrepreneurial founder must find ways to transfer knowledge in these key areas to others who will form the management team. If the business is to grow, the concentration of knowledge must shift gradually to the employees of the firm. Entrepreneurs need to learn to step back and let go. This will require shifting to a more participative and then delegating leadership style.

Learning to step back and let go requires the entrepreneur to identify clearly where they wish the business to go over the longer term, and then to develop a blueprint for the business accompanied by staff training and development (Bates 1999). Once such basic human resource (HR) policy is in place, the entrepreneur can set about adequately managing growth. (Sharlit and McConnell 1989) point to a staged process of how a small firm grows. In the first stage of this process – i.e. creativity – communication is informal and jobs, roles and functions are equally flexible and unstructured. Owners frequently realise that they lack the skills to effectively manage their HR function and look to build a management team to assist them. During the second stage – i.e. direction – a newly-developed management team changes the company structure and sets more defined job descriptions. Employee training is then implemented, and supervisory jobs are created. Communication thus becomes less spontaneous and more formal.

A further study of 364 small firms examined problems experienced over their lifecycle (Dodge and Robbins 1992). This found significant differences between the types of problems facing the firm during the various stages of its lifecycle. During the growth stage, one finds that accounting, inventory control and cash flow issues often dominate. This suggests the need for a strong focus on operational and financial management as well as the necessary ongoing focus on marketing, sales and new product development.

For most entrepreneurs with small, fast growing firms, the key challenge is to learn how to delegate while simultaneously creating a team-learning environment within the organisation. A longitudinal study undertaken with 576 start-up firms in the US over a 10-year period examined owners' ability to delegate various functions (Ardichvili et al. 1998). This study found that formal HR programs and policies did not emerge until turnover exceeded US $ten million for manufacturers and US $three million for service-based firms. Delegation of different business activities commenced first with the accounting functions and less so with production or information systems. Delegation of HR functions did not take place until much later, and the owners also largely retained the role of planning. Training was required fairly early among these firms and across a range of different functional areas. If the entrepreneur cannot learn to delegate responsibilities, they may risk becoming overextended which can have a detrimental impact on their capacity to plan and successfully develop market opportunities (Cronin 1991). The ability to delegate is an important step in the entrepreneur's transition from a small entrepreneurial business to a larger mature one (Weiner 1985). According to Baker (1994), the challenge for entrepreneurs is to create a suitable environment in which their employees can learn to assume responsibilities.

11.7.1 Lessons from Successful Entrepreneurs

The Kauffman Centre for Entrepreneurial Leadership is one of the largest centres of its kind in the world. On a regular basis, the centre holds discussion forums where successful entrepreneurs can exchange ideas and build knowledge through sharing experiences. In 1997, the centre held a gathering of 12 entrepreneurs who discussed leadership, micro-management and the challenges of developing a team. This gathering highlighted the importance of motivation and inspiration for successful entrepreneurial leadership. Leaders of fast-growing small firms must be motivators, and able to offer positive reinforcement and empowerment to their employees.

Of importance is the ability to be flexible in leadership style and to adapt to the needs of the growing organisation. During the early life of the business, the entrepreneur or owner-manager is able to lead by being an expert as they know how to do the business better than most others. The need to be a *jack of all trades* is also a requirement of this stage. Success in growing a firm is the ability to demonstrate leadership by having a clear vision, by setting goals for people, by having confidence in where things are going, and by being the driving force for the company (Kauffman Centre 1997). Some key tips these entrepreneurs suggested to help overcome the problems of delegation and to help avoid the traps of micro-management included:

- hiring people who are smarter, better and more efficient than you;
- asking questions first and trying not to jump in with an answer;
- constantly measuring the downsides of all your decisions (e.g. will a bad decision break the business?);
- recognising the problems of being the 'expert' in the business, and learning to delegate and transfer knowledge to the team;
- getting a mentor or someone who can teach or coach you; and
- changing your management structure as you grow.

11.8 Strategic Partnering

Part of the team building that the entrepreneur will need to undertake is the formation of strategic partnerships and alliances with third parties who are outside the business. This may include lead customers, key suppliers, sub-contractors and other outsiders who provide specialist services to the business. Many innovation projects that small firms seek to undertake cannot be progressed without the involvement of outsiders, but even large firms are now actively engaging in strategic partnering.

Strategic Partnering is one of the biggest issues that many new ventures face. As discussed in Chap. 9, a small firm seeking to commercialise an innovation that lacks the resources and competencies to do so alone, will need to either *develop in partnership* via a joint venture, *delegate development* through licensing agreements, *transfer development* via trade sale, or *withdraw* and abandon the project. The need to form strategic partnerships such as joint ventures, or even licencing agreements, will require the firm to learn the skills and develop the competencies associated with this process.

While a small, technology-based firm may have excellent technical skills, a wide range of skills to successfully commercialise new technology will be lacking. The innovation chain shown in Fig. 11.6 illustrates the full skill-set required, and how strategic partnering can be used to help overcome the shortcomings within the new venture.

11.8.1 Reasons for Small Firms to Partner

The key reason for small entrepreneurial firms to seek partnerships is clearly the lack of resources in their innovation chain along with financial constraints. Many elements of the innovation chain may not be readily available, such as manufacturing know-how, market credibility and distribution networks (Hull and Slowinski 1990). Thus, partnering with large corporations can offer many technological entrepreneurs attractive alternatives to venture capitalists. The goal of the small company is to obtain various types of financial and non-financial assistance while at the same time giving up as little independence as possible.

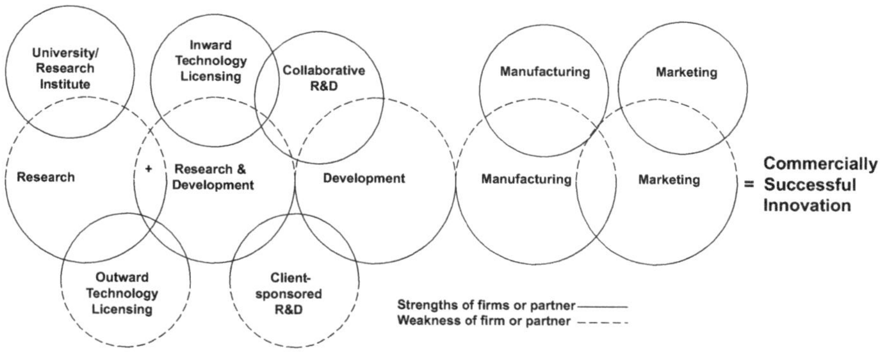

Fig. 11.6 The innovation chain & strategic partnering. (Source: Forrest 1990)

Lasagni (2012) suggests that small firms can secure significant enhancements in their innovation performance through the formation of strategic alliances. This can take a variety of forms, such as alliances with R&D centres at universities, as well as collaboration with customers and suppliers.

> **For example,** ... when small firms are able to strengthen their customers-supplier linkages, product innovation can accelerate because this type of partnership allows SMEs to reach new product development in shorter times. In particular, the fostering of closer relationships within the supply chain can be regarded as important source of new ideas for the design stages...SMEs will have better new product development results if they improve their collaborations and relationships with laboratories and research institutes. (Lasagni 2012, p. 330)

11.8.2 Reasons for Large Firms to Partner

For large companies, the main alternative to partnering is that of acquiring a small technology-based firm (Slowinski et al. 1996). The founders of the small company, who are also the key employees and owners, are made offers they can't refuse. They sell their companies and become rich employees of the large company. Within a short time, the former entrepreneurs become frustrated with the bureaucracy of the large company and leave. In too many cases the objective of the acquisition is not realized, primarily because the entrepreneurial spirit and incentives of the small company are incompatible with the culture of the large firm.

However, large firms can secure benefits from collaboration with small firms. This can typically involve the opportunity to access innovations such as new technology that the small firm has developed or is developing. Many large firms have begun to shift from *closed innovation* processes, where they rely primarily on in-house or existing customer and supplier engagements for new product or service ideas, to *open innovation* processes (see Chap. 10) (Chesbrough 2006). These involve opening up their R&D to a wide range of collaborators across almost all stages of the NPD process. Engagement not only with customers, but universities, small firms and research centres. The *open innovation* process involves sourcing ideas and innovations, collaborating and co-creating in their development, and sharing the knowledge and benefits with the wider network (West and Bogers 2014). This can have substantially enhanced the firm's innovation process.

> **For example,** ... Kimberley-Clark's "Insight Driven Innovation" program uses multiple linkages and stakeholders to leverage the expertise and capabilities of others to rapidly develop new product innovations. This has seen such ideas as "Huggies Little Swimmers" swim-pants for toddlers to partner with SunHealth Solutions to apply UV sensors to help parents monitor children's UV-B radiation. (Cooper and Edgett 2009)

In the 1990s Proctor & Gamble (P&G) adopted an *open innovation* process known as *Connect+Develop*. This helped to significantly transform their success at NPD and commercialisation through the opening up of their R&D process to universities, small firms and other larger firms. It was also a two-way flow of ideas with many of P&G's patents that had been sitting unused *on the shelf*, licensed to other firms to help disseminate these innovations and recoup value. It required the company to develop new ways to work, and to learn how to manage a large, global network of collaborative partners (Sakkab 2002).

> **For example,** ... P&G is not unique in commercializing only 10 percent of its patents – our benchmarking indicates that we are typical. Until recently, the 90 percent of unused technologies have been virtually "sitting on the shelf". We were very protective of our patents and know-how. We treated them as "corporate secrets". Licensing was seldom, if ever, considered, and if it was, it was viewed as the avenue of last resort...[but] We have opened the door to see our innovations in the marketplace, not only in our products but also in unexpected applications in totally unrelated fields. And all of it generates real dollars for our shareholders. (Sakkab 2002, p. 43)

11.8.3 The Process of Strategic Partnering

Unfortunately, large corporations are unlikely to form any partnership with small ventures at a very early stage, e.g. while the innovation is still evolving in somebody's garage. In such a case, obtaining government grants or angel investor funding significantly improves the credibility of a venture, and also helps obtaining access to specialist expertise needed at that point in time.

Creating a partnership with another organisation is a complex process in itself. Many partnerships are formed where neither party has any experience in this process, especially on the side of the new venture entrepreneur. There must be a good fit of business strategies of both partners, and available resources should complement each other, while an overlap in resources can easily threaten the job security of existing staff and seriously disturb overall staff morale. While the written partnership agreement provides a formal basis for implementation, a psychological contract (i.e. buy in by involved staff) is just as important. Table 11.2 lists a number of possible strategic partnerships that can be used in the commercialisation process.

As in any other negotiation, having a viable alternative is crucial in order to achieve a worthwhile outcome. Without such an alternative, the partner organisation can easily dictate unfavourable contract terms.

Table 11.2 Examples of strategic partnership types

Strategic partnership type	Description
Operating joint venture	An independent, third enterprise is formed by the company with another firm. Assets are contributed by both parties
Equity investment	An investment by a large established company in the venture
Client sponsored research contract	The small venture is paid to conduct research on particular products or processes for another organisation
Marketing/distribution agreement	Agreements whereby another company will market and distribute products for the venture
Manufacturing agreement	Agreements whereby another company agrees to manufacture products for the venture
Collaborative R&D	An agreement between the venture and another company to collaborate on the development of specific products or processes.
Technology licensing (inward)	A contractual arrangement by which the venture is granted access to another company's patents or technology for a fee (usually royalties)
Technology licensing (outward)	The reverse of the above. In this case the venture receives the fee/ royalties from another company for allowing it to use its technology

Source: Forrest (1990)

11.8.4 The Risks of Strategic Partnering

One of the biggest risks for a small firm partnering with a large one is to become dependent on the partner (Assens and Cherbib 2010; Garrette 1989). While the goals of the alliance are in alignment with both parties, this may not be a problem in the short term, but strategic objectives do change over time and the more powerful partner will either neglect or impose its will on the alliance. To protect against such a situation, partnership agreements should include exit clauses that allow terminating an unacceptable relationship. The exit clauses should be fair to, and protect the resources of both parties (Schnepple 2005). The success of partnerships relies on good relationships between key staff in the respective companies. Problems can occur if an *alliance champion* leaves and is replaced by no more than a *caretaker*. It should also be recognised that not everybody is necessarily happy when an alliance is first formed, especially if there are overlaps in competencies leading to a *wounded prince or princess* problem that must be carefully managed. The loss of intellectual property to a partner is one of the most difficult risks to protect against. Partnership agreements can easily deal with existing IP, but agreeing how to share newly created IP is the problem. Unless the relationship between the partners is good, there is a strong temptation to keep new IP secret at least until provisional patent applications have been lodged. A good working relationship between partners can easily be destroyed by the issues above which quickly turn a cooperative partnership into one of competition and hidden agendas.

11.8.5 How Small Firms Can Deal with Large Firms in Alliances

As discussed above, large firms have now embraced *open innovation* as a way to enhance the speed and success of their commercialisation process. This offers the potential for significant opportunities to small firms wanting to partner with larger ones over the commercialisation of their innovations. However, small firms can be vulnerable in such alliances because large firms typically have a greater capacity to absorb technology faster than their small counterparts. This requires small firms to learn how to engage and get the best out of the relationship. The first partner that learns what it needs to learn from the relationship can subsequently withdraw at relatively low cost (Alvarez and Barney 2001).

10 Principles for Managing Strategic Partnerships

If a single thread can be drawn through the fabric of strategic partnerships it would be that win-win means exactly what it says. It does not mean our firm wins and their firm loses. A strategic partnership is a cooperative, not competitive, relationship.

During partnership formation:

1. Partnerships need clearly defined strategic, operational, and business goals that are tied to each partner's corporate strategy.
2. An accurate mutual understanding of each partner's strengths and weaknesses is critical to success.
3. Staff personnel should be briefed as to the history, goals and value of this relationship to the corporation prior to their involvement with the partner.
4. The ownership of intellectual property must be clearly defined.
5. Prudence requires that exit strategies be written into partnership agreements. These strategies should meet the test of fairness, while protecting the resources of both firms.

During the ongoing relationship:

6. A partnership is not an event, it is a process; and managing the process is key.
7. Partnering is highly people-oriented. The relationship between operating managers is a critical factor that is often undervalued.
8. The loss of a key person can be traumatic. Dealing effectively with such transitions is necessary to the maintenance of the relationship.
9. Cooperation involves each partner adapting to the other's operating style.
10. Senior management commitment and the early inclusion of key groups in the planning process can counteract the corporate "immune response".

Source: Slowinski et al. (1993).

Table 11.3 Options for small firms in innovation alliances with larger firms

Alternatives	Firm execution	Advantages	Disadvantages
Go it alone	Acquire and build internal resources and capabilities	Retains value and benefits of commercialisation and R&D	Costly and time consuming
Slow down the large firm's rate of learning	Limit large firm's access to the small firm's technology. Only selected parts disclosed	Keeps the large firm from approaching the small firm's technology and IP	Slows down the rate of commercialisation and flow of case to small firm
Use detailed & elaborate legal contracts to define the alliance relationship	Engage lawyers with alliance, or JV expertise to set up contracts. Perform due diligence	Provides milestone timeline and specific terms and goals	Contracts cannot address all likely contingencies and can be costly to enforce
Build a relationship of trust	Keep communication lines open with partners. Do not promise to deliver more than can be delivered	Enhances the value of the alliance by not having to depend on legal contracts. May provide incentive for large firm to invest in relationship	Relies heavily on trust and might expose small firm to future exploitation by larger firm
Bring other resources to the alliance besides a single technology	Maintain the ability to be inventive and produce a stream of new technologies	Provides strong incentive for large firm to keep investing in relationship	Provides large investments in basic R&D

Source: Alvarez and Barney (2001)

For a small, entrepreneurial firm seeking to form a strategic partnership with a larger firm there are a number of things to consider. Table 11.3 provides a list of the options available as well as the means by which that option can be executed, plus the advantages and disadvantages of the option. It can be seen that the options are to proceed alone, or seek to employ one of four alternative strategies. The *DIY* (do it yourself) option will only be viable if the small firm has the necessary resources to commercialise alone. It may also be very time consuming and risky.

The other options can be broadly described as: *slow down*, *lawyer up*, *build trust* and *add value*. As shown in Table 11.3, the *slow down* option requires a gradual revealing of the small firm's IP assets and related knowledge. However, this option is likely to be very difficult to sustain and risks not only slowing down the entire process of commercialisation, but also breaching trust and permanently harming the alliance relationship. Adopting the *lawyer up* strategy can help to protect the interests of both parties and is a sensible way to set-up a formal joint venture or licensing agreement. However, it cannot address all foreseeable situations or contingencies and once the two parties have to enforce their rights under the contracts it will probably signal the death throes of the relationship.

Even if legal contracts are in place, the *build trust* option remains of value. Few partnerships can be sustained if there is a lack of trust between the participants. This requires the two parties to show integrity and a willingness to honour their agreements, benevolence towards the other partner, and competence in delivering their side of the partnership (Schoorman et al. 1996). Finally, the *add value* option is a sensible, albeit costly, strategy if the partnership is to be viewed as a long term sustainable one. Although it might involve the need to keep investing in R&D, if the alliance is generating significant value to the small firm it is a worthwhile investment.

11.8.6 Getting the Best from the Alliance

Any strategic partnership will require commitment and considered management. Table 11.4 summarises a list of the prescriptions suggested by Alvarez and Barney (2001) for both small and large firms that engage in partnerships focusing on innovation and commercialisation. As can be seen there are at least four key issues than need to be considered and actively managed: *technology*, *learning rates*, *needs* and *risk*.

In the management of *technology,* the small firm should consider bringing to the alliance a range of technological innovations that it can potentially deliver and work with its larger partner(s) to commercialise. Here it is important that the small firm is fully committed to ongoing R&D and NPD. In response, the large firm should look to partner with entrepreneurial small firms that have such commitment and can make a long-term contribution of innovations. If the small firm lacks this commitment and longer-term capacity it might be best to simply acquire the innovation via trade sale, or have it delegated via a licensing agreement.

The issue of mutual *learning rates* is important as the two partners should appreciate that they may have different levels of *absorptive capacity* (ACAP) (See Chap. 8). Small firms that have concerns over their large partner's ACAP may wish to

Table 11.4 How large and small firms can benefit from alliances

Issues	Small firm	Large firm
Manage technology carefully	Bring a string of technologies to the alliance or have the potential to generate a string of technologies	Choose entrepreneurial partners capable of generating several technology streams
Recognise the different rates of learning between firms	Slow down the large firm's rate of learning about the technology. Do not over expose the firm's technological capabilities too early in the partnership	Select entrepreneurial firms that have management skills to learn large firm organisational capabilities
Understand the need each firm is trying to fill via the alliance	Large firms often need the inventiveness of small firms. Once the large firm has the new technology it can usually exploit it	Dos the entrepreneurial small firm want to remain independent or be acquired? Does it want to remain small or grow?
Reduce risk	Perform due diligence on the large firm, be cautious to prevent excessive appropriation of alliance benefits by the larger firm	Form alliances with small firms that have managers capable of understanding what is required to make an alliance successful

Source: Alvarez and Barney (2001)

adopt the *slow down* strategy described above. The large firm that has strong ACAP needs to seek alliances with small firms that can demonstrate equivalent levels of ACAP. In that way both partners will move at a similar pace through the relationship.

It is also important for any sustainable partnership to have both parties understand each other *needs* and what they are seeking from the alliance. Here the small firm and its large partner should enter the relationship with an open and frank dialogue over what their respective goals are. Ideally both partners will have equally strong and mutually supportive goals. Where this is not the case caution should be applied to the alliance as it might not be sustainable. Questions like the small firm's plans in relation to an exit strategy (i.e. remain independent or trade sale; grow or not) should be explored. The large firm should also outline its aims and what it would hope to get by way of technology transfer.

Finally, the *risk* management requirements of a strategic alliance are important. There should be appropriate due diligence undertaken and both sides need to develop their managerial skills in working within a partnership such as a joint venture or more informal alliance.

11.8.7 Financial Partnering in Commercialisation

The decision for a large firm to partner with a smaller one requires consideration of a number of strategic issues. Of particular importance is the assessment of risk and return in any collaboration. As illustrated in Fig. 11.7: Venturing strategy

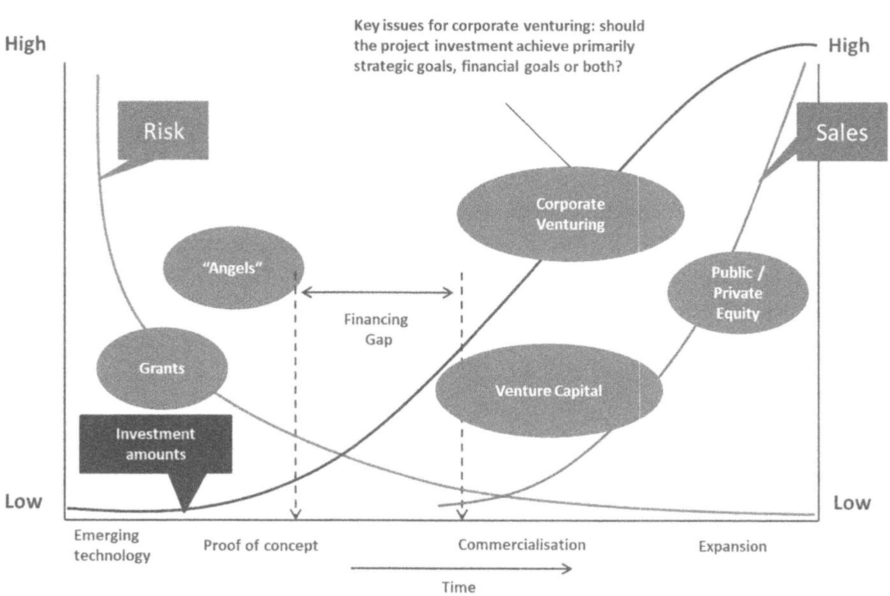

Fig. 11.7 Venturing strategy framework. (Source: Van Leen and Lubben 2013)

framework, the earlier the venture is in its lifecycle the higher the risk. This creates a dilemma for both start-up ventures and large firms that might consider engaging with such venture. At this early stage, the technology is typically still underdeveloped and a good deal of R&D remains to be completed. Some large firms are willing to invest in such R&D, but this is usually not viewed as part of a more coordinated corporate venturing process, which comes later.

As shown in Fig. 11.7, the evolution of a typical innovation project through its lifecycle commences with the initial R&D, then into prototyping and proof of concept. These early stages can a considerable amount of time and incur substantial costs. For example, the full process of a new drug approval (NDA) process in biotechnology involves an average of two and half years, with pre-clinical, clinical and full NDA review and final approval costing significant amounts of money (FDA 2018). Within the offshore liquid natural gas (LNG) and oil industry the full process of technology qualification via proof of concept can take an average of 3–4 years and run into high costs as field trials are undertaken, technology assessments made and modifications to the design completed and approved (DNV 2012).

These costs of R&D and proof of concept will either have to be carried by the smaller firm pursuing the project, and/or supported by publicly available R&D grants, as well as informal investors or *Business Angels* (see Chap. 12). There is a *financing gap* typically found between the proof of concept stage and the mainstream scaling-up of the company and its products in the commercialisation stage. Here the funding is either sourced from more formal venture capital investors, and/or initial public offering (IPO) on the stock market (see Chap. 12 for more detail). However, large firms can play a key role in assisting this scale-up process by investing in, or collaborating with the smaller, entrepreneurial company. However, as noted above, this strategic partnership is not without its risks and complexities.

11.8.8 Leading Customers as Strategic Partners

One of the most significant strategic partners for a small, entrepreneurial firm engaged in commercialisation of innovation is the leading customer or lead user (Von Hippel et al. 1999). To listen carefully to the voice of the customer is clearly a key ingredient in successfully developing new products. Many significant innovations are thought of and developed by users rather than by the manufacturers that first to bring them to market. Leading customers (lead users) can be characterised as follows:

- Lead users are ahead of a target market in an important dimension, they have needs that will become general in a marketplace either months or years later.
- Lead users have a high motivation to solve a problem; they stand to gain substantial benefits from a solution to the need they have encountered.
- Lead users may be found in the target market, but also in related markets.

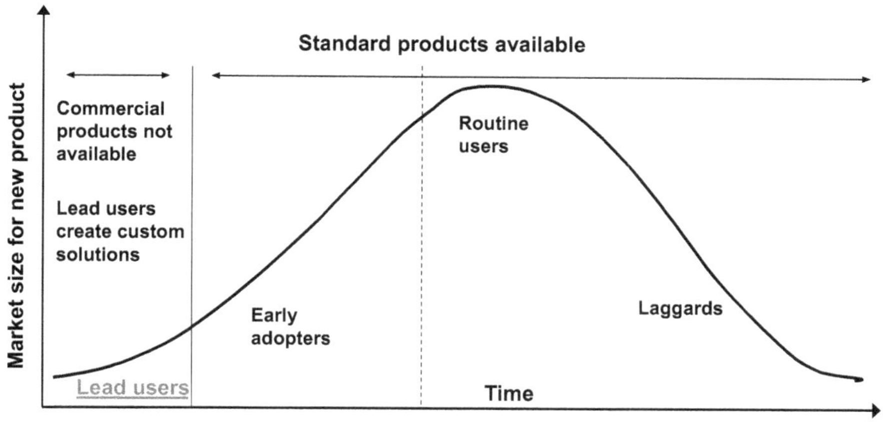

Fig. 11.8 Lead users at the 'leading edge' of the market. (Source: Von Hippel et al. 1999)

As shown in Fig. 11.8, lead users are found almost exclusively in the very early part of the market and the lead user method sets out to systematically identify such lead users. While leading users can be used as a *needs-forecasting laboratory*, regular users may not have the real-world experience needed to problem solve and provide accurate data to market researchers. This is particularly true for very novel or high technology products. The lead user or leading customer is often the primary source of market feedback that will encourage the entrepreneur to invest in the commercialisation of an innovation (Choi and Shepherd 2004; Mazzarol and Reboud 2005).

11.9 The Decision to Partner

In Chap. 8 the commercialisation pathways for the management of disruptive innovation were discussed along with the analysis of the *innovation rent*. It was suggested that there are at least five generic commercialisation pathways: (i) proceed alone; (ii) form an alliance, partnership or joint venture; (iii) license the technology; (iv) trade sale the technology; and (v) abandon the project or withdraw it from the firm's strategic planning. Each of these pathways has a different risk-return profile, with the highest risk and return generally residing with autonomous development, followed by partnership, then delegation via licensing, transfer through trade sale, and finally to withdrawal. The second, third and fourth pathways all involve a close engagement with third parties, and as such, a decision to partner. For small firms, this decision to seek outside assistance in the commercialisation of a new innovation is likely to be motivated by a lack of resources. These are typically within the areas of marketing, technology or technical competencies, and financial resources.

11.9.1 Considerations of Marketing Resources

One of the most significant costs associated with commercialisation is that relating to marketing and market development. This is particularly the case where the innovation has a global or significant market opportunity, but faces a high commercial or market risk due to the need to secure market share in circumstances where the market window of opportunity may not be open for long. Figure 11.9 provides a decision-making framework for SMEs facing resource management issues in relation to marketing.

As illustrated in Fig. 11.9, the first question to consider is whether the firm has sufficient resources and competencies within its own proprietary control to fully commercialise the innovation without outside assistance. If this is the case, then the project team should proceed. However, if this is not the case, the project team will need to make a strategic decision. At least two questions are important. First, can it buy the necessary resources and competencies, or develop them internally? Second, is partnering with other parties to acquire such resources possible?

It can be seen that if the answer to both questions is "yes", the firm will need to make a strategic choice as to whether to buy, build or partner. If the firm cannot buy or build the necessary marketing resources and competencies it will be forced into a partnership, and if it cannot partner, but can proceed alone, will be compelled to do so. However, if the firm has no option of partnering, or proceeding alone, it is likely to be forced to either delegate the commercialisation (e.g. via licencing), transfer it via trade sale, or withdraw and abandon the project.

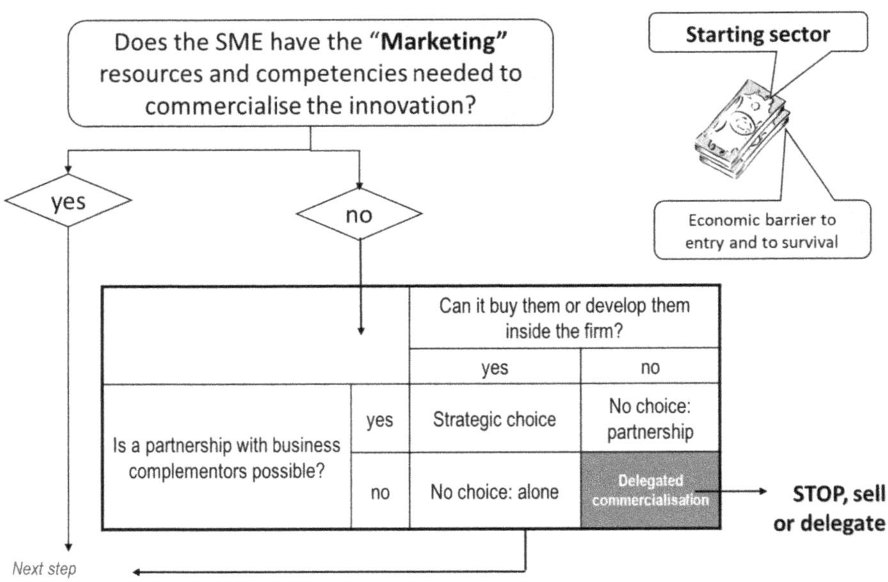

Fig. 11.9 Marketing resources and competencies of the firm. (Source: With permission Santi et al. 2003)

11.9.2 Considerations of Technological Resources

A similar situation can face the SME in relation to technological resources and competencies. Figure 11.10 illustrates this situation, and it can be seen that if the SME project team has all the necessary resources it should proceed, but if not, it will need to consider whether they are sufficient to sustain the full commercialisation of the innovation. If it seeks to proceed within the necessary resources, it will need to again ascertain whether it can buy or build them over time, or form a partnership with other complementary actors. Here the strategic choices of partnership, delegation, transfer or withdraw will need to be examined.

Table 11.5 summarises some of the advantages and disadvantages of strategic partnering for SMEs. These issues need to be considered by the project team working on the commercialisation and a well-considered assessment made as to the risks and benefits of strategic partnering before entering into such relationships. For many SMEs, particularly those who need third-party assistance to commercialise due to lack of technological resources and competencies, the formation of strategic partnerships is highly valuable. However, like any relationship it must be approached with consideration of the other party, and an appropriate due diligence before proceeding.

11.9.3 Considerations of Financial Resources

This process of strategic decision making applies equally to the ability of the SME to secure all the necessary financial resources that it needs. Figure 11.11 illustrates

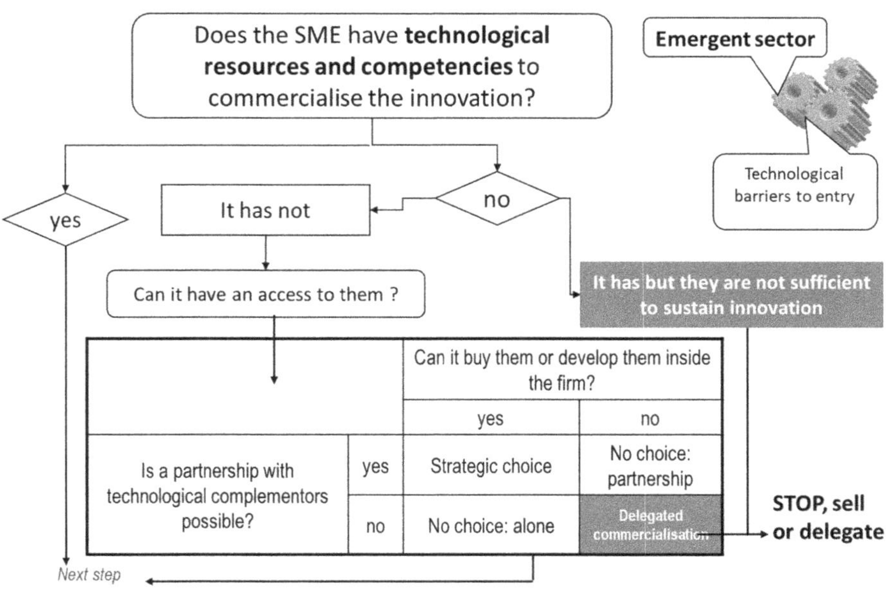

Fig. 11.10 Technical resources and competencies of the firm. (Source: With permission Santi et al. 2003)

Table 11.5 Advantages and disadvantages of strategic partnering for SMEs

Advantages	Disadvantages
Access to partners' resources	Loss of independence
Risks are shared by partner	Risk of strategic objectives of partners to go out of alignment
Access to technology	Requirement to surrender proportion of value created
Access to R&D expertise	Overlapping of resources – eroding power of existing people
Access to manufacturing facilities	Danger of losing (new) intellectual property to partners
Access to market knowledge	Over reliance on a partnership "champion"
Access to distribution networks	
Access to brand image of partner	

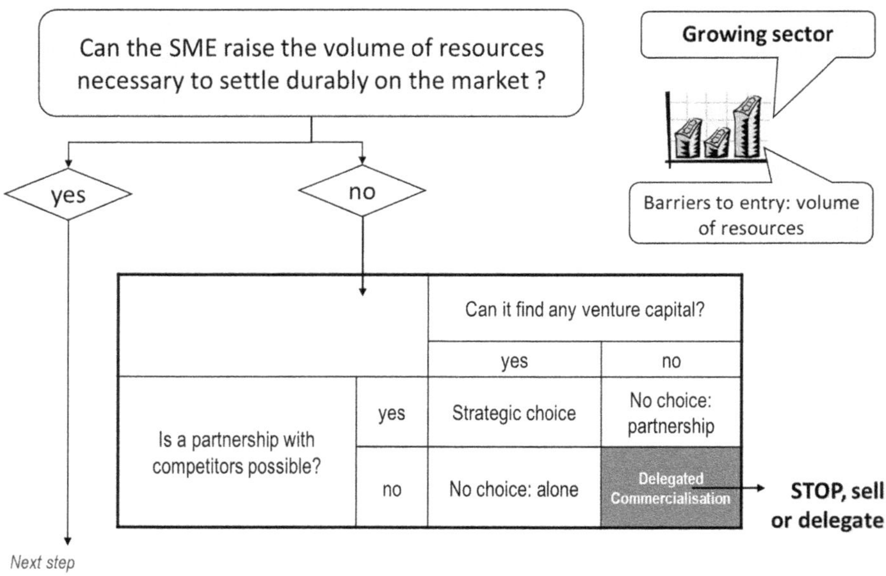

Fig. 11.11 Financial resources and competencies of the firm. (Source: With permission Santi et al. 2003)

the process for decisions over partnering in relation to financial resources. As discussed in Chap. 12, there are many options for financing a venture, and the use of venture capital or public listing, are not the most common. However, innovation commercialisation projects that require a significant expansion and large investments in marketing, market development, R&D and operations, will quickly outstrip the capabilities of most SMEs. Whether or not the firm can secure equity investment, or third-party funding from strategic partners, will determine not only how fast the commercialisation process can proceed, but whether or not it may have to be delegated, transferred or abandoned.

The formation of strategic alliances and partnerships can be a highly valuable way for firms of all sizes, but particularly SMEs, to secure access to resources and competencies that they either don't possess, or that might take them too long to develop alone. However, several considerations should be made in relation to any partnering process. First, both partners should ensure that they have *clearly defined and compatible business strategies*. The parties entering into the relationship must have well-defined and compatible strategic goals. If this is not the case there is the risk that the two parties will end up in conflict or be forced to abandon the relationship. Second, there should be a *mutual understanding of each other's' strengths and weaknesses*. Third, all *background IP rights* brought to the alliance should be identified, and agreements over how new IP rights generated as a result of the partnership will be determined (Harbison and Pekar 1999).

Another important issue that should be address prior to the formation of the partnership is to ask whether there is any alternative to a partnership? If the firm seeking a partnership has no alternative options, it may find itself in a weak bargaining position with the other partner. Consideration should also be given to how the partnership might be wound-up. This should involve establishing mutually beneficial and fair exit clauses for both partners right from the start of the relationship. Finally, it is important to realise that any agreement, regardless of how well its legal and contractual details are drafted, will depend on the establishment and maintenance of the personal relationships between the people in both partner organisations. There needs to be a strong sense of commitment from both sides to making the relationship work (Harbison and Pekar 1999).

11.10 Strategic Assets and Organisational Rent in the Context of Strategic Alliances

Entrepreneurial management and innovation within organisations of any size is focused on the configuration and deployment of specialised and co-specialised resources and capabilities in order to generate sustainable competitive advantage within target markets (Teece 1986). As the company grows by navigating the often-challenging process of commercialisation, the senior management team and its board will need to develop a set of unique capabilities and strategic assets and to understand how to use them to generate organisational rents.

11.10.1 The Relationship Between Firm Strategic Assets and Strategic Industry Factors

This process is illustrated in Fig. 11.12, first proposed by Amit and Schoemaker (1993), which shows the firm as being in possession of a portfolio of resources and capabilities, that when combined can form strategic assets that can be deployed to create organisational rents. Within this framework *resources* are defined as "*stocks of available factors that are owned or controlled by the firm*" (p. 35). By contrast

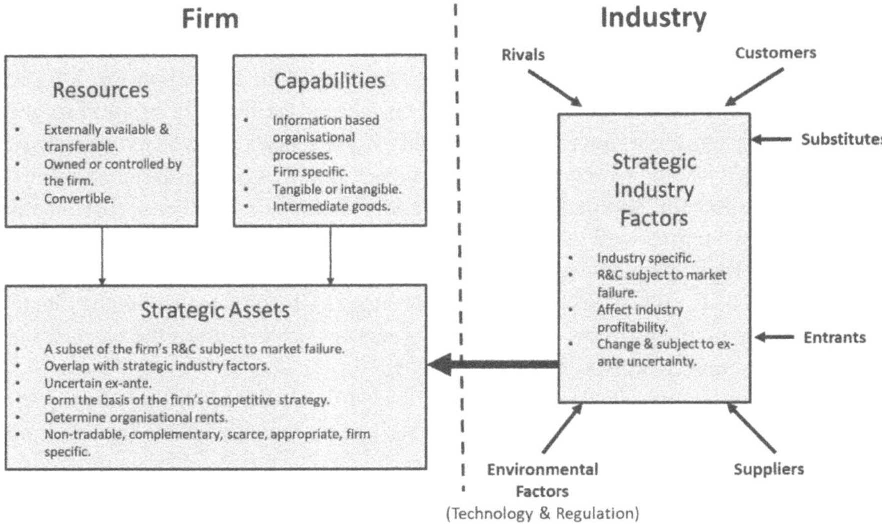

Fig. 11.12 Strategic assets and organisational rent – key constructs. (Source: Amit and Schoemaker 1993)

capabilities are defined as "*a firm's capacity to deploy resources, usually in combination, using organizational processes, to effect a desired end*" (p. 35). When combined, these resources and capabilities generate *strategic assets*, which are defined as, "*the set of difficult to trade and imitate, scarce, appropriable and specialised Resources and Capabilities that bestow the firm's competitive advantage*" (p. 36).

The deployment of these strategic assets will enable the firm to generate above average organisational rents and thereby build a competitive advantage. However, their deployment into the market will require the firm to consider how these strategic assets best exploit opportunities or mitigate threats identified within the industry sector where they are seeking to compete. As shown in Fig. 11.12, a range of issues will impact on the *strategic industry factors* and in-turn how best to deploy the firm's strategic assets. The strategic industry factors must be monitored and assessed on a regular basis. The techniques for this can be found with reference to Chaps. 7, 9, and 10.

11.10.2 Configuring the Firm's Resources and Capabilities to Generate Organisational Rents

The ability for an organisation to sustainably generate above average rents from the configuration and deployment of its strategic assets is contingent on at least eight key attributes, which are illustrated in Fig. 11.13. According to Amit and Schoemaker (1993), these eight attributes are essential for the following reasons:

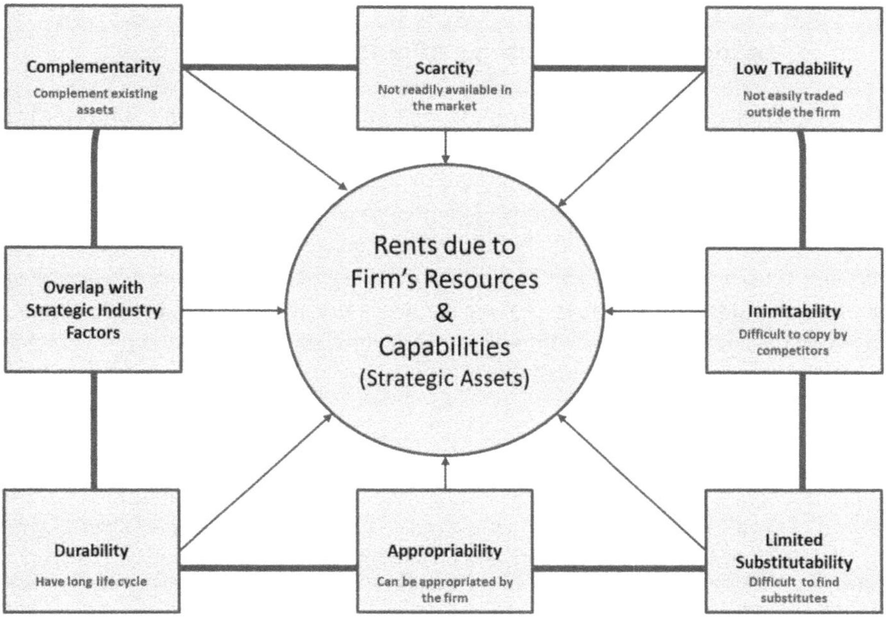

Fig. 11.13 Desired characteristics of the firm's resources and capabilities. (Source: Amit and Schoemaker 1993)

1. *Complementarity*: Resources and capabilities that offer good synergies and complement each other generate more value than those that operate in isolation. These are co-specialised assets that deliver more value when operating in concert with each other.
2. *Scarcity*: Any strategic assets that are unique to the firm, or that cannot be readily or easily acquired by customers, suppliers or competitors offer the basis for a sustainable competitive advantage.
3. *Low Tradeability:* Strategic assets that cannot be readily transferred outside the firm, e.g. via sub-contracting or outsourcing also provide a strong foundation for generating organisational rents.
4. *Imitability:* Another important attribute for strategic assets is that they should not be easily copied or replicated by competitors.
5. *Limited Substitutability:* In addition to how easily an asset can be imitated, is the ease or difficulty in it being substituted by alternatives by customers.
6. *Appropriability:* Strategic assets that might not be proprietary, but that can be appropriated by the firm, are also valuable.
7. *Durability:* A strategic asset must also be durable and possess a long lifecycle.
8. *Overlap with strategic industry factors:* Finally, the full value of any strategic asset is well it overlaps with the strategic industry factors described in Fig. 11.11. Unless these assets can be deployed to exploit opportunities or mitigate threats within the firm's industry, they may be of limited value.

11.10.3 Developing Strategic Assets via Team Building, Company Leadership and Strategic Alliances

The competitive success of any business venture will depend on the ability of the leadership team to acquire, develop and sustain the right mix of human, financial, physical and IP assets, and then configure its resources and capabilities into strategic assets that can be suitably deployed in order to address strategic industry factors. This process commences with building the management and staff capabilities through training, coaching and leadership. Making sure that the firm's board of directors has the right people to provide the necessary strategic guidance, and making wise decisions over how with who to forge strategic alliances and partnerships along the commercialisation pathway.

References

Alvarez, S. A., & Barney, J. B. (2001). How entrepreneurial firms can benefit from alliances with large partners. *The Academy of Management Executive, 15*(1), 139–148.

Amit, R., & Schoemaker, P. J. H. (1993). Strategic assets and organizational rent. *Strategic Management Journal, 14*(1), 33–46.

Ardichvili, A., Harmon, B., Cardozo, R. N., Reynolds, P. D., & Williams, M. L. (1998). The new venture growth: Functional differentiation and the need for human resource development interventions. *Human Resource Development Quarterly, 9*(1), 55–70.

Assens, C., & Cherbib, J. (2010). L'Alliance asymétrique: une stratégie durable ? *La Revue des Sciences de Gestion, 243–244*(3), 111–119.

Avolio, B. J., & Bass, B. M. (2011). *Full range leadership development: Manual for the multifactor leadership questionnaire*. Thousand Oaks/London: Sage Publications.

Baker, W. (1994). *The paradox of empowerment*. Chief Executive, April (93), 62–65.

Bass, B. M. (1990). *Bass and Stodgill's handbook of leadership development: Manual for the multi-factor leadership questionnaire*. Binghamton: Bass, Avolio and Associates.

Bass, B. M., & Avolio, B. J. (1994). *Improving organizational effectiveness through managerial applications* (3rd ed.). New York: Free Press.

Bates, S. (1999). Put emphasis on results before and after hiring. *Nation's Business, 87*(1), 13.

Chandler, G. N., Keller, C., & Lyon, D. W. (2000). Unraveling the determinants and consequences of an innovation-supportive organizational culture. *Entrepreneurship Theory and Practice(Fall), 25*, 59–76.

Chesbrough, H. W. (2006). *Open innovation: The new imperative for creating and profiting from technology*. Boston: Harvard Business Press.

Choi, Y. R., & Shepherd, D. A. (2004). Entrepreneurs' decisions to exploit opportunities. *Journal of Management, 30*(3), 377–395.

Cooper, R. G., & Edgett, S. J. (2009). *Generating breakthrough new product ideas: Feeding the innovation funnel*. Ancaster: Product Development Institute.

Cronin, T. (1991). Early warning signals. *Small Business Reports, 16*(9), 53–62.

Dingee, A. L., Haslett, B., & Smollen, L. E. (1995). *Characteristics of a successful entrepreneurial management team* (Pratts Guide to Venture Capital Sources) (pp. 23–21). New York: Securities Data Publishing.

DNV. (2012). *Qualification of new technology, DNV-RP-A203*. Det Norske Veritas AS. Retrieved from www.dnv.com

Dodge, R., & Robbins, J. (1992). An empirical investigation of the organisational lifecycle model for small business development and survival. *Journal of Small Business Management, 30*(1), 27–37.

Drew, S., & Coulson-Thomas, C. (1996). Transformation through teamwork: The path to the new organization? *Management Decision, 34*(1), 7–17.

Edwards, L. (2002). *Building a winning team*. Canberra: AusIndustry, Department of Industry, Tourism and Resources, Commonwealth of Australia.

FDA. (2018). *Development & approval process (Drugs)*. U.S. Food & Drug Administration. Retrieved from www.fda.gov

Forrest, J. (1990). Strategic alliances and the small technology-based firm. *Journal of Small Business Management, 28*(3), 37–45.

Garrette, B. (1989). Actifs spécifiques et coopération: une analyse des stratégies d'alliance. *Revue d'Économie Industrielle, 50*(1), 15–31.

Goodale, M. (2001). Establishing organizational structure. *Civil Engineering*, (August), 70–71.

Harbison, J. R., & Pekar, J. (1999). Harnessing the power of alliances and acquisitions. *Directorship, 25*(3), 6–8.

Harvey, P., & Butcher, D. (1998). Those who make a difference: Developing businesses through developing individuals. *Industrial and Commercial Training, 30*(1), 12–15.

Hersey, P., & Blanchard, K. H. (1982). Leadership style: Attitudes and behaviors. *Training & Development Journal, 36*(5), 50–52.

Hull, F., & Slowinski, E. (1990). Partnering with technology entrepreneurs. *Research-Technology Management, 33*(6), 16–20.

Kauffman Centre. (1997). *Tapping in: Attracting and retaining awesome people*. Kauffman Centre for Entrepreneurial Leadership. Retrieved from Kansas City:

Kauffman Centre. (1998). *Tapping in: Attracting, recruiting and retaining awesome people*. Kauffman Centre for Entrepreneurial Leadership. Retrieved from Kansas City:

Kauffman Centre. (1999). *Building the awesome organization: Kauffman gathering of entrepreneurs*. Kauffman Centre for Entrepreneurial Leadership. Retrieved from May 1999 Kansas City:

Kaufman, B. (2002). Grappling with dysfunctional board relationships. *Journal of Business Strategy*,. November/December, *23*, 26–31.

Lasagni, A. (2012). How can external relationships enhance innovation in SMEs? New evidence for Europe*. *Journal of Small Business Management, 50*(2), 310–339.

Mazzarol, T. (2002). Innovativeness in small firms: An exploratory study of the perspectives of growth oriented owner-managers. *Innovations, 4*(1–3), 30–40.

Mazzarol, T., & Reboud, S. (2005). Customers as predictors of rent returns to innovation in small firms – An exploratory study. *International Journal of Entrepreneurship and Innovation Management, 5*(5/6), 483–494.

Sakkab, N. Y. (2002, March–April). Connect & develop compliments research & develop at P&G. *Research Technology Management, 45*, 38–45.

Santi, M., Reboud, S., Gasiglia, H., & Sabouret, A. (2003). *Modèle de valorisation et de protection intellectuelle des innovations des PEI. HEC-INPI Research Report*. Retrieved from Paris.

Schnepple, T. (2005). *Managing commercialisation risk*. University of Western Australia: Innovation Excellence Program, Centre for Entrepreneurial Management and Innovation.

Schoorman, F. D., Mayer, R. C., & Davis, J. H. (1996). *Organizational trust: Philosophical perspectives and conceptual definitions*. JSTOR.

Sexton, D., & Seale, F. (1997). *Leading practices of fast growth entrepreneurs: Pathways for high performance*. Kansas City: National Centre for Entrepreneurship Research.

Sharlit, B., & McConnell, C. (1989). Managing growth. *Small Business Reports, 14*(7), 27–33.

Slowinski, G., Farris, F., & Jones, D. (1993). Strategic partnering: Process instead of event. *Research Technology Management, 36*(3), 22–26.

Slowinski, G., Seelig, G., & Hull, F. (1996). Managing technology-based strategic alliances between large and small firms. *SAM Advanced Management Journal, 61*(2), 42–48.

Teece, D. J. (1986). Profiting from technological innovation: Implications for integration, collaboration, licensing and public policy. *Research Policy, 15*(6), 285–305.

Van Leen, R., & Lubben, M. (2013). Open innovation and successful venturing. In K. B. Kahn (Ed.), *The PDMA handbook of new product development, Product Development & Management Association (PDMA)* (pp. 82–98). Hoboken: Wiley.

Von Hippel, E., Thomke, S., & Sonnack, M. (1999). Creating breakthroughs at 3M. *Harvard Business Review, 77*, 47–57.

Weiner, A. (1985). From the ground up. *The Executive, 27*(2), 21–27.

West, J., & Bogers, M. (2014). Leveraging external sources of innovation: A review of research on open innovation. *Journal of Product Innovation Management, 31*(4), 814–831.

12 Financing the Venture

12.1 Introduction

Trying to secure the funding required to take an innovation through to market is our biggest challenge. The Australian capital market is currently chasing dust and dollars; we need it to focus on DNA not dust and dollars.

Source: Australian biotech entrepreneur.

This chapter examines the financing options available to entrepreneurs from initial start-up through growth and expansion. It examines the key sources of finance with attention to debt, equity and retained profit. While much of the popular focus of entrepreneurial financing has been placed on venture capital, this is only one of many options available to entrepreneurs, and it is not always the most appropriate or popular. Furthermore, as we will show, securing venture capital financing is quite difficult and most new ventures will not be eligible for such financing.

12.2 The Financing Gap for Entrepreneurial Firms

Entrepreneurial firms experiencing rapid periods of growth frequently find themselves outstripping the amount of capital that most banks are willing to supply. Debt financing from banks usually requires security against tangible assets, and many fast-growing small firms cannot find sufficient assets against which to secure their loans. This is likely to be of particular concern to service firms and high technology companies that frequently have their wealth tied up in intellectual property rather than physical assets.

According to some theorists, there is a *financing gap* that exists within most economies whereby banks and suppliers of venture capital (equity financing)

T. Mazzarol, S. Reboud, *Entrepreneurship and Innovation*, Springer Texts in Business and Economics, https://doi.org/10.1007/978-981-13-9412-6_12

essentially ration credit and deny funding to entrepreneurial ventures, particularly start-ups and small firms (OECD 2006). This financing gap is attributed to financing institutions lacking adequate information with which to make rational assessments of the risks associated with small and entrepreneurial ventures. This leads them to either deny funding, or to place high costs of capital on such funds that reflect their risk premium (Stiglitz and Weiss 1981). Many banks will actually just deny funding, as they may feel that to raise interest rates could deter lower risk applicants and raise the overall risk profile of their loans portfolios (OECD 2006).

Since the *Global Financial Crisis* (GFC) of 2008–2009, the availability of investment capital has declined, and many small to medium enterprises (SMEs) and entrepreneurs are experiencing problems with financing. A study undertaken by the OECD (2009) found that many small firms were experiencing delays in payments from customers, shortages of working capital, reduced liquidity and an increase in creditor payment defaults, insolvencies, and bankruptcies. In addition to these operating issues, there was a significant slowdown in global venture capital fundraising during the period 2007–2008. Institutional investors were simply less willing to provide the funding for entrepreneurial ventures. Since the GFC the economic conditions across most of the world's economies have improved, however the financing gap has remained (OECD 2016a).

A study by the OECD (2006) into the *financing gap* found that there were several kinds of *gaps* around the world. In some countries, the lack of funding for small firms was caused by structural weaknesses in the financial systems – usually the banks – which is common in developing economies. Another problem was the relative absence of a venture capital market or sector within some economies, which tend to be overly reliant on banks provided debt financing. This is common in Europe. In some countries, the SME sector is very large but there is a lack of a high growth or *high-tech* sector. Other countries have much larger high-tech sectors. In short, each national economy has a different set of circumstances.

12.3 The OECD Scoreboard of SME and Entrepreneurial Financing

In 2012 the OECD commenced the publication of an annual scoreboard on SME and entrepreneurship financing (OECD 2012). This comprises a number of indicators with data collected from a range of countries drawn from within the OECD. These indicators are listed in Table 12.1 along with their meanings. The data for the *OECD Scoreboard* is drawn from a range of sources across participating countries. At time of writing this data was available for the period 2007–2014 and therefore offers a longitudinal assessment of the impact of the GFC. It also provides a valuable source of information on government policy and its impact on SMEs and entrepreneurs, as well as cross-country comparisons.

The OECD notes that the ability to make reliable global comparisons of this kind is challenging due to a range of factors. Amongst these is the different ways that each country defines what an SME or small firm is (see Chap. 5), as well as the

Table 12.1 Core indicators of the OECD Scoreboard on SME and entrepreneurship finance

Core indicators:	What they show
1. Share of SME loans in total business loans	SME's access to finance compared to larger firms
2. SME short-term loans in total SME loans	Debt structure of SMEs; % used for operations versus % used for expansion
3. SME loan guarantees	Extent of public support for SME finance
4. SME guaranteed loans	Extent to which such public support is used
5. SME direct government loans	Extent of public support for SME finance
6. SME rejection rate	Tightness of credit conditions and willingness of banks to lend
7. SME loans used/SME loan authorised	Sometimes used in addition or instead of the rejection rate to gauge credit conditions. A decrease indicates that conditions are loosening
8. SME non-performing loans/ SME loans	When compared to the ratio of non-performing loans (NPLs) for all business loans, it indicates if SMEs are less creditworthy than larger firms
9. SME interest rates	Tightness of credit conditions and willingness of banks to lend
10. Interest rates spread between large and small enterprises	Tightness of credit conditions; indicates how closely interest rates are correlated with firm size
11. Percent of SMEs required to provide collateral on their last bank loan	Tightness of credit conditions
12. Venture capital and growth capital	Ability to access external equity for start-up, early development and expansion stages
13. Asset-based finance	The take-up of non-bank finance instruments such as leasing, hire purchase, factoring and invoice discounting by SMEs
14. Payment delays	Cash flow problems; difficulty in paying and being paid
15. Bankruptcies	Rough indicator of the impact of a crisis, cash flow problems

Source: OECD (2012)

sheer logistical problems of collecting reliable data from a large number of countries. For this reason, the *OECD Scoreboard*, while able to provide a valuable overall picture, has some limitations when inter-country comparisons are made.

12.3.1 Key Findings from the OECD Scoreboard on SME Financing

Over the period 2007–2014 the *OECD Scoreboard of 2016* analysis suggested that the impact of the GFC, whilst severe, has largely abated as the years have passed (OECD 2016a). This has had a generally positive impact on SME financing with 59% of countries showing rising volumes of lending to small firms. However, for most SMEs across the OECD, credit remained tight. On a more positive note the rate of business bankruptcies declined over the period for the majority (80%) of countries. Despite this, around 44% of countries showed a rise in the number of non-performing loans (NPL).

Another noticeable trend found in the *OECD Scoreboard of 2016* was the increased use of alternative financial instruments by SMEs. This included the use of crowdfunding, factoring and *business angels* (discussed below). The provision of informal venture capital investors or *business angels* offers a source of funding for young, innovative, high growth firms. This type of financing also offers the potential for these *angel* investors to also provide mentoring, networks and strategic guidance to these small, entrepreneurial firms (OECD 2016a).

Government policy responses to the GFC, and the subsequent requirement for greater economic stimulation, has been to help ease access to finance, particularly for SMEs. In general, the SME sector is heavily reliant on bank debt financing. As discussed below, this has some positive and negative effects. A key problem is the limitation that this can place on firm's seeking growth, but lacking sufficient borrowing capacity. Throughout the world government policy has been targeting ways to increase the level of equity financing available to SMEs. This typically involves ways to stimulate venture capital investment and public listing on the stock exchange. Assisting SMEs to gain access to funding for international expansion and securing access into global supply chains is also an area of focus for government policy (OECD 2016a). Although the *OECD Scoreboard of 2016* was generally positive about the global trend in SME and entrepreneurial financing to that time it did raise a note of caution.

> **For example,** ... SME access to finance will remain a concern in the years to come. Despite recent improvements in SME lending, financial conditions often remain tight and many SMEs continue to face credit constraints. A number of factors persist which could jeopardise the economic recovery, with potential repercussions on SME lending. Furthermore, many financial institutions continue to deleverage and, due to tightened regulatory requirements, this will likely impact small businesses disproportionately. Governments should continue to monitor closely SME access to finance and take actions which enable them to access a broader range of financing instruments. (OECD 2016a, p.27)

These predictions have largely come true and the *OECD Scoreboard of 2018* has shown that over the period from 2014 to 2017 the median level of growth in new lending to SMEs across 15 countries declined from an annual rate of 2.6% to −5.6% (OECD 2018). Not all countries experienced negative trends, with only 15 out of 25 nations reporting this, and 24 out of 35 countries reporting growth. Many factors influenced these trends. In some countries (e.g. Australia, Austria, the Czech Republic, the Netherlands and the United Kingdom) there was a general decline in the demand for credit. In other countries (e.g. Greece, Slovenia, Portugal), the banks were reportedly more risk-averse, due to a high proportion of non-performing loans within the SME sector. Declining lending to SMEs within some countries (e.g. Russia and Brazil) was attributed to poor macro-economic conditions.

According to the OECD (2018), the overall trend from 2007 to 2016 has seen a steady decline in short-term lending and concurrent increase in long-term lending. Other good indicators have been an improvement in credit conditions, and a decline in the number of SME bankruptcies. In fact, from the peak of 2009 to 2009 during the height of the GFC, the number of small businesses declaring bankruptcy has steadily declined across all 36 OECD countries (OECD 2018).

12.4 Sources of Entrepreneurial Capital

Access to financing is one of the most significant challenges facing entrepreneurs (OECD 2009). Entrepreneurial capital – for the formation of new business ventures – is usually available from at least three sources:

- *Bootstrap financing;* The funding provided from the entrepreneur's savings and what can be retained through cash flow management and retained profits.
- *Debt financing:* The funding borrowed over the short and long-term from banks, other financial institutions and credit cards.
- *Equity financing:* The funding obtained from informal and formal investors who take part ownership in the business for a return on capital.

Each of these sources has quite a different dynamic and requires the entrepreneur to consider different issues. As the venture grows, it will continue to rely in retained profits and combinations of debt and equity financing, depending on the nature of the business and how large it seeks to grow.

It is important to note some basic differences between SMEs and large firms in relation to financing. Compared to large firms, most SMEs rely more heavily on *bootstrap* financing in the form of personal savings and retained profits. As a general rule, SMEs retain a higher proportion of earnings, which they use as working capital and to fund future growth (Keasey and McGuinness 1990). SMEs also obtain more funding from private debt and equity markets than large firms that generally operate within the public domain of the stock exchange (OECD 2004). SMEs also don't generally seek equity financing. This is due in part to the cost and difficulty of securing equity financing for a small firm, but also the desire by many entrepreneurs and small business owners to retain control over their venture and to not dilute equity control (Hughes 2001).

12.4.1 Bootstrap Financing

Bootstrap financing involves raising capital from internal sources. It can encompass personal savings accumulated by the entrepreneur, money borrowed from family and friends, or funds accumulated from trading (retained profits). An important part of bootstrap financing is the ability to retain earnings within the business for working capital. The concept of *working capital* refers to the cash and other short-term assets (e.g. receivables) that can be applied to pay short-term liabilities. A lack of working capital can be a serious problem for even the best business with good products and healthy profit margins.

A common cause of small business failure in the initial years after start-up is a lack of working capital. This is caused by such things as the lag between when money can be recovered from customers and put at bank, and the need to pay creditors, employee wages, taxes and overhead costs such as rent payments. During the GFC many SMEs found it difficult to secure finance from banks or private equity sources. As cash flow became squeezed with the slowing down of the economy this impacted their ability to maintain sufficient working capital to remain solvent (OECD 2009). Historically, a lack of working capital has been identified as a major source of business bankruptcies in Australia (ABS 2002).

The majority of small businesses start-up with funds derived from personal sources (Productivity Commission 2015). In the 1990s research in Australia found that approximately 59% of financing for new small business start-ups came from the personal savings or borrowings of the founders (ABS 1998). Subsequent research over the period 2007–2011 found that this pattern had not changed, with 66% of new business start-ups reporting that they had sought external finance for their venture (Productivity Commission 2015 p.122).

12.4.2 Benefits of Bootstrap Financing

The important benefit of bootstrap financing is that it costs little or nothing. Use of bank or venture capital financing will incur a cost of capital requirement on the business. However, the small business owner that uses the company's own cash for growth avoids this cost (Stevenson et al. 1999). Further, the owner-manager can have total control over the funds and their use. There are also no applications to worry about and, for many owner-managers who have been rejected by banks, this is important. Finally, many banks and venture capitalists have minimum amounts of money that they will lend. Use of the firm's own capital or money drawn from the entrepreneur's savings or from family and friends carry no such minimums. However, if borrowing from family or friends, it is important that the owner-manager deal with this money in a professional manner; it should be correctly recorded and repaid. Seeking legal assistance in drawing up a loan agreement may be worthwhile (Fraser 1999).

Checklist for Bootstrap Financing

- *Implement proven market ideas*. This will assist in getting sales moving quickly.
- *Look for a quick break-even*. The project or new venture should break-even and return a profit as quickly as possible. If not, the business will be forced to seek alternative sources of capital.
- *Look for high gross profit*. The higher the profit margin of a new product or service, the more retained earnings that can be generated.

- *Sell directly*. The bootstrap process is assisted if the product can be sold directly by personal selling. This assists sales growth and allows control of cash flows.
- *Keep the team lean*. Bootstrap financing does not usually permit the entrepreneur the luxury of hiring a large management team. The company must get what it can from the existing staff with everyone mucking-in.
- *Control growth*. Because capital is limited to cash flow, the firm cannot afford to allow expansion to get out of control. Live within your means is the rule.
- *Focus on cash flow*. Cash is king, as this feeds any growth.
- *Cultivate banks early*. Learn how to deal with bankers and what they want before you need them.

Source: Stevenson et al. (1999).

12.4.3 Cash Flow Financing

An important aspect of bootstrap financing is the ability to effectively manage the cash flow of the venture. Cash is required to buy stock and raw materials, fund work in progress, and pay for finished goods that go into inventory. As illustrated in Fig. 12.1, the cash that the business receives from its customers (*receivables*) is available to fund the purchase of inventory and equipment. Sale of inventory or use of equipment is used to generate new sales, which should have sufficient profit margins to leave enough cash to pay for purchasing, production costs and the cost of sales and distribution.

There can be delays between the time an invoice to a customer (*debtor*) is issued and the bill is paid. During this lag time, suppliers (*creditors*) will need to be paid – along with wages and other overheads (e.g. rent). A business that cannot raise debt

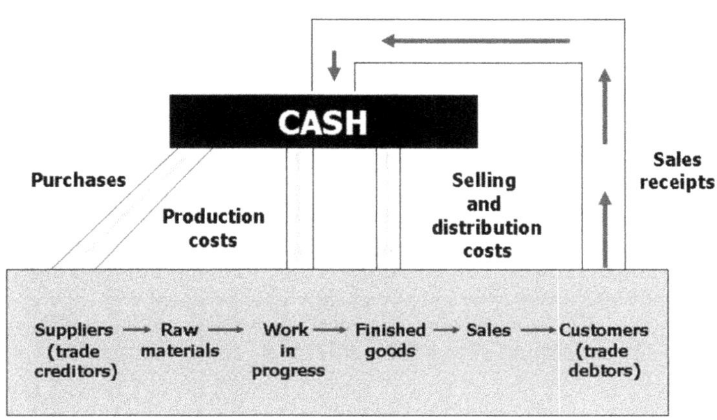

Fig. 12.1 The working capital cycle. (Source: Snaith and Walker 1999)

or equity to cover its working capital short fall has only one place to go – to its *creditors*. This can result in delays to paying creditors and this is referred to as *creditor strain*.

The cash flow cycle needs to be carefully managed, particularly where the business is growing, because this will place more demand on working capital. A key to improving the firm's cash position is the increase the *gross profit margin* on sales, as this means that there is more cash created from every sale made. The gross profit can be increased by raising prices or finding more efficient ways to work, and this can lower variable costs. The cash cycle time can also be improved by seeking to recover debts faster, or have customers pay deposits and instalments rather than waiting until the work has been completed.

The firm's *break-even* also needs to be closely monitored. Break-even is where the total costs are equal to the total revenues. Improving gross profit margins can help the firm reach break-even faster, but keeping overhead costs down will be of major importance. This may require that salaries – particularly for directors – are kept at a modest level, and that the business only leases sufficient building space or employs staff as is necessary.

12.4.4 Debt Financing

Debt financing is that which is obtained from banks and related financial institutions on either a short or long-term basis. The main characteristic of debt financing is that it is money obtained from a lender at a cost, usually associated with an interest charge on the repayments. The lender is keen to see the loan principal repaid, but also seeks to make money from the interest charges. Such debt financing is also secured – particularly long-term debts – by legal contracts that offset the lender's risk against assets owned by the borrower.

A study undertaken by the European Commission (2001) found that debt financing comprised the majority of funding used by SMEs. Half of these firms had bank loans or overdraughts, about 40% had some form of leasing finance and 11% were employing debtor financing or *factoring*. Only 9% reported using equity investment. The OECD *Scoreboard* of SME and entrepreneurial financing reports that over the period from 2007 to 2016 the share of SME loans as a proportion of total business loans across 37 countries was around 40% (OECD 2016a, 2018). As noted above, the general trend was away from short-term to long-term lending.

> **According to the OECD,** … Various factors may play a role. Recent improvements in cash flow and profitability may be allowing small firms to rely on internally generated revenues for their day-to-day operations, thus leading to a decline in external short-term financing. In addition, some SMEs may want to borrow on longer terms as interest rates decline, so as to 'lock-in' low rates. Finally, the recovery in corporate investments has been relatively weak and uneven since the financial crisis. (OECD 2018, p. 2)

Most debt financing in Australia is undertaken by the major banks and takes the form of credit cards, short and long-term loans, and overdraughts. The majority of debt financing for SMEs is undertaken by banks on the basis of loans secured against the family home.

> **For example,** … Most lending to new businesses in Australia is collateral based (often secured against the personal real estate of the business owner). There is evidence that banks adopt a relatively formulaic approach to lending and are less willing to lend on the basis of business prospects alone, but there are no impediments to lending on such bases other than the need to provide additional capital for prudential regulation purposes. Declining rates of home ownership amongst younger Australians present a challenge for collateral-based business lending models in the future. (Productivity Commission 2015, p. 177)

In France, the micro firms (e.g. those with fewer than ten employees) appear to have the most difficulty in securing bank financing. A study by the *Observatoire du financement des entreprises* published in 2014 found that the micro-business sector was highly turbulent with one-third of businesses failing after 3 years from start-up and half of them failing within 5 years. Bank financing was made more difficult due to the lack of working capital and equity in the firm, with one-third of micro-businesses having either zero or negative equity. Many of these firms also faced cash flow problems. However, most French micro-businesses used overdrafts to finance their cash flow, these were found to be relatively easily established and flexible, with benefits to both the banker and entrepreneur. Despite this, overdrafts were generally more expensive than conventional loans (OECD 2006).

12.4.5 Benefits of Debt Financing

Debt financing requires the entrepreneur to guarantee the debt and thereby risk the potential loss of not just the borrowed amount but also of their assets (e.g. home). It also has the cost of interest payments that must be made. Despite these shortcomings, debt financing has several benefits when compared to equity financing. Megginson et al. (2000) identify at least four main benefits:

- lower cost of capital;
- greater borrowing ability;
- no loss of equity or profits; and
- no loss of control.

- Lower Cost of Capital

The majority of debt financing is less expensive than the equivalent cost of raising equity – despite the interest payments. Further, the interest charges that must be paid on the money borrowed are a tax deduction to the business, thereby reducing the overall burden to the entrepreneur.

- Greater Borrowing Ability

In many cases the entrepreneur may be able to secure more of the total proportion of required capital from debt financing than through equity arrangements with venture funding sources. If the entrepreneur can secure the loans against other assets (e.g. property), then they can borrow substantial amounts of money. By comparison, many venture capitalists will be reluctant to take more than a proportion of the total equity in a business, and will usually seek to feed the capital to the business over time with a view to monitoring progress.

- No Loss of Equity or Profits

A further reason for the attraction of debt financing is the fact that the entrepreneur does not risk losing control of the business or any profits that are made. Debt capital is a fixed cost and does not erode the profits generated by the business. By comparison, equity partners may be seeking to share in profits. Debt funding sources also do not seek to take equity in the firm and are only concerned with recovering their principal and any interest charges.

- No Loss of Control

Just as debt financing does not erode the equity held by the entrepreneur, it also does not reduce the level of control the owner has in their business. Most venture capital investors will seek some influence in the management of the company, usually a seat or seats on the board and a veto over major decision-making such as capital expenditure or significant shifts in strategy. This level of influence is reasonable given the fact that venture financing involves the part ownership of the company and its associate risk sharing. However, many owner-managers resent such control and prefer to remain totally in control of their firms. While carrying some level of interference from mortgage holders and other major creditors, debt financing is less likely to see the entrepreneur losing control over the company unless they default on debt repayments.

12.4.6 Short-Term Debt Financing

Short-term debt financing consists of loans that must usually be paid within 1 year. The majority of this type of debt is self-liquidating, meaning that it repays itself over time. It is therefore used to finance such things as trade debtors or trading stock. Common types of short-term debt include: trade credit, overdrafts, accounts receivable, floor plans, bridging finance, commercial bills and import-export finance (English 1998).

- Trade Credit

Trade credit is where suppliers offer the firm the opportunity to secure goods or services without immediate payment. The longer the credit terms can be extended, the more attractive it is to the firm. This can be of particular assistance to retailers or manufacturers that need to acquire stock and who may experience long time delays before making sales. However, care must be taken to ensure that the business has the necessary cash flow to pay trade creditors when required. It is important for owner-managers to watch their level of *creditor strain* (e.g. the amount of trade credit owed by the business beyond reasonable terms). The amount of trade credit being used by small firms has increased significantly in recent years. For example, in Canada during 2000 nearly 40% of the outstanding debt owed by SMEs was in the form of trade credit (OECD 2006). It is also a major source of financing for Australian businesses with many SMEs using it to fund operations through customers paying a proportion of cost of the goods or services in advance to help the firm commence the work, and then making progress payments until the work is completed (Productivity Commission 2015).

- Bank Overdraft Facilities

Overdraft facilities are a common means of short-term debt where the firm secures a certain amount of credit from the bank within their company cheque account. The bank will normally set a limit on the overdraft in a similar way to a credit card limit, and may either secure the loan against assets in the business or not. The advantage of overdraft facilities is that they only become drawn when the money is required and interest is only paid on the money drawn not the entire loan. The cost of maintaining an overdraft facility can be high with establishment fees and administration charges. Approximately half of all SMEs in the European Union have some form of overdraft facility (OECD 2006).

- Factoring

Accounts receivable financing – also called *factoring* or *debtor financing* – is another form of short-term debt. In this method, the accounts receivables ledger is essentially purchased by a bank or specialist factoring company that advances a percentage (usually up to 80%) of the total outstanding invoices. With *factoring*, the lender secures the firm's debtors and provides a cash advance. Banks are a common source of this type of funding and usually insist on the firm having a system of debtor management before securing the loan. Factoring companies generally buy the debtor account at a discount and advance a proportion of the money up front, and the remainder – less fees and commissions – upon receipt of the money from the firm's debtors.

Factoring is not suitable for all firms and is usually appropriate for trade debtors rather than debts owed by the general public. There has been an increase in the use of factoring since the 1990s. For example, in 1998 the total amount of factoring funding provided across the European Union was €29.6 billion, while in 2004 this had grown to €61.3 billion. This compared to €70 billion in 1998 and €81.9 billion in 2004 within the US (OECD 2006). In Australia, total debtor financing in 2015 was estimated to be worth over AUD $60 billion (DIFA 2015). According to the OECD (2018), in 2016 the total volume of factoring deals for SMEs was up across two-thirds of the 34 countries surveyed within their global network. Along with leasing and hire purchase, factoring has become a common source of financing for SMEs.

- Floor Plan Loans

Typically used by retailers or wholesalers, this type of financing involves securing cash advances against high value stock (e.g. cars, boats, caravans) that can be placed on the showroom floor until sale. Once sold, the money is repaid to the lender plus any interest or commissions (English 1998).

- Bridging Finance

This type of loan is common within the property development industry. It involves borrowing money for a short time until the proceeds of another sale can be released or until alternative financing of a more permanent nature can be secured.

- Commercial Bills

Issued for periods ranging from 14 to 180 days, a commercial bill is a written promise to pay the business an amount of money on a particular date. The bills are sold on the short-term money market and cash is issued to the business after sale. Such bills are available from financial institutions and incur fees for their services (English 1998).

The Real Cost of Borrowing Money

Once, when my mother mentioned an amount and I realised I didn't understand, she had to explain to me: 'That's like three Mercedes.' Then I understood. — Brooke Shields.

The final cost of borrowing money often involves much more than just the interest rate. A variety of other monetary and non-monetary costs should be considered in determining the real cost of borrowing. For example, a loan that requires you to maintain certain financial ratios may be unrealistic for your particular business. Your checklist for reviewing the costs of a bank loan should include:

- Direct financial costs, such as interest rates, points, penalties, and required account balances;
- Indirect costs and loan conditions, such as periodic financial reporting, maintenance of certain financial covenants, and subordination agreements; and
- Personal guarantees needed to obtain the loan.

Source: CCH Business Owner's Toolkit, www.toolkit.cch.com.

12.4.7 Intermediate-Term Loans

Intermediate-term loans are so called because they offer financing over a period from 1 to 10 years' duration. These loans frequently have the requirement to be paid back in large instalments over a short time period and can incur higher rates of interest. Examples of this are personal loans, hire purchase agreements and leasing.

- Personal Loans

While most personal loans are used for individual household needs, it is common for small business owner-managers to acquire such loans for the financing of business activities. Personal loans frequently finance motor vehicles and office equipment.

- Hire Purchase and Leasing Agreements

Finance companies rather than banks are more likely to provide hire purchase deals, and such agreements can carry high costs. One negative aspect of hire purchase is that the ownership of the property or goods purchased under the agreement remains with the lender until the payments have been made. A lease agreement is beneficial to the small business as it does not tie up large sums of money for capital items. A lease – while technically not debt – is a contract that permits the owner-manager to use someone else's property (e.g. land or equipment) for a period of time and at a determined cost, and operates much like a debt contract. Leasing is attractive because the lease payments are tax deductible, and it often allows the firm to acquire assets that would be difficult to finance via other means (Megginson et al. 2000). Leasing and hire purchase agreements have grown steadily around the world as a source of financing for SMEs (OECD 2018).

12.4.8 Long-Term Loans

The long-term loan generally has a period of contract lasting in excess of 10 years. Because such loans are so long term, it is usual for the bank or other financial institution to require the business to demonstrate that it has a good track record of trading and is stable. Such loans also require collateral, usually in the form of a mortgage against property or other assets. Should the business go bankrupt, the lender or mortgage holder can step in and take control of the business and seek to recover its money from the sale of assets (Hodgetts and Kuratko 2001). Banks provide much of the mortgage lending, but finance companies and mortgage brokers are also common sources. Repayment of the mortgage requires principal plus interest, and interest rate terms can be both fixed and variable. It is possible to secure a second or even a third mortgage on the same property so long as there is sufficient equity available (English 1998).

- Peer-to-Peer Lending

A new emerging source of debt financing is peer-to-peer (P2P) lending. This is currently still in an early stage of development, but has been growing strongly in recent years with around USD $8.9 billion P2P loans issued in the United States in 2014 alone (Wei and Lin 2016). In Australia, P2P lending is still evolving and in 2015 was estimated to be worth less than AUD $25 million, although it is expected to grow strongly (Productivity Commission 2015).

P2P lending typically operates via an online platform that represents a market place for matching borrowers to lenders. At least two approaches can be taken to

Table 12.2 Comparison of auction versus price posting strategies in P2P Lending

	Auctions	Posted prices
Initial interest rate:	Chosen by the borrower	Pre=set by Prosper.com
Contract interest rate:	Prevailing interest rate at the end of the auction	Initial interest rate

Source: Wei and Lin (2016)

P2P lending. The first is that of an *auction* or *posted prices*, much the same as occurs within real estate markets. Most P2P online lending platforms adopt one of these two strategies (Wei and Lin 2016).

As shown in Table 12.2, there are different characteristics of the *auction* versus *posted prices* strategies in P2P lending. In the case of the *auction* model the borrower can have more control over the setting of the interest rate, but this will be finally determined as a result of the auction process and therefore it might be possible to secure a lower rate or have the rate negotiated up by the lenders. By contrast the *posted prices* approach uses an intermediary such as Prosper.com who set the rates, usually based on their assessment of the borrower's credit worthiness. Under this model the broker (i.e. Prosper.com) predetermines the rate for the loan and the borrower has to accept or reject the offer. Once agreed all potential lenders use this rate for their loans (Wei and Lin 2016).

The emergence of new forms of debt financing such as P2P lending is that it will require government regulations to ensure that it protects both the lenders and the borrowers. In Australia, this is something that the corporate regulator, the Australian Securities and Investments Commission (ASIC) is currently undertaking.

> **For example,** … ASIC has recently been working with peer-to-peer (P2P) lenders to develop appropriate regulation. Entrants in the nascent Australian P2P lending market submit that regulation is valuable in ensuring the industry begins with and maintains high standards. Existing regulation is not seen as an inappropriate barrier to entry, but rather a mechanism for ensuring new operators are competent. (Productivity Commission 2015, p. 182)

P2P lending can operate in either a wholesale or retail market. The *wholesale* model is targeted at professional and sophisticated investors and are currently not regulated in Australia. However, the operator does require a Financial Services License, and may also require an Australian Credit License. Their role is to act as a broker between the investors and the borrower. This is the most common form of P2P lending currently operating in Australia (Productivity Commission 2015).

The *retail* model of P2P lending is open to the general public and managed via the *posted prices* system described earlier. This type of P2P lending model requires much greater regulation and licensing of the operator. Within Australia this will also require the P2P lending scheme to be registered as a managed investment scheme with ASIC and the issuing of product disclosure statements for investors (Productivity Commission 2015).

12.5 Securing Debt Financing

As discussed above, debt financing can be sourced from a variety of providers. In Australia, this can include major banks, credit unions and building societies (including customer-owned banks), foreign subsidiary banks and bank branches, and other banks such as community banks (Productivity Commission 2015). However, the main source of debt financing for SMEs has traditionally been banks (Storey 1994). This is the case in Australia and also in the European Union (EU) where around 79% of debt financing for SMEs comes from banks (OECD 2009).

Entrepreneurs, particularly small business owner-managers, frequently view bankers as lacking sufficient understanding of their business, being inflexible and lacking creativity. Like many entrepreneurs, the owner-manager views him or herself as a *possibility thinker* while the banker sees him or herself as *bringing realism to the situation* (Petty and Upton 1997). A major cause of failure in bank loan applications by small firms is the existence of information asymmetries, where the information available to owner-manager and banker are not identical (Binks and Ennew 1996). As noted earlier, there is a tendency for banks to view start-ups and small firms as being risky.

To approve a loan the banker usually requires at least two sources of repayment. The first is a primary source of repayment such as cash flows from trading. The second is a guarantee against the possibility of business failure or collateral. Banks frequently adopt a *carcass mentality* when assessing business loan applications considering what the firm will be worth if liquidated. By comparison, the small business owner-manager adopts the most optimistic outlook (Petty and Upton 1997). Much has been made of the need for entrepreneurs and bankers to be better able to understand and appreciate each other's perspectives (Lister 1991; Larry 1990).

The importance of a good business plan to achieving bank financing has also been highlighted (Landsberg 1986; Bardell 1988), as has the need for cash flow projections to be prepared by professional accountants (Nichols 1991). However, service-based firms and those engaged in high technology industries lack the tangible assets available to manufacturers or other capital-intensive industries. Such firms are likely to find it more difficult meeting bank risk assessment criteria when seeking funding (Taylor 1989). Banks are beginning to consider cash flow and the valuation of intangibles in their assessments of business loan applications but difficulties remain. Most banks will seek assurance in the form of loan security such as personal property such as housing or land.

12.5.1 Business Banks

A range of sources can provide financing for entrepreneurial ventures. Business or commercial banks are the most commonly used and offer entrepreneurs a comprehensive range of services. One of the most frequently-used bank services is an

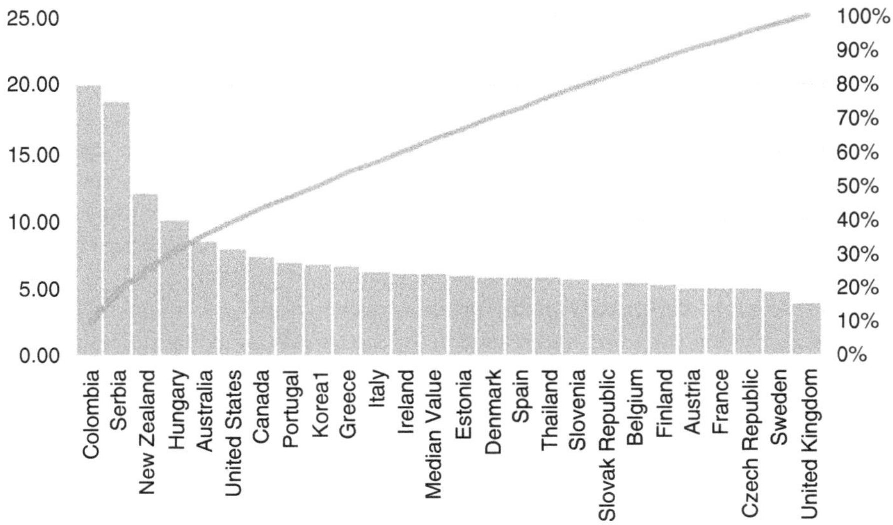

Fig. 12.2 Average bank interest rates for loans to SMEs 2007–2014 selected countries. (Source: OECD 2016a)

overdraft facility. This represents a flexible line of credit enabling the business to overdraw accounts to an agreed limit over a particular period of time. The bank will usually require some form of security and this is often real estate or some other form of tangible business asset. Banks also offer tailored business loans comprising specific sums of money over given time periods and secured against tangible assets. Such loans are frequently employed to finance the purchase of new plant, equipment or other fixed assets. Interest only repayments are sometimes negotiated by businesses to ease the impact of the loans on cash flow.

As shown in Fig. 12.2, over the period 2007–2014 interest rates charged by business banks for loans to SMEs have averaged at around 5.41% across many countries (OECD 2016a). The United Kingdom has maintained one of the lowest rates at 3.7%, while Columbia has had one of the highest levels at 20.7%. In Australia, this rate of interest on SME business loans has been running at an average of 7.5%. Bank lending to SMEs generally requires collateral and more than half of all loans issued by banks across most countries are secured against collateral assets such as property. However, the OECD (2016) notes that collateral requirements for SME loans amongst banks vary considerably country by country, with "no discernible pattern".

> **For example,** … Differences in businesses' access to credit across different economies are influenced by a range of factors such as macroeconomic conditions (that can affect the supply and demand of credit) and government policies around taxation and SME finance. The extent that countries embrace innovative lending models (such as P2P lending) can also have an impact. (Productivity Commission 2015, p. 189)

It should be noted that over the period from 2013 to 2016, interest rates for SMEs declined in all but two of the 36 countries that comprise the OECD. These were Ireland and Switzerland. In 2016 France had the lowest average interest rate charged to SMEs at 1.5%, and Chile had the highest, at 9.25% (OECD 2018).

12.5.2 Factoring, Leasing and Financing Companies

In addition to the business banks there are specialised factoring companies that offer accounts receivable financing or *factoring*. These firms acquire a business debt and take the responsibility to collect it. The money released by this transaction can be used to pay suppliers. Factoring companies usually provide finance for between 80% and 100% of approved debtors, less any charges. Large firms frequently use factoring to assist in their financing of large projects as they can increase their liquidity over the short term. The process can also free up staff who might otherwise be involved in the collection of account receivables. A business that has reliable customers who simply pay their bills slowly – e.g. printers who supply government agencies – can take advantage of factoring to speed up cash flow.

For ventures with higher risks than many conventional banks will accept, a finance company is an alternative. These firms can provide finance in the form of leases and hire purchase agreements for plant and equipment at higher than average interest rates. While such companies often require less collateral security than banks, they take a stronger interest in the ability of the client firm to repay the loan. Such loans are also likely to carry higher interest and charges than might be the case with banks. In 2015 it was estimated that total debt financing via *factoring* in Australia was over AUD $60 billion (DIFA 2015).

In addition to *factoring* other asset-based financing for SMEs and entrepreneurial firms can include leasing and hire-purchase financing. *Leasing* usually involves the business acquiring an asset (e.g. motor vehicle, plant and equipment) and renting it with finance from the leasing company. This usually takes place over a specific time period and may result in the business having the option or obligation to own the asset at the end of the contractual period. Although leasing is not strictly a debt financing structure it has some similarities. According to the OECD (2016a) *factoring* and *leasing* have become the most widely used forms of asset-based financing among SMEs. Over the period 2009–2014 *factoring* as a source of financing grew at a compound annual rate of 13% (OECD 2016a).

12.5.3 Insurance Companies and Merchant Banks

Insurance companies and merchant banks can also be sources of funding. Insurance companies have offered financing through the security of life insurance policies with a cash value for many years. More recently, such firms have obtained banking licenses. Merchant banks are another useful source of venture capital and can assist in a variety of other financial arrangements such as restructuring and amalgamations. As with venture capitalists, the merchant banker will be more concerned with the overall potential of the small business as a sound investment than with its collateral security. A down side for such banks is that they will seek to secure part-ownership of the business, thereby diluting the owner's equity and control.

12.5.4 Trade Creditors

Faced with difficulties in obtaining finance, many entrepreneurs seek to raise funding from other sources. This can include securing trade credit from suppliers or government agencies in the case of exporters. In Mexico, around 60% of the financing received by SMEs is sourced from suppliers as trade credit (OECD 2016a). It is also an important in Australia and has been estimated by the Reserve Bank as being worth around AUD $80 billion in 2013 (Fitzpatrick and Lien 2013). Throughout the OECD almost half of all countries provide trade credit to assist exporters (OECD 2016a).

Trade credit is important to SMEs with around 28% of all liabilities taking that form within Australian small businesses (ABS 1997). However, it is generally easier for larger firms to negotiate trade credit terms with suppliers than SMEs as they have greater bargaining power (Fitzpatrick and Lien 2013). What is not commonly appreciated is that, if the business is unable to secure funding from either debt or equity to provide its working capital requirements, the only source of financing available is usually trade creditors. When a business experiences rapid growth without sufficient working capital to fund its operations, and cannot obtain additional funding from other sources, it invariably increases its *creditor strain*, i.e. the time taken to pay the suppliers.

While the process of straining creditors is frequently viewed as a legitimate business practice among some entrepreneurs – that is, receive money quickly and pay creditors slowly – it is a risky strategy. Once a business gets a reputation for being slow to pay, it is likely that trade creditors will begin to raise the cost of doing business with them and key suppliers may suddenly refuse to provide goods or services at critical times, thereby placing increased strain on the venture.

However, late payment to trade creditors is a fairly common problem. For example, a survey of 211 small firms in the United Kingdom found that 89% reported paying their suppliers late, with 13.3% indicating that this was a common occurrence. Average creditor days were 46.3 and average debtor days were 52.6. Interestingly, large firms were the worst offenders in paying their smaller counterparts slowly (Peel et al. 2000).

It is worth noting that cash flow is frequently ranked as being among the top three problems facing small firms in the quarterly *Sensis Small Business Index* (Sensis 2017). Cash flow management is a critical area for successful financing of a small firm (Rowan 1994). Credit management techniques designed to speed up the collection of payments from customers and to reduce bad and doubtful debtors – e.g. checks on credit worthiness and tighter credit policies – are likely to ease cash flow problems for small firms (Peel et al. 2000).

12.6 What Are Banks Seeking?

Entrepreneurs and small business owner-managers frequently accuse the banks of being unwilling to lend to them or of placing unfair restrictions on how much funding they will supply. The level of hostility toward banks among the small business community is often high. However, banks remain a most important source of financing for the majority of small firms. It is therefore desirable that entrepreneurs and owner-managers understand what bankers are seeking and respond by preparing themselves and their firms appropriately.

Unlike venture capital, the banker is not seeking to achieve rapid return on investment and an early exit strategy. Most banks want clients and are usually seeking to establish and maintain a long-term relationship with the borrower. Bankers are generally highly risk adverse by nature, and are keen to see a steady and reliable repayment plan with security against possible business failure or default of loans. Banks are seeking evidence of a business having an established financial track record. When approaching a bank for financing, it is important to prepare a full financial history for presentation. According to some accountants, the borrower should prepare financial records displaying up to 3 years if available (Martin 1999).

The lending criteria used by different banks is subject to substantial variation. However, most banks will be seeking evidence of the same key things. This includes a track record of good cash flow to allow for repayments plus adequate shareholder funds or working capital that can cover any short-term cash requirements and ensure solvency. The bank will also be interested in the reputation and trading history of the business and the management team. This includes no evidence of having been at default on other loans. Finally, they will want to know how the money is to be used. While some banks may be less concerned with this than others, it is more likely that money will be lent for capital equipment or new product or market expansion than repayment of pre-existing business debts (Cattani and Mills 1998).

What Banks Look for

Most banks and other financial institutions to which the small firm is likely to turn for debt financing will seek the following:

- *Credit history.* What is the credit history of the borrower?
- *Cash flow.* How has the business been trading over recent years?
- *Collateral.* Are there tangible assets to secure the loan?
- *Character.* Who is borrowing the money and do they have a good track record in business?
- *Documentation.* Can the borrower provide business and personal financial records, income tax returns, and a business plan to support any claims?

Source: CCH Business Owner's Toolkit, www.toolkit.cch.com.

12.6.1 How to Deal with the Bank

A study undertaken in the United Kingdom in the 1990s into banks and small business owner-managers found that while most banks were seeking to enhance their relationship with their small business clients, dissatisfaction continues to exist on the part of the small businesses (Gammie 1995). This study highlighted several things that small business owner-managers should do to improve the relationship between themselves and their bank.

- Keep the Bank Fully Informed

The first recommendation was for the owner-manager to keep the bank fully informed of their overall financial position. This was particularly important with respect to cash flow and its management. It is often too late when the business has already started to experience cash flow problems to go to the bank seeking additional funding. Openness and honesty in dealing with a bank is important.

- Accept Advice and Build a Relationship

A second recommendation was for the small business owner-manager to be more willing to accept advice from the banker. While many small business owners feel that banks are unhelpful and can offer them little but money, the majority of business bankers are experienced professionals with the ability to make recommendations that can help a small business. Relationship banking has emerged in recent years as a major channel for most business banks.

The *Relationship Manager* is typically a personal business banker who is trained to work closely with their clients to assist them in business development. It is an expensive channel for most banks to operate and many banks require that client accounts be over a certain size before providing a relationship manager, however, alternative models can apply. Some banks use a structure involving banker support delivered via telephone and other indirect means for small accounts, and personal relationship managers for larger accounts.

- Negotiate Carefully

A third recommendation was for the owner-manager to negotiate carefully with the bank over charges, seeking clear explanations as to what the total cost of the bank services would be. Once again, the key was to maintain a close working relationship with the bank and engage in regular dialogue and openness. Banks want the business of small firms and operate in a highly competitive market environment. The owner-manager should see their business as important and not feel afraid to shop around for banking services if required.

It has been argued that shopping around is sometimes counterproductive because bankers may become annoyed if they are put to a lot of trouble for nothing (Cattani and Mills 1998), but this ignores the highly competitive nature of business banking. It is sometimes advisable for the business owner-manager to regularly tender out the banking contract, allowing various banks to bid for their business. While they may not change banks, this helps to keep them informed of the competitiveness of their own bank, and allows their banker to realise that their accounts should not be taken for granted.

12.6.2 What Information Should Be Presented to the Bank?

Each bank will have its own particular lending criteria and will generally outline the type of information that a small business owner seeking funding should prepare when making an application. It is best to talk to the bank well in advance, and ensure that all the necessary information is prepared prior to actually seeking the funds. Cattani and Mills (1998) outline a detailed list of the documents and information that is likely to be important for a banker to see when seeking to secure funding.

- Personal Profile of the Owner-Manager

The banker may be less interested in the owner than a venture capitalist, but they still want to know whom they are dealing with. A brief resume should be included in any presentation to the bank. This resume might be only 1–2 pages in length, but it should outline educational qualifications, professional training, past work experience (in particular management experience), and other relevant achievements. Personal references from employers may also be useful if the owner has a limited history of operating their own business.

- Information on the Company

A brochure or other information on the company and its products or services is useful in providing the bank with an understanding of how long the firm has been in business, the scale and scope of its activities, and the overall quality of its operations. This information might also include a list of customers and biographical details on any board members or directors. This can assist in giving the bank a sense of the reputation the company has within the market, and within the wider community. High profile customers and directors or board members can enhance the image for the firm.

- Evidence of a Good Credit Rating

If the company has previously had borrowings from other financial institutions and has established a good credit rating, it will be useful to include in the application letters of reference from other banks stating that payments on past loans have been regular and reliable. Where possible the names and address of the company's lawyers or accountants should be provided.

- Proof of Company Ownership or Registration

Where the business is a private company, there may be some requirement by certain banks for the owner-manager to prove that they own the company, and share certificates or registration documents will need to be shown. If company-owned assets are to be used as collateral, there may be a requirement to provide proof of ownership. This may involve an audited set of accounts or a statutory declaration listing assets and liabilities.

- Financial Statements

The most crucial information for most banks will be the company's accounts, and the three key documents will be the balance sheet, profit and loss account, and cash flow statement. At least 3 years of accounting information should be provided if such information is available. Where a substantial amount of funding is being sought, it may be prudent to have these audited by a charted accounting firm or certified accountant and approved by the company board of directors. Doing this in advance may avoid the trouble of having to respond to a request from the bank at short notice, or having to submit to the bank auditing the books themselves.

- Future Earnings Potential

The company budget for the forthcoming year and sales or cash flow forecasts should also be included in the documents provided to the bank. Letters of contract or order book data demonstrating agreements may support these forecasts. This may require the owner-manager to provide documentation that shows contracts with suppliers and customers. It may be necessary to defend cash flow and earnings forecasts, so the owner-manager should be ready to explain how they have derived these figures.

- Business Plan

The longer-term outlook for the business will interest the banker as much as the venture capitalist. The owner-manager seeking debt financing should provide an up-to-date business plan that clearly outlines where and how the new capital expenditure will be applied, and the anticipated revenue and expenditure over a period of up to 3–5 years. Such formal business planning should be viewed as being of benefit to the company – regardless of whether the bank lends or not. If the plan is a genuine attempt by the owner-manager to map out a future for their business, rather than a cynical exercise in raising capital, it is likely to stand out and reassure the bank that the debt will be repaid.

- Feasibility Assessments

If the funding being sought from the bank is to be used for a major business expansion, it is likely to be useful for the owner-manager to demonstrate the feasibility of the project or programs being financed. For example, the purchase of capital equipment should be evaluated to demonstrate that returns on investment will be achieved and that growth plans can be fulfilled. Market research studies or information would also be appropriate here if they assist in demonstrating the merits of an expansion program.

- Security or Collateral

Finally, the owner-manager is likely to need evidence of security or collateral against which a loan can be secured. While not all debt financing is secured by a mortgage, the majority of long-term debt will require security of some kind. This usually involves property or such fixed assets as plant and equipment. If a personal home is to be used to secure a mortgage, the documentation should include proof of ownership and recent valuation certificates if possible. It should be remembered that banks and other financial institutions are unlikely to lend against the full value of any collateral, and assets worth substantially more than the loan may need to be pledged. This is often viewed as unfair by small business owner-managers, but this is often beyond the control of the individual banker.

It should also be noted that, while the size of a firm's balance sheet and shareholder equity may be attractive, these items alone might be insufficient to secure significant funding from a bank. The banker will be interested in how the money will be applied and how repayments will be achieved. Care should be taken to ensure that the size of the borrowing is appropriate for what is required. Over borrowing only raises the level of debt held by the business and places excess interest burdens on the company. Negotiate the deal over interest charges and fees. It is frequently within the banker's power to reduce interest charges and fees to secure a competitive loan. The world of small business banking can sometimes be a buyers' market if the owner-manager operates a quality company.

12.7 Equity Financing

Despite the best cash flow management, and even with support from a banker, most entrepreneurs usually reach the limits of bootstrap or debt financing over time. To fully expand the business, they require large sums of money that must come in the form of equity capital. Equity financing – or venture capital (VC) – is often difficult for small firms to acquire as it tends to involve higher risk, than debt financing, and because the owner is forced to dilute their equity and to share control with other investors. According to the OECD (2018) entrepreneurs seeking exits from their business ventures are more likely to do so via mergers and acquisitions (e.g. trade sales), than by public listing on the stock market through an initial public offer (IPO). This is due in part to the difficulties that an IPO poses for the majority of small firms. In fact, the total number of IPOs across both the United States and Europe has been steadily declining (OECD 2018).

Venture capital investments in the United States in 2015 were estimated to be worth around USD $59.7 billion, which comprised 85% of all VC investments across the entire OECD group of companies. By contrast, the total VC investment in the European Union was USD 4.2 billion for the same year (OECD 2016b). In Australia, the amount of VC investment during 2015 was only around AUD $8.8 million (ABS 2016). While the United States and Israel have VC industries that comprise respectively 38% and 33% of their national GDP, this is a rare situation.

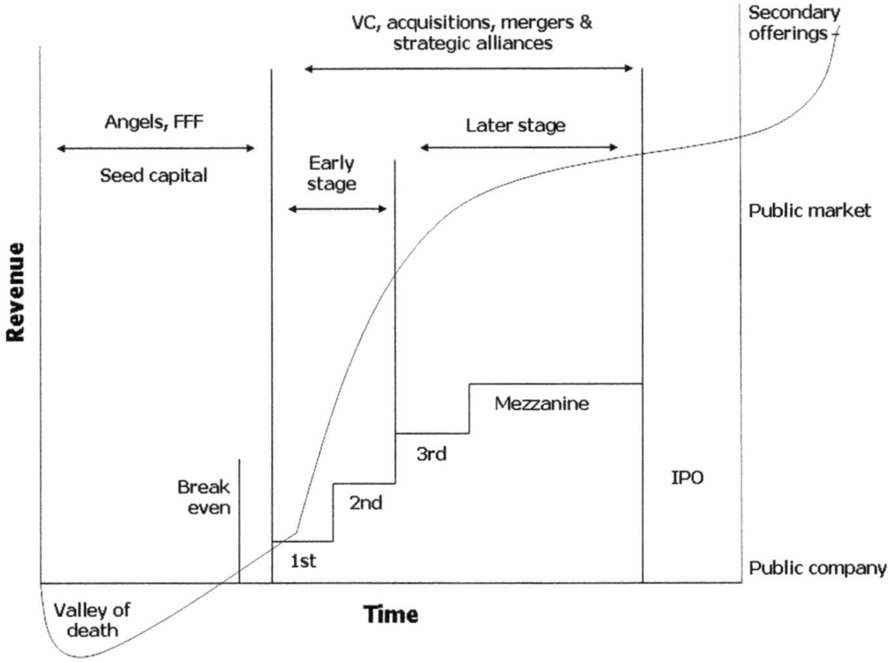

Fig. 12.3 The financing lifecycle. (Source: Cardullo 1999)

For most countries, VC financing comprises less than 0.05% of GDP (OECD 2016b). As such, VC is a highly-specialised form of business financing with its own dynamics.

Figure 12.3 illustrates the financing lifecycle through which small firms typically pass if they follow a VC-funded growth path. As shown, there are several distinct stages that the firm must pass, commencing with early stage seed capital funding, then moving on to early stage and later stage VC funding until it is either sold to a larger organisation via a trade sale or listed on the stock exchange via an initial public offering (IPO).

12.7.1 Seed Capital Funding-Family, Friends and Fools

Initial funding for small firms typically starts with the personal savings of the owner-manager and perhaps the provision of loans or other borrowings from family and friends. These informal sources of equity financing have been found to be among the most important to small firms, particularly highly innovative SMEs. The fast growing, high technology or high innovative firm is inherently risky and may not find it easy to attract debt financing from banks. Small firms are also often too small to secure investment from formal venture capital funds (OECD 2004).

The most common type of initial equity capital accessed by small firms is private equity. This is typically supplied by the *Three Fs* – namely family, friends and fools (FFF) – who provide informal funding to the business and usually don't seek substantial returns or demand high levels of due diligence. This type of funding may only be a few thousand dollars. The reference to *fools* is not meant as a derogatory term, but it reflects the fact that such investors don't normally undertake much due diligence prior to making their investments.

12.7.2 Business Angels

Once the business needs larger amounts of investment, the owner may need to turn to more substantial sources of equity funding which is frequently supplied by business angels. These are typically wealthy individuals willing to invest their money into business ventures in the expectation that a better-than-average return can be obtained. The term 'business angel' was reported to have originated from the United States theatre when Broadway musicals – frequently high risk and cash starved – were saved from disaster by wealthy private investors who appeared like angels from heaven to provide much needed funding to allow new shows to go on (Oats 1992).

In recent times the business angel is a wealthy private investor who puts up early stage financing to assist entrepreneurs to develop ventures that might otherwise fail to attract formal venture capital. They are considered one of the most important sources of risk capital available to early stage technology companies (Dwight 1999).

Such people can be difficult to find and usually don't advertise their interest in offering money for venture capital. Most business angels operate via a network of accountants or lawyers who refer them to entrepreneurs. Social contacts can therefore become highly important in this process. Most business angels don't wish to run the business, but can demand a lot of the entrepreneur's time in keeping them informed and happy.

> **Business angels may be defined as,** … high net-worth, non-institutional, private equity investors; that is, individuals who have the desire and sufficiently high net-worth to enable them to invest part of their net worth into high risk – high return entrepreneurial ventures in return for a share of voting control, income and ultimately capital gain. (Hindle and Wenban 1999)

Business angels have been identified as the largest single source of risk capital for entrepreneurial companies (Wetzel and Freear 1994). In the US, angels have been estimated to finance 30–40 times as many early stage companies as formal venture capital funds (Van Osnabrugge 1998; Gaston 1989). Within Australia, business angels were estimated in the 1990s to contribute about \$9.3 billion in investment capital (Coopers and Lybrand 1997).

The typical business angel is a middle-aged male of high net worth with annual income of around \$180,000 and personal wealth of around \$2 million. They are likely to have 10–14% of their investments within small entrepreneurial ventures, and usually invest an average of $200,000 in each deal (Hindle and Wenban 1999). Business angels are often engaged in investments that are close to home, or located in their local region or city and in industries that are familiar to them (Wiltbank and Sarasvathy 2002). In the US, it is sometimes said that business angels operate within a radius of 50 miles (80 km) of their homes. They will also frequently ask for a seat on the board so as to closely oversee the work done by the team (OECD 2006).

Angel investors have been identified as playing three broad roles within the ventures in which they invest. The first is a strategic one, providing guidance to the entrepreneurs seeking to develop the venture. The second role is an operational one, frequently networking the venture to a wider market or management talent pool, and assisting the entrepreneurs in finding additional resources. Finally, the angel can play a personal role guiding the entrepreneur as a mentor or friend (Sapienza and De Clercq 2000).

However, while business angels are an important source of financing for entrepreneurial investments, it is difficult to get reliable information on their activity due to differences in definitions and data collection methods. While business angels are commonly described as wealthy private individuals who invest part of their personal assets in a start-up and also share their personal management experience with the entrepreneur, definitions from different sources vary (OECD 2009).

The business angels' market is much larger in some countries than others. For example, in 2014 it was estimated that there were around 316,600 active business angels who each invested an average of USD $328,500. Over the period from 2012 to 2014 a total of USD $24.1 billion of business angel investments were made in the United States (OECD 2016b). By comparison total business angel investment from the EU, UK, Canada and Turkey in the same time period was a total of only USD $408.9 million (OECD 2016b). The USA has been noted as a larger and more vibrant business angel market than EU or most other countries for some time (OECD 2009).

A study of 15 business angels located in Western Australia found that the typical profile of an 'angel' in Perth was 50–59 years of age with an above average level of education – usually a postgraduate degree. These people had invested in an average of 12 deals, contributing between $50,000 and $100,000 to each venture. Key motivations for such investments were to make money, but also to contribute to the development of a worthwhile venture and assist the local economy. The idea that a venture might be 'fun' was also a consideration. However, levels of direct involvement in the management of the ventures in which such investments were made were generally quite low, although these angels did serve as a 'sounding board' for the entrepreneurs in whose businesses they had taken equity (Callahan and Mazzarol 2003).

This is a similar profile to that found in other countries where the typical business angel is a middle-aged male, with above average education and past experience in business or management. Such individuals also have high net-worth from a financial perspective. However, there is now evidence of a gradual change in the profile of business angels. For example, in the United Kingdom the proportion of women who are business angels has increased significantly over the past decade, although it still remains are only 14%, and the median age is slowly falling from the mid-50s to the mid-40s. This is a similar pattern as found in the United States where around 26% of business angels are women (OEDC 2016a).

12.7.3 Crowdfunding

As with P2P lending in the debt financing area, a new developing in equity financing is *crowdfunding* or crowd-sourced financing. This occurs when a business or entrepreneur raises capital from a large number of investors to either launch a new venture, or commercialise a product. It is usually undertaken via online platforms and has been popularised through the activities of crowdfunding online entities such as Kickstarter, Quirky or Indiegogo. The volume of online fundraising and *crowdfunding* activity around the world has doubled over the period from 2013 to 2016, with China, the United States and the United Kingdom demonstrating some of the highest levels of activity (OECD 2018).

According to the Australian Productivity Commission (2015), *crowdfunding* typically takes four major forms:

1. *Donation crowdfunding:* where the money is donated to a project without any anticipation by donors of getting a return.
2. *Reward crowdfunding:* where the providers of the funding receive a benefit, usually in the form of a product or service generated with the money. This can occur with music or artistic projects where the musicians give those who provide funding special editions of their new album, or seats at their performances.
3. *Debt crowdfunding:* this is a similar model to P2P lending but takes place on a large scale, such as retail P2P lending.
4. *Equity crowdfunding:* in this case the investors acquire shares in the business and receive dividends and capital gains.

Crowdfunding is becoming a mechanism for business angels to find investment opportunities. For example, in the UK a survey of business angels found that around 45% had invested through crowdfunding platforms. However, these investors were typically younger and less experienced business angels (Wright et al. 2015). In Canada and the United States *equity crowdfunding* requires investors to be high net-worth *accredited investors*, who are similar to business angels (OECD 2016a, b).

12.8 The Nature of Venture Capital

While there is no clear definition of the term venture capital, there appears to be at least four common elements associated with most venture capital deals (Barnett and Mazzarol 2002a, b):

- The investment in the venture is facilitated by equity or equity related instruments.
- The investment in the venture involves higher than average risk.
- The investor adds non-financial value to the venture by the provision of management skills or advice.
- The purpose of the investment is to secure above average returns through capital appreciation.

Venture capital providers come in a variety of forms but their role is to invest in new and rapidly growing smaller companies by taking an equity stake in the venture. In return for their investment, it is common for venture capital providers to also seek some control or influence over the management of the business. This is one of the major issues for entrepreneurs, who often fear losing control over their business as venture capital providers seek to control the direction of the company. It is important to note that venture capital investment is largely private, and can be both formal and informal in nature. The following quotation from Kenney (2001) provides a good definition of the nature of the venture capitalist and their motivations:

> **The venture capitalist** … the venture capitalist aims to invest in newly established firms capable of growing quickly and thereby creating capital gains of at least ten times their investment in less than five years. The difference between venture capitalists and bankers and other investors is that the venture capitalist actively monitors the venture and assists in its growth. (Kenney 2001)

As illustrated in Fig. 12.4, the decision-making process undertaken by formal venture capital providers is rigorous and can involve a high level of rejection at any stage during the evaluation process. In fact, the screening process employed by venture capital firms typically involves reviewing 80 opportunities, selecting only 20 to hold initial meetings with the management teams, then weeding this list down

Fig. 12.4 The venture capital screen. (Source: Teten and Farmer 2010)

to short list of about 4 deals, subjecting three of these to due diligence reviews before finally selecting one deal (Teten and Farmer 2010).

One perspective describes venture capital financing as a dynamic process that adapts and shifts in response to the surrounding environment and changing nature of industry (Meglio et al. 2017). Another view sees it more as a process involving the investment of financial resources into the business venture at various stages of its development cycle, and in which the investor accepts high relative risk in expectation of significant capital gain (Golis 2002). Venture capital is frequently viewed as relating to a particular class of financial asset associated with unlisted or non-public share capital (Smith 2000).

The non-public nature of venture capital financing highlights the importance within the venture capital process of the investor. This individual – the venture capitalist – plays a critical and largely non-financial role in assisting newly emerging companies to grow and develop (BVCA 2001). This non-financial function is a process of screening and monitoring fledgling firms, as well as providing financing (Anand and Galetovic 2000). Whereas the typical investor in a publicly listed company is seeking an income yield that complements capital gain, the VC investor is motivated almost exclusively by capital gain (Wright and Robbie 1997).

Venture capital is therefore a process involving relatively high risk, due to the fact that the business venture into which the capital is being invested is usually unproven or underdeveloped either in terms of its commercialisation or market growth. Further, there is usually no immediate mechanism for the disposal of the investment, as is typical within the public share market. A key element of the venture capital process is the VC investor who adds value to the venture, and partly mitigates his or her investment risk by playing an active role in the management of the venture to some degree and in some direct capacity (Leonard and Swap 2000). Their main investment objective is to achieve returns on the investment by capital appreciation. It should be noted that while VC investors are commonly perceived to be professionals managing venture capital funds, the term can also be used to describe any person or corporate entity that makes an investment involving risk and early stage business ventures.

12.8.1 Formal Venture Capital Financing

By contrast with business angels, the venture capitalist is usually a professional funds manager who is willing to invest in a business if the returns are high enough. Returns of about 25% are usually expected, although some may demand ROI of as much as 50 or 60%. As professionals, these venture capitalists will demand good management from the entrepreneur and will usually put a higher priority on this than the product or market potential (Mason and Stark 2004).

The amount of venture capital available within an economy varies considerably from country to country. Table 12.3 lists the venture capital investments made across a number of selected countries in 2015. It can be seen that the United States remains the world's largest and most vibrant VC market, with nearly USD $60 billion

Table 12.3 Venture capital investments 2015 – selected countries

Country	US $	Country	US $	Country	US $
Greece	0	Norway	$62.20 m	Switzerland	$289.29 m
Slovenia	$1.50 m	Portugal	$65.08 m	South Africa	$352.72 m
Czech Republic	$1.85 m	Belgium	$68.30 m	France	$757.86 m
Estonia	$4.12 m	Ireland	$84.03 m	Germany	$958.47 m
Luxembourg	$5.94 m	Denmark	$86.34 m	United Kingdom	$951.93 m
Slovak Republic	$9.91 m	Finland	$118.19 m	Korea	$1,087.46 m
Poland	$21.72 m	Austria	$122.87 m	Japan	$1,105.29 m
Hungary	$27.67 m	Spain	$173.55 m	Israel	$1,165.00 m
New Zealand	$43.59 m	Netherlands	$180.50 m	Canada	$1,825.63 m
Italy	$51.33 m	Sweden	$180.84 m	Total Europe	$4,220.13 m
Russian Fed.	$59.00 m	Australia	$288.49 m	United States	$59,698.50 m

Source: OECD (2016b)

invested. This is more than 14 times the size of all the venture capital invested within Europe during the same period. As noted above, only relatively few companies receive venture capital financing and it is rarely issued to start-up ventures, although Austria and Sweden are exceptions (OECD 2016b).

Finally, the largest source of equity capital is the public equity market. This requires the entrepreneur to prepare their company for public listing on the stock exchange. They will therefore become exposed to high levels of government regulation and scrutiny. Many entrepreneurs fear potential loss of ownership or control through such a process. However, this is usually the only way a company can get access to substantial capital funds.

12.9 The Venture Capital Process

As a process, venture capital financing can be viewed as moving through several distinct stages that broadly equate to the developmental cycle of the business venture (see Fig. 12.2). Each stage usually requires increasing levels of investment and involves differing levels of risk and return. Although there remains some debate within academic circles as to the number of stages within the venture capital process, five distinct stages can be identified, namely (Golis 2002; Humphrey 2000; Barnett and Mazzarol 2002):

1. *Seed capital* – typically $50,000–$500,000 applied to R&D, prototype development and incorporation costs.
2. *Start-up capital* – typically between $500,000 and $2 m, applied to commencement of initial commercial operations.
3. *Early expansion capital* – typically between $2 m and $10 m, applied to marketing and market development, plus the building of a management team.

4. *Development capital* – typically between \$2 m and \$10 m, used for market expansion and adjustments to the product design or process re-engineering.
5. *Mezzanine capital* – typically between \$10 m and \$50 m, used for IPO and related expenses, acquisitions or major capital funding.

As illustrated in Fig. 12.5, the process that occurs within the VC firm when dealing with an investment deal takes at least eight stages. If the proposal survives the initial screening it will be moved into a more rigorous multi-stage process of screening with the possibility of rejection at each stage. This process involves increasing time and costs to the two parties seeking to negotiate the deal, and requires a willingness to share information and build trust and common purpose. The deal can be rejected at any stage and requires patience and a willingness to seek mutually beneficial "win-win" outcomes by both the investor and the investee.

12.9.1 The Nature of Venture Capitalists

The typical venture capitalist is a member of a small, independent partnership with a professional staff of between six and 12 people, including a few general partners and a small number of associates who are venture capitalists in training. Venture capital firms are small. Studies undertaken in the US in the late 1990s found that a typical venture capital partnership managed between US\$50 and US\$99 million in assets. Nearly three-quarters of all venture capital firms managed between US\$25 million and US\$250 m in assets (Onorato 1997). In comparison, in 1996 the average

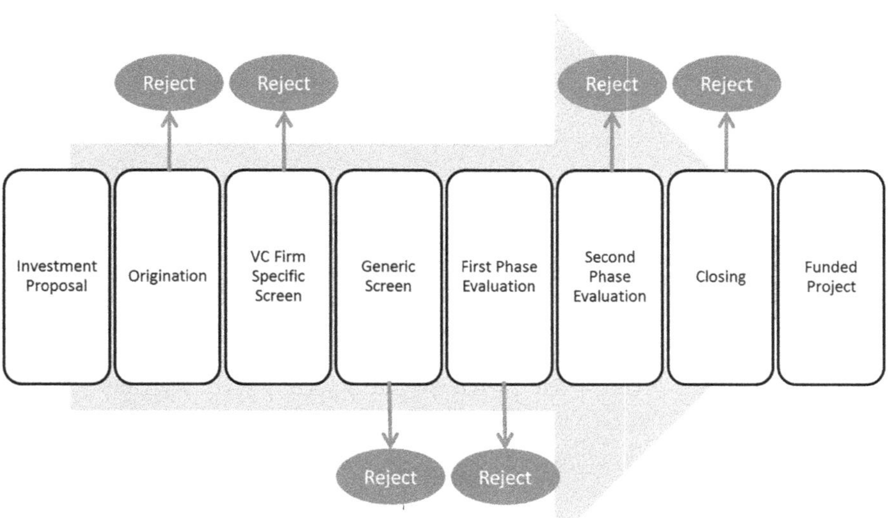

Fig. 12.5 The venture capital process. (Source: Fried and Hisrich 1994)

US commercial bank had a portfolio of more than US$481 m, and the 100th largest bank had more than US$7 billion in assets (Berlin 1998).

The venture capitalist doesn't make his or her investment all at once. Instead, funds are always provided in stages, and the entrepreneur receives only enough funding to reach the next stage. Each stage has well defined performance objectives, and more funds are provided if performance objectives are met. If performance objectives are not met, the venture capitalist must make a decision. Should the portfolio firm's strategy be reconsidered? Should the firm's management team be changed? And, in the worst case, should funding be cut off completely? Even if the venture capitalist decides to provide more funds, the entrepreneur will pay a price. The venture capitalist inevitably demands a larger share of the firm's stock in return for additional funding to meet some objective (Berlin 1998).

12.9.2 The Nature of Venture Capital Investors in Australia

In 2015 there were around 121 active venture capital and late stage private equity (VC&LSPE) managers operating in Australia, managing 210 VC&LSPE investment funds (ABS 2016). The VC&LSPE managers in Australia are professional investors who are either individuals with high net-worth, or institutional investors such as superannuation (pension) funds (Jones 2008).

Figure 12.6 illustrates the general operation of the Australian venture capital sector. The VC&LSPE managers control the venture capital investment through two types of investment vehicles: direct and indirect. The first of these invests directly into investee companies, while the second pools funds and then places the money

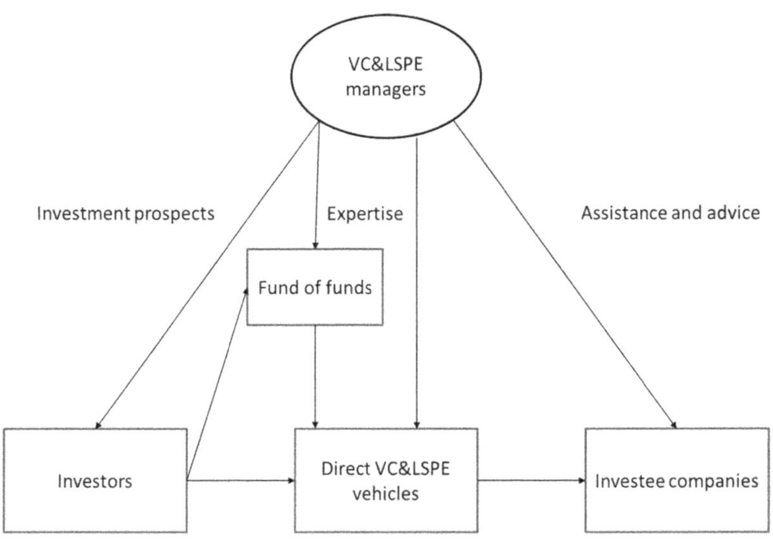

Fig. 12.6 The venture capital and late stage private equity (VC&LSPE) sector in Australia. (Source: ABS 2016)

into the direct vehicles. Investors place their money into either of these two vehicles and rely on the VC&LSPE managers for their expertise in managing the investment and getting an attractive return on the funds committed. The investee companies that receive this venture capital rely on the VC&LSPE mangers for assistance and advice to help them secure the funding they need, and assist with strategic decision making required to enable the business to grow. It is worth noting that the majority of VC funding (68%) in Australia is sourced locally with 42% sourced from superannuation (pension) funds (ABS 2016).

Pitching for Venture Capital

According to recent analysis of the climate for hunting venture capital financing in North America, the following things should be considered when pitching for venture capital.

Leave the shot gun at home:

Don't waste time using a scatter gun to target every VC in town. Target your approach carefully and approach those funding providers who are most likely to support your kind of deal. In doing so:

- Ensure that you know as much about this VC as you can *before* you make your pitch;
- Tailor the pitch to suit their track record of doing similar or previous deals; and
- Seek to sell your deal to them as a compliment to their existing investment portfolio.

Don't sell your technology:

The focus should be on the financial deal and the benefits to the VC, and *not* on the product or how smart it is. Focus the pitch on the 5 Ps:

1. *People.* Who is behind the company and who will run the venture?
2. *Product.* What is the product and why is it so good for the market?
3. *Problem.* What is the problem that this product or technology solves?
4. *Placement.* Where will the product be initially placed (target market) and is there a lead customer(s)?
5. *Plan.* How will all this work, how will you go to market, and how will you manage growth?

(continued)

Timing is everything:

Make sure that your venture is ready to go to market and that you have the product, the team and the customers ready – or nearly ready – before making the pitch. Long lead times for R&D may not be attractive, and time-sensitive technology needs to be ready to go to ensure that its window of opportunity is not closing or closed.
Source: Watson (2003).

12.9.3 What Do Venture Capital Investors Look for?

A study of venture capital investors found that the top five things that they looked for when deciding whether or not to invest in a deal were (McMillan et al. 1985):

- The Entrepreneur's Personality

Of importance was the entrepreneur's personality, in particular whether or not they seemed to be capable of sustained, intense effort and had an ability to evaluate and react to risk. Also important was their ability to explain their venture or business model clearly and understand its detail. Finally, they needed to have a personality that was viewed as compatible with the venture capital investor to allow for a good working relationship.

- The Entrepreneur's Experience

Of importance was the entrepreneur's experience, and specifically whether they were thoroughly familiar with the target market and had demonstrated leadership ability as well as a relevant track record. Also, of importance was whether the entrepreneur was either referred by a trustworthy source or had a reputation for past success.

- Characteristics of the Product or Service

The third factor was the product or service being developed. This included whether the product was proprietary or able to be formally protected via patent, and if it had been sold into the market. It if had not been fully commercialised, it was important to determine if there was a working prototype and if the technology was 'high-tech' in nature. The ability to protect the IP rights associated with the product or secure the proprietary rights of the product was of the most importance in this area.

- Characteristics of the Market

The fourth consideration was whether there was evidence that the target market was likely to enjoy significant rates of growth, or if the new venture would stimulate an existing market. Also, of importance was if the industry was familiar to the venture capital investor and the anticipated reaction from competitors.

- Financial Considerations

The fifth area of consideration was the financials associated with the venture, in particular the ability of the investment to return at least ten times the capital contributed within 5–10 years. The ability to have the investment taken public – or some exit strategy – was also of importance.

12.9.4 Deal Structures

In order to do a deal over securing finance, the entrepreneur needs to understand three key things: (i) they must understand their business; (ii) they must understand the viewpoint of the venture financier; and (iii) they must understand what their own needs are in relation to the money being sought.

- Understand the Business

This is usually transmitted via a business plan. Such a plan should demonstrate to the reader that the entrepreneur understands:

- the amount of funds required (both the absolute amount and the timing of the requirement),
- the level of risk associated with the venture (both the absolute level of risk and the factors that determine risk), and
- the timing and potential magnitude of returns.

- Understand the Viewpoint of Financiers

Different sources of funds have different needs and expectations. Banks will view things differently from venture capitalists. Entrepreneurs should consider:

- the size of the returns expected,
- how much risk will be tolerated?
- the size of funds that can be supplied,
- when 'returns' will be expected, and
- the degree of control that will be expected.

- Understand the Entrepreneur's Own Needs

The entrepreneur should also assess their own needs from any financing deal. How much control do they want or will they agree to give up? How will their control be exercised and how much finance do they need? What risk will they tolerate?

12.9.5 Preparing a Terms Sheet and Structuring the Deal

An essential element in the structuring of a venture capital deal is the preparation of a 'terms sheet', which is a document that outlines the details of how the deal will be structured. While a terms sheet is not generally a legally binding document, it does provide the basis for future legal agreements and is often the first step in setting up the deal. The contents of a terms sheet can vary from deal to deal as a result of differing legal environments. However, according to the National Venture Capital Association (NVCA 2004) in the US, a typical (Series A) terms sheet might contain:[1]

1. *Offering terms.* These detail the closing date for the deal to expire, who the investors will be, the amount of money to be raised, the price per share, the pre-money valuation of the share capital, and the capital structure of the venture before and after financing.
2. *Charter of shareholder rights.* This outlines any dividends policy the venture will adopt and liquidation preferences in the case of dissolution, including what might happen in a merger. Also, included in the charter would be the voting rights of shareholders, the provisions to protect their shareholdings in the case of liquidation, and details of things such as anti-dilution provisions, conversion options and redemption rights (allowing the investors to force the company to redeem their shares at cost plus and dividends).
3. *Stock purchase agreement.* This specifies any representations and warranties made by the company to the investors, conditions of closing the deal, who the legal counsel is handling the deal, and any costs associated with settlement.
4. *Investor rights agreement.* This outlines the rights of the initial investors in terms of their shareholding should the company list on the stock market via an IPO. It also outlines the rights of shareholders to have seats on the company board and their right to access company information. It might also contain details of employee stock options, key person insurance and the frequency of board meetings.
5. *Right of first refusal/co-sale agreement and voting agreement.* This describes the right of initial investors to have the right of first refusal with respect to any shares of capital stock that might be sold by the founders of the company. It also details the composition of the board of directors, and might specify the chairperson, CEO and any representatives of the founders or other investors.
6. *Drag along provisions.* Where 75% or more of the shareholders agree to sell the company at a given price, the remaining shareholders will agree to also selling under the same conditions.
7. *Other matters.* The terms sheet might also outline the rights of the founders to have their stock bought back by the company should they choose to exit as well as how preference shares will be handled.
8. *Confidentiality and expiration.* There should also be a statement agreeing that all parties will work in good faith during the execution of the deal and not seek to gain benefit by selling company stock at an advantage. The need to maintain confidentiality will also be noted along with a date when the terms sheet expires.

[1] See www.bvca.co.uk for a 'guide to venture capital term sheets,'

12.9.6 Exit Strategy

It is important to remember that, while the venture capital investor is taking equity in the business, they will generally want to have a clear exit strategy. This should be determined in advance of any investment deal and might include a range of options including a merger or trade sale to another company, or seeking to publicly list the business on the stock market. According to the Australian Venture Capital Association Ltd. (AVCAL), during the period 1997–2000, of 335 venture capital exits: 31% were write-offs, 31% were trade sales, and only 3% were public floats (Golis 2002, p.235). In 2008–2009 the value of exits from trade sales, IPOs and buybacks was $682 million (ABS 2010). This indicates not only the risks associated with venture capital, but also the preference many VCs have for trade sales. Public listings are generally complex, involve high costs and require careful timing.

An alternative to an IPO is the 'back door listing', where an existing listed firm is identified that has lost most of its value and can be acquired as a shell company without going through the rigors of a new listing. The shell company is essentially taken over by the newly emerging venture through a recapitalisation of its stock and with the consent of the existing shareholders of the shell. Within Australia, the typical shell company for a backdoor listing will have a market capitalisation of approximately $300,000, and following the deal the new venture would be worth over $5 million (Golis 2002).

12.9.7 Due Diligence

Prior to the venture capital investor settling, they will want to subject the deal to a process of due diligence. This typically involves checks by accountants and lawyers working for the VC who will examine the financial status of the venture, the validity of any patents or other IP, and even the backgrounds of the management team and employees of the business. Due diligence might also involve interviews with leading customers and key suppliers (McKaskill 2006).

The range of things that might be examined in a due diligence process includes (Camp 2002):

- *Annual company reports* and shareholder meetings minutes;
- *An audit of computers*, software and websites including computer security and back-up policy;
- what are the core competencies of the business and how vulnerable they are through loss of key personnel;
- *Engineering, R&D and IP policies* including patents and their currency;
- *plant and equipment,* fixtures & fittings, and property – and in particular, condition, security and title ownership;
- *Financials & accounting* – including bookkeeping, creditor/debtor policy, bad debts and contingent liabilities, previous audits, banking and cash flow management, working capital requirements and use of factoring, and mortgages and unsecured loans;

- *Human resources* – including absenteeism, staff turnover figures, skills, training and development, outstanding workers compensation and superannuation claims;
- *legal issues* relating to insurance policies and outstanding claims as well as legal contracts with third parties;
- *Management structure* – who are in the management team, their roles, responsibilities and their performance measures, and whether there a succession plan for any loss of key personnel;
- production and operations – specifically the quality of products, any dependence on key suppliers, and the efficiency of systems; and
- *Sales & marketing* – including the existence of registered brand names or trademarks, direct marketing and ecommerce strategies, leading customers and the risks associated with the loss of any key customers.

References

ABS. (1997). *Portrait of Australian business, 1995 business longitudinal survey*. Canberra: Australian Bureau of Statistics, AGPS.

ABS. (1998). *Small business in Australia 1997* (Cat. No. 1321.0). Canberra: Australian Bureau of Statistics, Commonwealth of Australia.

ABS. (2002). *Small business in Australia 2001* (Cat. 1321.0, Commonwealth of Australia). Canberra: Australian Bureau of Statistics.

ABS. (2010). *Venture capital and later stage private equity, Australia*. Canberra: Australian Bureau of Statistics AGPS.

ABS. (2016). *Venture capital and later stage private equity, 2014–2015* (Cat. No. 5678.0. AGPS). Canberra: Australian Bureau of Statistics.

Anand, B. N., & Galetovic, A. (2000). Information, non-excludability and financial market structure. *Journal of Business, 73*(3), 357–402.

Bardell, R. (1988). Banking on the business plan. *Accountancy, 102*(1134), 65.

Barnett, R. J., & Mazzarol, T.W. (2002a, December 5–8). *The social process of venture capital: The case of Western Australia. Developing Regional Communities*, ANZAM 2002 conference, Beechworth.

Barnett, R., & Mazzarol, T. W. (2002b). *Creating an effective venture capital environment in Western Australia*. Perth: Graduate School of Management, University of Western Australia.

Berlin, M. (1998). That thing venture capitalists do. *Business Review – Federal Reserve Bank of Philadelphia*, January–February, 15–26.

Binks, M., & Ennew, C. (1996). Growing firms and the credit constraint. *Small Business Economics, 8*(1), 17–25.

BVCA. (2001). *Terms sheets*. British Venture Capital Association. https://www.bvca.co.uk

BVCA. (2004). *A Guide to Venture Capital Term Sheets*. British Venture Capital Association (BVCA), www.bvca.co.uk. London.

Callahan, M., & Mazzarol, T. (2003). *Business angels in WA – Are they like angels everywhere?* ANZAM 2003 Conference. 2–5 December, Fremantle.

Camp, J. (2002). *Venture capital due diligence: A guide to making smart investment choices and increasing your portfolio returns*. New York: Wiley.

Cardullo, M. W. (1999). *Technological entrepreneurialism: Enterprise formation, financing and growth*. Baldock: Research Studies Press Ltd.

Cattani, C., & Mills, G. (1998). How to approach banks. *International Trade Forum, 2*(2), 20–25.

Coopers & Lybrand (1997). *The economic impact of venture capital, Department of Industry*, Science and Tourism, Coopers & Lybrand, Australian Venture Capital Association Ltd.

DIFA (2015). *DIFA update*. Debtor and Invoice Finance Association March.
Dwight, D. (1999, November 17). *The venture catalyst,* unpublished research paper prepared for Advanced Corporate Finance MBAF 6200.
English, J. (1998). *How to organise and operate a small business in Australia*. Sydney: Allen & Unwin.
European Commission. (2001). *Enterprises access to finance* (Commission Staff Working Paper SEC (2001) 1667). Brussels: Commission for the European Communities.
Fitzpatrick, A., & Lien, B. (2013). The use of trade credit by businesses. *RBA Bulletin Reserve Bank of Australia* (September Quarter), 39–46.
Fraser, J. A. (1999). How to finance anything. *Incorporated, 21*(3), 32–48.
Fried, V. H., & Hisrich, R. D. (1994). Toward a model of venture capital investment decision making. *Financial Management, 23*(2), 28–37.
Gammie, B. (1995). Small businesses and their banks: A post-charter analysis. *Management Decision, 33*(7), 47–52.
Gaston, R. J. (1989). *Finding private venture capital for your firm: A complete guide*. New York: Wiley.
Golis, C. (2002). *Enterprise and venture capital: A business builder's and investor's handbook* (4th ed.). Sydney: Allen & Unwin.
Hindle, K., & Wenban, R. (1999). Australia's informal venture capitalists: An exploratory profile. *Venture Capital, 1*(2), 169–186.
Hodgetts, R., & Kuratko, D. (2001). *Effective small business management*. New York: Harcourt College Publishers.
Hughes. (2001). The 'problems' of finance for smaller businesses. In N. Dimsdale & M. Prevezer (Eds.), *Capital markets and corporate governance* (pp. 209–234). New York: Oxford UP.
Humphrey, N. (2000). Worth the risk: How to win venture capital funding. *Journal of the Securities Institute of Australia, 3*(Spring), 2–6.
Jones, A. (2008). Venture capital in Australia. *Chemistry in Australia, 75*(6), 12–14.
Keasey, K., & McGuinness, P. (1990). Small new firms and the return to alternative sources of finance. *Small Business Economics, 2*(3), 213–222.
Kenney, M. (2001). *Regional clusters, venture capital and entrepreneurship: What can the social sciences tell us about Silicon Valley?* (OECD Workshop Proceedings). Davis: University of California.
Landsberg, R. (1986). Negotiating loans for small businesses. *Journal of the Institute of Certified Financial Planners, 7*(4), 215–219.
Larry, J. (1990). How to obtain a small business loan. *Business & Economic Review, 37*(1), 21–25.
Leonard, D., & Swap, W. (2000). Gurus in the garage. *Harvard Business Review, 78*(6), 71–82.
Lister, C. (1991). Borrower's viewpoint: Are bankers and borrowers speaking the same language? *Journal of Commercial Bank Lending, 73*(5), 21–27.
MacMillan, I. C., Siegel, R., & Narsimha. (1985). Criteria used by venture capitalists to evaluate new venture proposals. *Journal of Business Venturing, 1*(1), 119–128.
Martin, F. (1999). Forgotten reforms: The non-GST ANTS [A New Tax System] bills. *Taxation in Australia, 33*(7), 375–380.
Mason, C., & Stark, M. (2004). What do investors look for in a business plan? A comparison of the investment criteria of bankers, venture capitalists and business angels. *International Small Business Journal, 22*(6), 227–248.
McKaskill, T. (2006). *Finding the money: How to raise venture capital*. Melbourne: Wilkinson Publishing Pty Ltd.
Megginson, W., Byrd, M., & Megginson, L. (2000). *Small business management: An entrepreneur's guidebook*. Boston: McGraw-Hill.
Meglio, O., Destri, A. M. L., & Capasso, A. (2017). Fostering dynamic growth in new ventures through venture capital: Conceptualizing venture capital capabilities. *Long Range Planning, 50*(4), 518–530.
Nichols, D. (1991). How to woo your banker. *Small Business Reports, 16*(6), 41–43.
NCVA. (2004). *Venture Impact 2004: Venture Capital Benefits to the U.S. Economy*, National Venture Capital Association, www.nvca.org. Arlington Virginia.

Oats, D. (1992). Vision of angels. *Director, 45*(11), 34.
OECD. (2004). *Financing innovative SMEs in a global economy*. Istanbul. 3–5 June: Organisation for Economic Cooperation and Development.
OECD. (2006). *The SME financing gap: Theory and evidence volume 1*. Paris: Organisation for Economic Co-operation and Development.
OECD. (2009). *The impact of the global crisis on SME and entrepreneurship financing and policy responses*. Paris: Organisation for Economic Co-operation and Development.
OECD. (2012). *Financing SMEs and entrepreneurs 2012: An OECD scoreboard*. Paris: Organisation for Economic Co-operation and Development (OECD) Publishing.
OECD. (2016a). *Financing SMEs and entrepreneurs 2016: An OECD scoreboard*. Paris: Organisation for Economic Co-operation and Development (OECD) Publishing.
OECD. (2016b). *Entrepreneurship at a glance 2016*. Paris: Organisation of Economic Cooperation and Development (OECD).
OECD. (2018). *Financing SMEs and entrepreneurs 2018: An OECD scoreboard*. Paris: Organisation for Economic Co-operation and Development (OECD) Publishing.
Onorato, N. R. (1997). *Trends in venture capital funding in the 1990s*. Washington, DC: U.S. Small Business Administration Office of Advocacy.
Peel, M. J., Wilson, N., & Howorth, C. (2000). Late payment and credit management in the small firm sector: Some empirical evidence. *International Small Business Journal, 18*(2), 17–37.
Petty, J. W., & Upton, N. (1997). *The Entrepreneur and the Banker: A comparative study of perceptions*. Waco: Hankamer School of Business, Baylor University.
Productivity Commission. (2015). *Business set-up, transfer and closure: Productivity commission inquiry report no. 75*,. 30 September 2015. Canberra: AGPS.
Rowan, M. (1994). Cash flow is king. *Australian Accountant*, August, 17–19.
Sapienza, H. J., & De Clercq, D. (2000). Venture capital-entrepreneur relationships in technology-based ventures. *Enterprise and Innovation Management Studies, 1*(1), 57–71.
Sensis (2017). *Sensis business index December 2016: A survey of confidence and behaviour of Australian small and medium businesses*. https://www.sensis.com.au. Telstra Sensis.
Smith, J. (2000). *What is venture capital*, Australian Venture Capital Association (AVCAL) www.avcal.com.au.
Snaith, W., & Walker, J. (1999). *Planning and financing growth*. Durham: Financial Management Program, University of Durham.
Stevenson, H., Grousbeck, I., Roberts, M., & Bhide, A. (1999). *New business ventures and the entrepreneur*. Boston: McGraw-Hill International.
Stiglitz, J., & Weiss, A. (1981). Credit rationing in markets with incomplete information. *American Economic Review, 71*(3), 393–410.
Storey, D. (1994). New firm growth and Bank financing. *Small Business Economics, 6*(2), 139–150.
Taylor, L. (1989). How to succeed at bank financing. *Journal of Business Strategy, 10*(2), 58–61.
Teten, D., & Farmer, C. (2010). Time for investors to get social. *Harvard Business Review, 88*(6), 28.
Van Osnabrugge, M. (1998). Do serial and non-serial investors behave differently? An empirical and theoretical analysis. *Entrepreneurship Theory and Practice, 22*(4), 23–42.
Watson, T. (2003). How to shake the money tree. *Canadian Business, 76*(23), 147.
Wei, Z., & Lin, M. (2016). Market mechanisms in online peer-to-peer lending. *Management Science, 59*(1), 1–22.
Wetzel, W. E., & Freear, J. (1994). Promoting informal venture capital in the United States: Reflections on the history of the venture capital network. In R. Harrison & C. M. Mason (Eds.), *Informal venture capital: Information, networks and public policy*. Hempel-Hempstead: Woodhead Faulkner.
Wiltbank, R. & Sarasvathy, S. (2002). *Selection and return in angel investment*, Unpublished paper submitted to the Babson Conference, MA: Babson College.
Wright, M., & Robbie, K. (Eds.). (1997). *Venture capital*. UK: Dartmouth Publishing.
Wright, M., Hart, M. & Fu, K. (2015). *A nation of angels: Assessing the impact of angel investing across the UK*. The Centre for Entrepreneurs, European Research Centre, UK Business Angels Association.

Intellectual Property Management 13

13.1 Introduction

> The patent process is like a baby, you have to feed it all the time – the expected length of time is likely to be 20 years…the design is constantly challenged by others that claim their products are similar.
>
> Source: Chris Speight, inventor Smartaflow Chlorisafe system.

Commercialisation has been described as the process of preparing and taking an established product, process or service to market (DITR 2003). The process ends when the product, process or service is finally marketed successfully to the customer. It is typically the costliest part of the innovation process, requires the most entrepreneurial effort and involves the most commercial risk. At the heart of the commercialisation process is the development and economic leverage of IP, which is the ability of creative ideas to be identified and protected for future commercial benefit. In this chapter, we explore the nature of IP and IP rights as well as how such IP can be brought to market via the commercialisation process. The chapter examines the role of intellectual property (IP) in the innovation process including: types of IP, the protection of IP, and how to assess the technical feasibility of an innovation. Also considered is the process of licensing and the valuation of IP in the commercialisation of an innovation.

13.2 The Nature of Intellectual Property

According to the World Intellectual Property Organisation (WIPO), *intellectual property* (IP) refers to '*creations of the mind, such as inventions; literary and artistic works; designs; and symbols, names and images used in commerce*' (WIPO

T. Mazzarol, S. Reboud, *Entrepreneurship and Innovation*, Springer Texts in Business and Economics, https://doi.org/10.1007/978-981-13-9412-6_13

2019). Ownership of IP – or the rights associated with IP – allows individuals or companies to enjoy financial benefits from the sale or licencing of this IP. This is similar to how the ownership of physical property allows it to be sold or leased. In a world that is increasingly yielding value from knowledge-based assets, the role of IP is becoming crucial to future economic success. However, before IP rights can be used for commercial purposes, they must be formally recognised through a process of registration and protection. This is typically the case with many forms of IP, although some IP rights arise automatically as soon as a piece of work is created so long as there is a record of this creation process (Intellectual-Property UK 2005). IP can be formally listed within the balance sheet of a business and requires a business to develop a formal strategy for its protection in a similar way that physical assets might be protected from loss or damage (SBDC 2005).

There are several types of IP, some of which must be formally registered before rights can be legally assigned. Intellectual property is divided into two categories: Industrial Property includes patents for inventions, trademarks, industrial designs and geographical indications. Copyright covers literary works (such as novels, poems and plays), films, music, artistic works (e.g., drawings, paintings, photographs and sculptures) and architectural design (WIPO 2019). Thus, the following types of IP are generally recognised (IP Australia 2016):

- *Patents:* For new or improved products or processes capable of commercial or industrial application, requiring formal registration;
- *Trademarks:* For words, symbols, pictures, sounds, smells or a combination of these, to distinguish the goods and services of one trader from those of another, and requiring formal registration;
- *Designs:* For the shape or appearance of manufactured goods of the whole or a part of a product resulting from the features of, in particular, the lines, contours, colours, shape, texture or materials of the product itself or its ornamentation, and requiring formal registration;
- *Copyright:* For original material in literary, artistic, dramatic or musical works, films, broadcasts, multimedia and computer programs, and requiring no formal registration;
- *Circuit layout rights:* For the three-dimensional configuration of electronic circuits in integrated circuit products or layout designs, and requiring no formal registration;
- *Plant breeder's rights:* For new plant varieties, and requiring formal registration; and
- *Confidentiality/trade secrets:* Including know-how and other confidential or proprietary information, and requiring no formal registration process.

While copyright and circuit layout rights occur automatically upon creation of the original piece of work, patents, plant breeder's rights, trademarks and designs all need formal registration before IP rights can be recognised. Such registration incurs a cost and is generally only able to afford protection within the jurisdiction where it

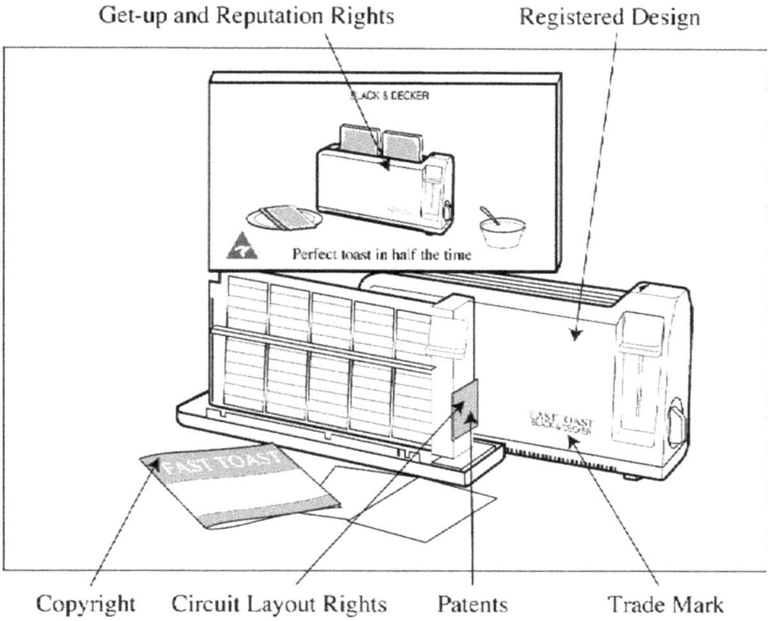

Fig. 13.1 What are intellectual property rights? (The Black & Decker Fast Toast)

is registered. For example, Registration of a patent in Australia will not automatically guarantee its protection in other countries.

To illustrate the application of IP rights in a product, the example of a toaster can be given. Figure 13.1 illustrates the Black & Decker Fast Toast electric toaster. As shown, even this relatively simple household appliance contains a lot of IP rights. These include patents over the technology behind the sensors for the toaster's browning system, and circuit layout rights for the computer board. The overall design of the toaster is registered, as is the trademark. In addition to these formal IP rights, there is also the copyright for the product booklet and general 'get up' and reputation rights for the device.

13.3 Formal IP Rights

Formal IP rights are conferred by government authorities in each jurisdiction. These rights require the rights holder to formally register their IP with the appropriate authority and pay a fee. Because these rights are conferred by different governments, it is usual that any business seeking to have its IP rights protected within international markets will need to register its IP in each country or group of countries (e.g. the European Patent Office or the African Intellectual Property Organization), where it seeks to do business. It is common for global patents and cross-border trademarks to be registered with the three major patents office systems of the European Patent Office (EPO), the Japanese Patent Office (JPO) and the US Patent and Trademark Office (USPTO) to protect the same invention. Thus, it can involve quite high costs for the registration and maintenance of such IP rights. The WIPO-administered Patent Cooperation Treaty (PCT) provides for the filing of a single international patent application that has the same effect as national applications filed in the designated countries. An applicant seeking protection may file one application and request protection in as many signatory states as needed (WIPO 2017).

13.3.1 Patents

> **A patent is,** … an exclusive right granted for an invention – a product or process that provides a new way of doing something, or that offers a new technical solution to a problem. A patent provides patent owners with protection for their inventions. Protection is granted for a limited period, generally 20 years. (WIPO 2017 p. 5)

This official right is granted to the patent owner by the sovereign state for exclusive title to the use, sale and licencing of a device, substance, method or process. This legally enforceable right provides the patent owner with the exclusive right to commercially exploit the invention for the life of the patent once it has been registered and granted to them. Patents are not automatically granted upon application and must meet the legal requirements for approval. It is not possible to patent artistic works, mathematical models, plans, schemes or other processes of a purely mental nature (IP Australia 2016).

Patents are associated with the functional and technical aspects of a process or product and are generally highly specific about what is being registered. Most patents are incremental in nature and involve evolutionary rather than revolutionary changes to existing technologies or processes. Before a patent can be registered, it must be demonstrated that the invention or process is able to meet three general criteria (WIPO 2019):

1. *It must be new.* The process or invention must demonstrate that it is genuinely new and does not form part of the 'state of the art', or what was already available to the public prior to the patent application. This means that if the idea has been published, presented at conferences, illustrated in a public display or generally disseminated prior to the patent application, it would not qualify;
2. *It must involve an inventive step.* It should not be 'obvious' from the perspective of a person skilled or knowledgeable in the discipline or area of technology from which the invention is derived;
3. *It must have industrial application.* The invention or process should be able to be made use of in industry in some demonstrable way.

This suggests that the invention or process that is to be described in the patent must be all or part of a product, process or chemical composition that offers something new and innovative for application within industry (SBDC 2005). It is also important to note that disclosure of the process in the public domain is likely to void the right to a patent. While it is acceptable to discuss patents with employees, business partners and advisors prior to the filing of a patent, this must be undertaken on a confidential basis.

It is advisable to make use of written confidentiality agreements in such discussions to protect patentable IP (IP Australia 2016). While this can create a good deal of legal red tape, it is often better to be safe than sorry. The case of electrical products, manufacturer Kambrook is illustrative of this. Their power board multi-point electrical product was a highly successful innovation when it was first invented in the early 1970s. However, the company failed to patent the technology, allowing others to quickly copy the design and erode its market share with the loss of millions of dollars of potential revenue (IP Australia 2016).

Kambrook – A Lesson Learned

In 1972, Frank Bannigan, Managing Director of Kambrook, developed the electrical power board. The product was hugely successful, and was the basis for Kambrook's growth to become a major producer of electrical appliances. However, the power board was not patented and Kambrook ended up sharing the market with many other manufacturers. According to Mr. Bannigan:

> *I've probably lost millions of dollars in royalties alone. Whenever I go into a department store and see the wide range of power boards on offer, it always comes back to haunt me.*

Today, Kambrook has a number of patents and pending applications for improvements in a range of consumer goods.
Source: IP Australia (2005)

Patents do not last forever. A standard patent is generally for a period of 20 years from date of registration. Annual maintenance fees are likely to apply after 5 years. Like all other patents pharmaceutical patents are issued for a period of 20 years from the date of deposit and upon payment of the annuities. However, pharmaceutical products require authorizations in order to be marketed. This authorization can take several years before being given. To compensate for this period when the patent cannot be exploited, a special title has been created for example in France or in the UK, the Supplementary Protection Certificate which extends the rights of the owner of a pharmaceutical patent (INPI 2019; Intellectual-Property UK 2005).

- Innovation Patents

In Australia, it is also possible to lodge an innovation patent that covers incremental developments in products or processes and needs to demonstrate that the new device or technology is 'innovative' rather than 'inventive'. This type of patent can provide protection for up to 8 years and can be applied for online (SBDC 2005).

Innovation patents offer a protection option designed specifically to protect inventions that do not meet the inventive threshold required for standard patents. Introduced into Australia in 2001, they are targeted at small firms and local industries. An innovation patent is a relatively fast way to obtain protection for a new device, substance, method or process.

However, an innovation patent doesn't allow you to legally stop others from copying your innovation unless you have your innovation patent examined.

An Innovation Patent – Boardsling

Boardsling is the brainchild of inventor and surfer Nick Kent who developed the device to make it easier for him to carry his surfboard to the Queensland beaches. With smaller waves in the area near his home, he started riding a long board, but this is heavy piece of equipment to carry. As Nick explained:

> *It was a half mile's walk to the surf break, and carrying a big board was awkward and hard on the arms, shoulders and back. People don't like to take their board bags because they can be stolen, or they get full of sand that then mixes with the wax on their board.*
> *So, I started looking at a way to create a sling-type surfboard carrier that would do the job.*

Nick's Boardsling prototype was a 'simple heavy-duty strap that hooks around the surfboard, allowing the carrier to simply sling it over a shoulder'. The device is both simple and ergonomic. It holds the board in place without bouncing, jarring or other injury.

Having created the prototype, Nick spoke to a patent attorney who helped him secure two innovation patents to give his device protection from imitation in Australia. It was a new and useful invention, but at the time would not have qualified for the more rigorous tests of a standard patent.

(continued)

IP Australia examined both patents and certified them to be legally enforceable. It offered Boardsling the necessary protection while the product became established in the market. Later, the patent can be upgraded to a standard patent. According to Nick:

> *Once this Boardsling wave is finished we want to come up with another invention to get on a new wave, and then we will ride that one, and then the next and then the next.*

Source: IP Australia (2010)

Examination of an innovation patent will only occur if requested by the patentee, a third party or the commissioner of patents. An innovation patent is only legally enforceable and certified if it has been examined by IP Australia and has met the requirements of the Patents Act (IP Australia 2010). This is similar in other countries. For example, in France, there are several categories of patents. They are subject to the same legal regime, but the extent of the right of the owner varies according to the nature of the invention, subject of the patent (INPI 2019):

- The "application patent" is a patent covering the new application of a patented product or process. The invention, object of the patent, consists in the use of known means, for a result that can also be known: the novelty does not rely on the means or on the result but on the average-result ratio.
- The "improvement patent" relates to an invention which is a technical improvement of another invention, itself protected by a patent. It therefore relates to an invention which consists of an improvement (a new element or a simplification) of at least one claim of another patent of invention.
- The "dominant patent is a patent" (also referred to as a "main title"), the claims of which must be reproduced, in whole or in part, for the exploitation of another invention, then referred to as a "dependent invention".

- Patent Registration

When a patent is registered, the documentation generally must have a clear description of the invention, including drawings that provide sufficient detail for a skilled person in the area of technology to perform the invention themselves. It should also make claims to define the scope of protection that is being sought. These details are then used to determine future claims made for or against the legal protection offered by the patent.

Once registered, the patent documentation is published by the patent office, making it available to the general public. The patent then becomes recognised as part of the 'state of the art' associated with the field of science or technology within which the patent lies. Anyone can then access the patent documentation and comment on it. It is not uncommon for a patent application to involve public comment, and for the application to be modified or amended to meet concerns of other parties before the patent is granted. Once accepted, the patent is re-published in a final form. Subsequently, if new information is made available after the patent is granted that requires the patent to be changed, this will take place and the patent will be republished again (WIPO 2019).

Patent Example – Orbital Engine

The Orbital engine was a new concept in internal combustion engines designed by Western Australian inventor Ralph Sarich. Having developed several agricultural equipment products, Ralph produced the prototype Orbital engine in the late 1960s.

In 1973 Ralph appeared with his engine on the ABC TV show *The Inventors*. He was then approached by BHP Ltd., with whom he formed a joint venture. The Orbital Engineering Co, now Orbital Technologies, now holds some 540 patents and licencing agreements with a number of major overseas automotive and marine engineering firms.

Sarich Australian Patent No: 467415 lodged 6 July 1970.

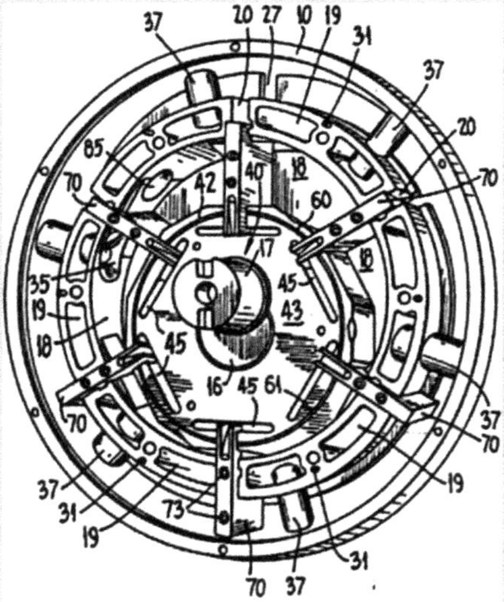

FIG. 2.

While the Orbital engine did not become a success from a commercialisation perspective, the company created a number of breakthrough engineering solutions in the area of fuel injection technologies. These were diffused into a range of outboard motor and motor vehicle applications. The original patent for the Orbital engine is 16 pages long with 4 drawings.

Source: IP Australia.

- Patent Costs and Coverage

In Australia, a patent is registered through the IP Australia patents office, which determines if the patent meets the appropriate criteria. In other countries, there are different patent laws and regulations. It is generally advisable to register a patent internationally to fully protect IP rights. Australia is a signatory to a number of international agreements relating to IP rights and patents.

A patent registered in Australia is therefore useful in establishing patent rights in other countries in subsequent years (IP Australia 2010). According to IP Australia (2010), the cost of registering a standard patent in Australia is \$6000–\$10,000 – inclusive of patent attorney fees and registration costs. Over the 20-year life of the patent, there are likely to be additional fees of approximately \$8600. Internationally registered patents will cost substantially more than this, and all patents are only a protection if they can be defended legally. Defending an alleged breach of a patent may cost tens of thousands of dollars in legal fees. The Patent Office does not take sides in patent disputes, so there is no automatic legal protection from the authorities.

There is an international agreement that exists between national patent offices. For example, IP Australia is a receiving office, searching authority and *International Preliminary Examining Authority* (IPEA) for international patents. This allows patents to be searched and initially examined by IP Australia at an international level. This ensures that inventions to be lodged within Australia are not likely to be at risk of breeching those that have already been registered in other countries. However, there are many differences between patent registration systems in each country, and it is advisable to use a professional patent attorney to assist with international patent applications.

A Patent Must Be Useful

To qualify for a patent, the invention must be useful for some purpose – however this hurdle is relatively easy to overcome; to be denied a patent under this requirement, the invention has to be totally incapable of achieving any useful result. This does not, however, mean that inventions *always* meet this requirement. A patent application can be denied under the usefulness requirement if the applicant fails to disclose enough information about the patent to make its utility apparent, or if the applicant asserted that the invention could do something that it obviously could not.

Source: Legal Database www.legal-database.com/patent.htm.

- Patent Rights

While a patent can protect the inventor of a new device or process and allow them to licence or sell the IP rights associated with it, the patents system is also a means of avoiding duplication. It is not widely recognised that the purpose of the patents system is to make public the 'state of the art' of the technology or scientific field in which the patent is located. By reviewing the patents register, it is possible for inventors to avoid replicating what has already been developed. Competitors can see what others are doing, or can build on what has already been developed. Once a patent is expired, it is possible to replicate the process or device without risk of legal challenge (Intellectual-Property UK 2005).

What Rights Does a Patent Give Me?

A patent gives you the right to stop others from using your invention. Alternatively, you can choose to let others use it under agreed terms. A patent also brings the right to take legal action against others who might be infringing the invention and to claim damages. The mere existence of a patent may be enough to deter a potential infringer. The Patent Office, however, does not take sides in any dispute.

A patent empowers the owner, or the proprietor, of an invention to take legal action against others to prevent the unlicensed manufacture, use, importation or sale of the patented invention. This right can be used to give the proprietor breathing space to develop a business based on the invention; or, another person or company may be allowed to exploit the invention and pay royalties under a licencing agreement.

Source: Intellectual-Property UK (2005).

A patent is essentially a negative right in that it is designed to stop someone else from exploiting an invention developed by the patent owner without the owner's permission. It is no legal defence to claim that you breeched a patent right because you were unaware of the patent. This means that inventors and innovative firms should be checking regularly with the patents register to ensure an idea has not already been registered.

Further, it is not compulsory for a patent to be registered but, once it is, the inventor must accept the risk that the publication of the patent will result in others copying the idea and thereby breeching their patent rights. A patent can also be challenged and revocation ordered by a court or by the patent's office. Finally, just because an invention is patented does not guarantee that it has commercial value.

13.3.2 Trademarks

A trademark, … is a distinctive sign that identifies certain goods or services produced or provided by an individual or a company. Its origin dates back to ancient times when craftsmen reproduced their signatures, or marks, on their artistic works or products of a functional or practical nature. Over the years, these marks have evolved into today's system of trademark registration and protection. The system helps consumers to identify and purchase a product or service based on whether its specific characteristics and quality – as indicated by its unique trademark – meet their needs (WIPO (2017) p 8).

It can be a letter, number, word, phrase, sound, smell, shape, logo, picture, aspect of packaging or any combination of these. It is thus impossible to register *generic* products (e.g. lawnmowers) or services (e.g. dentistry). Geographic place names, surnames and given names are often difficult to register as trademarks, although these can be registered if they have been used in the market place for a long period of time (IP Australia 2016). In the US, it is possible to register 'service marks' for services with the US Patent and Trademark Office (Williams and Bukowitz 2001).

Trademark Case – Redheads

The opening of Bryant and May's first Australian match factory was on the 15 December 1909 in Richmond, Victoria. The name 'Redheads' was derived from the red striking head of the 'safety match' and the famous Redheads logo was created in 1946. Soon the woman featured in the logo assumed a personality of her own, and became affectionately known as 'Miss Redhead'. Instantly recognisable as the Redhead's brand, the trademark has only had four major updates since its launch in 1946.

The first change to the trademark was in 1958, which gave 'Miss Redhead' a new hairdo. The next change was in 1975, which saw a red background introduced to the logo to give the product greater visibility on market shelves. This was also the year the word 'Redheads' was first registered as a trademark. Later, in 1980, the image of 'Miss Redheads' was also registered as a trademark. This design, with only minor typestyle and positioning changes, is still used today and can be seen not only on matches but also a huge range of other products including fire-lighters, barbeque accessories, gas matches and fire assist products.

Source: (IP Australia 2010).

While it is not compulsory to register a trademark or trade name prior to using it in the market, it is advisable to do so if you wish to have exclusive rights to its use, or if you wish to licence the rights to using a particular brand name (SBDC 2005). If a business has used a trademark or brand name in the market for a period of time without formally registering it and then finds that another business has begun to make use of the same trademark, they might still have a legal claim. If the original user of the trademark can prove prior and extended use, they may have legal protection under common law rights. However, this will usually require a court case and a judicial ruling that is likely to be expensive both in time and in monetary terms (IP Australia 2016).

Registration of a trademark provides the owner exclusive legal rights to use the trademark or to licence or sell it within Australia for the goods and services for which it is registered. It is advisable that trademarks be searched prior to any registration, as a legal claim might be triggered by those seeking to protect their existing trademarks. Costs associated with such registration can vary from a few hundred dollars if registration is done by you to approximately $3000 if legal services are used. A trademark is legally protected for 10 years in Australia, and can then be renewed for periods of up to 10 years at a time for additional fees. However, if a trademark is not used it can be subject to challenge and rights may be revoked (IP Australia 2010).

- International Trademarks

To avoid the need to register separate applications with each national or regional office, WIPO administers an international registration system for trademarks. Two treaties enable WIPO to run the system: the Madrid Agreement Concerning the International Registration of Marks and the Madrid Protocol. This international agreement was originally established in Madrid, Spain in 1891. According to WIPO, "persons with a link (be it through nationality, domicile or establishment) to a country party to one or both of these treaties may, on the basis of a registration or application with the trademark office of that country (or related region), obtain an international registration having effect in some or all of the other countries of the Madrid Union" (WIPO (2017), p. 11). Australia became a signatory to the Madrid Protocol in July 2001.The Madrid Protocol has been amended six times from 1900 to 1967.

13.3.3 Designs

An industrial design is "the ornamental or aesthetic aspects of an article. A design may consist of three-dimensional features, such as the shape or surface of an article, or two-dimensional features, such as patterns, lines or colour" (WIPO (2017), p.12). It often refers to the visual aspects of a logo or product resulting from, in particular, the features of the lines, contours, colours, shape, texture or materials of the product or its ornamentation. The registration of a design grants the owner the exclusive rights to make use of a product design, and to licence the use of this design or to sell it. Design rights are generally viewed as additional rights to any copyright protection that might automatically exist in a design (Intellectual-Property UK 2005). So, while a patent relates to the *function* of a device or product, a registered design relates to its *form* or appearance (SBDC 2005).

Design Case – Sebel Metal Frame Chair

Harry Sebel, founder of Sebels (Australia) Ltd was the designer of the stackable Sebel Metal Frame Chair. This chair holds the Australian Registered Design AU-S-35886 which was lodged 16 October 1956 and formally registered in October 1957.

This tubular metal frame chair design that stacks neatly inside another chair has received an international design registration and was a highly successful product for Sebels (Australia) Ltd. The chairs proved particularly popular in schools and large halls where they could be stacked neatly on top of each other to save space when not required.

The first prototype for the chair was produced by Sebel as the 'Stak-a-bye' chair of 1953. An example of this chair is now held at the Powerhouse Museum in Sydney.

Source: IP Australia (2010).

To be eligible for registration the design must be *new*, meaning that there is no identical design already in public use in Australia, or published in a document either in Australia or overseas. It must also be *distinctive*, in that it is not similar to any existing designs in terms of its overall appearance. If a design has already been published or perhaps posted on the internet prior to the date that it is filed with IP Australia, it may be deemed not to be new (IP Australia 2016).

Within Australia, a registered design lasts for 5 years from the date of its initial filing, and can be renewed for a further 5 years or up to a maximum of 10 years from date of application. IP Australia offers a reminder for design owners 2 months prior to the expiry date, and allows 6 months after the expiry date before allowing the registration to lapse. In the event of an infringement, IP Australia will provide advice after examining the claim and, if certified as a potential infringement, legal action can be taken.

13.3.4 Geographical Indication

According to WIPO, a geographical indication is "a sign used on goods that have a specific geographical origin and possess qualities or a reputation due to that place of origin". Generally speaking, a geographical indication consists of the name of the place of origin of the goods. It is common for agricultural products which typically have qualities that derive from their place of production or are influenced by specific local geographical conditions (e.g. climate and soil). Geographical indications are used for a wide variety of agricultural products, such as, for example, "Tuscany" for olive oil produced in a specific area of Italy, or "Roquefort" for cheese produced in that region of France (WIPO (2017) p. 15). This system has been widely developed and is intensively used in Europe, especially in France. The protected geographical indications (PGI) identify an agricultural product, raw or processed, which quality, reputation or other characteristics are linked to its geographical origin. The PGI applies to agricultural, agro-food and wine sectors[1].

However, the use of geographical indications is not limited to agricultural products. According to WIPO, they may also highlight specific qualities of a product that are due to human factors found in the product's place of origin, such as specific manufacturing skills and traditions: the place of origin may be a village or town, a region or a country. An example of the latter is "Switzerland" or "Swiss", perceived as a geographical indication in many countries for products made in Switzerland and, in particular, for watches (WIPO (2017) p. 16).

13.3.5 Plant Breeders' Rights

It is also possible within Australia for plant breeders to secure protection over the development of new varieties of plants that they have created. To do so, the plant breeder must be able to demonstrate that they have created an entirely new variety of plant that is distinct, uniform and stable. Through comparative trials, the breeder must be able to show that the new plant variety can be clearly distinguished from other plant varieties already commonly known in the market. This allows them to benefit from the commercial sale of this plant and its reproductive material, or the securing of royalties from the licencing of the plant to other producers as well as the ability to sell these rights to another party. Registration of the plant variety is undertaken with IP Australia, and protection lasts for 25 years for trees or vines and 20 years for other species. However, growers do not have to pay the breeder royalties

[1] https://www.inao.gouv.fr/eng/Official-signs-identifying-quality-and-origin/Protected-Geographical-Indications

on crops produced or seeds retained for future production on their land. Protection is also not provided that would restrict other breeders using that variety in future plant breeding (IP Australia 2010). Some examples of plant breeder rights include:

- *The 'Shalistin':* A white cabernet sauvignon grape variety bred by Malcolm 'Mac' Cleggett of Cleggett Wines in South Australia.
- *The 'bollgard II' cotton plant:* Developed by Australia's CSIRO, it has a resistance to the helicoverpa or bollworm, which is the primary insect pest for cotton. This species significantly reduces the need for pesticides.
- *The 'Drysdale' drought resistant wheat variety:* Developed by the CSIRO, this species of wheat offers significant drought and disease resistance to conventional varieties. Yields in dry areas are 10% higher than standard wheat species.
- *The 'pink iceberg' rose:* Bred by Tasmanian plant breeder Lilia Weatherley, this rose came from her identifying a pink mutation in her white 'iceberg' roses.

13.4 Automatically Granted IP Rights

In addition to the abovementioned IP rights that need to be formally registered, there a number of IP rights categories that do not require any formal registration. These are copyright, circuit layout rights, trade secrets and confidentiality.

13.4.1 Copyright

Unlike patents, trademarks or registered designs, copyright does not require formal registration. Copyright does not offer protection for creative ideas, only for the original expression or manifestation of these ideas. Once a work of art, music, film, broadcast, literature or computer programming has been created and placed onto media, it is protected under copyright. This prevents its unlawful copying or duplication without the permission of the originator or copyright owner. Australia is a signatory to the Universal Copyright Convention, thereby granting reciprocal protection internationally within those countries that are co-signatories (IP Australia 2016).

What Is Copyright?

Copyright gives the creators of a wide range of material – such as literature, art, music, sound recordings, films and broadcasts – economic rights enabling them to control the use of their material in a number of ways, such as by making copies, issuing copies to the public, performing in public, broadcasting and using the material online. It also gives the moral right to be identified as the creator of certain kinds of material, and to object to the distortion or mutilation of it. Material protected by copyright is termed a 'work'. However, copyright does not protect ideas *per se*, or things such as names or titles.

Source: Intellectual-Property UK (2005).

Copyright protection is provided under the *Copyright Act* 1968 and gives exclusive rights to licence others in regard to copying the work, performing it in public, broadcasting it, publishing it and making an adaptation of the work. Rights vary according to the nature of the work. Those for artistic works, for instance, are different to those for literary and musical works. Although making copies of copyright material can infringe exclusive rights, a certain amount of copying is permissible under the fair dealing provisions of Australian legislation (IP Australia 2010).

Creative works such as music, literary or artistic output is a product of a significant investment in human labour and intellectual talent, and is afforded protection under copyright laws to restrict the capacity of others to exploit it without paying royalties to the creators. Without such protection, it would be impossible for creative talent to be rewarded, and there would be little incentive for future new material to be generated. Copyright law does allow some limited reproduction without permission, but in most cases duplication of works without prior consent from the copyright owner is illegal (Intellectual-Property UK 2005). Unfortunately, the reproduction of music, artworks, software and literary works has become commonplace due to the capacity of modern technology to allow such reproduction.

It is not unknown for two creators to generate identical or similar works independently of each other. Under these circumstances copyright cannot provide protection to the concerned parties. While it is not necessary for copyright to be registered officially, it is advisable that copyright notices be placed on all creative works. This notice should list the copyright owner's name and date of creation and is a means by which copyright can be demonstrated – particularly when seeking to secure copyright overseas. It also serves as a warning to others to avoid any potential infringement (IP Australia 2010).

Copyright is generally recognised within Australia as lasting for the life of the author plus 70 years for literary and artistic works from the year of the author's death, or from the year of first publication after the author's death. For films and sound recordings, this time limit is 70 years from publication or production (IP Australia 2010). The Attorney-General's department is responsible in Australia for administering the *Copyright Act 1968*. In the US, the *Copyright Act 1976* provides similar protection and lasts for the duration of the author's life plus 50 years.

13.4.2 Copyright Changes Since the Australia-US Free Trade Agreement

The copyright laws in the US are administered by the Copyright Office of the Library of Congress (Williams and Bukowitz 2001). When Australia and the United States entered into a Free Trade Agreement in 2005, it became necessary for amendments to be made the Australian copyright and general IP protection system. In 2004, Australia's Federal Parliament passed the *US Free Trade Agreement Implementation Act*. The main changes that impacted on copyright laws for Australia included the following points (IP Australia 2005). New rights were introduced for musicians and performers in the area of sound recordings that offer economic and moral benefits. Copyright protection was extended from 50 to 70 years. A scheme for limitation of remedies available against Carriage Service Providers for copyright infringement was implemented. Wider criminal provisions for copyright infringement were introduced, along with broader protections for electronic rights management. There was also a wider range of protection against unauthorised reproductions. This example illustrates both the impact that free trade agreements can have on IP laws, but also the importance that is placed on securing IP rights, given their increasingly valuable role in underpinning the economies of most developed nations.

Using a Copyright Notice

Copyright notices that use the owner's name and date (e.g. ©Mazzarol and Reboud 2019 all rights reserved) are not necessary in some countries such as Australia, but they can make it easier to prove the ownership of the copyright at a later date. Copyright notices are necessary to establish copyright in some countries, however, and may serve as a deterrent to people who might seek to infringe the copyright.

IP Australia note that where a copyright owner applies a 3D artistic work in an industrial application – as might occur with some visual rendering in software programs – it will result in a loss of copyright. In this case the owner will need to register their creation as a design.

Source: IP Australia (2010).

13.4.3 Circuit Layout Rights

The design and layout of integrated circuits and computer chips is critical to the operation of computer equipment and electronic devices, and usually involves a high degree of complex intellectual effort. Where a computer chip or integrated circuit is designed in an original manner, the layout design can be afforded legal protection via circuit layout rights. These are an evolved form of copyright and, like copyright; there is no requirement for formal registration to ensure protection as circuit layout rights are essentially generated automatically as the circuit layout is created (IP Australia 2010).

Time Limit for Circuit Layout Rights

The maximum possible protection period is 20 years. Accordingly, rights in an original layout subsist for 10 years from the first commercial exploitation provided this occurs within 10 years from creation of the layout or 10 years from the year in which it was made – if not commercially exploited.

Source: IP Australia (2010).

The owner of an original circuit layout has exclusive right to copy the layout in a material form, construct integrated circuits from the layout, and commercially exploit the design within Australia for a period of 20 years. Commercial exploitation may occur by importation, sale, hire or distribution of a layout or an integrated circuit made according to the layout (SBDC 2005). As with copyright, it is the Attorney-General's department that administers circuit layout rights in Australia.

13.4.4 Confidentiality and Trade Secrets

In addition to the methods of IP protection listed above, there is also the option of employing confidentiality and secrecy within the business to secure IP rights. It is generally recommended that such provisions be employed in conjunction with other means of IP protection. The usual approach is for the company to require all employees and third-party actors (e.g. suppliers, sub-contractors) to sign confidentiality or non-disclosure agreements, thereby restricting their right to reveal trade secrets or proprietary knowledge during their employment or association with the business. Although these legal agreements do not by themselves stop a person revealing confidential or secret information, they provide evidence of what that person has agreed to and can form the basis of future legal action against them.

Use of confidentiality or secrecy provisions may be appropriate where IP cannot be easily patented or registered, or where the process associated with the production of the product or process is particularly complex and where reverse engineering is less likely. However, it can be a difficult process to maintain trade secrets over the long term, and the wider the circle of people who become aware of the process the greater the chance of leakage. Secrecy and confidentiality arrangements also will not prevent another company or individual independently developing the same product or process (IP Australia 2016).

Protecting Trade Secrets

Proving a breach of confidentiality under common law can be complex, and is potentially costlier than defending registered rights.

Ask contractors and employees to provide written undertakings not to compete with your business after they leave – in addition to signing a confidentiality agreement. It is often much easier to prove this than to prove breach of confidentiality. These undertakings, however, are difficult to enforce and need to be prepared by your legal adviser, as you need to be careful that the undertaking does not restrict the contractor's or employee's right to earn a living.

Source: IP Australia (2010).

Where a breach of confidentiality or an infringement of trade secrecy has occurred, the only legal recourse is under common law provisions. This would require the firm who feels that their secrecy has been violated to sue the offender, and it would be useful to have signed agreements over non-disclosure or non-competition to support the case. However, such agreements can be challenged if they are thought to restrict the rights of the other party to meaningfully earn their living.

It is important to recognise that if you or your organisation have not taken appropriate steps to protect IP rights, such as using non-disclosure agreements (NDA) or trade secrecy procedures, it may be very difficult to seek remedy from a court should you feel that a breach of your IP rights has occurred. The court is likely to take a more favourable view of the claim for remedy where there is evidence that some prior attempt was made to protect commercially valuable IP.

13.4.5 What Should an NDA Contract Look Like?

A non-disclosure agreement (NDA) creates a confidential relationship between a person that holds a trade secret or secrets, and the person to whom the secret is disclosed. As a formal agreement, an NDA legally binds the two parties to keep the information a secret. Under common law it is possible to seek damages for a breach of confidentiality, even if there is no formal NDA in place. However, the NDA provides greater evidence and helps clarify the nature of the agreement and the stated obligations of both parties. It is therefore more likely that a successful court action can proceed.

In developing an NDA, you should consider if the agreement is to be mutually binding or one-way. Also, of importance is that the NDA clarifies why the information that is being held in confidence is proprietary, and to adequately define what this information is. The overall purpose of the NDA should therefore be stated so as to avoid any future confusion. Another consideration in the design of an NDA is whether the parties that are entering into the agreement are individuals or legal entities (e.g. businesses). The authority of the person who is signing the NDA also needs to be considered, and all their contact details should be correct.

In some NDAs, there may be details relating to such things as: the action to be taken in the case of inadvertent disclosure; whether information to be transferred is to be marketed as 'confidential' or 'proprietary'; whether there is an indemnification against third party liability: and what the time period or duration of the obligation is to be. Some NDA may also specify whether it is possible for the information to be disclosed to specific people such as other employees within the organisation or sub-contractor organisations. They may also stipulate the need for documents or data to be stored in secure or locked facilities.

13.5 Developing an IP Strategy

Any IP strategy should be integrated into the overall business strategy, and should be included in business and marketing plans. A wide range of different measures is generally preferable to employing only one or two. Patents and other more formal IP protection measures – such as registered designs – should be supported by registered trademarks, copyright on manuals and other documents as well as

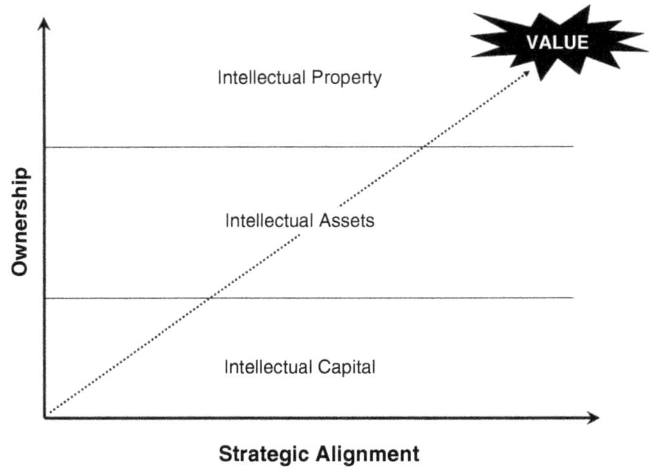

Fig. 13.2 IC, IA, IP degrees of ownership and strategic alignment. (Source: Williams and Bukowitz 2001)

confidentiality and trade secrecy provisions (IP Australia 2016). For many companies, the most valuable long-term protection for their products and services is the development of a well-recognised brand name. The end result of a well-considered branding strategy is the generation of substantial 'goodwill' in the market. 'Goodwill' is the intangible asset value inherent in a business after a period of trading. It can be difficult to accurately measure, but is easier to demonstrate with the presence of well-known brand names.

According to Williams and Bukowitz (2001), there are three separate categories of knowledge that can be found within a business organisation. The first kind is that of intellectual capital (IC), essentially all forms of knowledge – whether held in people's minds (tacit knowledge) or within an organisation's culture. It cannot be owned or appropriated by the organisation, but only borrowed or leveraged. The second type of knowledge is intellectual assets (IA), or such knowledge as can be identified as the exclusive right to the creators. This includes material (explicit knowledge) such as software, databases, algorithms, images, documents or manuscripts. Finally, there is intellectual property (IP) that comprises patents, trademarks, copyright and trade secrets as outlined above and that can be afforded exclusive legal rights. As shown in Fig. 13.2, the value lies with IP that has clearly defined ownership and that is aligned with the strategic directions being followed by the company.

The value of IP within most innovation intensive companies is now recognised as of sufficient importance to justify the development of formal strategies to systematically identify and protect that IP. Recommended strategies for the protection of IP include the avoidance of the public disclosure of sensitive information relating to products or processes until a patent application has been lodged. This is often a challenge for some organisations – and particularly of universities where it is a requirement of academic staff and students to publish findings. It is advisable to always use a non-disclosure agreement when engaging in discussions with potential investors or collaborative alliance partners. A patent attorney or IP lawyer should also be consulted to ensure that all appropriate legal issues have been considered.

All laboratory notes or documentations for processes should be recorded, with each page dated and signed by the person doing the work and countersigned by a witness who is technically competent to understand the work being performed. Any grant applications should be carefully reviewed by IP lawyers to ensure that they don't make any future patent applications a problem. All documentation and related materials should be secured and employees asked to sign confidentiality agreements. If new employees are contracted, they should be asked to sign deeds of confidentiality and non-disclosure and any background IP that they claim to bring with them should be discussed and formally acknowledged. This same process should be followed for collaborative agreements with third party organisations with which the company works in research or development. It is also advisable for due diligence to be undertaken on any IP that is to be licenced into the company or out of the company in order to ascertain its market value and the potential levels of commercial risk (Industry Week 2003).

It is important not only to protect IP, but to also value it appropriately. Williams (1999) suggests that companies make at least five common mistakes in relation to the valuation of their IP. The first of these is to enter into negotiations with a third party over a joint venture, merger or acquisition without first properly valuing their IP assets. A second mistake is to undervalue the IP assets, looking at what they are worth today rather than what they might be worth in future alignment with the assets of another partner. The third mistake is that of undervaluing corporate brands that have been created over many years and would cost substantial amounts to generate from scratch. For many firms, the fourth mistake is to value IP assets only *after* the deal has been negotiated. Finally, there is the mistake of valuing all IP assets collectively rather than individually. Each asset should be separately valued and this value recorded.

13.5.1 IP Assets Register

The value of IP assets is often greater than the value of physical assets, and it is advisable to have IP assets formally valued and their value recorded within the firm's assets register and balance sheet. An IP assets register can list a wide range of 'items', including: trademarks, brand names, patents, databases, registered designs and copyright materials (IP Australia 2016).

An IP assets register can take a variety of forms. It is essentially a database that lists all the IP assets and can be developed in a spreadsheet program or other document containing the following information for each asset:

- *Description*. This is a description or ID number for each item.
- *The nature of the IP asset.* This is a description of the nature of the IP asset, e.g. patent, registered design, copyright, etc.
- *Filing date.* This is the date that the asset was filed or lodged with IP Australia or the appropriate authority if applicable.
- *Publication date.* For copyright, this can include the date the document was published (e.g. either formally via a publisher, or onto the firm's website).
- *The creators.* The creator is the person or persons responsible for the creation of the asset. This can be the author(s) of the document or the creators of the design.
- *The owner.* Where the creators and the owners of the IP asset are not the same, this should be recorded. In some cases, an employee can be the creator but their IP rights are automatically assigned to the company or employer who becomes the owner.
- *Can it be formally registered?* Here you should note if the asset is a patent, trademark or design that can be registered, or if it is something that requires NDA and trade secrecy.
- *It is registered?* If it can be formally registered, here you record whether it has already been registered already, or what the outcomes were of any application for registration.
- *Applicable countries.* In this section, you record whether the asset has been formally registered in one or more countries. This can be important when seeking to develop a new technology or product for use in international markets.
- *Is it in use?* Another important point to note is whether asset is already in use, or if it is still in development.
- *How is it used?* If the asset is already in use you should note in the register how it is being used.
- *Rights to use third party assets.* If you don't own the IP rights but wish to use them, you will need to indicate in the register how you can prove that you have permission to use the asset.
- *Do contracts exist?* If NDA contracts or licence agreements have been signed, these should be noted. This can include contracts signed with employees and sub-contractors.
- *Has the IP been valued?* It is important to try to place a value on the asset. This may be difficult but some attempt should be made. Where an asset has been purchased or formally valued, the value should be recorded. If no valuation has been made, you should seek to estimate the value using a separate valuation process. This might include the cost of R&D to date, plus a forecast for future sales or profits. Valuations can be complex and are discussed below.
- *Term of protection.* Here the life of the IP rights protection should be noted. For example, if it is a design and needs to be renewed every 5 years, its anniversary should be recorded.
- *Summary of costs.* Any costs associated with the registration and renewal of the IP rights protection should be recorded.
- *Next date for payment.* Here the expiry date for any formal IP rights should be recorded.

- *Is it in the business plan?* If you are seeking to write a business plan to secure venture capital financing, you may wish to note these assets in the plan. A formal venture financing agreement will usually involve a due diligence process in which the IP assets will be examined and valued. Your IP assets register will prove a very important document at that time.

13.5.2 Checklist for Protecting IP Assets

According to IP Australia (2010), the following is a useful checklist for firms seeking to protect their IP assets:

1. Identify all IP associated with your business and itemise them in your business plan.
2. Check that you really do own all IP used in your business or that you have the right to use it.
3. List registered IP and place a dollar value on identified assets.
4. List unregistered IP and give it a dollar value.
5. List other valuable assets such as client lists and corporate knowledge.
6. Identify key staff involved in developing, maintaining and protecting your IP, and get them to sign agreements relating to confidentiality and competition.
7. Educate staff on the nature of IP, on how to protect it, and on their responsibilities.
8. Consider ways you can use the IP system in your overall business strategy. Decide which markets – including overseas ones – you may wish to pursue before going public.
9. Develop an infringement strategy. Consider insuring your IP against infringement, and against you infringing someone else's IP.
10. Search the patent, trademark and design databases as well as other literature and the internet to ensure that your ideas are new, and to avoid infringing the rights of others. You can also search for new business opportunities as well as keep a tab on what your competitors are doing.
11. Maintain secrecy and be first to market.
12. Make effective trademarks the core of your brand and image building strategy.

13.6 Innovation Management for Business Growth

The formal recognition of IP and its value within businesses has grown strongly in recent decades. During the late 1990s, the US Patent and Trademark Office recorded a major increase in the number of patents registered (Williams and Bukowitz 2001). A similar trend was noticed in Europe over the same period, with a major shift to online patent and trademark registrations in all OECD countries further driving the process (Hering 2002). At a national level, there is evidence of a positive

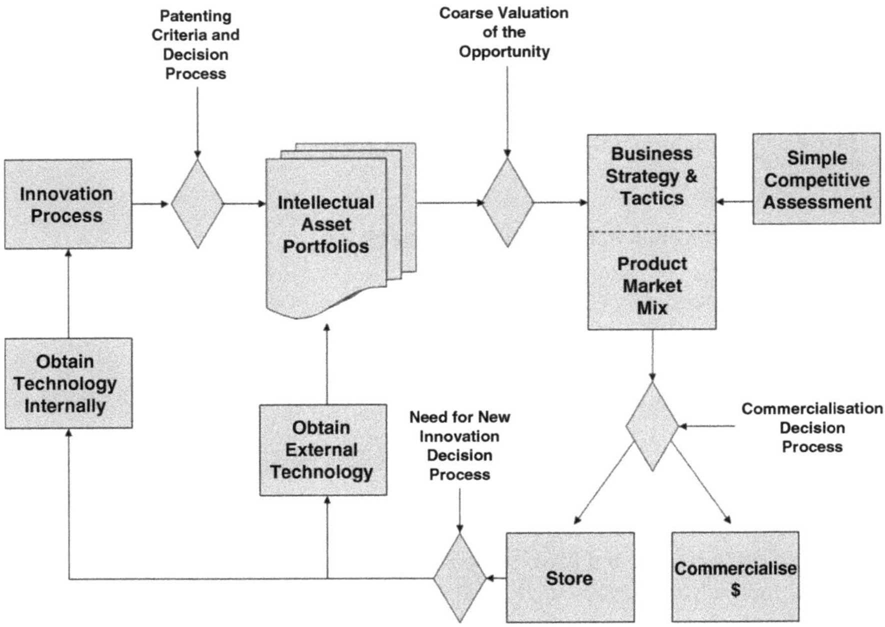

Fig. 13.3 Intellectual asset management system. (Source: Harrison and Sullivan 2000)

relationship between patent registration, labour productivity and economic growth (Crosby 2000).

The process of managing innovation for overall business growth requires attention on the customer within the context of the firm's competitive environment and on how to leverage IP assets and strategic alliance to deliver maximum value to customer. The ability to develop a systematic approach to innovation management and to new product development that is in concert with leading customers is likely to see the emergence of dominant designs that can capture market share (Miller 2001). An examination of innovation management systems of over two dozen companies noted for their leadership in successful commercialisation, as illustrated in Fig. 13.3, suggests a staged process to IP management and commercialisation. According to Harrison and Sullivan (2000), this system commences with the firm's innovation process. Each company would have its own individual system of managing innovation focused around their employees and R&D policies.

The creative ideas that are generated from the innovation process are subsequently screened through a stage-gating procedure that might involve early stage screening through to more advanced evaluations where full cost-benefit analysis is undertaken. Once an idea is able to pass this screening process, it will be included in the company's portfolio of intellectual assets. Decisions relating to whether a new process or technology is to be patented are usually decided at this stage. The cost of patent applications – particularly worldwide – is estimated to be around US$200,000, which is why a screening mechanism is desirable. Innovations that are not directly aligned with the firm's strategic goals may not be taken to patent but might be retained as trade secrets (Harrison and Sullivan 2000).

The intellectual assets portfolio held by the company contains a wide range of assets, including: registered patents, trademarks, designs and less formally acknowledged assets such as copyright material (e.g. corporate manuals and records) and customer databases. It is recommended that each asset be formally valued and this valuation recorded in the IP assets register. According to Harrison and Sullivan (2000), this valuation process commences with a description of how the asset is expected to bring value to the firm, e.g. via sales and marketing applications or via cost controls in processes. This stage is largely qualitative and, once completed, the next stage is to place a quantitative valuation on the asset. With some IP assets, their future value is often greater than their present value. Justification of how the valuation process is undertaken and of all assumptions used should also be recorded.

13.7 IP Rights as an "Isolating Mechanism"

Intellectual Property (IP) rights provide the firm with an ability to generate "*isolating mechanisms*" that can prevent competitors from securing a similar opportunity in the use of the innovation (Alvarez and Busenitz 2001). Where the entrepreneurial firm has the ability to create effective isolating mechanisms it can secure a market opportunity and effectively block out competition. Further, if it lacks sufficient resources to commercialise the innovation alone, it can use its control over IP rights to strengthen its bargaining position in any negotiations.

As illustrated in Fig. 13.4, where the firm has control over all the necessary resources required to fully commercialise an innovation it can proceed alone and in doing so capture or "arbitrage" all potential value. However, where it does not have all the resources it needs for commercialisation, which is common for small and start-up firms, its ability to successfully commercialise the innovation may depend on its ability to generate effective *isolating mechanisms* such as forma IP Rights.

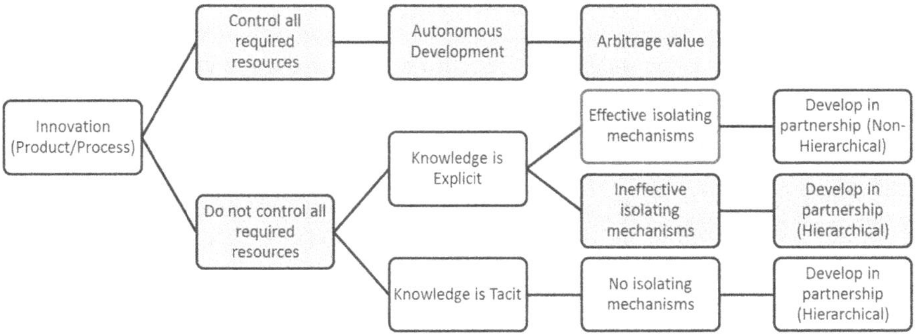

Fig. 13.4 Resources as isolating mechanisms in commercialisation. (Source: Alvarez and Barney 2004)

The ability to generate effective *isolating mechanisms* will depend on whether it can convert the ideas it has from *tacit knowledge* (e.g. held within the minds of its people), into *explicit knowledge* (e.g. able to be codified and disseminated) (Polanyi 1958). If the knowledge remains *tacit* there will be no *isolating mechanisms,* and the ability to secure a strong bargaining position with any future partners is likely to be limited. This weakness will make any relationship *hierarchical* (i.e. not-equal) (Alvarez and Barney 2004).

Formal IP Rights such as patents, can generate effective isolating mechanisms and give the entrepreneurial firm a *non-hierarchical* relationship with any third-parties. This can include investors (e.g. venture capital providers), customers, strategic alliance partners and other firms who need to be engaged in the co-development of the innovation. However, it should be noted that the possession of formal IP rights may not be sufficient to maintain a sustainable competitive advantage. Formal IP Rights such as patents or design registrations incur costs and need registration across multiple jurisdictions, which can become increasingly expensive if the innovation is to be commercialised within international markets. Patents and other similar formal IP Rights also become publicly disclosed and can therefore be at risk of imitation. This may require the firm that owns these IP Rights to engage in protracted and expensive civil litigation.

13.7.1 Causal Ambiguity

One way to secure *isolating mechanisms* without formal disclosure is the adoption of *Trade Secrets* which generate causally ambiguous competencies (Lippman and Rumelt 1982). As noted above, the use confidentiality and NDA can help to protect valuable IP. The *Coca Cola* corporation has maintained trade secrecy over its *Formula X* ingredients for *Coke* for over 100 years. There are at least three key sources of *causal ambiguity* (Reed and Defillippi 1990):

1. *Tacitness:* This is the implicit and non-codifiable accumulation of skills and knowledge that is generated from learning by doing;
2. *Complexity:* This is the possession of a large number of interdependent skills and assets (resource bundles); and
3. *Specificity:* This is the transaction-specific skills and assets that are utilized in the production processes and service delivery of products or services.

Each of these working together or in isolation can help to generate barriers to imitation and thereby create *isolating mechanisms*. They do this by increasing the level of *causal ambiguity* and make it harder for competitors to copy. Firm's that operate in highly competitive markets will need to create greater levels of causal ambiguity in order to compete through differentiation. How long a firm can retain these barriers will depend on many factors. A patent has a legal life of only 20 years, but new product development and innovation can quickly erode the value of a patent. Firm's seeking to sustain a competitive market position will need to maintain continuous investment in R&D to generate new ideas and retain causally ambiguous core competencies (Reed and Defillippi 1990).

13.7.2 The Boundaries of IP Rights

Although the possession of IP Rights is an advantage it has its boundaries. For example, it is important that any new invention be examined against existing patent databases to ensure that it is not already registered within other jurisdictions, or with important overlaps with existing technologies. In many cases IP Rights, in particular patents, may have similar properties to those already registered and in use. A professional adviser such as a Patent Attorney will be able to examine this and avoid the risk of subsequent legal challenges from competitors or owners of these conflicting IP Rights (Ambrozy 2013).

As shown in Fig. 13.5 there may be cases where the IP Rights are closely overlapped, as is the case with the situation on the left. This is an unfavourable situation because it may block any potential development of the innovation, or require a legal negotiation with the other IP Rights owners over licencing. However, if the overlap is modest (as is the case on the right), a more favourable situation arises. Here it may not be necessary to negotiate licencing agreements or even consider unrestricted development of the innovation. Legal advice from a Patent Attorney is recommended and if the overlap is considered too great a redesign of the technology may be required.

An important consideration is whether the speed of change within a market or field of technology is so rapid that it might not be worthwhile formally registering the IP Rights associated with the innovation.

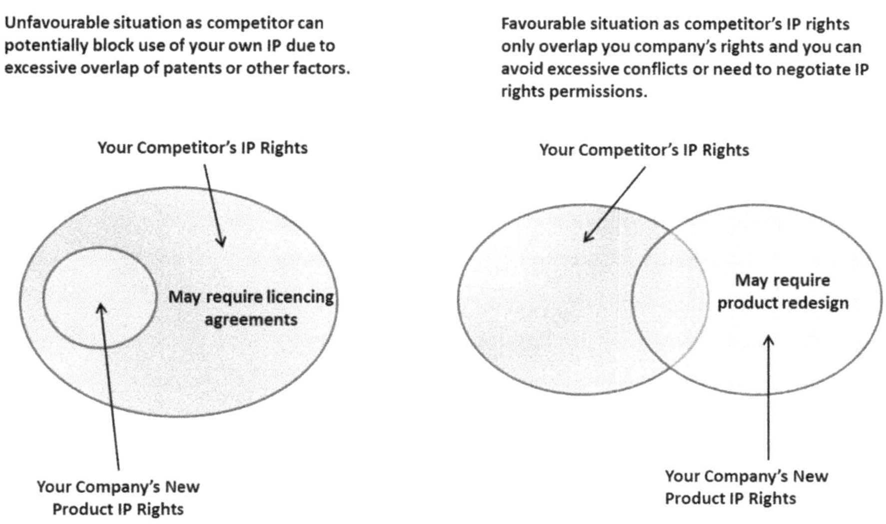

Fig. 13.5 The boundaries of IP rights. (Source: Ambrozy 2013)

> **For example,** … One consideration is whether the technology is in such a fast-changing marketplace that it will become obsolete within two or three years. If so, then it may not be worth the cost of pursuing a patent, and maintaining the invention as a trade secret might suffice. On the other hand, if the new technology can be easily reverse engineered, then a patent is the best source of protection, especially if the technology is likely to be valuable in the marketplace. (Ambrozy 2013)

13.8 How IP Rights Impact NPD Using Stage-Gate®

The management of IP rights throughout the commercialisation process is a strategic issue that should be an important part of any NPD project team's considerations from initial R&D to product launch and beyond. The relationship between IP rights management and the NPD process is illustrated in Fig. 13.6, with *Stage-Gate®* used as a framework.

13.8.1 Idea Screen: From Discovery to Scoping

During the first stage-gate transitioning from the early *discovery* or *idea stage* to the *scoping* stage, the main considerations should be whether the technology can or should be patented, and what additional IP rights need to be secured (e.g. registered designs, trademarks). The decision here will lead to an invention disclosure process and the tasking of a patent attorney to commenced the process of patent registration. This will need to be widened to examine any other IP rights that need to be registered. In a large organisation there is usually an *invention screening committee* that

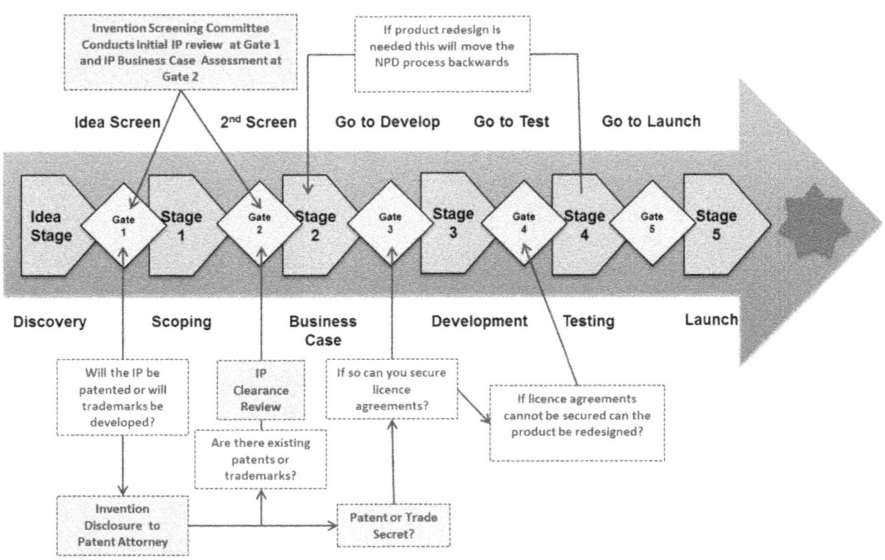

Fig. 13.6 How IP rights impact NPD using Stage-Gate®. (Source: developed from Ambrozy 2013)

is responsible for this initial review of the IP and they will typically require an *IP review* for stage-gate 1, and a *business case assessment* for stage-gate 2.

13.8.2 Second Screen: From Scoping to Business Case

The development from the *scoping* (stage 1) to the *business case* (stage 2) phases will require the technology to pass an *IP clearance review* within a large firm, and the advice from a sub-contracted patent attorney and/or IP legal counsel before the business case can proceed. This will ascertain if there are any existing patents or other formal IP rights registered within the country, or countries, where the firm wishes to commercialise the technology. Depending on what it found, the decision may be made to either not proceed, to redesign the technology to avoid any potential patent infringements, or to seek licencing agreements from the identified holders of the existing patents. In some cases, the decision might be to avoid registration of a patent, and to employ trade secrecy. This is common in some recipe or formula-based technologies (e.g. Coca Cola "formula X", KFC "secret herbs and spices) where any formal disclosure of the technology (as required under patent regulations) will make it too easy for competitors to replicate the original product.

13.8.3 Go to Develop: From Business Case to Development

For the product's business case to successfully pass stage-gate 3 the ability to secure the IP rights (e.g. proprietary or third-party) will be important. The determination of these issues will then influence the way in which the *development* phase (stage 3) proceeds. It may require the product to be redesigned to account for any inability to secure licence agreements from third-party IP owners.

13.8.4 Go to Test: From Development to Testing

How the IP rights to any third-party patents are resolved may influence the ability of the project to move through stage-gate 4 and proceed from *development* to *testing* the proof of concept of the new product or process innovation. As shown in Fig. 13.6, if it is deemed necessary for the product to be redesigned, the entire NPD process may need to move back to stage 2.

13.8.5 Go to Launch: From Testing to Launch

If all IP rights issues are resolved, and the proof-of-concept testing has been successful, the NPD project can move from *testing* (stage 4) to *launch* (stage 5). By that time all major IP rights issues should have been resolved, but as has been seen in recent high-profile cases (e.g. Apple v. Samsung), even large firms with quite mature product technologies, can end up in legal disputes over IP rights.

13.9 Licencing

13.9.1 The Factors

In many cases the ability to secure access to or value from IP Rights requires some form of licencing agreement. The process of licencing involves a legal agreement between the *licensee* (party who obtains the licence to use the technology) and the *licensor* (party who issues the licence). A variety of different types of IP Rights can be the subject of licencing agreements. The right to use or reproduce literary or artistic works (i.e. music, theatre, film, photographs) can be subject to licence agreements. However, it can also be applied to patents, registered designs, copyright, trademarks and plant breeder rights patents and technical designs. Table 13.1 summarises some of the factors that favour either the licensee or the licensor.

In high-technology industries licencing can play an important role. It can allow new innovations to be readily diffused through the industry and provide the basis of common industry or technology standards. This occurred with the case of *Dolby*, a company that developed noise reduction technologies that became a standard throughout the audio recording and reproduction industries. *Dolby* charged other firms a licence fee to use its patented technology within their products (Kazmi 2009).

Licences for the use of IP Rights can take many forms. However, a typical licence offers and exclusive or non-exclusive right conferred by the *licensor* to the *licensee* to use and sell the rights to the IP in a given geographic area, industry or field of use. Under an *exclusive licence* the rights to the IP are transferred from the IP owner to the licensee granting them the right to commercialise the IP to the exclusion of all others, including the licensor. This type of licence agreement occurs when the licensor cannot or does not wish to commercialise the IP. In this case, they will seek payment for their IP Rights and leave the licensee the task of commercialisation (IP Australia 2016).

Table 13.1 Factors favouring licencing parties

Factors favouring the licensor	Factors favouring the licensee
Broad, valid, assignable patents	Substantial NPD and product commercialisation work required
Related know-how and trade secrets	Substantial investment in plant and personnel required
Marketing contacts and potential customers	Existing strong competition in both market and product segment
Existing brand names	Existing plant and capacity
Company reputation in the market	Existing skilled workforce
Well-funded and resourced	Existing sales and distribution channels
Productive R&D pipeline for NPD.	Substantial NPD and product commercialisation work required
History of successful licensing	Substantial investment in plant and personnel required

Source: QPSX (2005)

Exclusive licences are the most common form found in commercialisation. However, non-exclusive licences can also be found. These may limit or restrict the use of the IP to a particular product, within a specific field of technology or industry application, or even within a given geographic area (i.e. within a country). This approach, while more complex to manage, offers the licensor the ability to secure multiple income streams from their IP Rights, as well as making greater use of the IP and continuing to develop the IP for future innovations.

When entering a licence agreement at least four key issues need to be addressed (Kazmi 2009):

- *Specifying the agreement boundaries* – both parties need to agree on what the licence agreement permits each party to do or not do. What rights each party has (i.e. exclusive or non-exclusive rights), is a major consideration. These issues should be clearly outlined in the licence agreement.
- *Determining the compensation* – this is a process of negotiating the best value for both sides. Usually a licence agreement involves the payment of royalties, which can be negotiated as a flat fee, fixed amount or percentage of a sale or usage.
- *Establishing rights, privileges and constraints* – what the rights, duties and obligations of each party are under the licencing agreement must also be clearly outlined. This is deigned to avoid later disputes; and
- *Specifying the duration of the agreement* – there should also be an agreement over the duration of the agreement. This might be a once-off complete transfer of IP Rights, or a shorter period. Much depends on the needs of both parties.

It should be recognised that there are no "standard royalties" and many factors need to be considered. This can involve royalties on sales, with consideration of sales taxes, customs and excise duties, income tax and even freight and insurance costs factored into the negotiations (IP Australia 2016). The key to a successful licence agreement is the ability to negotiate in good faith and consider the following:

- *The technology;* Scope, strengths and weaknesses and whether it can be redesigned or reengineered to overcome the original IP Rights.
- *The competition;* What other options exist to secure similar IP Rights and how much of a potential threat does this create?
- *Mutual benefits;* What do the two parties – licensee and licensor – want from the deal?

It should also be understood that the royalties paid by the licensee to the licensor under a licence agreement are allocations of future profit derived from the commercialisation of the IP. They are not a payment for the inherent value of the licensor's IP. Neither are they a means of recovering the costs of developing the IP, or a standard percentage of net sales.

13.9.2 Risks and Benefits of Licencing

Kazmi (2009) suggests that there are both risks and benefits to both parties in a licencing deal. The licensee benefits by getting access to the IP and any value they can derive from its use without the cost of having to develop the technology. They may also get access to IP that might be essential to their ability to enter some markets. In return the licensor can secure royalties from the use of their IP without the cost of having to commercialise.

However, both license and licensor surrender some of their future opportunities through the legal agreement. This might take the form of excluding one of the parties from operating in a given market. Another risk of licencing is that even the best legal agreements can be subject to disagreements. This can result in expensive legal disputes and it is potentially why exclusive licence agreements are more common because they involve a once-off payment and no further engagement between the two parties.

13.10 Valuing IP Assets

There are many different techniques that can be used to value an IP asset, and this is still an emerging field of activity (Steffens and Douglas 2007). As an intangible asset, IP creates significant problems in its valuation, which is made more complicated in situations where the IP asset is unproven and has no clearly-defined revenue stream.

A starting point for any IP valuation is the assumption that the IP assets have a market value, and therefore what needs to be determined are the conditions under which the asset can be bought and sold at a 'fair market' value. Of importance, is whether there is an alternative asset that the buyer might choose, and whether there is another potential buyer. Clearly, where an asset is unique, rare, valuable and cannot be easily imitated, its price is going to be higher. Also, of importance is whether the IP asset is to be sold in isolation or as part of a bundle of assets within a business that is a going concern. It may also be relevant to what purpose the IP asset is to be put and the scope of IP rights that the sale confers to the buyer (Tenenbaum 2002).

13.10.1 The IP Valuation Process

The process of IP asset valuation involves defining and classifying the IP and then assessing it to ensure that it can be easily identified and has the capacity to be separated from any other assets that are employed in the business. It should also be non-physical in nature and also capable of generating future economic benefits for its owner. Such IP assets should be protected legally or via a *de facto* right of ownership. If the IP asset is not able to satisfy these requirements, then the valuation is not worthwhile and should not proceed (Bertolotti 1995).

A number of different approaches to the valuation of IP assets have been identified. These include the cost, market, income, relief from royalty and real options approaches, which are discussed below. However, consideration needs to be given to whether the valuation is being undertaken with the intention of selling the asset on the open market, with the intention of using it within the business to generate future sales, or to ascertain what it might be worth at time of liquidation.

Considerations in IP Assets Valuation

- What is the lifecycle of the technology in which the IP asset resides?
- Is their legal protection of the IP asset (e.g. patents)?
- What is the economic life of the IP asset?
- How transferable is the IP asset from one owner to the next?
- Are there any restrictions on the exploitation of the IP asset?
- What is the level of R&D required to maintain the IP asset?
- What is the nature of the competitive environment?
- What is the normal financial return associated with the development of such an IP asset?
- What is the extent of functional and/or technological obsolescence?
- What are the forecasts for economic and technological trends in the industry?
- What is the likely cost of developing competing IP assets?

Source: Bertolotti (1995).

- Cost-Based Valuations

The cost-based approach to valuation takes into consideration the cost of creating or developing the IP asset. For example, it could include all the costs of R&D, prototype development, patent registration and legal fees – and potentially any marketing costs – to develop the brand. It is a very useful method where an IP asset is new and has no clear trading history or market comparison (Tenenbaum 2002). It assumes that the buyer would need to spend at least the same about of money to replicate the IP asset if they were to try to go it alone.

In undertaking a cost-based valuation, it is important to have data relating to the actual expenditure on the IP asset over the period from its inception. This can include the actual expenditure plus any taxation paid less any R&D tax offsets, and may also have an inflation factor included (Bertolotti 1995). It is clearly very important that good records are kept of any inventions at they move through the R&D process. This may include the hours spent on its development through to monitoring laboratory or workshop time sheets.

- Market-Based Valuations

A market-based approach follows a similar logic to that used in the way residential real estate valuations are undertaken. It requires a market equivalent asset against which the IP asset can be compared. Considerations may also include the size of the market, the bargaining power of buyer and seller, the anticipated growth for the products or services that the IP asset underpins, and the likelihood that new substitutes will emerge to challenge it in the market. The profitability of the IP asset when commercialised and the potential risk from legal or regulatory environmental changes might also need to be taken into account (Tenenbaum 2002).

Obtaining comparable market equivalents against which to base the valuation can be difficult. It may involve analysis of recent mergers or acquisitions where IP assets were included in the purchase agreements. The valuation will look at the price paid for these assets and how equivalent they were to the assets being valued in order to determine the estimated price. Stock market transactions that involve share trading may also provide useful market-based data, but it is likely to be difficult to isolate the IP assets from the rest of the venture. In some cases, the multiple of earnings at which the business is sold can be a reference point to strike a rate that can be used to estimate the value of the IP assets earnings (Bertolotti 1995).

- Income-Based Valuations

The third approach used to value IP assets is the income-based methods that follow a net present value (NPV) analysis of future income streams that might be expected from the IP asset over future years. This is one of the most common approaches used, but it relies on being able to identify, with reliability, the future income streams. Further, the revenues for the specific IP asset will need to be separated from any other tangible or intangible assets that may be contributing to income generation. This can be difficult in situations where the IP asset is part of a complex system or one of several intangible assets that comprise the overall product. It also requires being able to predict with some accuracy the anticipated lifecycle of the IP asset, and to determine an appropriate discount rate to account for risk (Tenenbaum 2002).

Income-based valuation methods are difficult in circumstances where an innovation is in its very early stages of commercialisation. Many IP assets form a 'platform IP' that can be applied to a range of potential products and target markets. In some cases, one option will see the IP converted into what is sometimes called a 'champion' innovation with mass market sales, significant profits and a long lifecycle. However, another option may produce a 'joker' with high sales and long lifecycle but low rates of profit.

13.10.2 The Measures

Some of the measures used in undertaking income-based valuations include: gross and net income, net operating income, pre-tax income, net income after tax, operating cash flow, net cash flow, and incremental income. A critical aspect of achieving a reliable outcome is the use of a consistent discount rate (Mard 2000).

In some income-based valuations, the contribution of the product's brand may need to be separately calculated from that of the overall business in which the IP asset is being produced. The gross contribution of the IP asset must be identified and separated from the gross contribution of any other tangible or intangible assets being employed within the firm. This is often undertaken using one of three ways (Bertolotti 1995):

1. By identifying the premium price of the IP asset over and above the retail price that might be obtained by a comparable product that has no brand or a generic brand;
2. By comparing the profit generated by a business with the brand versus an equivalent business that lacks this brand; or
3. By identifying a benchmark price charged by manufacturers and distributors of unbranded products, or by providers of unbranded services, and using this as a baseline.

Other variations of the income-based approaches can be found. The first of these is the *postulated loss of income method* in which the owner of the IP asset determines what the total amount of income that would be lost or foregone if they did not possess the asset. A second is the *residual earnings method*, which separates the firm's various tangible and intangible assets and deducts the earnings – or required rate of return – from all other assets from those of the IP asset being valued. This is a very complex method to apply and requires accurate data on revenue, costs and risk for all assets employed. A third approach is the *excess earnings method*, which assumes that the value of the IP asset can be measured by comparing the incremental earnings achieved by a proprietary product (e.g. patented or trademarked asset) against those generated by a non-proprietary product. It assumes that the existence of the trademark or patent will allow the asset to command a premium price. This is a very complex method to use as it may be difficult to isolate the true effects of the proprietary rights of the asset (Tenenbaum 2002).

- Relief from Royalty Valuations and the 25% "Rule of Thumb"

The method known as 'relief from royalty' assumes that the owners of an IP asset are relieved from having to pay a royalty to use their own IP. Under these conditions a royalty rate can be determined and the income stream for the IP asset estimated using an NPV approach. What is needed for this method is a projection of sales for the IP over its future forecast lifecycle (e.g. 10–20 years). Also needed is an estimate of the pre-tax royalty rate, the tax rate and a discount rate, plus a long-term growth rate if the fixed lifecycle cannot be estimated (Sausmer 2010).

Determining the royalty rate that might be applied to the IP asset is a key part of this method. One approach is the *25% Rule* commonly used for licencing. Here the net profit of a revenue-generating patent is multiplied by 25% and then divided by the total sales that can be expected. This produces a royalty rate for use in agreements (Berkman 2002).

Table 13.2 provides a simple example of how the 25% Rule might be applied in a licensing case. The rule is based on the assumption that the licensee is taking on three-times the commercial risk than the licensor, and therefore they should be

Table 13.2 The 25% rule simple example

Income statement of licensee		Estimated IP royalty rate using 25% Rule	
Revenue	\$100 m	Multiply profit by 25%	=10%*25%
Cost of sales	\$50 m	Extrapolated royalty rate	=2.5%
Gross margin	\$50 m	Multiply revenue by royalty rate	=\$100 m * 2.5%
Operating expenses	\$40 m	*Estimated royalty payment*	\$2.5 m
Operating profits	\$10 m		
Operating profit margin	10%		

Source: Bulakowski and Nesbitt (2012)

adequately compensated for their efforts. A key issue for assessing how to establish royalties for the use of patents, is whether to apply them to total revenues (e.g. percentage of sales), or profits. This creates a degree of complexity as the determination of what "profit" is can be open to debate. For example, the firm's gross profit or *gross margin*, as shown in Table 13.2 is the money remaining after variable costs or cost of sales (sometimes also called cost of goods sold "COGS"). Depending on what type of "profit" is chosen will determine the total size of any royalty payment.

In 2011 a U.S. Federal Court of Appeals case of Uniloc USA Inc. v. Microsoft Corp. resulted in a ruling that the 25% Rule cannot be used anymore as a starting-point for assessing damages claims for patent infringements. Their judgement was that the 25% Rule "does not rise to an admissible level of evidence, and may not be relied upon in a patent lawsuit in a U.S. Federal Court (Goldscheider 2011). This has generated a substantial debate over the value and worth of the 25% Rule.

The method used must consider the realities of licencing negotiations and not just a simplified royalty rate. For example, what will be the likely rate that a licensee might be willing to pay? A rate of 15% royalty is unlikely to be justified on an IP asset that is only capable of generating 5% profit margins (Mard 2000). It has also been argued that this method may underestimate the value of IP assets, as there may be more benefit to owning them than what the estimated royalty rate suggests as the owners could apply the IP asset to a number of opportunities (Sausmer 2010). Benchmark licencing "rules of thumb" such as the 25% Rule are useful but offer only a starting point for negotiations. There are some positive and negative issues associated with using net sales-based allocations of anticipated profits as a guide to setting licencing valuations.

First, licensees usually like it because they can avoid having to disclose commercially sensitive issues such as gross profit margins to their licensor. Second, licensors generally like them because they involve a royalty payment for any sales made even if no profit was actually generated. This of course is undesirable from the licensee's perspective. A third issue is that net sales-based allocations can restrict the licensee's flexibility in setting prices at they must factor in the royalty fees. This can make it difficult for them to adjust pricing strategies in highly competitive and price sensitive markets and may erode their profitability. Finally, such valuation

Table 13.3 Scenario 1: licensing the patent enhances or improves the product revenue

	No patent available	Revenue enhancing patent
Revenue	\$200,000	\$210,000
Cost of sales	\$80,000	\$80,000
Gross margin	\$120,000	\$130,000
Operating expenses	\$60,000	\$60,000
Operating profits	\$60,000	\$70,000
Operating profit margin	30%	33%
25% rule	(\$70,000∗25%) ÷ \$210,000 = 8.3%	

Source: QPSX (2005)

Table 13.4 Scenario 2: licensing the patent reduces the product costs

	No patent available	Revenue enhancing patent
Revenue	\$200,000	\$200,000
Cost of sales	\$80,000	\$70,000
Gross margin	\$120,000	\$130,000
Operating expenses	\$60,000	\$60,000
Operating profits	\$60,000	\$70,000
Operating profit margin	30%	33%
25% rule	(\$70,000∗25%) ÷ \$200,000 = 8.75%	

Source: QPSX (2005)

methods tend to push down the percentage of sales for any royalty, due to uncertainty over future profits.

Some legal advisers suggest estimating royalty rates by calculating the specific economic impact from the licencing. This suggests that the rate will be greater where the acquisition of the patented technology is able to generate higher revenues or lowers the product costs of production. Table 13.3 and Table 13.4 provide examples of this. The first shows the case of a patent that boosts total revenues from \$200,000 to \$210,000, while the second shows the benefits from a patent that lowers production costs and lowers variable costs from \$80,000 to \$70,000.

The decision to base licencing royalty payments on gross sales revenue or operating profits has several positive and negative perspectives depending on whether it is viewed from the licensee or licensor perspective. In general, licensees like to base the royalty on net-sales as it does not require them to disclose their profitability to the licensor. However, the downside for the licensee is that they have to make royalty payments regardless as to whether they are making any profit. By contrast, the licensor is usually happy to get payments immediately and not have to wait for the licensee to make profit. Further, as noted above, the sales revenue is usually much easier and more transparent than the profit. Another concern for licensees in relation to applying royalties to the sales revenue is that it may reduce their flexibility in setting prices when competing in price sensitive markets. This can in turn erode their profit margins. The allocation of royalties against sales rather than profits is also likely to reduce the total royalty percentage because of the uncertainty over future profits. Where the royalty is allocated against profits, and therefore carries higher potential risk, the percentage rate allocated is likely to be higher than against sales.

Despite the questions that have surrounded the 25% Rule, it remains a useful tool in the valuation of IP rights, in particular licensing agreements. For example, Robert Goldscheider, who was one of the founders of the concept during his time as an IP legal counsel to the Philco Corporation in Switzerland in 1959, has argued in favour of the 25% Rule, so long as it is used appropriately and not treated just as "rule of thumb".

> **For example,** ... The Rule's prominence has been accompanied by unfortunate misunderstandings about its form and substance. It is not, as some suggest, intended to be a simple shortcut to determine patent royalties. Rather, it was developed as, and remains, a meticulous methodology inspired by significant private transactions and ultimately refined by brilliant judicial interpretation. As such, it is inappropriate to condescendingly diminish it to a mere "rule of thumb." When properly understood and applied, the Classic 25% Rule is an effective discipline that achieves the high standards of reliability demanded by the U.S. Supreme Court in the Daubert and Kumho Tire cases (Goldscheider (2011) p.1).

According to Goldscheider (2011), 25% Rule should never be considered a "rule of thumb" by which the royalty split is always a 25:75 ratio in favour of the licensee. This is nothing more than a starting point for further negotiations. In reaching a final agreement, the two parties must consider a wide range of factors that relate to the nature of the technology being patented, and the conditions of the market into which it is to be employed. In doing so the use can be made of the *royalty/relief from royalty* approach mentioned at the start of this sub-section. This focuses on addressing the question: *What would the proprietor itself pay for its intangibles being measured at this time and under present circumstance?* In determining the value of the asset is the value of the royalty payments from which the company is relieved due to its ownership of the asset. The appropriate royalty rate is therefore determined by the calculation of the net present value (NPV) of the asset based on the future royalty income stream.

- Real Options Valuations

The real option valuation method has emerged in recent years as a novel and sophisticated approach to valuing IP assets. It is particularly useful in situations where there is a high degree of uncertainty as to the technical and market outcomes for the IP asset. The method is derived from financial market analysis and modelled on the approach taken when investors buy options to get a right – but not the obligation – to buy or sell the asset within a particular time period. A premium is paid for the right to have the ability to wait and exercise the option to buy or sell when the investor desires. Where the stock's market price is higher than the exercise price less the premium paid, the investor receives a payoff. However, if the stock price is lower than the exercise price, the investor is not obliged to exercise the option and only loses the premium originally paid (Tenenbaum 2002).

In the 1970s, Fischer Black and Myron Scholes developed the 'Black-Scholes formula' that has become a key tool in the financial derivatives investment market. Key variables that are needed to undertake the real options analysis are the current stock price, the exercise or 'strike' price, the dividends paid by the stock, the risk-free interest rate (e.g. government bond rates), the time to expiry of the option, and an estimate of the uncertainty of future stock price movements (Tenenbaum 2002) However, the real options approach is complex and requires an "*options thinking*" mindset. An, *options thinking* mindset emphasises the uncertainty of the future and encourages an adaptive approach that monitors the resolution of future uncertainties and anticipates that course adjustments will be required. It directs managerial attention toward a continual redefinition of the opportunities that are created by the resolution of uncertainty (Miller and Morris 1999).

References

Alvarez, S. A., & Barney, J. B. (2004). Organizing rent generation and appropriation: Toward a theory of the entrepreneurial firm. *Journal of Business Venturing, 19*(5), 621–635.

Alvarez, S. A., & Busenitz, L. W. (2001). The entrepreneurship of resource-based theory. *Journal of Management, 27*(6), 755–775.

Ambrozy, R. S. (2013). Understanding the Most common types of intellectual property rights and applying them to the product development process. In K. B. Khan, S. E. Kay, R. J. Slotegraaf, & S. Uban (Eds.), *The PDMA handbook of new product development* (3rd ed., pp. 368–384). Hoboken: Wyley.

Berkman, M. (2002). Valuing intellectual property assets for licensing transactions. *The Licensing Journal, 22*(4), 16–23.

Bertolotti, N. (1995). Valuing intellectual property. *Managing Intellectual Property, 46*, 28–32.

Bulakowski, A., & Nesbitt, B. (2012). *IP valuation: Is the "25% Rule" still relevant?* ipCG Blog, ipCapital Group. Retrieved from www.ipcg.com

Crosby, M. (2000). Patents, innovation and growth. *Economic Record, 76*(234), 255–262.

DITR. (2003). *Science and innovation mapping experts workshop: commercialisation, utilisation and intellectual property*. Department of Industry, Tourism and Resources: Science and Innovation Mapping Taskforce. Retrieved from Rydges Capital Hill.

Goldscheider, R. (2011). The classic 25% rule and the art of intellectual property licensing. *Duke Law & Technology Review, 2011*(6), 1–22.

Harrison, S., & Sullivan, P. H. (2000). Profiting from intellectual capital: Learning from leading companies. *Industrial and Commercial Training, 32*(4), 139–148.

Hering, I. (2002). Integrating IP Management. *Managing Intellectual Property, 117*(12), 25–27.

Industry Week. (2003). *Preserving intellectual property*. Retrieved from www.industryweek.com

INPI. (2019). *Que signifient "brevet dominant", "brevet de perfectionnement" et "brevet d'application"?* Retrieved from https://www.inpi.fr/fr/faq/que-signifient-brevet-dominant-brevet-de-perfectionnement-et-brevet-d-application

Intellectual-Property UK. (2005). What is intellectual property or IP? Retrieved from Intellectual-property UK [Online]. http://www.intellectual-property.gov.uk/

IP Australia. (2005). *Australia – United States free trade agreement: Examining the impact on intellectual property*. IP Australia, Australian Government. Retrieved from http://www.ipaustralia.gov.au

IP Australia. (2010). *An introduction to intellectual property*. IP Australia. Retrieved from http://www.ipaustralia.gov.au/

IP Australia. (2016). An introduction to intellectual property. Retrieved from IP Australia, [Online] <http://www.ipaustralia.gov.au/>.
Kazmi, A. (2009). Licencing. In C. Wankel (Ed.), *Encyclopedia of business in today's world* (pp. 1010–1011). Thousand Oaks: Sage.
Lippman, S. A., & Rumelt, R. P. (1982). Uncertain imitability: An analysis of interfirm differences in efficiency under competition. *The Bell Journal of Economics, 13*(2), 418–438.
Mard, M. (2000). Financial Factors. *Licencing Journal, 20*(8), 25–30.
Miller, W. L. (2001). Innovation for business growth. *Research-Technology Management, 44*(5), 26–41.
Miller, W. L., & Morris, L. (1999). *4th Generation R&D: Managing knowledge, technology, and innovation*. New York: Wiley.
Polanyi, M. (1958). *Personal knowledge: Towards a post-critical philosophy*. Chicago: University of Chicago Press.
QPSX (2005). *Intellectual property strategy*. Perth: QPSX Pty Ltd.
Reed, R., & Defillippi, R. J. (1990). Causal ambiguity, barriers to imitation, and sustainable competitive advantage. *Academy of Management Review, 15*(1), 88–102.
Sausmer, J. (2010). The income approach to valuing intellectual property. *New Jersey CPA, May/June*(2010), 28.
SBDC. (2005). *Intellectual property, small business brief*. Retrieved from small business development corporation, [Online]. www.sbdc.com.au
Steffens, P. R., & Douglas, E. J. (2007). Valuing technology investments: Use real options thinking but forget real options valuation. *International Journal of Technoentrepreneurship, 1*(1), 58–77.
Tenenbaum, D. (2002). Valuing intellectual property assets. *The Computer & Internet Lawyer, 19*(2), 1–8.
Williams, K. (1999, October). Are you valuing your intellectual assets correctly? *Strategic Finance*, pp. 76–77.
Williams, R. L., & Bukowitz, W. R. (2001). The Yin and Yang of intellectual capital management: The impact of ownership on realizing value from intellectual capital. *Journal of Intellectual Capital, 2*(2), 96–108.
WIPO. (2017). *What is IP?*, 23 pages. Retrieved from http://www.wipo.int/edocs/pubdocs/en/intproperty/450/wipo_pub_450.pdf
WIPO. (2019). *Applying for patent protection; What conditions must be met to obtain patent protection?* Retrieved from https://www.wipo.int/patents/en/faq_patents.html

14 Social Entrepreneurship and Co-operative and Mutual Enterprise

14.1 Introduction

> Social capital is more important than material capital. The solution involves the simple principle that social bonds and norms are of paramount importance for all people and communities.
>
> Source: Williams (2007), p. 179.

This chapter provides an overview of the emerging field of social entrepreneurship and innovation, with a specific focus on co-operative enterprise as a distinct business model. While entrepreneurship has been viewed as a process of self-directed, individualistic and profit maximising opportunism, the reality is that many entrepreneurs and innovators are not totally focused on personal wealth creation. Money is just a necessary tool that can be used to purchase assets with which to develop new products or services and deliver value to customers.

> **For example,** … New concepts such as social innovation, frugal innovation, inclusive innovation and social entrepreneurship are leading to new innovative business models and can contribute to a more inclusive approach to innovation. (OECD 2016, p. 65)

The behavioural skills of entrepreneurship and innovation can be applied readily in environments where a wider group or community benefit is the primary objective. This can be amply illustrated in the case of the co-operative enterprise, which is a business model that has been around for centuries. Today, many of the world's largest and most enduring business organisations are co-operatives.

T. Mazzarol, S. Reboud, *Entrepreneurship and Innovation*, Springer Texts in Business and Economics, https://doi.org/10.1007/978-981-13-9412-6_14

14.2 Social Entrepreneurship and Innovation

Social entrepreneurship and innovation have emerged in recent years as something of a new frontier for academics and public sector policy makers. However, these concepts remain poorly defined and encompass a wide range of activities that don't comfortably fit together under single definition.

While entrepreneurship is often characterised by profit-seeking and profit-maximising, social entrepreneurship is concerned with enhancing the welfare and betterment of others. As an outcome of this, social enterprises and social entrepreneurs have been identified as existing initially within the non-profit and voluntary sector (Thompson 2002).

Social Entrepreneurship and Innovation

Social entrepreneurship can be defined as entrepreneurship that aims to provide innovative solutions to unsolved social problems… Social entrepreneurship is, therefore, about solving social problems rather than about exploiting market opportunities.

Social innovation seeks new answers to social problems by identifying and delivering new services that improve the quality of life of individuals and communities, and by identifying and implementing new labour market integration processes, new competencies, new jobs, and new forms of participation. These diverse elements, then, each contribute to improving the position of individuals in the workforce.

Source: OECD (2010).

There remains no common agreement over the definition of social entrepreneurship or social innovation, and the theoretical foundations of this field have not been fully developed (Weerawardena and Sullivan-Mort 2006). While some definitions have focused on the individual level, others have attempted to explain social entrepreneurship in process terms. It has been viewed as revolving around a social problem that needs to be solved or addressed, and as a process that can occur in all sectors, not only the non-profit arena. We define social entrepreneurship as innovative, social value creating activity that can occur within or across the non-profit, business or government sectors (Austin et al. 2006).

14.2.1 Not Just Non-profit

Rather than a dichotomous separation into *for-profit* and *not-for-profit* forms of entrepreneurship, the process should be viewed as a continuum that ranges from the *purely social* to the *purely economic* (Austin et al. 2006).

What distinguishes the social entrepreneur from their more traditional counterparts is their social mission. They are focused not on wealth creation but on creating outcomes of social value (Dees 1998). If business activities are necessary to generate sufficient economic capital to allow the social mission to be undertaken, that is all the social entrepreneur is concerned with.

This notion that social entrepreneurship can take place within the for-profit sector and is not solely the preserve of the not-for-profit sector is embraced by a number of academics. For example, Mair and Marti (2006) note that the Grameen Bank of Muhammand Yunus, which provides micro-financing for the very poor, is a for-profit business model. They suggest that social entrepreneurship is not restricted to not-for-profit, and that the focus is on social wealth creation as opposed to economic wealth creation.

As illustrated in Fig. 14.1, the social enterprise resides in the arena (quadrant 1) in which the venture's mission is social but the primary market impact it is seeking to generate is economic. By comparison the traditional for-profit venture (quadrant 2) is established for economic purposes on both fronts. The non-profit or more correctly 'not-for-profit' venture (quadrant 4) is focused on social impacts and mission. The social consequence venture (quadrant 3) is one in which the mission remains economic in focus but its actions have a social impact. This is where the corporate social responsibility (CSR) that some businesses engage in through the establishment of social benefit programs comes into play (Neck et al. 2009).

The continuum of social enterprise can range from a non-government organisation (NGO), such as Médecins Sans Frontières that has no commercial exchange and has an exclusively social mission, to a for-profit organisation that is using social and environmental themes in its marketing and branding activities (Peredo and McLean 2006). The Body Shop cosmetics retail chain founded by entrepreneur Anita Roddick in 1976 lies somewhere in between. When it was first established, the Body Shop did not promote itself as an exclusively social enterprise. Its products were focused on being 'natural' – or based on natural ingredients that avoided the use of petrochemicals and inorganic elements commonly found in other cosmetics. It was not until the mid-1980s, when the Body Shop united with Greenpeace in a campaign to ban whaling, that its social activism began to emerge.

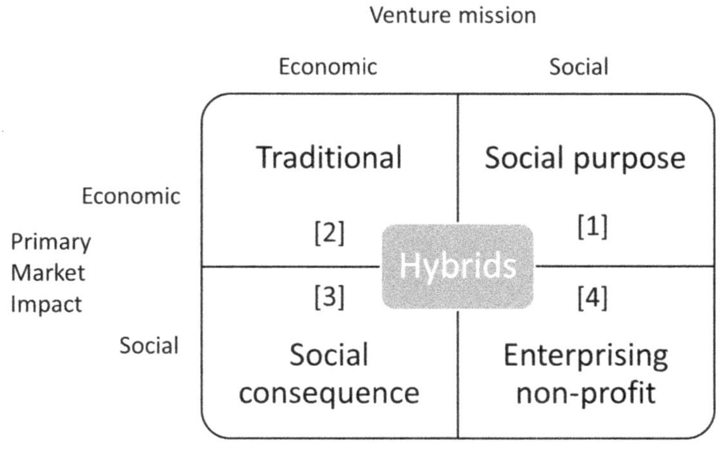

Fig. 14.1 Entrepreneurial venture typology. (Source: Neck et al. 2009)

14.2.2 The Realm of Social Entrepreneurship

Austin et al. (2006) suggest that the realm of the social entrepreneur differs from that of the traditional entrepreneur in several ways. First, they point to the context in which the social enterprise venture is taking place. Social enterprises have a different mission to their counterparts in the for-profit sector, and this impacts their performance measures. For example, while profitability and return on investment may be appropriate measures of the performance of a traditional entrepreneurial venture, they are not appropriate for a social enterprise, which may choose a lower rate of profit in order to deliver social benefits to the wider community.

A second point of difference between social enterprises and conventional ones may lie in their deployment of resources. This is best illustrated in the way social enterprises use voluntary labour. While traditional for-profit ventures will seek to hire people with the necessary skills and will pay market rates, this is often not possible for social enterprises. Pay rates may be more modest, and much of the work force may be voluntary. This can include the members of the board, who may donate their time to the social enterprise out of a desire to make a contribution.

Social enterprises also differ from traditional ones in terms of the deals they do. While a traditional enterprise will seek to do deals to exchange assets of economic value, a social enterprise may seek to exchange assets of a non-economic value. What most social enterprises are focused on is the creation of *social* value rather than *economic* value. This is illustrated in Fig. 14.2, which shows the *social entrepreneurship framework* in which the social enterprise operates. It draws people and

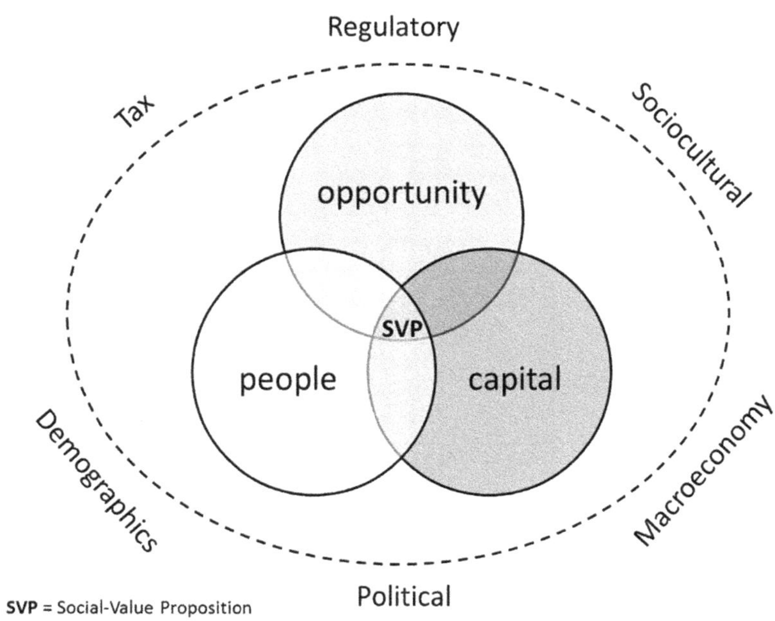

Fig. 14.2 Social entrepreneurship framework. (Source: Austin et al. 2006)

capital together to exploit an opportunity to deliver products and services of social value (the social-value proposition or SVP). This takes place within the wide context of the community, the economy and the regulatory environment surrounding the venture.

14.2.3 Social Innovation as an Emerging Concept

In addition to the emergence of social entrepreneurship as a concept, the idea of social innovation has also started to take hold within academic and public policy circles. For example, in 2000 the Local Economic and Employment Development Committee (LEED) of the OECD formally announced a *Framework on Social Innovations* (FSI). It aims to facilitate international dialogue and the transfer of best practice policies in social innovation (OECD 2010).

As with any innovation, a social innovation can be radical and disruptive in nature, or it can be incremental. It might include programs to reduce carbon emissions, or policies to improve the criminal justice system in a country (Caulier-Grice and Mulgan 2009). There are many forms that social innovation might take. These can include innovations in government or within government agencies that may deliver enhanced services to the community or reduce the cost of government. The formation of alliances between government, private sector and non-profit organisations to solve problems of a social, economic or environmental nature may also be part of the social innovation process.

The micro-financing business model developed by Muhammad Yunus in the Grameen Bank has been identified as an example of a social innovation. By its nature, a social innovation must meet the test of innovation by being new or novel and also by being primarily for the wider social benefit. It can be defined as a novel solution to a social problem that is more effective, efficient, sustainable or just than existing solutions and for which the value created accrues primarily to society as a whole rather than private individuals (Phills et al. 2008).

14.3 Developing a Social Economy

The concept of the *social economy* traces its origins back to at least the early nineteenth century, and now encompasses voluntary and non-profit organisations, charities, philanthropic organisations and foundations (Rowe 1893). It is distinguished from the private and public sectors in its role as a *third sector* (Birch and Whittam 2008). The work of Italian economist Achille Loria (1857–1943) was influential in recognising that a market-based economy would result in the unequal distribution of land into the hands of some to the disadvantage of others. This was, according to Rabbeno (1892), the cause of much of the world's tensions and conflicts.

According to Phills et al. (2008), the Great Depression of the 1930s was a period in which there was significant focus on social innovation. The *New Deal* of US President Franklin D Roosevelt saw a major shift in the role of the US federal government, and its intervention in the economy via numerous public agencies. Much of the architecture that was put in place by the *New Deal* continued on into the 1960s. The economic shock of the 1930s led many economists to start questioning the merits of a totally free market economy, and to consider the benefits of a more social or collective response to economic organisation (Berle and Means 1932; Miller 1937).

14.3.1 Economic Rationalism and the Third Way

The *New Deal* remains a contentious political issue for many conservative American politicians, and when Republican President Ronald Regan came to office in the 1980s there was a move to reduce the role played by the state and to privatise many areas of what were previously state-owned and operated services such as prisons, hospitals, health care and even military services. Regan's *New Federalism* was a reaction to rising costs of delivering social services and to the relative economic stagnation that was affecting the US at the time. The focus was on devolution of responsibility from the state or government sector to the community (Lasprogata and Cotten 2003).

This pattern of *economic rationalism* was echoed in the UK under Prime Minister Margaret Thatcher, and in Australia under the Australian Labor Party government of Robert (Bob) Hawke, and in New Zealand under the New Zealand Labour Party government of David Lange. The rise of the *economic rationalism* of the 1980s and its privatisation of public assets and quest for enhanced efficiency and productivity did not meet with universal approval. There was something of a counter-response from social activists and environmentalists who believed that these policies were not beneficial for the disadvantaged and for those in the Third World.

In the business community, companies like the Body Shop, Ben & Jerry's and Patagonia began to embrace a strong social purpose with an emphasis on social or environmental causes. The notion of *corporate social responsibility* (CSR), which had been in use since at least the 1960s, became more common. It was entrepreneurs such as Anita Roddick of Body Shop, Ben Cohen and Jerry Greenfield of Ben & Jerry's, and Yvon Chouinard of Patagonia, who led the social enterprise and CSR movement by using their success to promote environmental causes, fair trade and global labour standards (Phills et al. 2008).

During the 1990s, the political landscape shifted again with the election of President Bill Clinton in the US and Prime Minister Tony Blair in the UK. Clinton and Blair embraced what became known as 'the third way', a loosely defined concept that sought to balance the traditional left-wing and right-wing perspectives into a centrist model. The *New Labour Party* government of Tony Blair developed a policy platform that encompassed the idea of a *social economy* and what was referred to as the *new mutualism*, designed to boost the role of the co-operative enterprise movement within the UK. The role of social enterprise was viewed as being significant, with estimates in the late 1990s that there were around 1.7 million employed in the co-operatives, mutual enterprise and non-profits sectors (Passey and Lyons 2004).

14.3.2 Rise of the Social Economy

The 1990s saw the emergence of a greater recognition of the social economy that included co-operative enterprises, non-profit organisations and the role of voluntary, community and philanthropic activities. By the mid-1990s, the conservative Australian Liberal-National Party Government of Prime Minister John Howard continued to promote the idea of building up the social economy, and fostered philanthropy via tax incentives, the outsourcing of government social services to non-profit organisations, and programs to encourage volunteering. The Prime Minister's *Community Business Partnerships* program sought to generate a greater collaboration between the business and non-profit sectors (Passey and Lyons 2004). By 2007, the social economy in Australia was estimated to be worth around A$33 billion annually and to comprise 750,000 organisations. Of these, at least 35,000 were employing organisations with 3500 employing more than 20 people (Morrow et al. 2007). Within the UK, the *third sector* had become identified as an important part of the wider economy.

As illustrated in Fig. 14.3, the *third sector* exists in parallel to the private and public sectors of the economy. Within the *third sector* are a range of different organisations that include households, informal voluntary and charitable or benevolent activities, and the social economy. This social economy includes the formally

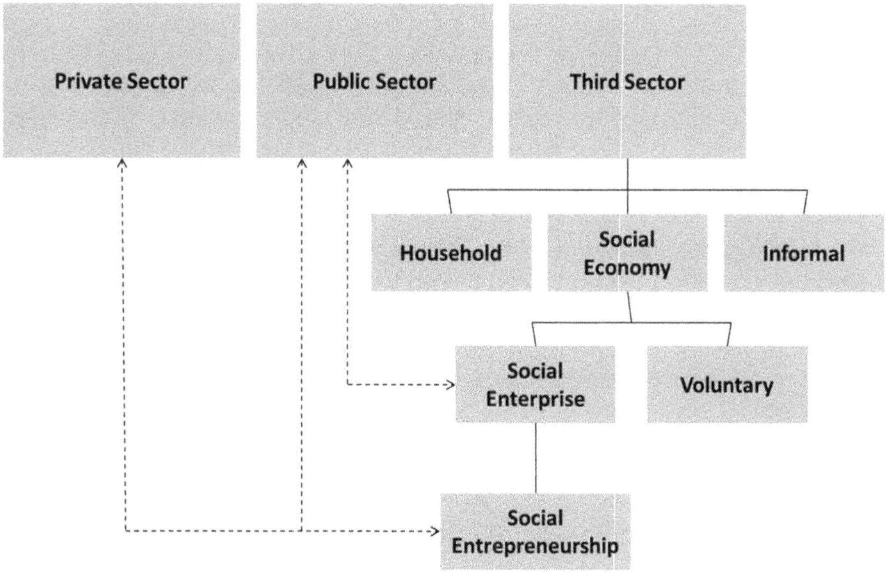

Fig. 14.3 The private, public and third sectors. (Source: Birch and Whittam 2008)

structured non-profits and voluntary organisations as well as the social enterprises, which encompass social entrepreneurship. According to Birch and Whittam (2008), the social economy remains poorly defined and, while it is recognised as a specific form of activity, it is characterised as having a business orientation, and the as using innovation, but with a social purpose. Hagen (2007) suggests that a definition of the social economy should focus on a common view, that most participants have, that money is not the only thing that matters.

> **For example,** … What unites people who categorise themselves as working in or for the social economy is their repugnance of a 'money only' way of catering for human needs, which translates into their unwillingness to accept that ever more needs remain unmet. Especially in the health and social service sectors, growing dehumanisation and bureaucratic procedures are increasingly being resented. In general, producers and users want a greater say in the decision-making processes that affect their lives. (Hagen 2007, p. 4)

Under the *European Charter of the Social Economy*, an organisation falls within this arena when it is an autonomous enterprise and where its members join voluntarily, are responsible, have equal rights and obligations, and are focused on self-help interest. Social economy enterprises must also be democratic (e.g. one-member-one-vote), and members must own at part of the assets. They should also be designed to provide services for the exclusive benefit of their members, and be member not investment focused. The creation of employment and the enhancement of member welfare and education are features that define these organisations. Finally, they should be independent and autonomous from the state (Hagen 2007).

14.4 The Social Enterprise

An important element within the social economy is the *social enterprise*. These are organisations that seek to replace traditional government-controlled welfare agencies with a combination of private, public and third sector providers. According to Bidet and Spear (2003), the features that define a social enterprise are fourfold:

- *First, the organisation needs to be focused on the production of goods and services on a continuous basis and in a direct way*. This contrasts with some philanthropic, non-profit organisations that simply provide grants or given policy advice.
- *A second feature of a social enterprise is that it must be voluntarily created by people who have autonomy from government or private sector control*. They must also be free to enter and leave the organisation at will.
- *Third, a social enterprise must place on its members a significant level of economic risk*, as compared to a publicly-funded agency where no personal financial risk is borne by those who manage it.
- Finally, *a social enterprise must employ those who work within* it for a minimum amount of paid time. In this way the social enterprise is differentiated from the purely volunteer enterprise.

Social Enterprise

A social enterprise is a business with primarily social objectives whose surpluses are principally reinvested for that purpose in the business or in the community rather than being driven by the need to maximise profit for shareholders and owners.

Source: DTI 2002.

Social enterprise is a well-established and generally well-recognised sector in Europe, and the foundations of social enterprise and the social economy remain strong in countries such as Italy, France, Belgium, Portugal and Germany (Bidet and Spear 2003).

Mancino and Thomas (2005) suggest that the social enterprise, particularly in the form of co-operatives, have played a significant role in the development of the social economy in Italy, with the model spreading to other European countries, particularly France. In 2003, there were an estimated 7400 social co-operatives in operation in Italy, established under an Act of Parliament of 1991. The majority of these social co-operatives (58%) provide services in the areas of health care, education, and home and residential care for the disabled or elderly, as well as child care and environmental protection. There focus is on the delivery of services to areas of need rather than to benefit members as in a normal co-operative. Most have around 40–50 members who are shareholders (only 10% have over 100 members), and have annual incomes of between €0.5 million and €3.7 billion. At least half of all members in these co-operatives are also employees.

Social enterprises can be not-for-profit organisations established for social and charitable purposes; however, as noted above, they can also be profit seeking enterprises, although their mission is primarily the delivery of social benefits and the development of social capital rather than wealth creation for shareholders.

Not-for-Profit Organisations

A not-for-profit (non-profit) organisation is an organisation established and operated for some benevolent purpose completely unrelated to the economic advancement of its founders and those who support it financially... Non-profit organisations can and often do earn a profit, but they are not permitted to distribute those earnings to their directors, officers, members or any other interested party in their private capacity.

Source: Lasprogata and Cotten (2003).

Not-for-profit and charitable organisations obtain special tax exemptions or concessions in most countries (Lasprogata and Cotten 2003). The donations and philanthropy often associated with the charities and non-profit sector are usually tax deductible for the donors.

14.5 The Social Entrepreneur

Despite the importance of non-profits, much of the focus of social entrepreneurship has been on more unconventional forms of enterprise that apply innovation and entrepreneurship to achieve socially beneficial outcomes. As noted above, many entrepreneurs who founded successful ventures of a conventional nature later became closely involved with social enterprise and CSR programs. However, there are examples of others who set out with a social mission in mind. Martin and Osberg (2007) provide the following list of such social entrepreneurs.

14.5.1 Robert Redford and the Sundance Institute

Robert Redford was a successful film actor and later a film director and producer. He made a series of highly successful films, commencing with *Butch Cassidy and the Sundance Kid* (1969), *The Sting* (1973), *All the President's Men* (1976), *Out of Africa* (1985), and *Sneakers* (1992). He later produced and directed several successful movies through the 1980s and 1990s. In 1981 he founded the Sundance Institute in Park City, Utah as a support for new and emerging independent film makers who might otherwise be locked out of the main stream film production companies. A non-profit organisation, the Sundance Institute assists film makers, directors, producers, screen writers, playwrights and theatre artists from around the world. The Sundance Film Festival was priced to appeal to a wide audience and to help showcase the films to a mass market. Redford's social entrepreneurship has been recognised as the foundation for the 'indie' (independent) film industry.

14.5.2 Muhammad Yunus and the Grameen Bank

Bangladeshi economist Muhammad Yunus founded the Grameen Bank as a lender of micro-finance for the poor. A Fulbright scholar and graduate of Vanderbilt University, Yunus became a Professor at the University of Chittagong following an academic career as an Assistant Professor of Economics at Tennessee State University. During the 1972 famine in Bangladesh, Yunus became involved in lending micro-loans of around US$27.00 to 42 poor women from the village of Jobra to help them into self-employment and out of the hands of unscrupulous money lenders. All the women repaid the loans, and it became clear that even tiny amounts of money could make a significant difference for such people. The women could use a sewing machine to make clothing for sale and earn enough to support their families and also repay the loan. The Grameen Bank charged tiny rates of interest on these loans, and used the profits to create a pool of capital to lend out to others. It is worth noting that 98% of the bank's customers are women.

14.5.3 Victoria Hale and the Institute for One World Health

Dr. Victoria Hale founded the non-profit pharmaceutical company The Institute for One World Health (IOWH) in 2000 with the purpose of developing safe, effective and affordable medicines for people in the developing economies of the world. A pharmaceutical scientist, Hale was unhappy with the profit-oriented mainstream pharmaceuticals industry that held patents on important drugs but priced them out of the reach of poor people. Her focus was on infectious diseases and the ability to offer affordable drugs to the world's poor. IOWH has developed two drugs that are targeted at Latin America and India. Her work has been supported by the Bill and Melinda Gates Foundation, which in 2006 provided the bulk of the organisation's R&D funding during its formative years.

Hale, Redford and Yunus are all examples of social entrepreneurs who have used the same basic characteristics of entrepreneurship and innovation, common to conventional businesses, to achieve social outcomes. Their motivation was a desire to help fill gaps in the existing economic structure created by market failure or the concentration of monopoly power into the hands of a relatively small number of large corporations. In each case, the industry and the motivation were different, but in each case their mission was social and not economic in nature. Further, while the Sundance Institute and the IOWH are non-profit organisations, Grameen Bank is a for-profit entity that ploughs its profits back into the social capital it seeks to foster.

14.6 Co-operative and Mutual Enterprise

One of the oldest and most enduring forms of social enterprise is the co-operative or mutual business. One of the earliest recorded co-operatives is the Shore Porters Society of Aberdeen, Scotland, which was founded in 1498 (Shore Porters 2007). Other early co-operatives include the Fenwick Weaver's Society, also from Scotland, that was formed in 1761 with the purpose of encouraging professional standards amongst weavers and collectively buying food and books (McFadzean 2008). In France, the co-operative movement can be traced back to at least 1750 with the foundation of one of the world's first consumer co-operatives, formed by a group of cheese makers (Williams 2007). The co-operative bakery *Caisse de Pain* was later established in Alsace at Guebwiller in 1828. By 1867 there were around 50 producer co-operatives, 100 credit unions, and 5 or 6 retail co-operatives operating in France (Gide 1922).

During the 1840s in Germany, Friedrich Raiffeisen led the development of agricultural co-operatives in order to assist impoverished farmers. He also helped to found a series of rural credit unions designed to break the grip of loan sharks taking advantage of small-scale German farmers. Elsewhere in Europe there were co-operatives formed by workers, farmers, tradesmen and small business owners with the purpose of collaborating in order to secure enhanced market power. Compared to other forms of social enterprise, the co-operative is a unique entity as it is essentially a creation of the middle class, or *bourgeoisie*, with an economic purpose that benefits its members (Gide 1922; Birchall 2003).

The *Rochdale Society of Equitable Pioneers* (Rochdale Society) was a co-operative founded in 1844 in the town of Rochdale, England, by self-employed weavers (Drury 1937; Fairbairn 1994). Its purpose was to provide its members with a range of economic and social benefits including a cooperative store for the purchase of food and other products (Wilson et al. 2012). Both social and economic objectives were listed in its constitution (Rochdale Society 1877, 21). However, it enshrined a set of guiding principles that have, with only a few minor changes, provided the foundation of what are today the key principles of the global co-operative movement (ICA 2015; Nelson et al. 2016).

The history of the mutual enterprise sector is also long and can be traced back to the middle ages. It has a strong foundation in financial services sectors such as banks, credit unions, building societies (saving and loan in the United States), friendly societies and insurance mutual firms (Grijpstra et al. 2011). They include the friendly societies, that emerged in the United Kingdom, including such organisations as the *Independent Order of Oddfellows*, *Independent Order of Rechabites*, *United Ancient Order of Druids*, and the *Ancient Order of Foresters* that provided pharmaceutical, financial, funeral and insurance services for their members (Lyons 2001). There are many insurance mutual enterprises that offer general, life and health insurance to their members. Automotive clubs such as the American Automobile Association (AAA) in the United States or the NRMA and Royal Automobile Clubs in Australia are also mutual.

Co-operative Enterprise

A co-operative is an autonomous association of persons united voluntarily to meet their common economic, social and cultural needs and aspirations through a jointly-owned and democratically-controlled enterprise.
Source: International Co-operative Alliance (2010).

Mutual Enterprise

A mutual is a private company whose ownership base is made of its clients or policyholders. The defining feature of a mutual company is since its customers are also its owners, they are entitled to receive profits or income generated by the mutual company. It is owned by, and run for the benefit of its members.
Source: UK Government (2011); Grijpstra et al. (2011).

Co-operative and Mutual Enterprises

A co-operative or mutual enterprise (CME) is a member-owned organisation with five or more active members and one or more economic or social purposes. Governance is democratic and based on sharing, democracy and delegation for the benefit of all its members.
Source: Mazzarol et al. (2018).

Mutual enterprises are not as easy to define as Co-operatives and are often less easily identified. Despite many having been founded in the nineteenth and early twentieth Centuries, many mutual enterprises have been demutualised and converted into *investor owned firms*. This has particularly occurred in the banking and financial services sector, where many Building Societies, Credit Unions and Insurance Mutual firms have undergone a demutualisation process (Wu 2015, 2016a, b). In Australia, in recent years, Credit Unions and Building Societies have started to establish themselves as *Member Owned Banks*, which are a mutual enterprise aimed to enable them to retain their mutuality while operating as competitive businesses within the financial services sector (Mazzarol et al. 2016a, b). In Europe, the mutual societies expanded strongly in the nineteenth and early twentieth centuries, and today are found predominately in two forms: (i) those that offer *mutual benefit* or *health providence* societies, and (ii) those that are *mutual insurance* societies. The first, of these provide welfare and health relate services (e.g. pharmacies, hospitals and medical services). The second, provide insurance protection (e.g. life and general). There are also mutual enterprises in Europe that provide financial credit and housing services (Grijpstra et al. 2011).

Although co-operative and mutual enterprises (CMEs) encompass a wide-variety of otherwise diverse types of business, they share sufficient common attributes to be recognised as a distinct form of enterprise known as a "CME". The acronym *CME* is thought to have its origins in a paper published by Co-operative Futures (2000), and has been used since by others to help unite the otherwise disparate sector of member-owned and focused enterprises (Yeo 2002; Ridley-Duff 2012, 2015; Mazzarol et al. 2018). All share a common focus on the social and economic benefit of their members, and a commitment to advancing trade through democratic and inclusive enterprise (Ridley-Duff 2015).

14.6.1 Co-operative and Mutual Enterprises (CMEs): A Global Network

At an international level, co-operative and mutual enterprises (CMEs) are represented by the International Co-operative Alliance (ICA), the peak body of the world Co-operative movement, which was founded in 1895. In 2019, the ICA had over 300-member organisations from 100 countries. These firms were found across eight industry sectors and had an estimated 1 billion memberships (ICA 2019). According to the ICA (2019), over 12% of the world's population are members of an estimated three million co-operative and mutual enterprises. The largest 300 CMEs by annual turnover have been estimated to generate in excess of US $2.1 trillion and employ around 280 million people (ICA-Euricse 2018). Table 14.1 lists the top 10 largest (by annual turnover) CMEs in the world. It can be seen that they are predominately from France, Germany, Japan and the United States, and in banking and financial services, insurance, wholesaling and retailing, as well as agriculture and food. However, CMEs can be found across numerous industries and countries.

Table 14.1 Top 10 co-operative and mutual enterprises by turnover

Organisation	Country	Industry sector	Annual turnover 2016 US $
1. Groupe Crédit Agricole	France	Banking and financial services	$ 90.16 bn
2. Groupe BPCE	France	Banking and financial services	$ 67.78 bn
3. BVR	Germany	Banking and financial services	$ 55.36 bn
4. Zenkyoren	Japan	Insurance services	$ 54.62 bn
5. REWE group	Germany	Wholesale and retail trade	$ 54.57 bn
6. Nippon life	Japan	Insurance services	$ 48.17 bn
7. ACDLEC – E. Leclerc	France	Wholesale and retail trade	$ 48.10 bn
8. Groupe Crédit Mutuel	France	Banking and financial services	$ 46.35 bn
9. Zen-Noh	Japan	Agriculture and food industries	$ 44.06 bn
10. State Farm	USA	Insurance	$40.80 bn

Source: ICA-Euricse (2018)

The following sub-sections overview a number of the world's largest co-operative and mutual enterprises across a range of industry sectors.

The National Agricultural Co-operative Federation (NH Nonghyup) of Korea provides around half the food marketing in South Korea. It encompasses most agricultural sectors, but specialises in beef, pork and poultry products. It also encompasses banking and financial services via two district banking networks offering financial service for its member co-operatives. Japan's Zen-Noh is a co-operative federation that represents a national network of over 1173 agricultural co-operatives and federations. It undertakes marketing, tracking and quality assurance of the member co-operative's farm products. It reportedly controls around 70% of all chemical fertiliser distribution in Japan, and in 2016 had an annual turnover of more than US $44 billion and a workforce of 12,557 people. The other major Japanese co-operative, Zenkyoren or 'National Mutual Insurance Federation of Agricultural Co-operatives' (established 1951), is a large financial mutual that provides property, liability and life insurance products for other co-operatives across Japan. New Zealand's Fonterra is a dairy co-operative that employs 17,400 people, and in 2016 had an annual turnover of US $13.4 billion (ICA-Euricse 2018). It is now a global business with a range of overseas subsidiaries, and holds a substantial share of the world trade in dairy products. Australia's largest co-operative enterprise is Co-operative Bulk Handling (CBH) from Western Australia. In 2017, CBH had an annual turnover of A$3.48 billion (Mazzarol 2018).

In France, the Crédit Agricole Group or Crédit Agricole S.A. (CASA) is the largest retail banking group in France, and the second largest such enterprise in Europe. It was also the largest CME by annual turnover at the global level (ICA-Euricse 2018)). In 2009, it employed around 160,000 people. The Groupe des Assurances Mutuellés Agricoles (Group of Mutual Agricultural Insurances) is an international insurance group headquartered in Paris. It has subsidiaries in the UK (Groupama Insurances), and is one of the largest mutual insurers in the world. Within the US the Nationwide Mutual Insurance is one of the largest financial services enterprises in that country. Founded in 1926, Nationwide is a financial service mutual based in Columbus, Ohio. It is primarily an insurance company, although it has a wide portfolio of financial services companies within its business portfolio with nationwide coverage.

In the field of retailing, there are Migross, Edeka Zentrale AG, and the Co-operative Group. Switzerland's Migross is one of that country's largest enterprises with a chain of supermarkets, petrol, electronics, books and homeware retail operations across the country. Founded in 1925, Migross had an annual turnover in 2016 of US$ 29.17 billion and a workforce of 79,000. Edeka Zentrale AG 'Edeka' is the largest supermarket business in Germany with around 26% of the total market share. Founded in 1898, it is a composite group of several independent co-operatives that work together under the Edeka group name. It is headquartered in Hamburg and has a network of 4100 stores ranging from small strip shops to hypermarkets. In 2016 it had an annual turnover of US $34.23 billion and employed around 250,000 people. The Co-operative Group is a consumer co-operative headquartered in Manchester, England. It was founded in 1863 and is generally known as *The Co-operative*. Its activities encompass retail groceries, banking, insurance, travel agency, farming, motoring, funeral directors and pharmacies. In 2016, it had an annual turnover of US $12.84 billion. In 2010, it operated 4900 stores and employed around 123,000 people throughout the UK.

The Mondragon Co-operative Corporation is a federation of worker co-operatives based in the Basque region of Spain. It was founded in the Spanish town of Mondragon in 1956. Its activities encompass finance, industry, retailing and education. In 2016 it had an annual turnover of US $13.32 billion (ICA-Euricse 2018), and has employed around 85,056 people. Mondragon has production centres at 60 locations throughout the world (Errasti et al. 2003).

14.7 CMEs as a Unique Form of Enterprise

Each of the Co-operative and Mutual Enterprises (CMEs) describe in the previous section is a substantial business, and it can be seen from the above that they encompass many different industry sectors and employ large numbers of people. CMEs should not be confused with non-profit organisations, and they are in many respects not really part of the *Third Sector* as outlined in Fig. 14.3. In fact, the CME is a different form of enterprise and forms what might be described as the *Fourth Sector* (Sabeti 2009). CMEs are generally established either for the economic or social benefits they can provide to their members, with both of these playing an important role (Novkovic 2008, 2014).

As shown in Fig. 14.4, the CME is a hybrid or *dual-function* enterprise that has both an economic and social purpose. They can be oriented more towards economic benefits, and in that case configured to distribute share capital amongst members

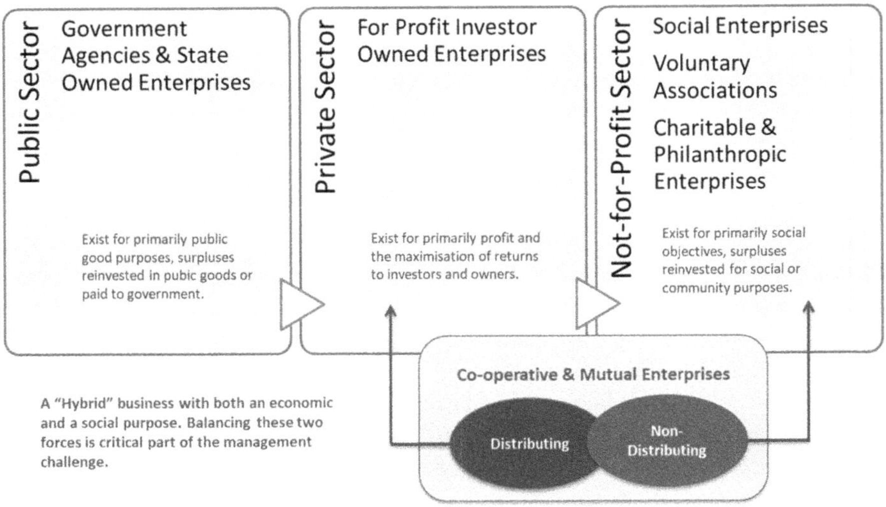

Fig. 14.4 The CME is a fourth-sector

and pay dividends as per a conventional *investor-owned enterprise*. Such CMEs are referred to as *distributing* and are usually co-operatives rather than mutual enterprises. By contrast, many CMEs are primarily focused on addressing social purposes, and as such they are not-for-profit businesses that don't distribute dividends from share capital. These CMEs, are referred to as *non-distributing* and can be found in both the co-operative and mutual enterprise forms.

Table 14.2 lists the key differences between the CME and the investor-owned firm (IOF), where it can be seen that the former is differentiated by its focus on the economic and social benefits of the members, who are the patrons, investors and owners of the enterprise, as well as members of a community of purpose that has been formed in order to solve economic and/or social problems that cannot be solved as effectively by any of the other business forms (e.g. IOFs, not-for-profit, state owned enterprises) (Mamouni Limnios et al. 2018). This need to maintain a balance between the economic and social objectives of the CME has been identified as an important point of difference that distinguishes this type of business as unique (Levi 2006; Levi and Davis 2008). This focus on more than just the member's is best illustrated with reference to the Rochdale Society and Co-operative principles.

14.7.1 The Rochdale Society and Co-operative Principles

As noted above, the contemporary co-operative movement traces its origins back to the establishment of the Rochdale Society in 1844. The co-operative was established on a set of principles – often referred to as the *Rochdale principles* – that continue to be the focus of co-operative enterprise throughout the world today. They are the key guiding principles of the international co-operative's movement. The

Table 14.2 Comparison of business decision making in co-operative and mutual enterprises and investor-owned firms

Business decision making	Co-operative and Mutual Enterprises (CMEs)	Investor-owned firms IOFs
Identify purpose	Embed mission and co-operative principles to meet member needs	Focus on outcomes for investors
Articulate the value proposition	Maximise member benefits	Satisfy customer needs and maximise shareholder returns.
Identify the market segments	Target areas of greatest member need	Target most lucrative opportunities
Define the value chain configuration	Suppliers and customers are owner-members of the firm	Suppliers and customers are outsiders to the firm
Estimate the cost and profit potential	Offer higher prices to suppliers and lower prices to customers	Reduce supplier costs and premium price customers
Define the position within the vale chain	Block substitution threats and form strategic partnerships within the co-op membership	Block substitution threats and form strategic partnerships within complementary actors
Formulate a competitive strategy	Offer members best value	Exploit future opportunities with existing resources
Evaluate performance	Economic value and social capital	Primarily economic value

Source: Mazzarol et al. (2018)

original principles of the Rochdale Society have only been amended twice, once in 1937 and once in 1966. They provide a means of identifying a co-operative, and in Australia, they have been enshrined into the *Co-operatives National Law and National Regulations 2012*, as well as state and territory Co-operatives Acts such as the 2009 *Co-operatives Act WA, 2009*. The co-operative principles are: (i) voluntary and open membership; (ii) democratic member control; (iii) member economic participation; (iv) autonomy and independence; (v) education, training and information; (vi) co-operation among co-operatives; and (vii) concern for community (International Co-operative Alliance 2010).

- Voluntary and Open Membership with Democratic Control

The co-operative enterprise is defined by voluntary and open membership that does not discriminate on the grounds of gender, social, racial, political or religious differences. Unlike a government organisation, membership is purely voluntary. The co-operative is also democratic, and members are in control of the enterprise. Both men and women can hold authority, and all members have equal voting rights. The rule of *one-member-one-vote* is a key distinguishing feature of the co-operative enterprise when compared to the investor-owned firm (IOF) where those with the majority of shares generally have the most voting rights.

- Member Economic Participation

All members of a co-operative contribute equitably and democratically to the enterprise, and at least part of the share capital is used for the common benefit of members. The co-operative generally does not distribute profits back to members in the same way as an IOF. As noted, while some co-operatives are *distributing,* and do return financial benefits to members, they are not generally designed as generators of high investment returns on share capital or major dividend payments. The *non-distributing*, co-operatives re-invest all their profits back into the enterprise in order to give better services to members in the future.

- Independent, Autonomous, Non-political and Secular

Co-operatives are also independent and autonomous entities. They are generally not funded by governments, nor do they seek government financial assistance as is often the case for non-profit and charitable organisations. Co-operatives are also traditionally non-religious in nature, and do not usually have affiliations with churches or religious organisations. The co-operative is, or should be, also non-political. However, in some countries the level of government engagement with a and control over co-operatives has been very high (Birchall 2011). In fact, too much government interference in Co-operatives has been the cause of their failure, as happened in Russia in recent years (Golovina and Nilsson 2011).

- Member Education, Collaboration and Community Concern

A key principle of co-operatives is their focus on the self-improvement of their members through education, training and the dissemination of information. This can include the establishment and operation of schools, academies and training institutions, or the provision of market and economic information to members. Co-operatives also seek to collaborate with other co-operatives and to strengthen the entire co-operative movement around the world. Finally, co-operatives have, as a key principle, concern for the community. They are committed to the enhancement of their members and the local communities in which they live.

14.8 The CME Business Model

The CME is a unique business model and as a result it can be described by use of a business model canvas as previously discussed in Chap. 7. Figure 14.5 illustrates this CME business model canvas and its nine elements. Each of these is discussed in the following sub-sections.

14.8.1 Purpose

One of three pillars of the CME business model is the clarification of the *purpose* for which the enterprise was founded. The co-operative and mutual enterprise is usually established to provide a solution to a market failure and provide economic and social benefits to its members that are not being, or cannot be provided by other forms of business model (LeVay 1983). The *purpose* is a clear statement of the organisation's mission and provides justification of why it exists, as well as a

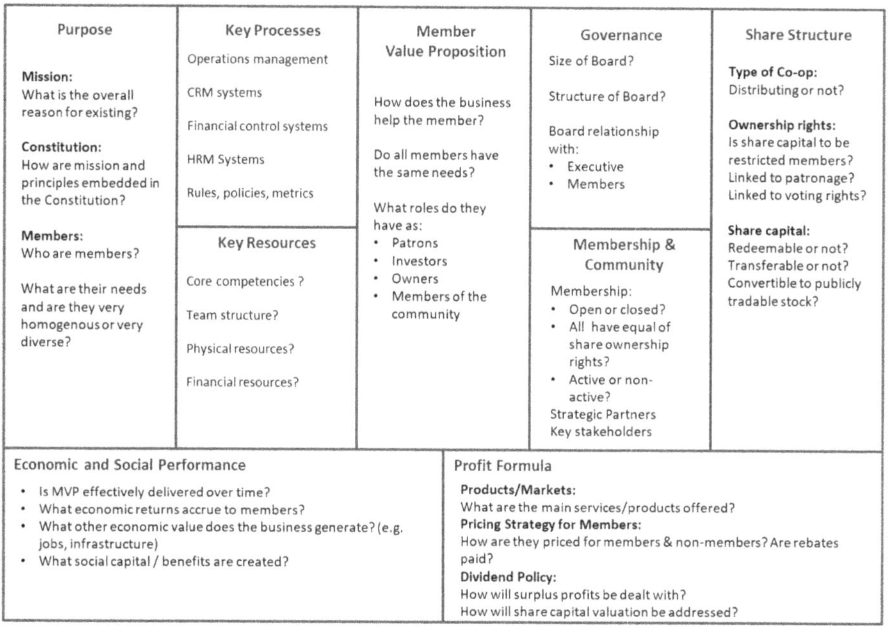

Fig. 14.5 The co-operative and mutual enterprise (CME) business model canvas. (Source: Mazzarol et al. 2018)

rallying point for its members. In developing the CME business model, it is important to start with this statement of purpose, and then to formally enshrine the purpose statement into the firm's constitution. This typically appears on the first page of the document. It should be designed to encompass the members' and their needs and generate a common purpose amongst not only the founders, but all future members (Staatz 1987). The following examples can be seen in the cases of customer-owned Bank Australia, and Australian housing co-operative Common Equity Housing Ltd.

> **Bank Australia,** … Our purpose is to create mutual prosperity for our customers in the form of positive, economic, personal, social, environmental and cultural outcomes.
> **Common Equity Housing Ltd (CEHL),** … Provide affordable, secure, well-managed housing to people wishing to access co-operative housing. Source: Mazzarol et al. (2018)

14.8.2 Member Value Proposition

The second main pillar of the CME business model is the *member value proposition* (MVP). This fulfils the same role as the *customer value proposition* (CVP) within the business model of an investor-owned firm (see Chap. 7). It can be developed by drawing together a range of economic and social benefits that membership can offer. In designing the MVP, consideration should be given to ensuring that these benefits can be provided over time in a sustainable manner, and against any competition or substitutes that might emerge (Nha 2006). The CME, regardless of what it trades (e.g. physical goods), is essentially a service business, and it is via patronage and value in use that the MVP will be created (Talonen et al. 2016; Vago and Lusch 2004; 2008). Some examples of MVP statements can be found in the cases of U.S. dairy co-operative Dairy Farmers of America and the Health Insurance Fund of Australia.

> **Dairy Farmers of America (DFA),** … Through superior performance, sound operations and integrity-based relationships, DFA will be the marketplace of choice for dairy farmers, the workplace of choice for employees, the supplier of choice for customers and the partner of choice for businesses.
> **Health Insurance Fund of Australia,** … Unlike many Australian health funds, we do not have shareholders. Moreover, cash dividends are not paid directly to our fund members. Instead, we return any surpluses to our members in the form of lower premiums, increased rebates and new benefits and services. This is our way of rewarding our loyal members.
> Source: Mazzarol et al. (2018).

The relationship between the CME and its members needs to be built on the basis that the member has at least four key roles or "hats" that they wear (Mamouni Limnios et al. 2018). The first of these is that of the *patron* hat, which is associated with their trading relationship with the CME. This can be either as a supplier (e.g. farmers supplying milk, grains), or as a buyer (e.g. retail customers buying goods or banking services). The second, is the *investor* hat, which encompasses their relationship with CMEs that issue shares that accumulate residual value and can be redeemed, traded or transferred. The third, is the *owner* hat, which reflects the fact that CMEs are owned in mutual by their members, who have the right to vote at general meetings and seek board positions. Finally, there is the role or "hat" they wear as a *member of a community of purpose*. This reflects the common purpose for which the CME was set up and how this remains a unifying goal for all members.

14.8.3 Share Structure

The third pillar within the CME business model is the management of share capital. As noted earlier, CMEs can be deemed to be either *distributing* or *non-distributing* in relation to how they distribute shares and dividends. Within the investor-owned firm (IOF), the fundamental model of share structure is for the founders to own the share capital of the incorporated venture, and trade via this enterprise to create strong returns to equity for all shareholders. Any raising of new capital in the case of an IOF, requires the issuing of new shares to investors, or the dilution of existing share ownership through the sale of shares. The IOF also operates on the formula of *one-share-one-vote*, so that any shareholder who accumulates 51% of more of the total shares will effectively own the company. By contrast, the CME, particularly the co-operatives, operate on a *one-member-one-vote*. As such, it does not matter how many shares an individual member owns, they still only get the same voting control over the company as any other member. How share capital is dealt with in the CME business model is therefore strategically very important. Many of the *generic problems* discussed below, are caused by this issue of how shares are allocated, redeemed or transferred by members, as well as how they are valued and how dividends are paid (Cook 1995; Nilsson 2001; Chaddad and Cook 2004).

14.8.4 Governance

Governance is one of the four interconnecting building blocks of the CME business model. It is also an area of major weakness for many CMEs, primarily due to the appointment to the board of members who may not have the experience required to manage large organisations. It is important that the democratic nature of the CME is protected, but good governance is essential regardless of the type of business (Prakash 2003; Birchall and Simmons 2007). Key issues to consider are the size of the board, who gets to become a director, and what will the ongoing relationship be between the members, the board and the executive management team? Some CME boards get too large as the organisation grows and there is a desire for more members to participate in running the enterprise. Most boards of even the largest CMEs, are rarely more than 12 people (Chaddad and Iliopoulos 2013). It should also be considered as to whether the board will appoint *independent directors*, who are non-members, but who possess specialist skills (e.g. finance, strategy, marketing) that can help to guide the non-expert member directors in decision making. The nature of the relationship between the board, the members and the executive managers is also an important area for consideration. In general, the board must see itself as the representatives of the members and the overseers of the members' interests, guiding the executive managers. However, they should not try to interfere in the daily operations of the executive team (Cornforth 2004). Their role is to also ensure active voice democracy for the members (Simmons 2015).

14.8.5 Membership and Community

Another important building block within the CME business model is the ability of the business to mobilise the membership and here the issues that need to be addressed are whether the membership is open or closed, how much equality of governance do members enjoy, whether patronage of the enterprise is contingent upon being a member, and what level of activity is required from members? Here, it may be prudent for the CME to define within its constitution these provisions. Not all CMEs are open to anyone who wishes to become a member. For example, the *New Generation Co-operative* (discussed below), is not open to anyone, and has restrictions on how membership is accessed, and the costs of exit. This is an important area.

For example, … As a mutually owned enterprise it is important that the CME business model considers how it will design its relationship with its membership base. Will the membership be open or closed? Will all members have equal share ownership rights, and will membership be contingent on active patronage? These issues have been largely addressed in the previous discussion over share capital structure and governance. How the CME approaches its membership and engenders a sense of shared values, identity, trust and mutually beneficial reciprocal engagement will determine its success and sustainability. (Mazzarol et al. 2018, p. 17)

Professor Alfred Marshall's Inaugural Address to the Co-operatives Congress 1889

Co-operation is many sided, and can be looked at from many points of view. There are, in consequence, many definitions of it, all having much in common, but each brining into special prominence some aspect of it which appeals with special strength to someone or other of the many different classes of mind who are attracted by it.

It has points of affinity with many other movements; but it is like no other.

Other schemes for developing the world's material resources are equally practical and equally business-like, but they have not the same direct aim to improve the quality of man himself.

Other schemes for social reform have equally high aspirations, but they have not the same broad basis of patient action and practical wisdom.

What distinguishes co-operation from all other movements is that it is at once a strong and calm and wise business, and a strong and fervent and proselytising faith.

Source: Alfred Marshall 1889 cited in Gide (1922, p. 28).

14.8.6 Key Resources and Processes

The key resources and processes that form the last two building blocks in the CME business model address the same areas as found in most other business models (see

Chap. 7). These will depend on the nature of the business that is being developed, and will evolve over time as the enterprise grows and matures. The attention given to these areas within the business model design are important, because they will determine how the CME functions as a business, and ensure that it offers an efficient operation and quality service level for its members. It should also use its members' capital in a wise and prudent manner to ensure that the best value for membership is returned back to members.

14.8.7 Outputs: Profits and Economic and Social Performance

The final two areas within the business model canvas relate to the *profit formula* and the *economic and social performance* of the CME. While the profitability of the CME remains as important as for any other business, the primary focus of these enterprises is not the maximisation of profits, but the economic and social value that they can generate for their members (Giannakas and Fulton 2005). What is needed in setting useful metrics for assessing the economic and social performance of the CME are not just financial measures for the venture, but measures of how it has helped grow the economic and social capital of its membership. This might include the number of jobs that the CME has created, the enhanced productivity of members, savings and profit growth within its members' households and/or businesses, and the enhancement of well-being, lifestyle and community or environmental sustainability as a result of the business existing (Birchall 2004; Novkovic 2008, 2014; Simmons and Birchall 2008).

14.9 Social Enterprise and the Role of Co-operatives

Most of the features of social enterprise are consistent with principles that underlie the co-operative. This includes a focus on community or member benefit, limited profit distribution, decision-making power not based on ownership of equity, and participation in the organisation by its customers or beneficiaries. While not all social enterprises are co-operatives, there is a strong correlation between the CMEs sector and the social enterprise (Ingram and McEvily 2007).

Compared with conventional non-profit organisations, Italy's social co-operatives have shown a greater capacity for strategic networking and partnering with other organisations in their region. They appear to engender more trust in such alliances. For their size they also appear to be able to deliver superior economic benefits, which have been attributed to enhanced synergies and efficiencies. They not only seek to address problems in their communities, but also to identify new problems, and their members display a greater focus on achieving social benefits as this is their primary mission. Compared to non-profits, these social co-operatives also seem to have better access to financial institutions when seeking to raise money (Mancino and Thomas 2005).

Within the developing world, the co-operative is viewed as an important social enterprise. As previously discussed in relation to the Grameen Bank, a key element in the alleviation of poverty in developing economies has been the provision of micro-financing in the form of small loans for start-up capital that enables otherwise very poor people to move into self-employment and break the poverty cycle. With over 2.8 billion people living on less than US $2 a day, and 97% of the world's population living in developing economies, this type of social enterprise initiative is of critical importance. The co-operative business model is viewed as offering an ideal balance between the objectives of profit and self-interest, with the capacity to provide services where they are required (Patel 2002).

The co-operative enterprise is therefore a unique form of social enterprise. The great English economist Alfred Marshall (1842–1924) was a major supporter of co-operative enterprise, and was President of the international Co-operative Congress movement in the late nineteenth century. In a speech to the Congress in 1889, he described the Co-operatives movement as one of many schemes design to help improve the world and affect social reform. However, he highlighted the key difference of the co-operative enterprise was its dual function of being both a sustainable business and an instrument of social change with a clear purpose to benefit its members.

14.9.1 Strengths of the Co-operative Enterprise

Although co-operative enterprise is strategically different from its mainstream counterparts, the co-operative business model has survived for centuries and has created many of the world's largest enterprises. Unlike investor-owned firms, the co-operative is not strategically focused on shareholder return on investment. Instead, the strategic focus of the co-operative enterprise is on patronage dividends, or the patron's share of the co-operative business (Bradley and McMaster 1980). As discussed earlier, the New Zealand dairy co-operative Fonterra has emerged as one of world's major international players in that sector (Ferrier 2004), while Spain's Mondragon Co-operative Corporation (MCC) has grown into a global business operation (Errasti et al. 2003).

In the US, the National Co-operative Business Association (NCBA) seeks to provide leadership for the American co-operative movement. At the 2006 Summit of the International Co-operative Association, representatives from 20 countries came together to identify common issues facing their movements. It was acknowledged that the co-operative was under challenge for both identity and relevancy in the face of international growth of alternative business models. NCBA President Paul Hazen, in a keynote speech, noted that the co-operative was a superior business model because:

1. Co-operatives provide a much wider and more equitable distribution of capital within the community.
2. Co-operatives keep the capital in the local community rather than siphoning it off to a few centres of financial power as is the case in public corporations.

3. Co-operatives 'exemplify the ownership society' rather than a shareholding class.
4. Co-operative governance is more open and democratic than the closed world of the public corporation.
5. A co-operative pursues both economic and social objectives, while public corporations are driven primarily for profit and shareholder wealth (NCBA 2006).

14.9.2 Blueprint for a Co-operative Decade

The year 2012 was the UN International Year of the Co-operative and this served to unite the CME community at a global level, as well as triggering many key initiatives at regional and country level. For example, in Australia an outcome of the UN International Year of the Co-operative was the creation of the Business Council of Co-operative and Mutuals (BCCM), the peak body of the CME sector[1]. Established in 2013, the BCCM provides a focal point and public "voice" for the nearly 2000 CMEs operating in Australia across a wider range of industry sectors. At the global level the International Co-operative Alliance has set out a *Blueprint for a Co-operative Decade* agenda. This is a global strategy focused on building up the CME sector and promoting the CME business model.

> **For example,** … The Blueprint for a Co-operative Decade is a global strategy of and for co-operatives…the Blueprint strategy, aims for the co-operative form of business – by 2020 – to become: i) the acknowledged leader in economic, social, and environmental sustainability; ii) the model preferred by people; and iii) the fastest growing form of enterprise. The 2020 Vision rests on five pillars, where co-operatives must make significant strides in order to reach their full potential. The first two – Participation and Sustainability – are differentiators. These traits set co-operatives apart from other business models in the marketplace. The third – identity – takes the core and backbone of the co-operative model into our digital and virtual age. The fourth and fifth – Legal Frameworks and Capital – are exogenous factors that can inhibit or facilitate co-operative economy. (ICA 2013)

The Case of America's Rural Electric Co-operatives

An example of the role that co-operatives can play in regional and community development is illustrated by the case of the rural electricity co-operatives established in the US in the 1930s.

In the early 1930s, the majority of rural communities in the US did not have electric power, telephones, water or sewerage services. In 1932, as many as 90% of rural households lacked access to the electricity grid, and it took the *Rural Electrification Act* of 1936 to start the roll out of large-scale electricity services.

This process was led by the Rural Electrification Administration (REA), working via the US Department of Agriculture (USDA), and a large number

(continued)

[1] See http://bccm.coop/

of rural electric co-operatives who drew loans from the REA to fund the electrification process. Loans to these rural electricity co-operatives funded the generation, power grids and transmission facilities. Around 100 such co-operatives had been established by the end of 1936 across 26 states. The success of this program is evidenced by the fact that approximately 98% of all rural households in the US were connected to the electricity grids by the early 1970s.

In 2006 there were 883 rural electric co-operatives in operation in 48 states across America. This network comprises approximately half of the total national electricity grid and three-fourths of the national land area. Compared to their larger, privately-held counterparts, the rural electric co-operatives earn approximately US$7000 per mile of line from approximately 5.8 consumers, rather than US$59,000 per mile of line from 35 consumers. As such, they are able to service communities that would otherwise be considered unprofitable by the mainstream, investor-owned power companies.

Source: Heriot and Campbell (2006).

14.9.3 Benefits of Co-operative Membership

A review of the international literature relating to agricultural co-operatives undertaken by Krivokapic-Skoko (2002) found that the main benefits identified by members could be grouped into at least five key areas:

1. *Market access and market risk reduction.* Members joined agricultural co-operatives in order to gain access to value-added markets, or to establish a local market for their produce. They also sought to reduce market risk by creating the co-operative as a buyer for their produce.
2. *Financial benefits from enhanced pricing.* Members sought a better financial deal from their co-operative membership. They were seeking lower input costs for supplies through price discounts. The co-operative was also aimed at strengthening their bargaining power with buyers so as to secure premium prices for their produce. They also sought access to better services via the co-operative.
3. *Improved productivity.* Membership of the co-operative was also viewed as offering members enhanced productivity through the pooling of marketing resources and bulk purchasing. This could provide access to more value-added services, as well as increasing farm income, efficiency and productivity.
4. *Access to resources.* The co-operative was also seen as a source of access to enhanced information, knowledge and resources. This might include access to new technology for the farm, or improved networking to help expand the farmer's sources of information.
5. *Community building.* Co-operative membership was also viewed as offering a greater opportunity to develop the local community and engage in self-help.

Collaboration via the co-operative could provide new services to the community and increase the benefits to members.

The co-operative enterprise is, therefore, an entity that seeks to generate benefits for its members in the form of enhance access to markets or to goods and services. It is also designed to offer financial benefits to its members through improved pricing, and achieve increased productivity from greater economies of scale and scope. A co-operative enterprise should also improve access to knowledge and information for its members as well as making a significant contribution to the local community in which it is based (Skurnik 2002).

14.9.4 Weaknesses of the Co-operative Enterprise

Using farmer co-operatives as an example, Staatz (1987) argues that the business model employed by the co-operative has two limitations. The first is the way in which individual co-operative members are able to enjoy incentives for membership. The second is the lack of common interest among what is often a highly heterogeneous membership. Because so many co-operatives involve a collective of smaller entities (e.g. farm business units) that operate independently of each other, it is usually impossible for the co-operative to leverage fully the potential synergies of the collective membership. The more heterogeneous the membership, the more difficult this process becomes. It is for this reason that many co-operatives find it hard to reach consensus amongst members and therefore to set clear strategic goals for the business.

Another key difference between the co-operative and the investor-owned enterprise is the relative points of focus for the members. For example, in the typical investor-owned enterprise, the focus for shareholders is the profitability of the entity and the return on the invested share capital. Prices charged by the investor-owned enterprises are important in their ability to deliver superior profits. Shareholders are therefore likely to be interested in the internal control of costs or the distribution of costs within the entity. By comparison, the members of a co-operative are more likely to be interested in cost allocation and pricing, and in its effects on their own individual participation in the entity. They are also likely to be more interested in the distribution of costs or pricing decisions amongst fellow members.

Compared to investor-owned businesses, these operational issues typically become more important to members, and they often create more problems for co-operative managers as a result. At the same time, the co-operative is well placed to enjoy enhanced communication flows between members, and this can result in the co-operative being more responsive to member needs.

For these reasons, the co-operative is often more constrained than the investor-owned enterprise in proactively seeking to exploit new market opportunities where competitive pricing is required, or to raise new share capital quickly to expand the equity base for future growth. Co-operatives are more likely than investor-owned enterprises to suffer from risk aversion in decision-making, under-financing or under-investment, and the absence of a secondary market for the share capital of the members exacerbates this. While the shareholder in an investor-owned business can sell their shares and secure either a capital gain or loss, the member of a co-operative is typically unable to do this. Shareholding in a co-operative only returns value to the member while they maintain patronage of the co-operative; this is the 'horizon' problem (Hardesty 2005).

14.10 The Five Generic Problems of Co-operative Enterprise

Although co-operatives have proven to be a successful and enduring business model they suffer from what have been defined as the five generic problems, most of which relate to the issue of vaguely defined property rights (Cook and Iliopoulos 1999).

14.10.1 The Free Rider Problem

The free rider problem emerges wherever property rights cannot be traded, or where they are insecure or unassigned. It is particularly common in co-operative enterprises that have open membership (Cook 1995). The free rider problem is caused by the fact that in an investor owned firm the early investors typically buy in at a low price and sell out at a high price after building up the enterprise. Any late entry investors must pay a premium price for the value-adding and reduction in risk that the early investors have created. This is not the case for the traditional co-operative, where the value of early or late entry is the same. An important outcome of the free rider problem is the unwillingness of the members of a co-operative to invest in the enterprise.

14.10.2 The Horizon Problem

The horizon problem emerges where the residual claims a member of a co-operative might make over the net income generated by an asset is shorter than the productive life of that asset (Cook 1995). This is caused by the inability of members within traditional co-operatives to transfer their ownership rights, and the absence of a secondary market for their rights such as is common with conventional shareholding.

In an investor-owned enterprise, because the investor can see their share equity appreciate in value over time, they tend to have a long-term horizon. In the case of publicly listed firms, they also have the comfort of being able to sell their share equity to another party via the stock exchange. This is not the case for the average co-operative whose members are more likely to be focused on year-by-year patronage issues that impact negatively on their capacity to develop strategic vision. The net result is a short-term perspective by co-operative members and an unwillingness to invest in the enterprise over the longer term.

According to Cook (1995), this horizon problem often leads to the membership placing pressure on the co-operative enterprise management to make cash flow distributions from profits in the short term rather than reinvesting this back into the business. Members may also seek to redeem their equity rather than retaining profits for long-term growth.

14.10.3 The Portfolio Problem

The portfolio problem emerges from the lack of transferability and liquidity of the members' equity in the co-operative enterprise. Any decision to invest in the co-operative by members is tied to their level of patronage of the co-operative.

> **For example,** ... The lack of transferability, liquidity, and appreciation mechanisms for exchange of residual claims prevents members from adjusting their co-operative asset portfolios to match their personal risk preferences. The cause of this problem is again the tied-equity issue – the investment decision is 'tied' to the patronage decision. Therefore, members hold suboptimal portfolios, and those who are forced to accept more risk than they prefer will pressure co-operative decision-makers to rearrange the co-operative's investment portfolio, even if the reduced risk portfolio means lower expected returns…In many co-ops, the members have not invested in the enterprise as part of a wider portfolio; they have invested in their own business and they lack the finance or interest to see the co-operative as part of their investment portfolio. (Cook 1995, p. 1157)

14.10.4 The Control Problem

The control problem emerges from the divergence of interests that takes place between the co-operative membership and its management. Investors in a conventional firm seek to maximise shareholder returns via the successful performance of the enterprise, which is a similar objective for the firm's management. By comparison, the members of a co-operative are seeking patronage benefits and lack any 'skin in the game' in the form of significant capital investment. While the investors in a convention business have, money tied up and are interested in what happens to it, the co-operative member is less easily engaged or controlled by the co-operative management.

14.10.5 The Influence Cost Problem

For many co-operatives, the strategic focus becomes fuzzy and the enterprise seeks to engage in a wide range of diverse activities. This can result in disputes over the allocation of costs or the distribution of profits or benefits within the enterprise, rather than a strategic reinvestment in the business. The extent of this problem varies depending on the level of central authority within the co-operative, the degree of homogeneity or conflict that exists between members, and the governance structure of the enterprise (Cook 1995).

14.11 The New Generation Co-operative

Cook and Iliopoulos (1999) suggest that the co-operative enterprise that wishes to overcome the problems arising from ill-defined property rights will need to offer equity shareholding to members that can be transferred, and that appreciate in value over time. Membership of the co-operative enterprise will also need to be adequately defined, and legally enforceable ownership rights protected via contracts associated with specific terms of patronage (e.g. supply or purchase). There should also be a minimum up-front equity investment requirement for all members.

Hardesty (2005) points to the so-called *New Generation Co-operative'* (NGC) as the business model that will overcome the generic problems inherent in the co-operative enterprise. Emerging in the US in the 1990s, the NGC was a response to the severe economic downturn experience in the American agricultural sector in early 1980s that adversely impacted on the viability of many producer co-operatives then operating in the US (Cook and Iliopoulos 1999).

The NGC business model seeks to overcome the weaknesses of traditional co-operatives through contracting with members over specific delivery rights based on the number of shares each member holds in the enterprise. The NGC is thus a one-vote, one-member democratic organisation in keeping with the principles of the co-operative, but where earnings are distributed based on shares owned by members. Unlike the traditional co-operative, membership is restricted. The financing of the NGC often involves the issuing of preference shares to augment the capital base of the enterprise and foster community involvement (Downing et al. 2005). Table 14.3 illustrates the differences between the NGC and the traditional co-operative, and how the NGC seeks to address each of the five generic problems inherent in the co-operative business model.

According to Katz and Boland (2002), the NGC differs from the traditional co-operative primarily in five ways. First, while the traditional producer co-operative is focused on the marketing of commodities, the NGC seeks to add value to such products to secure better prices. Second, while the traditional producer co-operative seeks to sell largely raw produce into a marketing supply chain, the NGC aims to develop value-added products it can target into niche markets. The third difference lies in the restricting of membership in the NGC as opposed to open membership of the traditional co-operative. This leads to the fourth area of difference. Because the traditional co-operative is open to all producers seeking to sell their produce, they are often faced with slack productive capacity as producers switch to other supply chains where they feel they can obtain better prices. This does not occur as readily within the NGC where supply chain relationships are controlled by 'delivery rights' contracts with producers. Finally, the ownership structure of the traditional co-operative is *one member, one vote* in pure democratic terms. This is not the case in the NGC model, where members do not have to own the same number of shares and

Table 14.3 The traditional versus new generation co-operative

Generic problems	Traditional co-operative	New generation co-operative
Free rider problem	Individual benefits and property rights are poorly aligned to ensure members get full benefits and bear full costs	Investment and optimal levels of product flows are determined before the firm begins conducting business
Horizon problem	Lack of liquidity through secondary market for shares	Stock can be traded to allow entry and exit from co-op as desired
Portfolio problem	Investment decision is tied to patronage. Members often pressure co-op board to structure assets to reduce risk	Risk is aligned with members' strategic goals as the risk profile is agreed prior to the formation of the co-op. Members can trade shares and risk
Control problem	Information and external pressure from public share trading are absent	NGC seek greater property rights and alignment of risk via patronage-based voting
Influence cost problem	Influence depends on centralisation of authority and member homogeneity	NGC are centralised and limited to specific purpose

Source: Katz and Boland (2002)

where shareholding is based directly on the level of patronage or supply contracts agreed.

Since their emergence in the 1990s, the NGC have been formed in a wide range of different industries including beef, pork, grains, dairy, fruit and vegetables, and particle board products (Downing et al. 2005). Despite their apparent strengths, they have evoked criticism from some for their exclusivity of membership and high up-front investments to new members, which are viewed as against the spirit of true co-operative enterprise (Torgerson 2001). Not all NGCs have succeeded. Like any other business enterprise, the co-operative must survive within its targeted markets and the NGC is no different. Competent leadership, sound financials and effective marketing are all keys to their success as with any business (Hardesty 2005).

14.12 The Co-operative Lifecycle Model

A question relating to co-operative enterprises is how sustainable are they as a business model. While many co-operatives are amongst the oldest and most enduring business enterprises in the world, many have abandoned their co-operative principles and converted into investor owned firms. Cook (1995) has proposed a five-stage co-operative lifecycle model that seeks to explain the stages a co-operative might move through and why.

Table 14.4 shows an adapted version of the lifecycle model developed by Brewin et al. (2008). In the first stage the co-operative is established for a purpose that can either be a market failure or some other trigger for a co-operative to be formed. They give the example of the Australian grains industry co-operatives. During the period from the 1920s to the 1950s, the Great Depression and the Second World War

Table 14.4 The five-stage co-operative lifecycle model

Lifecycle stages	Characteristics
Stage one	A co-operative is formed as a response to market failure; individual producers act collectively
	Co-operative's strategy is defensive in nature
Stage two	The co-operative provides net benefits by marketing products or providing services on more favourable terms than original investor-owned firms (IOFs) or oligopolies
Stage three	The market changes and co-operative benefits relative to IOFs are less certain. Focus turns inward to examine the co-operative's own transaction costs, especially free rider, horizon, portfolio, control and influence cost problems
Stage four	Managing the co-operative becomes exceedingly difficult and co-operative leaders consider strategic alternatives: exit, continue or a transition to new ownership
Stage five	The co-operative leaders implement a new strategy:
	Exit by liquidation, merger or conversion to an IOF
	Continue but address tendency to undercapitalise by:
	Seeking outside equity without complete restructure to IOF, or
	Pursuing proportionality strategy of internally generated capital
	Transition into a new generation co-operative
	Co-operative's strategy is more offensive in nature

Source: Brewin et al. (2008)

created an environment where farmers concerned about being exploited by the middlemen and grains processors. They formed co-operatives such as CBH in Western Australia, and the single-desk marketing agencies such as the Australian Wheat Board (AWB) and Australian Barley Board (ABB).

These grower co-operatives and state government agencies established statutory arrangements that saw all bulk grains handling and storage coordinated via these co-operatives, and all marketing centralised via single-desk authorities. In the 1950s, 1960s and 1970s, during what was a *stage two* of the lifecycle, the co-operatives grew, and farmers were generally supportive of these arrangements.

By the 1980s, the third stage had been entered, with a national movement across Australia for greater deregulation and efficiency. The co-operatives were placed under pressure from two levels. At the national level, the Federal Parliament introduced the *Wheat Marketing Act* 1989 that deregulated domestic wheat grain handling and threatened the monopoly enjoyed by the co-operatives. At the state government level, similar trends were occurring. This led to the sort of inward-looking review of costs and efficiencies within the grains co-operatives of the kind outlined in Cook's (1995) third stage.

During the 1990s, the pressure for greater cost efficiencies and economies of scale, plus the need for more responsiveness to a deregulated market environment, saw the co-operatives enter the fourth stage. Mergers took place between co-operatives and some of the single-desk marketing authorities. For example, in the early 1990s the ABB controlled 90% of barley exports from Australia (Dong et al. 2005). By 1999, ABB had moved towards privatisation, becoming ABB Grain Ltd. In the same year it lost its monopoly over domestic malting barley (Bielik 2004).

The period from the mid-1990s to 2010 saw the 'fifth stage' of the lifecycle with ABB Grain, CBH and AWB undergoing restructures and transitions. For example, AWB and ABB Grain issued different classes of shares, with ABB Grain listing on the Australian Stock Exchange and raising $22 million. By 2004, ABB Grain had merged with the grower co-operatives AusBulk and UGH, moving along a growth path that involved further acquisitions and expansion offshore into the Ukraine and New Zealand. By this stage, ABB Grain had retained a high proportion of grower shareholders, but was essentially operating as an investor-owned firm (IOF). Following a series of droughts that weakened its financial position, it was acquired by the Canadian agribusiness giant Viterra in 2009. AWB also became an IOF under the name AWB Ltd.

By comparison, CBH retained its traditional co-operative status, although it also went through a series of internal restructures. It merged with the Grain Pool of WA in 2002, and established international joint ventures. However, during the period from 2000 to 2010, it has also considered restructuring.

This history of the Australian grain co-operatives supports the five-stage co-operative lifecycle model and highlights the challenges that co-operatives face as a business model when confronted by the need to respond to environmental change such as deregulation, and the need to raise external capital.

14.13 The Theory of Community-Based Enterprise

For many co-operatives in the developed world, the pressures of having to conform to the norms of a free market and investor-focused economy have forced an abandoning of many of the traditional values which underlay their original foundations. According to Mooney (2004), this has impacted on the democratic principles of the co-operative. He argues that the co-operative enterprise remains one of the few institutions in the US that has a "*semblance of democratic governance*". The lack of democracy within large investor-owned firms means that most minority shareholders have little power or influence, often to their detriment. By comparison the co-operative, if allowed to retain its fundamental structure and governance, is a truly democratic enterprise.

Levin (2001), as a representative of the International Labour Organisation (ILO), suggested that the co-operative movement could play a key role in the alleviation of poverty. However, this would require a strengthening of the co-operative identity through education, plus the strengthening of member services. Co-operatives were also requested to build stronger business alliances at the regional, national and international level. The role of women in the developing world was also acknowledged to be a key area for attention, and the co-operative movement was asked to promote gender equality. Given the right legislative environment for the operation of co-operatives, there was a view expressed that co-operatives could employ the internet to facilitate education, social networking and e-commerce.

This potential role for the co-operative enterprise has led Peredo and Chrisman (2006) to propose the *theory of community-based enterprise*:

> **For example,** … At the centre of our argument is the concept of community-based enterprise (CBE), which we define as a community acting corporately as both entrepreneur and enterprise in pursuit of the common good. (Peredo and Chrisman 2006)

Community-based enterprise (CBE) occurs where a community acts in an entrepreneurial way to create a new enterprise that remains embedded in the existing social structure. Such CBEs are formed and managed in order to pursue the community's economic and social goals in a way that offers sustainable benefits for both the individual and the group.

According to Peredo and Chrisman (2006), the conditions that lead to the formation of CBEs are social and economic stress, and a process of incremental learning in which collective behaviour has become a feature of community life. The CBE is also dependent on social capital in the form of community members willing to devote time to these ventures. The community in which the CBE is to form must also be of a sufficient size to create the necessary critical mass for the resources required, but not so large as to become fragmented. The characteristics of the CBE are:

- Based on available community skills. A CBE will tend to focus on activities that are already part of the skills found within the community (e.g. cheese making, farming, mining, crafts).
- A multiplicity of goals. A CBE will have multiple objectives that will include economic, social, cultural and environmental as reflective of the interests of the wider community.
- Dependent on community participation. A CBE will also be built on the social capital that is available within the community, and will thrive or fail depending on how strong this community support and engagement is.

14.14 Enhancing Social Enterprise and Innovation

Social entrepreneurship and innovation are now recognised as important elements for a healthy and well-balanced economy. Governments from around the world are engaged in the promotion of policies designed to encourage social enterprise and innovation. The OECD (2010) has proposed several recommendations for the enhancement of these two areas.

14.15 Strategies for Enhancing Social Entrepreneurship

An initial starting point for the enhancement of social entrepreneurship is to 'build enabling environments and implement supporting policies' (OECD 2010). The *enabling environments* within a country comprise the regulatory, legal and fiscal policies and frameworks that either impede or encourage social enterprise. This can include appropriate taxation regimes to foster philanthropic and charitable fundraising as well as legislation to allow co-operative and community-based enterprises to be established and to grow.

Another important issue is the provision of sustainable finance that will allow community and social enterprise projects to be seed funded. This might include the establishment of tax exemption status for social enterprises as well as the micro-financing of organisations such as Grameen Bank. There is also a need for better education and training for social entrepreneurs and the OECD (2010) recommend such programs be taught within school and university programs. The aim is to foster pools successful social entrepreneurs and create a series of role models for others. More research is also needed into social entrepreneurship and it is important that government agencies officially recognise its value ensure that such enterprises are assisted.

14.16 Strategies for Enhancing Social Innovation

In the field of social innovation, the OECD (2010) also recommend that more research be conducted to better define the concept, to better understand how it works, and to determine the most effective policies to foster its emergence. They also suggest the formation of innovation funds for social innovation, or dedicated funding to permit communities to engage in innovative projects at the national, state and local levels.

The OECD (2010) also recommends the establishment of incubators for social innovation. These centres would work in a similar manner to technology incubators, and would bring together the skills and expertise that is needed to assist social entrepreneurs and innovators who are seeking to create and build a social enterprise. Such incubators would offer training and facilities, advice and networking opportunities. Finally, there is a need for the better measurement of the impact of social innovation to determine the returns that investment in such activities has. However, this should not be restricted to narrow economic or financial measures. It also needs to incorporate measures of social capital development, community benefit, and environmental sustainability.

References

Austin, J., Stevenson, H., & Wei-Skillem, J. (2006). Social and commercial entrepreneurship: Same, different or both? *Entrepreneurship Theory and Practice, 31*(1), 1–22.

Berle, A. A., & Means, G. C. (1932). *The modern corporation and private property*. New York: Macmillan.

Bidet, E., & Spear, R. (2003 October). *The role of social enterprise in European labour markets*. EMES Network Working Paper No. 03/10. Available at SSRN: https://ssrn.com/abstract=1352411 or https://doi.org/10.2139/ssrn.1352411

Bielik, M. (2004). *Organisational change in the Australian grain industry: A cooperative life cycle approach*. MSc thesis, University of Manitoba.

Birch, K., & Whittam, G. (2008). The third sector and the regional development of social capital. *Regional Studies, 42*(3), 437–450.

Birchall, J. (2003). *Rediscovering the cooperative advantage: Poverty reduction through self-help*. Geneva: Cooperative Branch, International Labour Office, International Labour Organization.
Birchall, J. (2004). *Cooperatives and the millennium development goals*. Geneva: International Labour Organization.
Birchall, J. (2011). *People-centred businesses: Co-operatives, mutuals and the idea of membership*. London: Palgrave MacMillan.
Birchall, J., & Simmons, R. (2007). The role and potential of co-operatives in the poverty reduction process: A research agenda. *Journal of Co-operative Studies, 40*(1), 43–51.
Bradley, F. L., & McMaster, R. C. (1980). A history of cooperatives and how they work. *WORLD, 14*(3), 23–25.
Brewin, D., Bielik, M., & Oleson, B. (2008). The evolution of grain trading organizations in Australia: Applying the cooperative life cycle. *Current Agriculture, Food & Resource Issues, Journal of the Canadian Agricultural Economics Society, 9*(2008), 9–17.
Caulier-Grice, J. & Mulgan G. (2009). *Exploring the Links between Social Enterprises*. Social Entrepreneurship and Social Innovation, paper prepared for the OECD LEED Programme, Paris.
Chaddad, F. H., & Cook, M. L. (2004). Understanding new cooperative models: An ownership–control rights typology. *Review of Agricultural Economics, 26*(3), 348–360.
Chaddad, F., & Iliopoulos, C. (2013). Control rights, governance, and the costs of ownership in agricultural cooperatives. *Agribusiness, 29*(1), 3–22.
Cook, M. (1995). The future of U.S. agricultural cooperatives: A neo-institutional approach. *American Journal of Agricultural Economics, 77*(5), 1153–1159.
Cook, M. L., & Iliopoulos, C. (1999). Beginning to inform the theory of the cooperative firm: Emergence of the new generation cooperative. *Finnish Journal of Business Economics, 4*(99), 525–535.
Cornforth, C. (2004). The governance of cooperatives and mutual associations: A paradox perspective. *Annals of Public & Cooperative Economics, 75*(1), 11–32.
Dees, J. G. (1998). Enterprising nonprofits. *Harvard Business Review, 76*(1), 55–66.
Dong, F., Marsh, T., & Stiegert, K. (2005, January). *State trading enterprises in a differentiated product environment: The case of global malting barley markets* (Food Systems Research Group Working Paper Series, FSWP2005-01). University of Wisconsin-Madison [available online] www.aae.wisc.edu/fsrg/
Downing, M., Volk, T. A., & Schmidt, D. A. (2005). Development of new generation cooperatives in agriculture for renewable energy research, development, and demonstration projects. *Biomass and Bioenergy, 28*(5), 425–434.
Drury, C. M. (1937). Marcus Whitman, MD: Pioneer and Martyr. Caxton Printers.
DTI. (2002). *Social enterprise: A strategy for success*. London: Department of Trade and Industry (DTI).
Errasti, A. M., Heras, I., Bakaikoa, B., & Elgoibar, P. (2003). The internationalisation of cooperatives: The case of the Mondragon Cooperative Corporation. *Annals of Public and Cooperative Economics, 74*(4), 553–584.
Fairbairn, B. (1994). *The meaning of Rochdale: The Rochdale pioneers and the co-operative principles*. University of Saskatchewan, Centre for the Study of Co-operatives, Occasional Papers, 55p. Retrieved from http://purl.umn.edu/31778
Ferrier, A. (2004). Opportunities and challenges of the co-operative model. *University of Auckland Business Review, 6*(2), 20–27.
Giannakas, K., & Fulton, M. (2005). Process innovation activity in a mixed oligopoly: The role of cooperatives. *American Journal of Agricultural Economics, 87*(2), 406–422.
Gide, C. (1922). *Consumers' co-operative societies*. New York: Alfred A Knopf.
Golovina, S., & Nilsson, J. (2011). The Russian top-down organised co-operatives – reasons behind the failure. *Post-Communist Economies, 23*(1), 55–67.
Grijpstra, D., Broek, S., & Plooij, M. (2011). *The role of mutual societies in the 21st century*. Brussels: European Parliament.
Hagen, H. (2007). *Social economy and its organization*. Geneva: International Labour Organization.

Hardesty, S. (2005). *Positioning California's agricultural cooperatives for the future*. Giannini Foundation of Agricultural Economics agmrc.org, pp. 7–10.

Heriot, K. C., & Campbell, N. D. (2006). Searching for Wortman's rural economic development zones: A case study of three rural electric cooperatives. *Journal of Developmental Entrepreneurship, 11*(3), 233–253.

ICA. (2013). *Blueprint for a co-operative decade*. International Co-operative Alliance. www.ica.coop

ICA. (2015). Co-operative governance fit to build resilience in the face of complexity. http://ica.coop/en/co-operative-governance-fit-build-resilience-face-complexity, International Co-operative Alliance.

ICA. (2019). *The alliance: The alliance represents....* International Co-operative Alliance, www.ica.coop

ICA-Euricse. (2018). *World co-operative monitor report 2018: Exploring the co-operative economy*. www.monitor.coop. International Co-operative Alliance and Euricse.

Ingram, P., & McEvily, B. (2007). *Sharper in relief: Opposition, identity and the maintenance of social movement organizations*. mitsloan.mit.edu

International Co-operative Alliance. (2010). *What is a co-operative*. www.ica.coop

Katz, J. P., & Boland, M. A. (2002). One for all and all for one? A new generation of co-operatives emerges. *Long Range Planning, 35*(1), 73–89.

Krivokapic-Skoko, B. (2002). *The concept and classifications of agricultural co-operatives* (ACCORD Paper No. 8). Bathurst: Australian Centre for Co-operative Research & Development, Charles Sturt University.

Lasprogata, G., & Cotten, M. (2003). Contemplating enterprise: The business and legal challenges of social entrepreneurship. *American Business Law Journal, 41*(1), 67–113.

LeVay, C. (1983). Agricultural co-operative theory: A review. *Journal of Agricultural Economics, 34*(1), 1–4.

Levi, Y. (2006). From the 'double nature' of cooperation to the social economy: Fifty years of associationalism. *International Review of Sociology, 16*(1), 149–163.

Levi, Y., & Davis, P. (2008). Cooperatives as the "enfants terribles" of economics: Some implications for the social economy. *Journal of Socio-Economics, 37*(6), 2178–2188.

Levin, M. (2001). *The role of cooperatives in providing local answers to globalization*. Keynote Speech to 10th National Cooperative Congress, San Jose, Costa Rica 29 March, ILO Cooperative Branch, Geneva.

Lyons, M. (2001). *Third sector the contribution of non-profit and cooperative Enterprise in Australia*. Allen & Unwin: Sydney.

Mair, J., & Marti, I. (2006). Social entrepreneurship research: A source of explanation, prediction and delight. *Journal of World Business, 41*(1), 36–44.

Mamouni Limnios, E. A., Mazzarol, T., Soutar, G. N., & Siddique, K. H. (2018). The member wears four hats: A member identification framework for cooperative enterprises. *Journal of Co-operative Organization and Management, 6*, 20–33.

Mancino, A., & Thomas, A. (2005). An Italian pattern of social enterprise: The social cooperative. *Non-profit Management & Leadership, 15*(3), 357–369.

Martin, R., & Osberg, S. (2007). Social entrepreneurship: The case for definitions. *Social Innovation Review, 5*(2), 28–39.

Mazzarol, T. (2018). *Australia's leading co-operative and mutual enterprises in 2018*: CEMI Discussion Paper Series, DP 1801. www.cemi.com.au. Centre for Entrepreneurial Management and Innovation.

Mazzarol, T., Clark, D., Reboud, S., & Mamouni Limnios, E. (2018). Developing a conceptual framework for the co-operative and mutual enterprise business model. *Journal of Management and Organization, 24*(4), 551–581.

Mazzarol, T., Mamouni Limnios, E., Soutar, G. N., & Kresling, J. (2016a). *Australia's Leading Co-operative and Mutual Enterprises in 2016: CEMI Discussion Paper Series*, DP 1601. www.cemi.com.au. Centre for Entrepreneurial Management and Innovation.

Mazzarol, T., Mamouni Limnios, E., Soutar, G. N., & Kresling, J. (2016b). *National Mutual Economy Report 2016: Incorporating the Top 100*. www.bccm.coop. Business Council of Co-operatives and Mutuals.

McFadzean, J. (2008). *The co-operators – A history of the Fenwick weavers*. East Ayrshire North Communities Federation Ltd..

Miller, M. G. (1937). The democratic theory of cooperation. *Annals of the American Academy of Political and Social Science, 191*(2), 29–37.

Mooney, P. (2004). Democratizing rural economy: Institutional friction, sustainable struggle and the cooperative movement. *Rural Sociology, 69*(1), 76–98.

Morrow, H., Bartlett, L., & Silaghi, L. (2007). *Contrary and congruent: Views of leadership and management in the Australian social economy*. Sydney: Perpetual – Social Economy Executive Education Network (SEEN).

NCBA. (2006). Summit focuses on common challenges, opportunities facing all co-op sectors. *Rural Cooperatives, 73*(4), 10–12.

Neck, H., Brush, C., & Allen, E. (2009). The landscape of social entrepreneurship. *Business Horizons, 52*(1), 13–19.

Nelson, T., Nelson, D., Huybrechts, B., Dufays, F., O'Shea, N., & Trasciani, G. (2016). Emergent identity formation and the cooperative: Theory building in relation to alternative organizational forms. *Entrepreneurship & regional development, 28*(3–4), 286–309.

Nha, N. (2006). The perceived image of service cooperatives: An investigation in Canada and Mexico. *Corporate Reputation Review, 19*(1), 62–78.

Nilsson, J. (2001). Organisational principles for co-operative firms. *Scandinavian Journal of Management, 17*(3), 329–356.

Novkovic, S. (2008). Defining the co-operative difference. *Journal of Socio-Economics, 37*(6), 2168–2177.

Novkovic, S. (2014). *The balancing act: Reconciling the economic and social goals of co-operatives* (International Summit of Co-operatives). Quebec: Desjardins and International Co-operative Alliance.

OECD. (2010). *SMEs, entrepreneurship and innovation*. Paris: Organisation for Economic Co-operation and Development.

OECD. (2016). *OECD science, technology and innovation outlook 2016*. Paris: Organisation for Economic Co-operation and Development (OECD) Publishing.

Passey, A., & Lyons, M. (2004). *Government initiatives to develop the UK social economy* (ACCORD Paper No. 12). Sydney: University of Technology Sydney.

Patel, S. (2002). *Insurance and poverty alleviation: The cooperative advantage*. Cheshire: ICMIF.

Peredo, A. M., & Chrisman, J. J. (2006). Toward a theory of community-based enterprise. *Academy of Management Review, 31*(2), 309–328.

Peredo, A. M., & McLean, M. (2006). Social entrepreneurship: A critical review of the concept. *Journal of World Business, 41*(1), 56–65.

Phills, J., Deiglmeier, K., & Miller, D. (2008). Rediscovering social innovation. *Social Innovation Review, 6*(4), 1–11.

Prakash, D. (2003). *The principles of cooperation: A look at the IGA cooperative identity statement*. New Delhi: Pamda-Network International.

Rabbeno, U. (1892). Loria's landed system of social economy. *Political Science Quarterly, 7*(2), 258–293.

Ridley-Duff, R. (2012). New frontiers in democratic self-management. In D. McDonnell & E. MacKnight (Eds.), *The co-operative model in practice* (pp. 99–118). Glasgow: Co-operative Education Trust Scotland.

Ridley-Duff, R. (2015). The Fairshares model: An ethical approach to social Enterprise development? *Ekonomski Vjesnik / Econviews, 28*(1), 43–66.

Rochdale Society. (1877). *Rules of the Rochdale Society of Equitable Pioneers' society*. Rochdale UK: Gilbert Haworth.

Rowe, L. (1893). Annual Congress of the Society of Social Economy, at Paris, May 29 to June 4. *Annals of the American Academy of Political and Social Science*. *4*(May), 102–105.

Sabeti, H. (2009). *The emerging fourth sector*. Washington, DC: Fourth Sector Network, W.K. Kellogg Foundation and The Aspen Institute.
Shore Porters Society. (2007). *Our history*. Aberdeen: Shore Porters Society. www.shoreporters.com.
Simmons, R. (2015). Measuring member engagement: Building a model of change? In L. Brown, C. Carini, J. Gordon Nembhard, L. Hammond Ketilson, E. Hicks, J. McNamara, S. Novkovic, D. Rixon, & R. Simmons (Eds.), *Co-operatives for sustainable communities: Tools to measure co-operative impact and performance* (pp. 239–265). Ottawa: Co-operatives and Mutuals Canada: Centre for the Study of Co-operatives.
Simmons, R., & Birchall, J. (2008). The role of co-operatives in poverty reduction: Network perspectives. *Journal of Socio-Economics, 37*(6), 2131–2140.
Skurnik, S. (2002). The role of cooperative entrepreneurship and firms in organising economic activities – past, present and future. *The Finnish Journal of Business Economics, 1*(02), 103–124.
Staatz, J. M. (1987). Recent developments in the theory of agricultural cooperation. *Journal of Agricultural Cooperation, 2*(20), 74–95.
Talonen, A., Jussila, I., Saarijavi, H., & Rintamaki, T. (2016). Consumer cooperatives: Uncovering the value potential of customer ownership. *AMS Review, 6*(3), 142–156.
Thompson, J. L. (2002). The world of the social entrepreneur. *International Journal of Public Sector Management, 15*(4/5), 412–431.
Torgerson, R. E. (2001). A new take on cooperatives. *American Vegetable Grower, 49*(11), 23–25.
Vargo, S. L., & Lusch, R. F. (2004). Evolving to a new dominant logic for marketing. *The Journal of Marketing, 68*(1), 1–17.
Vargo, S. L., & Lusch, R. F. (2008). Service-dominant logic: Continuing the evolution. *Journal of the Academy of Marketing Science, 36*(1), 1–10.
Weerawardena, J., & Mort, G. (2006). Investigating social entrepreneurship: A multidimensional model. *Journal of World Business, 41*(1), 21–35.
Williams, R. C. (2007). *The cooperative movement: Globalization from below*. London: Ashgate Publishing Ltd.
Wilson, M., Shaw, L., & Lonergan, G. (2012). *Our story: Rochdale pioneers museum*. Oldham, UK: Co-operative Heritage Trust.
Wu, T. (2015). *IBISWorld industry report K6222: Building societies in Australia*. www.ibisworld.com.au, IBISWorld.
Wu, T. (2016a). *IBISWorld industry report K6223: Credit unions in Australia*. www.ibisworld.com.au. IBISWorld.
Wu, T. (2016b). *IBISWorld industry report K6200: Finance in Australia*. www.ibisworld.com.au. IBISWorld.
Yeo, S. (2002). *Co-operative and mutual Enterprises in Britain: Ideas from a usable past for a modern future*. London: Centre for Civil Society, London School of Economics.

GPSR Compliance
The European Union's (EU) General Product Safety Regulation (GPSR) is a set of rules that requires consumer products to be safe and our obligations to ensure this.

If you have any concerns about our products, you can contact us on

ProductSafety@springernature.com

In case Publisher is established outside the EU, the EU authorized representative is:

Springer Nature Customer Service Center GmbH
Europaplatz 3
69115 Heidelberg, Germany

www.ingramcontent.com/pod-product-compliance
Ingram Content Group UK Ltd.
Pitfield, Milton Keynes, MK11 3LW, UK
UKHW020257051026
15470UKWH00020B/383
9789811394119